Courtesy Wm. Collins Sons & Company, Ltd.

"LET THERE BE LIGHT. . . ."—*GENESIS 1:3*

THE SACRAMENT OF LIGHT

In that far-off dim dawn,
When chaos reigned, and earth was still
A formless void in darkness dight,
The Spirit, brooding o'er the deep,
Awoke Creation from its sleep
With the High Call—
"Let—There—Be—Light!"
And instant from the tomb of night
Sprang forth the mystic seven-fold beam,
Ablaze with splendours bright.
God, in His Wisdom all supreme,
As His first act made—Light.

So, unto Him give praise!
Praise without ceasing! Praise!—
That in His Wisdom Infinite,
When making Man for His delight,
Before He dowered him with sight,
He filled the world with radiance bright,
Lest, dulled with fear and void of hope,
With stumbling footsteps he should grope,
Through an eternal night.
To God eternal praise!
Praise without ceasing! Praise!—
That in His Goodness Infinite
He blessed the world with Light.
Subserve it to His high employ
And see thou use it right!*

—*John Oxenham*

✠

* From *Sacraments* by John Oxenham. Copyright, 1928, by Pilgrim Press, Boston, Mass. Used by special permission of Miss Erica Oxenham.

THE OLD TESTAMENT
AND THE FINE ARTS

AN ANTHOLOGY OF
PICTURES, POETRY, MUSIC, AND STORIES
COVERING
THE OLD TESTAMENT

by

CYNTHIA PEARL MAUS

Fully Illustrated

1817

HARPER & ROW, PUBLISHERS
New York, Hagerstown, San Francisco, London

DEDICATED TO
MISSIONARY AND RELIGIOUS LEADERS
OF THE CHURCH ECUMENICAL THAT IN
ALL LANDS ARE GIVING THEIR LIVES
TO THE EDUCATION OF PEOPLE OF ALL
RACES, AGES, CLASSES, AND CULTURES
IN CHRISTIAN HISTORY AND
TRADITIONS

✢

THE OLD TESTAMENT AND THE FINE ARTS. Copyright © 1954 by Cynthia Pearl Maus. All rights reserved. Printed in the United States of America. For information address Harper & Row, Publishers, Inc., 10 East 53rd Street, New York, N.Y. 10022. Published simultaneously in Canada by Fitzhenry & Whiteside Limited, Toronto.

First Harper & Row paperback edition published in 1977.

Library of Congress Catalog card number: 54-8970
ISBN: 0-06-065511-9
77 78 79 80 81 10 9 8 7 6 5 4 3 2 1

CONTENTS

A detailed contents page will be found preceding each of the several sections listed below

INTRODUCTION

✣

THE research and compilation of this anthology on *The Old Testament and the Fine Arts* has been a challenging and worth-while experience. My restudy of the Old Testament from the fourfold viewpoint of great stories, great music, great poetry, and great art has been compensating indeed, because that portion of the Bible which we call the Old Testament dates back in its history and traditions to the beginning of human history among the Semitic peoples.

The Bible is a collection of sixty-six books, thirty-nine of which constitute the Old Testament, and twenty-seven the New. Biblical scholars almost universally agree that the Old Testament, except for a few portions written in Aramaic, was originally written in Hebrew. Since printing was not invented until A.D. 1454, the Old Testament in its original form was quite different from present-day editions of the Bible.

To many people the retention of the Old Testament is a stumbling-block, and they ask why we continue to read it? If anyone has the patience to read the whole of this book he will, it is hoped, realize that the O.T. is indispensable. We content ourselves here with giving a few reasons. First, the New Testament is often incomprehensible without a knowledge of the Old, or at least a great deal of its meaning is lost. Secondly, the Christian Church has arisen out of the Israel of the O.T. by a normal process of growth —a study of the Sacraments will show that even these, generally considered to be distinctly Christian. have a Jewish basis—you would not expect the biography of some great hero to omit his childhood. Thirdly, the New Testament by itself is not complete; many things were said so well in the O.T. that they did not need to be said again. Fourthly, in the prophets and the psalmists we have the classic presentation of the soul's meeting with God, rendered all the more striking when we realize that they had only the dimmest conception, if any at all, of a life after death.*

No one knows exactly when the first collection of sacred writings was made. One of the earliest references to the Books of the Law is to be found in Deuteronomy 28:58-61. While Joshua 8:32 indicates that "he wrote there upon the stones a copy of the law of Moses . . . in the presence of the children of Israel."

These early transcripts of the law of Moses were not written in Latin or Greek or English as they are today. From comparatively recent discoveries made by famous archaeologists among the ruins of ancient Assyria, we know that the history of primitive peoples was written on tablets of baked clay before the time when Abraham left Ur of the Chaldees for the country which we now call Palestine. Scholars,

---

* Adapted from *Concise Bible Commentary* by W. K. Lowther Clarke, pp. 1-2, Introduction. Copyright, 1953, by The Macmillan Company. Used by special permission of the publisher.

therefore, believe that the earliest writings of the Old Testament were written on tablets of baked clay and preserved to us in that way.

The Hebrew language is but a branch of the great Semitic family of languages spoken by the people of Arabia, Babylonia, Syria, and Mesopotamia. These early writings were probably in cuneiform, wedge-shaped characters, that were widely known and used throughout the ancient empires of Babylonia, Egypt, and Mesopotamia.

Tablets discovered in Egypt in A.D. 1887 contributed greatly to the modern world's understanding of these early sacred writings, because these wedge-shaped cuneiform characters date back to the days of Joshua. The Bible in ancient times consisted only of the first five books of the Old Testament, which we often hear called the Pentateuch. These five books have always been regarded as the Hebrew Bible and are held sacred by the Jewish people. To the Pentateuch were later added the historical books, the messages of the prophets, the poetic writings, several stories such as Job, Ruth, Esther, and Daniel, and the Books of Lamentations, Ecclesiastes, and the Chronicles.

Through the centuries Egypt has played a vital part in Jewish history; and it was in Egypt that use was first made of papyrus rolls. The fibers of the papyrus plant, grown in the region of the Nile, were laid in two layers running horizontally and perpendicularly. These layers after being treated with glue were pressed into sheets, and these sheets were attached together in the form of a roll or scroll.

Isaiah 8:1 indicates that the Lord spoke to Isaiah saying: "Take thee a great roll and write upon it"; and Jeremiah 36:2 says the word of the Lord came unto Jeremiah saying :"Take thee a roll of a book, and write therein all the words that I have spoken unto thee." We do not know definitely whether or not these rolls were made from papyrus, or the prepared skins of sheep or goats. It is possible that both methods and materials were used.

These rolls or scrolls were made up with a stick at each end, and could be unrolled from one end and rolled around the other end as the reading continued. It was in this form that the sacred Scriptures came into common usage in the days of Joshua and the Judges. This form continued to about the end of the third century after the birth of Jesus, so that scrolls or rolls of Sacred Writings were the form that Jesus Himself was familiar with when He read from the Law and the Prophets in the presence of the people.

In about the third century after the birth of Christ vellum or parchment for manuscripts became general throughout the region of the eastern Mediterranean. This vellum, made from the skins of sheep, goats, and other animals, was found to be more lasting than the Egyptian papyrus.

No one can tell when all the books of the Old Testament were written. Scholars generally agree, however, that the structure of that portion of the Bible which we call the Old Testament dates back to somewhere between the tenth and the second centuries B.C. In its present form the date given by most Modern Biblical scholars is 160 B.C.

A word needs to be said in this Introduction about the geography of Palestine.

This little country, not much larger than Wales or the State of Vermont, is geographically a microcosm—a world in miniature—for its climatic variations are those we should expect to find in a continent. Unlike other religions, Judaism and Christianity are rooted in history, which, in its turn, cannot be dissociated from geography, and the uniqueness of the land has a bearing on the part it has played in the development of mankind . . . for Palestine lay at the centre of the ancient world, between the sea and the desert; it formed a bridge joining the great civilizations of Egypt and Mesopotamia. South of Mt. Carmel there were no natural harbours so that the Hebrews had no reason to essay a seafaring life. . . . Though close to the centres of civilization, they could generally, if they wished, keep out of international politics, for the route connecting the great Powers ran through the Maritime Plain, and remaining in their hills, they could avoid being involved in wars, if they were wise. They were sufficiently in touch with the great world to be influenced by it, sufficiently detached to develop along their own lines during the centuries that formed their national character.*

For the purpose of aiding your understanding of the unique geography of Palestine in relation to the great world powers of ancient days *two maps*** are included in this anthology: one showing the Two Kingdoms, Judah and Israel (page 404); and one showing the extent of the Babylonian Empire in the time of Nebuchadnezzar (page 620). You will find these maps helpful in relation to the stories and art interpretations contained in this resource volume.

This anthology is dedicated to that host of missionaries and religious leaders of the Church ecumenical that in all lands are giving their lives to the education of people of all races, ages, classes, and cultures the world around in Christian history and traditions.

There are six major Parts in this anthology on *The Old Testament and the Fine Arts,* and each Part has from two to four Sections. In order to make this volume readily usable in planning worship services, devotional and special-day programs as well as for Church-school, Weekday and Vacation Church-school teaching periods, a general Table of Contents is provided just preceding the Introduction giving the page numbers of the following items: Introduction, Parts and Sections, Appendix article on "Origin and Content of the Old Testament," four Indexes, and Acknowledgments.

Then each separate Section begins with a Table of Contents listing the page number of each and every art interpretation, poem, story, and musical composition included in that Section, thus providing a comprehensive resource volume on Old Testament history and traditions from the viewpoint of the four major *fine arts* that is readily accessible in program building.

The Appendix (p. 801) contains an article on "Origin and Content of the Old Testament" which I hope you will take the time to read, that you may be fully informed concerning the structure and content of the thirty-nine books which we call the Old Testament. Your intelligent use of the materials in this volume will be greatly enhanced by giving time to a careful perusal of this article from the pen of Professor Robert H. Pfeiffer of Harvard University.

Among the sixty-three stories contained in this anthology, you will find four by outstanding English authors:

* *Ibid.,* p. 28.
** *Idem.*

"Moses, the Leader of a People," by Sir Winston S. Churchill.

"Abraham and Isaac," by Warwick Deeping, one of England's great contemporary writers who passed away during the time when the author-compiler of this volume was clearing copyright permissions.

"Joseph, the Poor Boy Who Saved His Country," by Lord Dunsany.

"David, the Hero with the Feet of Clay" (in two parts), by Sir Philip Gibbs.

Two hundred and forty-four poems find their place in this resource volume, several by contemporary American poets who composed, each of them, two or more poems especially for inclusion in this anthology on their favorite character, theme, or historical event in the Old Testament: The late Thomas Curtis Clark wrote several on the Old Testament prophets. The late William L. Stidger spent some time during his Easter vacation in 1949 to write and contribute three original poems. Grace Noll Crowell, Leslie Savage Clark, Madeleine S. Miller, Lola Echard, Ruth Ricklefs and others have contributed original poems to the enrichment of this anthology.

Among the original musical compositions are four hymns by William L. Stidger. A number of Jewish canticles and hymns emphasizing Old Testament events with accompanying music score are included. Several Negro spirituals stressing Old Testament history and traditions are also included in this third volume in the trilogy of anthologies: *Christ and the Fine Arts* (1938), *The World's Great Madonnas* (1947) and *The Old Testament and the Fine Arts* (1954), which the author has compiled during the past twenty years for the enrichment of the religious education program of the Church ecumenical.

One hundred full-page reproductions of great masterpieces of religious art are included with their interpretations covering the entire Old Testament from Creation's story in Genesis to the return of a remnant to Jerusalem, the uprising of the Maccabees, the work of the scribes in copying the fragmentary documents of the Old Testament, and the awaiting of the coming of the Messiah in which every devout Jew believed.

Whenever possible in the use of the materials in this anthology, couple with the art interpretations visual, eye-gate reproductions of the *one hundred* pictures contained in this volume. Both kodachrome slides and film strip are now available on the art in this volume through Miss Ruth Lister, Department of Visual Education, Oberlin-Schauffler College, Oberlin, Ohio. Link with the oral interpretations of these great masterpieces of art not only the visual presentation of the picture, but, whenever possible, either vocal or instrumental music of some of the great hymns, canticles, and spirituals included herein which suggest the same message to human hearts.

It is not important that the interpreter of the music, picture, or poem shall be *seen.* It is much more important that he shall be *heard,* and that he shall infuse into his oral interpretation of the hymn, poem, story, or picture such an appreciation of its message as will make it *live* in the minds and hearts of all who see the masterpiece or hear the interpretation that is being given. Remember that many a devotional service, special-day program, Sunday or Weekday lesson, or for that matter Women's Club program has been redeemed from mediocrity through the intelligent use of great pictures, great stories, great poetry, and great music artistically interpreted.

The author sends out this, her eighth book, in the hope that it will make a permanent and abiding contribution to the enrichment of Church and Church-school literature, as well as to the Biblical departments of church colleges and universities and to public libraries.

God, in the beginning, said: "Let there be light, and there was *light*." And John Oxenham in his poem "The Sacrament of Light," says:

> God, in His Wisdom all supreme,
> As His first act made—Light!
>
> . . .
>
> Subserve it to His high employ
> And see thou use it right!

Cynthia Pearl Maus

Long Beach, California

PART I

HIGH LIGHTS OF THE PENTATEUCH

CONTENTS

PART I SECTION 1

OLD TESTAMENT BEGINNINGS

✛

In the beginning God created the heaven and the earth. . . . So God created man in his own image, in the image of God created he him; male and female created he them. GENESIS 1:1, 27

✛

Music:

THE OLD TESTAMENT

Artist Unknown

FRONTISPIECE

(Interpretation)

THE story of Creation is told in the first chapter of Genesis. No one knows who the author may have been—it was once thought to have been Moses—nor when or where the story was first written.

No attempt is made to explain the process of Creation. Instead, the narrative is a simple, terse, and dramatic recital of the acts of Creation. It begins with the simple sentence, "In the beginning God created the heaven and the earth." Thus the creative process occurred "in the beginning," whenever and wherever that may have been; and God is the Creator.

"And the earth was without form, and void; and darkness was upon the face of the deep. And the spirit of God moved upon the face of the waters." As one looks at this frontispiece, "The Old Testament," one can almost see the first trembling movement of the waters. "And God said, 'Let there be light': and there was light." Again one studies the picture and sees the first glistening, gleaming sheen of light upon the face of the waters.

"And God saw the light, that it was good: and God divided the light from the darkness." The picture shows the clouds gathering in the heavens above. "And God called the light Day, and the darkness he called Night. And the evening and the morning were the first day.

"And God said, 'Let there be a firmament in the midst of the waters, and let it divide the waters from the waters.'

"And God made the firmament, and divided the waters which were under the firmament from the waters which were above the firmament: and it was so.

"And God called the firmament Heaven. And the evening and the morning were the second day.

"And God said, 'Let the waters under the heaven be gathered together unto one place, and let the dry land appear': and it was so.

"And God called the dry land Earth; and the gathering together of the waters called he Seas: and God saw that it was good.

"And God said, 'Let the earth bring forth grass, the herb yielding seed, and the fruit tree yielding fruit after his kind, whose seed is in itself, upon the earth': and it was so . . . and God saw that it was good.

"And the evening and the morning were the third day.

"And God said, 'Let there be lights in the firmament of the heaven to divide the day from the night; and let them be for signs, and for seasons, and for days, and years: and let them be for lights in the firmament of the heaven to give light upon the earth': and it was so. And God made two great lights; the greater light to rule the day, and the lesser light [the Moon] to rule the night: he made the stars also. And God set them in the firmament of the heaven to give light upon the earth, and to rule over the day and over the night, and to divide the light from the darkness: and God saw that it was good. And the evening and the morning were the fourth day."

Read again the entire first chapter of Genesis and then as you look at this frontispiece imagine that you are watching God in the actual work of Creation. *Light* will then have new meaning for you. Now read John Oxenham's poem "The Sacrament of Light" (page ii) and you will feel your own responsibility to use *light,* not only physical, but also spiritual, as the gift from the hand of God to the children of men. You will develop a new appreciation both for *light* and for *darkness,* which provides relaxation for tired minds and hearts in preparation for each new day.

All things were made by the hand of God; and all of them are His gifts to earth's children. You too were created in the image of God, and endowed with His spiritual capacities *to create,* to bring to pass a "new heaven and a new earth" which will reflect the mind and heart and soul of its Creator, God. This is the message of the frontispiece, "The Old Testament."

✣

GOD DIVIDING THE LAND FROM THE SEA

By

Raphael Sanzio

(Interpretation)

RAPHAEL was born in the city of Urbino, Italy, on Good Friday, 1483. Giovanni Sanzio, his father, was a painter who was held in high esteem in his native city. Raphael's mother, Magia, passed away when he was only eight years old, but his father's second wife, Bernardina, supplied his mother's place and loved and cared for young Raphael as if he had been her own son.

His father was his first art instructor, but he died when Raphael was only eleven years old. The name of his second teacher is not known. However, when Raphael was sixteen, he was sent to study under Perugino, with whom he remained until he was twenty years old.

In 1504 Raphael visited Florence for the first time. He did not remain long, but he did see and study the works of such notable artists as Masaccio, Masolino, Signorelli, and Fra Bartolommeo. He also saw for the first time some full-size designs for paintings by Leonardo da Vinci and Michelangelo. These cartoons filled his mind with new and bold ideas of form and composition.

Raphael was the greatest master of the art of composition in the modern world. He saw all things in their proper relation, sometimes even forgetting detail in his passion to arrange a striking ensemble. *Masters of Art,* published in December, 1900, commented on Raphael's style as follows: "His excellency lay in the propriety, beauty, and majesty of his characters, in the judicious contrivance of his composition, his correctness of drawing, purity of taste, and skillful accommodation of other men's conceptions to his own purpose." He was endowed with a visual imagination which has never been surpassed for range, sweep, and variety.

GOD DIVIDING THE LAND FROM THE SEA—*RAPHAEL*

This range, sweep, and variety is easily apparent in his painting of "God Dividing the Land from the Sea," which appears in the first arcade of the Loggie in the Vatican. It was completed some time between 1517 and 1519 by Raphael's students from designs made by the master artist himself.

In it the majestic form of the creator God, gowned in a robe of coral red with a scarf of royal blue, may be seen flying low above the curve of the earth's surface tracing with His finger the shore line between land and sea. In the distance stands a grove of shapely trees. The left hand of this mighty Creator is outstretched in a gesture indicating that the beauty of the grass-covered meadows and the comforting shade of the leafy trees was created for men.

Behind and above this majestic form of the Eternal God in the act of dividing the land from the sea is the cerulean sky the lower portion of which is delicately tinted with the first streaks of the morning's dawn.

As one gazes at this majestic painting one can almost hear the voice of God saying: " 'Let the waters under the heaven be gathered together unto one place, and let the dry land appear': and it was so. And God called the dry land Earth; and the gathering together of the waters called he Seas: and God saw that it was good" (Gen. 1:9-10).

Raphael's gifts as an artist were different from those of Leonardo da Vinci or Michelangelo. He did not have the delicacy of Leonardo nor the strength of Michelangelo. But he was a very great illustrator with an unequaled ability to fill space. He brought all parts of a picture into harmonious relationship with the whole composition. His great personal charm, which so impressed his friends, still radiates from his pictures.

His very success and the great demand for his work had unfortunate consequences. So much of his time was spent in superintending the work of hordes of younger artists attached to his studio that, as a result, his own creative genius suffered.

Raphael's untimely death occurred on his thirty-seventh birthday, Good Friday, April 6, 1520. From his home near St. Peter's in Rome multitudes from all walks of life followed his bier in sad procession to the church of the Pantheon for burial in a spot that the artist himself had chosen during his lifetime. Though the world lost one of its greatest painters, he left to posterity several sublime masterpieces that are numbered among the world's Twelve Great Paintings.

✛

THE CREATION OF MAN

By

Michelangelo Buonarroti

(Interpretation)

MICHELANGELO Buonarroti was born in Caprese, Italy, March 6, 1475. His father, Ludovico Buonarroti, a respected merchant citizen of Florence for many years, was chief magistrate of Caprese at the time Michelangelo was born. His mother died

THE CREATION OF MAN—MICHELANGELO

when the lad was only six years old, and at thirteen years of age his father, much against his own desire, followed the advice of Michelangelo's schoolmaster and apprenticed him for three years to the brothers David and Domenico Ghirlandajo to learn the art of painting. For the first time in his life Michelangelo was permitted to follow his only interest, art; and the world has been immeasurably enriched as a result.

Michelangelo was already a famous sculptor when the pope commissioned him to decorate the ceiling of the Sistine Chapel in Rome. The great frescoes he painted there demonstrate the stupendous scope and power of this artist's genius. The ceiling covers an area of 10,000 square feet and this Michelangelo decorated with his mighty scenes of the Creation, the Fall of Man, and the Flood. These are to painting what Dante's *Divine Comedy* is to poetry. In conception, imagination, and design the ceiling of the Sistine Chapel is worthy to stand beside the great story of Creation in Genesis itself.

During more than four years Michelangelo lived with the absorbing theme of the Creation and into its portrayal he poured his deepest understanding of life. He was primarily a sculptor for whom there was no beauty so great as that of the human figure. He did not have Leonardo's joy in beautiful things nor Raphael's delight in colors. He subordinated decoration and color to a masterful portrayal of the human figure. To this he succeeded in giving endlessly varied movements and the impression of almost living power.

In "The Creation of Man" from the Sistine Chapel this great artist portrays God in the act of endowing man with life. The figure of God and His attendant spirits form a group that seems alive, so full is it of vigorous movement. The focus of action lies in the hands. The hand of God is charged with life. Adam's hand hangs helpless but full of latent power. The magnificent figure of Adam as he lies on the ground unable to rise until God shall touch him combines helplessness with a promise of immense energy. The earth from which his body was formed still holds him. At the same time he feels an upward pull of his soul's aspiration toward the Divine Spirit in whose image he is made. He gazes in wonder and gratitude at his Creator who is about to give him the gift of life by which he will become a "living soul."

✛

EXPULSION OF ADAM AND EVE FROM THE GARDEN

Artist Unknown

(Interpretation)

THIS picture shows a tapestry in the Antique and Modern Gallery in the city of Florence, Italy. The name of the artist who designed this remarkable piece of woven art has been lost.

The meaning of the tapestry, however, is clear. Adam and Eve are being driven from the garden of Eden by God because of their greed, their attempted deception of Him, and their disobedience of His commands.

EXPULSION OF ADAM AND EVE FROM THE GARDEN—*ARTIST UNKNOWN*

They had been given the right to eat the fruit of all the trees in the garden of Eden except the tree in the center of it. This they had been told by their Heavenly Father they must not eat, nor even touch. Now Satan, in the form of a serpent, said to Eve, "Ye shall not surely die: for God doth know that in the day ye eat thereof, then your eyes shall be opened, and ye shall be as gods, knowing good and evil" (Gen. 3:4-5).

That bit of information was too much for Eve's inquisitive nature. The fruit on that forbidden tree did look more tempting than any other fruit in the garden. It was a delight to the eyes; it was good for food; and it was especially desirable because it would make her "wise." But Eve was soon to discover that the knowledge offered to her was not what she expected and that it did not make her either happy or blessed.

On the subtle suggestion of the serpent Eve ate and gave her husband also of the fruit and he ate; and their eyes were opened, and they knew, for the first time, that they were naked and they were ashamed of their nudity. They knew now the difference between good and evil. In shame and humiliation they sewed fig leaves together to make aprons to cover their nakedness.

In the cool of the evening God called to Adam and said: "Where art thou?"; and Adam replied: "I heard thy voice in the garden, and I was afraid, because I was naked; and I hid myself."

Then God knew that they had partaken of the tree of knowledge of good and evil, and he said to Adam: "Who told thee that thou wast naked? Hast thou eaten of the tree, whereof I commanded thee that thou shouldest not eat?"

Then Adam blamed Eve, saying: "The woman whom thou gavest to be with me, she gave me of the tree, and I did eat." Eve, when God called to her for an explanation, laid the blame on the serpent saying: "The serpent beguiled me, and I did eat." (Placing the blame for one's wrongdoing on someone else is as old as the garden of Eden.)

So God said to the serpent: "Because thou hast done this, thou art cursed above all cattle, and above every beast of the field; upon thy belly shalt thou go, and dust shalt thou eat all the days of thy life: and I will put enmity between thee and the woman, and between thy seed and her seed; it shall bruise thy head, and thou shalt bruise his heel" (Gen. 3:14-15).

Then the Lord turned to Eve and said: "I will greatly multiply thy sorrow and thy conception; in sorrow thou shalt bring forth children; and thy desire shall be to thy husband, and he shall rule over thee" (3:16).

To Adam the Lord God said: "Because thou hast hearkened unto the voice of thy wife, and hast eaten of the tree, of which I commanded thee, saying, 'Thou shalt not eat of it': cursed is the ground for thy sake; in sorrow shalt thou eat of it all the days of thy life; thorns also and thistles shall it bring forth to thee; and thou shalt eat the herb of the field; in the sweat of thy face shalt thou eat bread, till thou return unto the ground; for out of it wast thou taken: for dust thou art, and unto dust shalt thou return" (3:17-19).

Then the Lord made for Adam and Eve coats of skins and clothed them. And because they had violated the law for residence in the spiritual realm of the guiltless,

He sent them forth from the garden of Eden to till the ground from which they had had been formed.

In the foreground of this tapestry are Adam and Eve. In a tree sits a wise old owl, while a monkey following them seems to jabber: "I told you so." Above them in a robe of red patterned in gold with a fold floating over His head is the figure of God. One hand seems almost to push the disobedient pair from the garden of Eden while the other hand points toward the winged cherub with his flaming sword who henceforth is to guard the way to the tree of life.

✛

THE BUILDING OF THE ARK

By

Raphael Sanzio

(Interpretation)

IN 1508 Raphael Sanzio, at the request of Pope Julius II, became a citizen of Rome and took up his residence in that city, the most beautiful and brilliant city in the civilized world. Although he was then only twenty-five years of age, his ability and great personal charm won for him a place with such renowned masters of art as Sodoma, Perugino, Pinturicchio, Bramantino, and Michelangelo. Indeed, he soon became the leader and foremost painter of the Renaissance.

"The Building of the Ark" occupies a place in the third arcade in the Raphael Loggie in the Vatican in Rome, along with three others, "The Deluge," "The Coming Forth from the Ark," and "Noah's Sacrifice." All of these paintings in the Loggie, sometimes referred to as Raphael's Bible, were painted from designs made by the master artist himself, although many of them were completed by student artists attached to his staff.

The picture portrays the aged Noah supervising the building of the ark according to the meticulous specifications given to him by the Lord. For God had said to Noah: "Make thee an ark of gopher wood; rooms shalt thou make in the ark, and shalt pitch it within and without with pitch. And this is the fashion which thou shalt make it of: The length of the ark shall be three hundred cubits, the breadth of it fifty cubits, and the height of it thirty cubits. A window shalt thou make to the ark, and in a cubit shalt thou finish it above; and the door of the ark shalt thou set in the side thereof; with lower, second, and third stories shalt thou make it" (Gen. 6:14-16).

Noah, a righteous man of faith, took the Lord at His word. Notwithstanding the scoffing and jeers of many of his neighbors, he built the ark as God had commanded him. Later events were to prove the wisdom of his strict obedience.

The hull of the ark dominates the picture. Laborers with saw and ax trim and fit the great timbers of gopher wood that are to be used in its completion. With his robes clutched in one hand, Noah stands with his other hand outstretched toward the powerful form of a laborer in the act of sawing a giant beam.

In the background mountains may be seen, with trees growing down their slopes and in the valley, while in the foreground chips of gopher wood lie scattered. The men work diligently that each beam may fit snugly into the place it is to occupy. In the concentration of the workmen on their task and their great exertions to accomplish it one can sense the need for haste to complete the ark before the rains descend.

Read again the Bible story of Noah's building of the ark in Genesis 6:13 through the seventh, eighth and ninth chapters. Recall the beautiful covenant which the Lord made with Noah and his sons when the frightening ordeal of the Deluge was over: "I do set my bow in the cloud, and it shall be for a token of a covenant between me and the earth. And it shall come to pass, when I bring a cloud over the earth, that the bow shall be seen in the cloud: and I will remember my covenant, which is between me and you and every living creature of all flesh; and the waters shall no more become a flood to destroy all flesh" (Gen. 9:13-15).

When we see God's rainbow in the sky, we are reminded of this eternal covenant between God and man, and rejoice in the feeling of security it brings.

✛

A SCENE AFTER THE DELUGE

By

Giuseppe Palizzi

(Interpretation)

THIS painting portrays the jagged summit of the mountains of Ararat on which Noah's ark alighted after the one-hundred-and-fifty-day Deluge which God sent to destroy wickedness from the earth. The rain having at last ceased, on the seventeenth day of the seventh month the ark rested on the top of the mountains. By the end of the tenth month the waters had sufficiently abated so that the tops of this range could be seen clearly.

Even then Noah waited forty days more before he released the first raven that flew to and fro in search of tree tops upon which it might alight. Later a dove was sent forth, but she could find no resting place for her foot, and returned to the ark where Noah took her in and cared for her. Noah and his family remained seven more days in the ark before the dove was again sent forth. This time she returned at eventide with an olive leaf in her beak, so Noah knew that the waters had subsided from the earth.

Nevertheless, he and his family and the host of animals in the ark remained yet another seven days, and this time when he sent out the dove, she did not return, and Noah knew that the earth was sufficiently dry for the dove to take care of herself.

Then Noah opened wide the door of the ark and looked upon the face of the earth, and he could see that the ground was dry. Then, as commanded by the Lord, he and his family and his sons' families went forth from the ark to build a new and a better world in which righteousness and justice might prevail. All the animals

THE BUILDING OF THE ARK—*RAPHAEL*

were released; and in Giuseppe Palizzi's portrayal of this scene after the Deluge we can see them, birds, beasts of prey, and work animals, all stretching their legs and learning again to accommodate themselves to the earth as their permanent home.

In distant mountain crevices the blue haze of vanishing clouds may be seen, and in the foreground there are great trunks of trees that had fallen during the prolonged Deluge. Some trees are still standing, and in these birds have alighted that they may take a look at the surrounding peaks. Flocks of birds have already taken flight in the blue sky and soar away to distant trees on faraway mountaintops. Soon they, too, will begin the mating and nesting season of new homes and a new life. Some hover about and above the ark, that for so long a time has been their crowded home, as if loath to leave its assured safety.

Near the ark can be seen the smoke of Noah's sacrifice arising toward the heavens, as he and his family give thanks to God for His protecting care during the long period of the Deluge.

The original of this great painting by Giuseppe Palizzi will be found in the Palazzo Reale di Capodimenta in Naples, Italy. There it is a graphic picture of the fruit of sin and greed, as well as of God's protecting care of the just and righteous men of the earth who, in every generation, give themselves to the building of a god-like civilization.

✛

THE TOWER OF BABEL

By

Jan Brueghel

(Interpretation)

THE Tower of Babel was a favorite subject with both French and Flemish painters of the fifteenth and sixteenth centuries. Many of the contemporaries of Pieter Brueghel, the Elder, or Peasant Brueghel, as he was sometimes called, as well as some of his followers portrayed this story. Among them was his son, the Flemish painter Jan Brueghel (1568-1625).

The story is found in the eleventh chapter of Genesis (1-9) and follows immediately the listing of the posterity of Noah. At that time, according to the Scriptures, "the whole earth was of one language, and of one speech" (11:1). After the Deluge the descendants of Noah journeyed eastward toward a plain in the land of Shinar, and there they dwelt.

No sooner had they become permanently settled in this new land than one of them suggested that they make bricks and burn them thoroughly. Then using burned brick for stone and bitumen for mortar they conceived the idea of building, not only a city, but a tower whose top was to reach the heavens. Thus they planned to make an enduring name for themselves.

However, when the Lord came down to see the city and the tower whose summit was to reach the sky, he said: "Behold, the people is one, and they have all one lan-

A SCENE AFTER THE DELUGE—*PALIZZI*

guage; and this they begin to do: and now nothing will be restrained from them, which they have imagined to do" (11:6).

So He decided that the best way to stop them was to "confound their language," so that they could not understand one another's speech. Then He scattered them abroad from that time forward over all the face of the earth; and of course, since they could not now understand one another, they ceased building the city and the Tower of Babel.

In Jan Brueghel's "The Tower of Babel" there is a picturesque landscape with rugged mountain peaks in the background, and the blue, blue waters of a river almost entirely surround the tower. The summit of the tower appears higher than the mountains and is lost in vapory clouds.

The buildings of the city itself may be seen in the foreground, on various levels of the tower, and in the middle distance. Small boats dot the shore line or are rowed down the stream. Men with vehicles are going about their daily tasks. Laden donkeys and camels are led through the streets. On the right there is a balcony and from it a crowned ruler raises his scepter as a scroll of dedication is unfurled before him. Near by stands his horse which he will later ride to his home.

Whether or not we consider the story of the Tower of Babel as fact or fiction, no one can deny man's compelling desire to build towers to the sky, or his soul's longing for the starry firmament. Upon these two powerful urges the progress of civilization depends.

✣

"AND GOD MOVED UPON THE FACE OF THE WATERS"

What beauty earth received, what majesty
Of plunging comber, tide and undertow,
And flying spume—when God created sea!
He made the Arctic berg, the drifting floe
Beneath the phantom flare of Northern Lights,
The dark and icy depths that lie below.
He made the coral sand and wave which writes
Its signature in foam, the calm lagoon,
And phosphorescent fish of tropic nights.
He found them good, His works,—with beaches strewn
With fluted shell, and sky with gull's soft breast
Or wings of frigate bird against the moon.
And yet, of all the seas in East and West
Did God, perhaps, love Galilee the best?*

—*Leslie Savage Clark*

* Used by special permission of the author.

THE TOWER OF BABEL—*BRUEGHEL*

A FOREST HYMN

The groves were God's first temples. Ere man learned
To hew the shaft, and lay the architrave,
And spread the roof above them; ere he framed
The lofty vault, to gather and roll back
The sound of anthems;—in the darkling wood,
Amid the cool and silence, he knelt down,
And offered to the Mightiest solemn thanks
And supplication. For his simple heart
Might not resist the sacred influences
Which, from the stilly twilight of the place,
And from the gray old trunks that high in heaven
Mingled their mossy boughs, and from the sound
Of the invisible breath that swayed at once
All their green tops, stole over him, and bowed
His spirit with the thought of boundless power
And inaccessible majesty. Ah, why
Should we, in the world's riper years, neglect
God's ancient sanctuaries, and adore
Only among the crowd, and under roofs
That our frail hands have raised? Let me, at least,
Here, in the shadow of this ancient wood,
Offer one hymn,—thrice happy, if it find
Acceptance in His ear.

—William Cullen Bryant

A PERFECT WORLD

The perfect world by Adam trod
Was the first temple built by God;
His fiat laid the corner-stone,
And heaved its pillars, one by one.
He hung its starry roof on high,—
The broad, illimitable sky;
He spread its pavement, green and bright,
And curtained it with morning light.
The mountains in their places stood,
The sea, the sky, and "all was good";
And when its first pure praises rang,
The "morning stars together sang."

—N. P. Willis

EARTH'S STORY

With primal void and cosmic night
Love had its way, and there was light.

A flaming waste, through aeons long
Took form, and chaos turned to song.

The sun embraced the virgin earth
And warmed the leafy plants to birth.

Slow ages passed, and patient time
Brought creeping reptiles from the slime.

Through vasty waters fishes sped,
In torrid jungles beasts were bred.

Then Beauty filled the land with flowers,
And lo! birds thronged the forest bowers.

Love yearned for answering love—the voice
Of thinking Man made God rejoice.

Then all the stars began to sing
As conscious Nature crowned its King.*

—Thomas Curtis Clark

GOD'S AUTOGRAPH

I stood upon a hill one night
And saw the great Creator write
His autograph across the sky
In lightning strokes, and there was I
To witness this magnificent
Tumultuous, Divine event!

I stood one morning by a stream
When night was fading to a dream.
The fields were bright as fields may be
At spring, in golden mystery
Of buttercups—then God came on
And wrote His autograph in dawn.

One afternoon long years ago,
Where glacial tides had ebb and flow,
I found a cliff which God had smitten;
I scanned its breast, where He had written
With some great glacier for a pen
His signature for time and men.

One night I stood and watched the stars;
The Milky Way and ranging Mars,

* From *1000 Quotable Poems* compiled by Thomas Curtis Clark, pp. 231-232. Copyright, 1937, by Harper & Brothers. Used by special permission of the author.

Where God in letters tipped with fire
The story of His tall desire
Had writ in rhyme and signed His name
A stellar signature of flame.

Creation's Dawn was deep in night,
When suddenly: "Let there be light!"
Awakened grass, and flower, and tree,
Chaotic skies, the earth, and sea;
Then, to complete creation's span
In His own image, God made man,
And signed His name, with stroke most sure—
Man is God's greatest signature!*

—*William L. Stidger*

GOD CREATED MAN

And God created man in his own image, in the image of God created he him; male and female created he them.—GENESIS 1:27

No chance hath brought this ill to me;
'Tis God's own hand, so let it be,
He seeth what I cannot see.
There is a need-be for each pain,
And He one day will make it plain
That earthly loss is heavenly gain.
Like as a piece of tapestry
Viewed from the back appears to be
Naught but threads tangled hopelessly;
But in the front a picture fair
Rewards the worker for his care,
Proving his skill and patience rare.
Thou art the Workman, I the frame.
Lord, for the glory of Thy name,
Perfect Thine image on the same.

—*Author Unknown*

THE HEAVENS DECLARE THE GLORY

Stars swing like censers slowly through the sky,
And from the lofty dome hangs down the chain
That sways the sun, where man can lift again
His prayerful hope illimitably high.
In whose great transepts he can glorify
His own compassion and reflected pain,
And in that sacred worshiping attain
An answer to his catechetic cry.

* From *I Saw God Wash the World* by William L. Stidger, p. 12. Published by the Rodeheaver Hall-Mack Co. Copyright, 1934, by William L. Stidger. Used by special permission of the author.

Forever building faith from what he knows
In his own heart, he opens secret gates
To the unknown; striving to guard, to nurse
The infinite idea he slowly grows
Into the very substance he creates,
And gains a foothold in the universe.*

—*Sara King Carleton*

I SAW GOD WASH THE WORLD

I saw God wash the world last night
   With His sweet showers on high;
And then when morning came
   I saw Him hang it out to dry.

He washed each slender blade of grass
   And every trembling tree;
He flung his showers against the hills
   And swept the rolling sea.

The white rose is a deeper white;
   The red, a richer red
Since God washed every fragrant face
   And put them all to bed.

There's not a bird, there's not a bee
   That wings along the way,
But is a cleaner bird and bee
   Than it was yesterday.

I saw God wash the world last night;
   Ah, would He had washed me
As clean of all my dust and dirt,
   As that old white birch tree!**

—*William L. Stidger*

IN THE VASTNESS, A GOD

Deathless, though godheads be dying,
   Surviving the creeds that expire,
Illogical, reason defying,
   Lives that passionate, primal desire;
Insistent, persistent, forever
   Man cries to the silence, "Never
Shall Death reign the Lord of the soul,
   Shall the dust be the ultimate goal—

*From *Poems for Life* compiled by Thomas Curtis Clark, p. 5. Copyright, 1941, by Harper & Brothers. Used by special permission of the author and the publisher.

** From *I Saw God Wash the World* by William L. Stidger, p. 11. Published by the Rodeheaver Hall-Mack Co. Copyright, 1934, by William L. Stidger. Used by special permission of the author.

I will storm the black bastions of Night,
    I will tread where my vision has trod,
I will set in the darkness a light,
    In the vastness, a god."

—*Author Unknown*

LABOR

(Genesis 3:19)

"In the sweat of thy brow shalt thou eat thy bread"
Was the curse man heard when the serpent's head
Thrust its soul-killing fangs into Eden's joy,
And despoiled it of light only sin could destroy.

But man turned his curse into something sweet,
'Til the earthly smell of the upturned sod
And the gold, warm glow of the ripened wheat
Were better than Eden's paths he had trod.
But he loved God less than he loved his task,
Until daily bread was all he would ask,
And the things he earned were his heart's first choice,
For his smothered soul had lost worship's voice.

So, the curse transformed is a curse again,
And a yearning God calls acquisitive men;
"Seek ye first my Kingdom of wealth unseen,
And more from your fields will you daily glean.
Be ye fed on my life-giving manna unpriced.
Lift your eyes from the dust to the glories of Christ."*

—*Madeleine S. Miller*

A LATIN HYMN

Thou bounteous Giver of the light,
    All-glorious, in whose light serene,
Now that the night has passed away,
    The day pours back her sunny sheen.
Thou art the world's true Morning Star!
    Not that which, on the edge of night,—
Faint herald of a little orb,
    Shines with a dim and narrow light;
Far brighter than our earthly sun,
    Thyself at once the Light and Day!
The inmost chambers of the heart
    Illumining with heavenly ray.

Be every evil lust repelled,
    By guard of inward purity,

* Used by special permission of the author.

That the pure body evermore
   The Spirit's holy shrine may be.
These are our votive offerings,
   This hope inspires us as we pray,
That this our holy matin light
   May guide us through the busy day.

—St. Hilary of Arles

NOAH

Forth from the ark on questing wings it flew,
The dove that looked for land amid the flood,
A speck of stone, a narrow ridge of mud
To tell of continents submerged from view.
And land was found! And burgeoning life anew
Would robe the hills in green, and quinces bud,
And men of loftier faith and nobler blood
Would build above the wave-torn residue.

Sometimes I wish another dove would fly
Out of a greater ark than Noah planned,
Where storms of hate and avarice wash high
And havoc's deluge may engulf the land.
Oh, for an olive branch to testify
The waters dwindle, and new shores expand!*

—Stanton A. Coblentz

PLOWMEN

God made a race of plowmen
   And gave them earth to till,
To mold and make and plow, then
   To harvest with a will.

He set a star to guide them,
   A green tree for its shade,
The cawing crows to chide them
   And steal what they had made.

He sent the sun to burn them,
   The cooling touch of rain;
Each waking dawn to turn them
   Back to their plows again.

He gave them seed for sowing,
   A day in which to sow,
Then sent them forth to mowing
   With mighty wills to mow.

* Used by special permission of the author.

God made a race of plowmen
And gave them earth to till,
To sow and reap and plow, then
Leave them plowmen still.*

—*Howard McKinley Corning*

A PSALM OF CONFIDENCE

The Spirit of Man shall triumph and reign o'er all the earth
The earth was made for Man, he is heir to all that therein is.
He is the end of creation, the purpose of the ages since the
    dawn of time.
He is the fulfillment of all prophecy and is himself the goal
    of every great hope born in high desire.
Who art thou, O Spirit of Man?
Thou art the Child of the Infinite, in thy nostrils is the
    breath of God.
Thou didst come at Love's behest, yea! to fulfill the Love of
    the Eternal didst thou come.

I will not despair, O Spirit of Man!
Thou canst not forever deny the God that is within thee;
    nor turn thy back upon the Ideal;
Though thou destroyest fairest hopes yet shall they live
    again.
Though thou returnest to the level of the beast thou shalt
    arise to the heights of thy divine humanity.
For the Spirit of Man breathes the untiring purpose of the
    Living God and to the fulfillment of that purpose the
    whole creation moves.**

—*Stanton Coit*

THE BEST THAT I CAN DO

"I cannot do much," said a little star,
    "To make the dark world bright;
My silver beams cannot struggle far
    Through the folding gloom of night;
But I am a part of God's great plan,
    And I'll cheerfully do the best that I
    can."

"What is the use," said a fleecy cloud,
    "Of these dew-drops that I hold?
They will hardly bend the lily proud,
    Though caught in her cup of gold;

Yet I am a part of God's great plan,
My treasures I'll give as well as I can."

A child went merrily forth to play,
But a thought, like a silver thread,
Kept winding in and out all day
Through the happy, busy head,
"Mother said, 'darling, do all you can,
For you are a part of God's great plan.' "

So she helped a younger child along,
When the road was rough to the feet;
And she sang from her heart a little song,
A song that was passing sweet;
And her father, a weary, toil-worn man,
Said, "I too will do the best that I can."

—Author Unknown

✛

HOW THE BIRDS LEARNED TO SING

Arranged by

Hallie R. Thresher

(A Southern Folk Tale)

And God said . . . let birds fly above the earth in the open firmament of heaven . . . and let birds multiply on the earth.—GENESIS 1:20, 22

HIT war a long wile ago. O, a *long, long* wile ago! Must a bin befo' Adam an' Eve wuz in de gyardin'. All de buds at dat time didn't sing no song, no mo' dan ole Turkey Buzzehr—de only bud what nevah did larn no song.

Now ole Mistah Owl he 'low he ain't gwine to hab sich a state of tings no longuh. So he git to wuk an' he done tuk up a collectshun. An' when he done got de collectshun tuk up, he git to wuk and build a powful big schoolhus. Den he notify all de buds to come an' git some edication an' larn some songs.

So de next day all de buds come to de schoolhus, an' ole Mistah Owl stan' up in front wid a stick in his han' an' call up de classes. Fust he call up de trush-bud class, an' he larn dem a song. Nex' he call up de robin class, an' he larn dem a song. Den, he call up de meadow latk class, an' larn dem a song. Den he call up de red-bud class, an' he larn dem a song. Den when he larn all de buds one song apiece, he tole 'em to come next day and git some mo' edication, and larn anuder song. Den he ring de bell and all de buds file down de aisle, an' out de doah, an' ole Mistah Owl he brung up de reah wid a stick in his han'.

Now when Mistah Owl git to dat doah, he cas' his eyes up in a tree kinda' kyaless-like—an' dah sit Ole Mis' Mockin' Bud! She ain't been neah dat schoolhus, nosuh! She jus' been playin' truant! An' when she see ole Mistah Owl standin' in dat doah wid dat stick in his han', she light in an' she sing ebery one ob dem songs.

Yessuh! Ebery one of dem! An' ole Mistah Owl, he so *mad* dat his eyes jus' swell right up wid passion, so dat they kotch dah! And dey nebah come right no mo'. An' all de udah buds, dey so mad dat dey jus' walk off, kinda stiffy-like an' dey nevah come back no mo', to larn nary an' udah song. Dey jus' go all fru life a singin' one ole song, ober and ober again an' again.

Now all you school teachuhs, let me gib you a word of adwice. Don' you git mad! Don' you let yo' angry passions rise. Else yo' eyes gwine to swell up, jus' like ole Mistah Owl's, an' dey nebah will come right no mo'!

An' you little chilluns! When you see yo' playmates a laffin' an' makin' fun ob you, fo' dem lessons you wiked so hahd to larn—don' you fro yo' book one side an' say: "I ain't gwine to study no mo'." You jus' keep on wid dem lessons! Else yous gwine all fru life a singin' one ole song ober, an' ober, an' ober again, an' again, til eberbody say when dey see you a-comin': "Yessuh, yessuh, good-day, suh, good-day."*

+

JABAL, JUBAL, AND TUBAL-CAIN

By

Grace West Staley

And Lamech took unto him two wives: the name of the one was Adah, and the name of the other Zillah. And Adah bare Jabal: he was the father of such as dwell in tents and have cattle. And his brother's name was Jubal: he was the father of all such as handle the harp and pipe. And Zillah, she also bare Tubal-cain, the forger of every cutting instrument of brass and iron.—GENESIS 4:19-22

WHEN the world was very young, there lived in a city in the Land of Nod a man called Lamech. Lamech was chief of the tribe of Cain. He had four children: Naamah, a little dark-eyed girl, and three sons, Jabal, Jubal and Tubal-cain.

When the children were young, they played hide-and-seek about the small sun-baked brick houses. As they grew older, Naamah's mother taught her to spin goat's hair into coarse cloth to make the family's clothes.

Jabal, Jubal and Tubal-cain were taught how to use the heavy bow and arrow. Lamech showed his sons how to tan the skins of the animals they shot, and how to stretch them for drums and water bottles.

The boys liked to watch the old knife-maker of the tribe mix copper and pound it into crude knives and weapons for the tribe. How proud they were of their first knives he made for them! They soon learned to whittle and make staffs and carve pictures on wood.

When the boys were approaching manhood, Lamech called them to him and said, "My Sons, you have grown tall and strong. It is time to make your own way in the world. It is the custom of our people to work for the good of the tribe. Already your sister Naamah is spinning goat's hair finer than that of any other woman. Go, my

* From *Story Art Magazine*, March-April, 1948. Used by special permission of the author and the publisher.

Sons, out into the world. At the end of seven years, return to me that I may see what you have done and what manner of men you have become. We shall see then which of you has proved himself worthy of being chief after me."

Jabal, Jubal and Tubal-cain took off their garments of woven goat's hair. They put on the hunter's costume of animal skins. They took a few crude weapons, slung their goat-skin water bottles over their shoulders, and set out to seek their fortunes.

Jabal traveled slowly through the countryside, driving his sheep before him. His hair became long, and his beard heavy. He was as fearless and powerful a man as roamed the countryside.

One late afternoon, he stopped to rest on a green hillside. He fell asleep and was awakened by the lowing of the cattle and the bleating of the sheep as they huddled together under the trees. The sky was black, thunder pealed its warning of an approaching storm.

Jabal sprang to his feet and searched for shelter. He looked everywhere for a cave, but could find none. As the rain poured down upon him, he sought the trees.

When the storm was passed, Jabal removed his dripping animal skin from his shoulder to dry it. Suddenly he had an idea.

"I use skins of animals to cover my body, why can I not use them as a roof for my head?" he asked.

Jabal tanned the skins of the wild animals he shot. With a piece of bone for a needle, and a goat's sinew for thread, he sewed the skins together. Then he carved a long pole and pounded it into the ground. He placed the skins over it. Then he made several pegs, and pounded them through the ends of the hides into the ground.

Jabal smiled, "Neither wind nor rain can touch me as I lie inside my new house. I can take it down as easily as I put it up. I will be like the turtle, who takes his house with him wherever he goes. Won't Jubal and Tubal-cain be surprised at my house of hides!"

While Jabal was building better and bigger houses of hides, Jubal was following the brook into the hills.

Jubal found music in everything. He heard music in the songs of the birds at daybreak. He listened for the melody of the rustle of the wind in the trees. In the call of the animals and the ripple of the brook he found rhythm. He lived on berries, nuts and wild honey that the bees had stored in the rock crevices by the brook.

Jubal did not like to kill animals, but one day a bear came too close. Jubal had to lift his bow. As the arrow left the bow, Jubal heard the twang of the string. *Zum, zum, zum* it sang.

"I have a singing bow," he laughed. "Is it not a shame that it is so heavy?"

He made a smaller bow of wood, and strung it with goat's sinew. When it was finished, he fitted an arrow and let it fly. *Zim, zim, zim,* it hummed, lighter and higher than the sound of the big bow string.

Then Jubal made a short, wider bow, and strung several strings across it. He plucked the strings with his fingers. Jubal cried aloud at the beautiful sounds that came from the strings.

He learned that by tightening and loosening the strings, he could make different tones.

"The sounds are like those of the murmuring brook," cried Jubal.

As Jubal stood watching the sparkling water, he heard the wind whistling through the reeds along the bank. He bent down and broke one off. He placed the reed to his mouth and blew through it. He was startled at the sound! "This is better than blowing a goat's horn," he said. Then he made a mouthpiece and placed it in the reed. Soon he fastened three reeds together with one mouthpiece.

"I can hear three different tones in my swinging reeds!" he exclaimed. "Like the trill of the birds. I wonder what Father and Jabal and Tubal-cain will say about my singing bow and tuneful reeds!"

All this time Tubal-cain was busy, too. He found a large cave by a stream where he built a fireplace and went to work. Tubal-cain knew exactly what he wanted. He wanted to make things with his hands.

He began as a knife-maker of the tribe had taught him. Soon Tubal-cain was mixing the tin and copper and pounding them into all kinds of shapes. He heated the metals and made round bowls and cups. And as time went by, he hammered the metal into water jugs and bracelets for Naamah, his sister.

"Jabal and Jubal will not have anything like this to show Father," he cried.

Seven years passed, and the brothers returned home. Lamech and Naamah received them with great joy.

"You have been gone seven long years, my Sons," said the old chief. "What have you done, Jabal, in all this time?"

Jabal brought the houses of hides he had made. Some were small, some oblong, some square. He showed how to put them up and take them down, and how to carry them about.

"They are very useful," said Lamech. "What do you call them?"

"I call them tents," said Jabal.

Lamech was much pleased. Then he asked Jubal what he had done.

Jubal brought forth his singing bow of five strings, and his set of swinging reeds.

"These are very beautiful, but of what use are they?" Lamech asked.

Then Jubal lifted the singing bow to his arm, and plucked the strings. His astonished father and brothers heard the song of the birds, and all the music of the great outdoors. When he picked up his set of reed pipes and blew, the sound was sweet to their ears.

"The singing bow I call a harp," said Jubal; "the reeds I call a shepherd's pipe."

Lamech then spoke to his third son. "You have seen the work of your brothers' hands. What have you done?"

Tubal-cain laid out his ornaments and utensils before his father. He put his knives in a row on the ground and wielded a wonderful two-edged sword the like of which had never been seen.

"You have done well, my Sons," said Lamech. "Each has given something of great value to the tribe—different and wonderful. It is hard to choose who shall be chief after me."

He turned to Jabal. "You are my eldest son."

But Jabal spoke up. "No, Father, I do not wish to be chief, to live in a city. I want to live among the hills where I can be free. My tent is my home, and my home is where I pitch my tent."

And so Lamech divided the leadership of the tribe between Jubal and Tubal-cain.

The Old Testament tells us that Jubal became known far and wide as master of the harp and organ.

And Tubal-cain became a teacher of men in the making of all kinds of implements of brass and iron.

But Jabal took his tents and his great herds of cattle and sheep into the hills. And from Jabal descended the wandering tribes of the world, like the Arabs, who to this day pitch their tented homes under the open sky.*

✧

A LEGEND OF THE BED OF STRAW

By

Margaret J. Wiggins

IN the far-away time when the world was new, the Creator still walked on the earth, sometimes in the dewy morning, sometimes in the cool twilight. One morning, as He walked in the Garden, He blessed the trees and said:

"You shall be the orchards of the earth and bear delicious food for man."

Then He walked in the forests of giant trees. These, also, He blessed and said:

"You shall be the forests of the earth, and shall bear fruit and foliage that shall be for the wild things that live away from man."

Then He went into the great grain fields and blessed them that they produce food for man and beast and bird.

In the cool of the evening He called all the great parade of flowers and blessed them, each one, that it should, with its beauty and its fragrance, feed the soul of man, and with its nectar and pollen, feed the butterflies and bees.

Then He blessed the ocean and the rivers and at last He came to the tiny brooks. The grass made a soft cover for the earth on which He walked, but as He came to the side of the brook the grass did not grow in the wet ground, so, ferns sprang up in the footprints of the Creator. Some grew tall and slender; some grew with lacy fronds; some with clinging, tendril-like leaves that were as beautiful as flowers. But they all drooped low, to shield the precious footsteps from anything that would defile them.

Among all the dense beauty of green tendrils and fronds, one fern grew nearest to the ground, spreading itself in a dense cover. It was not lacy or beautiful as the others, but its straw-like mass made a soft hiding place for the little wild things and when its stems were crushed or bruised, it gave forth a sweet, pungent fragrance that soothed and rested all who smelled it.

The Creator turned and looked back at the trail of green beauty.

* From *Junior Language and Arts Magazine,* April, 1947. Used by special permission of the author.

"You," He said, as He ran His fingers through the lacy fronds, "shall make cool, soft beds along every stream and waterfall, so that little wild creatures can find a sheltered home."

Then one of the tall ferns cried out:

"Shall we not bear fruit as the other things do? Are we not to have flowers or seed?"

"No," He said, "you are so lovely as you are, no blossom or seed pod could make you more beautiful."

The very tiniest fern reached out its tendrils to Him.

"I am not beautiful, or tall or lacy as the other ferns. Will I be of any use, tiny as I am?" it asked.

"Because you are so small and meek, you shall become the most blessed of all the plants in the world," the Creator said, lovingly.

So, for long centuries, Creation grew, blossomed and bore its seeds, fruits, and grains, for man and beast, bird and butterfly. Under the ferns along the brooksides, the violets and buttercups, wild roses and fragrant arbutus made homes along with the little wild creatures that lived beside the brooks.

Then, one day, a shepherd came. He pushed aside the ferns so that his sheep could get to the clear, fresh water. While they drank and rested, he drew his harp from his shoulder, and, lying down among the ferns, he sang—

The Lord is my Shepherd
I shall not want.
He maketh me to lie down in green pastures,
He leadeth me beside the still waters.

Often he came with his flocks. Sometimes, when storms or cold drove them to shelter, he herded them into a cave near the brook. Then, for a long time, he did not come, and the ferns whispered among themselves, wondering why he came no more to sing and rest. One day they saw him coming, running swiftly down the hillside, more swiftly across the valley, flinging himself down beside the brook to drink long, and deep, bathing his face in the cool water, running his hands longingly over the soft ferns, wishing to lie down to rest.

At last he rose to go, but he spied the old cave that had so often sheltered his flocks in the happy days. Turning to the ferns he stooped down and gathered a great armful of the tiniest fern and carried it inside the cave.

"Saul will not seek for me here, tonight," he muttered, making a bed beside the door.

The tiniest fern thought—"He looks like the little wild things when they are pursued by hunters, and flee to the brookside to find refuge"; so it shaped itself into a most comfortable bed and sent out its soothing, refreshing fragrance that soon lulled the weary King of Israel to sleep.

In the morning, when he awoke, ready now to go again on his way, he laid his hand for a moment on the bed of ferns, blessing it for its service to him.

"You are very small and not very beautiful, but you have served King David well."

The little mossy green plant was very proud and happy. It had remembered the promise of the Creator that it should be the most blest of plants, and now it felt that the promise had been fulfilled. It was anxious to keep on serving man, as it had been serving the birds and rabbits at the brookside, so it reached out and found a place to strike a root in the dirt of the old cave's wall, and soon the floor, the walls, and even the ceiling of the cave were covered with fern. Sheep and cows and goats wandered into the cave, ate the green plant, sweet and clean and moist, but the little plant always grew back as fast as it was eaten off.

Changes came to the country. A city grew up, and an Inn was built. The old cave became a stable, and a manger was made for the cattle of the Innkeeper. Still, the fern grew, abundantly.

One day all was confusion. Noise and people filled the place. The Inn was crowded, there was no more room there. The Innkeeper, worried and tired, led two people and a donkey to the cave-stable. He pushed aside the rude skin that covered the door, and leading the way, showed the large, warm, roomy cave, with the walls sweet with fern.

"This is the old cave our father David hid in when pursued by Saul," the Innkeeper said. "Here is his bed by the door and the manger is filled with sweet bed-straw that he brought from the brook, long, long ago."

"This will be a blessed place," Mary said.

Yes, it was: That was the night when the angels sang over the hills of Judea, and a glorious star hung low over the door of the stable. And, within, the Christ-Child was cradled on a bed of sweet-smelling bedstraw!

Shepherds came and knelt beside the manger, worshiping the Child.

Men, dressed in the robes of Princes and Kings, came from afar, bringing gifts, and asking:

"Where is He who is born King of the Jews?"

They, too, knelt in rapture and worshiped at the bed of the babe.

One of the Wise Men lifted a piece of the fern from the manger, near the Baby's head. He looked at it closely, then turned to Joseph and asked:

"What is the name of this straw?"

"It is called bedstraw. It is a sort of fern, and grows beside the brooks and streams. 'Tis said David brought it here."

The Wise Man took a piece in his fingers and said:

"Blessed art thou. Thou shalt be known the whole world over, because thou hast made a bed for the Promised One of Israel."

Then, each of the Wise Men took a piece of the straw, and folded it away in his robes, to be carried to his own country.

Then the tiniest fern remembered the promise of the Creator,

"Thou shalt be the most blessed of all the plants of the earth," and it lifted its small tendrils in praise.

There are some ferns that grow only in certain countries; there are some that thrive only in certain climates; but, if you search, you will find bedstraw in every country in the world.

So, the desire of the smallest plant had been fulfilled, for it had wished to be of service to mankind. King David had blessed it but He who had been born the King of Kings, said:

"Blessed are the meek, for they shall inherit the earth."*

☩

THE FORGIVING FATHER

By

Sally Craft

Introduction

FROM the beginning of Jewish history men thought of God as a living, creative heavenly personality, but not as a Heavenly Father. In the Old Testament He is often presented as a God of omnipotent power and might to be feared more than to be loved. Centuries later as Jesus sat talking with His friends one day, they began to ask Him questions: "What is God like? How does God love us? We have not always done the right thing. Will God forgive us?"

Jesus knew the answers to these questions, but how could He best help His friends to understand God's love and forgiveness? He would tell them a story— not a story about God, but a story of a father—a father whose love for his son was like God's love for them, and this is the story of The Forgiving Father that Jesus told them :

The Forgiving Father

A certain rich man had two sons. One day the younger son said, "Father, I wish to go away. I want to go to the city and live my own life. Give me the share of your wealth *now* which some day I would inherit so that I may leave and go where I will and do as I please."

The father felt very sad that his son wished to leave home, but seeing that he was determined to go, the father divided his wealth and gave the younger son his fair share. Immediately the boy, with the help of the servants, prepared to leave. The father and the household bade him goodbye and he set out for a distant city.

In the city the boy had a fine time. He spent his money lavishly and foolishly. He forgot all his father had taught him. His riotous parties brought people about him and the boy said, "Ah, this is the life I have wanted for myself. Why did I stay so long in my father's house? Now I have friends and I am surrounded by gaiety, now I can do just as I please."

Time passed and at last the boy had spent all of his money. Now he could no longer afford to give parties and, alas, he found the people, whom he had thought to be his friends, no longer sought him out. At last all of his money was gone, he had sold everything he possessed and he needed to find work in order to live.

* From *Story Art Magazine,* November-December, 1940. Used by special permission of the author and the publisher.

It so happened that a famine was in the land that year, and the young man had great difficulty in finding work to do. At last he was engaged to herd swine in payment for his food. But the fare given him was little better than that which the swine ate. Then the young man thought of his home, and said, "Even the servants in my father's house are better off than I. I wish I were back in my father's house."

The more he thought of home, the more he longed to return. "I have no right to go home," the young man thought. "I have squandered my money and my time—I have behaved badly—I have disobeyed my father's teaching. I have no right to call myself his son. I have no right to ask my father to forgive me. I shall go back and seek work as a servant in my father's house."

He started his journey home. It was a long way and he traveled on foot. After many days he was in sight of his father's house. The father had sighted the boy afar off and had recognized his son. He ran to meet him and threw his arms about him and kissed him.

The son said, "Oh, father, I have sinned against heaven and in thy sight. I am no more worthy to be called thy son: make me as one of thy hired servants."

But the father said to the servants, "Quickly, bring fresh clothing and put on him, and bring a ring for his finger and shoes for his feet. Prepare a feast, for my son was lost and is found again." And the household began to make merry.

Now the elder brother was in the field, and as he came near the house he heard music and dancing. He called a servant, and asked: "What is the celebration?"

"It is because your brother has returned that your father has ordered a celebration."

The older brother was angry and would not enter the house. His father came out and entreated him to come in, but the brother would not.

"Why should we celebrate his return?" the brother asked. "All these years I have stayed with you and have done your will. You have not given me a party that I might make merry with my friends. But now my brother, who disobeyed your will, who has squandered his life, has returned—and you are celebrating."

The father looked at his elder son and said, "You and I have had no need for a party. We have had each other all the time. But your brother has been hurt and he is sick and afraid. He needs to be sure that we love him and are glad to have him back again at home. Come, let us go in and make him welcome."*

✛

ADAM AND EVE WALKING IN THE GARDEN

(Interpretation)

SPIRITUALS are the religious folk songs of the American Negro. None of them was composed in the usual manner. Instead the spirituals sprang into life during the white heat of religious fervor experienced in some protracted meeting in a church or at a camp-meeting ground.

* From *Story Art Magazine*, January-February, 1949. Used by special permission of the author and the publisher.

They are in reality the simple, ecstatic utterances of untutored minds. They grew out of the deep emotional upheaval of the Negro who had been unwillingly brought to a strange land and forced into the bondage of human slavery. In his original home in Africa the Negro sang as he worked, as he played, in times of peace and during the sudden and furious battles of his tribe against other unfriendly natives. Religion permeated his entire life. He believed in good and evil spirits. He worshiped natural forces and phenomena; he saw divine manifestations in plants, animals, and in human beings. He thought of his gods as beings whose favor could be won and whose wrath could be placated.

When he was brought to America he came, for the first time, into contact with the Christian religion. Because of his condition of servitude he often interpreted the limited and fragmentary religious concepts he received as compensations in the life to come for the ills he had to suffer in his present slavery.

Thus in these "songs of the spirit," as spirituals are often called, he associated the Old Testament stories he heard in church meetings or in the "big house" of his master with his own personal experiences. He often compared the experiences of these Old Testament characters with his own trials and tribulations.

This characteristic is true of the spiritual, "Adam and Eve Walking in the Garden." Just as Adam and Eve were ashamed to meet their God, because they were conscious of their own disobedience, so also the Negro knew that he, too, was weak and many times did that which his own inner conscience told him was neither just nor right. Therefore, he felt himself to be part of the story of Adam and Eve and he sang: "Lord, I'm on My Way." It was not an easy way, and it was beset by many temptations.

Because these Negro spirituals nearly always represent a real and vital religious experience of the Negroes, they should always be sung sincerely and with genuine understanding and devotional feeling. They should never be burlesqued or sung in a ludicrous or comic way.

✟

DIDN'T IT RAIN

(Interpretation)

IN the days of slavery, visitors throughout the South often spoke of the singing of the Negroes. The folks in the "big house," as the mansion was usually called, listened with pleasure to the music which they heard coming from the Negro quarters, especially at eventide, on the Sabbath, and on holidays.

It was not until the Civil War, however, that Negro spirituals were really discovered, although they had long been sung throughout the South. No one there had attempted to write down this music. The first person to do so was a Northerner, Lucy McKim, who in 1862 had two of these spirituals published. In 1867 she, with two other Northerners who had collected some of these Negro songs, had the ones they knew, along with a few in the possession of others, published in a little book entitled *Slave Songs of the United States*. Some five years later another

Adam and Eve Walking in the Garden

A - dam and Eve was a - walk - ing in the gar - den,

A - dam and Eve was a - walk - ing in the gar - den, A - dam and

Eve was a - walk - ing in the gar - den, Lord, I'm on my way.

What you gwine do when the world on fire? (*3 times*)
Lord, I'm on my way.

Adam and Eve was walking in the garden (*3 times*)
Lord, I'm on my way.

Eve said to Adam the Lord God calling (*3 times*)
Lord, I'm on my way.

Adam say I hear him but I shame to answer (*3 times*)
Lord, I'm on my way.

I was afraid because I was naked (*3 times*)
Lord, I'm on my way.

* From *Old Songs Hymnal* collected by Dorothy G. Bolton and arranged by Harry T. Burleigh, No. 6. Copyright, 1945, by Fleming H. Revell Company. Used by special permission of the publisher.

collection called *Jubilee Songs* was published by Theodore F. Seward, a distinguished composer.

These spirituals or Jubilee Songs as they were sometimes called were first brought to the attention of the public in 1871 by a group of Negro singers from what is now Fisk University at Nashville, Tennessee. This group made Negro music known throughout the world, for, as W. E. B. DuBois says :"They sang these songs so deeply into the world's heart that they were never again able to forget them."

"The poignant beauty of the spirituals was unforgettably celebrated a decade later by Dr. DuBois, the well-known scholar and educator, in his moving essay, *Sorrow Songs*. He called attention to the fact that these songs are the music of an unhappy people, of the children of disappointment; they tell of the death and suffering and unvoiced longing toward a truer world of misty wonderings and hidden ways."*

"A year later Samuel Coleridge-Taylor, an outstanding English Negro composer, gave added emphasis to Negro folk songs in his publication *Twenty-four Negro Melodies Translated for the Piano*. It was derived partly from African and partly from American Negro sources. In the foreword to this publication, this musician says: "What Brahams has done for Hungarian folk music, Dvorák for the Bohemian, and Greig for the Norwegian, I have tried to do for these Negro Melodies. Coleridge-Taylor also pays tribute to Frederick J. Loudin, manager of the Jubilee Singers, through whom he first learned to appreciate the folk music of his own race."**

This spiritual, "Didn't It Rain," is another illustration of the Negro's associating his own vague and often inadequate knowledge of Old Testament events with his own struggles. His cabin, like the ark, was often cold and uncomfortable, especially during long periods of rain. He, too, needed the mountaintop as a hope of escape, and the rainbow in the sky as a sign of God's covenant with man. As he pondered over his own uncomfortable life and recalled the experiences of Noah and his family during the greatest deluge this old world has ever known, he compared his own experiences with theirs as he created the spiritual, "Didn't It Rain."

The Negro not only sang of Noah and the Ark which God commanded him to build, but also of his own plight in times of flood and fire, when about the only thing he could do was "to pray."

---

* From *Songs of Sorrow in the Souls of Black Folk* by W. E. B. DuBois, p. 252. Published, 1904, by McClurg Company. Used by special permission of the author.

** From *The Negro's Contribution to Music in America* by Rose K. Nelson and Dorothy L. Cole, p. 3. Published by the Service Bureau for Intercultural Education. Rev. Ed. 1941.

Didn't It Rain

Oh! did-n't it rain, Oh! did-n't it rain, Oh! did-n't it rain, Some

for-ty days and nights. They called old No-rah a fool-ish man, Oh! did-n't it

rain, 'Cause No-rah built the ark up-on dry land, Oh! did-n't it rain.

When it begun to rain,
Oh! didn't it rain!
Women and children begun to scream,
Oh! didn't it rain!

It rain all day and it rain all night,
Oh! didn't it rain!
It rain 'til mountain top was out of
sight,
Oh! didn't it rain!

God told Norah by the rainbow sign,
Oh! didn't it rain!
No more water but fire next time,
Oh! didn't it rain!

Judgment Day is a coming,
Coming in the Prophet's way;
Some folks say they never prayed a
prayer,
They sho will pray that day.

* From *Old Songs Hymnal* collected by Dorothy G. Bolton and arranged by Harry T. Burleigh, No. 8. Copyright, 1945, by Fleming H. Revell Company. Used by special permission of the publisher.

OUR GOD, OUR HELP IN AGES PAST

(Interpretation)

ISAAC WATTS is often called "the father of English hymnody," probably because he translated into modern verse many of the poetic psalms of the Old Testament. This hymn finds its inspiration in the 90th Psalm of which it is a paraphrase. The opening word "Our" was later changed by John Wesley to the now familiar "O."

Long a favorite among all English-speaking peoples, the hymn has been used on many national and special-day occasions. It was sung in the first thanksgiving for peace after World War I, and at the funeral of the Unknown Soldier in Westminster Abbey.

Speaking of this hymn, Professor Osbert W. Warmingham says: "It swells like an ocean; it sobs out the grief of the centuries." It was first published in 1719, and is always sung to the familiar and challenging tune of "St. Anne," which was composed in 1708 by William Croft.

Our God, Our Help in Ages Past

Isaac Watts, 1674-1748

ST. ANNE
William Croft, 1678-1727

HYMN, 1719   TUNE, 1708   METER, C.M.

With majesty

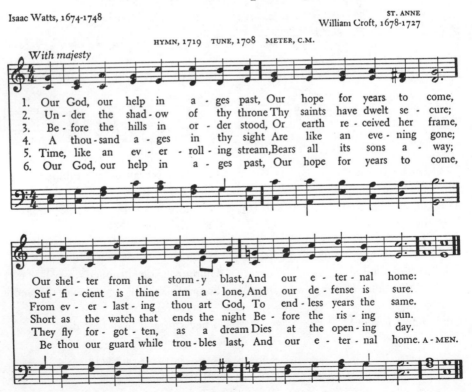

1. Our God, our help in a - ges past, Our hope for years to come,
2. Un - der the shad - ow of thy throne Thy saints have dwelt se - cure;
3. Be - fore the hills in or - der stood, Or earth re - ceived her frame,
4. A thou-sand a - ges in thy sight Are like an eve - ning gone;
5. Time, like an ev - er - roll - ing stream,Bears all its sons a - way;
6. Our God, our help in a - ges past, Our hope for years to come,

Our shel - ter from the storm - y blast, And our e - ter - nal home:
Suf - fi - cient is thine arm a - lone, And our de - fense is sure.
From ev - er - last - ing thou art God, To end - less years the same.
Short as the watch that ends the night Be - fore the ris - ing sun.
They fly for - got - ten, as a dream Dies at the open - ing day.
Be thou our guard while trou-bles last, And our e - ter - nal home. A - MEN.

O WORSHIP THE KING, ALL GLORIOUS ABOVE
(Interpretation)

SIR ROBERT GRANT was born in 1785 and died in 1838. He was a member of the British Parliament from Inverness, Scotland, and will be remembered in history for having introduced into Parliament the bill which granted civil rights to the Jew. He served as Governor of Bombay from 1834 to the time of his death.

It is as a hymn writer, however, that Sir Robert Grant is chiefly remembered by church people. He wrote twelve hymns, yet the only one that has lived on from generation to generation is "O Worship the King, All Glorious Above." It is constantly sung and is almost universally known and loved.

The hymn is a metrical version of the 104th Psalm. H. Augustine Smith in his *Lyric Religion* suggests that this Psalm and hymn provide a metrical commentary on the Six Days of Creation recorded in the first chapter of Genesis, and suggests an Antiphonal Service* which leaders of worship will find useful in program building.

Stereopticon slides of prints of the Burne-Jones panels of the Six Days of Creation and of some of Michelangelo's "Creation" pictures in the Sistine Chapel provide additional visual material with which to enrich the interpretation of this great hymn.

The tune "Lyons" to which this hymn is regularly sung was arranged from J. Michael Haydn, a less known musician than his famous brother Joseph Haydn. In his youth J. Michael Haydn was famous as an Austrian boy soprano, later as a violinist and pianist, and later still as a chorister and organist. He died the year that Robert Grant graduated from Cambridge University.

J. Michael Haydn composed some twenty masses, several offertories, and some one hundred and fourteen graduals. His best musical endeavors will be found in his religious compositions.

Lines from the 104th Psalm which provide the Biblical background for this great hymn are given below for the convenience of readers:

> Bless the Lord, O my soul.
> O Lord my God, thou art very great;
> Thou art clothed with honour and majesty.
> Who coverest thyself with light as with a garment;
> Who stretchest out the heavens like a curtain; . . .
>
> Who walketh upon the wings of the wind;
> Who maketh his angels spirits;
> His ministers a flaming fire;
> Who laid the foundations of the earth,
> That it should not be removed for ever.
>
> PSALM 104:1-5

---

* *Lyric Religion* by H. Augustine Smith, pp. 317-19. Copyright, 1931, by H. Augustine Smith. Used by special permission of Fleming H. Revell Company.

O, Worship the King, All Glorious Above

LYONS. 10, 10, 11, 11

ROBERT GRANT, 1833   Arr. from J. MICHAEL HAYDN, 1770

1. O, wor-ship the King, all glo-rious a-bove,
2. O, tell of his might, O, sing of his grace,
3. Thy boun-ti-ful care, what tongue can re-cite?
4. Frail chil-dren of dust, and fee-ble as frail,

O, grate-ful-ly sing his power and his love;
Whose robe is the light, whose can-o-py space;
It breathes in the air, it shines in the light;
In thee do we trust, nor find thee to fail;

Our Shield and De-fend-er, the An-cient of Days,
His char-iots of wrath the deep thun-der-clouds form,
It streams from the hills, it de-scends to the plain,
Thy mer-cies how ten-der, how firm to the end,

Pa-vil-ioned in splen-dor, and gird-ed with praise.
And dark is his path on the wings of the storm.
And sweet-ly dis-tils in the dew and the rain.
Our Ma-ker, De-fend-er, Re-deem-er, and Friend! A-men.

GOD OF THE EARTH, THE SKY, THE SEA
(Interpretation)

THE abiding faith of Samuel Longfellow in the omnipresence of God breathes through every line of this beautiful hymn-poem, "God of the Earth, the Sky, the Sea." It was first published, along with several others by the poet, in his *Hymns of the Spirit,* which was prepared for use in his vesper services in Brooklyn.

While Samuel Longfellow's fame as a poet was naturally overshadowed by that of his famous brother, Henry Wadsworth Longfellow, he was a poet of no mean ability. His unusual fondness of the sea is reflected in the small booklet he wrote entitled *Thalatta,* which contains charming bits of poetry about the sea and the seashore.

H. Augustine Smith in his *Lyric Religion* gives three Biblical texts which he feels provide the inspiration of this great hymn:

In him we live, and move, and have our being. [Acts 17:28]

One God and Father of all, who is over all, and through all, and in all.
[Ephesians 4:6]

In whose hand is the soul of every living thing,
And the breath of all mankind? . . .
With God is wisdom and might;
He hath counsel and understanding. . . .
He uncovereth deep things out of darkness,
And bringeth out to light the shadow of death.
[Job 12:10, 13, 22, A.S.V.]

Whether or not these Scripture passages were in the mind of Samuel Long-fellow as he penned the lines of this magnificent hymn, we cannot know; but we cannot read the first stanza of this great hymn without feeling that God is not absent from His created world.

As we read the lines of the second stanza we are made to feel the presence of God in the sunshine, the quickening air, the lightning's flash, and the power and might of the "storm winds" of God.

The third stanza emphasizes the presence of God in the calmness of the eventide, the grandeur and beauty of the oncoming night; the first breaking of the morning's dawn; and the ancient command of the Eternal God, "Let there be light!"

The fourth stanza of this sublime hymn emphasizes the indwelling of God's eternal spirit in the heart of man, His highest created form of life; while the refrain sung at the end of each stanza stresses the thankfulness of men's hearts to the Almighty God, Father and heavenly King.

This hymn may be sung to the tune "St. Catherine," which some prefer be-

God of the Earth, the Sky, the Sea

PATER OMNIUM. L.M. With Refrain

SAMUEL LONGFELLOW, 1864

HENRY J. E. HOLMES, 1875

1. God of the earth, the sky, the sea! Mak - er of all a -
2. Thy love is in the sun - shine's glow, Thy life is in the
3. We feel thy calm at eve - ning's hour, Thy gran-deur in the
4. But high - er far, and far more clear, Thee in man's spir it

bove, be - low! Cre - a - tion lives and moves in thee,
quick - 'ning air; When light-nings flash and storm-winds blow,
march of night; And, when thy morn - ing breaks in power,
we be - hold, Thine im - age and thy - self are there,—

REFRAIN

Thy pres - ent life through all doth flow. We give thee thanks, thy
There is thy power; thy law is there.
We hear thy word, "Let there be light."
Th' in-dwell-ing God, pro - claimed of old.

name we sing, Al - might - y Fa - ther, heav'n - ly King. A - men.

cause of its martial challenge; while others prefer the tune "Pater Omnium" which is included on the preceding page.

✛

A MIGHTY FORTRESS IS OUR GOD
(Interpretation)

THIS well-known hymn by Martin Luther was written in 1529 at Coburg. It was composed during the climax of Luther's struggle with the Roman Catholic Church. While Luther composed some thirty-seven hymns only ten of them have survived in English hymnals, and only one, "A Mighty Fortress Is Our God," has become a universal treasure that lives on from age to age.

Dr. Albert Edward Bailey in his *The Gospel in Hymns* summarizes Martin Luther's accomplishments in this way: "He established the Protestant Church in Germany known as Lutheran; he gave the people in their own language, the Bible, the Catechism, and the Hymnbook so that God might speak *directly* to them in His Word, and that they might directly answer Him in their songs. . . .

"Luther took the hymn out of a foreign tongue, away from the choir, away from an inelastic niche in a standardized liturgy; he gave it spontaneity, and, while requiring that the hymn be evangelical, he did not otherwise restrict the free imagination of any poet who was inspired to write."*

So magnificent is the power of this great hymn of faith that it has been the battle cry in many a national crisis. Dr. Louis Benson says of it:

"It was, as Heine said, the Marseillaise of the Reformation. . . . It was sung in the streets. . . . It was sung by poor Protestant emigrees on their way into exile, and by martyrs at their death. . . . Gustavus Adolphus ordered it sung by his army before the battle of Leipzig in 1631. . . . Again it was the battle hymn of his army at Lützen in 1632 in which the king was slain but his army won the victory. It has had a part in countless celebrations commemorating the men and events of the Reformation; and its first line is engraved on the base of Luther's monument at Wittenberg. . . . It is an imperishable hymn, not polished and artistically wrought, but rugged and strong like Luther himself, whose very words seem like deeds.**

This great hymn takes its title from the spirit of the 46th Psalm, "God is our refuge and strength." In 1852 it was translated into English by Frederick H. Hedge. The choral melody to which the hymn is regularly sung was probably developed by Luther himself from an old Gregorian chant.

* *The Gospel in Hymns* by Albert Edward Bailey, p. 313. Copyright, 1950, by Charles Scribner's Sons. Used by special permission of the publisher.

** *Studies in Familiar Hymns* by Louis F. Benson, First Series, pp. 159-60. Copyright, 1903, 1931, by Louis F. Benson. Used by special permission of the author.

A Mighty Fortress Is Our God

Martin Luther, 1483-1546
Trans. by Frederick H. Hedge, 1805-1890

EIN' FESTE BURG
Martin Luther, 1483-1546

HYMN, 1529, 1852   TUNE, 1529   METER, 8.7.8.7.6.6.6.6.7.

May be sung in unison. In majestic style

1. A might-y Fortress is our God, A Bul-wark nev-er fail - ing;
2. Did we in our own strength con-fide, Our striv - ing would be los - ing;
3. And though this world, with dev - ils filled, Should threat-en to un - do us;
4. That word a - bove all earth - ly powers, No thanks to them, a - bid - eth;

Our Help-er he a - mid the flood Of mor - tal ills pre - vail - ing:
Were not the right Man on our side, The Man of God's own choos - ing:
We will not fear, for God hath willed His truth to tri-umph through us:
The Spir - it and the gifts are ours Through him who with us sid - eth:

For still our an - cient Foe Doth seek to work us woe; His craft and power are great,
Dost ask who that may be? Christ Je - sus, it is he; Lord Sab - a - oth his Name,
The Prince of Dark - ness grim, We trem-ble not for him; His rage we can en - dure,
Let goods and kin - dred go, This mor-tal life al - so; The bod - y they may kill:

And, armed with cru - el hate, On earth is not his e - qual.
From age to age the same, And he must win the bat - tle.
For lo! his doom is sure, One lit - tle word shall fell him.
God's truth a - bid - eth still, His King-dom is for - ev - er. A - MEN.

TO THE GOD OF ALL CREATION

(Interpretation)

THE Book of Psalms, couched in beautiful, poetic form, contains some of the Church's richest devotional literature. It has come down to us through the centuries as one of the finest contributions to faith and trust that the languages of men can express.

The 95th Psalm represents the human heart's response of praise and thanksgiving to God for His loving care and guidance. Its four brief verses combine in a paean of praise to God, King of all nations, Creator of the earth, and Maker of man.

The first stanza confirms the faith that God is the "Rock of our salvation" in which human hearts everywhere rejoice. The second stanza expresses the need of the human heart to respond "with glad hearts and thankful lays." The third stanza expresses man's faith in the God that is "above all gods," the Ruler of Heaven and earth. The fourth stanza chants of God's creative power as evidenced in "land and oceans," and in the beauty with which He "clothes the sod"; and urges human hearts to "bow in deep devotion" and to bless their "Maker and God."

The poetic arrangement of the words of this beautiful Psalm is by W. W. Hull; the music is arranged from a melody by Ludwig van Beethoven.

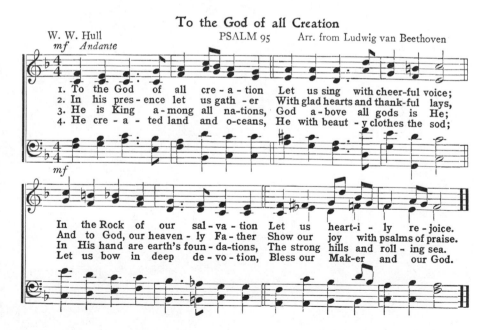

To the God of all Creation

W. W. Hull · PSALM 95 · Arr. from Ludwig van Beethoven

1. To the God of all cre-a-tion Let us sing with cheer-ful voice;
2. In his pres-ence let us gath-er With glad hearts and thank-ful lays,
3. He is King a-mong all na-tions, God a-bove all gods is He;
4. He cre-a-ted land and o-ceans, He with beaut-y clothes the sod;

In the Rock of our sal-va-tion Let us heart-i-ly re-joice.
And to God, our heaven-ly Fa-ther Show our joy with psalms of praise.
In His hand are earth's foun-da-tions, The strong hills and roll-ing sea.
Let us bow in deep de-vo-tion, Bless our Mak-er and our God.

CONTENTS

PART I SECTION 2

ABRAHAM AND HIS DESCENDANTS

✛

Now the Lord had said unto Abram, Get thee out of thy country, and from thy kindred, and from thy father's house, unto a land that I will shew thee: And I will make of thee a great nation.—GENESIS 12:1-2

✛

ABRAHAM

By

Saul Raskin

(Interpretation)

THE story of Abraham as we find it in Genesis 12-25 is the story of a man who left his home in the cosmopolitan city of Ur of the Chaldees at the command of his God to become a wanderer in strange lands and among unknown peoples. For it was to Abraham that the voice of the Lord came, saying:

"Get thee out of thy country, and from they kindred, and from thy father's house, unto a land that I will shew thee: and I will make of thee a great nation, and I will bless thee, and make thy name great; and thou shalt be a blessing: . . . and in thee shall all families of the earth be blessed" (12:1-3).

So Abraham gathered his family together, as the Lord had commanded him, with his nephew Lot also accompanying him, and ventured forth, not knowing whither he went. As they journeyed through strange lands and peoples on their way to the land which the Lord had promised them, Abraham, each night, built an altar, and as the smoke of his fire ascended heavenward so also did the prayers of this devout father of Israel lift themselves on the wings of night toward the throne of God.

The pioneers in every age have known the loneliness of separation from familiar people and places and this loneliness Abraham and his family knew as they journeyed ever onward among strange peoples speaking strange languages. But this Old Testament patriarch kept his sense of the nearness of his God, even though he could see Him only with the eyes of the spirit. For the God that Abraham knew and upon whom he centered his faith and devotion was not like the gods of wood and stone to be found, not only in Ur of the Chaldees, but also among the many strange peoples he and his family encountered.

One wonders if Abraham, in his aloneness, counted the silent stars in the blue-black of the nighttime sky for companionship. Was it out of his deep meditation and loneliness that the voice of the Lord came assuring him that someday his seed should be as the stars in the sky that could not be numbered because of their quantity and magnitude?

There were tragic hardships by day as well as weariness of body, mind, and soul in the lone watches of the night. There was famine in the lands through which they passed, so that they continued their course ever southward into Egypt were they tarried for a while. But in spite of the hardships of this pioneer life, Abraham and his family prospered in cattle, in silver, and in gold. At last they came in their wanderings to Bethel where he and Lot separated because the land immediately around them was not rich enough to provide food for all. So Lot chose the better land and pitched his tents near Sodom, while Abraham took the less fertile land as his abiding place.

After many long years of wilderness living, God visited Abraham with the promise that his wife Sarah, old now in years, should yet bear a son and that she would become a mother of nations. Though the promise of the Lord seemed far off, nevertheless with the coming of Isaac there was hope that it might be fulfilled.

It is a night sky filled with stars suggesting the promise of the Lord, "As the stars, so shall thy seed be," that Saul Raskin has chosen as the background of his etching of "Abraham."

The artist's own youthful pioneering helped him to catch the spirit of Abraham, the wanderer. Born in Nogaisk, Russia, August 15, 1878, he early evinced a strong interest in drawing, and his father took him to a neighboring town where he was apprenticed in a lithograph print shop. In his young manhood he went to Odessa where he attended his first art classes. Later, earning his living as a lithographer, he wandered throughout Europe dividing his spare time between reading and drawing. He then returned to Russia, but in 1904 he emigrated to the United States, where he has lived since. In New York City he made his first intimate contact with Jewish culture, and contributed to the liberal press.

During World War I he worked with the Jewish Welfare Board and in 1921 made the first of four journeys to Palestine. In Bible lands he traveled afoot drawing and painting; and it was here in the land of our Lord that he became convinced that painting was his true calling.

Back in New York at the age of forty-three he held his first art exhibit of about one hundred paintings and drawings. It heralded him as an artist of promise. Subsequently, he returned to Palestine in 1924, in 1929, and in 1937. His depictions in water colors and oils, his etchings and lithographs of life in Palestine's streets, synagogues, and harbors have won for him wide and merited acclaim. His etchings of the major and minor prophets of the Old Testament are unique in their presentation of the basic character that made each prophet distinctive.

Faithful always to his conception of a living God, ruler of earth and sky, guiding and controlling the destinies of men and of nations, Abraham has come down to us through the centuries as the "father of the faithful"—the father of all those who in every generation live by faith and not by sight. In his etching Saul Raskin has beautifully and feelingly portrayed this conception of Abraham, a man old in years, with arms flung upward in supplication to his God, while the myriad stars in the heavens above say in the deepest recesses of a man's soul, "The heavens declare the glory of God; and the firmament sheweth his handywork. Day unto day uttereth speech, and night unto night sheweth knowledge."

ABRAHAM—*RASKIN*

THE FLIGHT OF LOT

By

Raphael Sanzio

(Interpretation)

ALL Bible students are familiar with the story of how Abraham remonstrated with God on behalf of the wicked city of Sodom, as presented in Genesis 18:22-33; and of how the Lord finally agreed to spare this city from utter destruction if there were found in it as many as ten righteous men.

They know also that He sent two angels to Sodom and that Lot, Abraham's nephew, took them into his home, where at his insistence they remained as guests for the night. In the darkness of that night some of the wicked men of Sodom attempted to capture these representatives of the Most High God but were afflicted with blindness so that they could not find the door to Lot's house to enter it by force.

Later these messengers from the Lord urged Lot to flee with his wife and daughters, telling them that God purposed in His heart to destroy that city, notwithstanding Abraham's plea, because the outcry against its people had become so great.

When the morning came, these angels urged Lot to flee, saying: "Arise, take thy wife, and thy two daughters, which are here; lest thou be consumed in the iniquity of the city" (Gen. 19:15).

When Lot lingered, loth to leave his beautiful home, the two angels laid hold of his hand, and the hand of his wife and the hands of his two daughters, and brought them forth and set them without the city. And when they had brought them forth out of Sodom, the angels said: "Escape for thy life; look not behind thee, neither stay thou in all the plain; escape to the mountain, lest thou be consumed" (Gen. 19:17).

But Lot's wife looked back and she became as a pillar of salt.

In the foreground of Raphael's picture of "The Flight of Lot" is Lot himself, holding onto the hands of these two as yet unmarried daughters. Behind them is their mother in the act of looking backward at the burning city and the destruction of her home. She is robed in a pale blue gown, but the blotches that show from her head to her feet indicate that she has already begun to turn to salt, even as she watches the flames consuming her own home. The two young daughters are robed in gowns of pale pink and brilliant red. Lot wears a shirt of blue and a brown mantle. With the hands of his daughters clasped securely in his, they move rapidly, with downcast eyes, toward the distant mountains that are to be their sheltering home.

Wooded hills appear in the background. Immediately behind the fleeing family black clouds of smoke darken the sky as flames consume the doomed city.

This Old Testament painting adorns the fourth arcade of Raphael's Loggie in

THE FLIGHT OF LOT—*RAPHAEL*

the Vatican in Rome, along with pictures of "Abraham and Melchizedek," "God's Covenant with Abraham," and "The Visit of the Three Angels to Abraham."

✛

THE SACRIFICE OF ISAAC

By

Lorenzo Ghiberti

(Interpretation)

ONE day while Abraham was encamped in the plains of Mamre he looked out from his tent door and saw three men approaching. He ran to meet them and, bowing himself to the ground in greeting, he courteously offered the hospitality of his tent to the strangers. Unaware that they were messengers of God, he said to them: "Let a little water, I pray you, be fetched, and wash your feet, and rest yourselves under the tree. And I will fetch a morsel of bread, and comfort ye your hearts. After that ye shall pass on" (Gen. 18:4, 5).

While they were eating the meal that Sarah and Abraham set before them under the tree, the messengers of God promised Abraham that he and his wife Sarah would have a son. To Sarah, listening to this promise from her tent door, this seemed an impossible thing, for she was now old. However, before long a son was born to Sarah and Abraham whom they named Isaac. He was their only son and they loved him greatly. Through him they knew that the Lord would fulfill His promise that Abraham's descendants would be as numerous as the stars in the heavens.

Then came a severe testing of Abraham's faith in God. It is dramatically narrated in the twenty-second chapter of the Book of Genesis. Abraham believed that the Lord wanted him to offer up his only son Isaac as a burnt offering to God. Such sacrifices were not uncommon among the people with whom Abraham lived in those far-off days. But Abraham's heart must have been sad as he set about to obey what seemed to him to be the Lord's command and he must have wondered how God's promise to him could be fulfilled if his only son were to die.

Nevertheless, strong in his faith in God, "Abraham rose up early in the morning, and saddled his ass, and took two of his young men with him, and Isaac his son, and clave the wood for the burnt offering, and rose up, and went unto the place of which God had told him."

On the third day he reached the foot of the mountain and said to his two servants: "Abide ye here with the ass, and I and the lad will go yonder and worship, and come again to you."

Isaac saw his father's preparations, but was puzzled by the absence of one thing: "Behold the fire and the wood, but where is the lamb for a burnt offering?"

Abraham, still trusting in his Lord, replied: "My son, God will provide himself a lamb for a burnt offering."

THE SACRIFICE OF ISAAC—*GHIBERTI*

Then "Abraham built an altar there, and laid the wood in order, and bound Isaac his son, and laid him on the altar upon the wood. And Abraham stretched forth his hand, and took the knife to slay his son."

At that moment an angel of the Lord called to him: "Abraham! Abraham!"

"Here am I," replied Abraham.

"Lay not thine hand upon the lad, neither do thou anything unto him, for now I know that thou fearest God, seeing thou hast not withheld thy son, thine only son from me."

Looking behind him Abraham saw "a ram caught in a thicket by his horns. And Abraham went and took the ram, and offered him up for a burnt offering in the stead of his son."

This is the story Ghiberti portrayed in "The Sacrifice of Isaac." In this bronze panel where several episodes are brought easily and gracefully together into a unified design, our eye is led in sweeping curves first toward the left, then toward the right, inward and upward, from the high relief of the foreground to the low relief of the scene of the sacrifice. The action begins with the three lovely angel messengers of the Lord appearing to Abraham. He kneels to entreat them to be his guests. Before him is the basin of water in which they may wash their feet. Behind Abraham stands Sarah at the door of her tent unable to believe the angels' promise that she shall be the mother of a son.

The action is resumed in the lower right side of the panel where the ass, the provisions for the homeward journey, and the two servants all await Abraham's return from the mountain of sacrifice. Above them the culminating scene in Abraham's test of faith takes place. With his knife uplifted high above his head, Abraham prepares to sacrifice his kneeling, trusting son, Isaac. From the sky appears an angel who arrests Abraham's knife in mid-air and points toward the ram caught in the thicket at Abraham's feet.

This is one of the ten panels Ghiberti made for the eastern door of the Baptistery which stands opposite the Cathedral in Florence. The door, which is regarded as Ghiberti's masterpiece, was ordered in 1425 by the Florentine guilds, but all its panels were not finished and put in place for twenty-seven years. Ghiberti was aided by his assistants and especially by his son Vettorio, but he was a slow and painstaking artist and he was often interrupted in his work. During these years there were plagues and wars and tumults in Italy. But the Florentines gazed on these magnificent creations of Ghiberti and knew that they would outlive the upheavals of their own century. A hundred years after the completion of the doors while they still shone with the brightness of their original gilding, Michelangelo saw them and exclaimed: "They are so beautiful that they might fittingly stand at the gates of paradise!" Since that time this eastern door of the Baptistery in Florence has been known as the "Gates of Paradise."

REBEKAH AT THE WELL

By

Bartolomé Esteban Murillo

(Interpretation)

THIS painting of Rebekah and Eliezer at the well has a quality of real life about it, and is full of picturesque color. It is based on an incident in the story of how a wife was chosen for Isaac as narrated in Genesis 24.

Isaac was the son born to Abraham and Sarah during their old age. Now that Isaac had grown to young manhood his father wanted to see him happily married to a young maiden from among their own people and country. So he sent Eliezer, his faithful servant —a man who was at the head of his household—on the delicate task of finding a wife for his son Isaac.

Eliezer took ten camels and departed, and, as he drew near the city of Nahor, he made careful plans. He would take his place near the city's well, for he knew that at some time during the day, the maidens of the city would come thither to draw water.

He prayed to the Lord saying: "Let it come to pass, that the damsel to whom I shall say, 'Let down thy pitcher, I pray thee, that I may drink'; and she shall say, 'Drink, and I will give thy camels drink also': let the same be she that thou hast appointed for thy servant Isaac; and thereby shall I know that thou hast shewed kindness to my master" (Gen. 24:14).

Before Eliezer had finished his prayer, Rebekah, a maiden fair to look upon, appeared at the well, and he hastened to her with the words: "Let me, I pray thee, drink a little water of thy pitcher" (24:17). Rebekah acquiesced immediately and also drew water for his camels.

Abraham's old servant conversed with Rebekah at the well and learned that she was the daughter of Nahor and Bethuel, who were distant kinsfolk of Abraham; and he knew that this beautiful and gracious daughter was the one appointed to be Isaac's wife.

So Eliezer gave her gifts of a golden ring and two bracelets and accompanied her to the home of her father. The family received Abraham's old servant with gracious hospitality, and when he told them of his mission they replied: "Behold, Rebekah is before thee, take her, and go." Then they turned to Rebekah and said to her, "Wilt thou go with this man?" And she answered, "I will go."

Murillo in his painting of Rebekah and Eliezer at the well has portrayed the moment when the aged servant is drinking from the pitcher which Rebekah has offered him.

In the background the camels may be seen, while in the foreground, clustered about the well, are a group of village maidens watching with interest and curiosity this courteous old man who has just asked a special favor of Rebekah. She has turned her head toward the maidens as if on the point of answering their questions about the stranger, but her serene expression shows that she does not yet know what his mission is nor what her part in it will be.

Murillo was born in Seville, Spain, in 1618. He was a devout Catholic. His daughter Francisca became a Dominican nun, and one of his sons, Gaspar, became a priest. His other son was a seafaring man, and was in the West Indies at the time his father died.

This great Spanish painter was a keen observer of life. As he came and went through the streets of Seville he observed closely the habits and customs of the people as they chatted on doorsteps or conversed in the public market. His pictures reflect this love for, and appreciation of, the simple, charming customs of people in everyday life. His characters are all natural and lifelike in appearance.

✢

ISAAC BLESSING JACOB

By

Jan Victoors

(Interpretation)

THE painting "Isaac Blessing Jacob" (1640), by tht Dutch artist Jan Victoors, sometimes spelled Fictoors, hangs in the Louvre in Paris. This picture and the one which follows entitled "Esau Back from the Hunt Asks the Benediction" by Giulio Romano should be studied together, for both pictures complete the Bible story told in the 27th chapter of Genesis of how Jacob defrauded his brother of their father's blessing.

These two young brothers, Esau and Jacob, were opposites in character. Esau was a man of the present; Jacob, a man of the future. Esau rarely looked beyond his own immediate needs; Jacob, on the contrary, looked ahead to the future. Esau was absorbed in the pleasures of his senses; while Jacob was in constant pursuit of gain, both spiritual and temporal. Esau cared only for a happy, merry life from day to day; Jacob was willing to endure hardship and hard work to acquire material wealth. Esau had the disposition of a spendthrift; Jacob was willing even to be miserly for the sake of the future. Once when Esau returned home famished he asked for some of the food his younger brother Jacob was preparing. Jacob sold him the "mess of pottage" in exchange for Esau's birthright as his father's oldest son.

When Isaac, the father of these two lads, was an old man, and ill, he called his elder son Esau, who was a cunning hunter, to him and said: "Behold now, I am old, I know not the day of my death: Now therefore take, I pray thee, thy [hunting] weapons, thy quiver and thy bow, and go out to the field, and take me some venison; and make me savoury meat, such as I love, and bring it to me, that I may eat; that my soul may bless thee before I die" (Gen. 27:2-4). And Esau complied with his father's request.

But Rebekah, Isaac's wife, was listening, and when she heard her husband's

REBEKAH AT THE WELL—MURILLO

words she said to Jacob, her younger and her favorite son: "My son . . . go now to the flock, and fetch me from thence two good kids of the goats; and I will make them savoury meat for thy father, such as he loveth: and thou shalt bring it to thy father, that he may eat, and that he may bless thee before his death" (Gen. 27:8-10).

To Jacob's credit it must be said that he remonstrated with his mother. This, however, was not so much because of the deception which his mother had suggested, but for fear that this deception might be discovered by his father, and that he might receive a curse instead of a blessing. He replied to his mother: "Esau my brother is a hairy man, and I am a smooth man. My father peradventure will feel me, and I shall seem to him as a deceiver; and I shall bring a curse upon me and not a blessing" (Gen. 27:11-12).

But when his mother offered to take any curse meant for Jacob upon herself, the younger son complied with his mother's wishes. On his return from the flock with the two kids, his mother dressed Jacob in one of Esau's best robes, and she spread the skins of the kids over his hands and the smooth part of his neck so that he might successfully deceive his aged father. She prepared tasty food and when it was ready gave it to Jacob to offer to Isaac. After Isaac had eaten, he gave Jacob the blessing that rightfully belonged to Esau.

It is this incident at Isaac's bedside that is portrayed. Jacob is richly gowned in one of Esau's best robes, as he kneels by his father to receive the blessing. Near by stands Rebekah, Isaac's wife, with one finger raised to her lips. On a chair is the half-eaten plate of food.

The painting shows the rich fabrics, the Dutch costumes, and the carved furniture of the artist's own day. He has used the sharp contrasts of light and shade to emphasize the important parts of his picture. The drama of the moment is rendered by the expressions on the faces of the three figures. Rebekah is watching intently, almost anxiously. Will her trickery be discovered? Jacob smiles in pleased anticipation of winning the blessing that belongs to his older brother. Isaac's face shows that he is feeble and cannot see clearly. He is troubled as he tries to decide whether or not this boy is really his elder son Esau whom he must bless before he dies.

He failed to recognize Jacob, "because his hands were hairy, as his brother Esau's hands: so he blessed him" (Gen. 27:23).

Jan Victoors was born in Amsterdam in 1620 and died there about 1672. He was a pupil of Rembrandt and worked in his atelier from 1635 to 1640. Many of his picture themes were taken from the Old Testament, but he also painted genre, landscapes, peasant assemblies, and markets. In his Biblical pictures he adhered closely to the manner of Rembrandt. The masterpieces from the brush of Jan Victoors appear in the museums of Amsterdam, Antwerp, Copenhagen, Dresden, London, Munich, and Paris.

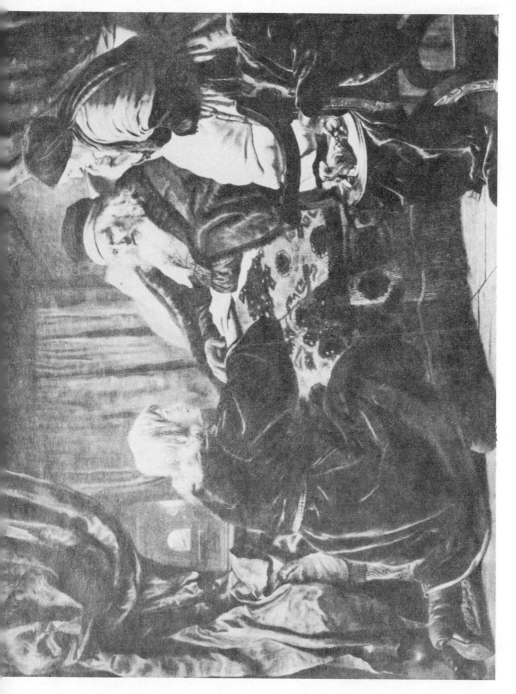

ISAAC BLESSING JACOB—*VICTOORS*

ESAU BACK FROM THE HUNT ASKS THE BENEDICTION
By
Giulio Romano
(Interpretation)

Isaac and Rebekah had two sons: Esau, "a cunning hunter, a man of the field," and Jacob, "a plain man, dwelling in tents." Isaac loved Esau, but Rebekah loved Jacob. Though Esau was the elder, he lost both his birthright and his father's blessing to his younger brother Jacob. His birthright he gave in exchange for food when he was hungry. But Jacob, coached by Rebekah, tricked him out of the blessing due by rights to the eldest son.

When Esau returned from the field with game he had hunted, expecting to receive his father's blessing, the deception which Rebekah and Jacob had practiced on the aged Isaac was disclosed. Isaac trembled and said to Esau: "Who? where is he that hath taken venison, and brought it me, and I have eaten of all before thou camest, and have blessed him? yea, and he shall be blessed" (Gen. 27:33).

In a burst of uncontrollable temper Esau said to his father: "He took away my birthright; and, behold, now he hath taken away my blessing." Then in bitterness he added: "Hast thou not reserved a blessing for me?" (Gen. 27:36).

Esau wept aloud, even though Isaac gave him a minor blessing. He hated his brother for this deception and vowed that he would seek Jacob out and slay him.

Rebekah, sensing his smoldering hatred, sent Jacob secretly to his uncle, Laban, in Haran. The years of separation, she hoped, might calm the anger which Esau bore his brother.

The incident of Esau, clad only in his hunter's robes, has been graphically pictured in Romano's painting, "Esau Back from the Hunt Asks the Benediction." At the hunter's feet is the young animal he has slain; but frustration and despair are in his gesture of surprise as Isaac reveals to him that he has already bestowed his blessing upon Jacob, thinking that he was his elder son.

In the background Rebekah and Jacob listen to the words of the aged Isaac as he reveals the deception that has been practiced on him, the half blind, ill head of his household.

This picture, like that of Jan Victoors of "Isaac Blessing Jacob," is full of dramatic action. Though the deceived father and the cheated brother at the moment of their discovery of the fraud are the chief figures, one's attention is drawn to Rebekah and Jacob half hidden in the background shadows. Their evil doing has succeeded. But human experience, in every generation, has found that "the wages of sin is death." The Bible story goes on to tell how Jacob, whose very name means "cheater," experienced years of discipline under Laban his uncle before his wicked deed could be blotted out and his sin purged through restitution to Esau. Just before his reunion with his brother an angel changed Jacob's name to "Is-

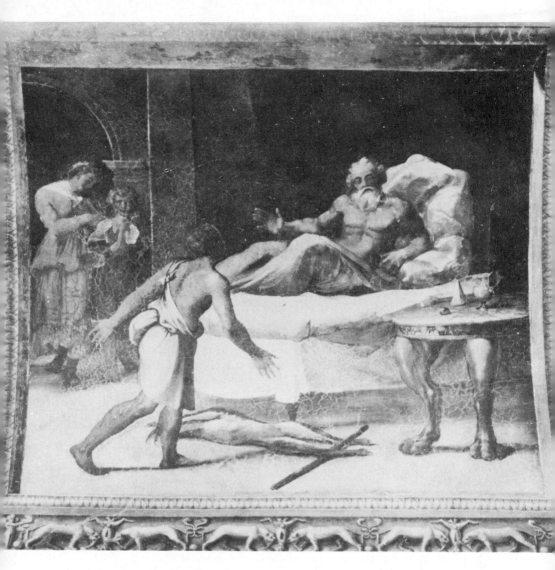

ESAU BACK FROM THE HUNT ASKS THE BENEDICTION—*ROMANO*

rael," saying "for as a prince hast thou power with God and with men, and hast prevailed" (Gen. 32:28).

Giulio Romano (1492-1546) was one of Raphael's most distinguished art pupils. More than any other pupil, he came nearer to his great master's style in manner, invention, design, and execution. To this younger student artist fell the task of completing many of Raphael's paintings in the Loggie, known as Raphael's Gallery in the Vatican in Rome. Shortly after Raphael's untimely death, Romano was acclaimed as one of the greatest of the Italian painters. He entered the service of the Duke of Mantua as an architect and designer in rebuilding and redecorating many of the cathedrals and palaces of that city.

✣

THE SELLING OF JOSEPH

By

Charles M. Relyea

(Interpretation)

JOSEPH is one of the best-loved Old Testament characters. His story is more familiar to the average reader than those of Abraham, Isaac, or Jacob, perhaps because it reads like a fairy tale. It is full of surprises and dramatic action, and despite many tragic disasters it has a happy and successful ending.

Joseph was the child of his father's old age. He was the favorite son of Jacob's best-loved wife, Rachel, and his father made him a coat of many colors. Thus at the beginning of his story we find a petted, spoiled boy.

From his grandfather, Abraham, Joseph had no doubt inherited his hopeful, optimistic nature. He believed that no evil could befall him. This confident spirit is characteristic of his entire life. From his father, Jacob, who had deceived his own father in an ambitious attempt to receive a blessing which did not rightfully belong to him, Joseph had no doubt received his ambition. He believed in himself and in his own happy destiny. His experiences in life taught him to be genuinely unselfish. He practiced "returning good for evil."

His first tragic experience began when, clad in his coat of many colors, he went on an errand for his doting father in search of his older brothers who kept watch over their father's sheep.

Not long before this the lad Joseph had had a dream which he guilelessly reported to his father and brothers. In this dream Joseph and his brethren were binding sheaves in a field when, according to Joseph, his sheaf arose and stood upright; and his brothers' sheaves came round about it and made obeisance to it. And again he dreamed another dream, and this time the sun and the moon and the eleven stars made obeisance to Joseph. When he told this second dream to his father and brothers, even his father rebuked him saying: "Shall I and thy mother and thy brethren indeed come to bow down ourselves to thee to the

THE SELLING OF JOSEPH—*RELYEA*

earth?" (Gen. 37:10). Nevertheless, his father kept this dream in memory, for the lad's dreams had a strange way of coming true.

It was not long afterward that Joseph's older brothers went to Shechem in search of better grazing lands for their father's flock; and when they did not return after the usual interval away, Jacob sent Joseph to find them and to bring him word that they were well and unharmed.

When the older brothers saw this young dreamer as he approached in his coat of many colors, they said among themselves, "Behold, this dreamer cometh. Come now therefore, and let us slay him, and cast him into some pit, and we will say, 'Some evil beast hath devoured him': and we shall see what will become of his dreams" (Gen. 37:19-20).

But Reuben, an older brother, when he heard this scheme, said, "Let us not kill him . . . but cast him into this pit that is in the wilderness, and lay no hand upon him" (Gen. 37:21-22). Later Reuben intended to rescue the lad and to return him safely to his father. So when Joseph came, he was stripped of his coat of many colors and cast into the pit.

After dinner, however, while Reuben was away, a band of traveling Ishmaelites coming from Gilead with their camels bearing spices, balm, and myrrh appeared. They were bound for Egypt. So Judah said to his brothers, " 'What profit is it if we slay our brother, and conceal his blood? Come, and let us sell him to the Ishmaelites, and let not our hand be upon him; for he is our brother and our flesh.' And his brethren were content . . . and they drew and lifted up Joseph out of the pit, and sold Joseph to the Ishmaelites for twenty pieces of silver. And they brought Joseph into Egypt" (Gen. 37:26-28).

The American artist Charles M. Relyea painted this picture to illustrate the story of the selling of Joseph by his brothers to Ishmaelite traders. In the background are five of Joseph's brothers. Four of them sit on the ground counting the money they have received in exchange for their brother. A fifth brother stands looking on and holding his shepherd's crook. The palm trees and the camel lend local color to the scene. In the left foreground can be seen the pit from which Joseph has just been taken and, lying on the ground, the rope by which he was raised. The central figure in this picture is young Joseph himself. He is being forcefully led away by two Ishmaelites who have purchased him. Joseph's face expresses his anguish at being torn away from his family and taken by strange men to an unknown land.

JOSEPH INTERPRETS PHARAOH'S DREAM

By.

Giulio Romano

(Interpretation)

JOSEPH'S life in Egypt reads like a fairy tale. When the traveling band of Ishmaelites to whom Joseph had been sold by his brothers reached Egypt, this young man was resold as a slave to Potiphar, an officer of Pharaoh and the captain of his guard.

Joseph was comely and well-favored and the blessing of the Lord was upon him as he served in Potiphar's house. His energy, intelligence, and optimistic good humor soon won Potiphar's admiration, so that he was made overseer in his master's household.

Later Potiphar's wife tried to induce this good-looking youth to sin against his master, but Joseph refused, saying: "Behold, my master . . . hath committed all that he hath to my hand; . . . because thou art his wife: how then can I do this great wickedness, and sin against God?" (Gen. 39:8-9).

Day after day Potiphar's wife still tried to entice Joseph, and still he refused to commit this sin against his master. Finally, she accused Joseph of forcing his attentions upon her and Joseph was imprisoned. But the Lord was with him, and showed kindness to him, and gave him favor in the eyes of the prisonkeeper.

Later both Pharaoh's butler and his baker were thrown into that same prison. There they each had a dream, which they were unable to interpret. Joseph, upon hearing the dreams, revealed to each their hidden meaning. Not many days later the revelation which he interpreted came true for both the butler and the baker.

Nearly two full years later Pharaoh himself had an unusual dream which none of his wise men and court advisers was able to interpret. Then Pharaoh's chief butler recalled Joseph's skill in dream interpretation, and he was sent for and appeared before Egypt's monarch. Genesis 41:25-36 records the interpretation which Joseph gave to Pharaoh:

"And Joseph said unto Pharaoh, 'The dream of Pharaoh is one: God hath shewed Pharaoh what he is about to do. The seven good kine are seven years; and the seven good ears are seven years: the dream is one. And the seven thin and ill favoured kine that came up after them are seven years; and the seven empty ears blasted with the east wind shall be seven years of famine. That is the thing which I have spoken unto Pharaoh: What God is about to do he sheweth unto Pharaoh. Behold, there come seven years of great plenty throughout all the land of Egypt; and there shall rise after them seven years of famine; and all the plenty shall be forgotten in the land of Egypt'; and the famine shall consume the land; and the plenty shall not be known in the land by reason of that famine following; for it shall be very grievous. And for that the dream was doubled unto Pharaoh twice; it is because the thing is established by God, and God will shortly bring it to pass. Now therefore let Pharaoh look out a man discreet and wise, and set him over the land of Egypt. Let Pharaoh do this, and let him appoint officers over the land, and take up the fifth part of the land of Egypt in the seven plenteous years. And let them gather all the food of those good years that come, and lay up corn under the hand of Pharaoh, and let them keep food in the cities. And that food shall be for store to the land against the seven years of famine, which shall be in the land of Egypt; that the land perish not through the famine."

Giulio Romano, an Italian artist of the sixteenth century (1492-1546), has chosen this incident as the theme of his picture, "Joseph Interprets Pharaoh's Dream."

In the background sits the king, his head bowed in deep thought, as he listens intently to Joseph's interpretation of this recurring and perplexing dream. Behind him is his chief adviser, also listening intently to Joseph's revelation. Above the monarch's crowned head two spheres appear. One shows the seven good kine and the seven lean kine, representing in turn the seven fat years and the seven lean years that are to come. The other sphere contains the seven full ears of wheat and the seven lean ears of wheat, foretelling the seven years of plenty and the seven years of famine. Both spheres symbolize the need to save and garner food during the seven plenteous years for the lean ones that will follow in Egypt's great famine.

Through the windows, waving trees and distant hills may be seen, while behind Joseph stand Pharaoh's prison guards, listening with undisguised admiration to the words of their famous prisoner as he interprets Pharaoh's dream.

In this picture the gestures of Pharaoh, his chief adviser, and the prison guards, and even the folds of the curtain in the background all lead toward the principal figure, Joseph. He stands, not frightened and cringing as a prisoner might who has just been led from a dungeon into the throne room, but poised and confident. The landscape beyond the windows indicates that what Joseph is saying concerns not merely Pharaoh himself, but all the fair land of Egypt.

✢

ABRAM

From homeland went he forth, with faith his guide,
   Unto an unknown land, assured that He
   Who brought him out, in sweet security
Would grant him rest beyond far Jordan's tide.

O Father of us all, give to each soul
   A faith that dares leave all that men count dear
   To travel unknown ways without a fear,
Assured Thy hand shall guide to worthy goal.*

—*Thomas Curtis Clark*

* Used by special permission of the author.

JOSEPH INTERPRETS PHARAOH'S DREAM—*ROMANO*

A WELL SIDE

A silver chiming broke the tranquil spell
    That broods above wide wastes of amber brown,
    Then at the green edge of a shining town
Knelt ten strange camels, and each bore a bell;
One after one thin topaz shadows fell,
    A star shone—Then a maiden wandered down
    Wearing her gleaming pitcher like a crown,
And pitied them so thirsty by the well.

When she gave drink, her tender unveiled face
    Was as a spring moon in the twilight hour
    Upon the earth-cooled water far below;
How little dreamed she of that unborn race—
    Mother of Israel, gathered like a flower
    From golden lands long centuries ago!*

                                            —*Thomas S. Jones, Jr.*

BITTER FRUIT

    Did Adam—exiled, sorrowful,—
    As he toiled where thorns took root
    To choke his parched and dusty fields,
    Find knowledge bitter fruit?

    Did Adam, when the slanting sun
    Lay hot on cursed sod,
    Remember—sadly—garden paths
    Where once he walked with God?**

                                            —*Leslie Savage Clark*

CHILDREN OF ESAU

From the dreamless sleep of the well-fed
They rise at the morning-time.
They feel no joy at the glory of the sunrise;
They see no heaven reflected in the drop of dew;
They hear no God clear speaking to the heart of man
In the freshly blown rose.

What care they to be called "the sons of God"
If the appetite of sense is satisfied?
What care they for Bethel dreams
If only the forests are filled with venison?

* From *Shadow of the Perfect Rose: Collected Poems of Thomas S. Jones, Jr.,* edited with a Memoir and Notes by John L. Foley. Copyright, 1937, by Rinehart & Co., Inc. Used by special permission of John L. Foley, literary executor for Thomas S. Jones, Jr.

** Used by special permission of the author.

What profits it to think?
Grows not the body lean with much thinking?
Why speculate on future years?
May not life's present good be lost in speculation?

This is their goal of life: To eat, to drink, to sleep;
To feel no gnawing of the appetite;
To strive not after things far distant.
Soon cometh death? Much more then must we haste
To find the good this world can give.
Spirit? The word falls dead upon their ears.
Flesh, let the flesh be satisfied!*

—*Thomas Curtis Clark*

THE CONVERSION OF ABRAHAM

At night, upon the silent plain,
Knelt Abraham and watched the sky:
When the bright evening star arose
He lifted up a joyful cry,—
"This is the Lord! This light shall shine
To mark the path for me and mine."
But suddenly the star's fair face
Sank down and left its darkened place.
Then Abraham cried in sore dismay,
"The Lord is not discovered yet,—
I cannot worship gods which set."
Then rose the moon, full orbed and clear,
And flooded all the plain with light,
And Abraham's heart again with joy
O'erflowed at the transcendent sight.
"This surely is the Lord," he cried;
"That other light was pale beside
This glorious one." But like the star
The moon in the horizon far
Sank low and vanished. Then again
Said Abraham, "This cannot be
My Lord: I am but lost, astray,
Unless one changeless guideth me."
Then came, unheralded, the dawn,
Rosy and swift from east to west;
High rode the great triumphant sun,
And Abraham cried, "O last and best
And sovereign Light! now I believe
This Lord will change not, nor deceive."
Each moment robbed the day's fair grace,—
The reddening sun went down apace;
And Abraham, left in rayless night,

* Used by special permission of the author.

Cried, "O my people, let us turn
And worship now the God who rules
These lesser lights, and makes them burn."

—Helen Hunt Jackson

FATHER ABRAHAM

God's chosen Child of Faith across the years
He fathered Nations, dauntless, unafraid—
And each command was but to be obeyed.
His trusting heart that knew no earthly fears,
Arose above all agony and tears,
And thus his sacrifice supreme he made,
And little Isaac on God's Altar laid,
Abiding in a Faith that calms and clears.

He walked with God,—this Patriarch of old,
The chosen Father of a chosen Race—
And all the richness that a life can hold
Was his,—for there is naught that can efface
That wealth of peace and harmony untold,—
To walk with God, in dignity and grace.*

—Lola F. Echard

IN THE LAND OF CANAAN

Perhaps when they reached Canaan Sarah wept
For home and kindred left in Ur's far land,
Perhaps she softly rose while Abram slept
And slipped, alone, outside their tent to stand
Beneath the jewelled sky and tried to read
Its mighty scroll. Had not Jehovah planned
That numberless as stars should be their seed?
How could she trust that promise when the years
Had brought but empty arms and aching need!
She turned, with bitter laughter through her tears;
Her beauty could not still the old unrest,
Nor wealth hold back her loneliness, her fears.
And yet, how soon—her son against her breast—
She, humbly kneeling, called Jehovah blest!**

—Leslie Savage Clark

LOT'S WIFE

A man is made of sterner stuff.
Lot, ready to depart,
Never dreamed how things she loved
Could bind a woman's heart:

* Used by special permission of the author.
** Used by special permission of the author.

Her lamp, her alabaster jar,
Her linen white as snow,
Her garden where the lilies bloomed
Shining row on row.
And while his steady eyes looked far
Across an alien loam,
Sobbing, she turned for one last glimpse
Of all her heart called home.*

—Leslie Savage Clark

ISHMAEL

How Abram must have loved that little son,—
The first of all the seed the Lord foretold—
That brown-skinned child who left his play to run
And proudly follow him from tent to fold.
Perhaps they sat together by the well
Or stopped to watch while new-born lambs were fed,
And Abram gently lifted Ishmael
When he grew tired, and smoothed his small dark head.
With what a heavy heart the father rose
To make his final gift of food the day
The two fled desertwards,—when Sarah chose
That Hagar's child must now be sent away.
Did Ishmael turn and wave,—and Abram stand
To watch, through blurring eyes, that little hand?**

—Leslie Savage Clark

ISAAC

No Abram he, no venturer to lands afar;
No Jacob-dreamer, siring sovereign tribes;
No Moses, bringing laws from Heaven down;
No Saul or David, kings and lords of war;
No rapt Isaiah, counselor to kings;
No fiery Amos, feared by vicious men.
He held no lofty place of power or fame,
He sought no prize for mighty traffickings.
For Isaac was a meek and quiet soul
Content to carry on his fathers' dreams.
He cleaned the wells his sires had digged in hope
Of Fairer realms. A Godly earth his goal.
That we might join the humble Isaac-clan—
Re-dig the Wells of Faith God meant for man!†

—Thomas Curtis Clark

* From *The Ave Maria* (Catholic Home Weekly). Used by special permission of the author and the publisher.
** Used by special permission of the author.
† Used by special permission of the author.

ISAAC'S BLESSING OF JACOB

(Genesis 27:27-29)

I. *The Translation*

Let Jacob be
blessed with
abundance of
corn and wine;
let him be
supreme over
brethren and
peoples.
(Gen. 27:27-29)

My son smells with the odor
Of field that Yahwe blesses.

Of heaven's dew let him give thee,
Of corn and wine in plenty.

Let nations be thy servants,
And peoples bow before thee.

Be lord over thy brothers,
Thy mother's sons bow to thee.

Who curses thee be cursed,
Who blesses thee be blessed.

ISAAC'S BLESSING OF ESAU

(Gen. 27:39, 40)

I. *The Translation*

Barrenness
of land and
servitude
shall be thy
lot, but at last
thou shalt free
thyself.
(Gen. 27:39, 40)

Far from the rich earth thou shalt dwell,
Far from the dew that falls from heaven.

Thou by thy sword shalt have to live,
And to thy brother be a slave.

But when at length thou shalt break loose,
Thou shalt shake from thy neck his yoke.*

JACOB AT THE JABBOK

(Genesis 33)

Jabbok, Jabbok, deep your rift
  In Transjordan's canyoned wall.
Yet your cleft is not so deep
  As that the twins felt pall.

---

* From *The Messages of the Poets,* Vol. II, by Nathaniel Schmidt, pp. 302-3. Copyright, 1911, by Charles Scribner's Sons. Used by special permission of the publisher.

Jabbok, Jabbok, strewn with rocks,
    Oleander lined,
Where the water trickles through
    Shepherds long to find.

Jabbok, Jabbok, where he came
    Whom Jacob feared to see—
Bringing gifts of peace, good-will,
    Flocks and family!

All the ruptured brotherhood,
    Healed since Jacob's dream
Showed him Godhead face to face
    And named him, "Israel."

No more barrier, Jabbok now,
    But a ford of meeting;
Brother reconciled to brother,
    Each the other greeting.

On to Seir, then, Esau strode,
    Flocks and family leading,
On to Shechem Jacob came,
    Keen for Canaan's feeding.

There he raised his altar-stone,
    Tented by a well,
Praising God at Jabbok known,
    Elohe—Israel!*

—Madeleine S. Miller

JACOB'S WELL

Between Mount Ebal and Mount Gerizim,
Where pass the caravans, lies Jacob's well,
Entrenched within a hoary past, Time's citadel.
Here travelers slake their thirst from flowing brim
Of water-pots; maids gossip round its rim
Of circling masonry. It casts a spell
That dims the Now and looses tongues to tell
Of happenings of old, tales glad and grim.

* Used by special permission of the author.

One narrative forever hallows it,
For here a woman of Samaria came
To fill her water jars. One sat there then
Who spoke to her of living water, lit
The dormant spark within her soul to flame,
Bade her to drink and never thirst again.*

—*Georgia Harkness*

WRESTLING JACOB

A masterpiece of religious poetry, based upon Genesis 32:26-31 and Hosea 12:4

Come, O thou Traveller unknown,
    Whom still I hold, but cannot see!
My company before is gone,
    And I am left alone with thee;
With thee all night I mean to stay,
    And wrestle till the break of day.

I need not tell thee who I am,
    My misery or sin declare.
Thyself has called me by my name:
    Look on thy hands, and read it there.
But who, I ask thee, who art thou?
    Tell me thy name, and tell me now.

In vain thou strugglest to get free;
    I never will unloose my hold.
Art thou the Man that died for me?
    The secret of thy love unfold:
Wrestling, I will not let thee go,
    Till I thy name, thy nature know.

Wilt thou not yet to me reveal
    Thy new, unutterable name?
Tell me, I still beseech thee, tell;
    To know it now resolved I am:
Wrestling, I will not let thee go,
    Till I thy name, thy nature know.

'Tis all in vain to hold thy tongue,
    Or touch the hollow of my thigh:
Though every sinew be unstrung,
    Out of my arms thou shalt not fly;
Wrestling, I will not let thee go,
    Till I thy name, thy nature know.

What though my shrinking flesh complain,
  And murmur to contend so long?
I rise superior to my pain:
  When I am weak, then I am strong:
And when my all of strength shall fail,
  I shall with the God-man prevail.

My strength is gone, my nature dies;
  I sink beneath thy weighty hand;
Faint to revive, and fall to rise:
  I fail, and yet by faith I stand.
I stand, and will not let thee go,
  Till I thy name, thy nature know.

Yield to me now, for I am weak,
  But confident in self-despair;
Speak to my heart, in blessings speak;
  Be conquered by my instant prayer:
Speak, or thou never hence shalt move,
  And tell me if thy name is Love.

'Tis Love! 'tis Love! thou didst for me;
  I hear thy whisper in my heart.
The morning breaks, the shadows flee;
  Pure, universal Love thou art:
To me, to all, thy bowels move;
  Thy nature and thy name is Love.

My prayer hath power with God; the grace
  Unspeakable I now receive;
Through faith I see thee face to face;
  I see thee face to face, and live.
In vain I have not wept and strove
  Thy nature and thy name is Love.

I know thee, Saviour, who thou art,
  Jesus, the feeble sinner's Friend;
Nor wilt thou with the night depart,
  But stay and love me to the end:
Thy mercies never shall remove;
  Thy nature and thy name is Love.

The Sun of Righteousness on me
  Hath rose with healing in his wings:
Withered my nature's strength; from thee
  My soul its life and succor brings.
My help is all laid up above,
  Thy nature and thy name is Love.

Contented now, upon my thigh
    I halt, till life's short journey end;
All helplessness, all weakness, I
    On thee alone for strength depend;
Nor have I power from thee to move:
    Thy nature and thy name is Love.

Lame as I am, I take the prey;
    Hell, earth, and sin, with ease o'ercome;
I leap for joy, pursue my way,
    And as a bounding hart fly home,
Through all eternity to prove
    Thy nature and thy name is Love.

—*Charles Wesley*

ON DOTHAN PLAIN (JUBB YUSUF)

(Genesis 37:28; II Kings 6:23)

The dusty plain of Dothan
    Still echoes Joseph's name,
Where age-old camel caravan
    The modern road became.

The cistern-pit where he was tossed
    Yet holds the winter rain,
Where shepherds still their fat sheep bring
    To crop the *Tell's** cut grain.

And brothers still their brothers sell,
    Though Ishmaelites are gone.
The land, the land! The yearned-for land—
    The contest still goes on.

Yet, slave-sold Joseph lived to rule
    At Pharaoh's golden court,
And lived to feast his brothers, starved,
    Though Jacob's years were short.

He fed their families and flocks,
    His love to demonstrate,
His many-colored coat exchanged
    For plaited kilts of state.

Forgiveness like to God's was his,
    And pity that did weep
While yet a power next in rank
    To Pharaoh's he did keep.

* Tell (the Arab word for mound) is a flat-topped mound which, when excavated, is found to contain layers of masonry, deposits of pottery, clay tablets, or other evidences of man's occupation in successive periods.

God, let us not resent our slight,
    Though justified the grudge.
For Thou alone dost see the right,
    And Thou alone canst judge.

Send us such chariots of resource
    As to Elisha came
While praying on old Dothan's Plain
    To check Ben-hadad's fame.

The forces that are with us prove
    Far more than those we dread.
The mountains are alive with friends—
    Our enemies have fled.*

—*Madeleine S. Miller*

THE DEATH OF JACOB

I saw the Syrian sunset's meteor-crown
    Hang over Bethel for a little space;
I saw a gentle wandering boy lie down,
    With tears upon his face.

Sheer up the fathomless, transparent blue,
    Rose jasper-battlement and crystal wall:
Rung all the night-air, pierced through and through
    With harps angelical.

And a great ladder was set up the while
    From earth to heaven, with angels on each round:
Barks, that bore precious freight to earth's far isle,
    Or sailed back homeward bound.

Ah! many a time we look on star-lit nights
    Up to the sky, as Jacob did of old,
Look longing up to the eternal lights,
    To spell their lines of gold.

But never more, as to the Hebrew boy,
    Each on his way, the angels walk abroad;
And never more we hear, with awful joy,
    The audible voice of God.

Yet to pure eyes the ladder still is set,
    And angel visitants still come and go;
Many bright messengers are moving yet
    From the dark world below.

* Used by special permission of the author.

Thoughts that are red-crossed Faith's outspreading wings;
    Prayers of the Church are keeping time and tryst;
Heart-wishes, making bee-like murmurings,
    Their flower the Eucharist;

Spirits elect, through suffering rendered meet
    For those high mansions; from the nursery door
Bright babies that climb up with their clay-cold feet,
    Upon the golden floor.

These are the messengers, forever wending
    From earth to heaven, that Faith alone may scan;
These are the angels of our God, ascending
    Upon the Son of man.*

—William Alexander

✠

ABRAM SON OF TERAH

By

Florence Marvyne Bauer

Now Jehovah said unto Abram, Get thee out of thy country, and from thy kindred, and from thy father's house, unto the land that I will show thee: and I will make of thee a great nation, and I will bless thee, and make thy name great; and be thou a blessing: and I will bless them that bless thee, and him that curseth thee will I curse: and in thee shall all the families of the earth be blessed. So Abram went, as Jehovah had spoken unto him; and Lot with him: . . . And Abram took Sarai his wife, and Lot his brother's son, and all their substance that they had gathered, and the souls that they had gotten in Haran; and they went forth to go into the land of Canaan.— GENESIS 12:1-5

AND so it came to pass that Terah with his youngest son, and Sarai, his son's wife, and Lot, Haran's son, joined themselves to the great company camped beyond the western walls of the city and began the long, long journey toward the moon god's city far to the northwest. . . .

Abram lay wide-eyed and sleepless in his black goat's-hair tent. The caravan encampment had not yet lost its animation, for occasional bleating of sheep or barking of dogs broke the cold silence of the desert night. At the entrance of his house of hair, his father's little ass shifted its weight, its dim outlines wavering in the silver moonlight. Beside Abram the old man Terah breathed lightly, and, beyond him, Haran's son slept the deep sleep of the young. On the other side of the curtain which separated her part of the tent from theirs, Abram could hear Sarai stirring restlessly.

<hr>

* On June 1, 1857, the University of Oxford selected "The Death of Jacob" for an award for the best poem on a sacred subject.

He sighed, appreciation of her loyalty lifting some of his dread of that which lay ahead of them. She had cooked for the four of them over dung fires and waited lovingly on the aged Terah. She had trudged cheerfully beside the little ass through long days of oppressive heat. To his demand that she wear a veil at all times, she had acquiesced, although it must often have been hot and irksome. She had been gentle and understanding with Haran's son and affectionate with her oftentimes irritable husband.

Abram, staring now at the gently undulating roof, wondered about the beautiful woman who was his wife. What were her thoughts as she plodded along the ancient trail? Did she secretly long for the comforts of the house of Ur and the luxuries of the palace at Marad? Was she mourning for Haran and Anah in the privacy of her veil? Was she weeping now perhaps—all alone on her pallet? How selfish was he! How far from those ideals Eber had taught him! He had been so wrapped up in his foreboding that he had not thought of anyone but himself.

He turned his face from the open doorway and closed his eyes. Out of the past rushed pictures that were precious to him, but they brought him no comfort, for the security they represented was lost to him. He saw himself a small boy again, watching the kinsmen gather to honor his brother Haran. What a crowd! His people and their servants.

He sighed. He was no longer a small boy in the security of his father's house. He was a man, responsible for the care and safety of a frail broken-hearted old man, a remarkably beautiful woman and a boy who was resentful of the hardships they must suffer. Four persons out of all that number who had come together to honor Haran! One by one he had lost them. Desolation settled on his spirit, and he covered his head with his cloak, hoping that sleep would come and blot out his sorrow for a time.

But his mind refused to slumber. One thought followed another, while he told himself that he must sleep, that dawn would soon come and bring another departure for the caravan. Would their supply of silver last them until he could find work in that distant city to which his father was determined to go? Would the men of that city be friendly to strangers? Would they take Sarai from him? Would his father live to see that city? Would Lot, now numbed by grief, later prove difficult?

Abram remembered how spoiled the boy was, recalled his arrogance in his father's palace. Would he call undesired attention to their little group by being supercilious and curt, or boastful of his past? The people in the caravan had so far given only casual heed to the members of Terah's party, no doubt assuming they were mushkinu like themselves. But if the boy bragged as boys are apt to do—what then? Abram wondered if Lot would obey his words of warning.

Suddenly the young man uncovered his head and turned to lie on his back again. Because his hands were hot against his sides he thrust them from him. One hand touched his father's warm skin and for an instant Abram felt that Eber was there beside him. Eber—beloved companion! Without his presence, the world was a frightening place, filled with ill omens and misfortune. Without him, his

God had seemed to retreat. Where was Yah? Had he forgotten Eber's friend? Where was the peace which came from knowing that the Lord Yah was his Patron, his Protector?

His thoughts went back to the days on his farm when he and Eber had worked side by side. Perhaps he dozed, dreaming of those times of companionship with his friend, for he thought he heard the Amorite's voice saying, "Abram, son of Terah."

He started up, his heart swelling with joy. "Here I am!"

But the voice that answered him was not Eber's. It lacked the gruff qualities he remembered. "Abram, son of Terah."

Abram opened his eyes and found the tent aglow with a peculiar radiance. It dazzled, yet warmed him. He shut his eyes against its brilliance, yet he felt no fear. His body seemed suddenly light, suspended in boundless space, which was somehow comforting. The world and its anxieties had dropped away from him. Every part of his being seemed suffused by tranquillity.

The voice spoke again. It was warm, compelling, musical. "Son of Terah, I am your Friend. I am Yah."

Filled with breathless exaltation, Abram heard himself ask, "O Lord Yah, what shall I do?"

"Believe that I am the most high God, Creator of all things, and I will bless you."

"O Lord most high, I do believe."

"Trust Me, and I will lead you to a land which your sons shall inherit."

"O Most High, I will trust Thee."

"If you will obey my words, I will prosper you and make your name great among men. Do you believe I am able to do this?"

Now Abram spoke with assurance. "Is anything too hard for Him Who created all things?" he asked. "O Lord Yah, Almighty God, I will obey thy voice."

Gradually the strange light vanished, but the wondrous peace remained in Abram's heart. Gone was his dread of the future. Gone were his grief and despair. Thanksgiving filled him like an overflowing cup. Yah had not forgotten him. He had made Himself the God of Abram, Terah's youngest son. He had promised him a dwelling place. He had said that sons would inherit that promised land.

All of his life Abram had yearned after a Patron whose power was limitless, Whose holiness and justice exceeded the understanding of men, Whose perfection inspired them to live in righteousness. He had longed for a God Who listened to man's prayers and understood his cravings, Who answered when man called to Him. And all the time Yah had been seeking him, he now realized. When he was a boy, the most high God had stated that He was his Patron. He had lingered near a scornful young man while his slave prayed, allowing Himself to be limited by Abram's doubts. He had revealed His glory to that young man as soon as His existence was acknowledged.

Now at last Abram knew the truth. Not only must he recognize the existence of Yah, but he must believe that the most high God possessed to a boundless degree every quality he had sought in a Patron. His doubts limited Yah. That had been the secret of Eber's strength. The Amorite had believed Yah able to arrange everything, no matter how gloomy the circumstances appeared in the view of mankind. Remembering his farm and those events that led to his loss of it, Abram wondered how the Most High would have saved it, but he no longer doubted that Yah could have done so.

"Believe . . . Trust Me . . . Believe I am able . . ." the Lord Yah had said.

And I promised to believe Him, thought Abram. We are friends. We have a covenant with each other. If I believe Him, if I refuse to doubt His power, He will bless me.

Again his thoughts drifted back into the past. He thought of his mother's ambition to give him an education, of the ideals in his father's house—Terah's and Amittai's had been widely separated, but each had its good quality—of his experiences in the palace of the king, of his life on his farm, of his friendship with Eber which had been built at first out of his love of Shuah, of the tenderness of Shelomith and its influence on her daughter who was to become his wife, of Haran's ideals of worship which had no doubt influenced his yearning after a God-Companion. How much had Yah had to do with the shaping of his life?

Surely, if the most high God had made a plan for the life of Terah's youngest son, He must have had a hand in arranging these things. The Potter had shaped the clay from the beginning, and would continue its development.

Now the future looked bright with promise to the young man lying under the black roof of the goat's-hair tent. His eyes closed and drowsiness took possession of him. Believe . . . trust . . . the most high God . . .*

✛

ABRAHAM AND ISAAC
By
Warwick Deeping
A Great Bible Drama of a Father's Love Retold

Now, in those days when men dwelt in walled cities, or wandered as nomads with their wealth in their flocks and herds, that woman was blessed who bore many children, and the male child was blessed in the eyes of the Lord. For the flocks and herds had to be watched and tended. The world was young and fierce, and pastures and wells were precious, and if a man would keep that which was his, he asked of his wife strong sons.

Now Abraham had riches, and much sheep and cattle, and many servants—but Sarah his wife was barren. Abraham had prayed to his God, and besought Him that Sarah might bear a child. Though his God listened to Abraham, no son was born.

Abraham was more than a flock-master and a merchant; he was a seer. He would commune with his God, and God promised Abraham that he should be the father of a great people. But still Abraham had no son, and he and Sarah his wife were troubled.

There came a famine in Canaan, where Abraham dwelt, and he led his people and his flocks into the land of Egypt, but when Abraham came into the land of the Pharaohs he feared the Egyptians. Cowardice smote him and he was afraid for his wealth and his wife —but his greatest fear was for himself.

Abraham said in his heart: "Lo, Sarah is beautiful, and I am at the mercy of the Egyptians. They will kill me because of my wife." So Abraham lied to the Egyptians and spoke of Sarah as his sister, and Sarah was silent for her husband's sake.

Then did Pharaoh see her beauty and desire it, and Sarah was taken to the palace, and for her sake Pharaoh treated Abraham well.

But what was in Sarah's heart? Was she woman and proud of this tribute to her beauty? Did she feel scorn for the coward in her husband? But the soul of Sarah was hidden; she was a woman.

Now Abraham's God was displeased, and he plagued Pharaoh and his house because of Sarah, and when Pharaoh's eyes were opened he was wrath with Abraham because of the deceit. "What hast thou done to me?" he cried.

And he scorned Abraham, and he commanded his men to take Abraham and his wife and people and thrust them out of Egypt, for Pharaoh was a great and magnanimous king.

Sarah Casts Out Hagar

It happened that Sarah took with her an Egyptian serving-maid named Hagar, and when Sarah knew that she was not to have a child her thoughts turned upon Hagar. A son there must be to fill the heart of her husband, and to bear his destiny, and Sarah was generous. She gave Hagar, her handmaid, to Abraham.

But Hagar was young and vain. She began to despise the mistress who was barren. She became insolent and proud in the presence of Sarah. "Lo, thy husband is mine. His child is mine. I shall be everything and thou—nothing."

And Hagar swaggered like a fool, not knowing the strength of Sarah, her mistress. And Sarah caused Hagar to be flung out into the desert, and the people obeyed Sarah, nor would Abraham save the wench. He feared Sarah's wrath, because the wrath of love can be terrible.

Now the forsaken Hagar bore a son—one Ishmael—and with the babe in her arms her pride was chastened. She was afraid for the child. She journeyed back to the tents of Abraham, and abased herself before Sarah. "I am afraid for the child in the wilderness, lest he should die."

And Sarah was merciful to Hagar at this time. She suffered her to bring her child into the tents of Abraham. So Abraham had his son—but it was Hagar's child.

One day three strangers came to Abraham's tent. They were Divine messengers sent for the destruction of Sodom. They said unto Abraham: "Sarah, thy wife, shall have a son." And Abraham laughed. "My wife is growing old. Do you mock me?"

Sodom was destroyed, and Gommorah with it, but not before Abraham had pleaded with his God for them to save the life of Lot and his people.

Then—once more—Abraham played the coward. He came into the land of a certain King Abimelech, and again Abraham feared for his life and riches because of Sarah. He called her his sister, and once more Sarah consented. There was bitterness in her. She was growing old; she had failed.

And Abimelech and his people afflicted by Abraham's God because of Sarah, learnt the truth and reproached Abraham and sent him forth from their land.

Did Abraham feel shame? Perhaps, God and Sarah knew.

Then, wonder of wonders, the thing happened, and Sarah bore her son Isaac. In her joy she cried out: "God hath made me to laugh, and all the world shall laugh with me."

And Abraham laughed. His joy was great in him. He had warriors and wealth, cattle and sheep—and a son, Sarah's son.

But what of Sarah, and what of Hagar, and the boy Ishmael?

Now was seen the ruthlessness of Sarah, the mother passion. There should be no rival to Isaac, no elder half-brother to contend for the inheritance. Her child—the wonder child—the God child, should be prince and lord.

When Sarah had had no child the world had been very different. But she had not forgotten Hagar's insolence. Again Sarah cast out Hagar and Ishmael into the desert, though Abraham's heart misgave him; he had love for Ishmael. Ishmael had been so much to him before Isaac had come, but Sarah, the ruthless mother, prevailed. Hagar and Ishmael were cast out.

But what of God? Through many years God had watched His chosen man, this creature called Abraham, and Abraham was a thing of contradictions. He was both brave and a coward; he loved his wealth, he loved his son. And God gazed upon Abraham and pondered:

This man is gold, and he is clay. Behold—I will lay a test upon him; I will try him to the death; I will wring his vitals. I will prove him. I will ask of him his son.

So God appeared unto Abraham in the night while Abraham and Sarah and all the people were asleep, and God called Abraham. And Abraham awoke in the tent:

"Who calls me?"

"It is thy God."

Abraham rose upon his knees and bowed himself, and in another part of the great tent the boy and Sarah and the women were sleeping.

Then God said unto Abraham:

"Take now thy son, thy only son Isaac, whom thou lovest, and get thee into the land of Morrah, and offer him there for a burnt offering upon one of the mountains of which I shall tell thee of."

And great fear came upon Abraham. He lifted his arms in the darkness, and called upon God. "My son, my only son Isaac! Will not my Lord be merciful? Let thy servant die—if only the child may live."

But there was silence, for God had withdrawn Himself, and Abraham covered his head and wept.

What strange sacrifice was this, his son, his beloved, the promised of the Lord? And the heart of Abraham rebelled in him, and in the bitterness of the moment, the man in him strove with God.

"O, Lord, lay not this thing upon me."

But there was silence.

Presently Abraham arose, and casting his mantle over him, he passed out of the great tent into the night. The sky was full of God's stars, and the night sealed with God's silence, and Abraham stood and gazed upon the stars. His people and his flocks slept, and yonder in the tent Sarah and the child slumbered.

And Abraham's heart smote him. What of Sarah, his wife? Should he speak to her of this dreadful thing, tell her that the flesh of Isaac was to be consumed upon the altar?

No, Sarah should sleep on. When God had been obeyed, then—she should know of the sacrifice.

So Abraham sat down outside the tent and covered his head with his mantle and waited for the dawn. Then he arose and called two of his young men and bade them saddle an ass and cleave wood for the burnt offering, but he himself went and stood in the doorway of the tent. And lo, Isaac his son was awake, and the women were still sleeping, and Abraham beckoned to the boy.

And Isaac arose and went to his father.

"Father what would you? It is early."

But Abraham laid a finger on his lip, and taking the boy by the hand, led him to where the two young men waited with the ass.

"My son, we go to make a burnt offering to the Lord our God."

The boy smiled at him, and to Abraham there was death in that smile.

To The Place of Sacrifice

So they set out together, Abraham and his little son, and the two young men and the ass, and for two days they journeyed, and each night the child slept, curled up against his father. But Abraham slept little, and in the night he yearned over Isaac, his son, and his heart was heavy in him.

Meanwhile, Sarah, his wife, sat alone in the tent in the midst of the flocks and the people, for the soul of Sarah was troubled. It was as though she felt a presence near her, and the shadow of some dreadful thing. She would neither eat nor speak, and Sarah was afraid.

Now on the third day of the journey Abraham lifted up his eyes and saw the place afar off, and in the silence of his heart Abraham cried out unto his God:

"Lord, I am weak: let this bitter thing pass from me. Lo, I have sinned much; take Thou my life and let the boy go to his mother."

But there was silence, and Abraham, holding the child by the hand, fared on.

Then Abraham said to the young men: "Abide here with the ass, and I and the lad will go yonder and worship, and come again to you."

The eyes of the young men troubled Abraham, and he took the wood of the burnt offering and laid it upon Isaac, his son, and he took the fire in his hand, and a knife; and they went both of them together.

The way was steep and stony, and Abraham's eyes looked up to the high place where the offering was to be made, and he thought in his heart—"Is God there?" But his eyes beheld nothing but the rocks and the sky.

And the wood lay heavy upon Isaac, and the child spoke to Abraham: "Father, do we climb to far?"

Abraham took the wood upon his shoulders. Then Isaac looked up to his father and smiled: "Behold the fire and the wood, but where is the lamb for the burnt offering?"

"My son, God will provide Himself a lamb for a burnt offering."

So they went both of them together, the child trusting and without fear, and they came to the place which God had appointed.

Abraham put the wood from off his shoulders, and set down the brazen bowl of fire. Then he said unto his son: "Bring stones and we will build the altar."

And Abraham and Isaac gathered stones and piled them, and to the boy it was but a game. Then Abraham laid the wood upon the altar and raised his eyes to heaven:

"O God, I am Thy servant."

There was silence. Then Abraham looked upon his son and laughed, and his laughter was for the child's sake:

"My son, let us play together before God. I will bind thee upon the altar, and we will pretend together that thou art the lamb."

Now, there was no fear in the child's eyes, and he suffered his father to bind him and to lay him upon the altar. And Abraham took the knife and then closed his eyes, and saw naught but a great blackness. For the boy trusted him and had no fear.

And then Abraham opened his eyes and stretched forth his hand to slay his son, and suddenly the angel of the Lord called to him out of heaven, "Abraham, Abraham."

And the angel said:

"Lay not thine hand upon the lad, neither do thou anything unto him; for now I know thou fearest God, seeing that thou hast not withheld thy son, thine only son, from me."

Abraham's Cry to Heaven

And Abraham stood and gazed into heaven, and lo—a great cry burst from him:

"Father, O Father, now I know that thou art my Father."

And thrusting the knife into his girdle, he fell upon the child and kissed him, and Abraham's face was wet.

"My son, my only son, this day hath God shown me that God is our Father."

And Abraham lifted up his eyes and looked and behold—behind him there was a ram caught in a thicket by his horns, and Abraham went and took the ram and offered him up for a burnt offering in the stead of his son.

Then, the angel of the Lord called to Abraham out of the heaven a second time and said: "By myself have I sworn, because thou hadst done this thing, and hadst withheld not thy son, thine only son, from me, that in blessing, I will bless thee, and in multiplying, I will multiply thy seed as the stars of heaven."

So Abraham returned to the young men, and they rose up and went together to Beersheba, where the flocks and the herds and the people tarried.

And Abraham gave back Isaac to Sarah his mother, and when Abraham spoke to Sarah of all that which was passed, Sarah was silent, gazing upon her child.*

✢

ISAAC TAKES A WIFE

By

Florence M. Earlle

ABRAHAM had lived in the land of Canaan for a long time. Here Isaac had been born and Sarah had died. Now Isaac was forty years old —old enough to marry, according to the custom of the times. Yet Abraham did not want him to marry a girl from the tribe of the Canaanites. He wanted him to have a wife from the same people from which he had come; if possible from his brother Nahor's family. And so one day Abraham called his head servant, Eliezer, and told him to go to his old home in Haran.

"You will find a wife for Isaac there. Swear to me that you will not take a wife for him from among these Canaanites."

"Perhaps the girl will not want to come with me," objected Eliezer. "If that is true, shall I come and take Isaac back with me?"

"No," said Abraham. "If she will not follow you, you shall be free from your oath. But I am sure you can find a wife among our kin in Haran."

Probably Isaac knew that his father had sent Eliezer·on that errand; but he would have nothing to say about the choice of the girl. The Oriental boy did not see his bride until after the wedding.

So Eliezer took ten camels burdened with all sorts of valuable things—for the bride must be bought—provisions for the journey, and several slaves. After a number of weeks of travel, for they could only journey in the early morning hours and in the late afternoon and evening on account of the heat, Eliezer arrived in Haran just at sunset. It was fortunate, for at that time of the day, the girls of the city would come to the public well for the water supply for the family. Now he would have opportunity to observe them and to choose one.

Before anyone came, he prayed, "Oh Lord, give me a sign. If I ask a girl for a

---

* From *The Sunday Chronicle*, Dec. 13, 1931. Used by special permission of the publisher and Mrs. M. P. Warwick Deeping.

drink and she not only gives me one, but offers to water the camels also, let that girl be the one for Isaac."

Almost before he had finished praying, a very pretty girl came to the spring, carrying her water pitcher on her head. Eliezer waited until she had filled the pitcher, then he said, "Will you give me to drink?"

"Of course!"

She let the pitcher down from her shoulder to her hand, and said, "Drink, and when you are through, I will water the camels, also. They must be thirsty, for you look as if you had traveled far."

Eliezer watched while she filled the trough for the animals. When she had finished, he took a heavy gold nose ring from his bag and put it in her nose. Then he put two heavy gold bracelets on her wrists, and said, "Whose daughter are you? And is there room in your father's house that I may spend the night?"

"I am Rebecca, the daughter of Bethuel and granddaughter of Nahor," she said. "And there is plenty of room in our house for you and all your animals and servants."

Then she turned and ran home to tell about the stranger and show the gifts she had received for watering his camels. But Eliezer did not follow her. He bowed his head and thanked God that he had been led to the home of his master's brother.

Now when Laban, the brother of Rebecca, saw the gifts, he knew that the stranger must be a man of wealth. He hurried to the well, and said, "Come in, the Lord's blessing on you," and brought Eliezer to the house of the men. The camels were unharnessed and fed. Water was given to Eliezer and his servants to wash their feet, and then food was set before them.

But Eliezer said, "I will not eat till I tell you who I am and why I am here. I am the servant of Abraham, your grandfather's brother, who went to the land of Canaan so many years ago. He is a very rich man, and in his old age, he had a son named Isaac. He is old enough now to marry; and my master sent me here to find him a wife among his own people. I prayed that the girl who gave me a drink and offered to water the camels might be the one, and Rebecca did just that. If you are willing, I would like to take her. If you are not, then I will hunt among other girls here in Haran."

And Laban said to his father, "This is the Lord's doing; we are willing, are we not, that she should be the wife of Isaac?"

Then Eliezer brought out gifts of gold and silver and rich robes for Rebecca as a part of her bridal clothing. He also gave beautiful presents to her mother and her brother, for these gifts were the price paid for the bride. That night there was feasting, music, and merriment.

The next morning Eliezer said, "Let us start for home."

"Oh, no!" begged Rebecca's mother and brother. "Let her stay at least ten days that we may have much feasting and rejoicing before she goes."

But Eliezer insisted until they said, "Well, let us ask her," and they called Rebecca and said to her: "Will you go at once with this man?" And Rebecca answered: "Yes, I will go."

So they gave her a nurse, her maid, and gifts and let her go, watching the little group as they rode away on the camels that Eliezer had brought.

Meanwhile at home in Canaan, Abraham wondered what good fortune Eliezer might be having; but he did not expect him to return for a long time.

One evening Isaac went out into the fields to think and perhaps to dream of his coming bride. Suddenly he saw a train of camels coming. As they drew nearer, he saw that they were his father's beasts and that Eliezer was riding at the head of the caravan. When he started to meet them, he saw a girl dismount from her camel and cover herself with her veil. This was his bride whose face he would not see until after the marriage ceremony was over.

Eliezer told him all that had happened, and Isaac took Rebecca by the hand and led her into his mother's tent which would be hers until they were married.

We have no record of the wedding, but we may be sure it was a magnificent one for the time, with music and dancing and feasting for a whole week or perhaps even longer. And when it was over, Isaac took his bride to his tent and loved her to the end of his life.*

✛

JOSEPH: THE POOR BOY WHO SAVED A COUNTRY

By

Lord Dunsany

IN a time so remote that it bridges, this story alone, the gap between the years of which we know anything and the long lost Egypt of Rameses, in wanderers' tents in the desert lived Jacob and all his sons.

Rather than desert it was that doubtful land, in which the flocks may be fed, but by moving them as soon as the scanty vegetation is eaten; only nomads can farm such lands.

And so it was that Jacob's sons had gone to Shechem to feed their flocks; all but Joseph, then only seventeen; and when Joseph was sent by his father to see if all were well with his brothers in Shechem he found that they had gone on to Dothan. And in Dothan Joseph found his brothers' welcome.

And because he never guessed what this welcome would be the sharps of the world will always deride him. There was reason enough for that welcome; firstly, he was his father's favourite son; secondly, he was a dreamer, and so his brothers despised him.

In utter trustfulness he went in that lonely land among eleven men, all jealous of his power to dream, and only hiding their jealousy with hatred. When his brothers saw him they said: "Behold this dreamer cometh. Come now, and let us slay him . . . and we shall see what will become of his dreams."

Reuben, the eldest son, had decent feelings, and told the rest not to kill the

* Used by special permission of the author.

boy but to put him into a pit, meaning himself to come and free him afterwards, and restore him to Jacob, their father. And that is what they did, first taking the boy's coloured coat that his father had given him.

"And they took him and cast him into a pit; and the pit was empty, there was no water in it." I think those words, "There was no water in it," show us that the pit was a well, and it was dry.

Sold by His Own Brothers

There his brothers left Joseph, "and they sat down to eat bread." And at this moment a company of Ishmaelites rode by, coming from Gilead with their camels on their way with spices to Egypt. And some kind of compunction stirred Judah.

And what he felt, and the course that he recommended, and what the others thought of it, may be found in verse twenty-seven of the thirty-seventh chapter of Genesis: "Come and let us sell him to the Ishmaelites, and let not our hand be upon him; for he is our brother and our flesh. And his brethren were content."

So they pulled him up from the well with the help of some Midianites, and sold him to the Ishmaelites, who took him with them to Egypt. And when Reuben came back, the boy was not to be found. And the rest took the bright coat and stained it with the blood of a kid, and told their father that Joseph had been killed by a wild beast, and left him to mourn. This happened among the sons of a man that had treated his own brother no better.

And so Joseph came into Egypt. He was sold to Potiphar, a captain of the guards. We are told little but that he found grace in Potiphar's sight. But in a very short time he ran the whole of Potiphar's household. Probably Potiphar had never had it well run before.

This lad who had seen crops won from the desert, and milk gained from the herds, and famine kept at a distance, knew something about the importance of provisions; and Potiphar, who commanded men, and at least knew when his household was being properly managed, though he could not do it himself, soon left everything to Joseph. "And he left all that he had in Joseph's hands; and he knew not ought he had, save the bread which he did eat."

The good are no more welcome among the bad, than the bad are among the good; and the putting of a large household upon a sound basis was probably resented by many, though the final blow came from Potiphar's wife. Joseph was true to his master in every detail, and when Potiphar's wife tried to make love to him he looked on this as a temptation to the greatest disloyalty he could commit.

About this temptation he used no more tact than he had used in telling his dreams to his brothers. Among bad women the device of Potiphar's wife is probably admired to this day. She merely accused Joseph of the disloyalty that he had refused to commit, showing such circumstantial evidence as she could collect to Potiphar, and Joseph was cast into prison.

There he had the opportunity of meeting, and even speaking with, the King's butler and the King's baker, who were also in prison. And both of these men dreamed. And Joseph was what his brothers had derisively called him, a dreamer: these strange and difficult things were familiar to him, for he knew the way of dreams.

Brought before Pharaoh

So they asked Joseph for the interpretation of their dreams, the King's butler first. And he told him that he should be butler again, and put the cup once more with his own hand into Pharaoh's.

The baker eagerly told his dream next, a dream not too unlike the butler's; and Joseph foretold from it that the baker would be hanged. And both of these things happened as Joseph had foretold, within three days.

Two years went by and then one night Pharaoh dreamed. But there was none to interpret his dream. And then the butler remembered Joseph. Not that he had exactly forgotten him; but it was one thing to have said: "I have a young friend in prison, who says he is innocent," and quite another to stand forth and say: "I know the man that Pharaoh needs, one whom I have seen interpret dreams."

So Joseph was taken out of prison at last, and brought before Pharaoh. And Pharaoh said: "I have had a curious dream. I dreamt that seven good fat cows came up out of the river. And afterwards seven lean ones came up, very lean indeed, and they ate the seven fat cows; and then the lean cows were no fatter for it. And I had another dream; I dreamt that there were seven ears of corn on one stalk, good full ears; and then seven thin ears, blasted with the East winds, sprung up after them; and then the thin ears devoured the seven good ears. And the magicians can make nothing of it."

And the first thing that Joseph said, who had shown so little tact as a boy when telling his dream to his brothers, and who had also offended Potiphar's wife, was: "God hath showed Pharaoh what He is about to do."

And then he gave the simple interpretations of the two dreams; they were one, said Joseph: the fat kine were seven good years, and the good ears of corn were seven good years; the lean kine that ate up the fat kine were seven years of famine, and the thin ears of corn also; and Pharaoh should appoint a man, with officers under him, to store grain in the good years and keep the food in the cities.

Pharaoh must have known the uncertainty of the Nile, on which Egypt depended more than any other country on any other river in the world. He had probably ordered them before now to store grain; but he had nobody with any idea of the magnitude of the need, or who was able to see the need during the abundant harvest, until it was too late.

Now, perhaps, he sought for a man with sufficient intelligence to imagine such a famine as must come some day, and to take precautions against it. However that be, he certainly found such a man, and immediately recognized him. And Pharaoh said to Joseph: "I am Pharaoh," and gave him absolute power over the whole of Egypt, and gave him a strange Egyptian name, and married him to a daughter of the Priest of On.

And then the Nile, from which the fat cows came in the dream, and the lean cows after them, must have begun to dwindle. And whatever narrowed the Nile, bringing famine to Egypt, parched the crops of neighbouring lands also; so that not only the Egyptians came to be fed to Joseph, but all the tribes that the Egyptians knew.

Joseph's Brethren Visit Egypt

And now we turn from such a story as history might tell, to one so human that in no bare chronicle of facts would one look for its like; rather in poetry we would search for such a tale as this, or find some such legend peeping out from the folk-lore of a wise and simple people. Old Jacob heard that there was corn in Egypt, and told his sons to go into Egypt and buy it, so that they should live; only Benjamin, his youngest son, he would not let go.

And these brothers came to the Governor of all the land, to pray him to sell them corn; and that governor was Joseph. And they did not know him; they never had known him truly; but Joseph knew them.

He pretended not to know them; he pretended to think they were spies; and when they told him who they were, and told him of their old father and of their youngest brother, Benjamin, his own full brother, then he told them to send one of their number to fetch Benjamin so as to prove their words, while the rest were held in prison, swearing by nothing less than the life of Pharaoh that unless he brought Benjamin they should die. Afterwards he relented and allowed all but one to go, and to take back corn to their homes, and he kept Simeon, only, as hostage in prison.

Then Reuben not knowing that the Governor would understand them, because they had been speaking through an interpreter, reproached the rest for what they had done to Joseph, believing that this evil had overtaken them because of the wrong they had done then. Then Joseph turned round from them and wept, and came back to them and took Simeon and bound him.

Found Money in Their Sacks

And the ten brothers went away with the corn loaded on their asses, and all the money they paid for the corn was put by command of Joseph into their sacks. So they went home to their father. And when they found the money in their sacks they were terrified, for they knew nothing of this strange play of Joseph.

And again hunger came to the tents of Jacob, and all the corn was gone. Then Jacob said to his sons: "Go again, buy us a little food." And Judah told him again that "the man" who was lord of Egypt would give them nothing unless they brought Benjamin with them; and this, Jacob had refused to allow, believing that death had overtaken Simeon and Joseph too, and that now his son Benjamin would go the same way if he let him go into Egypt.

But at last the famine being very severe, Jacob gave way; but insisted upon his sons taking a present to the man of balm, myrrh, spices and nuts. And again the brothers stood before Joseph.

When Joseph saw that Benjamin was really come with them he gave orders for a banquet to be prepared, and commanded that these men should be brought to his own house to dine with him.

But the rest of the brothers were afraid when they were brought into the great house; for they remembered the money that they had found in their sacks, and they told the steward all about it: and he only brought Simeon to them, and gave them water and gave food to their donkeys, and told them that he had duly received the money that they had paid for their food.

Then Joseph himself came in, and they gave him the myrrh and nuts that were to appease him, and prostrated themselves before him. And Joseph asked about the health of the old man, their father, of whom he remembered them speaking. Was he still alive? And they said he lived. Then Joseph saw his brother Benjamin; and at that he left them, looking for a place where he could weep alone; and he came to his own room and wept there. Then he washed his face and came back to them.

And after the dinner that they had, Joseph ordered that their sacks should be filled with food, and that his own silver cup should be put in Benjamin's sack, and his corn money, for he kept to his strange play. And as soon as it was light, they set forth on their journey, travelling through the cool hours.

Then Joseph sent his steward after them, telling him to accuse them of stealing the cup, the cup from which Joseph drank and whereby he divined. And this was done, and all the brothers came back to Joseph. And Joseph demanded that Benjamin, because of this, should remain in Egypt as his servant. Then Judah told his story, saying that if they went back without Benjamin it would kill their father, and Judah would see him die.

Then suddenly Joseph ordered that every man should leave them. And when all were gone from him and his brothers he wept aloud and said to them: "I am Joseph; doth my father yet live?" And while they stood silent he soothed their fears by telling them that when they sold him, God had sent him to Egypt to preserve life.

Saved with the People of Egypt

Then they parted again for a while, the brothers going back to bring their father, so that all should live together with Joseph in Egypt, where Joseph could save them all from the famine. There had now been two years of famine and there were five more years to come. And they told Jacob that Joseph lived and was lord of Egypt; and when they could get the old man to believe it, they all went with their wives and children together to Egypt, in carts that Joseph had provided for them.

And so all came back to Joseph, and he saw his father again. And he saved the people of Egypt from the famine, though he got all their lands for Pharaoh, excepting only the lands that the priests owned.

Joseph lived to the age of one hundred and ten years; and one day he said to his brothers, "I die," and took from them an oath such as he had sworn to their father, not to leave his body in Egypt, when they should go, as they one day would, into the land of Canaan. And they swore, and when Joseph died they embalmed his body; and the day came when Moses fulfilled their oath. So ends this great romance.

"Now there arose up a new king of Egypt, which knew not Joseph."*

✝

ANCIENT OF DAYS, THRONED IN GLORY
(Interpretation)

"ANCIENT of Days, Who Sittest Throned in Glory" was composed in 1886 by Bishop William Croswell Doane in honor of the bicentennial celebration of Albany, New York as the first chartered city in the United States of America. The sponsors of this celebration were men of faith who recognized the importance of the religious note in such a civic bicentennial.

Bishop Doane (1832-1913) came naturally by his hymn-writing ability. His father, Bishop George Washington Doane, was the author of several hymns among the most famous of which are "Softly Now the Light of Day" and "Fling Out the Banner." William Croswell Doane was ordained in 1856 and assisted his esteemed father in the church at Burlington, New Jersey, for a number of years. In 1869 he was made Bishop of the Protestant Episcopal Diocese of Albany, New York. Later he received the honorary degree of D.D. from Oxford University and his LL.D. degree from Cambridge University.

This hymn was written in praise of the Triune God for its verses describe vividly the work of each Person in the Trinity.

The title "Ancient of Days," which is found repeated three times in the seventh chapter of Daniel (7:9, 13, 22), provides an unusually challenging phrase for the opening line of this hymn.

The second stanza emphasizes the title "Holy Father," who in ancient days led the children of Israel with fire and cloud, dry shod through the Red Sea and the Jordan and in their years of weary wanderings in the wilderness.

The third stanza refers to Jesus, the Son of God, as Prince of Peace and the Saviour of mankind.

The fourth stanza speaks of the Holy Spirit, the Lord and Life-giver, who quickens the spirit of man, and from whom flows as from a pleasant river earthly bounties and the great gift of peace.

The fifth stanza is a paeon of praise to the Triune God, praise for the past and a prayer for the future of all those who are kept in His love and favor.

The tune "Ancient of Days," so named because of the opening phrase of this hymn, was composed in 1886 by J. Albert Jeffery (1855-1929) for the bicentennial celebration of the city of Albany. At that time he was organist for the Protestant Episcopal Cathedral of that city. He was an English musician, who later became an organist and teacher of music in the city of Boston.

* From *The Sunday Chronicle,* Dec. 20, 1931. Copyright, 1930, by Lord Dunsany. Used by special permission of the author and the publisher.

Ancient of Days, Throned in Glory

William Croswell Doane, 1832-1913

ANCIENT OF DAYS

John Albert Jeffery, 1855-1929, arr.

HYMN, 1886   TUNE, 1886   METER. 11.10.11.10.

Not too fast

1. An - cient of Days, who sit - test throned in glo - ry;
2. O Ho - ly Fa - ther, who hast led thy chil - dren
3. O Ho - ly Je - sus, Prince of Peace and Sav - iour,
4. O Ho - ly Ghost, the Lord and the Life Giv - er,
5. O Tri - une God, with heart and voice a - dor - ing,

To thee all knees are bent, all voi ces pray;
In all the a - ges, with the fire and cloud,
To thee we owe the peace that still pre - vails,
Thine is the quick - ening power that gives in - crease;
Praise we the good - ness that doth crown our days;

Thy love has blest the wide world's won - drous sto - ry
Through seas dry - shod, through wea - ry wastes be - wil - dering;
Still - ing the rude wills of men's wild be - hav - ior,
From thee have flowed, as from a pleas - ant riv - er,
Pray we that thou wilt hear us, still im - plor - ing

With light and life since E - den's dawn - ing day.
To thee, in rev - erent love, our hearts are bowed.
And calm - ing pas - sion's fierce and storm - y gales.
Our plen - ty, wealth, pros - per - i - ty, and peace.
Thy love and fa - vor, kept to us al - ways.   A - MEN.

BEFORE US, FATHER ABRAHAM

(Interpretation)

THE author of "Before Us, Father Abraham" is unknown; but the spirit and content of the hymn are true to the life and work of Abraham, the great patriarch of the Hebrew people, often referred to as "the Father of the Faithful."

The first stanza praises the leadership of Father Abraham, whose faith and devotion shine on through the centuries.

The second stanza not only stresses Abraham's leadership in tasks both great and small, but also challenges all those "who follow in his train" to a like courage and devotion as "we go marching on."

The third stanza emphasizes the continuity of the followers of the Lord in all ages as they lift the banner of faith, rising above the sorrows and triumphs which are but milestones along the way.

The fourth stanza returns to the theme, faith in and devotion to the God of Abraham, and pledges his followers of today to look upon all men as their brothers, to "cheer the bruised in spirit," as they, too, "go marching on."

This hymn is sung to the tune, "Battle Hymn of the Republic," adapted by Percy Shaw.

✤

THE GOD OF ABRAHAM PRAISE

(Interpretation)

LITTLE is known of Thomas Olivers, who in 1770 arranged this great hymn which was written in the fourteenth century by Daniel Ben Judah, and set to the traditional Hebrew melody entitled "Leoni." He was orphaned early, and became a reckless youth. Then one day in Bristol he heard Whitefield preach. That sermon changed his life. He paid up his debts with money earned as a shoemaker, and then joined John Wesley as an evangelist. He wrote several hymns, one of the best of which is "The God of Abraham Praise." A Jewish friend suggested the Hebrew melody "Leoni." This hymn is also sung to a tune by John Stainer. The hymn is in reality a rather free interpretation of the Hebrew doxology "Yigdal." It bears its own message to the God of Abraham, the great I AM of the Old Testament.

To appreciate the content of this hymn, one must have some knowledge of the place of high esteem which Abraham, the great Hebrew patriarch, holds in Hebrew life and thought. Abraham's deep and abiding faith in the Lord God of the Hebrew people to whom he erected altars during his years of wandering is well known. The Scripture says: "He went out, not knowing whither he went," guided only by his implicit faith in a God not made of wood or stone, but eternal in the

Before us, Father Abraham

Adaptation by PERCY SHAW

1. Be-fore us, Fa-ther Ab-ra-ham, a star-ry com-pass true,
2. No task too small to mas - ter, and no task too great to dare;
3. The ban-ner of the fu - ture flies a - bove our long ar-ray,
4. We are com-ing Fa-ther Ab-ra-ham, we heed your might-y call

Shines your mes-sage to the ag - es lead-ing on a-cross the blue,
No load too big to shoul - der and no grief too small to share;
Our steps are swift with cour - age while the fifes and bu-gles play,
To look up - on our fel-low men as broth-ers one and all,

To the glo-ry of a-chieve-ment and the good that man can do,
No hope too dim to bright - en and no pain too grim to bear,
And your tri-umphs and your sor - rows are our mile-stones on the way,
To cheer the bruised in spir-it and to raise the weak that fall,

REFRAIN

As Time goes march-ing on. Glo - ry! glo - ry! Hal - le - lu - jah!
As we go march-ing on.
As we go march-ing on.
As we go march-ing on.

* From *Services for the Open* arranged by Laura I. Mattoon and Helen D. Bragdon, No. 79. Copyright, 1923, by the Century Company. Used by special permission of Fleming H. Revell Company.

The God of Abraham Praise

LEONI. 6, 6, 8, 4, D.

THOMAS OLIVERS, c. 1770

Traditional Hebrew Melody

1. The God of A-braham praise, Who reigns en-thron'd a-bove,
2. The God of A-braham praise, At whose su-preme com-mand
3. He by him-self hath sworn, I on his oath de-pend;

An - cient of ev - er - last - ing days, And God of love.
From earth I rise and seek the joys At his right hand;
I shall, on ea - gle's wings up - borne, To heav'n as - cend;

Je - ho - vah! Great I AM! By earth and heav'n con - fess'd;
I all on earth for - sake, Its wis - dom, fame, and pow'r;
I shall be - hold his face, I shall his pow'r a - dore,

I bow and bless thy sa - cred name, For ev - er blest.
And him my on - ly por - tion make, My shield and tow'r.
And sing the won - ders of his grace For - ev - er - more. A-men.

heavens. His deep and abiding faith earned for this ancient patriarch the title "The father of the faithful."

The first stanza emphasizes the "God of love, the Great I AM" who sits enthroned above, the Creator of the Universe, who guards and guides the destinies of men.

The second stanza praises the God of ancient days at whose supreme command Abraham became a wilderness wanderer, forsaking the fame, wisdom, and power of earthly possessions to make the Lord the shield and defender, not alone of his own life, but also of the generations which succeeded him.

The third stanza stresses the faith both of Abraham and of his faithful followers down through the ages, who believe the Lord's promises: "In thee and thy seed shall all the nations of the earth be blest"; and who adore and obey Abraham's God, and sing forevermore of His wonders and grace.

So long as men and women read of the struggles and achievements of this ancient Hebrew patriarch, and are moved by his devotion and loyalty to the living God, just so long will they, too, join the host of the "faithful" who follow in Abraham's train, making faith, obedience, and devotion to God the touchstone of their lives.

One cannot read the eleventh chapter of Hebrews, the great faith chapter of the New Testament, with its frequent references to Abraham, without gratitude to this prophet-patriarch of ancient times who first conceived the idea of a God not made of wood or stone, but living eternally in the heavens and in men's hearts.

The Church today can and should often sing this song of praise to the God of Abraham as it renews its own faith in the living, timeless, ageless God of men and nations.

✣

GUIDE ME, O THOU GREAT JEHOVAH
(Interpretation)

THE imagery of "Guide Me, O Thou Great Jehovah," finds its inspiration in the vicissitudes and experiences of "followers of the way" in all ages from the days of Abraham down to the present time. The words were written by William Williams.

Just as Abraham, the ancient patriarch of the Hebrew people, prayed for the guidance of the Lord in the lone watches of the night, so in these later times men and women in their pilgrim wanderings "through this barren land" beseech God to "feed me till I want no more."

The second stanza refers to the "cloud of fire" that led the children of Israel in ancient times, and asserts that God is still the "strong Deliverer," the strength and shield of all those who abide in the faith and love of the God of Israel.

The third stanza refers to Jordan and the anxious fears of the Hebrew people

Guide Me, O Thou Great Jehovah.

William Williams.　　　　*Zion. 8. 7. 8. 7. 4. 7.*　　　　Thomas Hastings.

1. Guide me, O Thou great Je - ho - vah, Pil - grim thro' this bar - ren
2. O - pen now the crys - tal foun - tain Whence the heal - ing wa - ters
3. When I tread the verge of Jor - dan, Bid my anx - ious fears sub-

land; I am weak, but Thou art might - y, Hold me with Thy pow'r - ful
flow; Let the fi - er - y, cloud - y pil - lar Lead me all my jour - ney
side; Bear me thro' the swell - ing cur - rent, Land me safe on Ca - naan's

hand: Bread of Heav - en, Feed me till I want no more;
thro': Strong De - liv - 'rer, Be Thou still my Strength and Shield;
side: Songs of prais - es I will ev - er give to Thee;

Bread of Heav - en, Feed me till I want no more.
Strong De - liv - 'rer, Be Thou still my Strength and Shield.
Songs of prais - es I will ev - er give to Thee. A - MEN.

as they camped along its shores preparatory to crossing over Jordan into the Promised Land. Just as the Hebrews, guided by the faith of their patriarchal leaders in the Lord's word, walked dry shod through Jordan's swelling current into the safety of the Promised Land, so Christians today follow where the eternal God leads and give Him the praise as their "strong Deliv'rer," their "Strength and Shield."

As one sings this great hymn of the Church one feels a union of spirit with the faithful of all ages. Guidance is needed at all times and in all places; but faith in God and trust in His promises has and will guide the faltering footsteps of mankind through to victory and eventually to rest in the heart of the eternal God.

William Williams (1717-1791) was one of the great Welsh hymn writers of his century. Although medicine was his profession, he wrote hundreds of hymns. Such vital religious enthusiasm was kindled in him by the preaching of Whitefield that he became a minister, and spent the greater part of his adult life as an evangelist with the Methodists of Wales. He was also a gifted poet. Perhaps his greatest hymn, written in the Welsh dialect, is "Guide Me, O Thou Great Jehovah."

The tune "Zion" was composed by Thomas Hastings, and should be sung with fervor and in a spirit of deep reverence and devotion to the God of all nations, who still leads and guides the spirits of men.

CONTENTS

PART I SECTION 3

MOSES AND THE EXODUS

———————————————————— ✛ ————————————————————

Now there arose up a new king over Egypt, which knew not Joseph. . . . And the Egyptians made the children of Israel to serve with rigour.—EXODUS 1:8, 13

———————————————————— ✛ ————————————————————

FINDING THE BABY MOSES

By

Raffaelino dal Colle

(Interpretation)

RAFFAELINO dal Colle, sometimes called Raffaelino dal Borgo, was born at Borgo San Sepolcro about 1490. He was first a pupil of Raphael, but after Raphael's death he became the scholar of Giulio Romano, whom he assisted in his principal works in Rome.

Raffaelino was employed by Raphael in the decorations of the Raphael Loggie in the Vatican in Rome, and he painted one of the small cupolas in the roof with a portion of the life of Moses. He also completed the painting of "Finding the Baby Moses" from a design by Raphael in the eighth arcade of the Loggie.

Moses, the great deliverer and lawgiver of Israel, was born during the period of oppression of the children of Israel in Egypt. He was the son of Amram and Jochebed, and the younger brother of Miriam and Aaron. While just an infant he was placed in a homemade ark of bulrushes and hidden among the reeds along the banks of the river Nile, for Pharaoh, the ruler of Egypt, had decreed that all sons born to the Israelites be put to death. His sister, Miriam, was stationed some distance away to watch over him.

He was soon discovered by the daughter of Pharaoh when she and her maidens came down to the Nile to bathe. The princess named the infant Moses, because "she drew him out of the water." She took him to Pharaoh's palace and reared him as her own son. He was given a splendid education and became learned in "all the wisdom of the Egyptians."

In his fortieth year Moses fled to the Midian desert, fearing the wrath of Pharaoh because he had killed an Egyptian whom he had found ill-treating a Hebrew. In the Midian wilderness he married Zipporah, the daughter of a Midian priest and sheik, and lived in the desert caring for his father-in-law's sheep. There in the wilderness God appeared to Moses in a bush that "burned with fire" yet "was not consumed." He commanded Moses to return to Egypt to deliver the children of Israel from Egyptian bondage.

After ten miracles or plagues, the last of which was the death of the firstborn, in every Egyptian home, the children of Israel were allowed to depart from Egypt. Under the leadership of Moses, they set their faces toward Canaan, the promised land. For another period of approximately forty years, Moses led the Israelites in their desert wanderings. At Mount Sinai he received from the Lord the tables of the Law. He was even allowed to view the promised land from the top of Mount Pizgah, although he himself was not permitted to lead the children of Israel into it.

Moses was the greatest figure in Hebrew history. Under his leadership God made of the children of Israel a great nation, and established the national life of the Hebrews on a foundation of Laws which determined the entire future of that people, and through them, the life of the world.

The rescue of the infant Moses from the Nile has been strikingly portrayed in this painting by Raffaelino dal Colle. It shows the princess and her maidens on the bank of the river Nile. One of the maidens kneels as she draws to the shore the ark of bulrushes with its baby occupant. There is amazement and wonder on this girl's face as she gazes at the beautiful, sturdy child. His tiny arms are extended toward her in a touching little gesture as if he were seeking her protection. Behind the kneeling maiden and the child stands the princess wearing her coronet. Her hands express surprise, but the pose of her head and the expression on her face indicate a dawning tenderness and love for the helpless child. The princess's attendants crowd about to see the baby, their bodies assuming varied positions and their faces each registering interest and astonishment in a different way. The girl on the extreme right, looking over the attendants' shoulders, may represent Miriam, the sister of Moses.

Soft foliage enriches the banks of the river, while in the distance may be seen the houses of Egypt's capital which henceforth is to be the home of Moses, as the adopted son of Pharaoh's daughter.

✛

MOSES KEEPING JETHRO'S SHEEP

By

Sir Edward John Poynter

(Interpretation)

MOSES, the great lawgiver and deliverer of Israel, was the son of Amram and Jochebed of the tribe of Levi. He was the younger brother of Miriam and Aaron. In his fortieth year he fled from Egypt to the Midian wilderness because he feared the wrath of the king for having killed an Egyptian whom he had found ill-treating a Hebrew.

There in the Midian wilderness he sat down by a wayside well to rest and to think about his future. Shortly the seven daughters of Jethro, who was also called Reuel, a priest of Midian, arrived to fill the troughs with water in order to refresh their father's flocks. Burly shepherds came and drove the girls away and they were frightened. Moses, seeing their predicament, helped them to draw more water for their flocks.

When they returned home earlier than usual, their father, Reuel, asked: "How is it that ye are come so soon today?" (Ex. 2:18).

And they replied: "An Egyptian delivered us out of the hand of the shepherds, and also drew water enough for us, and watered the flock" (Ex. 2:19).

Then the father of these seven girls said: "And where is he? Why is it that ye have left the man? Call him, that he may eat bread" (Ex. 2:20).

So they called Moses, who readily accepted Jethro's invitation to live with

FINDING THE BABY MOSES—*DAL COLLE*

them and to tend the flocks. Later he married Zipporah, one of the daughters of the Midian priest, and dwelt in the Midian wilderness nearly forty years until God commissioned him to return to Egypt to deliver the Israelites out of the hands of Pharaoh.

This picture portraying "Moses Keeping Jethro's Sheep" presents a wilderness scene. Moses, the Midian shepherd, stands leaning against a boulder deep in thought. His eyes are raised to the distant horizon and there is a troubled sadness in them as he ponders the wrongs done to his people serving in bondage in Egypt. He has drawn his mantle over his head to protect himself from the burning rays of the sun. His shepherd's staff is close beside him ready to be used, should the need arise, to defend or guide his sheep. A ram of his flock trustingly licks his hand. These are the horned, short-wool sheep still found in Palestine.

The artist, Sir Edward J. Poynter, was born in Paris in 1836. He studied in England and Paris and exhibited his first picture at the Royal Academy in 1861. He designed this picture for Dalziel's *Bible Gallery,* a collection of Bible illustrations by some of the foremost artists of the day. The engraving was executed by the Dalziel brothers. Their signature appears in the lower left of the picture, while the artist's initials and the date, 1863, appear at the lower right. Poynter became director of the National Gallery of British Art. In 1902 he was made a baronet. He died in London in 1919.

✛

MOSES AND THE BURNING BUSH

By

Hans Holbein, the Younger

(Interpretation)

THE story of Moses and the burning bush is based on an incident recorded in Exodus 3:1-10. After slaying an Egyptian for the murder of a Hebrew, Moses fled to the Midian wilderness where he lived for years. There he married Zipporah, the daughter of Jethro, the priest of Midian. He saw no more of crowded cities, of magnificent temples and pyramids, nor of the great river Nile, whose annual overflow made the land of the Nile a rich and fertile valley. Moses wandered about in the Midian desert, much of the time living alone and tending the flock of his father-in-law, Jethro. At night he often slept on the ground; by day he gazed at the gray hills fading away in the distance. Meanwhile, in Egypt the children of Israel were still bearing heavy burdens as slaves, making brick, and building cities and monuments for the Pharaohs. The people of Israel cried out for help and God heard their cry, and "God remembered his covenant with Abraham, with Isaac, and with Jacob. And God looked upon the children of Israel, and God had respect unto them" (Ex. 2:24, 25).

One day while Moses was feeding his flock at Mount Horeb, he saw a bush which seemed to be on fire. As he watched it from a distance, he noticed that

MOSES KEEPING JETHRO'S SHEEP—*POYNTER*

while it burned, it was not consumed. Finally he said: "I will now turn aside, and see this great sight, why the bush is not burnt" (Ex. 3:3).

As he approached nearer to the fire a voice came to him, seemingly out of the fire, saying: "Moses, Moses," and he answered: "Here am I." Then the Lord said to Moses: "Draw not nigh hither: put off thy shoes from off thy feet, for the place whereon thou standest is holy ground" (Ex. 3:5).

So Moses removed his sandals and in humble reverence stood barefooted before the burning bush in the presence of God. Then the voice continued speaking from the bush: "'I am the God of thy father, the God of Abraham, the God of Isaac, and the God of Jacob.' And Moses hid his face; for he was afraid to look upon God.

"And the Lord said, 'I have surely seen the affliction of my people which are in Egypt, and have heard their cry by reason of their taskmasters; for I know their sorrows; and I am come down to deliver them out of the hand of the Egyptians, and to bring them up out of that land unto a good land and a large, unto a land flowing with milk and honey; unto the place of the Canaanites. . . . Come now therefore, and I will send thee unto Pharaoh, that thou mayest bring forth my people the children of Israel out of Egypt" (Ex. 3:6-10).

Hans Holbein, the great sixteenth-century German artist, designed this wood-cut, "Moses and the Burning Bush." It is one of the ninety-two woodcuts, all from drawings by Holbein, that appear in *Icones Historiarum Veteris Testamenti,* first published in 1547 by Jean Frellon at Lyons. The original of this picture is very small, but it shows Holbein's amazing skill in design and in execution. He tells an entire story with a few figures whose characters are made plain by masterful touches. Of Holbein's Old Testament woodcuts it has been said: "They have been expounded and praised in every century succeeding their publication and have fairly won their place among the great achievements of the graphic art." These woodcuts have about them a simplicity and directness which is completely suited to the style of the Old Testament narratives.

This woodcut shows Moses in the wilderness with Horeb, the mountain of God, in the background. A flock of flying birds are silhouetted against the distant sky. In the foreground the sheep huddle together, disturbed and frightened by the fire and the voice of the Lord, and completely unaware that they are present at one of the sublime moments of Hebrew history when God made himself manifest to Moses. The Lord speaks to Moses from the midst of the flaming bush that burns yet is not consumed. He is portrayed as the benign Father of His people Israel and His hand is outstretched in blessing. Moses has thrown down his shepherd's staff and kneels to put off his shoes, for this place where the Lord appears to him is holy ground. At this first moment of encounter Moses gazes upon his Lord with an expression of wonder and adoration and from his head come rays of light.

The call to Moses in the Midian desert marked the beginning of one of the longest and most notable careers in the Bible. Moses faced a life of self-sacrifice, hardship, and service to and for the children of Israel, until they came, as a host

MOSES AND THE BURNING BUSH—HOLBEIN

that could not be numbered, to the boundaries of Canaan, the promised land of their people.

✛

MIRIAM'S SONG

By

Sir Edward John Poynter

(Interpretation)

AFTER his meeting with God in the burning bush, Moses returned to Egypt, as the Lord commanded him, and became the leader of the Israelites serving there in bondage. At length he persuaded Pharaoh to let the children of Israel leave his country. Led by a pillar of fire by night and a pillar of cloud by day the great host of Moses' people escaped out of Egypt and encamped by the sea. But Pharaoh changed his mind about allowing his former slaves to leave and he set out with horses and chariots and his army to overtake them and bring them back.

Seeing the pursuing chariots of Pharaoh behind them and the waters of the sea before them, the Israelites knew that they were trapped. They bitterly upbraided Moses saying that it would have been better for them to continue serving the Egyptians than to die in the wilderness. But Moses said:

"Fear ye not, stand still and see the salvation of the Lord, which he will shew to you today; for the Egyptians whom ye have seen today, ye shall see them again no more for ever" (Ex. 14:13).

Then the Lord commanded Moses, saying: "Speak unto the children of Israel, that they go forward."

"And the Lord caused the sea to go back by a strong east wind all that night, and made the sea dry land, and the waters were divided. And the children of Israel went into the midst of the sea upon the dry ground; and the waters were a wall unto them on their right hand, and on their left" (14:21, 22).

Pharaoh with all his horses and chariots and horsemen pressed on after the Israelites, pursuing them across the dry bed of the sea. Here the wheels of their chariots became mired in the soft sand. "And the waters returned, and covered the chariots, and the horsemen, and all the host of Pharaoh. . . . But the children of Israel walked upon dry land in the midst of the sea. . . . Thus the Lord saved Israel that day out of the hand of the Egyptians" (14:28, 29, 30).

In the hour of their great deliverance Israel rejoiced, and gave thanks to God. "And Miriam, the prophetess, the sister of Aaron, took a timbrel in her hand; and all the women went out after her with timbrels and with dances" (15:20). Then Miriam sang a song:

> Sing ye to the Lord,
> For he hath triumphed gloriously;
> The horse and his rider
> Hath he thrown into the sea.   [15:21]

MIRIAM'S SONG—*POYNTER*

This memorable event lived forever in their hearts, for now for the first time the Israelites saw clearly that the Lord was with them, protecting and guiding them, and making of them a great nation. Their deliverance at the sea kindled their faith in a glorious destiny for Israel under the leadership of God. Again and again they were to remember the hour of Miriam's rejoicing, for it was the moment when their amazing faith and loyalty to God were born.

The English artist, Sir Edward John Poynter, portrays in "Miriam's Song" the rejoicing of the women of Israel after their great deliverance. Miriam leads the women, seeming almost to float in air as she dances joyfully. The women shake their timbrels and strum their lyres to mark the rhythms of the dance. Even the little girls join in with their own lively steps, clashing their cymbals together in excitement. In the background the host of Israel follow, driving their flocks of sheep before them and carrying their few possessions. In the distance can be seen the cliffs of Egypt where the Israelites so recently camped and feared that they were a doomed people. Below the cliffs lie the waters of the sea, smooth now as they cover the host of Pharaoh.

Sir Edward John Poynter designed this picture for *Dalziel's Bible Gallery* and Dalziel executed the engraving. It was made in 1864, as the date in the lower right-hand corner indicates, but the *Bible Gallery,* which is a collection of Biblical pictures by a number of English artists, was not published until 1880.

✝

MOSES SHOWING THE TABLETS OF THE LAW

By

Raphael Sanzio

(Interpretation)

THE Decalogue or Ten Commandments was given by God to Moses on Mount Sinai. This dramatic story is graphically told in the nineteenth and twentieth chapters of the book of Exodus.

Three months after the miraculous escape of the children of Israel from Egypt they encamped in the wilderness about Mount Sinai. Moses went up into the mountain that he might commune with the Lord. And the Lord said to Moses:

"Thus shalt thou say to the house of Jacob, and tell the children of Israel . . . 'if ye will obey my voice indeed, and keep my covenant, then ye shall be a peculiar treasure unto me above all people, for all the earth is mine. And ye shall be unto me a kingdom of priests, and an holy nation'" (Ex. 19:3, 5, 6).

When the people heard these words from Moses, they promised to do all that the Lord had commanded.

Then the Lord directed that the children of Israel sanctify themselves, wash their garments, and be ready on the third day, when He would appear to them in the clouds that covered the summit of Mount Sinai.

When the third day arrived, Moses brought the children of Israel out of the

MOSES SHOWING THE TABLETS OF THE LAW—*RAPHAEL*

camp to meet God. At the foot of the mountain they waited, listening to the thunder and watching the heavy clouds and the lightning as it played about the summit of Mount Sinai. The whole mountain smoked because the Lord descended upon it in fire. Hot smoke as though from a furnace ascended and the mountain quaked greatly as the trumpet of the Lord waxed louder and louder. And the children of Israel were afraid and stood afar off while Moses drew near to the thick darkness where God was.

Then the voice of God, whose face they could not see, called Moses to the crest of the peak that he might commune with Him. And Moses went up. There on Mount Sinai the Lord talked with Moses alone and gave to him two tablets of stone "written with the finger of God." On these tablets appeared the Decalogue or Ten Commandments which summarize man's duty toward God and toward his neighbor. These are the commandments which from that day forward the Israelites called the Law.

The original of the picture of "Moses Showing the Tablets of the Law" to the Israelites will be found in the ninth arcade of the Raphael Loggie in the Vatican in Rome, along with one showing "Moses Receiving the Tablets of the Law," one of "The Golden Calf," and one of the "Pillar of Cloud" that guided the children of Israel by day.

Moses with rays of light resting on his head is seen as the divinely inspired leader of Israel. He stands resolute and firm amid a tumultuous crowd of Israelites. He is on one of the lower levels of the mountainside, and holds in his strong hands, for all to see, the two tablets containing the Decalogue or Ten Commandments. He is wearing a robe of royal blue under which is a tunic of gold. Nearly every eye is turned toward the tablets of the Law. The crowd betrays various responses, but all their gestures and the motions of their bodies are directed toward the stone slabs on which the Lord has written. At the right an old man quietly ponders the meaning of these laws. In front of him stands one who is profoundly impressed by the event and raises his right arm as if assenting to the commandments and promising to obey them. The emotions portrayed reach a climax of vehemence in the next figure who raises both arms above his head and appears to be crying out his loyalty and gratitude to God. Beyond him the emotions become more subdued as the lovely, half-kneeling and kneeling figures express a deeper response of prayerful dedication to God.

Behind and at Moses' right hand stand three people who by their position show that they must have some special relation to their leader. The middle figure is clothed in blue and wears the white veil of a woman. She may be Moses' wife or his sister Miriam. The young man supporting her wears a green robe. The imperious twist of his head seems to denote one who rules in Israel. Perhaps this is Aaron.

The sky, from which the black clouds which enveloped the mountain are lifting, appears blue; and in the distance low hills, covered with the green foliage of trees in spring, may be seen.

MOSES STRIKING THE ROCK

By

Raphael Sanzio

(Interpretation)

ON the fifteenth day of the second month after the children of Israel departed out of Egypt, they came into the wilderness of Sin which is between Elim and Mount Sinai. In this region there was little or no food, and the whole congregation of Israel murmured against both Moses and Aaron, saying: "Would to God we had died by the hand of the Lord in the land of Egypt, when we sat by the flesh pots, and when we did eat bread to the full; for ye have brought us forth into this wilderness, to kill this whole assembly with hunger" (Ex. 16:3).

When God heard their complaints against His faithful servants, He said to Moses: "Behold, I will rain bread from heaven for you; and the people shall go out and gather a certain rate every day, that I may prove them, whether they will walk in my law, or not" (16:4).

And so to provide for the children of Israel during their stay in the wilderness, the Lord sent quails at eventide that the Israelites might have meat at night, and manna by day. God directed Moses to instruct them to eat the quail, which appeared each evening, at night, and the manna, which they found small as hoarfrost on the ground, by day.

Thus under God's protection the children of Israel journeyed through the wilderness of Sin until they encamped in Rephidim. Here there was no water to drink, and again the Israelites complained to Moses and murmured against him, saying: "Wherefore is this that thou hast brought us up out of Egypt, to kill us and our children and our cattle with thirst?" (Ex. 17:3).

Moses appealed to the Lord and asked: "What shall I do unto this people? They be almost ready to stone me" (17:4).

Then God instructed Moses to take with him the elders of Israel and stand before the rock in Horeb. God promised that He, too, would stand there with him. So Moses took his rod and struck the rock, as the Lord had commanded him, and behold water gushed from it. The children of Israel drank from this gushing spring and their thirst was satisfied.

The artist has graphically portrayed this scene in his painting, "Moses Striking the Rock," the original of which will be found in the eighth arcade of Raphael's Loggie in the Vatican in Rome.

Above the rock, hovering in the billowy clouds, the form of God may be seen, surrounded by the indistinct heads of cherubs. Behind Moses, who is the center of focus in this painting, stand the leaders or judges of the various tribes of Israel, their hands raised in joyous shouts as the living water gushes forth in a stream from the rock in Horeb. Tree trunks, bare of leaves, appear immediately behind these leaders; while in the near and far background green shrubs and trees in leaf relieve the waste of this desert wilderness. In the background are rugged peaks topped by rocks that seem to form castles in the air.

Henry Strachey in his *Raphael* writes: "In composition no one before or after has ever approached to within a distance which makes comparison possible. . . . It matters not to Raphael whether he is using one figure or twenty, whether his space is rectangular, circular, or both, and lopsided also. In every instance the given space is filled with a pattern of figures exactly suitable to the decorative requirements and to the true expression of the sentiment of the work."*

✛

MOSES SMITES WATER FROM THE ROCK

By

Luke Yuan Tu Chen

(Interpretation)

THE Catholic University in Peking, China, through its department of art, has made a significant contribution toward the development of Chinese Christian ideals.

When Luke Chen, one of China's greatest contemporary artists, became a professor in the Catholic University, several of his students began a study of the Bible and the catechism so that they might paint Biblical teachings on silk. Partly as a result of this, sooner or later almost all of these young students of art became Christians.

It is Luke Chen, the teacher of this group, who in this painting, "Moses Smites Water from the Rock," has given his conception of this significant Old Testament story. All the lines portraying the Bible story (Ex. 17:5-6) are distinctly Chinese—the rugged rocks of Mount Horeb rising almost perpendicularly, the abundant water which gushes from the rock and flows away in a swift stream, the Chinese women with their earthen water pots dipping up the life-giving water, the benign and venerable figure of Moses standing, with one hand on his staff and the other pointing to the waterfall. A young Chinese girl only half shown on the edge of the picture clasps her hands in prayerful thanksgiving for this gift from God. The entire scene is presented by a limited number of bold, sure strokes and dots yet they achieve an arresting and significant picture.

The lights and shadows in this painting are unique. The delicate coloring of pale chartreuse, blue, green, pink, and gray-green makes this an unforgettable picture. With skill, directness, and simplicity it tells the story of God's abounding goodness to a complaining and ungrateful people.

This Chinese picture is included in this anthology with the permission of the Reverend Father Ralph, S.V.D., National Director of Catholic Universities, Chicago, Illinois.

* *Raphael* by Henry Strachey, pp. 45-46. George Bell & Sons (1902).

MOSES STRIKING THE ROCK—*RAPHAEL*

MOSES SMITES WATER FROM THE ROCK—*TU CHEN*

BEGIN THE DAY WITH GOD

Be ready by the morning, and come up . . . present thyself there to me on the top of the mount. And no man shall come up with thee.—EXODUS 34:2, 3

Begin the day with God!
    He is thy Sun and Day!
His is the radiance of thy dawn;
    To Him address thy lay.

Sing a new song at morn!
    Join the glad woods and hills;
Join the fresh winds and seas and plains,
    Join the bright flowers and rills.

Sing the first song to God!
    Not to thy fellow men;
Not to the creatures of His hand,
    But to the glorious One.

Take thy first walk with God!
    Let Him go forth with thee;
By stream, or sea, or mountain path,
    Seek still His company.

Thy first transaction be
    With God himself above;
So shall thy business prosper well,
    And all thy day be love.

—Horatius Bonar

THE VOICE UNTO PHARAOH

And the children . . . sighed by reason of the bondage, and they cried, and their cry came up unto God.—EXODUS 2:23

Pharaoh, Pharaoh, let my people go!

My fettered children toil with aching limbs
    And wearied fingers, brain and spirit bound.
Their puny forms are bent; the shadow dims
    Their straining eyes; their ears are choked with
        sound
And thick with reek is every breath they draw.
    I gave them light to see and song to hear;
I gave them Truth for guide and Love for law;
    And *thou* hast given darkness, blight and fear.

Pharaoh, Pharaoh, let my people go!

In chains, unseen but strong, my children slave,
     Too dull for hopes or dreams, too dumb for prayers;
Thou, thou hast robbed them of the youth I gave,
     The world I made, the joy that should be theirs;
These lives are coined to swell thy glittering store;
     Then darest thou plead, "Nay, Lord, I did not
          know!"—
Still heaping up their burdens more and more?
     The sand is running. Let my people go!

Pharaoh, Pharaoh, let my people go!

Thy heart is hard. Be warned: The Plague shall come.
     This wrong thou dost shall breed yet fouler wrong.
Those lips shall speak in flame that now are dumb;
     Those feeble hands, through wrath and hatred
          strong,
Shall rend where they have wrought. Yea, once again
     Disease, Rebellion, Crime shall overthrow
The selfishness that bred them. Sons of men,
     For dread of vengeance, let my people go!*

                                        —*Arthur Guiterman*

GO FORWARD

Speak unto the children of Israel, that they go forward.—Exodus 14:15

Have you come to the Red Sea place in your life,
     Where, in spite of all you can do,
There is no way out, there is no way back,
     There is no other way but through?
Then wait on the Lord with a trust serene
     Till the night of your fear is gone;
He will send the wind, He will heap the floods,
     When He says to your soul, "Go on."

And His hand will lead you through—clear through—
     Ere the watery walls roll down,
No foe can reach you, no wave can touch,
     No mightiest sea can drown;
The tossing billows may rear their crests,
     Their foam at your feet may break,
But over their bed you will walk dry shod
     In the path that your Lord will make.

* Used by special permission of Mrs. Arthur Guiterman.

In the morning watch, 'neath the lifted cloud,
   You shall see but the Lord alone,
When He leads you on from the place of the sea
   To a land that you have not known;
And your fears shall pass as your foes have passed,
   You shall be no more afraid;
You shall sing His praise in a better place,
   A place that His hand has made.*

                                 —*Annie Johnson Flint*

MY BURNING BUSH FOR EVERY DAY

And the angel of the Lord appeared to him in a flaming fire out of the midst of a burning bush. —EXODUS 3:2

I have my Burning Bush each day
   As Moses had of old:
A sunrise on a mountain top,
   All crimson flame—and gold.

My Burning Bush of wild-rose bloom,
   Of Phlox and golden rod
In which I feel the presence of
   Creation and its God.

My angel of the Lord appears
   Each day when dawn is born
And I can hear the music of
   A far-off Elfland horn.

God's voice speaks to me every spring
   And I can hear His name
Where every crimson rose bush bursts
   Into a flash of flame.**

                              —*William L. Stidger*

GOOD NEWS FROM GOD

Good news, old world, good news;
The river and the winds refuse
To keep the matter still;
My soul!
The oriole
Is on the knoll!

* From *Flint Poems in One Volume.* Used by special permission of Evangelical Publishers.
** Used by special permission of the author.

Good morning, friend of mine, arise!
And hear God singing in the skies.
The fields are wet with dew,
The skies are cloudless, blue;
The dark
Has gone, and hark!
The meadowlark!

Hail, friend and foe, thrice hail!
I bring you news; a wondrous tale;
The story of a vast, sublime
Blossoming of tide and time.
It's spring!
The redwing
Blackbirds sing!

Hark, friend of mine, thrice hark!
You'll hear sweet singing in the dark,
Across the peaceful bay
Beyond the rim of day
When all is still.
His call and trill,
The whippoorwill!*

—*William L. Stidger*

JUST AS GOD LEADS

Just as God leads me I would go;
  I would not ask to choose my way;
Content with what he will bestow,
  Assured he will not let me stray.
So, as he leads, my path I make,
  And step by step I gladly take—
A child, in him confiding,

Just as God leads I am content;
  I rest me calmly in his hands;
That which he has decreed and sent—
  That which his will for me commands—
I would that he should all fulfill,
  That I should do his gracious will
In living or in dying.

Just as God leads, I all resign;
  I trust me to my Father's will;
When reason's rays deceptive shine,
  His counsel would I yet fulfill;

* From *I Saw God Wash the World* by William L. Stidger, p. 16. Published by The Rodeheaver Hall-Mack Co. Copyright, 1934, by William L. Stidger. Used by special permission of the author.

Before he brought me to the right
   My all to him resigning.

Just as God leads me, I abide
   In faith, in hope, in suffering true;
His strength is ever by my side—
   Can aught my hold on him undo?
I hold me firm in patience, knowing
   That God my life is still bestowing—
The best in kindness sending.

Just as God leads I onward go,
   Out amid thorns and briars keen;
God does not yet his guidance show—
   But in the end it shall be seen.
How, by a loving Father's will,
   Faithful and true, he leads me still.
And so my heart is resting.

Translated from the German; Author Unknown

MIRIAM'S SONG

Sound the loud timbrel o'er Egypt's dark sea!
Jehovah has triumphed, His people are free!
Sing, for the pride of the tyrant is broken;
   His chariots, his horsemen, all splendid and brave,—
How vain was their boast! for the Lord hath but spoken,
   And chariots and horsemen are sunk in the wave.
Sound the loud timbrel o'er Egypt's dark sea!
Jehovah has triumphed, His people are free!
Praise to the Conqueror, praise to the Lord!
His word was our arrow, His breath was our sword!
Who shall return to tell Egypt the story
   Of those she sent forth in the hour of her pride?
For the Lord hath looked out from His pillar of glory,
   And all her brave thousands are dashed in the tide.
Sound the loud timbrel o'er Egypt's dark sea!
Jehovah has triumphed, His people are free!

—Thomas Moore

REBECCA'S HYMN

When Israel of the Lord beloved,
   Out of the land of bondage came,
Her father's God before her moved,
   An awful guide in smoke and flame.
By day, along the astonished lands
   The cloudy pillar glided slow;

By night Arabia's crimson sands
    Returned the fiery column's glow.

There rose the choral hymn of praise,
    And trump and timbrel answered keen;
And Zion's daughters poured their lays,
    With priest's and warrior's voice between.
No portents now our foes amaze,—
    Forsaken Israel wanders lone:
Our fathers would not know thy ways,
    And thou hast left them to their own.

But, present still, though now unseen,
    When brightly shines the prosperous day,
Be thoughts of thee a cloudy screen,
    To temper the deceitful ray.
And oh, when stoops on Judah's path
    In shade and storm the frequent night,
Be thou, long-suffering, slow to wrath,
    A burning and a shining light.

Our harps we left by Babel's streams, —
    The tyrant's jest, the Gentile's scorn;
No censer round our altar beams,
    And mute are timbrel, trump, and horn.
But thou hast said, "The blood of goat,
    The flesh of rams, I will not prize,—
A contrite heart, a humble thought,
    Are mine accepted sacrifice."

                          —*Sir Walter Scott*

MOSES

Like a high mountain bathed in morning light,
Stands he above the tortuous centuries.
Nations have risen, grown to power and fame,
Then, cursed by fate, have vanished into night.
But still he stands, with his stern laws God-lent,
Challenging the peoples with their changeless truth—
Challenging the peoples, though they will not hear,
Hard and stiff-necked still, proud and insolent.
He still stands high above our petty men—
Sages and judges, regnant for a day,
Pouring out laws and wisdom sacrosanct;
Vain are the fruits of their blind brains and pen.
Still Moses stands, and God above his shade,
Pitying the nations for the world they've made.*

                          —*Thomas Curtis Clark*

* Used by special permission of the author.

PIONEER OF GOD
(The Exodus)

Moses was a shepherd
  Before he brought the Law.
On Jethro's range he grazed his sheep,
  His eyes the palm-wells saw.

Moses was a shepherd,
  He knew the way to lead
His flock of hungry people
  Where they might daily feed.

The manna and the fatted quail
  He saw his tribesmen eat,
And knew that should these fail them,
  God still would give them meat.

Moses was a mountain man
  Who Sinai crags endured,
To gain Jehovah's living truth
  That Israel's life ensured.

He brought Jehovah down to them
  From smoking-mountain talks,
And when they thirsted, Moses' rod
  Brought springs from flinty rocks.

And Moses saw the Promised Land,
  From salt Dead Sea to Dan,
From Pisgah's peak he saw it all,
  An aged and wistful man.

Yet, Canaan never entered he,
  Nor owned a foot of land.
He only led young Israel
  To homelands God had planned.*

—*Madeleine S. Miller*

PRAYER

I asked for bread; God gave a stone instead.
Yet, while I pillowed there my weary head,
The angels made a ladder of my dreams,
Which upward to celestial mountains led.
And when I woke beneath the morning's beams,

* Used by special permission of the author.

Around my resting place fresh manna lay;
And, praising God, I went upon my way.
   For I was fed.

God answers prayer; sometimes, when hearts are weak,
He gives the very gifts believers seek.
But often faith must learn a deeper rest,
And trust God's silence when He does not speak;
For He whose name is Love will send the best.
Stars may burn out, nor mountain walls endure,
But God is true, His promises are sure
   For those who seek.

—Author Unknown

SOME SINAI

And Moses went up unto God, and the Lord called unto him out of the mountain.
—EXODUS 19:3

Each soul must seek some Sinai
   Where God's great truths are told;
Must find God's revelations
   Writ on shining plates of gold.

Some high and sacred place, apart;
   Some sky-touched mountain peak
Where he may hear the thunders roll
   And all God's voices speak.

Each soul must find some silent place;
   Some high and holy shrine
Where all the stars and suns and moons
   And plunging planets shine.

Here are God's revelations;
   Here are His thoughts, sublime
To guide all human hearts and hopes
   Through space and tide and time.

Each soul must seek some Sinai;
   Some vision-haunted place;
Some silent, sacred, singing shrine
   To see His lighted face.*

—William L. Stidger

* Used by special permission of the author.

WHEN THOU PASSEST THROUGH

When thou passest through the waters . . . they shall not overflow thee.—ISAIAH 43:2

"When thou passest through the waters"
   Deep the waves may be and cold,
But Jehovah is our refuge,
   And His promise is our hold;
For the Lord himself hath said it,
   He, the faithful God and true:
"When thou comest to the waters
   Thou shalt not go down, but through."

Seas of sorrow, seas of trial,
   Bitterest anguish, fiercest pain,
Rolling surges of temptation
   Sweeping over heart and brain—
They shall never overflow us
   For He knows His word is true;
All His waves and all His billows
   He will lead us safely through.

Threatening breakers of destruction,
   Doubt's insidious undertow,
Shall not sink us, shall not drag us
   Out to ocean depths of woe;
For His promise shall sustain us,
   Praise the Lord, whose Word is true!
We shall not go down, or under,
   For He saith, "Thou passest through."*

—Annie Johnson Flint

WORSHIP OF IDOLS

Thou shalt have no other Gods before me.—EXODUS 20:3

Mankind has always feared the great unknown,
And felt a helplessness against the world;
And so in fear he bowed at every throne,
In hope no thunderbolts at him be hurled.
Man gives his loyalty to what sustains,
And worships what he thinks has power to save,
We see him bow to money, force and gains,
And give himself to state to be a slave.
There is a God to worship that's worth while,
Who has a love that's true and just and right,

* From *Songs of Faith and Comfort* by Annie Johnson Flint. Used by special permission of Evangelical Publishers.

Who puts within the heart of man a smile,
And saves him from the sin that tends to blight.
"Thou shalt not have another God than me,"
Obey that call and joy and peace you'll see.*

—*Henry C. Spear*

DIVINE PROTECTION

(Psalm 121)

Up to the hills I lift mine eyes,
The eternal hills beyond the skies;
Thence all her help my soul derives:
There my almighty refuge lives.

He lives! the everlasting God,
Who built the world, who spread the flood;
The heavens with all their hosts he made,
And the dark regions of the dead.

He guides our feet, he guards our way;
His morning smiles bless all the day;
He spreads the evening veil, and keeps
The silent hours while Israel sleeps.

Israel, a name divinely blest,
May rise secure, securely rest;
Thy holy Guardian's wakeful eyes
Admit no slumber or surprise.

No sun shall smite thy head by day;
Nor the pale moon, with sickly ray,
Shall blast thy couch; no baleful star
Dart his malignant fire so far.

Should earth and hell with malice burn,
Still thou shalt go, and still return,
Safe in the Lord; his heavenly care
Defends thy life from every snare.

On thee foul spirits have no power;
And, in thy last, departing hour,
Angels, who trace the airy road,
Shall bare thee homeward to thy God.

—*Isaac Watts*

* From *Sermon Sonnets* by Henry C. Spear, p. 16. Used by special permission of the author.

THE BURIAL OF MOSES

And he buried him in the valley in the land of Moab over against Beth-peor: but no man knoweth of his sepulchre unto this day.—DEUTERONOMY 34:6

By Nebo's lonely mountain,
    On this side Jordan's wave,
In a vale in the land of Moab,
    There lies a lonely grave;
But no man dug that sepulcher,
    And no man saw it e'er,
For the angels of God upturned the sod,
    And laid the dead man there.

That was the grandest funeral
    That ever passed on earth;
But no man heard the tramping,
    Or saw the train go forth;
Noiselessly as the daylight
    Comes when the night is done,
And the crimson streak on ocean's cheek
    Grows into the great sun,—

Noiselessly as the springtime
    Her crown of verdure weaves,
And all the trees on all the hills
    Open their thousand leaves, —
So, without sound of music,
    Or voice of them that wept,
Silently down the mountain crown
    The great procession swept.

Perchance the bald old eagle,
    On gray Beth-peor's height,
Out of his rocky eyrie,
    Looked on the wondrous sight.
Perchance the lion, stalking,
    Still shuns the hallowed spot;
For beast and bird have seen and heard
    That which man knoweth not.

Lo! when the warrior dieth,
    His comrades in the war,
With arms reversed, and muffled drum,
    Follow the funeral car.
They show the banners taken,
    They tell his battles won,
And after him lead his masterless steed,
    While peals the minute gun.

Amid the noblest of the land
  Men lay the sage to rest,
And give the bard an honored place
  With costly marble dressed.
In the great minster transept,
  Where lights like glories fall,
And the sweet choir sings, and the organ rings,
  Along the emblazoned wall.

This was the bravest warrior
  That ever buckled sword;
This the most gifted poet
  That ever breathed a word;
And never earth's philosopher
  Traced with his golden pen,
On the deathless page, truths half so sage,
  As he wrote down for men.

And had he not high honor,
  The hillside for his pall;
To lie in state while angels wait
  With stars for taper tall;
And the dark rock pines, like tossing plumes,
  Over his bier to wave;
And God's own hand, in that lonely land,
  To lay him in the grave—

In that deep grave, without a name.
  Whence his uncoffined clay
Shall break again—most wondrous thought—
  Before the judgment day,
And stand with glory wrapped around
  On the hills he never trod,
And speak of the strife that won our life
  With the Incarnate Son of God.

O, lonely tomb in Moab's land,
  O, dark Beth-peor's hill,
Speak to these curious hearts of ours,
  And teach them to be still.
God hath His mysteries of Grace—
  Ways that we cannot tell;
He hides them deep, like the secret sleep
  Of him he loved so well.

                                 —Cecil Frances Alexander

THE MAN WHO HARDENED HIS HEART

By

Florence M. Earlle

PHARAOH leaned back under his royal canopy and sneered:

"What have I to do with a Hebrew even though he does come from the desert and claim that he is sent by the Hebrew god? Who is the Hebrew god that I should heed him? Is he greater than Ra?" he sneered again. "No one is greater than Ra, our sun god."

"But my lord," said the slave timidly, "this man, who calls himself Moses, will not leave the palace until he has seen you. For three days now, he has been waiting."

"Well, let him come in then," said the Pharaoh. "He might be amusing."

When the slave drew the curtain aside, a tall man dressed in the clothing of a shepherd walked in boldly. His face was deeply tanned by the wind and sun of the desert, and his hair was white; but his eyes were bright and showed no fear. Another man, who seemed to be his brother, followed him.

"O Pharaoh," Moses began at once, "I am come from our great God to demand that you let the children of Israel go a three-day journey into the wilderness that they may worship, lest God send a pestilence upon them."

"Who is your god?" said Pharaoh. "I do not know him. Why do you want to make the people restless and keep them from their work? I will not let them go."

Then the other man, whose name was Aaron, threw down a staff, and it became a snake. Pharaoh called his court magicians, and by trickery they did the same, only Aaron's snake ate up the other ones. But the king would not let the people go. Indeed that very day, after Moses and Aaron had gone from the court, he said to his taskmaster over the Israelites, "The Hebrew slaves are to have no more straw for making bricks; they must hunt it for themselves. Yet the number of bricks they are to make every day will not be decreased. The people are lazy, or they would not be thinking about going into the wilderness for a religious feast."

The next morning when Pharaoh went down to the river Nile to bathe, there stood Moses and Aaron, and Moses called, "I have been sent to tell you to let the people go; you have not done it. Now watch and learn that the God of the Hebrews is powerful."

He stretched out his staff over the Nile, and before the very eyes of the king, the water in the river turned to blood. When Pharaoh hurried back to the palace, there was no jar or cup or bowl that held water; only blood. He demanded of his servants that he have water; so they dug in the sand and filtered it for him. For seven days this plague lasted.

On the eighth day Moses came again to the palace.

"Let the Hebrews go," he demanded, "or the land shall be plagued with frogs."

And it was so. An army of frogs came up from the river. They crawled into the ovens and the kneading bowls; they jumped over men's feet as they walked, and crept into bed with them at night. Then Pharaoh called Moses and Aaron and said, "Make your god take away the frogs, and I will let the people go. Ask for tomorrow."

The next day all the frogs died. The Egyptians gathered them into heaps and burned them, but the king did not keep his promise.

And now came other plagues upon the Egyptians, but strange to say, not on the Hebrews who lived in the land of Goshen on the other side of the river. There was a plague of lice, of flies, of disease among the cattle that killed off many of the royal herds. There was the plague of boils, also, among the people, and even the magicians of Pharaoh were too afflicted to stand before the king. Finally the king did make some compromises. He said, "You may worship in the land; the people may have a three-day holiday."

But Moses said, "No," again.

Weeks passed. Then came a plague of hail that destroyed all the crops that were in the fields and all the cattle that were not under cover; and Pharaoh was terrified. He had never seen hail that killed both men and cattle, or lightning that ran along the ground as balls of fire would run. He sent for Moses in haste.

"I have sinned that I have hardened my heart against your plea. Take away the hail and lightning, and I will let the Hebrews go."

And yet when the hail ceased, he took back his promise.

More months passed. The later crops began to show promise of harvest, when Moses again came to Pharaoh as he went to the river, and said, "Tomorrow, the locust will come."

Then the servants of Pharaoh knelt before him, "O master, don't you see that this man and his god are destroying Egypt? We beg of you, let the Hebrews go!"

But the compromise that Pharaoh offered of just the men going, Moses refused, and the locust came. There were hoards and hoards of them, so many that the sky was darkened. They ate everything; there was not a single green blade of grass, nor fruit on any tree. Then the king sent for Moses in haste, and acknowledged that he had sinned.

"Pray your god to forgive me, and take away the locust; and I will let the people go," he said.

But again when the locust had been driven into the sea by a strong wind, he hardened his heart.

Then suddenly a thick darkness fell upon the land; a darkness so black that the flaring torches in the palace cast only a dim light. Most of the people were so terrified that they refused to move about for the three days that it lasted. This time the compromise Pharaoh offered was that they might go—all the people and their children—but not their cattle.

"No," said Moses. "We shall need our cattle for sacrifices. When we go, not a hoof shall be left behind."

Pharaoh was very angry.

"Get out!" he said. "If you enter the palace again, I will have you killed."

Moses said quietly, "You are right; I shall not come again," but the king saw no significance in his answer.

He did not know of the preparations that went on in the Hebrew homes in the days that followed. Instead he felt that at last he was victor. Then on the night of the fourteenth of the month Abib, the tenth plague came. At midnight the son of Pharaoh suddenly died. But it was not he alone. In every home of the Egyptians all over the land wails arose, for the first-born in every home had died. Men and women rushed into streets, tearing their hair and their clothing, screaming and smearing mud on their hands and faces as signs of grief. The narrow streets were so crowded that Pharaoh's messengers who were hunting for Moses, wasted precious time trying to work their way through the people.

Suddenly someone realized that there were no lamentations from the huts of the Hebrews. Their doors were closed.

"Look!" cried the man, "the death angel has passed over their homes. Their god has given them a sign! See, there is blood on the door and the doorposts."

New cries rose from the Egyptians.

"Let the Hebrews go before their god kills all our children! before he kills all of us! Make Pharaoh let the people go! It is his fault that the Hebrew god has ruined our land; he must not let us be killed too!" and the crowd surged toward the palace gates.

Egyptian families that held Hebrew slaves as nurses for their children or for their households were now eager to let them go. They even bribed them with jewels of silver and jewels of gold; purple and scarlet and fine-twined linen and perfumes. Never had servants been treated so royally.

Meanwhile the messengers of Pharaoh had found Moses and hurried him to the palace, the chariot with its hard-driven horses racing through the streets that were not quite so congested as they had been at first. It was not a king, but a heartbroken father who greeted him.

"Go!" he cried hoarsely. "Go!" Your god has conquered, and my son—my son, lies dead. Go, and take your flocks and herds and your little ones and worship your god in the wilderness. And when you pray, ask a blessing for me also."

It was almost morning when at last the more than six hundred thousand Hebrew men—not counting the women and children—with their flocks and herds wound slowly out of Egypt, and started for the land of Canaan from which their ancestors had come more than four hundred years before. They were happy, and many of them sang as they marched along. Perhaps no one even thought of the ruler who with each plague had hardened his heart and kept them in bondage so long, as a heartbroken father who this day wept beside the bed of his dead son who would have been the next Pharaoh.*

* Used by special permission of the author.

MOSES, THE LEADER OF A PEOPLE

By

Sir Winston S. Churchill

And there arose not a prophet since in Israel like unto Moses, whom the Lord knew face to face, in all the signs and the wonders, which the Lord sent him to do in the land of Egypt to Pharaoh, and to all his servants, and to all his land, and in all that mighty hand, and in all the great terror which Moses shewed in the sight of all Israel.
—DEUTERONOMY 34:10-12

THESE closing words of the Book of Deuteronomy are an apt expression of the esteem in which the great leader and liberator of the Hebrew people was held by the generations that succeeded him. He was the greatest of prophets, who spoke in person to the God of Israel; he was the national hero who led the Chosen People out of the land of bondage, through the perils of the wilderness, and brought them to the very threshold of the Promised Land; he was the supreme law-giver, who received from God that remarkable code upon which the religious, moral, and social life of the nation was so securely founded. Tradition lastly ascribed to him the authorship of the whole Pentateuch, and the mystery that surrounded his death added to his prestige.

Let us first retell the Bible story.

The days were gone when Joseph ruled in Egypt. A century had passed. A new Pharaoh had arisen who knew not Joseph. The nomadic tribe of Bedouins who, in the years of dearth preceding the Great Famine, had sought asylum by the ever-fertile banks of the Nile, had increased and multiplied. From being a band of strangers hospitably received into the wealth of a powerful kingdom, they had become a social, political, and industrial problem. There they were in the "Land of Goshen," waxing exceedingly, and stretching out every day long arms and competent fingers into the whole life of Egypt. There must have arisen one of those movements with which the modern world is acquainted. A wave of anti-Semitism swept across the land. Gradually, year by year and inch by inch, the Children of Israel were reduced by the policy of the State and the prejudices of its citizens from guests to servants and from servants almost to slaves.

Building was the mania then, and here were strong, skilful, industrious builders. They were made to build. They built for Pharaoh by forced labour treasure cities or store cities, for the real treasure then was grain. Two such cities are mentioned in Exodus—Pithom and Rameses. The Egyptologist Naville has uncovered the city of Pithom, which was indeed built in the time of Rameses, and lies in that "Land of Goshen" on the north-east frontier, where the Children of Israel were settled. The fluctuations of the Nile could only be provided against by enormous granaries filled in good years. The possession of these granaries constituted the power of government. When a bad season came Pharaoh had the food and dealt it out to man and beast in return for plenary submission. By means of this hard leverage Egyptian civilization rose. Grim times! We may imagine these cities built by the Israelites in the capacity of state serfs as enormous food depots upon which the administration relied to preserve the obedience of the populace and the life of the nation.

The Israelites were serviceable folk. They paid their keep, and more. Nevertheless, their ceaseless multiplication became a growing embarrassment. There was a limit to the store depots that were required, and the available labourers soon exceeded the opportunities for their useful or economic employment. The Egyptian government fell back on birth control. By various measures which are bluntly described in the book of Exodus, they sought to arrest the increase of male Israelites. Finally they determined to have the male infants killed. There was evidently at this time a strong tension between the principle of Jewish life and the ruthless force of established Egyptian civilization. It was at this moment that Moses was born.

The laws were hard, and pity played little part in them. But his mother loved her baby dearly, and resolved to evade the laws. With immense difficulty she concealed him till he was three months old. Then the intense will-to-live in the coming generation led her to a bold stratagem. It has its parallels in various ancient legends about great men. Sargon, the famous Sumerian King, was abandoned by his mother in a basket of reeds, and rescued and brought up by a peasant. There are similar stories about the infancies of Romulus and Cyrus. In this case the only chance for the child was that he should be planted upon the Court. Pharaoh's daughter, the Princess Royal, was accustomed to bathe in the Nile. Her routine was studied. A little ark of bulrushes floated enticingly near the bank from which she took her morning swim. Servants were sent to retrieve it. Inside this floating cradle was a perfect baby . . . "and the babe wept!" ' The heart of the Princess melted and she took the little boy in her arms, and vowed he should not perish while her father's writ ran along the Nile. But a little sister of the infant Moses judiciously posted beforehand now approached. "I know where a nurse can be found." So the nurse was sought, and the mother came. In the wide economy of an Imperial household a niche was thus found where the baby could be reared.

The years pass. The child is a man, nurtured in the palace or its purlieus, ranking, no doubt, with the many bastards or polygamous offspring of Oriental thrones. But he is no Egyptian, no child of the sheltered progeny of the Nile valley. The wild blood of the desert, the potent blood of Beni Israel not yet mingled with the Hittite infusions, is in his veins. He walks abroad, he sees what is going on. He sees his own race exploited beyond all economic need or social justice. He sees them the drudge of Egypt, consuming their strong life and seed in the upholding of its grandeur, and even grudged the pittance which they earn. He sees them treated as a helot class; they, the free children of the wilderness who came as honoured guests and had worked every hour of their passage! Upon these general impressions he sees an Egyptian beating an Israelite; no doubt a common spectacle, an episode coming to be accepted as part of the daily social routine. But he has no doubts; not for a moment does he hesitate. He knows which side he is on, and the favours of the Court and the privileged attachments which he had with the ruling and possessing race vanish in a moment. The call of blood surges in him. He slays the Egyptian, amid the loud and continuing applause of the insurgents of the ages.

It was difficult to conceal the corpse; it was even more difficult to conceal the tale. No very lengthy interval seems to have elapsed before it was known throughout the palace that this somewhat nondescript and hitherto favoured denizen had bit the hand that fed him. How easily can we recreate their mood! The most cultured and civilized states and administrations of the present day would have felt with Pharaoh that this was going altogether too far. Very likely Egyptian public opinion—and there is always public opinion where there is the slightest pretence of civilization—fixed upon this act of violence as a final proof that the weakness of the government towards these overweening strangers and intruders had reached its limit. At any rate Pharaoh—which is as good a name as any other for the governing classes in any country at any time under any system—acted. He decreed death upon the murderer. We really cannot blame him; nor can we accuse the subsequent conduct of the slayer. His action also conformed to modern procedure. He fled.

In those days a little island of civilization had grown up under the peculiar physical stimulus of the Nile flood and the Nile mud with all the granary system to grip it together—a tiny island in a vast ocean of bleak and blank starvation. Few and far between were the human beings who were able to support life beyond its shores. There were, indeed, other similar islands in other parts of the world, in Mesopotamia, in Crete, in Mycenae; but to Moses the choice of Egypt or the wilderness, all that was now open, was, in fact, virtually a choice between swift execution and the barest existence which can be conceived.

Moses fled into the Sinai Peninsula. These are the most awful deserts where human life in any form can be supported. There are others, like the vast expanses of the Sahara, or the Polar ice, where human beings cannot exist at all. Still, always a very few people have been able to keep body and soul together amid the rigours of the Sinai Peninsula. There are nowadays a few hundred Bedouin inhabitants. But when an aeroplane makes a forced landing in the Sinai Peninsula the pilot nearly always perishes of thirst and starvation. In these dour recesses the fugitive Moses found a local chief and priest named Jethro. With him he took up his abode; he rendered him good service, married his daughter, Zipporah, and dwelt in extreme privation for many years. Every prophet has to come from civilization, but every prophet has to go into the wilderness. He must have a strong impression of a complex society and all that it has to give, and then he must serve periods of isolation and meditation. This is the process by which psychic dynamite is made.

Moses watched the skinny flocks which browsed upon a starveling herbage, and lived a life almost as materially restricted as theirs. He communed within himself, and then one day when the sun rode fierce in the heavens, and the dust-devils and mirages danced and flickered amid the scrub, he saw the Burning Bush. It burned, yet it was not consumed. It was a prodigy. The more it burned the less it was consumed; it seemed to renew itself from its own consumption. Perhaps it was not a bush at all, but his own heart that was aflame with a fire never to be quenched while the earth supports human beings.

God spoke to Moses from the Burning Bush. He said to him in effect: "You cannot leave your fellow-countrymen in bondage. Death or freedom! Better the wilderness than slavery. You must go back and bring them out. Let them live among this thorn-scrub, or die if they cannot live. But no more let them be chained in the house of bondage." God went a good deal further. He said from the Burning Bush, now surely inside the frame of Moses, "I will endow you with superhuman power. There is nothing that man cannot do, if he wills it with enough resolution. Man is the epitome of the universe. All moves and exists as a result of his invincible will, which is My Will."

Moses did not understand the bulk of this, and asked a great many questions and demanded all kinds of guarantees. God gave all the guarantees. Indeed, Moses persisted so much in his doubts and bargainings that we are told Jehovah (for that was the great new name of this God that spoke from the Burning Bush) became angry. However, in the end He made His contract with the man, and Moses got a fairly reasonable assurance in his own mind that he could work miracles. If he laid his staff upon the ground he was sure it would turn into a snake, and when he picked it up it would become a staff again. Moreover, he stipulated that he must have a spokesman. He was not himself eloquent; he could give the driving force, but he must have a competent orator, some man used to putting cases and dealing in high affairs, as his assistant. Otherwise how could he hold parley with Pharaoh and all the Ministers of the only known civilization his world could show? God met all these requests. A competent politician and trained speaker in the shape of one Aaron would be provided. Moses now remembered his kinsman Aaron, with whom he had been good friends before he had to flee from Egypt. Thereupon action! Jethro is told that his son-in-law intends to start on a great adventure. He gives his full consent. The donkey is saddled; Zipporah, the two children, and the family property are placed upon its back, and through the dust-clouds and blazing sunlight the smallest, most potent and most glorious of all the rescue forces of history starts upon its expedition.

Undue importance can easily be given to the records of the protracted duel between Moses and Pharaoh. The plagues of Egypt are famous, and most of them were the kind of plagues from which Egypt has frequently suffered—pollution of the Nile and the consequent destruction of its fish; multiplication of frogs and their invasion of the land; flies beyond all bearing; lice abounding (but some authorities say they were gnats); the death of cattle; darkness over the face of the earth such as is produced by prolonged sandstorms; the prodigy of hail in the Nile Valley; finally the death of the first-born by pestilence. The local magicians, entering fully into the spirit of the contest, kept going until the third round, measure for measure and step by step. But when the dust turned into lice they admitted with professional awe that this was "the finger of God."

Great interest attaches to the behaviour of Pharaoh. Across the centuries we feel the modernity of his actions. At first he was curious, and open to conviction.

Quite mild plagues brought him to reason. He was ready to let the Israelites depart into the wilderness and sacrifice to their potent God. This serious concession arrested all of his building plans and caused considerable derangement in the economic life of the country. It was very like a general strike. It was no doubt represented to him that the loss of the national income from this cessation of labour would be disastrous to the State. So he hardened his heart and took back in the evening what he had promised in the dawn, and in the morning that which he had promised the night before. The plagues continued; the magicians dropped out. It was a dead-lift struggle between Jehovah and Pharaoh. But Jehovah did not wish to win too easily. The liberation of the Children of Israel was only a part of His high Purpose. Their liberation had to be effected in such a manner as to convince them that they were the Chosen People, with the supreme forces of the universe enlisted in their special interest, should they show themselves faithful. So Jehovah laid on His plagues on the one hand, and hardened the heart of Pharaoh on the other.

It has often happened this way in later times. How often governments and peoples plunge into struggles most reluctantly, terrified of their small beginnings, but once swimming in the torrent go on desperately with immense unsuspected reserves and force in the hopes of emerging triumphantly on the other shore. So Pharaoh and the Egyptian government, once they had taken the plunge, got themselves into the mood that they would "see it through;" and this perhaps "hardened their hearts." However, the plagues continued and one misfortune after another fell upon the agonized State, until finally a collapse occurred. Pharaoh decided to "let the people go."

Amid the general confusion which followed this surrender the Chosen People spoiled the Egyptians. They begged, borrowed, and stole all they could lay their hands upon, and, gathering themselves together laden with treasure, equipment, and provender, launched out from the island of civilization into the awful desert. Their best chance was to cross the isthmus which joins Africa and Asia and make for the regions we now call Palestine. But two reasons which could not be neglected weighed against this. First, the Philistines barred the road. This formidable people had already carried their military organization to a high pitch. The Israelites after 150 years of domestic servitude in Egypt were in no condition to encounter the fierce warriors of the wilds. Secondly, and concurrently, Jehovah had told Moses he must lead the liberated tribe to the neighbourhood of Mount Sinai, where other revelations of the Divine Will would be made known to them.

They marched accordingly to the northern inlet of the Red Sea. There is much dispute as to their numbers. The Bible story says they were 600,000 men, with the women and children in addition. A clerical error may so easily have arisen. Even today a nought or two is sometimes misplaced. But more than two thousand years had yet to pass before the "nought" and all its conveniences was to be at the disposal of mankind. The earlier forms of notation were more liable to error than our own. Unless the climate was very different from the present it is difficult to see how even six thousand persons could have lived in the Sinai Peninsula with supernatural aid on a considerable and well-organized scale.

But now once again Pharaoh has changed his mind. No doubt the resentment aroused among the Egyptians by the wholesale pillage to which they had been subjected in their hour of panic, combined with the regrets of the government at the loss of so many capable labourers and subjects, constituted a kind of situation to which very few Parliaments of the present age would be insensible. The Egyptian army was mobilized; all the chariots set out in pursuit. The fugitive tribesmen, having reached the shore of a body of water called the "Yam Suph," at the extreme northern end of the Gulf of Akaba, were trapped between the sea and Pharaoh's overwhelming host. Their situation was forlorn, their only resource was flight, and flight was barred by salt water.

But Jehovah did not fail. A violent eruption occurred, of which the volcanic mountains in these regions still bear traces. The waters of the sea divided, and the Children of Israel passed dryshod across the inlet. Pharaoh and his host, hotly following them, were swallowed up by the returning waters. Thereafter, guided by a pillar of smoke by day and of fire by night, the Israelites reached the neighbourhood of Mount Sinai. Here Moses received from Jehovah the tables of those fundamental laws which were henceforward to be followed, with occasional lapses by the highest forms of human society.

We must, at this point, examine briefly the whole question of the miracles. Everyone knows that the pollution of rivers, the flies, frogs, lice, sandstorms and pestilence among men and cattle, are the well-known afflictions of the East. The most sceptical person can readily believe that they occurred with exceptional frequency at this juncture. The strong north wind which is said to have blown back the waters of the Red Sea may well have been assisted by a seismic and volcanic disturbance. Geologists tell us that the same fault in the earth's structure which cleft the depression of the Dead Sea in Palestine runs unbroken to the Rift Valley in what we now call the Kenya province of East Africa. The Sinai Peninsula was once volcanic, and the Bible descriptions of Mount Sinai both by day and by night are directly explicable by an eruption, which would have provided at once the pillar of cloud by daylight and of fire in the darkness. Flocks of quails frequently arrive exhausted in Egypt in their migrations, and some might well have alighted in the nick of time near the encampment of the Israelites. Renan has described the exudation by certain shrubs in the Sinai Peninsula of a white gummy substance which appears from time to time, and is undoubtedly capable of supplying a form of nourishment.

All these purely rationalistic and scientific explanations only prove the truth of the Bible story. It is silly to waste time arguing whether Jehovah broke His own natural laws to save His Chosen People, or whether He merely made them work in a favourable manner. At any rate there is no doubt about one miracle. This wandering tribe, in many respects indistinguishable from numberless nomadic communities, grasped and proclaimed an idea of which all the genius of Greece and all the power of Rome were incapable. There was to be only one God, a universal God, a God of nations, a just God, a God who would punish in another world a wicked man dying rich and prosperous; a God from whose service the god of the humble and of the weak and poor was inseparable.

Books are written in many languages upon the question of how much of this was due to Moses. Devastating, inexorable modern study and criticism have proved that the Pentateuch constitutes a body of narrative and doctrine which came into being over at least the compass of several centuries. We reject, however, with scorn all those learned and laboured myths that Moses was but a legendary figure upon whom the priesthood and the people hung their essential social, moral, and religious ordinances. We believe that the most scientific view, the most up-to-date and rationalistic conception, will find its fullest satisfaction in taking the Bible story literally, and in identifying one of the greatest of human beings with the most decisive leap-forward ever discernible in the human story. We remain unmoved by the tomes of Professor Gradgrind and Dr. Dryasdust. We may be sure that all these things happened just as they are set out according to Holy Writ. We may believe that they happened to people not so very different from ourselves, and that the impressions those people received were faithfully recorded and have been transmitted across the centuries with far more accuracy than many of the telegraphed accounts we read of the goings-on of today. In the words of a forgotten work of Mr. Gladstone, we rest with assurance upon "The impregnable rock of Holy Scripture."

Unluckily the stresses of the Exodus, the long forty years, or whatever the period may have been which was needed in the wilderness to sharpen the Children of Israel from a domesticated race into an armed force of conquering warriors, led them to make undue claims upon Jehovah. They forgot the older tradition which the Pentateuch enshrines. They forgot the enlightened monotheism which under the heretic Pharaoh Akhenaton had left its impression upon Egypt. They appropriated Jehovah to themselves. In Renan's words, they made Him revoltingly partial to the Chosen People. All Divine laws and ordinary equity were suspended or disallowed when they applied to a foreigner, especially to a foreigner whose land and property they required.

But these are the natural errors of the human heart under exceptional stresses. Many centuries were to pass before the God that spoke in the Burning Bush was to manifest Himself in a new revelation, which nevertheless was the oldest of all the inspirations of the Hebrew people—as the God not only of Israel, but of all mankind who wished to serve Him; a God not only of justice, but of mercy; a God not only of self-preservation and survival, but of pity, self-sacrifice, and ineffable love.

Let the men of science and of learning expand their knowledge and probe with their researches every detail of the records which have been preserved to us from these dim ages. All they will do is to fortify the grand simplicity and essential accuracy of the recorded truths which have lighted so far the pilgrimage of man.*

* From *Amid These Storms* by Sir Winston S. Churchill, pp. 283-94. Copyright, 1932, by Charles Scribner's Sons. Used by special permission of the publisher. British Empire copyright permission also granted by Oldhams Press, Ltd., from a volume by Sir Winston Churchill entitled *Thoughts and Adventures,* 1932.

SHEPHERD OF ISRAEL

By

Leonora Eyles

IN the days that followed, the deadness grew upon Moses like the deadness over the earth at the solstice, when no wind stirs, and the earth and the sun both seem to hang mute and motionless in the still sky. It was like the enchantment that had fallen upon him when he changed, in a moment, from prince to slave. But then he was young and full of the sap of life; now he was old and dried up with the carrying of burdens and the bearing of griefs. Then there had been, calling to the deeps of brain and heart, the crying of people in bondage, to mutter underground within him until it rose to a clamouring shout. Now there was no clamour to put ardour into him—only a further, ratifying task. The seed-time had been his, and the ploughing and the heat and burden of the day. The harvest he must leave for others to garner; and sometimes he feared for the harvest.

The Israelites traversed the plain of Moab, keeping from the towns and sometimes adventuring into the surrounding lands. At one camp Miriam died and was buried, and nobody save Moses felt a pang at her death. He thought of little things at this time—how, a little girl with big frightened eyes and beating heart, she had watched his mother give him a chance of life in his boat of rushes; how she had taught him, in the palace with a secret fierce insistence, the language of Israel; how she had bathed the Princess Meri in sweet waters when her death sickness came upon her; how she had lavished love upon Gershom and the sullen Eliezer—a twisted woman, her love more bitter than her hate. He saw the golden sand mingle with her grey hair, and left her there and went on his way. Then, on a day when their path had led for a month or more to the east of a range of mountains, they fell at night upon a great caravan of merchants coming from Damascus with rich stuffs for Egypt.

"Egypt buys greatly of us now," said the merchants, "for she has no slaves to weave for her."

They talked together that night, and presently Moses, coming upon the group, asked what land lay on the other side of the mountains.

"That is the land of Canaan. At the foot of the hills is the Dead Sea, into which the river you see in front drains."

For the first time in many days Moses felt a stirring of feeling within him.

"Then is that the river Jordan?" he asked, with a catch in his breath.

"No, it is only a small brook compared to the Jordan. If you journey for ten more days you will reach the North end of the Dea Sea, and then you will only be two days' journey from Jericho. There is a mountain at the edge of the salt sea called Pisgah, from which a man can see Canaan rolled out before him even to the sea."

When the merchants heard that they had stumbled across the encampment of the Israelites, who had by their going out of Egypt so increased the trade of Damascus in linen and cloth of gold and rich colours, they were eager for talk, and one of them, an old man who could read and write, talked long into the night with Moses.

"I once climbed to the top of Mount Pisgah," he said, with a sigh. "In those days I was a young man and had it in mind to be a priest, but men's ways with gods never satisfied me. So I became a merchant and found men's ways with men little more pleasing." He lowered his voice suddenly, and breathed in Moses' ear: "These men think that I am a man of Damascus, but on the day that my father died he told me that I was a circumcised Israelite even as he was, and a wanderer."

"Are all Israelites wanderers at heart?" asked Moses, speaking as much to himself as the merchant.

"Wanderers and fighters both. When they find a home they wander from it into strange lands, and are never content until they get back again, only to find that even then it never satisfies them. When they find God they fight with Him and flee from Him, and call on Him to gather them back again as a shepherd gathers his flock. When you climb Mount Pisgah, look to the north, where you will see another mountain. If you go up and wait for the dawn you will see the rocks on the crest of it turn to the likeness of a man's face with the sun shining upon it. That is Peniel, where our ancestor Jacob wrestled all night with the angel for a blessing, and in the morning saw God face to face."

So the old man rambled on, much as Jethro used to, until at last he fell asleep as he talked. The next day the children of Israel encamped by the side of the river and found good pasturage, fish in the river and dates on the trees in plenty. Moses went about amongst them, but although they treated him with fear and reverence, there were none of those looks of shy love from the children, of friendliness from the men, of worship from the women. "He spared not his own son," they said of him behind their hands as he passed. So, just as once they had followed him for the miracles he did not perform, now they avoided him for his very justice towards them. And he knew that his work was almost done, although still, perhaps even more than ever now, they would obey him, for at last they feared him for himself as once they had feared him for God.

He proclaimed a feast for three days hence, and bade the people make preparations for the Passover. In secret he went about amongst the people, choosing here and there one amongst the young men, those whom he had heard teaching the people worthily, and to them he gave robes of white and gold stitchery that he had bought from the men of Damascus, and to them, in the Tent of Justice, still secretly, he taught his plans. Some who did not agree went out, and others were chosen until there were threescore and ten. Knowing all he knew of the rot that enters into a man when he becomes a paid priest and makes knowledge of God into a trade, he had fought against priests in Israel, but the people must have teachers and they craved for ritual. Yet surely if he made of his priests men who went also about their daily work, the rot in their souls would be stayed! He bade the people be ready to waken at dawn on the third day to the sound of the ram's horn, and for a day and a night he shut himself away from them.

They awakened to the blast of the trumpet on a dawn still as a dream. The mists were just rising from the river, and birds in the trees that fringed it were twittering their excitement at the unwonted sound of a multitude. The coffin and the ark had been placed on a hillock so that all could see them, and beside them was a pile of stones, like the altar on which Jethro had sacrificed his lambs night and morning. The people stirred nearer, and nearer still as they saw the company of the seventy white-robed men that covered the hillock. Moses went from amongst them, robed in white as they were, and they noticed that he was taller than any, although he walked feebly, as though he were very weary. His voice was gentle when he spoke, but in the cool of the morning it reached to a great number of the people, and even those who could not hear saw him outlined against the blue sky and understood something of what he was doing.

"Children of Israel," he cried, leaning on his staff, "you have come, after great tribulation, to the very borders of the land of your inheritance. There are still sufferings for you to undergo, for you will have to fight for the land, but never again need you hunger for bread or thirst for water or for a cool pasture to lie down in. Now I am an old man and a weary man, and before long in the natural course of life I must leave you. But I would not leave you fatherless, and today from amongst you I choose one whom I have trained in the crafts of war, the arts of governance and the conquest of his own fears and desires. Joshua, son of Nun, stand forth!"

Moses had told Joshua nothing of what was to happen, but he was standing a little apart from the white-robed company, for wherever Moses was, Joshua was not far away. He came forward, his eyes shining, his mouth quivering, and Moses kissed him before the whole congregation. Then, laying his hand on the young man's head, he spoke in a voice so clear and loud that it penetrated almost to the hills of Moab. "Joshua, son of Nun, I choose you to be Shepherd of Israel. Be slow to fight and swift to make peace with your enemies. When you strike a blow, strike to kill, for it is an evil thing to leave a maimed man alive. In the Tent of Justice, purge your mind of all save the Law, and let neither pity nor anger sway you from the Law. But outside the Tent of Justice, let mercy temper your judgments and let compassion soften your strength, for the Lord our God is full of compassion and mercy, slow to anger and of great goodness. Think first of the good of the nation, for you are leader of a people chosen as the first-born of the Lord, and the sin of the child pierces the Father's heart, the suffering of the child takes the sap from His veins, but the steadfastness and courage of the child give life to the Father when He is failing. After the nation, take compassion on the individual. Last of all, think of your own good. And now, my son, I give the Law into your hands. Come with me." He led him to the ark, unlocked it with the key he carried on his girdle, and laid the stone tables in Joshua's arms. "I put them in the ark, and none but I have touched them. Lay them now in the ark again, my son, and until you give them to your successor, they are your guide and strength."

As Joshua, speechless with the great honour and the great burden that had come upon him, laid the tables back again, Moses took out of the ark his staff, and a quiver went through the people as they saw it, for a few who were old remembered the miracles it had wrought on the Egyptians, and those who had not seen the wonders made them more wonderful still. Just a light staff of shittim wood, very thin and strong, polished by much handling, scarred a little by knocks and blows. Moses leant on it a moment, and thought how once it had guided Jethro's sheep in the sweet days of peace and loving-kindness, when he had a father, a friend, a home, a wife and a child, before ever he took the bleak path of the lover and leader of men. Then he put it into Joshua's hand, and kissed him again and looked at him with compassion, for it was a heavy burden this staff was giving him. But Joshua was young and full of hope and strength, and he drew himself up to tiptoe height and said:

"The Lord do to me tenfold all the wrongs I do to His firstborn, whether wrongs of malice or false judgment, of haste or faint-heartedness."

So Moses blessed him with the old blessing: "The Lord be on your lips and in your heart; the Lord show His Face to you; the Lord be in your hands and in your feet and give you peace."

Then a great cry went up from the people, as they acclaimed Joshua as their leader, and after it had died away, Moses held up his hands for silence and pointed to the men who stood quiet beside him, looking in their white robes like a company of the Blest in the cool light of the morning.

"You are a people who crave for converse with God and earthly symbols of your union with God. I had thought to teach you to offer to your God and your Father the daily offering of your lives with a pure worship, but I have tried to make you run before you can walk. So now I have chosen from among the people men with clean hands and quiet minds, men able to read and interpret the Law, and these shall be your priests. At dawn one of them, in his order, shall slay a firstling lamb and burn it on the altar he shall build, and on the head of the lamb shall all the labours of your hands lie, to be offered up to God. When the smoke of the burning has passed, he shall burn gums of sweet calamus, of onycha and frankincense and galbanum, that shall give odours of pleasant and acceptable savour, and with their burning shall you offer to the Lord your God all the love wherewith you love your neighbours, the dreams wherewith you climb to His Presence. So each day shall your daily task, your love and your hopes, be offered to Him, a holy offering. And see that you keep your labours and your thoughts pure, for the Lord will cut off from before Him any that offend."

Then Moses took a lamb from the hands of Eleazar the son of Aaron, and sacrificed it there before the altar, and set coals of fire upon it until it was consumed. As the smoke of it rose, the people worshipped the Lord their God who had led them by paths they knew not of, and with the sweet uprising of the incense Moses lifted his voice in prayer, and the people repeated each sentence after him.

"Lord, thou hast been our dwelling-place from one generation to another.

"Before the mountains were brought forth out of the sea, or ever Thou hadst formed the earth and the world.

"Even from everlasting to everlasting Thou art God.

"O Lord our God, let Israel dwell in safety, and the fountain of Jacob, let it be upon a land of corn and wine.

"And let the heavens drop down dew upon it.

"And so teach Israel to regard the days that he may apply his heart to learning Thy wisdom.

"Let only righteousness appear in the children of Israel and Thy glory in his children.

"And may Thy beauty be in us so that the work of our hands is established on the face of the earth,

"Yea, let our handiwork not fade away from before Thee."

Then Moses took a skin of water and a cake of bread and went out from among the people, and none saw his going, for the feast had begun, and Joshua alone stood in his tent with his hands uplifted in prayer. For three days Moses journeyed, and his going was swift now, for he had dropped his burden, although he still felt weary. And at sunset of the third day he reached the head of a great sheet of water, and when he stooped to drink and found it salt, he knew it was the Dead Sea of which the merchant had spoken, and before him a hill that first sloped gently like the breast of a sleeping woman, and then rose in a steep ascent. He was very thirsty, but because he could not drink the water, he cast aside his garments and bathed in the lake to ease his tired limbs, and lay down to sleep. His sleep was as soft as a child's, and he awakened next morning to find the dew heavy upon him and his parched body revived. He would have sought for water with his rod, but he had left it behind in the camp. So he started to climb the hill, but had to rest often, for the shortness of breath that had troubled him during the past year seemed to have grown worse during the last few days. It was at first a wooded hill that he climbed, and the shade of the great trees was grateful and cool, the scents of their barks and gums like sweetest incense. As he penetrated deeper amongst the trees the air grew murmurous with the hum of insects and heavy like wine from the honey that dripped from overflowing honey combs, in the hollows of ancient branches. His feet crackled over fallen leaves and twigs that had lain for many years, and over his head birds sang their piercing songs in the branches while the day was yet cool, dropping to lazy murmurs in the heat of the sun. But always the voice of the turtle-dove was heard, its low note plaintive yet soothing, as the voice of one who comforts another for a great sorrow he comprehends and grieves for but knows must be borne. It was evening when Moses reached the naked top of the hill, and the landscape beneath him, rolled out like a coloured carpet, was dim with rising mists. But north, as the merchant had said, was a hill shaped like a man's face, the hill on which Jacob had wrestled with the angel all night, only to find with the morning light that it was the Lord he had fought for his blessing.

Moses lay down, pondering the old story of a man who fought with a God and won his way, although the finger of God had shrunk his body where it touched him. Yea, after all, Jacob had gone down the hillside in the radiance of human strength for all his wounding, when the sun rose upon him. Jacob had wrestled only one night, and Moses for many years, ever since the dawn on Mount

Horeb. Jacob had seen God face to face. Moses had never seen Him—only distant, elusive things that might have been echoes of His passing—a holy face that a man might worship —footsteps faint and far off that might have been His—murmurs of a voice so thrilling sweet that might have been God's voice. But never had he been sure. Never had he had any ratification that he could trust.

He lay down to sleep, fighting with his will to master the growing faintness of hunger, the pangs of thirst, and his weariness was so great that he could forget other pains. But a great doubt was in him, a great unrest and fear. Had he done righteously in giving the people a God he himself could not believe in? Had he done righteously in trying to wean them from this God even as he set Him up before them? Was there a God such as Jacob had wrestled with, who might shrivel a man's body with His touch, even as He blessed him? In the forest below, noises began as beasts went about seeking their food, and he listened to their many voices. But at last weariness overcame even his unrest, and when he wakened, the sun rose upon him, as upon Jacob.

He stood up and looked at a sight that made his heart leap, for the whole valley of the Jordan lay stretched before him in the crystal light of the morning. The river wound away to the north, golden now in the light of dawn, with rich pastures and lofty trees fringing its banks. Here and there a hill rose gently, here and there a city with roofs and towers gleaming, but for the most part man had done little to the country, and it lay there green and golden with a shimmer to the far west that might have been the sea. The cradle of his race, the home of the homeless sons of Abraham, towards which through desert and danger, set back by their own weaknesses, they had struggled, of which in the house of bondage as well as in the caravan of the merchant, every son of Abraham had dreamed. The land of the Covenant! Even as he said the words to himself, the mists that had been in his mind all these years rolled away as the mists were licked from the valley by the growing heat of the sun. God! the God of the Covenant! The God he had never seen but dimly followed, the God he had never heard speak, but whose echoed voice he had fearfully interpreted for a weak people. Moses' heart began to beat until it sounded in his ears like the thudding of waves on an ocean strand, but his body grew lighter and lighter as the knowledge flooded in with each wave. Osiris—and Horus— and Set! God in the Highest Heaven, shining serene in the beauty of unchanging holiness, yet dwelling in man to make him like Himself. God the Holy Immortal, wedding earth, the Mortal and Changing and bringing forth Man that he might tame Set and give the Kingdom into his Father's hands at the last.

As the certainty flooded him, he lifted his hands in prayer, and for the first time since he had ceased to be a priest of Egypt, they were not empty hands held up to lead a lost people. They were hands in which he held his whole being, and he knew to Whom he prayed at last.

He saw now why Moab had made an orgy of the thing of beauty, why the priests of Amen had made a release into a tyranny. The spirit of God would struggle through in men, giving here a vision, there a law, and men by their flesh would defile it. Yet ever friends of God, fighting as allies with Him for the

Kingdom of man, and in the end God would win. It all rested with the strength and courage of His ally.

"O my Father," he said, "you chose me to lead men to You, but You gave me no sure knowledge, so that I should feel in my own soul and body their weakness and doubt, and have compassion on it and lead them gently. For a man must grope his way towards You, and in his groping strengthen his hands and his feet. But all the time You have taught me by Your free spirit, and guided me by Your mighty hand. I have tried to make their bodies Your tabernacle, and spared not even my own son when he defiled the tabernacle. I have taught them that You are Holy and Awful in Your holiness, yet tender in Your compassion for Your children, for never can You, who are Truth, deny Your children. And yet it was not I who taught or led, but You in my lips and my hands, stronger than I, You in my spirit that was wiser than my mind—all the time when I was lost and lonely, longing for the touch of Your hand on mine. Never in my life, with all my questing, have I known anything. Now at last I know. I know I am Your Son—and I can doubt no more. Father, now that I have struggled through without You—show me Your face. Let me touch your hand."

He stopped speaking and sank to the ground, but raised himself to look again over the land, and as he looked it seemed that the corn had ripened that was not yet sown by earthly hands, the winepresses were flowing with the blood of grapes not yet gathered on earth. Was it his soul, wandering in the Fields of the Long-standing Corn? He seemed to be eating little cakes of wheat and drinking from a Cup, with all the people at peace around him. Was it a dream fed by his thirst and his hunger, or was he eating the bread of Maat, given of Her very body—eating and drinking the Wine and Bread of Very Truth that Man had won from Life for the nourishing and refreshing of God the Father?

The thudding of the waves grew to thunders, and beat his tired body to the earth, but he was too tired to struggle against them, and soon they strove with him no more, but changed to a peaceful lapping of a calm lake against its shores, and his soul, after its desert journeyings, had dominion over cool waters.

When Moses did not come back to the camp as the days passed, they sought him, and those who had heard him talk with the merchant, climbed the height of Pisgah and found him there. Already the seeds of death against which he had made a Law had done their corrupting work on his body, for the Law was but yet young. So they buried him there, with his face to the sky and his feet towards the Land of Canaan, and Joshua son of Nun took up the burden.*

* Abridged from *Shepherd of Israel* by Leonora Eyles, pp. 293-307. Copyright, 1929, by Harcourt, Brace and Company, Inc. Used by special permission of the publisher.

THROUGH THE RED SEA TO THE PROMISED LAND

By

Elizabeth Miller

THE Lawgiver laid his hand on the young man's shoulder but did not answer at once. The growing clamor about them had reached the acme of insistence. The nearest people pressed through the tribal lines and, rushing forward, began to throw themselves on their knees, tumbling in circles about the majestic Hebrew. Others kept their feet, and with arms and clenched hands above their heads, shouted vehemently. Their cries were partly in Egyptian, partly in their own tongue, but the cause of their terror and the burden of their supplications were the same. The Egyptians were upon them!

After a little sad contemplation of the clamoring horde about him, the Lawgiver drew nearer to Kenkenes* and said in his ear, because the tumult drowned his voice:

"The Lord will fight for thee; thine enemy cannot flee His strong hand. Wait upon Him and behold His triumph."

Kenkenes bowed his head in acquiescence.

The turmoil of Israel began to subside, growing fainter, ceasing among the ranks nearest the sea, failing toward the rear, dying away like a sigh up and down the long encampment. The people that had been on their knees rose slowly. The bleating of the flocks quieted into stillness. Commotion ceased and Israel held its breath.

The Lawgiver had passed from among them, and those that followed him with their eyes saw that he was moving toward the sea, seemingly at the very limit of the outer radiance and still going on. First to one and then to another, it became apparent that the extent of the illuminated beach was widening. . . . Ripple-worn sand, shells, barnacle-covered rocks, slowly came within the pale of the radiance and Moses moved with it. Eight stalwart Hebrews, bearing a funeral ark, shrouded with a purple pall, fringed with gold, emerged from among the people and, taking a place in front of the Lawgiver, walked confidently down the sand toward the east.

The radiance progressed step by step. Wet rocks entered the glow, lines of seaweed, immense drifts of debris, the brink of a ledge, the shadow before it, and then a sandy bottom.

A long line of old men, two abreast, the wind making the picture awesome as it tossed their beards and their gray robes, followed the Lawgiver. After these several litters, borne by young men, proceeded in imposing order.

Except for the raving of the tempest there was no sound in Israel.

A double file of camels with sumptuous housings moved with dignified and unhasty tread after the litters. By this time, the foremost ranks of the procession

* *Kenken'eez.*

were some distance ahead, the limit of radiance just in advance, and lighting with special tenderness the funeral ark. Here were the bones of that noblest son of Jacob. Having brought Israel into Egypt, Joseph was leading it forth again.

Pools, lighted by the ray, glowed like sheets of gold, darkling here and there with shadow; long ledges of rock, bearded with deep-water growth, sparkled rarely in the light; stretches of sodden sand, colored with salts of the waters, and littered with curious fish-life, lay between.

Where was the sea?

After the camels followed a score of mules, little and trim in contrast to the tall shaggy beasts ahead of them. They were burden-bearing animals, precious among Israel, for they were laden with the records of the tribes, much treasure in jewels and fine stuffs, incense, writing materials, and such things as the people would need, and were not to be had from among them, or like to be found in the places to which they might come. These passed and their drivers with them.

The next moment, Kenkenes was caught in the center of a rushing wave of humanity. He fought off the consternation that threatened to seize him and tried to care for himself, but a reed on the breast of the Nile at flood could not have been more helpless. Behind Israel were the Egyptians, ahead of it miraculous escape; the one impulse of the multitude was flight. . . .

Neither halt nor escape was possible. . . .

After the first moment of battle against the human sea, Kenkenes recognized the futility of resistance and suffered himself to be borne along. There was no turning back now, had he been so disposed. He had left behind him his purposes, unaccomplished.

He had received no explicit promise from Moses, and if he had given ear to the doubts of his own reason, he might have been sorely afraid, much troubled for Egypt and all he loved therein. But he went with the multitude passively, even contentedly; he did not speculate how his God would fight for him; his faith was perfect.

As for his presence with Israel, no one heeded him. Sometimes it came his way to be helpful; an old man lost his feet and becoming panic-stricken was soothed only when the young Egyptian put a strong arm about him and held him till his feet touched earth again. Children became heavy in the arms of parents and the little Hebrews had no fear of the young man who carried them, a while, instead. But no one stopped to take notice that this was an Egyptian, totally unlike those among the "mixed multitude" that had come to join Israel; nor did any wonder what a nobleman of the blood of the oppressors did among the fleeing slaves. Indeed, if the host had any thought beyond the impulse of self-preservation, it was only a dim realization that they were walking over a most rocky, oozy and untended road and that the smell of the sea was very strong about them.

In the early hours of the morning, having become so accustomed to the roar of the wind and the sound of the moving multitude, Kenkenes ceased to be conscious of it. . . .

He tried to think it one of the many voices of the storm, but the second time he heard it, he knew what it was. Far to the rear, a trumpet-call, beautiful and spirited, rose upon the air.

The Egyptian army was in pursuit!

Israel heard it, and crying aloud in its terror, swept forward, as if the trumpet-call had commanded it. Kenkenes felt a quickening of pulse, a momentary tremor, but no more.

He became conscious finally of a warmth penetrating his sandals. He knew that he had been struggling up a slope for a long time, and now he realized that he was again on the dry, sun-heated sand of the desert. The multitude ceased to crowd, the pressure about him diminished; the ranks began to widen to his left and right; the leaders halted altogether, and though there was still much movement among the body and the rear of the host, people turned to look upon their neighbors. . . .

Kenkenes, with many others, looked back and saw that the pillar, illuminated, but no longer illuminating, had halted above a solitary figure of seemingly superhuman stature in the morning gray, standing on an eminence, overlooking the sea.

The arm was uplifted and outstretched, tense and motionless.

From his superior height, Kenkenes saw, over the heads of the immense concourse, two lines of foam riding like the wind across the sea-bed toward each other. Between them was a great body of plunging horses; overhead a forest of fluttering banners; and faint from the commotion came shouts and wild notes of trumpets. Then the two lines of foam smote against each other with a fearful rush and a muffled report like the cannonading of surf. A mountain of water pitched high into the air and collapsed in a vast froth, which spread abroad over the churning, wallowing sea. The falling wind dashed a sheet of spray over the silent host on the eastern shore. Sharp against the white foam, dark objects and masses sank, arose, and sank again.

At that moment the sun thrust a broad shaft of light between the horizon and the lifted cloud.

It discovered only the sea, raving and stormy, and afar to the west a misty, vacant, lifeless line of shore.

"And the water returned and covered the chariots and the horsemen, and all the host of the Pharaoh that came into the sea after them; there remained not so much as one of them."

So perished Har-hat and the flower of the Egyptian army.

On the ensuing day Kenkenes had no very distinct memory. Very fair and beautiful, one recollection remained—a recollection of another figure on the eminence, and by the flash of white upthrown arms, and the blowing of a somber cloud of hair, this time it was a woman. . . .

Thereafter Israel moved inland and down the coast some distance, for the sea had begun to surrender its dead. Of the stir and method of the removal he did not remember, but of the encampment and the reassembling of the tribes he recalled several incidents. He was numb and sleep-heavy beyond words, and while leaning, in a semi-conscious condition, against some household goods, he was dis-covered by the owner, who was none other than the friendly son of Judah, his assistant in his search for Rachel in Pa-Ramesu. The man's honest joy over Ken-kenes' safety was good to look upon. A few words of explanation concerning his very apparent exhaustion were fruitful of some comfort to the young Egyptian. The Hebrew's wife had a motherly heart, and the weary face of the comely youth touched it. Therefore, she brought him bread and wine and made him a place in the shadow of her tent-furnishings where he might sleep till what time the family shelter could be raised.

But Kenkenes did not rest. He fell asleep only to dream of Rachel, and awoke asking himself why he had abandoned the search for her; why he had left Egypt without her; and why he had not gone to Moses at once for aid to further his seeking through Israel.

He arose from his place, sick with all the old suspense and heartache. He would begin now to look for Rachel and cease not till he found her or died in his weariness.

He stepped forth directly in the path of a party of women. He moved aside to give them room, and glancing at the foremost, recognized her immediately as the Lady Miriam. She stopped and looked at him.

"Thou are he who found Jehovah in Egypt?" she asked.

He bowed in assent.

"Thy faith is entire," she commented. "Also, have I cause to remember thee. Thou didst display a courteous spirit in Tape, a year agone."

"Thou hast repaid me with the flattery of thy remembrance, Lady Miriam," he replied.

"Thy speech publishes thee as noble," she went on calmly. "Thy name?"

"Kenkenes, the son of Mentu, the murket."

Her lips parted suddenly and her eyes gleamed.

"See yonder tent," she said, indicating a pavilion of new cloth, reared not far from the quarters of Moses. "Repair thither and await till I send to thee."

Without pausing for an answer she swept on, her maidens following, damp of brow and bright of eye.

Kenkenes turned toward the tent. A Hebrew at the entrance lifted the side without a word and signed him to enter.

The interior was not yet fully furnished. A rug of Memphian weave covered the sand and a taboret was placed in the center.

Presently the serving man entered with a laver of sea-water, and an Israelitish robe, fringed and bound at the selvage with blue. With the despatch and adroit-ness of one long used to personal service, he attended the young Egyptian, and dressed him in the stately garments of his own people. When his service was complete, he took up the bowl and cast-off dress and went forth.

After a time he brought in a couch-like divan, dressed it with fringed linen and strewed it with cushions; next, he suspended a cluster of lamps from the center-pole; set a tiny inlaid table close to the couch, and on the table put a bottle of wine and a beaker; and brought last a heap of fine rugs and coverings which he laid in one corner. The tent was furnished and nobly. The man bowed before Kenkenes, awaiting the Egyptian's further pleasure, but at a sign from the young man, bowed again and retired.

Kenkenes went over to the divan and sat down on it, to wait.

Presently some one entered behind him. He arose and turned. Before him was the most welcome picture his bereaved eyes could have looked upon. His visitor was all in shimmering white and wore no ornament except a collar of golden rings. What need of further adornment when she was mantled and crowned with a glory of golden hair? Except that the face was marble white and the eyes dark and large with quiet sorrow, it was the same divinely beautiful Rachel!

It may have been that he was beyond the recuperative influence of sudden joy . . . but whatever the cause, Kenkenes sank to his knees and forward into the eager arms flung out to receive him. Her cry of great joy seemed to come to him from afar.

"Kenkenes! O my love! Not dead; not dead!"

Then it was he learned that she had despaired, grieving beyond any comfort, for she had counted him with the first-born of Egypt. And even though thoughts came to him but slowly now, he said to himself:

"Praise God, I did not think of it, or I had gone distracted with her trouble."

How rich woman-love is in solicitude and ministering resource! It made Rachel strong enough to raise him, and having led him back to the divan, gently lay him down among the cushions. The wine was at hand, and she filled the beaker, and held it while he drank. Then she kissed him. . . . And though he held her very close and had in his heart a great longing to soothe her, he could not speak.

After a little she spoke:

"I had not dreamed that there was such artifice in Miriam. She told me of a nobleman that had served God and Israel, and was in need of comfort in his tent. But she bridled her tongue and governed her expression so cunningly, that I did not dream the hero was mine—mine!"

It is the love of riper years, that makes the lips of lovers silent. But Kenkenes and Rachel were very young and wholly demonstrative, and they had need of many words to supplement the testimony of caresses. They had much to tell and they left no avowal unmade.

But at last Kenkenes' voice wearied and Rachel noted it. So in her pretty authoritative way, she stroked his lashes down and bade him sleep . . .

As she bent over him, she noted with a great sweep of tenderness how young he was. In all her relations with Kenkenes she had seen him in the manliest roles. She had depended upon him, looked up to him, and had felt secure in his protection. Now she contemplated a face from which content had erased the mature lines that care had drawn. The curve of his lips, the length of the drooping lashes, the roundness of cheek, and the softness of throat, were youthful—boyish . . . the maternal element leaped to the fore; their positions were instantly reversed. It was hers to care for him!

After another space of rapt contemplation of his unconscious face she went forth and drew the entrance together behind her.

The next daybreak was the happiest Israel had known in a hundred years. Egypt, overthrown and humbled, was behind them; God was with them, and Canaan was just ahead—perhaps only beyond the horizon. Few but would have laughed at the glory of Babylonia, Assyria and the great powers.

For had it not been promised that out of Israel nations should be made, and kings should come?

The march was to be taken up immediately, and in the cool of the morning the host was ready to advance.

Rachel had not permitted herself to be seen until the tent of Miriam was struck. She knew that Kenkenes was without, waiting for her . . . and when the moment arrived she slipped across the open space to the camel that was to bear her into Canaan, but in the shadow of the faithful creature, Kenkenes overtook her and folded her in his arms.

"Didst thou sleep well?" she asked.

"Most industriously, since I made up what I lost and overlapped a little. And yet I was abroad at dawn prowling about thy tent lest thou shouldst flee me once again. Rachel—" his voice sobered and his face grew serious—"Rachel, wilt thou wed me this day?"

"If it were only 'aye' or 'nay' to be said, I should have said it long ago, . . . but there are many things that thou shouldst know, Kenkenes, before thou demandest the answer from me."

"Name them, Rachel," he said submissively.

"Art thou ready for the tent and shepherd life of Israel? . . . There is much to prosper thee in Egypt; there, thy state is high; there, thou hast opportunity and wealth. Israel can offer thee only God and me. . . . Thou art the murket's son, and building takes the place of carving for thee, now. But, here, O Kenkenes, thou must lay thy chisel down forever, for the faith of the multitude, so newly weaned from idolatry, is too feeble to be tried with the sight of images."

Kenkenes heard her with a passive countenance. . . .

"I am of Israel and whosoever weds with me, will be of Israel likewise. It may be that I shall escape my people's sorrows. Shall I bring them upon thy head, also, my Kenkenes?"

After a little he answered, sighing. . . .

"Thou speakest of the benefits of Egypt," he said. "What were Egypt without thee, save a great darkness haunted and vacant? Besides, there is no Egypt beyond this sea. She hath risen and crossed with Israel. . . . For thou art Egypt and shalt be to me all that I loved in Egypt."

He took her hands. . . .

"When wilt thou wed me, my love?"

"Thou knowest, my Kenkenes, the Hebrews are married simply. There is feasting and dancing and the bride is taken to the house of her father-in-law. Thereafter there is still much feasting, but the wedding ceremony is done at the home-bringing of the bride."

"I hear," said Kenkenes when she paused.

"I am without kindred; thou art without house. There can be no wedding feast for us, nor dancing nor singing, for Israel is on the march. . . . So there is only the essential portion of the ceremony left to us—the home-bringing of the bride."

"It is enough," said Kenkenes.

"Hur and Miriam brought me to thy tent last night. . . . From that moment, I have been thy wife!"

It must not be supposed that there was no serene life nor any happiness in the long wandering of forty years. . . . There were long stretches of peace and plenty. . . .

Kenkenes was among the chosen people but not of them . . . because most of Israel had nothing in common with the nobleman. But Moses loved him and found joy in his company. Joshua loved him and had him by his side when Israel warred. Caleb and Aaron loved him because he was godly, and Miriam was proud of him.

From the moment of his union with his beautiful wife, through the long years of semi-isolation that he knew thereafter, he grew closer and closer to Rachel. She filled all his needs as Israel failed to supply them, and he missed neither friend nor neighbor when she was near. Rachel knew wherein she was more fortunate than other women and her content and her devotion were beyond measure. So Kenkenes and Rachel were lovers all the days of their lives.

The genius of Kenkenes did not die. His voice enriched with age, and the rocky vales wherein his flocks wandered had melodious echoes whenever he followed the sheep. But he never used the chisel upon stone again. His sons were artists after him, but they were handicapped also. And so it continued for many generations until the Temple of Solomon was built. Then, though the plans came from the Lord, and artisans were brought from Tyre, it was the descendants of Kenkenes who made the Temple beautiful "with carved figures of cherubim and palm trees and open flowers, within and without."*

✛

GO DOWN, MOSES

(Interpretation)

MOST Negro spirituals show the influence of African music in the very form which the spiritual takes. Usually a typical African song begins with a line sung by a leader or soloist. This is followed by a response of one or more lines chanted by a chorus or group of voices.

This leading line followed by a response appears in many spirituals. They are, for the most part, spontaneous group compositions. They originated, not as written music, but with a solo line followed by a choral response. Often one person in a group began singing; the melody was caught up by another person adding a line or a thought; then a group picked up the thoughts already sung and added

* Abridged from *The Yoke* by Elizabeth Miller. Copyright, 1904, by The Bobbs-Merrill Company; 1932, by Elizabeth Miller. Used by special permission of the publisher.

Go Down, Moses.

1. When Is-rael was in E-gypt's land: Let my peo-ple go; Op-
2. Thus saith the Lord, bold Mo-ses said, Let my peo-ple go; If

pressed so hard they could not stand, Let my peo-ple go. Go down, Mo-ses,
not, I'll smite your first-born dead, Let my peo-ple go. Go down, Mo-ses,

'Way down in E-gypt land, Tell ole Pha-raoh, Let my peo-ple go.

3 No more shall they in bondage toil,
Let them come out with Egypt's spoil.

4 When Israel out of Egypt came,
And left the proud oppressive land.

5 O, 'twas a dark and dismal night,
When Moses led the Israelites.

6 'Twas good old Moses and Aaron, too,
'Twas they that led the armies through.

7 The Lord told Moses what to do,
To lead the children of Israel through.

8 O come along Moses, you'll not get lost,
Stretch out your rod and come across.

9 As Israel stood by the water side,
At the command of God it did divide.

10 When they had reached the other shore,
They sang the song of triumph o'er.

11 Pharaoh said he would go across,
But Pharaoh and his host were lost.

12 O Moses the cloud shall clear the way,
A fire by night, a shade by day.

13 You'll not get lost in the wilderness,
With a lighted candle in your breast.

14 Jordan shall stand up like a wall,
And the walls of Jericho shall fall.

15 Your foes shall not before you stand,
And you'll posess fair Canaan's land.

16 'Twas just about in harvest-time,
When Joshua led his host divine.

17 O let us all from bondage flee,
And let us all in Christ be free.

18 We need not always weep and moan,
And wear these slavery chains forlorn.

* From *Southland Spirituals,* No. 17. Copyright, 1936, by Homer Rodeheaver, Hall-Mack Company. Used by special permission of the publisher.

a response, and thus a spiritual was born. Sometimes only the theme and the verse would be created at a singing. Changes and additions were often made at later singings. Sometimes the former lines would be remembered; others, that were often original, were added. The final product was always a group experience and a group composition different from anything that had ever existed before. Thus most spirituals are intended to be sung by a soloist or leader with a chorus of responsive voices.

"Go Down, Moses" is another of those spirituals that relate in many stanzas the life experiences of Moses, the great lawgiver and deliverer of the Hebrew people from the bondage of Egypt.

One can understand why the stories of Moses should make such a deep impression on the Negro in America. They, too, were slaves in a foreign land, thousands of miles from their own country and people. They, too, yearned for the day when a saviour would appear to lead them out of their bondage. And so they sang with heartfelt sympathy and understanding of the experiences of Moses and the children of Israel in Egypt, adding their own deep-felt conviction expressed in the refrain "Tell ole Pharaoh, Let my people go."

These spirituals should be sung with deep fervor and understanding of the Negro's position and condition. Thus one will be able to appreciate the power and beauty of these American folk songs.

✠

SOME SINAI

(Interpretation)

WILLIAM L. STIDGER, for many years head of the Department of Homiletics in the Boston University School of Theology, wrote this beautiful hymn, "Some Sinai," in 1939. It was set to music by his friend, Frank R. White.

For more than twenty years William L. Stidger contributed to the enrichment of American life and thought through his prose and poetic volumes, alive with ideas and possessing unconventional energy of expression. His death during the summer of 1949 was a distinct loss to the young preachers of America for his writings and his teaching helped, not only to make preaching more attractive, but to make sermons more crisp and cogent.

His poetry abounds in a feeling for nature coupled with a persistent sense of moral values. In his poetic volume, *I Saw God Wash the World,* Dr. Stidger entered boldly into the realm of the lyric muse. All his poems possess swinging, ringing lines of courage and cheer that give the lift needed to carry one through those periods when the burdens of life grow heavy and the way ahead dark.

His poetic hymn, "Some Sinai," is a splendid illustration of the poet's ability to find a new challenge for himself and for everyone in the courageous life of Moses seeking the rugged heights of Sinai that he might banish the cares of the world below, and hear with a new distinctness the voice of the Most High God.

Some Sinai

William L. Stidger

Frank R. White

Each soul must seek some Sin - ai, as Mo-ses sought of old, And
Each soul must seek some Sin - ai, some se-cret place a - part, Where

find im-mort-al mu - sic writ on slabs of liv - ing gold. Each
he may be a - lone with God and New-Born Kingdoms chart. Each

soul must seek some Sin - ai, some high flung mount-ain peak Where
soul must seek some Sin - ai, where God's own voice is heard and

he may hear the thun-ders roll and time-less voi - ces speak.
he may see the myst - ic sign and hear the se - cret word.

Dr. Stidger believed devoutly that each soul in each generation must make a similar quest into high places where he can be alone with God, and unhindered by the noisy clamor that distracts and disturbs high thinking, listen *to* and *for* the "still small voice" that speaks to all men in times of stress, turmoil, and need.

As we read or sing this hymn, we hear again the challenge to high thinking and the call to heroic living that come to us in solitude when we seek to hear the voice of God as did Moses in the long ago. Each stanza stresses the importance of each soul's individual quest for the guidance of the living God.

✢

THE LAW

"THE TORAH"

(Interpretation)

THE music of the Hebrew people in the early years of their history was probably similar to that of people living in neighboring countries. It was bound up largely with the ritual of their worship of the one God in whom they believed.

King David assigned to one of the Hebrew tribes the sole duty of providing music for the temple worship, although there had been previously a special caste of "singers with instruments, psalteries, harps and cymbals." It was the tribe of the Levites who sang and played and danced before the Lord; and many of the words which they sang on these occasions are to be found in the Psalms.

This hymn, bearing the simple title of "The Torah" or Law, consists of five brief stanzas all stressing the importance of the Law in the life of the Hebrew people.

The first stanza stresses the importance of *teaching* the Law. It represents a paean of praise to "our fathers' God, for all the teaching of Thy Law," and for the way in which Israel has been led by God through the centuries.

The second stanza recalls the *suffering* through which Israel passed, the fire and flame through which they were led by the one God of the Hebrew people, and reveals the reverence of the Hebrews for the sanctity of "The Torah" in building human life and character.

The third stanza *gives thanks* for the prophets and sages of the Hebrew people who in times past led them on their way, giving all Israel strength and light.

The fourth stanza stresses the importance of a continuing *faith in God's law,* and urges Jewish people today to live their lives, as their patriotic forebears did, for Israel and for God.

The fifth stanza is a *prayer* to Israel's God to shield and guide the Jewish people, to uplift them through the Law, to unveil their eyes so that the children of Israel today may see in the Law the truth which has guided the Hebrew people in past centuries.

The Law
"The Torah"

Max D. Klein

Pinchos Jassinowsky

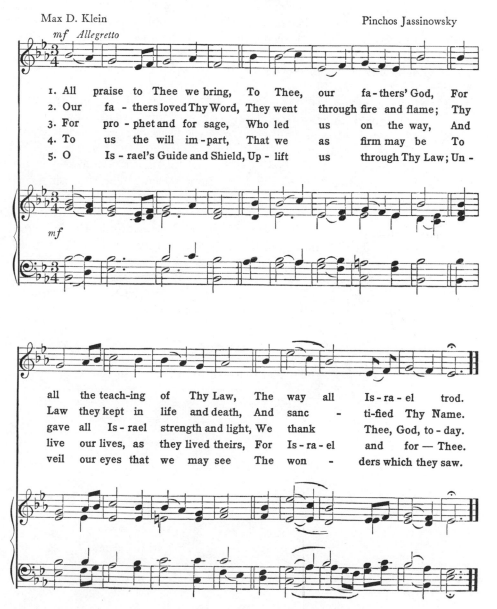

1. All praise to Thee we bring, To Thee, our fa-thers' God, For
2. Our fa - thers loved Thy Word, They went through fire and flame; Thy
3. For pro - phet and for sage, Who led us on the way, And
4. To us the will im-part, That we as firm may be To
5. O Is - rael's Guide and Shield, Up - lift us through Thy Law; Un -

all the teach-ing of Thy Law, The way all Is - ra - el trod.
Law they kept in life and death, And sanc - ti-fied Thy Name.
gave all Is - rael strength and light, We thank Thee, God, to - day.
live our lives, as they lived theirs, For Is - ra - el and for — Thee.
veil our eyes that we may see The won - ders which they saw.

* From *Union Hymnal,* No. 203. Copyright, 1932, by the Central Conference of American Rabbis. Used by special permission of the publisher.

WHEN ISRAEL TO THE WILDERNESS
(Interpretation)

THE absence of adequate records regarding ancient Hebrew music makes it difficult for us to learn a great deal about the vocal music of the Hebrew people. This example of Hebrew music, the words of which were composed by Max Meyerhardt, and the tune by Jacob Beimel, reviews the story of the wilderness wanderings of Israel after her miraculous escape from Pharaoh's cruel army. It was written, no doubt, for the commemoration of the feast of the Passover which to this day is regularly observed by devout Jews everywhere.

The first stanza of this hymn refers to the "cloud by day, a fire by night" which led and guided the children of Israel during their wilderness wanderings.

The second stanza continues the story, in poetic form, of how the children of Israel led by the cloud and fire eventually reached the Promised Land.

The third stanza stresses the continued guidance of Israel's God, not alone of the Hebrew people, but of all mankind, as with a glorious light He leads them on.

The fourth stanza emphasizes the contribution of the Jewish people in keeping alive in every land faith in a living God, and dependance on His love and mercy in leading them "through fire and flood, through tears and blood" to ultimate freedom.

The fifth and last stanza picks up the imagery of God's law "as a light unto one's feet and a lamp unto one's highway" in guiding humanity in their constant struggle onward and upward toward the eventual rule of justice, truth, and love.

It is a type of hymn to which human hearts everywhere can and do respond with thanksgiving. It stresses the progress which the races of men are making toward the reign of peace and justice that will one day be achieved in our world.

When Israel to the Wilderness

Max Meyerhardt

mf Andante moderato

Jacob Beimel

1. When Is - ra - el to the wil - - der - ness
2. And, guid - ed by that heav'n - ly flame,
3. Yet, not a - lone in days of yore,
4. A lamp of ra - diant, glow - ing hue,
5. Oh, heav'n - ly lamp! Thy light shall shine

Had fled from Pha - raoh's cru - - el might,
That bea - - con from the Lord's own hand,
Has God His won - - drous mer - - cy shown,
By Is - - rael borne in ev' - - ry clime,
'Till sin and hate from earth de - part,

Th' E - ter - - nal sent to lead them on,
The cho - - sen peo - - ple safe - - ly reached
For still He grants to all man - kind
Through fire and flood, through tears and blood,
'Till wrong shall fail and right pre - vail,

A cloud by day, a fire by night.
Their des - - tined goal,— the Prom - ised Land.
A glo - - - rious light to lead them on.
With cour - - age grand and faith sub - lime.
And jus - - - tice rule the hu - - - man heart.

PART II

HIGH LIGHTS OF THE PERIODS OF JOSHUA AND THE JUDGES

CONTENTS

PART II   SECTION 1

JOSHUA'S LEADERSHIP AND CONQUESTS

---✠---

And Joshua the son of Nun was full of the spirit of wisdom; for Moses had laid his hands upon him: and
the children of Israel hearkened unto him, and did as the Lord commanded Moses.—DEUTERONOMY 34:9

---✠---

MOSES' SUCCESSOR

By

Julius Schnorr von Carolsfeld

(Interpretation)

THE great German artist, Julius Schnorr von Carolsfeld, was born at Leipzig, Germany, in 1794 and died in Dresden in 1872. As a youth he studied with his father who was director of the Academy in Leipzig, and later at the Academy in Vienna. In 1817 he traveled to Italy where he joined a group of artists known as the Nazarenes because of the simple life they lived and the sincerity of their work. In 1827 Schnorr von Carolsfeld was called to Bavaria by the art-loving King Ludwig II to work in the Munich Academy of Art. During his residence in Bavaria he painted several series of murals for the royal castle, the themes of which were from German mythology and history. In 1847 he went to Dresden as instructor in the Academy and as director of the Art Gallery. In 1851 he visited London where he was enthusiastically received. There he was asked to illustrate a Bible which was later published in Leipzig. While in London he made designs for several windows of St. Paul's Cathedral. His art appears in many art galleries, churches, and castles of his native Germany.

This engraving, "Moses' Successor," is based on one of the closing verses of the last chapter of Deuteronomy. It reads: "And Joshua the son of Nun was full of the spirit of wisdom; for Moses had laid his hands upon him: and the children of Israel hearkened unto him, and did as the Lord commanded Moses" (34:9).

Moses had just descended from the summit of Mount Nebo which rises from the plains of Moab. From the pinnacle of this mountain Moses had viewed the Promised Land which the Lord had declared to Abraham He would give to the children of Israel. Moses himself was not to accompany the Israelites into the Promised Land. They would enter this longed-for country under the leadership of one whom Moses would choose to be his successor.

Moses knew that his lifework was done, and that very soon the children of Israel must go on under a new command and a new leadership. So he called the chief priests and the people together at the foot of Mount Nebo. In their presence, while the young soldier knelt at his feet, Moses laid his hands in blessing on Joshua their new leader.

In Schnorr von Carolsfeld's portrayal of this incident, Joshua, clad in armor, beneath his mantle, kneels before Moses, his hands clasped over his sword and his head bowed to receive his commission from Israel's great lawgiver and statesman. Behind the kneeling Joshua stands the high priest wearing the breastplate of righteousness with its twelve jewels each representing one of the twelve tribes. Elders of Israel, soldiers, and a group of youths looks on, as their aged leader, with one hand on Joshua's head and the other upraised, gives his blessing to this young soldier-statesman, who from this time forward is to be the earthly leader of the children of Israel. With his blessing Moses is bequeathing to his successor the nation he has created out of twelve tribes. By instilling in these people an undying loyalty to their God, Moses has shaped a nation.

Rays of light converge on the head of Moses as he performs his last act for the Israelites whom he had led from the slavery of Egypt through more than forty years of wandering in the wilderness. Before long he will go to his rest with Abraham, Isaac, and Jacob, having accomplished the task to which his God called him when He appeared to him in the burning bush in the Midian desert. The sadness of farewells here has added poignancy because Israel's great lawgiver was denied the privilege of leading his people into the Promised Land.

The verses that close Deuteronomy (34:10-12) praise him for "all the signs and the wonders, which the Lord sent him to do in the land of Egypt to Pharaoh, and to all his servants, and to all his land, and in all that mighty hand, and in all the great terror which Moses shewed in the sight of all Israel." But Israel was taught to regard him as their greatest prophet, not because of his noble character nor his supreme achievements, but because he obeyed God and lived in communion with Him: "There arose not a prophet since in Israel like unto Moses, whom the Lord knew face to face."

It was now Joshua's responsibility to lead the twelve tribes of Israel that Moses had brought from Egypt to the very borders of the Promised Land. The Lord said to Joshua: "Be strong and of a good courage, for unto this people shalt thou divide for an inheritance the land, which I sware unto their fathers to give them. Only be thou strong and very courageous, that thou mayest observe to do according to all the law, which Moses my servant commanded thee" (Josh. 1:6, 7).

✠

THE TABERNACLE IN THE WILDERNESS

(Woodcut)

Artist Unknown

(Interpretation)

THE Tabernacle was a movable sanctuary set up by Moses soon after the tables of Law were given. It was first erected in the wilderness of Sinai but served as a place of worship for the Israelites throughout the period of their sojourn in the Wilderness. The materials used in its construction were shittim or acacia wood, goats' hair, rams' skins, the skins of fish (perhaps porpoise), linen (possibly cotton), and gold, silver, and brass. It was called variously "the house of the Lord thy God," "the tabernacle of the congregation" for God and His people, and "the tent of the testimony" or the "tabernacle of witness" (Num. 9:15, 18:2).

The Tabernacle was an oblong tent, thirty cubits long, ten cubits broad, and ten cubits high (Ex. 26:15-20). It was placed at the western end of a long court measuring one hundred cubits by fifty (Ex. 27:9-19). A cubit was originally the

MOSES' SUCCESSOR—*VON CAROLSFELD*

length of a man's arm from the elbow to the end of the middle finger, or about eighteen inches.

The front or east end of the Tabernacle was a doorway of five pillars overlaid with gold, and hung with a curtain. The interior was divided into two apartments by four similar pillars supporting a curtain (Ex. 26:31-37). The western room, the Holy of Holies, measured ten cubits in every dimension; the eastern, the Sanctuary or Holy Place, was twenty cubits long by ten cubits breadth and height.

The hangings were of four kinds:

1. The ceiling, and apparently the walls, were hung with a curtain of fine linen, blue, purple, and scarlet, and figured with cherubim (Ex. 26:1-6).

2. The main external covering was made of a certain of goats' hair (Ex. 26:7-13).

3. The double roof of red-dyed rams' skins and goatskins (or perhaps badgers' skins [Ex. 26:14])

4. There were two veils of divers-colored fine linen, one at the entrance to the Sanctuary, and the other in front of the Holy of Holies (Ex. 26:31-37).

The Holy of Holies was empty except for the Ark of the Covenant which stood there. For a time a pot of manna, Aaron's rod that blossomed, and the book of the Law were placed beside the Ark (Heb. 9:4). The Ark itself was a chest two and a half cubits long by one and a half in breadth and height, made of acacia wood overlaid with gold, and covered by a lid of solid gold, which was the mercy seat (Ex. 25:17). Two cherubim of gold faced each other above the mercy seat and covered it with their outspread wings. Here the Lord had said: "I will commune with thee from above the mercy seat, from between the two cherubims which are upon the ark of the testimony" (Ex. 25:18-22). The cherubim were symbols of the presence of the Lord who was believed to dwell between them.

Attached to the Ark on each side were two rings. These were for the poles of acacia wood overlaid with gold by which the Ark was carried from one camp in the Wilderness to another and finally across the Jordan and into the Promised Land.

Outside the Holy of Holies, in the Sanctuary or Holy Place, stood the Golden Altar or the Altar of Incense, four cubits square and two cubits high, also of acacia wood covered with gold (Ex. 30:1-10, 40:5).

The table of Shewbread stood on the northern side of the Sanctuary. It was two cubits long, one cubit broad, and one and a half cubits high, made of acacia wood overlaid with gold. On it was displayed in two rows the twelve cakes, representing the twelve tribes of Israel. It was called the Shewbread or Bread of the Presence (Ex. 25:23-30; Lev. 24:5-9).

The Golden Candlestick stood on the south side of the Sanctuary. It consisted of a base and shaft with six branches and seven lamps (Ex. 25:31-40, 27:20, 30:7, 8; Lev. 24:2-4; I Sam. 3:3; Zech. 4).

The Brazen Altar or Altar of Burnt Offering, stood in the outer court, in front of the Tabernacle. It was five cubits square, and three cubits high, made of acacia

THE TABERNACLE IN THE WILDERNESS—ARTIST UNKNOWN

wood overlaid with brass. It was on this altar that the sacrifices were offered (Ex. 27:1-8).

The Laver of Brass stood upon a base of brass between the Altar of Burnt Offering and the door of the Tabernacle (Ex. 30:17-21, 38:8).

This woodcut gives an idea of how the Tabernacle in the Wilderness may have looked as it served the tribes of Israel during their desert sojourning. Thousands of tent homes for the children of Israel surround the Tabernacle on three sides. A cloud from which come bright rays covers the Holy of Holies into which only the High Priest might enter to make intercession for the people. When the Tabernacle was completed this cloud first appeared and "covered the tent of the congregation, and the glory of the Lord filled the tabernacle" (Ex. 40:34). It was this central yet movable place of worship, perhaps more than anything else, that welded the children of Israel into a united people during their more than forty years of wandering and prepared them for the dangers they must face under Joshua's leadership when they entered the Promised Land.

✢

THE FRIEZE OF THE PROPHETS

By

John Singer Sargent

(Interpretation)

CENTER SECTION

ALTHOUGH most of John Singer Sargent's life was devoted to the painting of portraits, his murals represent his greatest undertaking in America and brought him his greatest fame.

As early as 1890 Sargent had received a commission to decorate the walls of the great Hall in the Boston Public Library. He gave endless study and effort to the project that was in its entirety to illustrate the "History of Religion." His research included not only the reading of Bible history, but also special studies in Palestine and other parts of the Near East. The north end of the Hall was finally completed in 1919 with a series entitled "The Frieze of the Prophets." It consists of eighteen mural paintings of the prophets, nine on each side of the central figure of Moses. On the left side appear four prophets of despair, while on the right are the prophets of hope. These figures are in the nature of a Greek chorus interpreting the movement of a great drama. The entire mural illustrates the development of prophetic insight among the Hebrews and their final expectation of the Messiah.

The center section of this great mural presents Moses as the central figure, not painted, as are the other figures, but modeled in high relief with great golden wings folded about his shoulders and the Ten Commandments or Decalogue in the form of two tablets clasped securely in his strong hands. The face of this great prophet-statesman who led the children of Israel out of the bondage of Egypt is

THE FRIEZE OF THE PROPHETS (CENTER SECTION)—*SARGENT*

strong, his eyes far-seeing as, remembering the struggles of the past, he looks directly forward into the future. The tablets brought down from Sinai symbolize the foundation of the religion of Israel upon the structure of the Law.

At the right stands Joshua, who succeeded Moses as the leader of Israel and who led the tribes, after more than forty years of wandering in the wilderness, into the Promised Land. The children of Israel achieved for the first time in their history the status of a nation, with Canaan as their home. The artist has put Joshua's face in shadow and accented his arm and hand to portray him as a man of action rather than of words. His right arm unsheathing his sword characterizes Joshua as the military leader of the Hebrews during the period of their conquest of Canaan.

At the left of the picture stands Elijah who lived centuries after Moses and Joshua in the days of Ahab, king of Israel. This early Hebrew prophet stood for wholehearted loyalty and service to the God of Israel at a time when Queen Jezebel was doing her utmost to substitute the worship of her heathen god Baal for the worship of the God Abraham and of Isaac and of Jacob. Elijah condemned Ahab for the murder of Naboth and the stealing of his vineyard. He also brought to a successful conclusion the dramatic contest on Mount Carmel between Jezebel's heathen god Baal and the true God of the Hebrew people. He is here represented as a man of burning, denunciatory words, fearless in his championship of the cause of God. He together with Moses and Joshua are portrayed somewhat larger and more rugged and primitive than the others.

Sargent's figures are painted with incisiveness and directness. They are not mere wall decoration, but have a plastic feeling which gives them remarkable vitality. This artist not only possessed insight into a person's character, but he had the ability to render this in his paintings. He used these gifts in portraying the unique character of each prophet. Though all these spokesmen for God had similar careers, throughout this frieze they are all shown in different poses and with individual facial expressions. It is this individuality in the handling of the prophets that gives the frieze its rare and beautiful distinction.

✠

THE PASSAGE OF THE JORDAN

(Engraving)

By

Frederick Richard Pickersgill

(Interpretation)

THIS engraving, "The Passage of the Jordan," was designed by the English artist, Frederick Richard Pickersgill and engraved by Edward Dalziel for his book of Old Testament pictures entitled *Dalziel's Bible Gallery*, published in 1880. The artist was born in London in 1820 and studied at the Royal Academy where he

THE PASSAGE OF THE JORDAN—*PICKERSGILL*

exhibited his paintings. He specialized in historical scenes and his "Burial of Harold" was bought for a wall in the Houses of Parliament in London.

Edward Dalziel was born in 1817, the fifth of twelve sons of a famous Northumbrian artist. In 1839 he joined an older brother, George, in London, and gradually with a third brother, Thomas, they built up the great business soon to be known as Dalziel Brothers, wood engravers. They were artists of no mean ability.

After the death of Moses the leadership of the children of Israel fell upon Joshua. One of his first responsibilities was the preparation of the Israelites to cross the Jordan river that they might possess the Promised Land. The Biblical story of the Lord's charge to Joshua and of the crossing of the Jordan river reads as follows:

"Then Joshua commanded the officers of the people, saying, 'Pass through the host, and command the people, saying, "Prepare you victuals; for within three days ye shall pass over this Jordan, to go in to possess the land, which the Lord your God giveth you to possess it."'' [Josh. 1:10-11.]

"And Joshua rose early in the morning; and they removed from Shittim, and came to Jordan, he and all the children of Israel, and lodged there before they passed over. And it came to pass after three days, that the officers went through the host; and they commanded the people, saying, 'When ye see the ark of the covenant of the Lord your God, and the priests the Levites bearing it, then ye shall remove from your place, and go after it. Yet there shall be a space between you and it, about two thousand cubits by measure: come not near unto it, that ye may know the way by which ye must go: for ye have not passed this way heretofore.' And Joshua said unto the people, 'Sanctify yourselves: for tomorrow the Lord will do wonders among you.' And Joshua spake unto the priests, saying, 'Take up the ark of the covenant, and pass over before the people.' And they took up the ark of the covenant, and went before the people. [3:1-6.]

"And it came to pass, when the people removed from their tents, to pass over Jordan, and the priests bearing the ark of the covenant before the people; and as they that bare the ark were come unto Jordan, and the feet of the priests that bare the ark were dipped in the brim of the water . . . that the waters which came down from above stood and rose up upon an heap very far from the city. . . . And the priests that bare the ark of the covenant of the Lord stood firm on dry ground in the midst of Jordan, and all the Israelites passed over on dry ground, until all the people were passed clean over Jordan." [3:14-17.]

This portrayal shows a Hebrew family preparing an aged, blind father to follow the Ark of the Covenant into the surging stream. The patriarch perhaps remembers another time, during his youth, when Moses led the children of Israel in their crossing of the Red Sea, as they were pursued by a host of the Egyptian army ready to recapture and return them into the bondage of Egypt. Faith in God and in their leader, Moses, saved the children of Israel then, and he is ready to move forward again at the command of Joshua, Moses' successor. His sightless eyes are lifted up, and one hand is outstretched at the urging of his granddaughter who is helping him to his feet. He has not, as yet, grasped his staff. They wait for the advance of the Ark of the Covenant that they may see the direction they are to take.

Below them is the shrouded Ark of the Covenant borne on the shoulders of the priests. Already the down-rushing waters of the river have become dammed up so that the dry bed of the river has appeared on which the fearful yet faithful Israelites are to cross. In the background rise hills of the Promised Land.

This engraving portrays a wide range of human emotions. The man on the right, shading his eyes with his hand and perhaps remembering the dangers and difficulties through which the Israelites have already passed, cannot bear to look across the river where new hardships and dangers lie. The woman comforting her terrified daughter watches fearfully as the priests cross the river on dry land. She cannot believe that the waters will hold back for all the Israelites to cross. The second young woman's fear has been put aside as she faces the problem of helping her blind grandfather. The patriarch's sightless face, alone of the group, expresses confidence as he recalls Joshua's words: "Hereby ye shall know that the Living God is among you. . . . Behold, the ark of the covenant of the Lord of all the earth passeth over before you into Jordan" (Josh. 3:10, 11). He indeed walks by faith and not by sight.

✛

THE FALL OF JERICHO

By

Lorenzo Ghiberti

(Interpretation)

WHEN Joshua became leader of Israel after the death of Moses, the Lord spoke to him, saying: "Be strong and of a good courage; be not afraid; neither be thou dismayed, for the Lord thy God is with thee whithersoever thou goest" (Josh. 1:9). Strong in the Lord's strength and faithful to His commands Joshua led the children of Israel over the Jordan river to the Promised Land beyond. From the river's bed they carried twelve large stones and set them up on the bank as a memorial of their passage.

Joshua spoke these words to Israel: "When your children shall ask their fathers in time to come, saying, 'What mean these stones?' Then ye shall let your children know, saying, 'Israel came over this Jordan on dry land.' For the Lord your God dried up the waters of Jordan from before you, until ye were passed over . . . that all the people of the earth might know the hand of the Lord, that it is mighty; that ye might fear the Lord your God for ever" (4:21-24).

After their safe passage of the river the Israelites faced new dangers, for beyond their camp at Gilgal the Israelites saw the strong, walled city of Jericho blocking their way into the Promised Land. Then the Lord told Joshua how the city should be taken and Joshua prepared to march against it as the Lord commanded. First came the soldiers, followed by seven priests with trumpets of rams' horns. Next came the Ark of the Covenant borne aloft on the shoulders of the priests, and last came all the host of Israel.

In that order the Israelites marched around the walls of Jericho with the trumpets blaring, but the people did not shout nor make any noise. Then they all marched back to their camp at Gilgal. Every day for six days they marched thus around the walls of Jericho.

On the seventh day they set out at dawn and circled the walls seven times. "And it came to pass at the seventh time, when the priests blew the trumpets, Joshua said unto the people: 'Shout! For the Lord hath given you the city!' . . .

"So the people shouted when the priests blew with the trumpets. And it came to pass, when the people heard the sound of the trumpet, and the people shouted with a great shout, that the wall fell down flat, so that the people went up into the city, every man straight before him, and they took the city" (6:16, 20).

The theme of this bronze panel by Ghiberti is Israel under the leadership of Joshua safely passing over Jordan and triumphing over Jericho. The procession begins at the lower left of the panel where a group of graceful figures in sweeping draperies prepare to follow the Ark of the Covenant across the dry bed of the river. Dominating this scene is Joshua in full armor, holding his staff and standing in his horse-drawn chariot. Beyond the river men struggle to carry the twelve heavy stones which are to be set up in memory of this event. Beyond them, standing before the tents, some of the Israelites look toward the river and in their attitudes express their thanks to God for His care of them.

But new dangers still await them, for frowning down upon the camp at Gilgal are the strong walls of Jericho. Again under Joshua's leadership, and carrying out all the Lord's commands, they march around the city. The Ark is there, borne on the shoulders of the priests. Seven horns sound. Joshua raises his staff to bid the people shout. Walls crack, towers topple over, and Jericho is overcome.

This is one of the ten bronze panels of Ghiberti's "Gates of Paradise," the chief doors of the Baptistery in Florence. Ghiberti was born in 1378 in Florence, where he was taught the trade of a goldsmith. He became a painter and stonecutter as well. He left Florence in 1400 to escape an outbreak of the plague, but returned when he learned that there was to be a competition for a new set of bronze doors for the Baptistery, similar to those made by Andrea Pisano a hundred years before. The design he submitted had for its subject the sacrifice of Isaac and he won the commission over six other competitors. It took him twenty years to complete his first doors, but so greatly were they admired that a second set of doors were immediately ordered. These were completed in 1452 and included among their ten panels "The Fall of Jericho." Benvenuto Cellini, a goldsmith himself, said of Ghiberti: "He was a goldsmith indeed! Not only in the wonderfulness of his own peculiar style, but because of his unwearied power of marvellous finish and his exceeding diligence in execution."

THE FALL OF JERICHO—*GHIBERTI*

EVIDENCE OF GOD'S EXISTENCE

"There is no God," the fool in secret said:
"There is no God that rules o'er earth or sky."
Tear off the band that folds the wretch's head,
That God may burst upon his faithless eye!
Is there no God?—the stars in myriads spread,
If he look up, the blasphemy deny;
Whilst his own features, in the mirror read,
Reflect the image of Divinity.
Is there no God?—the stream that silver flows,
The air he breathes, the ground he treads, the trees,
The flowers, the grass, the sands, each wind
        that blows,
All speak of God; throughout one voice agrees,
And eloquent his dread existence shows:
Blind to thyself, ah, see him, fool, in these!*

—*Giovanni Battista Cotta*

A THOUGHT

"God wills but ill," the doubter said,
    "Lo, time doth evil only bear;
Give me a sign his love to prove,—
    His vaunted goodness to declare!"

The poet paused by where a flower,
    A simple daisy, starred the sod,
And answered, "Proof of love and power
    Behold—behold a smile of God!"

—*William Cox Bennett*

CHARACTER OF A CITIZEN OF ZION
(Psalm 15)

Who shall inhabit thy holy hill,
    O God of holiness?
Whom will the Lord admit to dwell
    So near his throne of grace?

The man who walks in pious ways,
    And works with pious hands?
Who trusts his Maker's promises,
    And follows his commands.

* Translator unknown.

He speaks the meaning of his heart,
Nor slanders with his tongue;
Will scarce believe an ill report,
Nor do his neighbor wrong.

The wealthy sinner he contemns,
Loves all who fear the Lord!
And though to his own hurt he swears,
Still he performs his word.

His hands disdain a golden bribe,
And never gripe the poor;
This man shall dwell with God on earth,
And find his heaven secure.

—Isaac Watts

A CONFESSION OF FAITH

I believe in God who is for me spirit, love, the principle
of all things.

I believe that God is in me as I am in Him.

I believe that the true welfare of man consists in fulfilling the will of God.

I believe that from the fulfillment of the will of God
there can follow nothing but that which is good for
me and for all men.

I believe that the will of God is that every man should
love his fellowmen and should act toward others as
he desires that they should act toward him.

I believe that the reason of life is for each of us simply
to grow in love.

I believe that this growth in love will contribute more
than any other force to establish the Kingdom of
God on earth—

To replace a social life in which division, falsehood and
violence are all-powerful with a new order in which
humanity, truth and brotherhood will reign.

—Leo Tolstoy

THE LORD OF HOSTS OUR REFUGE

God is our refuge and strength,
    A very present help in trouble.
Therefore will we not fear, though the earth do change,
    And though the mountains be moved in the heart of the seas;
Though the waters thereof roar and be troubled,
    Though the mountains shake with the swelling thereof.
        THE LORD OF HOSTS IS WITH US;
        THE GOD OF JACOB IS OUR REFUGE !

There is a river, the streams whereof make glad the city of God,
    The holy place of the tabernacles of the Most High.
God is in the midst of her; she shall not be moved:
    God shall help her at the dawn of morning.
The nations raged, the kingdoms were moved:
    He uttered his voice, the earth melted.
        THE LORD OF HOSTS IS WITH US;
        THE GOD OF JACOB IS OUR REFUGE!

Come, behold the works of the Lord,
    What desolations he hath made in the earth.
He maketh wars to cease unto the end of the earth;
    He breaketh the bow, and cutteth the spear in sunder;
    He burneth the chariots in the fire.
"Be still, and know that I am God:
    I will be exalted among the nations,
    I will be exalted in the earth."
        THE LORD OF HOSTS IS WITH US;
        THE GOD OF JACOB IS OUR REFUGE!*

—Psalm 46

From JEHOVAH

I sing the uplift and the upwelling,
I sing the yearning toward the sun,
And the blind sea that lifts white hands in prayer.
I sing the wild battle-cry of warriors
And the sweet whispers of lovers,
And the dear word of the hearth and the altar,
Aspiration, Inspiration, Compensation,
                God!

The hint of beauty behind the turbid cities,
The eternal laws that cleanse and cancel.
The pity through the savagery of nature,

* From *The Modern Reader's Bible* edited by Richard G. Moulton. Copyright, 1935, by The Macmillan Company. Used by special permission of the publisher.

The love atoning for the brothels,
The Master-Artist behind Hid tragedies,
Creator, Destroyer, Purifier, Avenger,
                    God!

—*Israel Zangwill*

GOD MEETS ME IN THE MOUNTAINS

God meets me in the mountains when I climb alone and high,
    Above the wrangling sinners and the jangling devotees,
Up where the tapered spruce will guide my glances to the sky
    And canyon walls will mutely preach their mighty homilies
In hush so dense that I can sense—is it my pulses drumming?
    Or God's light footfall, coming through the silvery aspen trees?

Some way I seem to lose him in the jostle of the street,
    But on a twisty deer trail, as I trudge along alone,
A mystic presence in the forest often stays my feet—
    No vision borrowed from a saint, but awesomely my own.
I feel it smite my spirit white, the prophet's taintless passion,
    As ancient as the fashion of the pine tree's rugged cone.

For me no school can give it life, as none can deal it death.
    Up through the pine's red pillars and across the snow and shale.
Where science and theology alike are but a breath,
    I follow marks that make the wisest book an idle tale.
Why should I squint at faded print to glimpse his timeword traces?
    God walks the lonely places yet, where men first found His trail,

Where pines reach up the mountains and the mountains up the blue,
    And, tense with some expectancy, the lifting ledges frown,
The high desire of the hills is my desire too,
    For there my spirit laughs to fling its worldly duffle down
And, shaking free exultantly, calls to its great companion!
    God meets me in the canyon when I miss Him in the town.*

—*Badger Clark*

THE GRACE OF GOD

(Psalm 36)

High in the heavens, eternal God,
    Thy goodness in full glory shines;
Thy truth shall break through every cloud,
    That veils and darkens thy designs.

* From *Sky Lines and Wood Smoke* by Badger Clark, pp. 16-17. Copyright, 1935, by Badger Clark. Used by special permission of the author.

Forever firm thy justice stands,
 As mountains their foundations keep;
Wise are the wonders of thy hands,
 Thy judgments are a mighty deep.

The Providence is kind and large,
 Both man and beast thy bounty share;
The whole creation is thy charge,
 But saints are thy peculiar care.

My God, how excellent thy grace,
 Whence all our hope and comfort springs!
The sons of Adam, in distress,
 Fly to the shadow of thy wings.

From the provisions of thy house,
 We shall be fed with sweet repast;
There mercy like a river flows,
 And brings salvation to our taste.

Life, like a fountain rich and free,
 Springs from the presence of my Lord;
And in thy light, our souls shall see
 The glories promised in thy word.

—Isaac Watts

JERICHO

(Joshua 6)

I

Around the walls of Jericho
The Israelitish army go.

With steady tramp, their spears in hand,
They follow out the Lord's command.

Six days, six journeys, now are past,
The sun has risen upon the last.

Scarce had the first flushings of the dawn
Announced that weary night had gone,

When, forth from every well-known tent,
The mighty hosts of Israel went

Thus early start they on their way;
Seven rounds must be fulfilled today.

II

Within the walls of Jericho
In stern indifference wait the foe.

What care they for these haggard men
Who have commenced their march again?

How can they hope to overthrow,
In such a way, proud Jericho?

And so with a laugh and a scornful glance
They join the wild mazes of the dance.

And pass around the ruddy wine,
Rarest of all in Palestine.

The sounds of revelry rise high
Beneath the glare of the noonday sky.

III

Outside the walls of Jericho
Steadily on the warriors go.

Six of the rounds are already past,
And they have now commenced the last.

Throughout those ranks no sound is heard,
No merry jest, no cheering word.

There rises up no other sound
Than the steady foot-beat on the ground.

Now suddenly they turn about,
And with one voice the people shout.

Down fall the walls of Jericho,
The heathen's power lieth low.

IV

Low lie the walls of Jericho,
And through her halls her foemen go.

All hope for the city proud hath fled,
For all her boasted host are dead;

And the ringing pavement of the street
Echoeth nought but the foemen's feet.

Thus did firm faith in God's commands
Prove mightier than human hands.

Thus did the strong right arm of God
Scatter the heathen hosts abroad.

Thus did he great honor lay
Upon the name of Joshua.

V

In the long march of every life,
Where there is much of toil and strife,

Remaineth still some Jericho,
Some firm stronghold where lurks the foe.

And as the Israelite of old,
Trusted the promise, we are told,

And had the patience to fulfil
The unknown mysteries of God's will;

So we, if we with patience wait,
Unbought by love, unmoved by hate,

Shall see the walls of error go
As went the walls of Jericho.

—*Frank Foxcroft*

THE PROVIDENCE OF GOD
(Psalm 78, Part 1)

Let children hear the mighty deeds,
  Which God performed of old;
Which in our younger years, we saw,
  And which our fathers told.

He bids us make his glories known,
  His works of power and grace;
And we'll convey his wonders down,
  Through every rising race.

Our lips shall tell them to our sons,
  And they again to theirs;
That generations, yet unborn
  May teach them to their heirs.

Thus shall they learn, in God alone
　　Their hope securely stands;
That they may ne'er forget his works,
　　But practise his commands.

　　　　　　　　　　　　—*Isaac Watts*

THE WEISSENBRUNN HYMN

This I have heard from ancient sages,
Men the chief of elder ages,
That in time of old gone by,
There was not the heaven on high,—
Heaven on high, nor earth below;
Then nor star was seen to glow;

Nor the sun was shining bright;
Nor the moon gave forth her light;
Nor was mountain then, nor tree;
Nor the interminable sea;
Of this universal round
Not a whit from bound to bound.

But though lower world was none,
Yet there wanted not the one
Almighty God in being then,
He, most merciful to men!
And with him there was of old
Godlike spirits manifold.

Holy God Almighty, thou
Heaven and earth hast fashioned now,
And thy creature, man, dost bless
With provisions numberless:
May thy way in mercy show,
And on me thy grace bestow.

Faith, to thy pure truth resigned;
Prompt to serve, a willing mind;
Prudent heart, and active hand,
Craft of Satan to withstand;
Evil ever to eschew,
And thy will, O God, to do.*

　　　　　　　　　　　　—*Author Unknown*

---

* This is one of the oldest poems extant in the German language.

WHO WILL LEAD ME INTO EDOM?

Who will lead me into Edom?—Psalm 60:9

Who will lead me into Edom?
    Who will take me by the hand?
Who will break the rugged pathway
    Leading through that unknown land?

Hope will lead me into Edom,
    Hope will guide me all the way
Like the morning star before me,
    Hope will bring me to the day.

Faith will lead me into Edom,
    Faith, eternal as the hills,
Faith which passeth understanding,
    And all prophecy fulfills.

Love will lead me into Edom
    Like a father leads a child,
Love as gentle as the breezes,
    As benign and undefiled.

Christ will lead me into Edom,
    Christ will guide and guard and keep,
Like a shepherd on the hillside
    Loves and leads his trusting sheep.

God will guide me into Edom
    And my splendid destiny;
God fulfilling every promise
    Of my Immortality.*

—*William L. Stidger*

CALEB, HERO OF FAITH

They shrank from giants and from men of might—
The ten whom Moses sent to view the land;
But Caleb, Joshua's peer, saw only God
Whose power had done great things for them. Their sight
Was sharpened by their faith and hope, and they
Could see, beyond the pagan tide, a land of dream
Prepared for those who yielded not to fear:
"Our God is with us, let no foe dismay!"
O that we might, as Caleb, trust in Him
Who bids us win the world from evil's blight!

* Used by special permission of the author.

What though the foe be strong, what though the world
Be blind to visions, choosing carnage grim!
Let us go up, possess the land for God,
Treading the path of faith that Caleb trod.*

—Thomas Curtis Clark

✛

HEWERS OF WOOD

By

Florence M. Earlle

NORTH and west of the smoke-blackened ruins of Jericho, on the summit of a great hill in the country of the Hevites, rose the royal city of Gibeon. Strong walls with watchtowers at regular intervals encompassed the city, and guards were stationed on those towers day and night. Of late the watch had been doubled, for rumors were coming from the south concerning the hordes of invaders that had appeared from the desert. Jericho had fallen—that great city of palm trees! And yet Jericho was not a warlike city. Its inhabitants were not noted for their bravery. Over and over again Jericho had fallen before her enemies. But the manner in which she had fallen this time was mysterious. Six days, so said the messenger, had the invaders marched about the city with no sound save the padding of bare feet.

But on the seventh day, they had encompassed the city seven times; and the seventh time all the people had shouted, and the walls of the city had fallen. Not one person had been spared save the harlot Rahab and her household. She had escaped because she had hidden the two spies who had come to search out the land some days before. The city itself had been given to the flames—nothing being taken by the invaders but the gold and silver.

Then Ai had been attacked by night, and repulsed the invaders. Their victory had been but temporary, for the second night attack had resulted in the entire destruction of Ai, even as Jericho had been destroyed. Who would be next? was the question that each city in the region was asking itself. A council of the princes and elders of the people of Gibeon had been set for tonight about a council fire.

Reca, the daughter of Prince Nadad, sat with her lover, Hixon, under a palm tree that shadowed the temple of Ashtaroth. He was telling her of the mighty events that had been told concerning these desert tribes.

"They are not great in stature, but they are mighty men of valor. Their God hath stopped rivers from flowing that they might cross over; and He plagued the Egyptians who had held them in captivity until the king let them go; yea, he drove them out of his country. They have a beautiful tent, so 'tis said, in which they worship their God whom they do not see. Our city is strongly fortified, yet I fear it will not be able to stand before these men. I shall plead with the elders and princes that they make peace with these tribes."

* Used by special permission of the author.

"But would they make peace with us?" questioned the girl.

"Nay, I know not. It seems that they want the country all for themselves. Yet I am sure that will be the only way we can be spared. If there were just some way that we might work wilily to deceive them as to where we dwell. Think, Reca, thou hast a wise head beyond thy years, think of some way whereby we may be saved."

"I shall try," answered Reca. "If I do think of a plan, I shall come to the council fire with my father. Do thou make thy speech, pleading for an effort to make peace, and then I shall give my plan—if I can think of one," she added smiling.

"Try!" urged her lover. "Thou dost not realize how serious our situation is. But look! is that not Barges, the scout thy father sent to spy upon the Israelites? Hail, Barges, what tidings of our foe?"

The man came toward them, and bowed low before Hikon.

"The tidings are evil, my lord. Our foes are but a few days' journey from us. Unless our gods help us, we too shall perish from the earth."

The man passed on to the tent of the father of Reca, and Hikon said, "I must see my father. Do thou pray the goddess that she whisper to thee some way of escape. I trust thee as I do none other."

The light from the council fire flared on the faces of the elders and princes of the people. Without the circle were the warriors, and such of the men and women who had wished to listen to the discussion of plans to protect themselves from this enemy that threatened them. Fear had fallen upon them all, and few believed that their walls, strong as they were, would be sufficient protection in this crisis. Hikon's suggestion that they try to deceive the enemy as to where they lived, had met with approval, but none had suggested a way whereby it might be accomplished.

Suddenly Reca rose from her place beside her father.

"Listen, O friends," she said, "I have a plan that will deceive our enemies. If they believe that we come from the far north, miles away from this region, they will make a treaty with us, and at least spare our lives. We would be glad to be their servants even, if it meant no loss of life. Is it not so?"

"Yes! Yes!" answered the people.

"Then hearken." Briefly she outlined a plan.

There was a murmur of approval when the girl ceased. Nadad, her father, glanced at her proudly. Five of the princes volunteered to go as ambassadors from a far country (among them Hikon and Nadad), and the journey was planned for the next day, since no time must be lost. Long before sunrise the next morning, the men started. Hikon held Reca close for a moment.

"I shall return, never fear. Thy plan will deceive them, I am sure, and we shall make our peace with them. Fare thee well!"

Into the camp of Israel at Gilgal early on the morning of the second day, came five strangers, wearily driving asses before them. They had walked throughout the night hours that they might appear tired out from their journey.

"Whence come ye?" questioned the men of Israel. "And why have ye come?"

"We be come from a far land," answered the Hevites, "and desire a league with you."

The five were brought to the tent of Joshua. Again he questioned them.

"Who are ye? And from whence come ye?"

And they said unto him, "From a very far country thy servants are come, because of the name of the Lord thy God, for we have heard the fame of Him, and all that He did in Egypt. And all that He did to the two kings of the Amorites, that were beyond Jordan, to Sihon, king of Hashbon, and to Og, king of Bashan, which was at Ashtareth. Therefore our elders and all the inhabitants of the country spake unto us, saying, "Take victuals with you for the journey, and go to meet them, and say unto them, 'We are thy servants.' Therefore now make a league with us. This our bread we took hot for our provision out of our houses on the day we came forth to go unto you. But now—behold it is dry, and it is moldy. And these bottles of wine which we filled were new; and behold they be rent; and these garments and our shoes are become old by reason of the very long journey."

"Let me taste of thy bread," said Nahor, one of the princes of Israel. "Yes, it is dry and moldy, and thy wineskin hath been bound up on account of the rents. Is it not wonderful that the tidings of the acts of our God hath been told in these far countries?"

"How didst thou know where we might be found?" questioned Joshua, turning to Nadad.

"A fugitive runner from the court of Og brought the news of the destruction of his city to us."

"How did he escape? All within the city of Bashan were put to death. Not one was allowed to live."

Nadad made an obeisance.

"He told thy servant that he had been sent by Og to Adonizedek, king of Jerusalem, with a message asking for help to defend the city against thee; but that when he returned, thou hadst already attacked and burnt it. He found naught but ruins where his home had stood, and fled for his life farther north telling the evil tidings to all the cities that he passed. And thy servants took council together, and appointed us to seek thee out and make a league with thee. We have journeyed far as thou canst see. Now, therefore, let thy servants be at peace with thee."

Then Joshua and the elders held a feast for their guests, and made a league with them, but they forgot to ask counsel of the Lord.

Early in the morning, Hikon came to the tent of Joshua.

"I pray thee, send us away, if we have found favor in thy sight."

"Nay," said Joshua. "Abide with us for a space, that thou mayest rest from thy long journey."

"Alas, my lord," said Hikon, "if we tarry, our people will think that we have perished on the way, or that thou hast destroyed thy servants. I pray thee, let us depart, and journey to our own land."

So Joshua allowed them to depart in peace.

Three days later, just at sunset, a scout appeared at the tent of the leader.

"What news of the country," asked Joshua, "for we are marching at the break of day?"

"Master, I have news indeed, for as I journeyed, I came upon a mighty city, a royal-looking city. It had strong walls, and guards kept the gates and watchtowers. I hid, that I might learn the name of the people who inhabited it. But alas, my hiding place was discovered, and I was brought before the princes of the people. I thought that my life was forfeited, but when I did make known my people, I was told that thou hadst made a league with them. Then did they release me, and I departed. Master, is it true that thou hast made a league with our enemies?"

"Nay," said Joshua. "Our only league hath been made with men who came from the faraway north, not our neighbors."

Meanwhile, the five ambassadors had reached Gibeon and reported their success.

"Joshua said that they would not march for three days. He had sent a scout to spy out the land," said Hikon to Reca.

"His scout was captured while thou wert gone," said Reca. "The elders held him captive until my father reported last night, and then they released him. He did not believe that a league had been made. Thou shouldst have seen his face, when he was told. Will not the leader of the Israelites be surprised when he discovers that we are his neighbors?" and the girl laughed merrily.

"I am not so sure that all will be well with us," said Hikon, "but whatever punishment he will give us, we will at least have our lives. He dare not go back on an oath; the gods would punish him."

And the children of Israel journeyed, and on the third day they came to Gibeon. The same five princes who had been the ambassadors went out to meet Joshua.

"Why did ye beguile us, saying, 'We are very far from you,' when ye dwelt among us?"

And the princes answered, "It was told thy servants how thy God commanded his servant, Moses, to give you all the land before you; therefore, we were afraid for our lives, and we have done this thing. And now we are in thy hands; as seemeth good and right unto thee to do unto us, do."

And Joshua said, "There shall never fail to be of you bondmen."

And he made them hewers of wood and drawers of water for the tabernacle of the congregation.*

✢

OFFERINGS FOR THE TABERNACLE

By

Florence M. Earlle

FOR more than six weeks the Israelites had been in camp at the foot of Mount Sinai, while their leader, Moses, had been on the mountaintop talking with God. Now at their assembly he had told them that they were to build a place of worship for God. It was to be built in such a way that it might be taken apart and

* Used by special permission of the author.

carried with them on their march to the land of Canaan. Its materials were to be of shittim wood, purple and scarlet and fine-twined linen; spices, oil, gold, silver, and precious stones, ram skins, and strong leather. All these materials were to be voluntary gifts, and a Sabbath Day had been set aside to receive their offerings.

In their thin, patched tent, Abigail and Seth were talking in low tones:

"What can we offer unto the Lord for all His kindnesses to us?" Seth was saying.

Abigail bowed her head. "We have so very little," she murmured, yet in her heart she knew what they could give.

"There is Sara's bracelet!"

"It is all I have left of her! She was the light of my eyes, and now that light is withdrawn"; and Abigail buried her face in her robe and wept passionately. It had been so hard to leave that little grave in Egypt.

Seth rose and going to the corner, he took from a little bundle a massive gold bracelet, set with jewels.

"Do you remember how excited she was when she brought this home? How she turned it round and round on her thin little arm while she told how the lordly Egyptian had stopped in his chariot to watch her dance? And she had danced and danced until she had dropped from exhaustion. Then he had flung her the bracelet and ridden away."

"Oh, but I feared for her after that. I think he would have come back again; but the Lord took her in His arms as one snatches up a child around whom dogs are barking." Abigail's eyes saw things afar off. "Let us give it to the tent of the Lord." And she kissed the little bracelet and handed it back to Seth.

Moses accepted it and used it for one of the rings on the veil between the Holy Place and the Holy of Holies.

"If Sara could know it," said Abigail, "I think she would be glad.

Judah walked around the tent, completely around it before he went in and fastened the flap. From a hole in the ground, he lifted a leathern bag whose contents clinked. One by one he lifted out his treasures. A long chain of beaten gold set with emeralds; a brooch, sparkling with gems, once the pride of an Egyptian high priest; a beautiful seal ring; then another chain. Judah sighed as he laid each piece by as too beautiful to give away. He had nothing that he could give.

The Sabbath dawned bright and beautiful. Judah watched the long lines of people as they brought their gifts.

"Mine are not needed," he muttered; and yet, if he gave nothing people would notice and wonder. He was a rich man. He had been a freed man in Egypt.

Two onyx stones would do. They could be set on the shoulders of the high priest's robe and men would know that they were his gift. Once more he went to his tent and dug up his treasure. One of the onyx stones had a little crack; the other was not quite clear; but who would notice that? He joined the thinning procession of people.

Moses spoke his thanks; but it brought no joy to the heart of Judah. He might have given so much more than two onyx stones—one flawed, one dull!

"Mother, can't we hurry? I'm so afraid we won't see everything." Dinah smiled at her impatient little son.

"There is plenty of time. Joab said that they had just begun to set up the tabernacle. See, just one side and an end is up. It has taken a long time to fit the boards in their silver sockets and run the long gold poles through the rings in the center of each board. Look how they sparkle in the sunlight! I think it is wonderful that so many of us have had a part in the building and its furnishings. I am especially proud of the work I did on Aaron's clothes. 'Holiness unto the Lord' is engraven on his miter. His everyday clothes are so beautiful with their different colors and decoration of bells and pomegranates; but I do not understand his robes for the Day of Atonement. They are just plain white linen. I wonder why? Moses says we shall not see Aaron and his sons consecrated today, though all things are ready. That ceremony will come later."

"Look, Mother, they are setting up the pillars between the Holy Place and the Holy of Holies. Did you work on the curtain or the veil?"

"No. I wish I might have embroidered just one of the cherubim, they are so beautiful!" and Dinah sighed wistfully.

"A wonderful day for us, friends, is it not?"

"O Abigail, Seth, yes, wonderful indeed! What part have you had in the building?"

"Very little," said Abigail in a low tone. "My fingers are too stiff for embroidering and Seth's have no cunning. But we gave all we had. Sara's bracelet is one of the rings on the veil for the Holy of Holies."

Impulsively Dinah put her arm around Abigail's thin bowed shoulders as she glanced at her own small son.

"Look quickly, lad," said Seth. "Never again will you see the Ark of the Covenant uncovered. Once it is within the Holy of Holies, it will become sacred to our God, and when we travel and it is carried on the shoulders of the priests, it will always be veiled. That lid with the kneeling cherubim is very heavy, for it is solid gold."

"Why is it called the Ark of the Covenant?"

"Don't you know, son? Covenant means agreement, and the tables of stone on which the Ten Commandments are written are the agreement between God and us that so long as we obey them, we are His children and He is our God."

"Who brought the pot for the 'manna'?"

"I don't know, but I marvel that it keeps."

"Why marvel?" said Seth. "Does not our God keep it sweet for us over each Sabbath? Then why should He not keep it sweet in the pot forever?"

"Now they are bringing in the furniture for the Holy Place. Isn't that altar of incense beautiful with its golden bowl and golden crown? Moses says that the incense that is burned upon it is a type of our prayers that go up to God."

Abigail said softly, "Hagar told me that she and Keturah baked the shewbread. Moses was so pleased that he said they might bake it each week if they so desired. I could have done that. Perhaps Hagar will let me do it for her some week."

"The golden candlestick will furnish the only light in the tabernacle. Only the purest of olive oil and the best of sweet spices will be used in the lamps."

"Mother, let's push in closer."

"No, lad, you can see better right here. Look, now, here they come with the brazen laver. My! that must be heavy. Surely when we march that will be carried on an ox cart."

"Now I had a part in that too," said Abigail. "I gave my mirror which Seth gave me as a betrothal gift. It was very small, but Moses said if many women were willing to give their mirrors he would have enough."

"How large the altar of sacrifice is! Joab told me it was large, but I did not realize it would be that size. Yet I should have known, for I knew that it was to have a slanting platform for the priest to walk up to the altar on; and that it had to be large enough to hold a whole ox."

Now the workers began to place the coverings on the tabernacle. First came the lovely linen one, embroidered in purple and scarlet. It covered the ceiling and sides of the Holy Place and all of the Holy of Holies. Over this was a curtain of goat hair, then one of ramskin, dyed red, and finally one of strong leather.

Surrounding the tabernacle was the court, seventy-five feet wide and one hundred and fifty feet long. It was made of curtains hung on pillars of brass. The entrance of both the court and the tabernacle was to the east. When all these curtains had been hung, the people saw a marvelous sight. The pillar of cloud and fire that had been their leader from Egypt, rose, and came and hung directly over the Holy of Holies, filling it with a roseate light. Centuries later, scholars named this light the "Shekinah" but this day, the awe-stricken people bowed their faces to the ground and worshiped.*

✣

RAHAB**

By

Norah Lofts

IF THERE had survived, from the sack of Jericho, one Canaanitish historian who was subsequently inspired to write his version of the city's fall, the name of Rahab would have figured very blackly therein, and might have become a synonym for treachery. But Rahab's history has come down to us in the chronicles of Israel whose cause she adopted and whose spies she sheltered and so this Canaanitish woman who helped to betray her city to the enemy is presented to us as a Biblical heroine, recognized not only in the Old Testament but also in the New, where, twice at least, she is favourably mentioned. In history, as in war, there are some strange shiftings of standards.

* The source material for this story is from *Bible Character Stories* by William J. May (now out of print). Copyright, 1928, by the Fleming H. Revell Company. Used by special permission of the publisher.

** Josh. 2:1-24; 6:25.

Rahab's story is set in a very critical, and therefore interesting, period of Israel's history. A phase had ended. Moses, who had brought the tribes up from the Captivity in Egypt, had lived just long enough to stand upon the eminence of Pisgah and see with his earthly eyes the country so familiar to his spiritual sight. The Exodus was over, and with it the leadership of the wise, sorely tried, old man. Now was the time for conquest; and, as though symbolically, the reins of government fell from the hands of a diplomat and a saint into those of a soldier. Joshua had been chosen to drive out the Canaanites and establish the twelve tribes in the land which God had promised to Abraham, their forefather.

That was a legend which had never died through all the years of slavery in Egypt, all the years of wandering in the wilderness; and it was not as intruders or invaders that they looked down at last upon the fruitful valley of the Jordan river. They were coming home. There lay the land in which, before he died, Abraham had finally established himself, where Isaac, his son, had lived and begotten Jacob who in turn had reared his twelve sons. Famine had driven them out of their inheritance and the years of exile had been long, but they had come back, not a mere family, but twelve strong tribes with the making of a nation within them, ready to take possession.

From their hiding places in the mountains the Hebrews looked down upon the Jordan valley and saw it as the dream-come-true of land-hungry men fresh from the desert. Spies had crept down and come back with mouth-watering tales of its luxuriant fertility; but those tales, and the more tangible proofs which the spies carried back, had another, darker significance. Those grapes which swung so heavily between the poles of the spies had been planted and tended by men who would not easily abandon the soil over which they had sweated; the milk and honey with which the land was flowing told of settled, agricultural people who would take arms to guard their rights. This was no unpopulated island, no uninhabited oasis, and there at the head of the valley, a symbol of defiant guardianship stood the strong-walled city of Jericho. It had risen there as a protection against invasion from the mountains; it had repelled land-hungry raiders before and looked ready to do so again.

Joshua, looking down from the mountains, judged the walls to be twenty feet high, and sentries made their rounds along its top, so thick it was. Where the busy trade roads ended, the wall was pierced by gateways, overlooked by strong towers and fitted with gates which were closed at night, or in times of danger. It was a formidable obstacle in the Jews' path. But Joshua was less concerned with its appearance of impregnability than with its inward state. Before he moved he must know what kind of army the King of Jericho had at his command, what was the mind of the ordinary people and whether those outwardly unassailable walls had weaknesses within. To this end he sent out his spies again, and two men whose names are not even remembered stole down from the hills and entered the city.

They were not immediately noticed or suspected. The course of the story proves that they spoke a language understood in the city; their Semitic features were not remarkable in a Semitic city and, if their clothes and accents were strange, they were not alone in that, for Jericho was a busy trade centre where aliens were no novelty. But the presence of Joshua and his host in the hills was known to the people of the city, and the danger from spies was recognized; at a time when all strangers were subjected to nervous scrutiny something about Joshua's men did eventually give rise to comment and that in turn to suspicion. But before that happened the two spies had found a friend.

In both the Old Testament and the New, she is called bluntly a harlot; Josephus—not usually mealy-mouthed—says that she was an inn-keeper; other authorities have suggested that she was by trade a dyer because of the flax on her roof and the mention of the scarlet cord. But in those days of unspecialized industry there must have been flax drying on many a roof in Jericho, and a scarlet cord would be no rarity. It is possible that Rahab combined all three trades, but only the most tragic of them is a certainty. It was the motive force behind her behaviour.

The spies lodged with her, and were perhaps the first men to treat her respectfully in many years. At first, at least, as strangers, they would be unaware of the dreary trade to which the house that sheltered them and the woman who befriended them, were devoted. And later, when they knew the truth, they would not take advantage of it because they were dedicated to a mission. It is reasonable to suppose that Joshua had picked his spies carefully, choosing young men in the prime of life, with the physical fitness and keen wits which their task demanded and with the kind of manner that would be useful in an awkward situation should one arise; in this, as well as in their attitude towards her as a woman, they would make a striking contrast to Rahab's usual clientele. Those to whom the gift is denied, the callowly young, the unpalatably aging, the physically unattractive are the customers for bought love. Measuring the two young Israelites against the men she knew, the shrewd harlot would be inclined not only to regard them with favour, but to conclude that, if they were representative of the invaders, her city was doomed.

The length of time during which they "lodged" in her house is not mentioned; nor is any conversation until the last recorded; but when the spies returned to Joshua they reported verbatim Rahab's assessment of her fellow-citizens' state of mind, which rather indicates that upon other subjects they had invited her opinion and afterwards confirmed it from their own observations. And perhaps in exchange for the information she could give them they talked to her about the promise which had been made to their forefather and of the intricate and sometimes almost imperceptible stages of its fulfilment.

If she ever knew a moment of wavering indecision there is no hint of it in the story. The King of Jericho, warned of the presence of Israelite spies within his walls, sent to Rahab and demanded that she should bring them forth and instantly she had chosen her course, uttered her lie and sent her fellow-countrymen on their futile search of the river fords while the men for whom they were looking lay snugly hidden under the flax upon her roof. But that decision was not made then; an impulse however momentary it may seem is the result of influences and tendencies that reach back through the years. Rahab sheltered the spies because she had no love of her native city or of her fellow-citizens. Joshua's spies were safe in that house because the respectable people of Jericho had pointed to it with derisory fingers, looked at it with sneers. In that betrayal is indicated the whole story of the woman; there are the skirts drawn aside in the public places, the whispers, the outspoken insults, there are the men whose lust had used her and whose hypocrisy had passed her, slant-eyed, in the streets; there are the women whose scorn had stung. A lifetime of outlawry, concomitant with her profession, had demoralized Rahab. Owing loyalty to no man, how could she be loyal to a city?

Her trade served her now. It was likely enough that to such a house men might come and be asked no questions, and leave again without disclosing either their identities or their nationalities. The King's messengers were so little suspicious that they did not even wait to search the house. Why should she lie? What was one man more than another to Rahab the harlot?

They clattered away and the gates of the city were closed and barred. In the very heart of the night, when Jericho slept and only the drowsy sentries made their perfunctory rounds, Rahab climbed up to her roof with a stout rope in her hand. She roused the spies from their hiding place under the flax and conversed with them in hurried whispers. She professed her faith in their God and her belief that Joshua's host would conquer the city. Without a single plaintive, patriotic word she spoke of her country's doom. And then she disassociated herself from it and struck her bargain. A greater woman, convinced of the Israelite's victory, or sentimentally pushed into treason by her personal liking for the spies, might have been prepared to let her own chance rest upon the fortune of war; or even have been resigned to sharing the fate of her fellows. But Rahab was a trader, and a cynic. She did not trust the spies to remember her service to them. Before they left she had extracted their promise that in the event of a Hebrew victory she and her family should be spared.

When the promise was given and the sign—a scarlet cord hung from the window of the house on the wall—arranged, she let the men down, one after the other, into the darkness. Then she drew in the rope and stood for a few moments listening. There was no outcry, no sound of running feet. The spies stole away to hide in the hills until the alarm had died down and the fords of Jordan were no longer watched for their passing.

Once they were gone and the rope withdrawn, Rahab was safe. No woman in the whole of Jericho, no cherished woman in any of its palaces or mansions was so safe as Rahab in her little mud house of ill-repute on the city wall. Standing, the ramparts afford her their unquestioning shelter; breached, they but admit friends.

Everyone knows the result of the siege of Jericho; how the priests blew on their trumpets and all the people shouted and the walls, as the Negro spiritual has it, "came tumbling down." The scarlet thread hung in Rahab's window and was matched that day by the scarlet streams that ran in the streets, for not only was every man, woman and child in Jericho put to the sword but every sheep and ox and ass as well. Only the harlot and her family were spared. She lived to take an honoured place in Israel; legend whispered that she married Joshua.

Her memory lives in two oddly paradoxical references in the New Testament. And man's woman while she lived, she seems to serve, after death, as a peg for any man's argument. When the superior merits of faith or works formed the subject of hot altercations she is quoted, in the Epistle to the Hebrews, as a supreme example of faith; a mere two pages on, in the Epistle of James, she is held up as an instance of the supremacy of works. But in each case she is "Rahab the harlot." The meditations and searchings of centuries leave only one thing certain about her—her profession.*

☩

THE SIN OF THE FATHER

By

Florence M. Earlle

JUDITH stood on a little knoll, watching the last rays of the setting sun. She felt that surely before the twilight settled down her lover, Benoi, would appear. Of course the journey to Ai might have ended in the capture of the spies, but Judith believed Benoi was too good a scout to be captured. Had he not been one of the two that Joshua had sent to Jericho, and had he not returned safely from that most dangerous trip? There was no anxiety in her soft brown eyes as she brushed back a heavy braid of hair. Behind her were the black goat-hair tents, for the Israelites had been in camp now since a few weeks before the fall of Jericho. Suddenly there was a sound of running steps, and in a moment, Rachel, Benoi's little sister, appeared.

"Benoi has come," she called as soon as she saw Judith. "He is with Joshua right now; but he saw me as he went to the tent, and told me to tell you that he would meet you as the moon rose at the trysting place. Where is your trysting place, Judith? Benoi will not tell me; he says I would tell. You know I never tell anything I am told to keep. Please tell me, Judith!"

Judith smiled at the little girl. "Very soon I will tell you, little one; just as soon as Benoi is my husband."

Rachel pouted: "Why then it won't be a trysting place, when you are married."

Then her face cleared. "It is tomorrow. Just one more night to wait. Aren't you excited, Judith? I'm sure I would be if I were to be married tomorrow. Will you live in our tent now instead of your father's?"

"No, your father and mine have agreed that we shall have a tent of our own, although but a few steps from your father's tent. He will count us as a part of his family. I think it will be much joy to belong to a family all my own. You know I have no brothers and sisters as you have. And still I shall not be very far from my father and mother's tent. Let's go back now and wait till moonrise."

*From *Women in the Old Testament* by Norah Lofts, pp. 51-56. Copyright, 1949, by Norah Lofts. Used by special permission of The Macmillan Company.

"Then may I go with you to the trysting place?"

"No, little sister. The moon rises late and you will be asleep; but I will keep my promise. I will show you our trysting place, as soon as we are married."

Leaving the child at the door of the tent, Judith went swiftly away from the encampment toward the smoke-blackened ruins of Jericho. Although night had fallen, she felt no fear. She sought the bank of a little stream; such a tiny one that it was scarcely more than a brook that would be dry when the rainy season was over. Here, close to an old palm tree, was a large rock, so large that one could not see around it. Quietly she seated herself here to wait for the rising of the moon and the coming of Benoi. She dozed a little, but suddenly she was wide awake, every nerve strained in an attitude of listening. Could she have been dreaming? No, there it was again! a slight rustling, then all was quiet. Judith was about to breathe easily again, deciding that she had been mistaken after all, when she heard a groan, and then a man's voice lifted in prayer.

"Lord God of Israel, look upon me and forgive! I have taken the accursed thing and hidden it away! Yet the robe was so beautiful, how could I see it consumed in the flames? There was much spoil in the city. Into thy treasury Joshua put the silver and the gold. He will never miss the two hundred shekels of silver and the wedge of gold that I took. I have broken Thy law in that I have coveted and stolen; yet no man knows. How shall I restore and not be cast out of the camp? The family of the Zarhites are a family of honor and I have dishonored them, for I am a thief!"

Judith listened with horror on her face. The family of the Zarhites? Why that was the family to which Benoi belonged and of which she would be a member after tomorrow! She must see this man who had disgraced them. With the utmost caution, she began to creep around the rock. The moon was beginning to rise now, and Benoi would be coming soon. She must see who it was, for the man, if surprised in his guilty secret, might attack her lover. But before she reached the place where she could see his face, he began to speak again.

"Beautiful! beautiful!" he murmured, and Judith shrank back as she realized that the man had stood up. He took a step forward, and the girl caught her breath as the first rays of the rising moon revealed the most beautiful garment she had ever seen. It was made of silk, though Judith had never seen silk, and could not have named the material. The long folds that swept the ground were embroidered with gold and silver threads and sparkled with gems that caught the light in a thousand rays. A feeling of sympathy swept over the girl. She, too, loved beauty in whatever form she saw it. She could understand how easily that love had conquered the man's common sense and the commands of Joshua, and how, on the impulse of the moment, he had taken it for his own. Now he did not know what to do about it. He dared not confess, as he had said; yet he could not wear the robe or spend the money. His only hope lay in no one discovering what he had done. He had ceased to pray. The sight of the robe seemed to have made him feel that he could not give it up, and he recognized that there would be no forgiveness without restitution. Slowly he folded it and putting it under his own somber robe, he turned to go. Judith shrank back for fear the man would see her; yet she must know who he was. As he turned away, the rays of the moon fell full on his face, and Judith with difficulty suppressed a cry; for the man was Achan, father of Benoi. There could be no mistake, for he walked with a slight limp that identified him. She sank down on the grass and watched him go. What should she do? If she told what she knew it would break her lover's heart that his father was a thief? She loved him too much to give him up or hurt him if she could help it. He would be coming soon, and she must make her decision. She would keep the secret. No one should know from her that which she had so unwittingly stumbled upon.

"Judith! Judith! Where are you, loved one?"

It was Benoi.

"I am here," she answered, and went into his arms.

"Why are you trembling! What is it? You are cold even in this hot air?"

She shook her head.

"You were afraid that I had not come back? But no, Rachel was sent with the message. What is it?"

Her only answer at first was her passionate sobbing, while he held her close. Then she dried her eyes and laughed at herself, trying to make him laugh too.

"You are a man, not a maid; and do not know what it means to a girl to leave her home for a strange tent, even though it be with the man she has chosen. Even your little sister knew that and asked me if I were not excited. You must pay no attention to a girl's tears on the even of her wedding day."

He held her close, but she could see that he was not altogether satisfied.

"Tell me of your journey today?"

His face lighted up with eagerness.

"We made the journey without any trouble, and found that Ai is poorly fortified, and but small. I have suggested to Joshua that he send only three or four thousand men to capture the city, for their fighting men are few. He has set the battle for day after tomorrow."

"Will you be one of the three thousand fighting men?"

"Yes. You need not fear for me. I shall return to you when the battle is over. You are not afraid to be a warrior's wife?"

She shook her head and he took her in his arms again.

Thirty-six hours later, Judith stood in the door of her new tent, shading her eyes against the rays of the rising sun. At sunset on her wedding day, Benoi had marched proudly away with the three thousand, as it was to be a night attack on Ai. The camp of Israel had not been worried that the warriors had not returned sooner. They would wait until daybreak of course to spoil the battlefield and come singing home, laden with such booty as Joshua had commanded them to bring—gold, silver, and other precious metals. But now it was sunrise and still they had not come. Then far off in the distance, Judith saw a cloud of dust. She hurried over to call Rachel and her sister Sara, that they might run to meet the victors. But before they could snatch up timbrels, the foremost of the army appeared, not as victors, but in a flight of panic. Quickly they panted out the tidings: "We met defeat in our night attack, and have fled for hours before our pursuers. We do not know how many have been killed, but we left some behind."

Wails and lamentations filled the air, as the people beat their breasts, tore their hair and clothing, and strewed dust and ashes on their heads. The Elders of the people quickly gathered to Joshua's tent and for hours lay on their faces in prayer and lamentation. But God seemed deaf to their cries. The day dragged wearily on. A roll call of the army showed a loss of thirty-six. Benoi's pride lay in the dust, and even Judith had no power to quicken his spirit. At sunset the trumpet blew, and the people gathered together. Then Joshua told how the Lord had commanded him to stand on his feet and listen.

"Israel has taken of the accursed thing," the Lord said to me. "Someone has stolen and dissembled also, and hidden it among his own stuff. Therefore the children of Israel could not stand before their enemies. Neither will I be with you any more till you destroy the accursed thing from among you."

Judith drew nearer to Benoi, her face paling, and he put his arm around her. She looked at her father-in-law, but the man's face was set, and he stared straight at Joshua who was speaking again.

"You are to sanctify yourselves against tomorrow, for in the morning you are to be brought according to your tribes; and it shall be that the tribe which the Lord taketh, shall come by families; and the family that the Lord taketh shall come by households; and the household that the Lord taketh shall come, man by man."

A murmur ran through the assembled people, dying down as Joshua continued: "He that has taken the accursed thing, shall be burnt with fire—he and all that he has, because he has transgressed the covenant of the Lord, and because he has wrought folly in Israel."

In the outburst of wails and lamentations that followed Joshua's speech, Judith's cry of horror was lost. Even Benoi thought it but the cry of a tender heart that could not bear to look upon suffering.

"Beloved, you need not be in the congregation tomorrow. You shall stay in the tent, and need not see upon whom the lot falleth. And you need not take part in the stoning; that would be more than your tender heart could bear."

Thus he tried to comfort the passionate sobbing of the girl.

The people departed, silent for the most part, or speaking only in whispers of who the guilty man might be. Achan seated himself in the door of the tent, refusing food when it was offered. Late in the evening, he rose, and started toward the old ruins of Jericho. Benoi had gone on an errand for Joshua, and Judith was alone, so she followed her father-in-law at a little distance, until she was certain he was going to the rock beside the stream. She lingered until it was dark, before she made her way swiftly to the old trysting place. Cautiously she approached the back of the rock, and as before she heard the man's voice lifted in prayer.

"Lord God of Israel, forgive, oh forgive a wretched man! I did not know that the sin of one man would bring defeat upon the camp, or that the innocent must suffer with the guilty. My precious wife, my sons, my daughters, my grandchil-

dren—all must suffer on account of my sin! Why, oh why did I covet that garment? Its beauty must have made me mad! Forgive, oh forgive, Lord God!"

"He will forgive, even as I also forgive you," said the clear voice of Judith.
Achan started up in terror.

"Judith! What are you doing here? What do you know? What have you
heard?"

"I know all," she answered calmly, "and have heard all."

Then she told him of hearing his prayer three days before, and of her decision
to keep his secret.

"But you would have saved your life, had you told then and refused to marry
the son of a thief. Now nothing can save you. You must die as a member of my
family. And yet you say that the Lord will forgive me, even as you forgive. Why
do you forgive me?"

"Because in my heart also is the love of the beautiful. I, too, would have coveted the Babylonish garment, and perhaps I, too, would have taken it. Our God
must deal harshly with us when we break His laws, yet I believe He pities and
forgives us, since I have pity and forgiveness in my heart."

Achan threw himself at the girl's feet, sobbing like a child. Judith knelt beside
him and tried to comfort him as she would have comforted a child. When he
was calmer, he said, "My own family I cannot save; they must die for the sin of
their father; but I may be able to save you. I shall go to Joshua and beg for your
life. Since you have been one of us such a brief time, he may grant my prayer."

But Judith shook her head.

"No, I would rather die with Benoi, for what would life be without him? I
beg of you, believe that God has forgiven you, but let me die with you and
Benoi."

Achan said no more as they walked back to the tent, but he resolved to save
the life of this daughter-in-law if it were at all possible.

Early in the morning the casting of the lots began, for it might prove to be a
long process. On the first lot, the tribe of Judah was taken. The second brought
the families of the Zarhites. Achan stood seemingly unmoved as the lots dropped
down to the family of Zabdi; then the households, and he knew that the next
time the lot would fall upon him, and that he and his children would be cursed
forever among the tribes. Once more the lot was passed, and every man except
Achan held his breath and looked fearfully at his kinsman. Then the marked
stone lay in the hand of Achan, the son of Carmi, the son of Zabdi, the son of
Zerah of the tribe of Judah. Above the wails of the family and friends of Achan,
rose the cry of Benoi, "My father! My father! Oh my beloved Judith!"

Then Joshua said to Achan, "My son, give glory to the God of Israel and
make confession to Him. Tell me now what you have done. Do not hide it from
me."

And Achan said, "Indeed I have sinned against the Lord God of Israel. On
that day when the walls of Jericho fell, and every man went straight up before him,
I came to a wonderfully beautiful house. Such beauty as my eyes had never seen
was spread out before me and my heart smote me that all this beauty must be

destroyed. Yet I remembered the word of the Lord that everything was accursed except the metals; so I applied my torch to the house, though I had to turn away my eyes from the destruction of such beauty. Then as it burned, I spied in one corner of the room a small chest that I had overlooked in my haste. It was my duty to see if it had gold or silver in it. I lifted the lid, and there lay the most beautiful Babylonish garment that my eyes had ever seen. It glittered as I have never seen a garment glitter not even in my childhood in Egypt. It rustled as I lifted it, and the gems with which it was adorned, sparkled. I could not give it to the flames; I hid it under my cloak. Beneath the garment was a wedge of gold of some fifty shekels weight, and two hundred shekels of silver; and I coveted and took them. They are hidden in the earth under the floor of my tent house—the garment, the gold, and the silver. God has forgiven my sin against Him. Do with me now as you will."

The messengers whom Joshua sent to the tent of Achan found the garment and the gold and the silver even as he had said. They brought them and laid them at the feet of Joshua. Then Achan said to Joshua.

"Grant me one request. Grant that Judith, bride of but a day of my son, Benoi, be allowed to live. She has done no harm, and is, as yet, scarcely a member of my family. She is the only child of Elidad, and the light of his eyes."

And Joshua answered, "She is innocent, and she shall live; but tomorrow, you and your family, your flocks, your herds of asses, your tent, and the accursed thing that you took shall be destroyed."

And so it came to pass that at sunset a messenger from Joshua came to the tent of Benoi and took Judith back to the tent of her father. Her pleas and wails were not heeded. It was the command of Joshua.

"Nay, go, beloved," begged Benoi. "I am so glad that you can live. Do not come to the Valley of Achor, but stay in your father's tent till there is only a heap of stones to mark our resting place. God grant you peace."

Judith's only answer was sobbing as she was hurried away. Through the long hours of the night, Elidad and his wife kept watch over Judith. The girl had been stonily silent, since the messenger had brought her to their tent; but when daylight came, she turned to her father.

"How long will it be before the stoning takes place?"

"It will be the third hour," answered Elidad, "but I shall not go."

"Oh go!" begged Judith. "I want you to take a message for me to Benoi. They will not let him come to see me again; but they will let you tell him that my love reaches beyond the grave, and that I shall come to him before long. Hurry, for the sun has already risen and the Valley of Achor is far from here."

When he had gone, she persuaded her mother to lie down on the sleeping mat for a little rest. "You have watched with me all night; you can do no more."

When she was sure that her mother was asleep, she slipped quietly from the tent and hurried in the direction of the Valley of Achor. As she neared the place she could hear the noise of both shouts and lamentations. Hands were outstretched to grasp her robe as she darted through the crowd, and into the circle of stoners, but she managed to elude them all. As she darted into the ring, one glance showed that her Benoi was already dead, but Achan, though fallen to his knees and bleeding, was still conscious. She ran to him and threw her arms about him.

"Stop throwing, stop throwing!" rose the cry, but one stone struck Judith as she tried to shield Achan. She was carried from the circle and willing hands helped her father to bear her home.

It was evening when Judith regained consciousness to find her parents weeping beside her.

"Do not weep," she said softly. "I failed to go with Benoi, but now I shall never leave you."

A few weeks later the Israelites broke camp, and started on their expedition to conquer the cities farther north. Judith made a last visit to the heap of stones in the Valley of Achor. As the last rays of the sun began to be withdrawn from the top of the pile, she rose to go.

"Fairwell, Beloved," she whispered; "you can never come to me again, but someday I shall come to you. Someday, too, I believe that men will understand God as we do not *now*. Then I am sure that they will know that as a father pities his children, even as Achan pitied me and tried to save me, so 'the Lord pitieth them that fear him.' "*

+

GOD OF OUR FATHERS, WHOSE ALMIGHTY HAND

(Interpretation)

THE Reverend Daniel C. Roberts (1841-1907), author of this hymn, was born in Bridgehampton, New York. In 1866 he was ordained as an Episcopal clergyman, and held several important pastorates in Vermont and Massachusetts, and in Concord, New Hampshire.

He was a veteran of the Civil War, having enlisted with the 84th Regiment of Ohio volunteers. Dr. Roberts tells his own story of the writing and publishing of this hymn in a personal letter to Dr. Louis F. Benson. It reads:

"This hymn was written in 1876 for a celebration of the centennial of the Fourth of July, and sung first at Brandon, Vermont to a tune entitled 'Russian Hymn'! When our General Convention appointed a Commission to revise the Hymnal, I sent it, without my name, promising to send my name later if the hymn was accepted. It was accepted and printed anonymously in the report of the Commission. Before the Hymnal was printed, the Reverend Dr. Tucker, late of Troy, editor of our best musical Hymnal, and Mr. George William Warren, organist of St. Thomas Church, New York, were appointed a committee to choose a hymn for the centennial celebration of the adoption of the Constitution [of New York State]. They selected this hymn, then anonymous, and, wanting a tune, Mr. Warren composed a tune to which it has since been set in the *Tucker Hymnal*."**

* Used by special permission of the author.
** *Lyric Religion* by H. Augustine Smith, pp. 122-23. Copyright, 1931, by H. Augustine Smith. Used by special permission of the Fleming H. Revell Company.

God of Our Fathers, Whose Almighty Hand

Daniel C. Roberts, 1841-1907

NATIONAL HYMN
George William Warren, 1828-1902

HYMN, 1876   TUNE, 1892   METER, 10.10.10.10.

Trumpets, before each stanza

1. God of our fa-thers, whose al-might-y hand
2. Thy love di-vine hath led us in the past;
3. From war's a-larms, from dead-ly pes-ti-lence,
4. Re-fresh thy peo-ple on their toil-some way,

Leads forth in beau-ty all the star-ry band
In this free land by thee our lot is cast;
Be thy strong arm our ev-er sure de-fense;
Lead us from night to nev-er-end-ing day;

Of shin-ing worlds in splen-dor through the skies,
Be thou our Rul-er, Guard-ian, Guide, and Stay;
Thy true re-li-gion in our hearts in-crease,
Fill all our lives with love and grace di-vine,

Our grate-ful songs be-fore thy throne a-rise.
Thy word our law, thy paths our cho-sen way.
Thy boun-teous good-ness nour-ish us in peace.
And glo-ry, laud, and praise be ev-er thine. A-MEN.

This hymn is particularly appropriate for national anniversaries. The first stanza expresses a paeon of praise to God "whose almighty hand leads forth in beauty all the starry band." The second stanza expresses gratitude for past favors, thanksgiving for the present, and confidence in the future guidance of the God of our fathers to whom four distinguished names are applied: "ruler, guardian, guide and stay." The third stanza is a prayer for peace, and emphasizes the importance of religious faith in national life. The fourth stanza expresses a confidence in the continued leadership of the Eternal God to whom the human race must ever offer never-ending "glory, laud, and praise."

George William Warren was born in 1828 in Albany, New York, and his musical career began as organist for St. Peter's Church when he was eighteen years of age. For twelve years he served that church, and then went to the Church of the Holy Trinity in Brooklyn, New York, and still later to St. Thomas Church in New York City. He died in 1902.

Several bars of trumpet music usually precede each stanza and provide effective interludes which help to create the feeling of patriotism characteristic of this hymn. It is a majestic melody expressing patriotism, purpose, and power.

✝

JONAH AND JOSHUA

(Interpretation)

SPIRITUALS are spontaneous group creations, originating, not as written, but as vocal music sung by a leader and chorus. Many times one person begins to sing, then the tune and words are caught up by others, a line or two added, and sometimes within a few minutes a new spiritual has been created. Changes and additions may be added later, but the final product is usually a composition of many minds and hearts.

Often the tunes of spirituals are variations of those that the Negro had heard in his native Africa. Both the music and the words, however, are original, and are the outgrowth of a people who absorbed much musically as well as culturally from the country of their enforced adoption. The Negro singer nearly always improved the original tune.

It has often been said that the United States has no folk songs. In only one sense is this true, for we are a people of European and Asiatic backgrounds. But Negro spirituals are folk songs. They are both American and African.

This spiritual, sometimes entitled merely "Jonah," is another of those folk songs that couple Old Testament historical events with the experiences of a conquered people far removed from their own native land and race. It sings of the trials and troubles of Jonah and Joshua. Like Jonah and Joshua these Negro slaves did not want to die in bondage in a strange land. They found release for their conquered bodies and minds in singing of the victories and defeats of Jonah,

Jonah and Joshua

* From *Old Songs Hymnal* collected by Dorothy G. Bolton and arranged by Harry T. Burleigh, No. 16. Copyright, 1945, by Fleming H. Revell Company. Used by special permission of the publisher.

God told Jonah go to Nineveh and preach;
Jonah would not — he went down to de Beach —
He found a boat that was ready to go,
He got on board fer the Joppa shore.
    CHORUS

The wind it blowed and the storm it ride
And tossed the ship from side to side;
The Captain of the ship got trouble in mind,
He searched the ship before and behind.
    CHORUS

He found Brother Jonah in the deck asleep,
Say man we's goin ter de bottom of de deep!
Jonah riz up, begun fer ter shout,
De fault's in me — you kin cast me out!
    CHORUS

They throwed Brother Jonah overboard,
The whale grabbed Jonah and swallowed him whole;
The whale made away to Neneveh land
And cast Brother Jonah up on dry land.
    CHORUS

The gourd vine growed around Jonah's head,
The inch worm smarted and cut it down dead,
The inch worm smarted and cut it down
And that left a cross on Jonah's crown.
    CHORUS

Joshuay was the son of Nun,
God was with him when the Battle was won;
The Battle of one was the battle two,
The Battle of two was the Battle three,
The Battle of three was the Battle four,
The Battle of four was the Battle five,
The Battle five was the Battle six,
The Battle six was the Battle seven,
The wall fell down — God heard it in Heaven!

who would not obey his Lord and go to Nineveh; and of Joshua and his battles before the walls of Jericho, and of his leadership of the children of Israel after their release from Egyptian slavery.

✢

IMMORTAL LOVE, FOREVER FULL

(Interpretation)

ACCORDING to John Greenleaf Whittier, author of this hymn, "a good hymn is the best use to which poetry can be put." It would seem that editors and hymn-book publishers confirm Whittier's conviction, for they have selected from his poems enough verse to create some seventy or more hymns.

John Greenleaf Whittier was a Quaker poet. His genuine love of nature, and his feeling of the abiding nearness of God is apparent in all his verse. The longer poem, "Our Master," from which the stanzas of this hymn were taken, was composed in 1866, after the strenuous days of the poet's active life had passed. The sentiment of this poem reflects Whittier's faith in the nearness of God, and His continuing help in all the problems and perplexities of our daily lives.

The poet's broad understanding of the frailties of men and nations breathes through the last stanza of this great hymn:

> The letter fails, the systems fall,
>   And ev'ry symbol wanes:
> The Spirit over-brooding all,
>   Eternal Love, remains.

One of the melodies to which Whittier's hymn-poem is sung is "Beatitudo," written in 1875 by John B. Dykes. It is also sung to a tune entitled "Dundee" which dates back to the *Scottish Psalter* published in 1615.

Immortal Love, Forever Full

FIRST TUNE. BEATITUDO. C.M.

JOHN G. WHITTIER, 1859

JOHN B. DYKES, 1875

1. Im - mor - tal Love, for - ev - er full, For - ev - er flow - ing free,
2. Our out-ward lips con - fess the name All oth - er names a - bove;
3. Blow, winds of God, a - wake and blow The mists of earth a - way!
4. The let - ter fails, the sys - tems fall, And ev - 'ry sym - bol wanes:

For - ev - er shared, for - ev - er whole, A nev - er - ebb - ing sea!
But love a - lone knows whence it came, And com - pre-hend-eth love.
Shine out, O Light di - vine, and show How wide and far we stray!
The Spir-it o - ver-brood-ing all, E - ter - nal Love, re-mains. A - men.

YOU'LL BE A WITNESS FOR THE LORD

(Interpretation)

ALTHOUGH Negro spirituals have been appropriately called "songs of sorrow," few are written in a minor strain. Instead, they often express a profound hope for ultimate freedom.

Some of the early collectors of spirituals erroneously believed these songs were not sung in harmony. However, Negroes in group singing have four-part harmony, and sometimes six- and even eight-part harmony.

In Negro schools, the girls usually sit in a body on one side of the assembly, while the boys sit on the other side. Yet each student will pick up his own part and harmonize without discord with the entire student group. For as Natalie Curtis Burton says: "The Negro sings by nature, not by training; by ear and heart, not by rote, in perfect pitch and without accompaniment."* Each person takes the part he likes and harmonizes naturally with the rest. To test this, James

* From *Hampton Series Negro Folk Songs,* Bk. I, p. 4.

You'll be a Witness for the Lord

Mo-ses was a man of God, God called Mo-ses from the
burn-ing bush, Go on down in E-gypt's land, And
bring my chil-dren out of Phar-aoh's hand. And
you'll be a wit-ness for the Lord, And you'll be a wit-ness
for the Lord, And you'll be a wit-ness for the Lord,

* From *Old Songs Hymnal* collected by Dorothy G. Bolton and arranged by Harry T. Burleigh, No. 23. Copyright, 1945, by Fleming H. Revell Company. Used by special permission of the publisher.

You'll be a Witness for the Lord

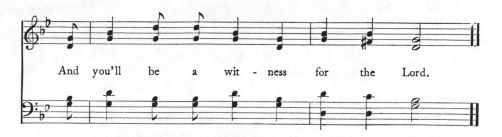

And you'll be a wit - ness for the Lord.

Moses! Moses! come and see,
I'll tell you what you do for me.
I want you to let them idols alone,
Place my law on the tables of stone,
And you'll be a witness for the Lord.
    Chorus

Moses went down in Egypt land,
Sung and prayed for wicked man,
Having God at his right hand,
He brought the children out of Pharoah's land,
Moses was a witness for the Lord.
    Chorus

When my soul is burden down,
I ask the Lord to turn me around.
Jesus washed my sins away,
Taught me how to watch and pray,
My soul was a witness for the Lord.
    Chorus

Just about time I thought I was lost,
My dungeon shook and my chains fell off,
My soul was a witness for the Lord.

Weldon Johnson suggests that one select four Negro boys or young men, almost anywhere, and "the chances are ninety to one hundred that you will have a perfect quartette, for Negro voices are almost never discordant." And Mrs. Burton, speaking of Negro youth, says: "They seem to possess an intuitive gift for part singing."*

The Negro had a limited and often fragmentary knowledge of Old Testament events to which he likened his own experience. Thus in this spiritual, "You'll Be a Witness for the Lord," he sings of Moses in Egypt's land dealing with the cruel and vindictive ruler of an enslaved people. Just as Moses in his troublesome experience was a "witness for the Lord," so he too, the Negro, when his heart was burdened by the trials of an enslaved people, turned in thought and prayer to God, beseeching Him to "turn me round" and "teach me how to watch and pray"; for his soul also longed to be a "witness for the Lord."

This spiritual is rich in devotional appeal, and should be sung with deep and genuine religious fervor.

* *Ibid.*, p. 33.

CONTENTS

PART II SECTION 2

THE PERIOD OF THE JUDGES

— ✠ —

And the people served the Lord all the days of Joshua, and all the days of the elders that outlived Joshua, who had seen all the great works of the Lord, that he did for Israel.—JUDGES 2:7

— ✠ —

DEBORAH

By

Paul Gustave Doré

(Interpretation)

DEBORAH has a unique place in Hebrew history because she is the only woman of whom it is recorded that she exercised political power over Israel and led the tribes to victory. She lived in the hill country of Ephraim where her people had been settled for half a century since the conquest of Canaan under Joshua. This was the period when the "judges" ruled Israel. Deborah was the wife of an obscure man. She first became known as a prophetess to whom the Lord spoke. As she taught people the messages she had received from God, there developed in her a concern for the people and she took upon herself the troubles of all. The men and women of Israel who came to her for guidance and received wise counsel spread tidings of her unusual ability until the name of Deborah became a talisman that drew people to her from far and near. Thus her power grew until it could be said of her that "she judged Israel at that time. And she dwelt under the palm tree of Deborah between Ramah and Beth-el in mount Ephraim. And the children of Israel came up to her for judgment" (Judg. 4:4, 5).

In those days the children of Israel cried unto God, for they were being oppressed by Jabin, King of Canaan. Sisera, the captain of Jabin's troops, commanded nine hundred iron chariots. With these he threatened the entire countryside. Roads became unsafe; travelers used hidden trails; outlying Israelite villages were abandoned. Then there arose in Deborah anxiety for her people. At the command of the Lord she became "a mother in Israel."

Thereupon she summoned Barak to lead the Israelites against their oppressor. She addressed Barak in prophetic words:

"Hath not the Lord God of Israel commanded, saying, 'Go and draw toward mount Tabor, and take with thee ten thousand men of the children of Naphtali and of the children of Zebulun? And I will draw unto thee to the river Kishon Sisera, the captain of Jabin's army, with his chariots and his multitude; and I will deliver him into thine hand.'" (Judg. 4:6, 7.)

"Deborah" by Paul Gustave Doré portrays the moment when the voice of Deborah rang out like a trumpet call urging Barak and the men of Israel to rise up to defeat Sisera. Deborah the "judge" and prophetess is the focus of the composition. Beads decorate her forehead and fall in graceful loops from her head. One hand is upraised in exhortation while the other covers her heart. The men surrounding her listen attentively to her challenging words, but not one has yet been stirred to action against the enemy of God and His people.

Barak hesitated to summon the tribes and lead them against Sisera until Deborah had promised to go with him even into battle. So great was her power over the people that only she could unite the scattered tribes and by her presence inspire them to victory. The amazing triumph over Sisera is celebrated in the Ode of Deborah in Judges 5, one of the greatest masterpieces of ancient Hebrew poetry.

Paul Gustave Doré, the French artist, was born in Strasbourg in 1832. He went to Paris at the age of sixteen and soon became known as an unusual draughtsman. His facility was extraordinary. His drawings were admired for their sureness and their originality. Among the books he illustrated were Dante's *Inferno,* Milton's *Paradise Lost,* and La Fontaine's *Fables.* His many Bible illustrations became very popular, especially in England and America. He died in Paris in 1883.

✛

GIDEON DESTROYS THE MIDIANITES

(Woodcut)

Artist Unknown

(Interpretation)

THE call of Gideon, the son of Joash the Abiezrite, is a story of the "victory of Faith" which is told in the sixth, seventh, and eighth chapters of the book of Judges.

The children of Israel, because of their wickedness, were oppressed by the Midianites, a nomadic people from Arabia who invaded Canaan with their camels, their cattle, and their tents. They seized the crops planted by the Israelites and stripped them of all their possessions. Many of the Israelites fled before the invader, making their homes in the caves and deserted animal dens of the mountains, and threshing their wheat in wine presses by night to hide their movements from the Midianites.

Gideon was one of these Israelites. His family was one of the poorest of the tribe of Manasseh, and he was the least of his household. Nevertheless, as Gideon was threshing wheat in his father's wine press in Ophrah, an angel of the Lord appeared unto him and said:

" 'The Lord is with thee, thou mighty man of valour. . . . Go in this thy might, and thou shalt save Israel from the hand of the Midianites. Have not I sent thee?'

"And Gideon said unto God, 'If thou wilt save Israel by mine hand, as thou hast said, behold, I will put a fleece of wool in the floor; and if the dew be on the fleece only, and it be dry upon all the earth beside, then shall I know that thou wilt save Israel by mine hand, as thou hast said.' And it was so; for he rose up early on the morrow, and thrust the fleece together, and wringed the dew out of the fleece, a bowl full of water" (6:12, 14, 36-38).

Then Gideon blew a trumpet and sent messengers to summon men from the tribes of Manasseh, Asher, Zebulun, and Naphtali. Many thousands responded to his call to battle against the camp of the Midianites. But the Lord said to Gideon: "The people that are with thee are too many for me to give the Midian-

DEBORAH—*DORÉ*

ites into their hands, lest Israel vaunt themselves against me, saying, 'Mine own hand hath saved me'" (7:2).

Then all the "fearful and trembling" were told to return to their homes, but ten thousand still remained.

"And the Lord said unto Gideon, 'The people are yet too many; bring them down unto the water, and I will try them for thee. . . .' So he brought down the people unto the water; and the Lord said unto Gideon, 'Every one that lappeth of the water with his tongue, as a dog lappeth, him shalt thou set by himself; likewise every one that boweth down upon his knees to drink.' And the number of them that lapped, putting their hand to their mouth, was three hundred men: but all the rest of the people bowed down upon their knees to drink water. And the Lord said unto Gideon, 'By the three hundred men that lapped will I save you, and deliver the Midianites into thine hand: and let all the other people go every man unto his place'" (7:4, 5-7).

That same night the voice of the Lord said to Gideon: "Arise, get thee down unto the host; for I have delivered it into thine hand" (7:9). And Gideon "divided the three hundred men into three companies, and he put a trumpet in every man's hand, with empty pitchers, and lamps within the pitchers. And he said unto them, 'Look on me, and do likewise; and, behold, when I come to the outside of the camp, it shall be that, as I do, so shall ye do. When I blow with a trumpet, I and all that are with me, then blow ye the trumpets also on every side of all the camp, and say, "The sword of the Lord, and of Gideon."'

"So Gideon, and the hundred men that were with him, came unto the outside of the camp in the beginning of the middle watch; and they had but newly set the watch. And they blew the trumpets, and brake the pitchers that were in their hands. And the three companies blew the trumpets, and brake the pitchers, and held the lamps in their left hands, and the trumpets in their right hands to blow withal; and they cried, 'The sword of the Lord, and of Gideon.' And they stood every man in his place round about the camp; and all the host ran. . . . And the Lord set every man's sword against his fellow, even throughout all the host; and the host fled to Beth-shittah in Zererath, and to the border of Abel-meholah, unto Tabbath" (7:16-24).

Thus three bands of Israelites attacking from different directions surprised the camp of the Midianites and threw them into a panic. Confusion reigned in the midst of this sudden attack of blaring trumpets, glowing torches, and shouting men. The Midianites lost their heads and attacked each other. They were overpowered and fled in defeat.

An unknown artist has portrayed this incident in the woodcut entitled "Gideon's Army Destroying the Midianites." It illustrates a unique strategy in battle coupled with implicit faith in the God of the Israelites.

Gideon returned victorious and then the men of Israel said to him: "Rule thou over us, both thou, and thy son, and thy son's son also; for thou hast delivered us from the hand of Midian."

But Gideon refused the kingship of Israel when it was thus offered to him for he believed that as God's chosen people they were to be ruled directly by God.

GIDEON DESTROYS THE MIDIANITES—*ARTIST UNKNOWN*

He replied to them: "I will not rule over you, neither shall my son rule over you: the Lord shall rule over you" (8:22-23).

✠

JEPHTHAH'S DAUGHTER

(Woodcut)

Artist Unknown

(Interpretation)

THE story of Jephtha's daughter and the fulfillment of the father's vow is one of the tragedies of the Old Testament. Jephthah was a mighty man of valor. He was the son of Gilead by a harlot. Later Gilead married and his wife bore other sons. They, when they were grown to manhood, drove Jephthah out saying to him: "Thou shalt not inherit in our father's house; for thou art the son of a strange woman" (Judg. 11:2).

Years later, when the children of Ammon made war against Israel, the elders in Gilead sought out Jephthah in the land of Tob, saying to him: "Come, and be our captain, that we may fight with the children of Ammon" (11:6).

The elders assured Jephthah that if he would be with them and fight against the Ammonites, then they would make him their chief and leader. Jephthah returned to his people to become their leader in the struggle against the Ammonites. He "vowed a vow unto the Lord, and said, 'If thou shalt without fail deliver the children of Ammon into mine hands, then it shall be, that whatsoever cometh forth of the doors of my house to meet me, when I return in peace from the children of Ammon, shall surely be the Lord's, and I will offer it up for a burnt offering" (11:30-31). And Jephthah and the children of Israel fought against the Ammonites. The Lord delivered the enemy into Jephthah's hands, and the children of Ammon were subdued.

Although victory in battle was Jephthah's reward, a tragedy awaited him when he returned victorious. For when he came to his house in Mizpah, his only daughter, whom he loved dearly, was the first to come out of his house to meet him with timbrels and with dances. When Jephthah saw her he rent his clothes and cried: "'Alas, my daughter! thou hast brought me very low, and thou art one of them that trouble me; for I have opened my mouth unto the Lord, and I cannot go back.'

"And she said unto him, 'My father, if thou hast opened thy mouth unto the Lord, do to me according to that which hath proceeded out of thy mouth; forasmuch as the Lord hath taken vengeance for thee of thine enemies, even of the children of Ammon.' And she said unto her father, 'Let this thing be done for me: let me alone two months, that I may go up and down upon the mountains, and bewail my virginity, I and my fellows.' And he said, 'Go.' And he sent her away for two months: and she went with her companions, and bewailed her virginity upon the mountains. And it came to pass at the end of two months, that she

JEPHTHAH'S DAUGHTER—*ARTIST UNKNOWN*

returned unto her father, who did with her according to his vow which he had vowed" (11:35-39).

Thereafter it was the custom of the daughters of Israel to go once each year for four days to the mountains to celebrate the loyalty and devotion of the daughter of Jephthah (11:40).

An unknown artist has portrayed this incident in the woodcut, "Jephthah's Daughter." She, accompanied by other maidens, comes out to meet her father with timbrels, castanets, and drums. In the center stands Jephthah, his head bowed in utter dejection as he remembers his vow. Behind him are two of his victorious warriors, followed by manacled captives. In the background stand aged elders of Israel who had heard his vow and know that its fulfillment means the death of his only daughter. In this picture there is dancing, music, and rejoicing to celebrate a great victory, but the victor is plunged in sorrow and regret.

✜

SAMSON AND DELILAH

By

Alessandro Turchi

(Interpretation)

ALESSANDRO TURCHI, also called L' Orbetto and Alessandro Veronese, was born in Verona in 1582. It is said that in his childhood he was employed to conduct a blind beggar; hence he acquired the name L' Orbetto.

On leaving the school of Riccio he went to Venice, where he worked for a time under Carlo Cagliari. Afterward he went to Rome where he painted pictures for the church of La Concezione, as well as altar pieces for several other churches. Among the best of these pictures are "Flight into Egypt" and "The Holy Family." Throughout his life Turchi was much employed on small, beautifully detailed pictures representing historical subjects, which he often painted on black marble. He died in 1648.

Turchi's style of painting frequently combined Roman design with Venetian coloring. Most of his pictures are unusually well executed, care being equally bestowed on all figures. His picture entitled "Samson and Delilah" hangs in the Louvre in Paris, along with his "Death of Cleopatra," "The Deluge," "The Marriage of St. Catherine," and "The Woman Taken in Adultery."

The basis for "Samson in the Hands of the Philistines" is Judges 16:4-21. Samson whose almost superhuman strength was feared by his enemies, the Philistines, loved a woman named Delilah. The Philistines came to her and offered her a bribe, saying: "Entice him, and see wherein his great strength lieth, and by what means we may prevail against him."

Three times Samson deceived her, telling her he could be bound with seven new bowstrings, by new ropes, and by woven locks of his hair. Each time she tried to bind him he always shook himself free. But Delilah continued to press

SAMSON AND DELILAH—TURCHI

him to tell her the secret of his strength. Finally he revealed to her that he had been pledged to God since his birth in the Nazirite vow and according to the requirements of this vow he had never cut his hair. Herein lay his amazing strength. "If I be shaven, then my strength will go from me, and I shall become weak, and be like any other man."

Delilah promptly revealed his secret to the Philistines. "And she made him sleep upon her knees; and she called for a man, and caused him to shave off the seven locks of his head. . . . And he awoke out his sleep, and said, 'I will go out as at other times before, and shake myself.' And he wist not that the Lord was departed from him.

"But the Philistines took him, and put out his eyes, and brought him down to Gaza, and bound him with fetters of brass; and he did grind in the prison house."

In Turchi's portrayal, Delilah sits in the center. Samson is asleep, his head resting on his arm which is upon Delilah's knees. Her hand is on his shoulders. She has heard his deep, rhythmic breathing and knows he is sleeping soundly. So she has called to a secreted Philistine servant who stealthily clips off seven locks of his hair believing that the giant strength of Samson will thus be overcome.

In the background on one side are the half-concealed faces of Philistine soldiers ready to pounce upon and bind this giant, that he may be taken into captivity and made to serve his enemies.

On the opposite side of the picture two children play with each other. One of them has picked up Samson's jaw bone of an ass. The other is trying to lift his heavy sword.

In this portrayal the interest centers in the deft fingers of the servant clipping the seven woven locks from Samson's head. Delilah has half turned away. One cannot be sure whether she is merely making a sign to the soldier to be quiet, or whether she shrinks from witnessing the downfall of a strong man through her treachery.

✛

SAMSON BRINGS DOWN THE PILLARS OF THE TEMPLE

By

Paul Gustave Doré

(Interpretation)

PAUL GUSTAVE DORÉ was an Alsatian by birth, but a Parisian by training and environment. He is often referred to as "of the French school" though in reality he belonged to no school at all.

During his childhood he very often accompanied his father up and down the Rhine river, and came to know intimately every wild crag, fortress, and bend in the river which in childish fancy he repeopled with weird and often grotesque personalities. The background of many of his pictures is a deep woods, a moun-

SAMSON BRINGS DOWN THE PILLARS OF THE TEMPLE—*DORÉ*

tain pass, or a deep ravine, undoubtedly resulting from his memories of these rides.

His father unsuccessfully tried to divert his attention from drawing by ridiculing him and even offering bribes. In his early manhood Doré drew a series of sketches of the Parisian opera, the circus, and the Odéon that were candidly and comically good. Later, however, he turned to mythological, historical, and religious subjects.

He seldom, if ever, used a model, almost never sketched from nature, never asked for nor accepted advice from anyone, and never retouched a sketch after he had completed it. He was an individualist in every sense of the word, though not an egotist. Since no one else could see the mental picture as he saw it, he felt the criticism of friends and fellow artists was useless. His drawings were unequaled in Paris. He was both original and inventive, appropriating and adapting his ideas from many sources. He illustrated serial after serial with great ease and surety, creating illustrations that were weird, wild, and sometimes ludicrous.

Doré found the Bible a rich source of inspiration, as his engraving, "Samson Brings Down the Pillars of the Temple," illustrates. This is one of his many Biblical illustrations. One notes the painstaking care which he gave to every detail of this picture.

In Judges 16:23-30 one reads of the lofty magnitude of the Temple of Dagon, the god of the Philistines. Indeed, Doré has not exaggerated its size, for the Biblical narrative reveals:

"Now the house was full of men and women; and all the lords of the Philistines were there; and there were upon the roof about three thousand men and women."

They had assembled to offer a great sacrifice to Dagon their god, and to rejoice because they had at last captured and blinded Samson. In high spirits they called for him to be brought out of prison and set between the pillars of the temple that they might mock him and make sport of him.

"And Samson called unto the Lord, and said, 'O Lord God, remember me, I pray thee, and strengthen me, I pray thee, only this once, O God, that I may be at once avenged of the Philistines for my two eyes.'

"And Samson took hold of the two middle pillars upon which the house stood, and he leaned on them, of the one with his right hand, and of the other with his left. And Samson said, 'Let me die with the Philistines.'

"And he bowed himself with all his might; and the house fell upon the lords, and upon all the people that were therein."

RUTH GLEANING

By

Ludwig Bruck-Lajos

(Interpretation)

WE are indebted to the Hungarian artist, Ludwig Bruck-Lajos, for this unusually attractive painting of Ruth. Born in Poza, Hungary November 3, 1846, Bruck-Lajos studied in the Academy of Art in Vienna with Michael Munkacsy and later traveled widely throughout Italy and France. In 1897 he exhibited in the Royal Academy in London and later in both Paris and New York City, and received merited recognition. He died in 1910.

This painting realistically portrays the young widowed gleaner, who just a few weeks before had made the supreme decision of her life. She had renounced her own kin and country to remain with her mother-in-law because of the love and respect she bore for this woman twice her age who had been bereaved of her husband and both her sons in a foreign land.

Down through the centuries Ruth's great decision and the stirring words in which she announced it have been remembered: "Entreat me not to leave thee, or to return from following after thee: for whither thou goest, I will go; and where thou lodgest, I will lodge: thy people shall be my people, and thy God my God. Where thou diest, will I die, and there will I be buried: the Lord do so to me, and more also, if aught but death part thee and me" (Ruth 1:16-17).

Following this vow, Ruth accompanied Naomi, her mother-in-law, to Bethlehem. They arrived at the time of the barley harvest. The season itself, as well as their poverty, suggested to this young Moabitess her opportunity to prove her sincerity. She would become a gleaner in the barley fields. Naomi was aware that Ruth would be the subject of much curiosity and gossip among the Hebrew maidens who also would be gleaning. Both her dress and her speech would proclaim her foreign origin and nationality. Therefore, in assenting to her daughter-in-law's request that she be allowed to glean, Naomi wisely sent her into the fields of the rich Boaz, because she knew he was a distant kinsman. Boaz came to the field one morning and saluted his reapers in friendly welcome. He was about to give his head servant instructions for the day when his eyes lighted upon this new damsel in her flowing, Oriental costume. He inquired of his chief servant, "Whose damsel is this?" Upon learning that she was the widowed daughter-in-law of Naomi, his kinswoman, he ordered his chief servant to instruct the reapers to allow additional gleanings purposefully to fall so that this young widow might not go home empty-handed at the end of the day.

Then he cordially invited Ruth to glean along with his own maidens until the end of the barley harvest, and to partake of the common meal provided for all who served him.

In his interpretation of Ruth the gleaner, Ludwig Bruck-Lajos portrays a young, girlish figure in picturesque Oriental costume. A long, flowing veil is brought forward on one side, but is thrown carelessly back over her shoulder on the other side. This young Moabitess is, indeed, an attractive figure as she stands, barefooted, by a large sheaf of grain which she has just bound and seems ready to carry away. Ruth's face and eyes are downcast, perhaps in reminiscence of her homeland, and of the kin from whom she has become permanently separated.

In the background stands Boaz and one of his chief servants of whom the master has just asked, "Whose damsel is this?" Farther away are other reapers, near the field of standing grain.

One recalls Thomas Hood's description* of this young damsel from a foreign land who showed love and loyalty to her widowed mother-in-law. Her son, Obed, was David's grandfather and David was an ancestor of Jesus of Nazareth.

✛

RUTH AND BOAZ

In Stained Glass

Designed by William R. Jack

(Interpretation)

THE story of Ruth and Boaz, as related in the Book of Ruth, is one of the most unusual love stories in history. It is the tale of a girl from Moab who sacrificed her home and kindred to relieve the loneliness of her bereaved mother-in-law. Against this background of unusual devotion Ruth's love story unfolds. We learn how Ruth, who seemed to have given up everything, became the wife of the noble and generous Boaz and the ancestress of King David.

George Matheson, the blind Scottish preacher, has entitled his character sketch of this Biblical woman "Ruth the Decided," because her heroic decision changed not only the life of this young widow, but also the lineage of God's only-begotten Son. For as a result of the marriage of Ruth and Boaz, they became the ancestors of the Messiah.

Interpreting the significance of Ruth's choice Matheson says:

"I thank Thee, O God, that amid the women in Thy Great Gallery there is one that shines only by her heart. There are those, like Miriam, who shine by genius; there are those, like Deborah, who shine by work; there are those, like Rebekah, who shine by foresight; and there are those, like Rachel, who shine by beauty. But I am glad Thou hast set apart a corner for the heart alone. I am glad Thou hast chosen Thy specimen of female decidedness from a simple act of love. I am glad Thou hast revealed a type of womanly heroism in one who was not clever, not gifted, not sparkling, not loud or showy, not even strong in practical working, but merely a domesticated girl clinging to a domestic affection."

Let this Old Testament story reveal to women everywhere and in all ages that:

"Thou has a sphere of women's heroism distinct from any of these, the sphere

* See the poem "Ruth" on p. 248.

RUTH GLEANING—*BRUCK-LAJOS*

of those who simply *will* to do! Let it tell them that though they may not be Sarahs, or Rebekahs, or Miriams, or Deborahs, there remains for them another mansion in Thy house, the mansion where Ruth abides! Let it tell them that Thou hast a wreath for the choice of the heart even though the hand be feeble, that Thou hast a crown for the resolute will even though the mind be slender, that Thou hast a place for love's devotion even though the sphere be humble!"*

This lovely story inspired William R. Jack to design and create an unusual stained-glass window entitled "Ruth and Boaz," which is in the Second Congregational Church at Attleboro, Massachusetts. The window is made of antique and cathedral glass. This process was perfected by Louis C. Tiffany and John La-Farge of England by fusing layer upon layer of stained glass to achieve certain color effects unsurpassed in Europe from 1875 to 1915.

The United States has taken the lead in the antique glass field, which was made possible by the arrival of many noted English artists during and following World War I. This type of antique glass has been used for centuries in the old cathedrals of Europe, and may be seen in the United States in the stained-glass windows of the Cathedral of St. John the Divine and of the Riverside Church, both in New York City.

William R. Jack has devoted his life to designing and creating stained-glass windows. He came to the United States from England in 1925 as the chief designer for an important American firm. He maintained that position until the close of World War II, at which time he became associated with the firm of Whittemore Associates, Inc. of Boston, Massachusetts, as supervisor of their studios and chief designer of all their stained-glass windows.

Occasionally it is necessary to blend opalescent and antique glass in order to match designs already present in church or cathedral. In this distinctive window portraying Ruth and Boaz in the wheat field, the border is of opalescent glass of pale opal and gold stains, while the main portion of the window is in the traditional antique glass colors of ruby, blue, purple, green, and white. Ruth is dressed in a gown of gold with white and gold headdress. In her arms is a sheaf of grain. Boaz wears a robe of rich blue. The entire effect is one of simplicity and unaffected dignity.

✛

THE CAVES OF WADI EL-MUGHARAH

(Prehistoric Palestinians)

Deep ancient caves of Carmel
  Above Philistia's Plain,
Ten thousand years ago you saw
  The cavemen fight the rain,
Where hunters first to farming turned,
And homes first comforts learned.

* From *Representative Women of the Bible* by George Matheson, pp. 190-91. Published by Hodder & Stoughton, Ltd., London, E. C. 4, England. Used by special permission of the publisher.

IN LOVING MEMORY OF
MARY A. MONROE & GEORGE A. MONROE
PRESENTED BY THEIR DAUGHTER

Courtesy William R. Jack, designer, and Carroll E. Whittemore Associates, Inc., Boston, Mass.

RUTH AND BOAZ—*JACK*

Such caves for homes are strong and cool,
  Such caves last long and sure.
For nothing can dislodge the men
  Who hold them—they endure.

Natufians* here made sharp their flints,
  Here watched their fires' first glints.
Here women netted caps of bead
  To meet their beauty's need—
Poor relics that are priceless clues
  To scientists they gave.

Although Natufians have gone,
  Yet by their lowest rung
Of laddered progress men have climbed
  To God, and reared their young.**

—*Madeleine S. Miller*

CONCERNING USURY

To him who is of kin to thee give his due and to the
  poor and to the wayfarer: this will be best for those
  who seek the face of God: and with them it shall be
  well.

Whatever ye put out at usury to increase it with the
  substance of others shall have no increase from God:
  but whatever ye shall give in alms as seeking the
  face of God shall be doubled to you.

—*The Koran*

THE NEARNESS

O Might beyond the utmost suns and stars
  That fixed their orbits and majestic pace,
O Core of life and light, there are no bars,
  For all the veil of blue before Thy face,
To separate Thee from my yearning heart;
  I feel how near to me, how near Thou art!

I hear Thy sacred heartbeat in the rain
  Whose rhythm summons life within the sod;
I hear Thy footsteps on the earth again
  In blessed winds that waft the spring, O God;

---

* Natufians were ancient people who inhabited caves in the face of Mount Carmel, overlooking the Maritime Plain. They represented the oldest race of modern man yet found in Palestine. The flints with which they worked the terraces outside their caves have been excavated, and their ways of living studied by Biblical archaeologists. Their hearths and tombs have also been found in and about these ancient Carmel caves.

** Used by special permission of the author.

I mark in every sunrise of the land
  The golden benediction of Thy hand.

And when my wells of hope and strength run dry,
  O deep exhaustless Source, I call on Thee,
And feel the Living Waters surge close by
  That flow to fill my empty wells for me.
I pray to One beyond the farthest sphere,
  And He who answers is so near, so near!*

—Adelaide Love

WHEN IS THE TIME TO TRUST?

Let me prove, I pray thee, but this once with the fleece.—JUDGES 6:39

When is the time to trust?
  Is it when all is calm,
  When waves the victor's palm,
  And life is one glad psalm
    Of joy and praise?
Nay! but the time to trust
  Is when the waves beat high,
  When storm clouds fill the sky,
  And prayer is one long cry,
    O help and save!

When is the time to trust?
  Is it when friends are true?
  Is it when comforts woo,
  And in all we say and do
    We meet but praise?
Nay! but the time to trust
  Is when we stand alone,
  And summer birds have flown,
  And every drop is gone,
    All else but God.

What is the time to trust?
  Is it some future day,
  When you have tried your way,
  And learned to trust and pray
    By bitter woe?
Nay! but the time to trust
  Is in this moment's need,
  Poor, broken, bruised reed!
  Poor, troubled soul, make speed
    To trust thy God.

* From *Poems for Life* compiled by Thomas Curtis Clark, p. 29. Copyright, :941, by Harper & Brothers. Used by special permission of the author and the publisher.

What is the time to trust?
Is it when hopes beat high,
When sunshine gilds the sky,
And joy and ecstasy
Fill all the heart?
Nay! but the time to trust
Is when our joy is fled,
When sorrow bows the head,
And all is cold and dead,
All else but God.

— *Author Unknown*

FOR SAMSON AT GAZA

(Judges 16)

Samson was a strong man
Who found it naught to lift
The mighty gates of Gaza
Or bolted doors to shift.

Samson was a weak man,
Unable to resist
Philistine-born Delilah
When once their lips had kissed.

Then he who tore a lion's frame,
As blinded prisoner ground
While pagan cultists mocked at him
In Gaza's dungeon bound.

The lives he crushed when temple walls
He tumbled to the Plain,
Were more than those in battle
His giant hands had slain.

And yet the crash was not so much
That temple pillars fell,
But that *he* fell who twenty years
Had judged all Israel!*

— *Madeleine S. Miller*

* Used by special permission of the author.

SIT STILL

(Ruth 3:18)

Sit still, my child, 'Tis no great thing I
    ask,
No glorious deed, no mighty task;
But just to sit and patiently abide.
Wait in my presence, in my word confide.

"But oh! dear Lord, I long the sword to
    wield,
Forward to go, and in the battle field
To fight for thee, thine enemies o'er-
    throw,
And in thy strength to vanquish every
    foe.

"The harvest-fields spread out before
    me lie,
The reapers toward me look, and vainly
    cry—
'The field is white, the laborers are few;
Our Lord's command is also sent to
    you.' "

My child, it is a sweet and blessed thing
To rest beneath the shadow of my wing;
To feel thy doings and thy words are
    naught,
To trust to me each restless, longing
    thought.

"Dear Lord, help me this lesson sweet
    to learn,
To sit at thy pierced feet and only yearn
To love thee better, Lord, and feel that
    still
Waiting is working, if it be thy will."

—Author Unknown

RUTH AND NAOMI

Three weeping women in the Moab land:
For death had robbed them of the men they loved;
Three widows left to face the world, which proved,
For all it held, a maze of desert sand.
But fate was kind: to Bethlehem returned,

Naomi, Ruth found comfort for their woes.
Good Boaz, kinsman, smiled as in the rows
Of corn the daughter gleaned; and as he yearned
To soothe her grief, Naomi dreamed that he
Should through the lowly Ruth raise up once more
From wreck the family name. The shining door
Of hope stood wide: her dream came true and she
Who sorrowed now was glad. Ruth then could sing—
She knew not that through her should come Earth's King!*

—*Thomas Curtis Clark*

RUTH

She stood breast-high among the corn,
Clasped by the golden light of morn,
Like the sweetheart of the sun,
Who many a glowing kiss had won.

On her cheek an autumn flush
Deeply ripened; such a blush
In the midst of brown was born,—
Like red poppies grown with corn.

Round her eyes her tresses fell,
Which were blackest none could tell;
But long lashes veiled a light
That had else been all too bright;

And her hat with shady brim,
Made her tressy forehead dim:
Thus she stood amid the stooks
Praising God with sweetest looks.

Sure, I said, Heaven did not mean
Where I reap thou should'st but glean;
Lay thy sheaf adown, and come,
Share my harvest and my home.

—*Thomas Hood*

THE GLEANERS

I like to think of gentle Ruth
    As beautiful indeed—
The love of God within her heart,
    The Golden Rule her creed.

* Used by special permission of the author.

Her course was charted in a world
  So very strange and new . . .
But God was leading her alway—
  One of the chosen few.

Naomi begged her to return
  With Orpah . . . but she said . . .
"Entreat me not to leave thee,
  But go with you instead—

"Thy God shall be my God alway,
  Thy people shall be mine—"
And so to Bethlehem they went,
  This maiden so divine.

Perhaps she longed to see the land
  Her husband knew in youth . . .
But Naomi's heart was very glad
  For loving, trusting Ruth.

Now Boaz was a kinsman,
  A wealthy man and good . . .
So Ruth went forth into his field
  To glean her daily food.

And he was very pleased with her,
  As she gathered grain each day . . .
He showed her every kindness
  'Til the harvest was away.

Then for his wife he took her,
  And Obed was their son—
Thus, through David's generation,
  Christ's lineage was begun.

In one of the greatest dramas,
  With connecting, vital roles—
Ruth, the gleaner of barley and corn . . .
  And Christ, the gleaner of souls!*

                                       —*Ruth Ricklefs*

THE BETHLEHEM OF BOAZ

Bethlehem of David,
  Of Ruth and Boaz' love,
Sweetly still you shining live
  Their fertile fields above.

* Used by special permission of the author.

"House of Bread" eternal,
  You nourish stalwart men,
While mothers in their homes of stone
  Toil with the strength of ten.

Far more than rubies are they worth.
  They fear not rain or snow.
They spin and weave and toiling, pray,
  As worthily they go.

The earth has many gentle towns,
  But just one Bethlehem.
Forever down the centuries,
  It wears love's diadem.*

—*Madeleine S. Miller*

☩

GIDEON, A MAN WHO WAS UNAFRAID

Anonymous

And the angel of the Lord appeared unto him [Gideon], and said unto him, The Lord is with thee, thou mighty man of valour.—JUDGES 6:12

DURING the period of the Judges the Israelites forgot their God and began to worship idols. In their midst, however, was a young man who thought that it was silly to believe that a piece of painted wood could either help or harm a person. Yet in spite of the fact that God became angry with His people, they continued to put their faith in the idol. If their luck was good, they thanked the idol and burned incense or the leg of a goat before it. If misfortune befell them, they said the idol was angry with them and promised to do better.

As punishment for their idolatry, Jehovah allowed His people to fall into the hands of their enemy, the Midianites, who took possession of all the land and drove the Israelites to caves and dens in the mountainside. Their towns were captured, their homes burned and their fields and orchards robbed, so that there was little peace or safety for them anywhere.

For seven years things went from bad to worse, for in all the land there didn't seem to be even one man brave enough to lead the people against their foes. However, Jehovah took pity on his people, decided that they had had sufficient punishment and that the time had come to deliver them from their enemy.

One day the young man who thought it was silly to worship idols ventured out of his hiding place in the mountains and crept down to his father's farm to see how things there were getting along. He found that the wheat in the field was ripe. There wasn't an enemy in sight, so he decided that he would harvest some of the grain.

He found a small sickle and soon had cut down as many sheaves as he could

* Used by special permission of the author.

carry. He remembered an old wine press which stood behind some trees; so he carried the sheaves to that place and began to tramp upon them with his feet. All day long he carried on his work of cutting down the sheaves and tramping out the grain. That evening as he was about to put the grain into a sack, he looked toward his father's house, and there saw someone sitting in the shadow of a great oak tree.

He wondered who this man could be, but since he was not a Midianite he wasn't afraid. Just then the stranger came toward him and spoke, "The Lord has chosen thee to 'go in your might and to set your people free.'"

At first the young man tried to excuse himself, saying that he was neither worthy of such an honor nor capable of winning it. But the stranger repeated his command. Then the young man realized that he was talking to a messenger from God and that he must obey.

He went from cave to cave and from mountainside to mountainside calling upon the Israelite men to arm themselves and to follow him; and it wasn't long until he found himself at the head of an army of thirty-two thousand men. With these men he marched off to overwhelm the Midianites.

But all of these men were not needed, for Jehovah wished to prove to His people that what they needed was to rely upon Him and all would be well. So He spoke to Gideon, saying, "The people that are with thee are too many."

Just as the sun arose over the hills the young general blew his trumpet. His army arose at his call and followed him down into the valley. Gideon pointed to the army of the enemy which was encamped not far away and said: "The foes that you have come out to meet are many, and the battle will be a hard one. If any of you are afraid, I will give you leave to return to your homes." Twenty-two thousand men gladly seized this opportunity to leave the army and return to a place of safety.

Seeing that the army of the Israelites was still too large, Jehovah told the young general to lead his remaining men down to the river's edge, and to select as his army only those who "lapped the water with his tongue, as a dog lappeth." Among all that remaining army there were only three hundred who dipped water up with their hands, without bending the knee, and lapped it. With this small band young Gideon was to drive away the enemy, allowing the other soldiers to return to their homes.

The young general then led his three hundred men a little farther down the valley and waited there far into the night. When everything was still he roused his men, saying, "Now do as I bid you and we will be victorious." Then he put into the hand of each man a deep pitcher. Next he gave to each man a candle, told him to light it and place it in the pitcher. Then in the right hand of each man he placed a trumpet. The men were naturally puzzled and asked, "How shall we fight with these things?"

"Just follow me and do as I do," was the commander's reply. Then he divided the small company into three bands of one hundred men each. He told one band to go to the right, another to the left. The third he told to creep up to the center. This was achieved so quietly that not a sound was heard. They reached the camp of the enemy at midnight. Suddenly the young general dashed his pitcher against a stone, blew his trumpet and shouted, "The sword of the Lord and of Gideon is upon thee."

Every man of the three hundred did the same thing, and the lights of the three hundred candles shone forth in the darkness as the three hundred men rushed into the camp of the Midianites shouting, "The sword of the Lord and of Gideon is upon thee."

The enemy awoke; sprang up in alarm; and when they saw three hundred twinkling lights and heard the noise of three hundred blaring trumpet, they thought they were surrounded by a great army. Disorganized they fell in fear, making no effort to defend themselves or their possessions; and soon the entire army of the Midianites was in flight.

In their joy over their success, the Israelites wanted Gideon to become their king; but he refused, saying, "No, I will not be your king. The God of our fathers, He is your King."

✛

JOTHAM'S FABLE OF THE TREES

(Judges 9:6–21)

AND all the men of Shechem gathered together, and all the house of Millo, and went, and made Abimelech king, by the plain of the pillar that was in Shechem.

And when they told it to Jotham, he went and stood in the top of mount Gerizim, and lifted up his voice, and cried, and said unto them, "Hearken unto me, ye men of Shechem, that God may hearken unto you.

"The trees went forth on a time to anoint a king over them; and they said unto the olive tree, 'Reign thou over us.' But the olive tree said unto them, 'Should I leave my fatness, wherewith by me they honour God and man, and go to be promoted over the trees?'

"And the trees said to the fig tree, 'Come thou, and reign over us.' But the fig tree said unto them, 'Should I forsake my sweetness, and my good fruit, and go to be promoted over the trees?'

"Then said the trees unto the vine, 'Come thou, and reign over us.' And the vine said unto them, 'Should I leave my wine, which cheereth God and man, and go to be promoted over the trees?'

"Then said all the trees unto the bramble, 'Come thou, and reign over us.' And the bramble said unto the trees, 'If in truth ye anoint me king over you, then come and put your trust in my shadow: and if not, let fire come out of the bramble, and devour the cedars of Lebanon.'

"Now therefore, if ye have done truly and sincerely, in that ye have made Abimelech king, and if ye have dealt well with Jerubbaal and his house, and have done unto him according to the deserving of his hands (for my father fought for you, and adventured his life far, and delivered you out of the hand of Midian: and ye are risen up against my father's house this day, and have slain his sons, threescore and ten persons, upon one stone, and have made Abimelech, the son of his maid-servant, king over the men of Shechem, because he is your brother); if ye then have dealt truly and sincerely with Jerubbaal and with his house this day, then rejoice ye in Abimelech, and let him also rejoice in you. But if not, let fire come out from Abimelech, and devour the men of Shechem, and the house of Millo; and let fire come out from the men of Shechem, and from the house of Millo, and devour Abimelech."

And Jotham ran away, and fled, and went to Beer, and dwelt there, for fear of Abimelech his brother.

+

RUTH, THE MOABITESS

By

Cynthia Pearl Maus

THE Old Testament story of Ruth belongs to the period when the Judges ruled Israel and defended her from her enemies. This was before the people felt a need for a king to reign over them. In those days men of wisdom and judgment, known as Elders, ruled over the cities and tribes of Israel.

Ruth, the Moabitess, is unique not only among the women of Bible times, but also among the women of the world. Her claim to immortality rests not alone upon the unusual love of an alien daughter-in-law for her mother-in-law, but also upon her poetically expressed pledge of loyalty, "if aught but death part thee and me," to her lonely and bereft mother-in-law.

Naomi was a Hebrew woman from Bethlehem in the land of Judah. With her husband, Elimelech, and her two sons, Mahlon and Chilion, she had left Bethlehem during one of the prolonged famines which frequently occur in Canaan, and had gone to Moab, a land to the south and east of the Dead Sea between the river Arnon and the brook of Zereda, which land was under the control of an independent non-Jewish tribe.

Here the family of Elimelech found refuge, and here the two sons grew to young manhood and took for themselves brides from among the Moabitish women—two sisters, Ruth and Orpah. They were young, beautiful, and full of the vigor and ambition so characteristic of youth.

When Naomi went into the land of Moab she, according to her own words, "went out full." That is, she went out with a man's family, a husband, and two sons. There she found her own life increasingly fulfilled when her sons brought to her home as brides two lovely Moabitish girls. She welcomed these young wives into her household, and gave them her love and devotion and a place in her well-ordered and happy home.

Although we know little of Naomi, for the Book of Ruth which gives us this Old Testament story contains only four brief chapters, we know that she must have been a perfect wife and mother providing an unusually attractive home for these two young girls from a foreign tribe, who no doubt felt insecure in their marriage to men of another land and religion.

It is small wonder, therefore, that both Ruth and Orpah came to love Naomi devotedly and to share graciously with her the common daily household tasks necessary to the smooth running of a well-ordered home. And thus the three families —the father Elimelech and his wife, and the two sons and their Moabitish wives —lived happily and contentedly.

After a few years, however, Elimelech died. The story might have had a different ending if either of the two daughters-in-law had borne a child, but such was not the case. Some time later both the young men, Mahlon and Chilion, died also leaving the three widows alone in their grief and insecurity.

After the first fresh grief of their motherhood and wifehood was ended, Naomi, without making any effort to build around herself and her widowed daughters-in-law a new security for the years ahead, expressed her intention of returning to her own homeland in Judah, there to find whatever respite from her sorrows she might be able to secure in the homes of her kinsfolk, for news had come to her that "the Lord had visited his people in giving them bread."

When she announced this intention to Ruth and Orpah both of the young wives indicated their desire to accompany her, though she strove earnestly to dissuade them. When the day of departure arrived they even went a day's journey with her for they could not bear to see her take that long journey unaccompanied. Toward the end of the day, however, as they neared the border of Moab, Naomi said to them: "Go, return each to her mother's house: the Lord deal kindly with you, as ye have dealt with the dead, and with me." Then she kissed each of them and they lifted up their voices and wept.

After some persuasion Orpah turned her face homeward, but Ruth clung to her mother-in-law, giving voice to that poetic declaration of loyalty even unto death which has come ringing down to us through the centuries:

> Entreat me not to leave thee,
> or to return from following after thee;
> for whither thou goest, I will go;
> and where thou lodgest, I will lodge;
> thy people shall be my people,
> and thy God my God;
> where thou diest, will I die,
> and there will I be buried:
> The Lord do so to me, and more also,
> if aught but death part thee and me.

When Naomi saw that Ruth was determined to go with her, no matter what sorrow and hardship it might entail, she ceased trying to dissuade her, and the two women set their faces toward Bethlehem in the land of Judah from which Naomi and her husband and her sons had come some ten years before.

They came at last, after many days of tiresome travel, to Naomi's native city, and were welcomed with joy by friends, neighbors, and relatives in the Hebrew community from which Naomi's roots sprang. But Naomi could not forget the fullness she had known a decade or more ago when she with her husband and sons had left Bethlehem, and in her sorrow she said to them: "Call me not Naomi, call me Mara; for the Almighty hath dealt very bitterly with me. I went out full, and the Lord hath brought me home again empty."

It was at the beginning of the barley harvest when Naomi and her daughter-in-law reached Bethlehem, the season when women were welcomed as gleaners in the harvest fields. As soon as they were settled in the little house which had formerly belonged to her husband Elimelech, Naomi remembered that she had a near kinsman on her husband's side of the family, whose name was Boaz, and that he was a man of wealth in the community. She shared this information with Ruth, who immediately answered, "Let me now go to the field, and glean ears of corn after him in whose sight I shall find grace." And Naomi replied: "Go, my daughter."

The laws of the Hebrews were not blind to the hardships of women left in widowhood in a primitive society, and expressly indicated that "kinsmen" should take such widows under their protective care. Thus it was that when Boaz noticed this strange girl from an alien land among the gleaners following his servants—for her devotion to Naomi, his relative by marriage, had already come to his ears—he immediately took her under his protection inviting Ruth to share the meal which he provided for his harvesters, even telling the young men in his employ to drop down a handful of grain every now and then that Ruth's gleaning might be a rich one.

When Ruth returned home at the end of the day, she had not only an abundant supply of grain as her reward, but also the news that Boaz had been unusually kind and generous to her. This pleased Naomi mightily and she began to make plans whereby Boaz should see Ruth not in the garb of a gleaner, but properly robed and anointed in such a way as to attract him. She waited patiently until the barley harvest was fully gathered, and the night for the threshing out of the grain came. Then she advised Ruth to put on her finest raiment and to go down to the barn where Boaz was threshing, but not to reveal herself to him until the work was done and the owner with his helpers, tired and happy, had eaten and drunken, and laid themselves down to sleep on the harvest floor. Then she, Ruth, was to go and lie at the feet of Boaz until he awakened and told her what to do.

No doubt Ruth was a little bewildered by the strange customs of this land to which she had come as an alien; but she followed Naomi's instructions to the letter saying, "All that thou sayest unto me I will do."

So Ruth came to the barn and carried out Naomi's instructions in claiming kinship to Boaz the wealthy landowner. When Boaz awakened in the early dawn he was delighted to find this young, beautiful Moabitish girl who was his kinswoman, at his feet. He was flattered also that she had chosen to reveal her kinship to him, an older man, rather than to some of the younger harvesters nearer her own age. He sent her away in the early morning, before the other harvesters awoke, but not until he had filled her veil with six measures of barley. This gift indicated that he, Boaz, intended to see that the Levitical right of a kinsman with a widow should in this case be fulfilled.

Boaz knew that there was a nearer relative, who according to the Levitical law must be given the first offer of this young Moabitess as a wife. With the dawn of the new day he set about the task of finding out whether or not the nearer relative had any intention of exercising his right. He gathered a quorum of ten elders at the city gate and in their presence asked the nearer relative of Naomi whether or not he was prepared to redeem the piece of land which had belonged to Elimelech and his dead sons. This redemption carried with it the right to wed Ruth, the widow of one of the rightful claimants. The nearer kinsman was taken by surprise. He probably already had more land than he cared to be responsible for, and, in the presence of these city elders, he handed over to Boaz, the next nearest kinsman, all his rights in this matter, going about thereafter with an unlaced shoe to indicate his abdication of his rights and responsibilities in the redemption of Elimelech's inheritance.

So Boaz took Ruth and she became his wife, thus providing security not only for herself in the home of this wealthy villager, but also for her aging mother-in-law. In due time Ruth achieved the crown so prized by all Eastern women. She bore a son to Boaz which Naomi took and became nurse to.

The women that were her neighbors called this son Obed. He was the father of Jesse, who was the father of David. Thus Ruth in her marriage to Boaz achieved immortality in another way, for it was from the line of David that Joseph, the earthly father of Jesus, God's only begotten Son, came into the world.

✛

DON'T GOD'S CHILDREN HAVE A HARD TIME

(Interpretation)

MOST Negro spirituals, and especially the earlier ones, were built upon a form common to African folk songs, composed of leading lines and a response. James Weldon Johnson says:

"The American Negro went a step beyond his original African music in the development of melody and harmony; he also went a step beyond in the development of form. The lead and the response are still maintained, but the response is often developed into a true chorus. This is true of 'Go Down, Moses.' Here the congregation opens with the powerful theme of the chorus, singing in unison down to the last line which is harmonized. . . .

"It is not, however, as solo singing that we should think of Spirituals—it is rather as communal music, singing in harmony. The harmonization of the spirituals by the folk group in singing them is what distinguished them among the folk songs of the world. It is only natural that spirituals should be sung in harmony, for the Negro's musical soul expresses itself instinctively in the communal spirit and in rich and varied harmonies.

"Of the words of the spirituals not so much, of course, can be said as of the

music. Both the Negro bard and his fellow singers worked under mental limitations that handicapped them. Many of the lines of the spirituals are trite, and
there is monotonous repetition. But there is an appealing simplicity—and in some
of the spirituals real poetry, the naïve poetry of a primitive race."*

"Don't God's Children Have a Hard Time" is an excellent illustration of a
spiritual that starts with a chorus, followed by innumerable stanzas, each of which
is followed by repeating the chorus. Just as Ezekiel in ancient days had a hard
time, so "God's children" in bondage in a strange land, remote from their race
and native home, also "have a hard time." God through Noah provided an Ark
to save His people. Moses, His statesman, led the children of Israel out of their
bondage in Egypt. Joshua led the children of Israel over the Jordan after Moses
died. All of these ancient Bible characters had "a hard time." The American Negro felt a bond of sympathy between them and him, and this produced in his
heart the spiritual, "Don't God's Children Have a Hard Time." He sings out his
longing for freedom and guidance in his troublesome world. He hopes, too, that
all Negro slaves in the United States might be released from their bondage by
the same God who guided Joshua, Ezekiel, Noah, and Moses, as well as other
patriarchs of ancient Bible times.

✣

FAITH OF OUR FATHERS, LIVING STILL

(Interpretation)

"FAITH of Our Fathers, Living Still" was written in 1849 by Frederick William
Faber (1814-1863). It is one of the best-loved and most deservedly popular hymns
of the Church, and continues to challenge the faith, love, and loyalty of devoutly
religious people of all ages.

This hymn recalls such Scripture passages as these:

"Now faith is the substance of things hoped for, the evidence of things not
seen. . . . Through faith we understand that the worlds were framed by the word
of God, so that things which are seen were not made of things which do appear. . . .

"These all died in faith, not having received the promises, but having seen
them afar off, and were persuaded of them, and embraced them, and confessed
that they were strangers and pilgrims on the earth . . . wherefore God is not ashamed
to be called their God. . . .

"And what shall I more say? for the time would fail me to tell of Gideon, and
of Barak, and of Samson, and of Jephthae; of David also, and Samuel, and of the
prophets: who through faith subdued kingdoms, wrought righteousness, obtained
promises, stopped the mouths of lions, quenched the violence of fire, escaped the
edge of the sword, out of weakness were made strong, waxed valiant in fight,
turned to flight the armies of the aliens. . . .

"They were stoned, they were sawn asunder, were tempted, were slain with the
sword: they wandered about in sheepskins and goatskins; being destitute, afflicted,

* From *The Mentor*, Feb., 1929, p. 52. Used by special permission of the publisher.

Don't God's Children Have a Hard Time

God tole Ezekial go one day,
Don't God's children have a hard time?
Down in the valley where the dry bones lay,
Don't God's children have a hard time?
CHORUS

Don't God's Children Have a Hard Time?

The wind did blow, the bones did rise,
Don't God's children have a hard time?
None can't enter but the sanctified,
Don't God's children have a hard time?
    CHORUS

Jes stop right still and steady yourself,
Don't God's children have a hard time?
God's gwine ter move this Ark hisself,
Don't God's children have a hard time?
    CHORUS

Joshuay was qualified,
Don't God's children have a hard time?
He led the children atter Moses died,
Don't God's children have a hard time?
    CHORUS

You don't believe I been redeemed,
Don't God's children have a hard time?
Follow me down by Jorden stream,
Don't God's children have a hard time?
    CHORUS

I'm gwine to Heaven on Angel's wings,
Don't God's children have a hard time?
Them don't see me gwine to hear me sing,
Don't God's children have a hard time?
    CHORUS

Religion am like a bloomin' rose,
Don't God's children have a hard time?
None can't tell it but them that knows,
Don't God's children have a hard time?
    CHORUS

See them old folks in that day,
Don't God's children have a hard time?
Throwin' their walkin' canes away,
Don't God's children have a hard time?

tormented; they wandered in deserts, and in mountains, and in dens and caves of the earth" (Heb. 11:1, 3, 13, 16, 32-34, 37-38).

"Fight the good fight of faith, lay hold on eternal life" (I Tim. 6:12).

Throughout its five stanzas and refrain this hymn is a constant affirmation of a living faith in the God of the centuries. It recalls the dark days when Christian martyrs, "followers of the Way," knelt in the arena praying to the unseen God of their fathers before hungry lions rushed upon them.

Its author may have been thinking of his French Huguenot ancestors on that terrible St. Bartholomew's Day in 1572 when seventy thousand of them perished within a few brief hours because of their unflinching faith in the God of their fathers.

Each line of this great hymn has a timely and a timeless message to human hearts. The author, a follower of John Henry Newman, wrote the words after undergoing a severe mental and spiritual struggle which resulted in his joining the Roman Catholic Church.

The third stanza of this hymn, written for reading and singing by loyal Catholics, in its original form reads:

> Faith of our fathers! Mary's prayers
> Shall win our country back to Thee:
> And through the truth that comes from God
> England shall then indeed be free.

It was later altered for Protestant worship to read:

> Faith of our fathers, God's great power
> Shall win all nations unto thee;
> And, through the truth that comes from God,
> Mankind shall then indeed be free.

The climax of this hymn appears in the fourth stanza which emphasizes that the most effective preaching is that of millions of humble followers of God who, day after day, express their faith in and love for their Heavenly Father "by kindly words and virtuous life."

The tune "St. Catherine" is the work of two composers, Henri Frederic Hemy (1818-1888) and James George Walton (1821-1905). This double credit for arrangement is undoubtedly due to the appearance of Mr. Walton's melody for this hymn in Mr. Hemy's book, *Crown of Jesus Music,* published in 1864. Mr. Hemy was an English composer and organist, born at Newcastle upon Tyne.

✛

GOD MOVES IN A MYSTERIOUS WAY

(Interpretation)

WILLIAM COWPER was a man of unusual temperament, a poet with a vivid imagination, the gift of logic, and an infinite sensitiveness toward everything related to his native England. He was one of the great English lyric poets, and has won

Faith of Our Fathers, Living Still

ST. CATHERINE. 8, 8, 8, 8, 8, 8

FREDERICK W. FABER, 1849   HENRI F. HEMY and JAMES G. WALTON, 1874

1. Faith of our fa - thers, liv - ing still   In spite of dun - geon,
2. Our fa - thers, chained in pris - ons dark,   Were still in heart and
3. Faith of our fa - thers, God's great pow'r   Shall win all na - tions
4. Faith of our fa - thers, we will love   Both friend and foe in
5. Faith of our fa - thers, faith and pray'r   Have kept our coun - try

fire and sword,   O, how our hearts beat high with joy
con - science free,   And blest would be their chil - dren's fate,
un - to thee;   And, through the truth that comes from God,
all our strife,   And preach thee, too, as love knows how,
brave and free,   And through the truth that comes from God,

When - e'er we hear that glo - rious word! Faith of our fa - thers,
Though they, like them, should die for thee: Faith of our fa - thers,
Man - kind shall then in - deed be free: Faith of our fa - thers,
By kind - ly words and vir - tuous life: Faith of our fa - thers,
Her chil - dren have true lib - er - ty. Faith of our fa - thers,

ho - ly faith, We will be true to thee till death. A - men.

an unforgettable place in the hymnody of the Church for his hymns of lasting worth and popularity.

As William Cowper read and studied his Bible, and observed the life about him, he was impressed by what is often called "the providence of God." He wondered why some people suffer, while others, less worthy, often prosper. Out of such reflections he wrote this hymn. In a day when many were attempting to prove that the Eternal God was not interested in the minutiae of men's lives this hymn brought comfort and peace to many a sorrowful and distraught heart.

The poet's own life was not without its trials. His delicate nervous system was overcome by attacks of insanity, which, while not of lasting duration, nevertheless made him sensitive to his fellow men. His own deep and abiding faith in, and love for, his heavenly Father is beautifully expressed in the stanzas of this hymn.

And down through the years men and women have been cheered and stimulated to fresh courage and determination to rise above their vicissitudes, and to see behind life's misfortunes the hand of God working out the destinies of men.

God Moves in a Mysterious Way

DUNDEE. C.M.

WILLIAM COWPER, 1774   Scottish Psalter, 1615

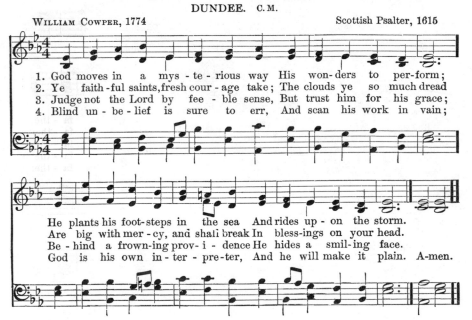

1. God moves in a mys - te - rious way His won - ders to per - form;
2. Ye faith - ful saints, fresh cour - age take; The clouds ye so much dread
3. Judge not the Lord by fee - ble sense, But trust him for his grace;
4. Blind un - be - lief is sure to err, And scan his work in vain;

He plants his foot-steps in the sea And rides up - on the storm.
Are big with mer - cy, and shall break In bless-ings on your head.
Be - hind a frown-ing prov - i - dence He hides a smil-ing face.
God is his own in - ter - pre - ter, And he will make it plain. A-men.

O LOVE OF GOD, HOW STRONG AND TRUE
(Interpretation)

THIS devotional hymn was written by Horatius Bonar (1808-1889). He has frequently been called "the prince of Scottish hymnists." He received his education in the high school and University of Edinburgh, and in 1838 was ordained as minister of the North Parish Church in Kelso. During this pastorate the "Disruption" of 1843 occurred which resulted in the organization of the Free Church of Scotland. Dr. Bonar's congregation went with the "Free Kirk" movement and for a time he edited a paper, *The Border Watch,* which promoted the ideals of the Free Church.

In the early years of his ministry his sermons were stern and unyielding; but his dogmatic theology mellowed as time went by. He remained with the Kelso "Free Kirk" for twenty-eight years, and then became pastor of a newly organized Chalmers Memorial Church in Edinburgh, his native city, remaining with this church until his death in 1881.

Dr. Bonar liked to sing, and his hymns depict his deep spiritual piety and yearning. "O Love of God, How Strong and True," written in 1861, reflects his sincere love for, and devotion to, the God he so unwaveringly served.

The first stanza emphasizes the boundless scope of God's love, "eternal and yet ever new," and beyond the knowledge and thought of men to comprehend. It is love that is given, not earned, for men are not worthy of it. The second stanza speaks of the all-embracing character of God's love to be observed in the starry skies above and in the richness of God's earth below. The third stanza tells of the healing comfort of God's all-enduring love for and to those who suffer in nights of pain and helplessness. The last stanza summarizes the eternal and abiding shield and stay which God's love provides for all those who trust in Him.

The tune "Duke Street" to which this hymn is sung was composed in 1793 by John Hatton. It is one of his most universally loved melodies, and was named for the street in St. Helens on which he lived. Mr. Hatton was born at Warrenton, near Liverpool, Scotland, and died in 1793 at St. Helens.

O Love of God, How Strong and True

Horatius Bonar, 1861 DUKE STREET John Hatton, 1793

1. O love of God, how strong and true,
   E - ter - nal and yet ev - er new,
   Un - com - pre - hend - ed and un - bought,
   Be - yond all knowl - edge and all thought.

2. O wide em - brac - ing, won - drous love!
   We read thee in the sky a - bove;
   We read thee in the earth be - low,
   In seas that swell and streams that flow.

3. O heaven - ly love, how pre - cious still,
   In days of wea - ri - ness and ill,
   In nights of pain and help - less - ness,
   To heal, to com - fort, and to bless!

4. O love of God, our shield and stay
   Thro' all the per - ils of our way,
   E - ter - nal love, in thee we rest,
   For - ev - er safe, for - ev - er blest. A - men.

* From *Services for the Open* arranged by Laura I. Mattoon and Helen D. Bragdon, No. 78. Copyright, 1923, by the Century Company. Used by special permission of Fleming H. Revell Company.

PART III

HIGH LIGHTS OF THE KINGDOMS OF SAUL, DAVID, AND SOLOMON

CONTENTS

PART III SECTION I

THE KINGDOM OF SAUL

✢

Then all the elders of Israel gathered themselves together, and came to Samuel . . . and said unto him . . . now make us a king to judge us like all the nations.—I SAMUEL 8:4-5

✢

267

SAMUEL ANOINTS SAUL TO BE KING

Hans Holbein the Younger

(Interpretation)

WHEN Samuel, one of Israel's greatest prophets, was an old man he appointed his two sons to succeed him as judges of the Israelites. However, these two young men "walked not in his ways, but turned aside after lucre [money], and took bribes, and perverted justice." Finally, their conduct brought its just reward, for the elders in Israel came to the aging Samuel in Ramah, saying: "Behold, thou art old, and thy sons walk not in thy ways: now make us a king to judge us like all the nations" (I Sam. 8:3, 5).

This demand for a king did not please Samuel; nevertheless, he took the matter to God in prayer, and He answered him thus: "Hearken unto the voice of the people in all that they say unto thee; for they have not rejected thee, but they have rejected me, that I should not reign over them" (8:7).

Then Samuel gathered the elders and the people together and told them the words which the Lord bade him speak in answer to their request for an earthly king to rule over them. But first he warned them of the evils this kingship would bring them, saying: "He will take your sons, and appoint them for himself, for his chariots, and to be his horsemen; and some shall run before his chariots. And he will appoint him captains over thousands, and captains over fifties; and will set them to ear his ground, and to reap his harvest, and to make his instruments of war, and instruments of his chariots. And he will take your daughters to be confectionaries, and to be cooks, and to be bakers. And he will take your fields, and your vineyards, and your oliveyards, even the best of them, and give them to his servants. And he will take the tenth of your seed, and of your vineyards, and give to his officers, and to his servants. And he will take your menservants, and your maidservants, and your goodliest young men, and your asses, and put them to his work. He will take the tenth of your sheep: and ye shall be his servants. And ye shall cry out in that day because of your king which ye shall have chosen you; and the Lord will not hear you in that day" (8:11-18).

But the people refused to listen to Samuel's words and persisted in demanding a king like the other nations round about them. So Samuel commanded every man to return to his own city and his own household. Then, following the counsel of the Lord, he went in search of a young man that he might anoint to be Israel's first earthly king.

God had revealed to Samuel that there was a young man of the tribe of Benjamin, whose name was Saul, the son of Kish, who was of goodly bearing, in stature standing head and shoulders above any of the other men of his tribe. This young man was, at that time, on a journey in search of his father's asses that had strayed away. The Lord indicated to Samuel that sooner or later this young man would visit him, seeking his aid in finding the lost asses; and that when he came Samuel was to anoint him as Israel's first king. For God had said to Samuel: "Tomorrow . . . I will send thee a man out of the land of Benjamin, and thou shalt anoint him to be captain over my people Israel" (9:16).

Thus on the "tomorrow" when young Saul appeared at Samuel's home in Ramah, the prophet knew this was the youth he should anoint. At first Saul remonstrated, saying: "Am not I a Benjamite, of the smallest of the tribes of Israel? and my family the least of all the families of the tribe of Benjamin? wherefore then speakest thou so to me?" (9:21).

Nevertheless, the young man, at Samuel's request, tarried with him for the night; and on the following morning Samuel accompanied his guest to the edge of the city and then said to him, "Bid the servant pass on before us (and he passed on), but stand thou still a while, that I may shew thee the word of God" (9:27).

Then Samuel took a vial of oil and poured it upon Saul's head as a sign of God's choice, and kissed him, saying: "Is it not because the Lord hath anointed thee to be captain over his inheritance?" (10:1).

After several days Samuel called the children of Israel together at Mizpah. He presented Saul, the son of Kish to them, saying: " 'See ye him whom the Lord hath chosen, that there is none like him among all the people?' And all the people shouted, . . . 'God save the king' " (10:24).

The incident of Samuel anointing young Saul to be king of Israel is the theme of this picture. In the background rise the hills of Judah while in the valley can be seen two houses of the city of Ramah. In the center is the figure of young Saul, tall even in this kneeling position. Before him stands the aged prophet wearing priestly robes, with a high priest's miter on his head. One hand is touching Saul's shoulder; the other pours the anointing oil on the young man's head. In order that we may not miss the high significance of this simple action, the artist has placed a crown on young Saul's head and put a scepter in his hands. These tokens of sovereignty mark this anointing as a consecration for kingship.

In the left background Saul's servant, who has been helping him search for the missing asses, turns to watch curiously, but uncomprehendingly, the scene in the foreground. He is so moved by it that he pays no attention to the infirm man who speaks querulously to him.

Hans Holbein the younger, who designed this woodcut for his series of Old Testament illustrations published in *Icones Historiarum Veteris Testamenti,* was born in 1497 at Augsburg. His father, Hans Holbein the elder, gave him his first lessons in drawing and painting. From 1528 to 1543 he made eighty-seven drawings and an equal number of portraits of important people of England. These are still preserved in Windsor Castle and indicate his popularity as a portrait painter. It has been said that his portraits at Windsor stamp him as one of the "greatest of all masters of portraiture." His drawings show delicacy and an unrivaled power and subtlety. His Bible illustrations were made about 1526 in Basle where he had a home. In 1543, while in London working on a picture of Henry VIII, he became sick with the plague and died. Examples of his work can be seen in the art galleries of Europe, England, and America and countless reproductions of his drawings and woodcuts have been made.

SAMUEL ANOINTS SAUL TO BE KING—HOLBEIN

YOUNG DAVID, THE SHEPHERD

By

Mme. Elizabeth Jane Bouguereau

(Interpretation)

RARELY is there to be found a person like David who possessed so many attributes of greatness. Not only did he become Israel's greatest king, but he was a man great in everything. He has been called "David, the Many-sided." He was a poet and a musician, a ferocious and resourceful fighter and a wise ruler with a real concern for his people. He was above all a man with a deeply religious nature; he was a man of repentance and a man of prayer.

At the outset of his life, during the reign of King Saul, David was a simple shepherd lad of Bethlehem. But even then he was beginning to show those qualities which later contributed to his greatness. His appearance was striking, for we read that "he was ruddy, and withal of a beautiful countenance, and goodly to look to" (I Sam. 16:12). He was a boy whom his father could trust to take care of the sheep and to protect them from robbers and from wild animals. Long before he met the enemies of Israel in battle he had learned to be a daring fighter. During the long hours while he guarded the sheep he developed his gift for music, singing songs of his own invention as he accompanied himself on the harp or lyre. Even as a boy there must have been some sign that he was to become a man of deep faith, for the prophet Samuel passed over David's seven older brothers and anointed him to be the future king of Israel.

George Matheson has written of him:

"Little David was, like little Israel, a pigmy among the giants; and the world said, 'He will never equal his brothers!' Yet little David had within that soul of his ambition, compared to which that of his brothers was a molehill. He, like his tiny country, had a dream of empire—that dream which had its beginning when Abraham heard his mission under the Chaldean stars. He, like Abraham, had received a prophetic voice, had felt the touch of an anointing hand. Ever, amid the bleating of the sheep, there had sounded in his ear a deep refrain, 'You will be king of Israel! you will be king of Israel!' He kept the dream in his heart, he told it not; but all the warmer did it burn because it could not be spoken. And though it could not be spoken, it could be sung; it made songs without words. It tuned the strings of his harp; it accompanied his music; it imparted to his notes a wild dash and daring which made them seem to strike the stars. He was unconscious of their power; he played spontaneously—played to relieve himself. But just on that account he was overheard; unconscious genius ever *is* overheard. Men stood and listened in the night to the great musician. They spread his fame. They spoke of a harp with chords inspired.

"And by and by the tidings reached the most august ear in all the land. They came to the royal palace; they were heard by Saul the King. . . . David is sent

YOUNG DAVID, THE SHEPHERD—*BOUGUEREAU*

for, and comes; and, as he comes, the Gallery repeats in him another of its past stages. He has already heard the call of *Abraham;* he is about to experience the call of Isaac. The call of Abraham was the summoning to a life of glory; the call of Isaac was the summoning to a life of domestic ministration. When David entered the house of Saul he abandoned, for the time, his *dream.* He laid aside his desire to rule; he tried to serve, to dig wells of comfort for the heart of another. And not without success. As he played, the malady of Saul subsided; the clouds parted, and a stream of sunshine burst upon his soul. If a pupil in a Sunday-school were asked, 'Who was the first man influenced by the Psalms of David?' he would not go very far wrong if he answered, 'Saul.' It is true, these melodies were songs without words; but they were not songs without thoughts. On the poor wandering soul of the monarch they had all the effect of a sweet and solemn prayer; they said, 'Peace! be still!' They were the *earliest* psalms of David—psalms of *unspoken* words, psalms of *undefined* comfort, psalms whose Divine message came only in music. When the critics have disposed of all the rest, they will leave to the minstrel these *first* chords."*

The youthful David, guarding his father's sheep in the rough hills and vales of Bethlehem, is beautifully portrayed in the picture, "Young David, the Shepherd," by Mme. Bouguereau. David has just killed a lion and rescued one of his father's young lambs from its murderous jaws. As he raises his hand to signal his victory in this unequal struggle, he looks toward the distant hills "from whence cometh my strength," and offers his thanks to God.

No one might have known of this dangerous encounter had not David himself told of it to Saul when he was trying to persuade the doubtful king that he was able to fight Goliath. "Thy servant kept his father's sheep, and there came a lion, and a bear, and took a lamb out of the flock: and I went out after him, and smote him, and delivered it out of his mouth; and when he arose against me, I caught him by his beard, and smote him, and slew him' (I Sam. 17:34, 35).

Mme. Bouguereau was an American girl, born in New Hampshire in 1851 and named Elizabeth Jane Gardner. From childhood she showed unusual talent, and in her young womanhood went to Paris to study art. There she met and later married her instructor, W. A. Bouguereau. She received a number of rewards including honorable mention in the Paris Salon in 1879, medals in the Paris Salon in 1887, and the bronze medal in the Paris exposition in 1889. She died in Paris in 1922.

---

* From *Representative Men of the Bible* by George Matheson, pp. 264-76. Published by Hodder & Stoughton, Ltd. Used by special permission of the publisher.

SAMUEL, THE MAKER OF KINGS

By

Saul Raskin

(Interpretation)

SAMUEL was one of the first of all the Hebrew prophets. The call of the Lord came to him in early childhood, as he served in the house of Eli, the Priest. Samuel was to live long, to do a great many things, and to suffer much. To him fell the difficult task of purifying public worship, of destroying the idolatry of his people, of judging the tribes of Israel, of humbling the pride of the Philistines, and of making and unmaking Israel's kings.

George Matheson has written: "There were three great functions in the Jewish nation whose simultaneous existence was contemporary with the life of Samuel—the Prophet, the Priest, and the King. . . . These three represent the three periods in the conception of time—yesterday, today and tomorrow. The Priest is the representative of the past . . . his sacrifices are efforts to wash man's sins away. The King represents the present. He exists to guide the hand at the actual hour, to give the law which shall regulate the immediate course of action. But the Prophet is the representative of the future. He exists to tell, not merely of forthcoming events, but of eternal principles. It is his mission to reveal the issues of right and wrong —to proclaim how, by an inevitable law, the one will bring joy and the other pain."*

It is this threefold function of Prophet, Priest, and King that Saul Raskin, perhaps the greatest contemporary Jewish artist has portrayed in his etching, "Samuel, the Maker of Kings."

In his old age Samuel heeded the demand of the children of Israel for a king and when the Lord indicated that His choice fell on Saul son of Kish, Samuel anointed him to be Israel's first king. But Saul would not hearken to the voice of the Lord. Instead he followed his own wishes and desires, and in the end God rejected him, saying to Samuel: "How long wilt thou mourn for Saul, seeing I have rejected him from reigning over Israel? Fill thine horn with oil, and go, I will send thee to Jesse the Bethlehemite: for I have provided me a king among his sons" (I Sam. 16:1).

When David was brought to Samuel, the aged prophet "took the horn of oil, and anointed him in the midst of his brethren. And the spirit of the Lord came upon David from that day forward" (I Sam. 16:13).

At the right of this etching by Saul Raskin stands the shepherd boy David. Behind him the sun rising over the Judean hills symbolized the glory of this king that is to be. David is in the midst of his flock and carries his harp in his hands.

---

* From *Representative Men of the Bible* by George Matheson, pp. 257-58. Published by Hodder & Stoughton, Ltd. Used by special permission of the publisher.

On his face there is an expression of awe as he realizes that he has been chosen by the Lord to be the future king of Israel.

In the background King Saul broods in shadows that are as dark as his own thoughts. His calculating, secretive, cruel expression is the outward manifestation of his character. He is a self-willed man who brooks no opposition from anyone, even from Samuel or from the Lord. He is a powerfully built man and in his hand there is a spear symbolizing the warlike nature of his achievements. In contrast to David's motion forward into the center of the picture, Saul's gaze and pose are both directed away from the center. Though Saul still wears the crown of Israel, Samuel has turned his back upon him and God has rejected him from being king.

Towering between the dark past and the king of the bright future stands Samuel the prophet and the maker of kings. He holds aloft the jar from which he pours the oil of anointing. This is the sign and seal of the divine choice. There is high seriousness in Samuel's expression as he performs his prophetic function. There is also a sternness that bodes ill for all who oppose God's will. He is an old man, but there is no frailty in him. The immense power of his frame and the lively motion of his garments denote one endowed with more than human strength. He was austere, uncompromising, persevering. He subordinated his selfish wishes to a burning desire for the welfare of Israel. When he died "all Israel had lamented him," for they knew that he was one of their chief men of God.

✛

DAVID PLAYING ON HIS HARP BEFORE SAUL

By

Ernest Normand

(Interpretation)

THE English artist, Ernest Normand, lived in Norwood, England, and began exhibiting in the Royal Academy in London in 1881. His works consist chiefly of Biblical pictures, genre, and portraits. His painting of "David Playing on His Harp before Saul" portrays a significant moment in the lives of two of Israel's kings.

Saul, wearing a kingly robe, sits on his throne. The sword at his belt is in its sheath. He is a king who has gained and kept his power by leading his people in battle against their foes. Now he is at war with himself. He knows that he has been both a wicked and a disobedient king. He has failed to do as God commanded him through Samuel the prophet. Instead he has gone his own willful way, vindictive when anyone thwarted his self-will.

One day Samuel came to Saul and said to him: "Because thou hast rejected the word of the Lord, he hath also rejected thee from being king" (I Sam. 15:23). And Samuel left the presence of the king, never to see him again.

The knowledge that God had rejected him filled Saul with dark thoughts and fear. And men knew that "the spirit of the Lord departed from Saul." He became subject to periods of depression and his servants said to him:

SAMUEL, THE MAKER OF KINGS—*RASKIN*

"Behold now, an evil spirit from God troubleth thee."

They suggested that a skillful player on the harp be found and brought to court that he might play music and so cure the king of his melancholy moods. Saul agreed to this and David was recommended to him as one "that is cunning in playing, and a mighty valiant man, and a man of war, and prudent in matters, and a comely person, and the Lord is with him" (16:18).

David, the shepherd boy, came from Bethlehem and stood before the king and Saul loved him. He sent a message to David's father, Jesse, requesting that the boy remain with Saul. "And it came to pass, when the evil spirit from God was upon Saul, that David took an harp, and played with his hand. So Saul was refreshed, and was well, and the evil spirit departed from him" (16:23).

In this picture the unhappy, troubled king leans forward and, grasping David's auburn hair, turns his face upward. Saul gazes intently, but with affection into the eyes of the lad whose music soothes him and whose charming nature has won his love. He seems to be trying to understand why this young shepherd at his feet is filled with serenity and joy while he, the king, sitting on his carved and elaborately inlaid chair, is so troubled. David looks up at him with undisguised loyalty which, in spite of all that later came between the two men, remained with David and led him to lament at Saul's death:

> Saul and Jonathan were lovely and pleasant in their lives,
> And in their death they were not divided.
> They were swifter than eagles;
> They were stronger than lions . . .
> How are the mighty fallen!   [II Sam. 1:23, 27]

✛

DAVID AND GOLIATH

By

J. F. Repin

(Interpretation)

THE German artist, J. F. Repin, has portrayed a tense moment in the fight between David and Goliath. The Philistines had advanced with their army against Israel. Saul and the men of Israel had taken to the field and were drawn up in battle array facing the Philistines, with only a valley separating the two armies. Out from the Philistine ranks came the giant Goliath shouting his taunt:

"I defy the armies of Israel this day. Give me a man, that we may fight together." (I Sam. 17:10).

But in Saul's army there was no man strong enough to pit his strength against the giant. Saul and all Israel were dismayed and greatly afraid.

When Saul and his army went out to meet the Philistines, David had doubtless returned to his home in Bethlehem, but three of his brothers were serving in the

DAVID PLAYING ON HIS HARP BEFORE SAUL—*NORMAND*

army. Their father sent David to them with provisions. David arrived at the Israel-
ite camp and heard Goliath's taunt ring across the valley. He said to Saul:
"Let no man's heart fail because of him. Thy servant will go and fight with this
Philistine" (17:32).

Saul finally assented to this apparently foolhardy plan. Instead of putting on the
king's own armor which was offered to him, David took merely his shepherd's
staff, his sling, and his bag containing five smooth stones.

Seeing the unarmed youth coming out to meet him, Goliath shouted his contemptuous scorn across the valley: "Come to me, and I will give thy flesh unto
the fowls of the air, and to the beasts of the field" (17:44).

David replied confidently: "Thou comest to me with a sword, and with a spear,
and with a shield. But I come to thee in the name of the Lord of hosts, the God
of the armies of Israel. . . . This day will the Lord deliver thee into mine hand . . .
that all the earth may know that there is a God in Israel" (vv. 45, 46).

Then David added for the army of Israel to hear: "and all this assembly shall
know that the Lord saveth not with sword and spear; for the battle is the Lord's"
(vs. 47).

This is the moment portrayed in the painting of "David and Goliath."

In the background is the desolate and empty valley separating the two armies.
The heavily armed giant Goliath taunts the young shepherd from the hills who
dares to come out, unarmed, to fight him. Near the giant stands his midget armor-
bearer holding an additional staff and sword which is so much too large for him
that its point touches the ground. He gazes in extravagant admiration at the boastful champion of the armies of the Philistines.

In the presence of his gigantic and heavily armed adversary young David looks
indeed an undefended victim. But there is splendid defiance in his pose. His upraised finger points to the skies signifying that it is the Lord in whom he puts
his trust in this unequal struggle. Over his shoulders is his shepherd's bag usually
filled with the daily provisions needed to care for one's flock but now filled with
five smooth, deadly stones. From his belt hangs his slingshot and a short knife
both of which he has often used against marauding beasts from the hills which
threatened his flocks. In his hand is his shepherd's staff. Armed thus with his
meager shepherd equipment he steps forward to accept the giant's challenge, shouting his confidence in victory for the battle is the Lord's.

The outcome of the contest between David and Goliath is too well known to
need recounting. The entire story, from which J. F. Repin chose one dramatic
moment, is told in I Samuel 17, perhaps one of the supreme narratives in the Old
Testament.

✛

HANNAH, SEWING

I like to think of Hannah at her window,
Stitching the little coat she was to take

DAVID AND GOLIATH—*REPIN*

To the small child Samuel housed within the temple,
And the yearly pilgrimage she was to make
Drawing near, until her preparations
Were all but ready, save this one small thing:
The little coat she made for her Beloved,
To bless and cheer him with its comforting.

Seam by tiny seam she did her stitching,
But often through her tears her eyes were dim.
For though she bravely kept her sacred promise
To give him up, she could but long for him.
Motherlike she yearned to hold her baby,
Close to her heart—to tuck him into bed—
She reached her arms across the miles to fold him,
Then knew the coat must warm her child, instead.*

—*Grace Noll Crowell*

A HOLY GOD TO BE WORSHIPPED WITH REVERENCE

(Psalm 99:5-9)

Exalt the Lord our God,
And worship at his feet;
His nature is all holiness,
And mercy is his seat.

When Israel was his church,
When Aaron was his priest,—
When Moses cried, when Samuel prayed,—
He gave his people rest.

Oft he forgave their sins,
Nor would destroy their race;
And oft he made his vengeance known,
When they abused his grace.

Exalt the Lord our God,
Whose grace is still the same;
Still he's a God of holiness,
And jealous for his name.

—*Isaac Watts*

* Used by special permission of the author.

A MEDITATION AND PRAYER

(Psalm 90:1-12*)

Sometimes entitled "The dirge of a world"

Lord, thou hast been our dwelling-place
In all generations.
Before the mountains were brought forth,
Or ever thou hadst formed the earth and the world,
Even from everlasting to everlasting thou art God.

Thou turnest man back to dust,
And sayest, Return, ye children of men.
For a thousand years in Thy sight
Are but as yesterday when it is past.
As a watch in the night thou dost flood them** away.

In the morning they are like grass which groweth up.
In the evening it is cut down and withereth.
For we are consumed in Thine anger, and in Thy wrath
   are we troubled.
Thou hast set our iniquities before thee,
Our secret sins in the light of Thy countenance.

For all our days do decline;
In Thy wrath we bring our years to an end;
As a sigh are the days of our years,
And their breadth is travail and trouble,
For it is soon gone and we fly away.

Who knoweth the power of thine anger,
Or can number the awful deeds of thy wrath!
So teach us to number our days,
That we may get a mind of wisdom.
Return, O Lord, how long!

Be sorry for Thy servants,
O satisfy us in the morning with Thy kindness,
That we may rejoice and be glad all our days.
Make us glad according to the days Thou hast afflicted us,
And the years wherein we have seen evil.

Let Thy work appear unto Thy servants,
And Thy glory unto their children.
And let the beauty of the Lord our God be upon us;
And establish Thou the work of our hands upon us;
Yea, the work of our hands establish Thou it.

* This is the translation of the Authorized Version with a few changes suggested in the *International Critical Commentary*.
**I.e., the years.

THE CONQUEROR'S SONG

(Psalm 18)

To thine almighty arm we owe
The triumphs of the day;
Thy terrors, Lord, confound the foe,
And melt their strength away.

'Tis by thy aid our troops prevail,
And break united powers;
Or burn their boasted fleets, or scale
The proudest of their towers.

How have we chased them through the field,
And trod them to the ground;
While thy salvation was our shield,
But they no shelter found!

In vain to idol saints they cry,
And perish in their blood:
Where is a rock so great, so high,
So powerful, as our God?

The Rock of Israel ever lives,
His name be ever blest;
'Tis his own arm the victory gives,
And gives his people rest.

On kings that reign as *David* did,
He pours his blessings down;
Secures their honours to their seed,
And well supports their crown.

—Isaac Watts

DAVID, THE YOUTH

A slim boy out in the windy weather,
Tending his father's wandering sheep,
Is a picture the world will ever remember:
A picture to hold and to keep.

A clean lad plucking his golden harp strings
Has added to music a wealth unpriced:
Music that dripped from the sensitive fingers
Of this young kinsman of Christ.

A slender Youth with the eyes of a dreamer,
Sharing the wind's wild rhythm and rhyme—
Has given to men the cleanest and finest
Poetry of all time.

O great musician, and flame-hearted poet,
Channel for color and light and song,
Little you knew that your work would out-last you,
Song, so very long.*

—*Grace Noll Crowell*

GOD IS HERE

In the church where John Wesley preached his first sermon are to be found these words, engraved on the floor:

Enter this door
As if the floor
Within were gold
And every wall
Of jewels, all
Of wealth untold;
As if a choir
In robes of fire
Were singing here
Nor shout, nor rush
  But hush—
For God is here.**

—*Author Unknown*

MEN OF ISRAEL

How bravely toiled, they, men of old,
    To build one Canaan town,
Where dates and palms and olives grow
    And vines the farm-lands crown.

From Joshua to Gideon
    And David's wiser son,
From good Uzziah, Asa, too,
    The worthy men did run.

Keen Hezekiah tunnelled rock
    For waters' safer flow,
And Nehemiah patched the walls
    Chaldeans had laid low.

* Used by special permission of the author.
** From "The Meetinghouse," a local church bulletin.

But all unlike his kinsmen, he,
   In country Nazareth reared,
Who heard Jerusalem's learned tell
   Of God whose laws they feared.

For through his veins the ancient blood
   Was flowing, young as dew.
He knew the God men talked about,
   He bridged the old and new.*

—*Madeleine S. Miller*

ONLY ONE WAY

However the battle is ended,
   Though proudly the victor comes,
With fluttering flags and prancing nags
   And echoing roll of drums,
Still truth proclaims this motto,
   In letters of living light:
No question is ever settled
   Until it is settled right.

Though the heel of the strong oppressor
   May grind the weak in the dust,
And the voices of fame with one acclaim
   May call him great and just,
Let those who applaud take warning,
   And keep this motto in sight:
No question is ever settled
   Until it is settled right.

Let those who have failed take courage;
   Though the enemy seemed to have won,
Though his ranks are strong, if in the wrong
   The battle is not yet done.
For, sure as the morning follows
   The darkest hour of the night,
No question is ever settled
   Until it is settled right.

—*Author Unknown*

* Used by special permission of the author.

THE ONE HUNDRED AND FOURTEENTH PSALM

(In Antistrophic Inversion form)

Strophe 1

When Israel went forth out of Egypt,
The house of Jacob from a people of strange language;
Judah became his sanctuary,
Israel his dominion.

Strophe 2

The sea saw it and fled;
Jordan was driven back.
The mountains skipped like rams,
The little hills like young sheep.

Antistrophe 2

What aileth thee, O thou sea, that thou fleest?
Thou Jordan, that thou turnest back?
Ye mountains, that ye skip like rams?
Ye little hills, like young sheep?

Antistrophe 1

Tremble, thou earth, at the presence of the Lord,
At the presence of the God of Jacob;
Which turn the rock into a pool of water,
The flint into a fountain of waters!*

PSALMIST

David's harp, once plucked for Saul,
Has long been still;
The centuries drift deep on courts
His strings could fill
With magic. Yet while music lives
And song is part
Of love and tears, his hand shall heal
The human heart.**

—Leslie Savage Clark

* From *The Literary Study of the Bible* by Richard G. Moulton, p. 55. Published by D. C. Heath & Company.
Used by special permission of the publisher.
** From *The Catholic World*, Nov., 1948. Used by special permission of the author and the publisher.

SAFETY IN GOD

(Psalm 61:1-6)

When overwhelmed with grief,
My heart within me dies;
Helpless and far from all relief,
To heaven I lift mine eyes.

O lead me to the Rock,
That's high above my head;
And make the covert of thy wings
My shelter and my shade.

Within thy presence, Lord,
Forever I'll abide;
Thou art the tower of my defence,
The refuge where I hide.

Thou givest me the lot
Of those that fear thy name;
If endless life be their reward,
I shall possess the same.

—*Isaac Watts*

THE TWENTIETH PSALM

(Dominated Strophic Form)

Strophe 1—The People

The Lord answer thee in the day of trouble;
The name of the God of Jacob set thee up on high;
Send thee help from the sanctuary,
And strengthen thee out of Zion;
Remember all thy offerings,
And accept thy burnt sacrifice;
Grant thee thy heart's desire,
And fulfil all thy counsel.
We will triumph in thy salvation,
And in the name of our God we will set up our banners:
The Lord fulfil all thy petitions.

Strophe 2—The King

Now know I that the Lord saveth his anointed;
He will answer him from his holy heaven
With the saving strength of his right hand.

Strophe 3—The People

Some trust in chariots, and some in horses:
But we will make mention of the name of the Lord our God.
They are bowed down and fallen:
But we are risen, and stand upright.
O Lord, save the king;
And answer us when we call.*

THE AGONY OF GOD

I listen to the agony of God—
   I who am fed,
   Who never yet went hungry for a day.
   I see the dead—
   The children starved for lack of bread—
   I see, and try to pray.

I listen to the agony of God—
   I who am warm,
   Who never yet have lacked a sheltering home.
   In dull alarm
   The dispossessed of hut and farm
   Aimless and "transient" roam.

I listen to the agony of God—
   I who am strong,
   With health, and love, and laughter in my soul.
   I see a throng
   Of stunted children reared in wrong,
   And wish to make them whole.

I listen to the agony of God—
   But know full well
   That not until I share their bitter cry—
   Earth's pain and hell—
   Can God within my spirit dwell
   To bring His Kingdom nigh.**

—*Georgia Harkness*

SONG OF TRIUMPH

Prepare! your festal rites prepare!
Let your triumphs rend the air!

Idol gods shall reign no more:
We the living Lord adore!
Let heathen hosts on human helps repose,
Since Israel's God has routed Israel's foes.

Let remotest nations know
Proud Goliath's overthrow.
Fallen, Philistia, is thy trust;
Dagon mingles with the dust!
Who fears the Lord of glory, need not fear
The brazen armor or the lifted spear.

See, the routed squadrons fly!
Hark! their clamors rend the sky!
Blood and carnage stain the field!
See, the vanquished nations yield!
Dismay and terror fill the frightened land,
While conquering David routs the trembling
    band.

Lo, upon the tented field
Royal Saul has thousands killed!
Lo, upon the ensanguined plain
David has ten thousand slain!
Let mighty Saul! his vanquished thousands tell,
While tenfold triumphs David's victories swell!

—*Hannah More*

✝

SAMUEL THE SEER

By

George Matheson

IN the days when the High Priest Eli was Judge of Israel, there appeared in the sanctuary of Shiloh a wonderful child; his name was Samuel. It was a dark and stormy time; there were fears within and fightings without. Israel was climbing a steep hill—arduously, painfully. Her progress was slow; she was alternately worsted and victorious—to-day left in the valley, to-morrow gaining a height. And the struggle was more arduous from the fact that there was no prophecy. It was an age of materialism. The hands of Moses were no longer uplifted on the mountain; the eyes of Moses no longer gazed on a promised glory. Religion had become a form; its *spirit* had fled. There were few remains left of that heroic time when Joshua had fought for God, and Deborah had sung for God. The nation had lost its poetry, and had lost its faith. These had to be recreated, kindled anew at the lamp of heaven. Where was the new kindling to begin? Where was the Divine Spirit to touch the world once more? In the heart of the sage? No. In the breast of the old man? No. In the leaders of the Jewish armies? No. It was to begin in the soul of a little child. Out of the mouth of a babe in knowledge, God was to ordain strength. All Israel was startled by the tidings that there had appeared a prophetic *child*. From Dan to Beersheba there ran a thrill of wonder. Israel had been asking when the next Moses would appear. Here he came—in the garb of a tiny boy! Men were speechless with surprise. It was a surprise that was never to be equalled until that day when Christ was to put a little child in the centre of the apostolic band.

Was he a miracle—this little Samuel? No—in the view characteristic of the Bible he is the real and normal aspect of humanity. So normal is he that Christ says we must all return to his state before we can become seers. . . . The true seer must ever be a child, that, however grown-up he be, it is by the survival of his childhood that he sees the kingdom of God! Little Samuel is *no* miracle. He reveals the normal law of faith. He is the first of the prophets because he is the first of inspired children. He is a representative *man* in religion because he is a representative child. All seers of God's kingdom have seen it by the light of their childhood. We do not drop our childhood when we become men; we carry it with us *into* the life of men. Every sage bears within his bosom a little Samuel— an instinctive child-life which concludes without reasoning, adores without arguments, worships without symbols, prays without words. The man who listens to *this* voice is a prophet of the Kingdom.

There are two things about Samuel's illumination which are very prominent in the Picture, and which seem to me to be typical of religious illumination in general. Let us glance at each of them as they are exhibited in the Great Gallery.

The first is that the call of Samuel does not come to him as a call from heaven, but as a voice from earth. This is all the more remarkable in the light of the fact that from the very outset Samuel was placed in a religious environment. His parents wished him to be a *pious* child. From the dawn of his intelligence they consigned him to the care of the High Priest Eli, in whose house he became a servant. His employment was in the things of the sanctuary. He ministered in the temple of Shiloh. What he did, we do not exactly know. Of course, it must have been work external to the actual service of the sanctuary; yet he wore a little ephod to mark the fact that he was engaged in temple duty. In any case, he was breathing every moment the atmosphere of the house of God and using every day the symbols of things Divine. We expect it will be in the discharge of these duties that his illumination will come. No. It is when the work of the day is done, when the little priest has retired to rest, that the message from heaven greets him. And it does not greet him *as* a message from heaven. A voice cries "Samuel!"—he never dreams it is any other voice than that of Eli. He rises from his couch to get his orders from *human* lips; "I did not call you," says his master. He lies down again; and again a voice cries, "Samuel!" A second time he deems it to be only human; a second time he is told there has been no human call. Once more he seeks his rest, and once more the voice cries "Samuel!" Even then he believes it to be human; even then he deems it a summons from earthly lips. The voice of God has assumed the accents of a man.

Now, in this feature of the Portrait the artist has recorded not an abnormal, but a universal symptom of the religious life. Our deepest impressions of spiritual things come to us indirectly. It is not by a voice from *heaven* that a man believes himself to be in the presence of God; it is by the blending of *earthly* voices. When two or three circumstances, distinctly different in origin and emanating from different points of the compass, appear to converge towards one definite result, we are constrained to say, "This is the will of God." How does a man get inspired with the belief that God has a mission for him? By imagining he hears voices from the sky? Very rarely has it been *thus*. In the large majority of cases the sense of a Divine mission has come from observing how independent events have conspired in place and time to further an individual destiny. An Egyptian princess happens to be passing when a child is floating on the Nile river; that child in after years will probably feel that his life was preserved for *something*. A band of Ishmaelites is on its journey at the very spot and hour in which a boy is about to experience violence; that boy in days to come will claim a special destiny. A ram is caught by the horns in a thicket at the very moment when a man is debating within himself what would be the most suitable burnt offering; that ram will assuredly be accepted as the object of sacrifice preferred by heaven.

There is a remarkable passage in the Jewish Scriptures, "Ye shall hear a voice *behind* you," saying, 'This is the way; walk ye in it!' " I believe that to the Jew the voice of God *ever* came from behind—from the region of past experience. He followed because he felt he had been already led—led by a stream of tendencies over which he had no control, and whose united currents had been produced by a connection he could not understand. He heard the Divine because he had first heard the human. The voice of God came to him as the voice of Eli—as the voice of *earthly* influences. It was in looking back that he saw their sacred character. It was in *retrospect* that he recognized the presence of the Spirit of God beneath those seemingly mechanical movements which had shaped his worldly way.

But there is a second feature in this call of Samuel which is worthy of our attention. From the moment in which he recognized the real origin of the message, he perceived it to be something which would disturb the calm of his life. It brought not peace, but a sword. What *was* this message which young Samuel received? It was the command to denounce the wickedness of the house of Eli. I do not suppose that he then heard of this wickedness for the first time; doubtless there had already rung in his ears many human complaints. But now for the first time it was borne in upon him that these human complaints were the voice of *God*. His conscience told him that, if he were a true minister at the Divine altar, it was incumbent on him to bring before the High Priest Eli the iniquity of his own family. When conscience spoke, Samuel resolved to obey; but consider what that resolve meant to him! To obey it, was to endanger all his worldly interests. It was likely to procure his dismissal from the service of the High Priest; and to be dismissed from the service of a High Priest would be, in the opinion of the Jewish race, to contract an indelible stain. The choice before Samuel was the choice between the rose and the thistle. On the one side was comfort for the present and an open door to the future; on the other there was a probable expulsion into the cold world and a shutting of all the gates which led to promotion.

Now, although the case of Samuel is an accentuated one, the call of duty is nearly always a call to struggle. The very idea of duty implies restraint or *constraint*. Duty is the middle term between compulsion and love; it is halfway between Egypt and Canaan; it is the desert. Outward force has passed, but spontaneity has not yet come. I move voluntarily; but I move with a burden, and I move slowly. I have met my angel, but I *struggle* with my angel; I have seen God face to face, but I halt upon my thigh. Our moments of duty are never unconscious moments, never light-hearted moments. They have always a sense of pressure, always an obstruction at the door. The life of Samuel is, from the dawn, a life of sacrifice. The path on which his childhood went forth was a path of thorns; and he took it knowing it to be so. All who have followed his steps have had to tread the same narrow way. In all ages Herod has sought the young child to kill it. The Divine life has always run counter to a worldly principle, and has required to make its way in conflict with that principle. The road of individual pleasure is not parallel with the road of virtue. They will diverge with you as they diverged with Samuel—at the very point where duty calls. The hour of his spiritual promotion was precisely that hour which presaged his material degradation. The experience of the first prophet will be the experience of all Christian seers.

I have confined myself to the opening of Samuel's life, because it is in the opening of his life that he is universally representative. He was to live long, to do much, to suffer many things. He was to purify public worship, to root out idolatry, to judge the tribes of Israel, to humble the pride of the Philistine, to be the maker and the unmaker of kings. The sense of his presence in the nation was to be so vivid that it was to outlast even his life, for, after he had passed away, men were to believe in the apparition of his spectre. But these things belong to the annals of Judaism, not to the annals of humanity. What belongs to humanity is the fact that the spirit of prophecy came to him through the spirit of a little child. This is the one abiding element in the life of Samuel. It is the one element which is not connected with Shiloh, with Ramah, with Gilgal, with any local haunt whatever, but which is found in every place and at every time. The name of Samuel is traditionally associated with the establishing of the prophetic school; and his spirit of prophecy came to him in *childhood*. That is the fact of permanent interest in this delineation of the Great Gallery; for it is still through the intuitions of child life that Man sees the kingdom of God.*

* Abridged from *Representative Men of the Bible* (First Series) by George Matheson, pp. 245-57. Published by Hodder & Stoughton, Ltd. Used by special permission of the publisher.

ISRAEL CHOOSES A KING

By

Florence M. Earlle

SAUL, the son of Kish, sat under a fig tree. It was very early in the morning; so early that few of the servants were stirring. Saul had risen early because he wanted to think about the wonderful thing that was soon to happen to his people. At last they were to have a king like other nations. A king who would lead them into battle, and to whom they could pay homage as other peoples did. No more would they have to confess when questioned about their ruler that they had none; that God was their leader. Of course the other nations had gods, too, but they could be seen. Sometimes they were even taken into battle by their kings; but the king was the actual ruler.

And who should be king? Those who had attended the meeting reported that the old prophet, Samuel, had not said. He wept instead and begged the people to listen to him. "A king will take the best lands for himself," Samuel had said. "He will take a goodly part of your crops. He will take your young men and your young women to serve in his court. And you will pay taxes far beyond what you pay into the Lord's tabernacle. The time will come when you will regret your decision to have a king. You are really rejecting God himself."

But the people had only cried louder, "Nay, we will have a king!"

So, at last, Samuel had sent them home, after setting a day when they should come together at Mizpah.

Saul wondered to himself, Who would be chosen king? He would be from among the young men, he was sure. That might mean anyone, for the choice would be by lot. "But the lot would never fall on me," thought Saul. "I am not so fortunate as that. But wait: would it be fortunate to be a king? To be envied by others; never to know who was really your friend; to have to carry such heavy responsibilities; to lead in battle and to be blamed if the victory was not theirs? No, I think I would not like to be chosen king. I shall stay at home and tend the asses that day, and let the servants go."

Saul looked up to see his father standing before him.

"My son, the asses have not been found, although I have sent Reuben and Asher to the east and to the west. Come now, take one of the servants with you and go hunt for them. They are too valuable to let escape."

So Saul took old Benoi and they started. They hunted first over Mount Ephraim, then in the land of Shalisha; then in the land of Shalim, and the land of Benjamin; but they found no trace of the missing animals. At last Saul said to Benoi, "Let's go home. My father will stop worrying about the asses and begin to worry about us if we do not return soon."

But the servant said, "We are only a little way from the city where the man of God lives a part of the time. Whatever he says surely comes to pass. Let us go and ask him where the asses are."

"But," objected Saul, "we have no present for him. We cannot ask a favor and give him nothing. We have eaten all our bread, and I have no money or anything else to give him."

"I have a little money," said Benoi. "It isn't much, but enough."

As they went up the hill into the city, they met some girls going to the well for water.

"Is the man of God in the city today?" asked Saul.

"He has just come," answered the girls. "If you hurry, you can catch up with him. This is a feast day and he will bless the sacrifices for the people before they eat."

When they came to the gate, they saw an old man, and Saul said, "Can you tell us where the man of God lives?"

"I am he," said Samuel. "I am going to the high place to bless the sacrifices. Come with me for you will eat with me today. Tomorrow I will tell you of what you are thinking. As for the asses, they have been found."

And then he said a strange thing. "On whom is all the desire of Israel? Is it not on you and on your father's house?"

Saul stared at him in amazement. He could only stammer, "Why—I—belong to the smallest tribe, and my family is the least in the tribe of Benjamin. Why do you speak thus to me?"

Samuel did not answer, but he took Saul and his servant to his house where they were given chief seats among thirty guests. Saul was honored, too, by the meat that was given him, for Samuel said to the cook, "Bring the left shoulder which I told you to save when I invited my guests." The cook brought it and set it before Saul. And from that time on, the left shoulder became the royal piece.

All afternoon and late into the night Samuel talked with Saul about the people of Israel and what a king should and should not do in governing them.

Early the next morning Samuel wakened Saul and together they went to the gate of the city. As they passed through, Samuel said to Saul, "Send the servant on ahead, but you wait. I want to show you the word of God."

Benoi went on. Then Samuel took a little bottle of olive oil and pouring it on the head of Saul, he said, "God has anointed you to be king over Israel. On the way home you will meet near Rachel's tomb, two men. They will tell you that the asses have been found, but that your father is worried about you. Later, you will meet three men going to a sacrifice. They will speak to you and give you three loaves of bread. When you come to the Philistine garrison, you will meet a band of prophets, and you, too, shall prophesy. After this whatever happens, use your own judgment. Go down to the city of Gilgal and wait there for me. I will come in a week, make sacrifices, and tell you what to do next."

And the journey home was just as Samuel had said it would be.

When they arrived, Saul's uncle said, "Where did you go?"

Benoi answered, "When we could not find the asses, we went to see Samuel."

"Oh! And what did he tell you?"

"He said the beasts were found," said Saul. But he was careful to say nothing about his having been anointed king.

Then Samuel called the people together at Mizpah as he had said he would. Once more he warned them. "You have made a mistake in demanding a king. But God has said that you may have one."

Then he called the tribes one by one, and the lot fell on the tribe of Benjamin. When the families were called, it fell on Matri. The third lot brought Kish, the father of Saul, and the fourth, Saul himself.

No one could find him at first, for overcome with the realization that he would be king, he had hidden himself among the pieces of baggage. When he was found, and brought up before the people, his appearance pleased them; for he stood head and shoulders taller than anyone else. And the people shouted, "God save the King!"

Samuel told them what kind of kingdom they were to have; and wrote their constitution for them, putting it in the Tabernacle at Shiloh. Then he sent the people home. Saul also went to his home in Gibeah; but with him went a group of young men who pledged themselves to be his loyal followers.

But there were certain ones, envious fellows, who said, "How can this man save us?" and they brought him no presents, although many others had. Of course Saul as king could have had these men punished. But he wisely paid no attention to them. He would wait the day when he could prove by deeds that he could save his people.*

✢

HOW A SHEPHERD BOY HELPED A KING

By

Grace West Staley

THOUGH it had not been a long journey, the little donkey was tired and the old man was also tired. How hot the sun was! It beat down unmercifully on the lonely road. Dust filled the traveler's throat, till his tongue felt parched and swollen, and his eyes were rimmed with red. He would be glad to reach home, and yet he dreaded it, too, for his master had been strange and wild these many days.

The old man sighed. The life of a servant was a hard one, and full of worries, even if one's master was the great King Saul. If only there was something he could do to help his loved master! Thus thought Saul's faithful servant as he rode along between the low hills, outside the town of Bethlehem.

Suddenly, a low sweet sound broke the stillness of the quiet countryside. The old man raised his head and listened. Tones, clear and bell-like, came from over a nearby hill. Someone was playing a harp!

* Used by special permission of the publisher.

Saul's servant stopped the little donkey and dismounted. "Strange," he muttered to himself. "Beautiful music, out here among the hills!"

He scrambled up the hill as the music continued, now gay, now sad. And as he neared the top he became aware of a voice singing to the music. A voice sweeter than any the old man had ever heard. He must see this musician! He reached the top of the hill and eagerly looked over.

Just below him, on the hillside, sat a young shepherd, dressed in goatskin, playing upon a small harp held in one arm, and singing to the sheep which crowded about him. The shepherd had not heard Saul's servant and continued his song to the sheep. The song told of a boy who had been sent away from his father and mother to watch the sheep on the hillside. The words related the boy's sadness on leaving his seven brothers, of his loneliness at work with no one to talk to but the sheep. The music grew gayer, then, and the shepherd's voice rang out with the joy that filled the boy's heart when his father had given him a harp. The song told how the boy had learned to play and sing of the beautiful world about him—the trees, the birds, the flowers, the brook. Next, the music became sweet and calm, describing the boy's happiness at finding that God was very close to him under the blue, blue sky; and of how the boy had lain awake at night studying the stars and the moon.

At last the voice stopped and the shepherd put down his harp. Saul's servant leaned forward to see the boy's face, and the shepherd turned and saw him.

"Be not surprised," said the old man. "As I was passing I heard thee and stopped to see what manner of man could make such music."

The shepherd smiled and then stood up. He was strong and handsome.

"Tell me," continued the king's servant, "was it of thyself that thee sang?"

The shepherd boy laughed. "Yes," he said.

"Then who art thou?" asked the elderly man.

The shepherd boy answered, "I am David, son of Jesse, the Bethlehemite."

During the rest of his journey that day, Saul's servant thought about the happy shepherd boy. David, a son of Jesse. Everyone knew of Jesse, a leading citizen of Bethlehem. Why, only last year Jesse had presided over the town's yearly feast. It was said that Jesse came from a family of great men, fearless, powerful, God-fearing.

At the feast, Saul's servant has seen seven of Jesse's handsome sons and had heard of their bravery in battle. He remembered now! He had heard of another son, who, because of his youth, had been sent to mind the sheep. This gifted David was that boy.

As he neared the town of Bethlehem, the old servant thought of his master, Saul, who had helped the Hebrews in a very dark hour. Saul had united the land of Israel when it needed a king. He had raised armies and subdued neighboring kings who were stealing the Hebrews' lands and cattle. Rich and powerful now, Saul was feared by the other nations. Yes, God had been with Saul once. But what had happened of late? Why was Saul unhappy and sick in mind? The old servant shook his head. He knew. Saul had thought himself so great that he had not listened to God's warnings. He had disobeyed God, and had grown vain and cruel. He thought only of growing more rich, and more powerful. So proud had he become that he would not ask God to forgive him! But the weight of his wrongs was always with him. The master was torn by doubts and worries which, at times, brought on spells of madness. His faithful followers, including the old servant, had tried vainly to help their king.

Suddenly, at this point in his thoughts, the old man on his way to Bethlehem stopped short. Perhaps there was a way that he could help Saul! The king was a lover of music. The old man thought again of David's nimble fingers moving on the harp strings. He remembered the sound of the boy's voice. It might be that this shepherd boy, with songs of peace and contentment, could help his master.

The old servant did not know how he could arrange a meeting between King Saul and David, the shepherd boy. His chance, however, came sooner than he expected. For, several days later, after the servant reached home, Saul had a severe attack of his illness, and when it was over, his followers gathered about him. The old servant, thinking this might be his opportunity, begged Saul to have a musician come. "Music," he said, "is soothing and restful. Perhaps we could *seek out a man who is a cunning player on an harp.*"

And Saul said, *"Provide me now a man that can play well, and bring him to me."*

Quickly the servant spoke up. *"Behold, I have seen a son of Jesse the Bethlehemite, that is cunning in playing."* And he told Saul of the afternoon he had seen David on the hillside. "He is *a comely person, and the Lord is with him."*

Saul nodded. He knew Jesse, and he knew his sons.

With a few other servants, the old man hastened to Jesse's house. He felt sure that David could help his master, yet he feared that Saul might change his mind.

Jesse was much surprised that Saul should want to see David. "Thou seekest David?" he asked. "In what way can the lad help Saul? He is too young for battle. He keepeth the sheep on the hillside."

"Find him, then," said the servant, "and send him to Saul, for this is the king's message, *'Send me David thy son, which is with the sheep.'* "

And so David was brought from the hillside and, taking his harp and gifts from his father to the king, he set off on a donkey to the court of King Saul. When he arrived, the servant said to him, "Fear not, my son. Be of good courage. Sing and play as thou didst for the sheep, and God will be with thee."

David's eyes were calm as he told the old servant, "I am not afraid, for God is here with me, even as He was on the hillside."

Then David was led before the king.

Saul sat on a low throne, looking dark and terrible with the weight of worries on his soul. But David smiled and drew his harp to his arm and began to play. Timidly at first, then, as his fingers touched the familiar strings, richer and deeper. He forgot the vain and cruel king before him and thought of his sheep under the blue, blue sky. He began to sing, not of war and evil, power and greed, but of the peacefulness of the hillside. He sang of birds at daybreak, he sang of the clear brook sparkling over the stones in the sunshine, he sang of the long nights under the stars with only the sheep for company. And, last of all, he sang of God's love for every living thing.

And the wild look left Saul's face and the trouble lifted from his heart and he felt at peace and slept.

"Thou art a brave lad, and noble," the old servant said to David, "but what thou hast done, thou must do again. Stay with the master."

David said, "I shall stay until Saul no longer needs me."

So Saul made David his armor-bearer and arranged a place for him in his court.

Thankful that David had helped Saul, everyone watched the boy with interest. As time went on, people saw how David grew in wisdom and courage, how he became a hero of war, and how he was praised as a poet and musician. Even the Hebrew leaders felt that David would one day be king of all Israel. As indeed he did become king, one of the greatest and wisest kings of all time.

Amidst all the glory that came to David, as poet, priest, soldier, musician and king, he remembered God. Sometimes, alone at night, harp in hand, he sang to God. Looking out over the starlit city of Jerusalem, he thought of the shepherd boy on the hillside. He thought of the patient sheep, of the long hot days. He remembered all these things and he sang the Psalm of David: *"The Lord is my shepherd; I shall not want."*

Always he kept his harp beside him and often he sang. So beautiful were his songs that the Hebrews wished to sing them also and asked him to write them down. Thus David gave his poems to the world. We read them, today, in our Bibles.*

PSALM 19

The heavens declare the glory of God; and the firmament sheweth his handiwork.

2. Day unto day uttereth speech, and night unto night sheweth knowledge.

3. There is no speech nor language, where their voice is not heard.

4. Their line is gone out through all the earth, and their words to the end of the world. In them hath he set a tabernacle for the sun,

5. Which is as a bridegroom coming out of his chamber, and rejoiceth as a strong man to run a race.

6. His going forth is from the end of heaven, and his circuit unto the ends of it: and there is nothing hid from the heat thereof.

7. The law of the Lord is perfect, converting the soul: the testimony of the Lord is sure, making wise the simple.

8. The statutes of the Lord are right, rejoicing the heart: the commandment of the Lord is pure, enlightening the eyes.

9. The fear of the Lord is clean, endur-ing forever: the judgments of the Lord are true and righteous altogether.

10. More to be desired are they than gold, yea, than much fine gold: sweeter also than honey and the honeycomb.

11. Moreover by them is thy servant warned: and in keeping of them there is great reward.

12. Who can understand his errors? cleanse thou me from secret faults.

13. Keep back thy servant also from presumptuous sins; let them not have dominion over me: then shall I be upright, and I shall be innocent from the great transgression.

14. Let the words of my mouth, and the meditation of my heart, be acceptable in thy sight, O Lord, my strength and my redeemer.

PSALM 27

The Lord is my light and my salvation; whom shall I fear? the Lord is the strength of my life; of whom shall I be afraid?

2. When the wicked, even mine ene-

* From *Jack and Jill,* 1946.

mies and my foes, came upon me to eat up my flesh, they stumbled and fell.

3. Though an host should encamp against me, my heart shall not fear: though war should rise against me, in this will I be confident.

4. One thing have I desired of the Lord, that will I seek after; that I may dwell in the house of the Lord all the days of my life, to behold the beauty of the Lord, and to inquire in his temple.

5. For in the time of trouble he shall hide me in his pavilion: in the secret of his tabernacle shall he hide me; he shall set me upon a rock.

6. And now shall mine head be lifted up above mine enemies round about me: therefore will I offer in his tabernacle sacrifices of joy; I will sing, yea, I will sing praises unto the Lord.

7. Hear, O Lord, when I cry with my voice: have mercy also upon me, and answer me.

8. When thou saidst, Seek ye my face; my heart said unto thee, Thy face, Lord, will I seek.

9. Hide not thy face far from me; put not thy servant away in anger: thou hast been my help; leave me not, neither forsake me, O God of my salvation.

10. When my father and my mother forsake me, then the Lord will take me up.

11. Teach me thy way, O Lord, and lead me in a plain path, because of mine enemies.

12. Deliver me not over unto the will of mine enemies: for false witnesses are risen up against me, and such as breathe out cruelty.

13. I had fainted, unless I had believed to see the goodness of the Lord in the land of the living.

14. Wait on the Lord: be of good courage, and he shall strengthen thine heart: wait, I say, on the Lord.

✛

DAVID, THE HERO WITH THE FEET OF CLAY

By

Sir Philip Gibbs

Part I. DAVID THE YOUTH

AFTER three thousand years the story of David, poet-king of Israel, still has a deathless interest. Across the bridge of time, through all the darkness of history, his figure stands out, vital and human.

It is the young David, strong in the grace of youth, and brave, who is sculptured still as a memorial to the valour of young manhood killed in modern wars.

The story begins with David as a boy tending the sheep and goats of his father Jesse on the outskirts of a village called Bethlehem, just about a thousand years before a man named Joseph, who was one of his descendants, came there with Mary, his wife, before the birth of the Christ Child.

As a shepherd David's ways were not soft and pastoral. He climbed with his goats to the high crags of wild and mountainous country where there was little grass among the rocks. He was a hunter as well as a shepherd. Alone he fought with a lion—a lion cub, perhaps—which he caught by the beard before he strangled it. Body to body he fought with a bear and gave thanks to God for being delivered out of its paws. He could run as fast as a young hind. He could leap over a high wall. He rejoiced in his strength of body.

Often, standing on high crags, he looked over a countryside where his own clan and friendly tribes among the people of Judah and Israel were surrounded by hostile people of different races.

Some of them were very close. Only twelve miles away he could see with his keen eyes the hill city of Jerusalem—then called Jabus, because it was held by the Jebusites, a Canaanite race who had come across the Mediterranean with sharp broadswords and round shields.

Young David, feeling the strength of his arm, the vitality and glory of his youth, waited for the day when he should strike a blow against the enemies of his own folk whom he hated worse than wild beasts.

His day came. It was when the Philistines gathered a great force together and advanced to battle array against the army of Saul, King of the Israelites, encamped on the borders of Judah. Three brothers of David were with Saul's army, which had taken up a position of defence with a deep valley between themselves and the enemy.

David was looking after the family flocks when he was sent for by his father, Jesse, who told him to take some loaves and cheese to his brothers and find out if they were well and with whom they were placed. Nothing loath, David left his flocks in charge of a keeper and went across country towards the fighting line.

He found it in the neighborhood of a place called Magala, and leaving his provisions in the baggage line ran to where the troops were in position, and inquired if all things went well with his brothers.

As he was talking to them there was a great excitement in the camp. One of the Philistines advanced to their lines with his armour-bearer and issued a challenge for a single combat. He was a rough fellow called Goliath, who looked about twelve feet high to his enemies.

Afterwards they may have added on an inch or two every time they told the story, as Falstaff counted his men in buckram. But he was tall and he wore a helmet of brass and a coat of mail and greaves of armour. He held a shield of brass on his shoulder and carried a tall spear. He called out abusive words to the Israelites and taunted them. But his offer was fair enough:

"Choose out a man of you, and let him come down and fight, hand-to-hand."

There was not a man among the Israelites ready to take on this gigantic fellow in a hand-to-hand fight until David heard about it. He spoke impatiently to the men about him:

"Who is this dog, that he should defy the armies of the living God?"

He was taken before Saul, the old chief who had led his tribes into many battles against the enemies of Israel, and David spoke up bravely:

"Let no man be dismayed. I, thy servant, will go and fight against the Philistine."

"Thou art but a boy!" said Saul, looking at this tall stripling, so fair and comely.

But David spoke proudly and eagerly, like a young savage rehearsing his exploits. He told about his fight with the lion, and the bear. He had strangled and killed them. So would he do with the Philistine who had cursed the army of the living God.

Saul was pleased with the boy, who was after his own heart. He lent his armour to David, and put a helmet of brass on his head, and clothed him in a coat of mail, and handed him a sword which David girded on.

In the narrative now there is one of those touches which give one a sure sense of reality. The young David, who had run barefoot up the mountain sides and had been free as the wind, tried to see if he could walk in this armour. He felt imprisoned.

"I cannot go thus, for I am not used to it," he protested sulkily.

He laid off his armour and took his staff which he always carried. Then he chose five smooth stones out of a brook near by and put them in his shepherd's wallet.

Three thousand years later a friend of mine who was the captain of a London regiment fighting in Palestine found two smooth stones in the same place, and kept them through the war in memory of David, who went out with his sling to meet the Philistine.

David's Conquest of Goliath

Goliath, that rough fellow, was very abusive when he saw David. "Am I a dog that thou should'st come to me with a staff?" he asked. In the manner of time (and later) he swore oaths, and promised to feed the vultures with this boy's flesh, and to feed the beasts with his bones.

David answered back with equal eloquence, jeering at Goliath's sword and spear and shield:

"I come to thee in the name of the Lord of hosts, the God of the armies of Israel, which thou hast defied. This day the Lord will deliver thee into my hand, and I will slay thee, and take away thy head from thee."

Goliath crouched and sprang. But David had put a stone into his sling, and "fetching it about" quick as a snake struck the Philistine in the forehead. He fell on his face, and David, taking his enemy's sword, cut off his head.

When the Philistines saw that their champion was dead, they fled in disorder, while the Israelites shouted and pursued them to the very gates of their strongholds.

About this time the servants of King Saul became anxious because of his dark moods of melancholy. They advised him to get some minstrel, skillful with the harp, who would play and sing to him, so that he could bear them more easily. Saul liked the idea:

"Provide me, then, with some man that can play well and bring him to me," he said.

It was David who was chosen.

He had now drawn near to his destiny. He was the King's favourite and his constant companion. When Saul fell into his melancholy moods David struck the notes of his harp and chanted his songs of glory to the Lord of life's happiness.

The Lord is my shepherd, I shall not want.
He maketh me to lie down in green pastures;
He leadeth me beside the still waters.
He restoreth my soul; He leadeth me in the
Paths of righteousness for His name's sake. . . .

One can see those two in the King's tent as a picture which still glows through the mists of time, that tall young man, fair, straight, and splendid in the beauty of manhood, striking the strings of his harp, while the old chief, troubled by memories of blood and horror, afraid of the wrath of God, with some poison in his brain, sits moodily with his eyes fixed upon his favourite until his spirit is touched by these words of sweetness and joy, this music, this enchantment of youth.

Jonathan, Saul's son, had no jealousy of David, his father's favourite. These two young men swore an eternal friendship with each other. Jonathan loved David as his own soul, and David had a love for Jonathan passing the love of women.

It is this comradeship between two young men, loyal to each other in a time of treachery, which makes the story of David so human and so appealing. It is rarer in history and legend than the love between man and woman.

David had been promised the hand of Saul's eldest daughter, but that young woman married another man; and it was Michal, a younger daughter, who fell in love with David and was eager to be his wife.

He could not afford the dowry for a king's daughter, but Saul was willing to release him from any dowry. He wanted rather the lives of two hundred Philistines.

It was a trap. Saul's disordered mind had become jealous of this young hero who was acquiring glory for himself. The old man had begun to hate his armourbearer, who had the gift of youth. It was constantly whispered to him that David aspired to be his successor. He desired the death of David and hoped the Philistines would kill him on one of his rash adventures.

But David thought the prize was worth the game and attacked one of the Philistine strongholds and killed two hundred of them, and had their bodies mutilated according to the horrible practice of his fighting men.

He claimed the hand of Michal who loved him, and Saul could not refuse, so that David, the shepherd of Bethlehem, became the son-in-law of the King and went out one morning to meet his bride.*

✛

GOD THE ALL-MERCIFUL

(Interpretation)

Two authors, Henry F. Chorley (1808-1872) and John Ellerton (1826-1893), wrote this hymn, also entitled "God the Omnipotent," twenty-eight years apart.

* From *The Sunday Chronicle* Nov. 22, 1931. Used by special permission of the author and the publisher. Part II, "Flight from the Wrath of Saul," is reprinted on p. 341.

It first appeared with four stanzas in 1842 under the title "In Time of War," and was written by Henry F. Chorley, music critic for the London *Athenaeum.*

Twenty-eight years later in 1870 John Ellerton, at that time vicar of Crew Green, composed an adaptation of Chorley's hymn. It was written during the Franco-Prussian War, which adds significance to the closing words of the first two stanzas, "Give to us peace in our time, O Lord." Just how these two hymns came to be joined is not fully known; but the hymn as it is usually sung today is a composite: the first verse is the work of Chorley, the second and third and doubtless the last were written by Ellerton.

John Ellerton (1826-1893) was a graduate of Trinity College at Cambridge. The major part of his life was spent as a country preacher. Yet he is best known to

God the All-Merciful

RUSSIAN HYMN. 11, 10, 11, 9

HENRY F. CHORLEY, 1842
JOHN ELLERTON, 1870

ALEXIS T. LWOFF, 1833

1. God the All-mer-ci-ful! earth hath for-sak-en Thy ways of bless-ed-ness, slight-ed thy word; Bid not thy wrath in its ter-rors a-wak-en; Give to us peace in our time, O Lord!
2. God the All-right-eous One! man hath de-fied thee, Yet to e-ter-ni-ty stand-eth thy word; False-hood and wrong shall not tar-ry be-side thee: Give to us peace in our time, O Lord!
3. God the All-wise! by the fire of thy chas-t'ning, Earth shall to free-dom and truth be re-stored; Thro' the thick dark-ness thy king-dom is has-t'ning: Thou wilt give peace in thy time, O Lord!
4. So shall thy chil-dren with thank-ful de-vo-tion Praise him who saved them from per-il and sword, Sing-ing in cho-rus from o-cean to o-cean, Peace to the na-tions and praise to the Lord. A-men.

succeeding generations as a hymnologist. He compiled and edited two important books, *Church Hymns* and *The Children's Hymn Book*. He was also a joint compiler of the 1889 edition of *Hymns Ancient and Modern,* which ranked high in affection and usage by the English Church. Not less than eighty-six hymns, original and translations, are the work of his genius.

The tune "Russian Hymn" to which this hymn is universally sung was originally the national anthem of Old Russia. It was composed in 1833 by Alexis T. Lwoff. He rose to the office of adjutant during the reign of Czar Nicholas I; but he left the army later to head the Imperial Choir. Among his many other musical compositions are three operas, several violin pieces, six settings for psalms, and other Church music.

✢

LEAD ON, O KING ETERNAL

(Interpretation)

ERNEST WARBURTON SHURTLEFF (1862-1917) wrote this hymn while he was a student at Andover Theological Seminary. It was written as a graduation hymn for the class of 1888 of which he was the acknowledged poet.

Upon his graduation he became a Congregational minister and held important pastorates at Buenaventura, California, Plymouth, Massachusetts, and Minneapolis, Minnesota. He later went to Europe where in 1895 he organized the American Church at Frankfort, Germany.

No doubt his own days of preparation during his student years at the Seminary are referred to in the first stanza. The hymn has a martial note but is devoid of the militaristic tone of "Onward Christian Soldiers." It is a battle song in the warfare against sin. The second stanza looks forward to the peace that is attained by holiness and the coming of the heavenly kingdom not by conquest of swords but by "deeds of love and mercy." The third stanza expresses the glorious optimism of youth and a sublime courage that wins the immediate response of young people everywhere. In every generation youth faces the future with courage and with the assurance that it provides for each unique opportunities for service.

Two familiar Scriptures come to our minds as we sing this great hymn: one in the Old Testament, and one in the New Testament:

"I saw also the Lord sitting upon a throne, high and lifted up: . . . then said I, 'Woe is me! for I am undone; because I am a man of unclean lips, and I dwell in the midst of a people of unclean lips: for mine eyes have seen the King, the Lord of Hosts.' . . . Also I heard the voice of the Lord, saying, 'Whom shall I send, and who will go for us?' Then said I, 'Here am I; send me'" (Isa. 6:1, 5, 8).

"Behold I send you forth . . .

"He that taketh not his cross, and followeth after me, is not worthy of me. He that findeth his life shall lose it: and he that loseth his life for my sake shall find it. He that receiveth you receiveth me, and he that receiveth me receiveth him that sent me" (Matt. 10:16, 38-40).

The tune "Lancashire," composed in 1836 by Henry Smart, provides an ideal melody for the challenge contained in this great hymn. Although originally writ-

Lead on, O King Eternal

Lancashire 7 6 7 6 D

ERNEST W. SHURTLEFF, 1888

HENRY SMART, 1836

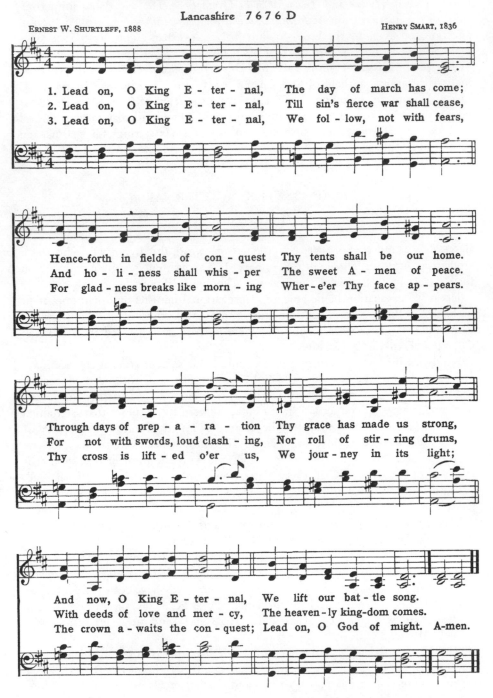

1. Lead on, O King E - ter - nal, The day of march has come;
Hence-forth in fields of con - quest Thy tents shall be our home.
Through days of prep - a - ra - tion Thy grace has made us strong,
And now, O King E - ter - nal, We lift our bat - tle song.

2. Lead on, O King E - ter - nal, Till sin's fierce war shall cease,
And ho - li - ness shall whis - per The sweet A - men of peace.
For not with swords, loud clash - ing, Nor roll of stir - ring drums,
With deeds of love and mer - cy, The heaven - ly king-dom comes.

3. Lead on, O King E - ter - nal, We fol - low, not with fears,
For glad - ness breaks like morn - ing Wher - e'er Thy face ap - pears.
Thy cross is lift - ed o'er us, We jour - ney in its light;
The crown a - waits the con - quest; Lead on, O God of might. A-men.

ten for "From Greenland's Icy Mountains," it was sung first at a musical festival in the parish church at Blackburn where Mr. Smart was the organist. The festival was in honor of the tercentenary of the Reformation.

The tune is vigorous and pre-eminently fitted to the marching words," Lead On, O King Eternal."

✛

MY GOD AND FATHER, WHILE I STRAY

(Interpretation)

THIS brief four-verse hymn was composed in 1834 by Charlotte Elliott. It expresses the devout yearnings of a heart, young in years, and buffeted by the winds of indecision, yet longing to remain staunch and true to the God and Father of her childhood.

The first stanza recognizes that "straying" is easy, and that life's pathway is rough and beset by many temptations. She pleads that while evil influences may play about her, God will teach her heart to say "Thy will be done."

The second stanza expresses a willingness to "resign" what her heart most yearns for, and to yield to the call of the spirit with the affirmative phrase, "Thy will be done."

My God and Father, While I Stray

ST. GABRIEL. 8, 8, 8, 4

CHARLOTTE ELLIOTT, 1834

FREDERICK A. G. OUSELEY, 1868

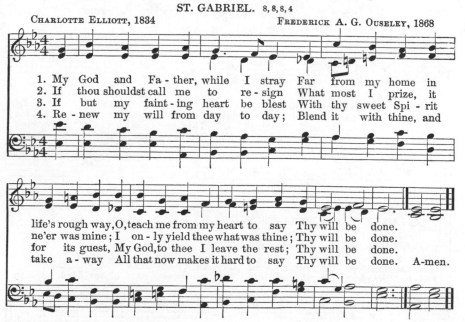

1. My God and Fa-ther, while I stray Far from my home in life's rough way, O, teach me from my heart to say Thy will be done.
2. If thou shouldst call me to re-sign What most I prize, it ne'er was mine; I on-ly yield thee what was thine; Thy will be done.
3. If but my faint-ing heart be blest With thy sweet Spi-rit for its guest, My God, to thee I leave the rest; Thy will be done.
4. Re-new my will from day to day; Blend it with thine, and take a-way All that now makes it hard to say Thy will be done. A-men.

The third stanza expresses confidence that if the Spirit of God dwells as a guest in her heart, His will will be accomplished in her life.

The fourth stanza acknowledges the need of renewed will power from day to day, and prays that her will may be blended with the will of God so that it will be increasingly easier as the years go by to say, "The will be done."

Frederick A. G. Ouseley (1868) composed the melody "St. Gabriel" to which this hymn is sung.

✣

THERE'S A WIDENESS IN GOD'S MERCY

(Interpretation)

THE lines of this immortal hymn, "There's a Wideness in God's Mercy," suggest two familiar Scripture passages, one in the Old Testament, and one in the New Testament:

"But though he cause grief, yet will he have compassion according to the multitude of his mercies. For he doth not afflict willingly nor grieve the children of men" (Lam. 3:32, 33).

"God is love. In this was manifested the love of God toward us, because that God sent his only begotten Son into the world, that we might live through him. Herein is love, not that we loved God, but that he loved us, and sent his Son to be the propitiation for our sins" (I John 4:8-10).

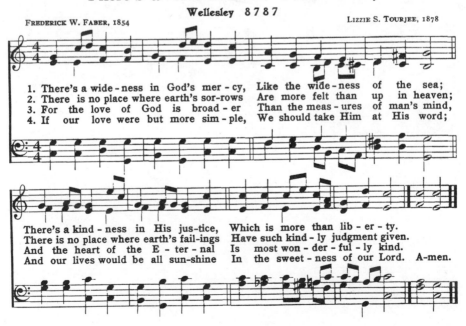

There's a Wideness in God's Mercy
Wellesley 8 7 8 7

FREDERICK W. FABER, 1854   LIZZIE S. TOURJEE, 1878

1. There's a wide-ness in God's mer-cy,   Like the wide-ness of   the sea;
2. There is no place where earth's sor-rows   Are more felt than up in heaven;
3. For the love of God is broad-er   Than the meas-ures of man's mind,
4. If   our love were but more sim-ple,   We should take Him at His word;

There's a kind-ness in His jus-tice,   Which is more than lib-er-ty.
There is no place where earth's fail-ings   Have such kind-ly judgment given.
And the heart of the E-ter-nal   Is most won-der-ful-ly kind.
And our lives would be all sun-shine   In the sweet-ness of our Lord. A-men.

The author, Frederick William Faber (1814-1863), lived as a boy in the wild and beautiful scenery of Durham, Westmorland, and in the Lake region. Lonely for the heather, crags, and streams of his boyhood home, he wrote: "It seems to me a home whence I have been exiled, but which only to think of is tranquility and peace."

He became an excellent rider and swimmer. He attended Harrow and Balliol College, Oxford, where he became a friend of John Henry Newman. Later he founded a religious community at Birmingham. There he sometimes fasted to the point of complete exhaustion. He partook of only one good meal a week, usually on Sunday, and died at the early age of forty-eight.

As a hymnist he was original, using simple words so effectively that they conveyed a deeper feeling and meaning than many more widely known poets were able to express.

This hymn-poem, the original of which had thirteen stanzas, is beautiful in content and meaning, and has long been popular in the services of the Church. The tune "Wellesley" is only one of the musical compositions to which it is sung. It also appears set to the melodies of "Ilsley" an "Erie."

Lizzie Shove Tourjée (1878), the composer of the tune "Wellesley," was the daughter of Dr. Eben Tourjée, the founder of the New England Conservatory of Music. She wrote this tune while she was a high school student in Newton, Massachusetts. Her father was the musical editor of the *Methodist Hymnal* (1878 edition). He included in it his daughter's tune "Wellesley," on the same page with Faber's hymn-poem "There's a Wideness in God's Mercy," and thus the two came to be associated.

CONTENTS

PART III SECTION 2

THE KINGDOM PASSES TO DAVID

---✛---

Then Samuel took the horn of oil, and anointed him in the midst of his brethren: and the spirit of the Lord came upon David from that day forward.—I SAMUEL 16:13

---✛---

MUSIC:

THE STATUE OF DAVID

By

Michelangelo Buonarroti

(Interpretation)

MICHELANGELO was born in Caprese, Italy, March 6, 1475. Early in life he was apprenticed to Ghirlandajo, and worked with him until he became a better draftsman than his teacher.

When he was sixteen he became a member of the household of Lorenzo de' Medici in Florence, Italy. There, amid the collection of antique sculptures, Michelangelo not only found his true calling, but became associated with the learned society of the Medici court. There also he came under the influence of the fiery preaching of Savonarola.

After Lorenzo de' Medici's death, Michelangelo went to Rome in 1496, where he carved his world-famous "Pieta." He then returned to Florence where he made his popular statue of David, and his cartoon, "The Bathing Soldiers."

In 1505 Pope Julius II summoned him to Rome and assigned to him the gigantic task of painting the ceiling of the Sistine Chapel. During the next four years this great artist conceived and executed, almost singlehandedly, a stupendous masterpiece of three hundred and forty-three major figures.

Michelangelo, however, regarded sculpture as his pre-eminent domain. The French sculptor Guillaume has written of his achievement in this field: "His works are sublime rather than beautiful. Power is more strongly expressed than order, and awe is commingled with our admiration." With his statues of Moses and of David he attained the highest degree of sculpture. He proved his consummate mastery of this art by cutting his magnificent statue of David from a huge block of marble that another sculptor thirty years or more earlier had attempted to carve but had discarded as useless. In that piece of marble Michelangelo saw David in the prime of his youth and manly strength, victorious in the first great crisis of his life. He contracted to complete his statue within two years for four hundred and twenty ducats, the sum needed to erect the necessary scaffolding and to pay the wages of his laborers. He began his work in September, 1501, and completed the statue early in 1504.

A commission of the most famous artists in Florence were then invited to view it and to choose a site for it. A place out in the open was suggested, but the artist's friend, Perugino, disapproved because the weather would, in time, deface it. The visiting artists could not agree, so the final selection was left to Michelangelo himself. He chose the entrance to the Palazzo Vecchio. It has since been removed to the Academy of Fine Arts in Florence where it is protected from the ravages caused by weather.

The figure is of noble proportions, like most of Michelangelo's productions, and should be viewed from a distance to be appreciated. There is sternness and confidence on young David's face as he defies the giant Goliath. The angular pose and the overgrown hands and feet suggest that David is no longer a boy but not yet a man. Every detail of this figure, which so faithfully reproduces nature, is remarkable and the entire work has an unusual feeling of elasticity. It gives the impression of immense but self-restrained power.

To the Florentines it suggested their new republic defying its enemies and it became the most popular statue in their city. For many years they reckoned events as happening "so long after the completion of Michelangelo's David"!

✠

SAUL HURLS HIS SPEAR AT DAVID

(A woodcut designed after a painting by Joseph Knight)

(Interpretation)

SAUL'S reign as the first king of Israel was a long one. He served forty years from approximately 1040 to 1000 B.C. according to Biblical historians. His reign was one of almost continuous warfare with the neighboring tribes surrounding the people of Israel. He fought against his enemies on every side: Moab, Ammon, Edom, Zobah, the Philistines, and the Amalekites. He vanquished many of his enemies, but over the Philistines he won no decisive victory. He was impulsive, wilful, jealous, and vindictive to those who served with and for him, even to the members of his own household. He preferred offering sacrifices to obeying the Lord's divine command before entering into a war with the Philistines. He disobeyed God's decree concerning the Amalekites. These are proof of his lack of complete allegiance to the Lord, the true spiritual leader of Israel. Samuel declared to Saul: "Because thou hast rejected the word of the Lord, he hath also rejected thee from being king" (I Sam. 15:23). The Bible tells us that "the spirit of the Lord departed from Saul, and an evil spirit . . . troubled him" (16:14).

Saul's massacres of the Gibeonites and the innocent priests of Nob were followed by the disastrous battle at Mount Gilboa where brave Jonathan and two other sons of Saul were slain by the Philistines; and where Saul himself, in despair, fell upon his own sword and perished.

Though he was stately and kingly in appearance, generous on impulse, heroic in action, Saul's acts of disobedience and unfaithfulness mark the beginning of his failure as a king set apart for high service to Israel and to Israel's God. The Bible historian Von Ranke says: "Saul is the first tragic figure in Biblical history." He enjoyed, for a time, the trust and favor of God and of Samuel, God's prophet; he won many victories for Israel; but when weighed in the balance of human history, he was found wanting. He lacked self-control and foresight. In a crisis he could not be depended upon to set aside his own self-will and obey the commands of God.

From the day of his amazing triumph David became one of Saul's most pop-

THE STATUE OF DAVID—*MICHELANGELO*

ular warriors. He "behaved himself wisely and Saul set him over the men of war, and he was accepted in the sight of all the people, and also in the sight of Saul's servants" (18:5).

One day when Saul was returning from a victory over the Philistines the women came out from all the cities of Israel singing and dancing to meet their king. They chanted a song:

> Saul hath slain his thousands,
> And David his ten thousands. [18:7]

Saul was furious when he heard the song. His pride was hurt and he became filled with jealousy and suspicion.

"They have ascribed unto David ten thousands, and to me they have ascribed but thousands; and what can he have more but the kingdom?" (18:8).

From that day on Saul eyed David with suspicion. And he continued to suffer from his dark moods.

This woodcut by an unknown artist was designed after a painting by Joseph Knight, a little-known English artist of the nineteenth century. It shows what happened one day as David played sweet strains on his lyre to soothe the king. Saul is seated on his throne. Suddenly and without provocation he lurches forward grasping his spear. He raises his arm intending to hurl the spear directly at the unsuspecting David. "And Saul cast the javelin, for he said, 'I will smite David even to the wall with it'" (18:11).

But David, swift and agile, fled unharmed from the king's presence. The people surrounding the king show their extreme dismay and even horror at Saul's mad attack. The king's armed bodyguard draws back in a gesture of vigorous protest. On Saul's face there is an expression of violent anger. "And Saul was afraid of David, because the Lord was with him, and was departed from Saul" (18:12).

✣

DAVID AND JONATHAN

Artist Unknown

(Interpretation)

THE Old Testament contains few stories more beautiful than that of the whole-hearted love of Jonathan, Saul's eldest son, for David, the shepherd lad from Bethlehem's plains. "The soul of Jonathan was knit with the soul of David, and Jonathan loved him as his own soul" (I Sam. 18:1). Of that unique love George Matheson has written:

"David's love for Jonathan had no barriers; it coincided with his interest. But the love of Jonathan for David had every prudential argument *against* it. He puts out his hand to save from the destroying hand of his father a man whom the popular voice had predicted to be his own supplanter. In this he is animated by a purely personal liking. Jonathan is an absolute spendthrift for the sake of love.

SAUL HURLS HIS SPEAR AT DAVID— *AFTER KNIGHT*

Nothing could more powerfully express the attitude of his mind than the passage in I Samuel 18:4, 'Jonathan stripped himself of the robe that was upon him, and gave it to David, and his garments, even to his sword, and to his bow, and to his girdle.' It is a typical statement; it describes in one sentence the whole trend of his heart. From beginning to end, the love of Jonathan for David was a disrobing, a divestiture. In every act of friendship, in every deed of devotion, in every outstretching of a protective hand, he was stripping himself of a royal garment. He was unarming himself, ungirding himself, sapping the foundations of his imperial strength—and all to gratify an impulse of human affection."*

Jonathan loved his home, he loved his father and his father's household, he loved his country. He proved that love because he died fighting for his country, fighting for his father's kingdom against the Philistines. The man who stripped himself of his own armor to serve David, put on his armor to die for a country whose kingship he knew he would never inherit. That fact reveals how great was his love for this shepherd lad from the hills of Bethlehem.

The love of Jonathan is in a way a prototype of Jesus' love for humanity. It was a stooping, bending, self-emptying love such as the Master of men expressed when he divested himself of glory, left his Heavenly Father's home, and came to this earth to become "the friend of man."

An unknown modern artist has portrayed this love in the painting, "Jonathan and David." In the springtime of their youth these two young men stand hand in hand in the shadow of a great oak tree. David has escaped into the country, for Jonathan has warned him of the wicked plot of King Saul. The hand of Jonathan rests upon David's shoulder and his eyes look directly into the face of his friend, but David's eyes gaze into the distance. David is reluctantly taking leave of Jonathan and about to go far away where he will be safe from the jealous anger of King Saul. Jonathan, who "loved him as he loved his own soul," knows that King Saul intends to kill David and he has just brought him word that he must flee.

"And Jonathan said to David, 'Go in peace, forasmuch as we have sworn both of us in the name of the Lord, saying, "The Lord be between me and thee, and between my seed and thy seed for ever."' And he rose and departed: and Jonathan went into the city" (I Sam. 20:42).

✢

SAUL VISITS THE WITCH OF ENDOR

By

Paul Gustave Doré

(Interpretation)

THROUGHOUT King Saul's tempestuous reign over the people of Israel he waged almost continuous war with the Philistines, a savage warlike people who pos-

---

* From "Jonathan the Generous" in *Representative Men of the Bible* (Second Series) by George Matheson, pp. 186-87. Published by Hodder & Stoughton, Ltd. Used by special permission of the publisher.

DAVID AND JONATHAN—*ARTIST UNKNOWN*

sessed the coast line of Palestine from the Plain of Sharon on the north to the Egyptian desert on the south. Though not of the Semitic race, they adopted the Semitic language of Canaan. Sometimes the armies of Saul prevailed, and at other times the Philistines won a victory which usually ended in a temporary truce.

King Saul rarely listened to the counsel of Samuel, the Lord's faithful prophet, preferring instead the advice of soothsayers and witches. But when Samuel abandoned Saul, he felt depressed and frustrated. Witnessing the sincere grief of his people at the time of Samuel's death, the king buried the prophet with great pomp in Ramah, his native city. He then expelled all the soothsayers, fortune-tellers, wizards, and mediums who claimed to have power to recall spirits from the dead.

When David was compelled to flee from Saul's presence, he had gathered about him a band of men and finally sought refuge for himself and his band among the Philistines. Israel was thus deprived of her foremost champion. It was at this juncture that Saul's enemies, the Philistines, decided that a favorable moment had arrived for them to renew their war against Israel.

They gathered together their armies and encamped at Shunem in the plain of Esdraelon in readiness to attack. Saul, upon learning of this move, mobilized his armies high above the plain on Mount Gilboa. But when he saw the host of the Philistines and knew that his own army was outnumbered, he was afraid and felt a dire need for the counsel of Samuel, God's prophet, that he had so often flouted. But Samuel was dead. In his distress he prayed to the God of the Israelites for guidance. "And when Saul inquired of the Lord, the Lord answered him not" (I Sam. 28:6).

Then Saul instructed his servants to find a woman who was a medium that he might go to her for the advice he so sorely needed. His servants told him about the witch of Endor, and Saul, disguising himself, visited her in the nighttime, accompanied by his servants. This witch, however, knowing that Saul had expelled all soothsayers and wizards and fearing that his visit might be a trap for her, at first refused him aid. He then swore that no punishment would come to her if she helped him with her occult powers. The woman asked: "Whom shall I bring up unto thee?" And Saul replied: "Bring me up Samuel" (28:11).

The witch then went into a trance and said: " 'I saw gods ascending out of the earth.' And he said unto her, 'What form is he of?' And she said, 'An old man cometh up; and he is covered with a mantle.' And Saul perceived that it was Samuel, and he stooped with his face to the ground, and bowed himself' " (28:13-14).

But the message which Saul received from Samuel's spirit was a message of doom. The prophet said: "The Lord will also deliver Israel with thee into the hand of the Philistines; and tomorrow shalt thou and thy sons be with me" (28:19). At these words Saul fell to the earth.

The artist, Paul Gustave Doré, has captured this dramatic moment in his engraving, "Saul Visits the Witch of Endor." The woman of Endor stands on a little rise of ground, with her back to her witch's pot and the snakes writhing around it. She points to the floating, insubstantial figure of Samuel, God's prophet,

SAUL VISITS THE WITCH OF ENDOR—*DORÉ*

whom she has recalled from the grave at Saul's command. Samuel gazes down at the king and, as he so often did when he was alive, delivers the Lord's stern condemnation of Saul. As the king hears Samuel's words and realizes that his fate is sealed, and that in the coming battle with the Philistines he will die, he sinks to the ground in despair. His attendants try to hold up his great, powerful body, but he is slipping from their grasp. Behind him one of his servants, with uplifted arms silhouetted against the darkness, expresses the ultimate woe of this scene.

✛

NATHAN DENOUNCING DAVID

By

Gebhardt Fügel

(Interpretation)

AFTER the deaths of Saul and Jonathan in the disastrous battle of Mount Gilboa, David became King of Israel. He captured Jerusalem and made it his capital. He built himself a palace in Jerusalem and brought the Ark of the Covenant into his royal city. There he planned to build a temple for the Ark, but Nathan, the prophet, forbade this, reminding David that the God of Israel had always dwelt in a tent.

Nathan is best known for his fearless denunciation of King David for having had Uriah the Hittite killed so that he might marry Bathsheba, Uriah's wife. The Biblical material which provides the theme for Fügel's painting, "Nathan Denouncing David," is found in II Samuel 12:1-15. It reads:

"And the Lord sent Nathan unto David. And he came unto him, and said, 'There were two men in one city; the one rich, and the other poor. The rich man had exceeding many flocks and herds; but the poor man had nothing, save one little ewe lamb, which he had brought and nourished up; and it grew up together with him, and with his children; it did eat of his own meat, and drank of his own cup, and lay in his bosom, and was unto him as a daughter. And there came a traveller unto the rich man, and he spared to take of his own flock and of his own herd, to dress for the wayfaring man that was come unto him; but took the poor man's lamb, and dressed it for the man that was come to him.' And David's anger was greatly kindled against the man; and he said to Nathan, 'As the Lord liveth, the man that hath done this thing shall surely die: and he shall restore the lamb fourfold, because he did this thing, and because he had no pity.'

"And Nathan said to David, 'Thou art the man. Thus saith the Lord God of Israel, I anointed thee king over Israel, and I delivered thee out of the hand of Saul; and I gave thee thy master's house, and thy master's wives into thy bosom, and gave thee the house of Israel and of Judah; and if that had been too little, I would moreover have given unto thee such and such things. Wherefore hast thou despised the commandment of the Lord, to do evil in his sight? thou hast killed

NATHAN DENOUNCING DAVID—FÜGEL

Uriah the Hittite with the sword, and hast taken his wife to be thy wife, and hast slain him with the sword of the children of Ammon. Now therefore the sword shall never depart from thine house; because thou hast despised me, and hast taken the wife of Uriah the Hittite to be thy wife.' . . . And David said unto Nathan, 'I have sinned against the Lord.' And Nathan said unto David, 'The Lord also hath put away thy sin; thou shalt not die. Howbeit, because by this deed thou hast given great occasion to the enemies of the Lord to blaspheme, the child also that is born unto thee shall surely die.' And Nathan departed unto his house."

The artist's portrayal of this incident is striking indeed in the contrast between the condemning prophet and the remorseful king. In the foreground sits David, his head bowed in shame, and his hands clasped in tense despair and regret. Nathan, the prophet, has just said: "Thou art the man," and consciousness of the enormity of his crime against Uriah is evident in every line and feature of the king's face. His staring eyes show that the prophet's story of "the poor man" and his one little ewe lamb has made him see himself as he really is and what he sees makes him ashamed. At his side is the harp with which, in bygone days, he had charmed away the melancholy of Saul. It stands silent now, for this scene has no place for singing and music. David wears a garment of white suggesting purity, and on his head is a golden crown denoting royal power. But David has neither purity nor power at this moment when Nathan stands confronting him. In one hand Nathan holds a scroll of the Law which says: "Thou shalt not covet thy neighbor's man-servant or maidservant." The index finger of his right hand is thrust out at David, to emphasize the depth of sin into which David's covetousness has led him.

Gebhardt Fügel was born in Ravensburg, Germany, in 1863.

✣

DAVID FORGIVING ABSALOM

Artist Unknown

(Interpretation)

ABSALOM was the third son of David. His mother was Maacah, the daughter of Talmai, king of Geshur. "Absalom" means "father of peace," yet David's third son spent most of his adult life in alienating people from his father's kingdom and in planning revolts. In maturity he was an unusually handsome man. II Samuel 14:25 reads: "But in all Israel there was none to be so much praised as Absalom for his beauty: from the sole of his foot even to the crown of his head there was no blemish in him."

Chapters fourteen through nineteen of II Samuel contain one incident after another revealing the treachery and plotting of Absalom against his father and his father's household. Yet David forgave him, even after he had slain his half-brother Amnon. After this revengeful murder Absalom fled to Talmai, king of Geshur, where he remained in hiding. But David mourned for his wayward son, and when Joab, his servant, saw this he went to Geshur and brought Absalom back to Jeru-

DAVID FORGIVING ABSALOM—*ARTIST UNKNOWN*

salem. There Absalom remained for two years but David would not allow him to come to see him.

Finally, since Absalom was unusually vain, he could bear the disgrace no longer, and so sent for Joab so that they might arrange some pretext by which he might be allowed to see the king. After three unsuccessful requests, when Joab still refused to come to him, Absalom said to his servants: " 'See, Joab's field is near mine and he hath barley there; go and set it on fire.' And Absalom's servants set the field on fire. Then Joab arose, and came to Absalom unto his house, and said unto him, 'Wherefore have thy servants set my field on fire?' And Absalom answered Joab, 'Behold, I sent unto thee, saying, "Come hither, that I may send thee to the king, to say, 'Wherefore am I come from Geshur? It had been good for me to have been there still.' Now therefore let me see the king's face; and if there be any iniquity in me, let him kill me." '

"So Joab came to the king, and told him; and when he had called for Absalom, he came to the king and bowed himself on his face to the ground before the king; and the king kissed Absalom" (II Sam. 14:30-33).

A realistic portrayal of this moment appears in a woodcut entitled "David Forgiving Absalom," by an unknown artist. Clad in kingly robes, David rises from his throne to receive the son he has not seen in more than two years. He forgives him, gives him his blessing, and with a kiss reinstates him to sonship. Absalom, his face hidden, clings to his aging father while David's general, Joab, looks on. There is in this scene a kinship with Jesus' parable of the prodigal son and the forgiving father.

Even after this reinstatement to love and confidence, Absalom stirred up another revolt against David. He was defeated by David's army, and finally slain by Joab as he hung from a tree in which his long hair caught as he was fleeing from the scene of battle. When David was informed of the death of this wayward son he wept and said: "O my son Absalom, my son, my son Absalom! would God I had died for thee, O Absalom, my son, my son!" (II Sam. 18:33).

✛

GOD'S CHOSEN KING

He was Jesse's youngest son—
A comely boy, and fair,
Yet brave and strong.
Untrampled by the heavy tread of Time
His life was on the Open—free, sublime—
Within his gentle soul he held the lilt of Spring,
And to the music of his harp-strings—loved to sing
In verse and song, the praises of his heavenly King.
He felt the hand of God within his own,
And tempted even death—stout-hearted and alone—
And knew the victory won

Ere the struggle had begun—
God's hand within his own—free, brave and strong.*

—Lola F. Echard

CAVE OF ADULLAM

David and his three captains bold
Kept ambush once within a hold.
It was in Adullam's cave,
Nigh which no water they could have,
Nor spring nor running brook was near
To quench the thirst that parched them there.
Then David, King of Israel,
Straight bethought him of a well,
Which stood beside the city gate
At Bethlehem; where, before his state
Of kingly dignity, he had
Oft drunk his fill, a shepherd lad;
But now his fierce Philistine foe
Encamped before it he does know.
Yet ne'er the less, with heart opprest,
Those three bold captains he addrest;
And wished that one to him would bring
Some water from his native spring.
His valiant captains instantly
To execute his will did fly.
The mighty three the ranks broke through
Of armed foes, and water drew
For David, their beloved King,
At his own sweet native spring.
Back through their armed foes they haste,
With the hard-earned treasure graced.
But when the good king David found
What they had done, he on the ground
The water poured. "Because," said he,
"That it was at the jeopardy
Of your three lives this thing ye did,
That I should drink it, God forbid."

—Charles Lamb

THE CALL OF DAVID

And the Lord said, "Arise, anoint him, for this is he."—I SAMUEL 16:12

Latest born of Jesse's race,
Wonder lights thy bashful face,

* Used by special permission of the author.

While the prophet's gifted oil
Seals thee for a path of toil.
We, thy angels circling round thee,
Ne'er shall find thee as we found thee,
When thy faith first brought us near,
In thy lion-fight severe.

Go! and mid thy flocks awhile
At thy doom of greatness smile;
Bold to bear God's heaviest load,
Dimly guessing of the road,—
Rocky road, and scarce ascended
Though thy foot be angel-tended!

Twofold praise thou shalt attain
In royal court and battle-plain:
Then come heart-ache, care, distress,
Blighted hope, and loneliness,
Wounds from friend, and gifts from foe,
Dizzied faith, and guilt and woe,
Loftiest aims by earth defiled,
Gleams of wisdom, sin-beguiled,
Sated power's tyrannic mood,
Counsels shared with men of blood.
Sad success, parental tears
And a dreary gift of years.

Strange that guileless face and form,
To lavish on the scarring storm!
Yet we take thee in thy blindness,
And we buffet thee in kindness;
Little chary of thy fame,—
Dust unborn may bless or blame,—
But we mould thee for the root
Of man's promised healing Fruit,
And we mould thee hence to rise
As our brother in the skies.

*—J. H. Newman**

DAVID'S LAMENT OVER SAUL AND JONATHAN

(2 Samuel 1:18-27)

I. *The Translation*

Weep O Judah,	Shed tears, O Judah, lament
over the sad fate	The sad fate of Israel's pride!
of Israel's heroes.	Thy heights are covered with slain.
(2 Sam. 1:18-21)	Alas, how the mighty are fallen!

* Lazaret, Malta, Jan. 18, 1833.

Let it not be told in Gath,
Nor proclaimed in Ashkelon's streets,
Lest Philistine cities rejoice,
The uncircumcised exult.

O Gilboa's mounts, let no dew,
Nor rain ever fall upon you,
Ye high spreading fields of death,
Where disgraced was the hero's shield!

Saul and
Jonathan were
notable warriors.
(2 Sam. 1:22, 23)

No oil wet the shield of Saul,
But the blood and the gore of the slain.
Never Jonathan's bow came back,
Nor the sword of Saul, without spoil.

Saul and Jonathan, pleasant, beloved,
Nor in life nor in death were parted.
They were swifter far than eagles,
They were stronger than lions both.

O women of
Israel, Saul
brought you
much spoil.
(2 Sam. 1:24)

O women of Israel, weep,
Lament ye the sad fate of Saul!
He gave you scarlet and linen,
Put jewels of gold on your dress.

O how are the heroes fallen!
They fell on the field of death.

O heroic
Jonathan,
how precious
to me was
thy love.
(2 Sam. 1:25-27)

On the hills lies Jonathan slain.
I am grieved for thee, O my brother!

My delight and rapture wert thou,
Thy love was sweeter than woman's.
O how are the mighty fallen!
The sons of war have perished.*

LAMENTATION OF DAVID OVER SAUL AND JONATHAN

A paraphrase of 2 Samuel 1:19-27

Thy beauty, Israel, is fled,
  Sunk to the dead;
How are the valiant fallen! The slain
  Thy mountains stain.
Oh, let it not in Gath be known,
Nor in the streets of Ascalon!

* From *The Messages of the Poets* by Nathaniel Schmidt, pp. 364-65. Copyright, 1911, by Charles Scribner's Sons. Used by special permission of the publisher.

Lest that sad story should excite
   Their dire delight;
Lest in the torrent of our woe
   Their pleasure flow;
Lest their triumphant daughters ring
Their cymbals, and their paeans sing.

You hills of Gilboa, never may
   You offerings pay;
No morning dew, nor fruitful showers,
   Clothe you with flowers:
Saul and his arms there made a spoil,
As if untoucht with sacred oil.

The bow of noble Jonathan
   Great battles won;
His arrows on the mighty fed,
   With slaughter red.
Saul never raised his arm in vain,
His sword still glutted with the slain.

How lovely, oh, how pleasant, when
   They lived with men!
Than eagles swifter; stronger far
   Than lions are;
Whom love in life so strangely tied,
The stroke of death could not divide.

Sad Israel's daughters, weep for Saul;
   Lament his fall,
Who fed you with the earth's increase,
   And crowned with peace;
With robes of Tyrian purple deckt,
And gems which sparkling light reflect.

How are thy worthies by the sword
   Of war devoured!
O Jonathan! the better part
   Of my torn heart!
The savage rocks have drunk thy blood:
My brother! oh, how kind! how good!

Thy love was great: oh, nevermore
   To man, man bore!
No woman when most passionate
   Loved at that rate!
How are the mighty fallen in fight!
They and their glory set in night!

—George Sandys

LORD OF THE MOUNTAIN

Lord of the mountain,
Reared with the mountain,
Young Man, Chieftain,
Hear a young man's prayer!

Hear a prayer for cleanness.
Keeper of the strong rain,
Drumming on the mountain;
Lord of the small rain
That restores the earth in newness;
Keeper of the clean rain,
Hear a prayer for wholeness.
Hear a prayer for courage.

Lord of the peaks,
Reared amid the thunders;
Keeper of the headlands
Holding up the harvest,
Keeper of the strong rocks,
Hear a prayer for staunchness,
Young Man, Chieftain,
Spirit of the mountain.

—Navajo Indian Poem

DAVID

THE THRESHING FLOOR

King's sons and captains over Israel, hark!
  The oxen low and fiery shapes draw near
  To him who veils his face in sudden fear
When voices answer from the altar spark;
For this is David, whom the patriarch
  Led from the sheep-folds by the rippling weir,
  He who braved lions without dart or spear,
Singing to God till Judah's hills grew dark.

There where he waits amid the harvest yield,
  His heart beholds the Temple which shall rise,
  Builded by hands that never swung the sword;
While shadowing Araunah's threshing field,
  As if in promise from the parted skies,
Full-armed shines forth the Angel of the Lord!*

—Thomas S. Jones, Jr.

* From *Shadow of the Perfect Rose: Collected Poems of Thomas S. Jones, Jr.*, edited with a Memoir and Notes by John L. Foley. Copyright, 1937, by Rinehart & Co., Inc. Used by special permission of John L. Foley, literary executor for Thomas S. Jones, Jr.

JERUSALEM MY HAPPY HOME

Jerusalem my happy home
  When shall I come to thee?
When shall my sorrows have an end?
  Thy joys when shall I see?
O happy harbor of the saints!
  O sweet and pleasant soil!
In thee no sorrow may be found
  No grief, no care, no toil

Thy gardens and thy gallant walks
  Continually are green;
There grow such sweet and pleasant flowers
  As nowhere else are seen;
Quite through the streets with silver sound
  The flood of life doth flow;
Upon whose banks on every side
  The wood of life doth grow

The saints are crowned with glory great
  They see God face to face;
They triumph still they still rejoice;
  Most happy is their case;
For there they live in such delight
  Such pleasure and such play
As that to them a thousand years
  Doth seem as yesterday

There Magdalene hath left her moan
  And cheerfully doth sing;
With blessed saints whose harmony
  In every street doth ring
Ah my sweet home Jerusalem
  Would God I were in thee!
Would God my woes were at an end
  Thy joys that I might see.

—Author Unknown; from the Latin

HILLS

"I will lift up mine eyes unto the hills,
From whence there cometh strength as from our God,"
So sang the Psalmist as of old he trod
Judea's rugged slopes, and found in rills
And waterfalls, in mountain crags, in trills
Of birds, in flaming trees, in every clod,

The splendor and the majesty of God
Who fashions all in age-long ceaseless mills.

Today I walked and lifted up my eyes
To other hills, to other mountain heights
Aglow with saffron radiance and calm
With Autumn's gentle potency, to skies
Serene. I saw a world that strength invites,
And in my soul, unvoiced, there stirred a psalm.*

—Georgia Harkness

THE LAST WORDS OF DAVID: GOD BLESSES THE RIGHTEOUS RULER

(2 Sam. 23:1-7)

I. *The Translation*

Through David,
the sweet singer
of Israel, Yahwe
hath spoken.
(2 Sam. 23:1-3a)

Says David, son of Jesse,
The man who was exalted,
Of Jacob's God anointed,
And Israel's sweet singer:

"Through me spoke Yahwe's spirit,
His word upon my tongue was;
Thus spoke the God of Jacob,
To me said Israel's rock:

A just ruler
brings happi-
ness.
(2 Sam. 23:3b-4)

" 'Who rules mankind in justice,
Who in the fear of God reigns,
Is like the light that breaks forth,
The sun on cloudless morning.'

God has
greatly
blessed my
reign. (2 Sam. 23:5)

"Is not my house with God so?
He made with me a covenant,
His watchcare has preserved me,
What I wished has succeeded.

He deals
roughly with
the wicked.
(2 Sam. 23:6, 7)

"Like thorns the bad are cast off,
They are not led by His hand.
Who touches them must armed be,
With spear of wood and iron."**

THE LORD THY KEEPER

I will lift up mine eyes unto the mountains:
From whence shall my help come?
My help cometh from the Lord,
Which made heaven and earth.

He will not suffer thy foot to be moved:
He that keepeth thee will not slumber.
Behold, he that keepeth Israel
Shall neither slumber nor sleep.

The Lord is thy keeper:
The Lord is thy shade upon thy right hand.
The sun shall not smite thee by day,
Nor the moon by night.

The Lord shall keep thee from all evil;
He shall keep thy soul.
The Lord shall keep thy going out and thy coming in,
From this time forth and for evermore.*

—*Psalm 121*

PSALM XIX

The Heavens declare Thy Glory, Lord;
Thy handiwork the starry skies;
Throughout all Time and Space they chant
Their silent litanies.

Day unto day, and night by night,
Their soundless voices still proclaim,
In one vast universal tongue,
The wonder of Thy name.

Like eager bridegroom, there the sun
Draws back the curtains of the night,
And sallies forth to bless the world
With Thy good gift of Light.

Then, with pale majesty, the moon
Takes up the tale, and all the stars
Repeat the message of Thy love—
"He sees! He knows! He cares!"

* From *The Modern Reader's Bible* edited by Richard G. Moulton. Copyright, 1935, by The Macmillan Company. Used by special permission of the publisher.

The Law of the Lord is perfect,
For it takes the souls of men,
And chisels and shapes and fashions them,
And gives them to Him again.
    It is wisdom to the wisest,
    It makes the simple wise,
    It makes men see the ways of God
    With clear unclouded eyes.

O, sweeter than sweetest honey,
And rarer than much fine gold,
Is that great unchanging Law of God
In its riches manifold.
    It is wisdom to the wisest,
    It makes the simple wise,
    It leads men up through life and death,
    To the love that never dies.

    .   .   .   .   .

The keeping of God's Law is in itself
A great reward.
Help us, O Lord—
For what man truly understands himself?
Help us to keep Thy Law!
Cleanse us from every secret fault,
From wilful and presumptuous sin!
Then shall we stand before Thee undismayed,
Upright and confident and free,
Freemen of God's most glorious Liberty.
    0, that my every thought this day
    May be acceptable to Thee!
    Then shall I go upon my way
    *Without offence, and joyfully.**

—*John Oxenham*

THE REMORSE OF DAVID

Did someone call me king—David, the king?
The lips spake false that spake thus for my ear.
King over men, but of his lust the slave!
Ill fares the throne on such foundation built.
Who ruleth self hath naught wherefrom to fear;
Who holdeth not the reins to appetite
Hath naught to guide save his wild, lustful will,
A charioteer to fiery steeds attached.
Death yawns for such, though life seems long to bless.

* Used by special permission of Miss Erica Oxenham.

O fatal night, in which the thought was born
Bearing in turn the deed that bound my soul
To this deep hell! No fires with this compare—
The pangs of conscience wronged, the will of God defied.
I know not now the peace that reigned within
When I, a lad on these Judean hills,
Led tender flocks by gently flowing streams,
Through pastures green, all innocent of wrong.

Sweet hours of youth, come ye but once again
To still this spirit groaning in its chains,
Where it, alas! must bide for evermore—
Except One come, in strength of purity,
To break these galling bonds and set me free.

My harp, once as my love, hangs idle now;
For music bideth not in souls depraved.
She dwelleth but on high, where God abides.
And if she comes to earth, she visits men
In holiness secure. O wretched fate,
To be bereft of that we once adored
As never womankind! Forget the past,
Beloved Music, be thou still my friend,
As when of old in grassy fields you walked with me
And doubted not my heart was true.
You pointed out the stars and bade me sing
Their matchless harmonies; nor did I halt,
But, tuning harp to voice, I sang to Him
And felt the heavens descend and lift me far
Beyond Judean hills to Jahweh's throne.

Alas! my power is gone, my harp is still,
And evermore shall be; for who would deign
To touch those magic strings with hands defiled!

Again the voices call, "King David—King!"
No more a king, but slave, a self-bound slave!
Who calls? Let him come in, but call not, "King."*

                                            —*Thomas Curtis Clark*

UNDER THE PROTECTION OF JEHOVAH

The Lord is my shepherd;
I shall not want.

He maketh me to lie down in green pastures:
He leadeth me beside the still waters.
He restoreth my soul:
He guideth me in the paths of righteousness for his name's sake.

* Used by special permission of the author.

Yea, though I walk through the valley of the shadow of death,
I will fear no evil;
For thou art with me:
Thy rod and thy staff, they comfort me.

Thou preparest a table before me
In the presence of mine enemies:
Thou hast anointed my head with oil;
My cup runneth over.

Surely goodness and mercy shall follow me all the days of my life:
And I will dwell in the house of the Lord for ever.*

—Psalm 23

"WHEN I CONSIDER THY HEAVENS"

How proudly bronzed young David wore the crown
And took its power in hands that once held sling
And five small stones to strike a giant down,—
Yet now received the honors due a king.
Instead of shepherd's crook, the flock, the fold,
The upland pasture where he watched alone,
He knew the royal robes, the jewels, the gold,
And fawning flatterers that haunt a throne.
But, still, at dusk he slipped away to keep
The old loved covenant with night and sky,
And kneeling there beside the huddled sheep
He traced in script of stars the Name Most High.
Nor did he care that earth's brief crowns grow dim,—
"For what is man that THOU rememberest him!"**

—Leslie Savage Clark

HERE'S A THOUGHT TO TUNE YOUR HARP TO

Here's a thought to tune your harp to,
　Here's a song that you can sing;
Here's a dream to play your pipe to:
　There is God in everything!

There is God in every dawning;
　God in every noon and night;
God in every roll of thunder,
　God in every flash of light.

There is God in every rose-bud,
　God in grass, and grain, and tree;

* From *The Modern Reader's Bible* edited by Richard G. Moulton. Copyright, 1935, by The Macmillan Company. Used by permission of the publisher.
** From *The Sign*, July, 1952. Used by special permission of the author and the publisher.

God in every planet, wheeling
    Through the dusky midnight sea.

There is God in song and laughter,
    God in loving hope and dream;
God in every dear child's sweetness;
    God in every silver stream.

God in growth and evolution,
    God in history and hope;
God in dim and distant mornings
    Where the poets dream and grope.

Here's a hope to tune your harp to,
    Here's a bell to boom and ring;
Here's a faith that will requite you
    There is God in everything!*

—William L. Stidger

✠

THE BASQUE SHEEPHERDER AND THE SHEPHERD PSALM

By

James K. Wallace

OLD Ferando D'Alfonso is a Basque herder employed by one of the big Nevada sheep outfits. He is rated as one of the best sheep rangers in the State, and he should be; for back of him are at least twenty generations of Iberian shepherds.

But D'Alfonso is more than a sheepherder; he is a patriarch of his guild, the traditions and secrets of which have been handed down from generation to generation, just as were those of the Damascus steel temperers and other trade guilds of the pre-medieval age. Despite a thirty-year absence from his homeland he is still full of the legends, the mysteries, the religious fervor of his native hills.

I sat with him one night under the clear, starry skies, his sheep bedded down beside a pool of sparkling water. As we were preparing to curl up in our blankets, he suddenly began a dissertation in a jargon of Greek and Basque. When he had finished, I asked him what he had said. In reply he began to quote in English the Twenty-third Psalm. There on the desert I learned the shepherd's literal interpretation of this beautiful poem.

"David and his ancestors," said D'Alfonso, "knew sheep and their ways, and David has translated a sheep's musing into simple words. The daily repetition of this Psalm fills the sheepherder with reverence for his calling. Our guild takes this poem as a lodestone to guide us. It is our bulwark when the days are hot and stormy, when the nights are dark; when wild animals surround our bands.

Many of its lines are the statements of the simple requirements and actual duties of a Holy Land shepherd, whether he lives today or followed the same calling six thousand years ago. Phrase by phrase, it has a well-understood meaning to us."

The Lord is my shepherd;
I shall not want.

"Sheep instinctively know," said D'Alfonso, "that ere they have been folded for the night the shepherd has planned out their grazing for the morrow. It may be that he will take them back over the same range; it may be that he will go to a new grazing ground. They do not worry. His guidance has been good in the past and they have faith in the future because they know he has their well-being in view."

He maketh me to lie down
in green pastures.

"Sheep graze from around 3:30 o'clock in the morning until about ten. They then lie down for three or four hours and rest," said D'Alfonso. "When they are contentedly chewing their cuds, the shepherd knows they are putting on fat. Consequently the good shepherd starts his flocks out in the early hours on the rougher herbage, moving on through the morning to the richer, sweeter grasses, and finally coming with the band to a shady place for its forenoon rest in fine green pastures, best grazing of the day. Sheep, while resting in such happy surroundings, feel contentment."

He leadeth me beside
the still waters.

"Every shepherd knows," said the Basque, "that sheep will not drink gurgling water. There are many small springs high in the hills of the Holy Land, whose waters run down the valleys only to evaporate in the desert sun. Although the sheep need the water, they will not drink from these fast-flowing streams. The shepherd must find a place where rocks or erosion have made a little pool, or else he fashions with his hands a pocket sufficient to hold at least a bucketful."

He restoreth my soul; He leadeth me
in the paths of righteousness for
His name's sake.

"Holy Land sheep exceed in herding instinct the Spanish Merino or the French Rambouillet," went on D'Alfonso. "Each takes his place in the grazing line in the morning and keeps the same position throughout the day. Once, however, during the day each sheep leaves its place and goes to the shepherd. Whereupon the shepherd stretches out his hand, as the sheep approaches with expectant eyes and mild little baas. The shepherd rubs its nose and ears, scratches its chin, whispers affectionately into its ears. The sheep, meanwhile, rubs against his leg or, if the shepherd is sitting down, nibbles at his ear, and rubs its cheek against his face. After a few minutes of this communion with the master, the sheep returns to its place in the feeding line."

Yea, though I walk through the
Valley of the Shadow of Death,
I will fear no evil. Thy rod
and Thy staff they comfort me.

"There is an actual Valley of the Shadow of Death in Palestine, and every shepherder from Spain to Dalmatia knows of it. It is south of the Jericho Road leading from Jerusalem to the Dead Sea and is a narrow defile through a mountain range. Climatic and grazing conditions make it necessary for the sheep to be moved through this valley for seasonal feeding each year.

"The valley is four and a half miles long. Its side walls are over fifteen hundred feet high in places and it is only ten or twelve feet wide at the bottom. Travel through the valley is dangerous, because its floor, badly eroded by cloudbursts, has gullies seven or eight feet deep. Actual footing on solid rock is so narrow in many places that a sheep cannot turn around, and it is an unwritten law of shepherds that flocks must go up the valley in the morning hours and down toward the eventide, lest flocks meet in the defile. Mules have not been able to make the trip for centuries, but sheep and goat herders from earliest Old Testament days have maintained a passage for their stock.

"About halfway through the valley the walk crosses from one side to the other at a place where the path is cut in two by an eight-foot gully. One section of the path is about eighteen inches higher than the other; the sheep must jump across it. The shepherd stands at this break and coaxes or forces the sheep to make the leap. If a sheep slips and lands in the gully, the shepherd's rod is brought into play. The old-style crook is encircled around a large sheep's neck or a small sheep's chest, and it is lifted to safety. If a more modern narrow crook is used, the sheep is caught about the hoofs and lifted up to the walk.

"Many wild dogs lurk in the shadow of the valley looking for prey. After a band of sheep has entered the defile, the leader may come upon such a dog. Unable to retreat, the leader baas a warning. The shepherd, skilled in throwing his staff, hurls it at the dog and knocks the animal into the washed-out gully where it is easily killed. Thus the sheep have learned to fear no evil even in the Valley of the Shadow of Death, for their master is there to aid them and protect them from harm."

Thou preparest a table before me
In the presence of mine enemies.

"David's meaning is a simple one," said D'Alfonso, "when conditions on the Holy Land sheep ranges are known. Poisonous plants abound which are fatal to grazing animals. Each spring the shepherd must be constantly alert. When he finds the plants he takes his mattock and goes on ahead of the flock, grubbing out every stock and root he can see. As he digs out the stocks, he lays them upon little stone pyres, some of which were built by shepherds in Old Testament days, and by the morrow they are dry enough to burn. In the meantime, the sheep are led into the newly prepared pasture, which is now free from poisonous plants, and, in the presence of their deadly plant enemies, they eat in peace."

Thou anointest my head with oil;
my cup runneth over.

"At every sheepfold there is a big earthen bowl of olive oil and a large stone jar of water. As the sheep come in for the night they are led to a gate. The shepherd lays his rod across the top of the gateway just higher than the backs of his sheep. As each sheep passes in single file, he quickly examines it for briers in the ears, snags in the cheek, or weeping of the eyes from dust or scratches. When such conditions are found, he drops the rod across the sheep's back and it steps out of the line.

"Each sheep's wounds are carefully cleaned. Then the shepherd dips his hand into the olive oil and anoints the injury. A large cup is dipped into the jar of water, kept cool by evaporation in the unglazed pottery, and is brought out— never half full but always overflowing. The sheep will sink its nose into the water clear to the eyes, if fevered, and drink until fully refreshed.

"When the sheep are at rest, the shepherd lays his staff on the ground within reach in case it is needed for protection of the flock during the night, wraps himself in his heavy woolen robe and lies down across the gateway, facing the sheep, for his night's repose.

"So," concluded D'Alfonso, "after all the care and protection the shepherd has given it, a sheep may well soliloquize in the twilight, as translated into words by David."

Surely goodness and mercy shall follow me
all the days of my life and I shall dwell
*in the house of the Lord forever.**

✢

DAVID, THE HERO WITH THE FEET OF CLAY

By

Sir Philip Gibbs

Part II. Flight from the Wrath of Saul

FROM this time on Saul hated David with greater intensity. This poet was getting all the glory. This harpist had made himself a hero. It was David . . . David . . . David. Soon he would claim the kingdom. Perhaps he had already claimed it.

David was kind to the old man. He played his harp to him again as in the days when he was favourite. But Saul listened moodily—and one day put his hand to his spear stealthily and flung it at David, thinking to nail him to the wall. David stepped to one side and the spear struck in the wall harmlessly.

After that, Saul spoke to his son and to others about him and asked them to kill David. But Jonathan loved David exceedingly and warned him of his danger. The war began again. David gained new victories and hero worship, and on

* From an article in *Reader's Digest* (June, 1950) reprinted from *The National Wool Growers* (Dec., 1949). Used by special permission of the publishers.

his return Saul's jealousy overtook him again, so that he made further attempts against David's life. One night he issued orders for his arrest and sent his body-guard to surround David's house. It was the beautiful Michal who warned her husband: "Unless thou save thyself this night tomorrow thou wilt die."

She let him down through a window, and he escaped from the King's body-guard in the darkness, and when the soldiers came into the house at dawn Michal pretended that David lay ill in bed, having stuffed something that looked like a body with a goat's skin, covering the head.

"Bring him to me in his bed!" shouted Saul, and he was furious with his daughter when her trick was discovered.

Jonathan knew there would be no peace between David and his father. He went to warn David again. There was a farewell meeting between the two com-rades, recorded in a few lines which still stir men's hearts because of this noble grief.

David fell on his face to the ground and adored thrice . . . "And kissing one another they wept, but David more."

And Jonathan said to David: "Go in peace. And let all stand we have sworn, both of us, in the name of the Lord." So David escaped into the wilds, leaving his wife and his friend, and his honours and his fortune, all that he had gained and loved.

For several years David was an outlaw, hunted like a beast by Saul and his men. Other men joined him, some of his own clansmen, and men escaping from debt, and others who had incurred the wrath of Saul, until he had a company of six hundred.

Among them were young, fighting men of knightly type who under the leader-ship of David, became his champions, like those of Arthur's court in *The Idylls of the King*. For a time their headquarters were in the stronghold, or cave, of Adul-lam, a Canaanite town twelve miles from Bethlehem, from which they made raids upon the Philistines and other hostile folk, seizing their cattle and treasures, which David distributed among friendly tribesmen to gain their allegiance and good will.

He was a kind of Rob Roy of Palestine, and in some ways a Robin Hood.

Later on David and his six hundred men returned to "safer places," and lived by taking tribute from neighboring chiefs in return for protection of their flocks and herds from marauding bands.

One of these chiefs who had his stronghold in Mount Carmel, in the south-west of the country beyond the wilderness, had three thousand sheep and one thousand goats. His name was Nabal, and he had a beautiful wife called Abigail. When David demanded the usual blackmail, Nabal refused with the bitter words that there were too many servants nowadays who had fled from their masters.

They were rash words to send back to David. He girded on his sword in great anger and, leaving two hundred of his men to guard the baggage, set off with four hundred men to take his tribute by force.

A massacre was prevented by the beautiful Abigail. One of her servants had warned her of the vengeance threatened against her husband and his clan. Abigail did not tell her husband, but set out with a caravan laden with tribute to intercept David, who was advancing with his freebooters. Meeting him coming up the mountain road, she got off her mule and fell on her face to the ground before him and then pleaded with him.

David regarded her beauty and saw also that her asses were well laden. Having taken her gifts, which he needed for the refreshments of his men, he spoke to her graciously:

"Go in peace to thy house. Behold I have heard thy voice and have honoured thy face."

It was a pretty face which lingered in his mind and blotted out the memory of Michal, his wife.

When Abigail returned to her husband he was giving a banquet and became very drunk, so that she said nothing of what she had done. But when he was sober the next morning she told him, and he was stricken with rage and his heart became like a stone.

Ten days later he had a stroke and died, and David, hearing the news, sent word to Abigail that he desired her as his wife. She was a wealthy young widow and came to David with five of her damsels, and they were married.

Away where Saul kept his court in Israel, Michal, who had loved David, was given by her father to the son of one of his officers, as women in those days had no rights or liberties under the tyranny of men.

Eventually the Philistines fell upon the army of Saul and utterly routed it, driving the remnants back to Mount Gilboa, where the Philistine archers surrounded them.

Saul, himself, was wounded with arrows and Jonathan was slain. The old King knew that he was doomed. Only a few days before he had been forewarned of his fate by the spirit of Samuel, called up by the witch of Endor—a "medium"—as she would now be called—and he was resolved not to fall into the hands of his enemies.

According to one account, he called to his armour-bearer: "Draw thy sword and kill me." But when the armour-bearer refused, being stricken with fear, Saul took his own sword and fell upon it, as afterwards many a Roman did, and as his armour-bearer did then.

The old hunter of men had fallen at last. In his youth he had obeyed the God of Israel, and had been among the prophets. He had welded the tribes of Israel into a nation. He had been their *first King* and with a fierce patriotism had thrust back their enemies time and time again before madness overtook him. Now he lay dead among the bodies of his spearmen, and Jonathan was slain not far away.

A Messenger came from the camp of the Israelites, fell at the feet of David and told him what had happened in the battle, and that Saul and Jonathan were dead. David was incredulous at first: "How knowest thou that Saul and Jonathan, his son, are dead?"

The young man told a strange tale. It contradicts the account of Saul falling on his own sword, but reads like truth:

"I came by chance upon Mount Gilboa and Saul leaned upon his spear and the chariots and horsemen drew nigh to him. Looking behind him and seeing me he called me. And I answered, 'Here I am.' And he said to me, 'Who are thou?' And I said to him, 'I am an Amalekite.' And he said to me, 'Stand over and kill me, for anguish is come upon me and as yet my whole life is in me.' So standing over him I killed him. And I took the diadem that was on his head and the bracelet that was on his arm, and have brought them hither to thee, my lord."

It sounds as matter of fact as a man giving evidence of murder in some police court of today.

David listened, and spoke calmly at first, asking the young man whether he had not been afraid to kill the Lord's anointed. Then like a sultan he called to one of his servants to slay the man then and there. And looking down at the poor wretch as he lay dead, he spoke to him, as a defense to this act to his own conscience.

"Thy blood be upon thy own head. For thy mouth hath spoken against thee, saying: 'I have slain the Lord's anointed.'"

Then he made that dirge for the death of Saul, who had been his enemy, and for Jonathan, his friend, which is one of the most beautiful of all laments in the history of the world, or in the books of poets:

Saul and Jonathan, lovely and comely in their life, even in death they were not divided; they were swifter than eagles, stronger than lions.

Ye daughters of Israel, weep over Saul who clothed you with scarlet, who gave you ornaments of gold for your attire.

How are the valiant fallen in battle! Jonathan slain in the high places! . . . I grieve for thee, my brother Jonathan, exceedingly beautiful and amiable to me above the love of a woman. As a mother who loveth her only son so did I love thee.

Overthrown by a Rebel Son

After the death of Saul, David went to Mount Hebron with his wives and clansmen, and here, by an assembly of the men of Judea, he was anointed King over that country, where he reigned for eleven years, and later, at thirty years of age, became King over all Israel.

He was engaged in incessant fighting against the Philistines and gained many victories over their strongholds, his most important act being the capture of Jerusalem. Until then it had never been in Hebrew hands, although so close—no more than twelve miles away—to the town of Bethlehem. David chose Jerusalem as his capital, and in his hands it became no mean city.

During one of the campaigns against the Israelites' other great enemies, the Ammonites, commanded by Joab, his chief of staff, David, remaining behind in Jerusalem, committed a sin which wounded his own conscience and offended the Commandments of God as written down by Moses, and as they stand in the hearts of all just men.

As he walked one morning on the roof of his house, he saw a woman down below, washing herself, and was taken by her beauty. He discovered that she was a woman named Bathsheba and the wife of a man named Uriah the Hittite, who was a mercenary soldier serving in his army under Joab.

He sent for Bathsheba and made love to her. Then he sent for Uriah and tried to bribe him to keep quiet about this affair, but the man refused to acquiesce in his wife's misconduct with the King, and would not even go inside his house, so that people were scandalized.

"Tarry here today," said David, "and tomorrow I will send thee away."

Then David did an unpardonable thing, against all the laws of God and man. He wrote a note to Joab, his commander-in-chief, telling him to put this man Uriah in the forefront of the battle where the fighting was hottest, so that he would be wounded and would die.

Messengers came back from Joab, telling David that his orders had been carried out, and when Bathsheba heard, she wept for her husband. But David made her his wife.

"And the thing which David had done was displeasing to the Lord."

For forty years David reigned over Israel, fighting many wars and maintaining his power until he became enfeebled with age. Towards the end of his life quarrels broke out among his sons, and one of them, named Absalom, set up a standard of revolt in Hebron (where David had made his stronghold in his early days), declaring war against the King and gaining the allegiance of many clans because of his gallantry and spirit.

The conspiracy seems to have reached Jerusalem, and David in his old age, after all his years of rule, was compelled to escape. It was a tragic procession which went slowly away from Jerusalem and wound up the hillside of the Mount of Olives. David, old now and weak, walked barefoot, with his head covered to hide his agony, and all of his followers covered their heads in grief.

In this hour of misfortune David drank the cup of bitterness to the dregs. Many of those whom he had most befriended were treacherous to him. In Jerusalem, Absalom, whom he most loved, ill-used his father's wives. The crippled son of Jonathan, whom he had taken into his court, had stayed behind in Jerusalem, saying: "Today the house of Israel will restore to me the Kingdom of my father."

One of Saul's kinsmen stood on the hillside as the King passed and flung down stones as well as curses at him, accusing him of having usurped the kingdom.

News was brought presently that Absalom's army was advancing on the fugitives and they retreated across the Jordan and came in to the country of their old enemies the Ammonites. Here many of the clans who had followed Absalom rallied around the King, and Joab reconstituted his army and prepared to advance upon the traitors, who by this time had also crossed the Jordan.

David was induced to remain behind, and he gave only one command to Joab and the other captains: "Save me the boy Absalom."

The battle took place in the wood of Ephraim, and the Israelites under Absalom were utterly defeated. Absalom himself was caught in the branches of a tree as he fled on a mule which ran from under him. A runner came back to Joab with this news of David's son.

"Why did you not stab him?" asked Joab. "I would have given thee ten pieces of silver and a girdle." The man was shocked by these words and said: "If thou hadst paid down into my hands a thousand pieces of silver, I would not lay my hands on the King's son. For in our hearing the King charged thee, saying: 'Spare me the boy, Absalom.'"

"I will set upon him," said Joab sternly, and he went to where Absalom was caught in a tree, and thrust a lance into him and his two armour-bearers finished him off.

Meanwhile David was waiting for the news in the hilltop fortress where he had taken refuge. The two messengers fell at his feet telling him of the victory, but several times David interrupted them by one question: "Is the young man Absalom safe?"

For a time they prevaricated, until one of the messengers told the truth in cryptic words :"Let the enemies of my lord and king and all that rise against him be as this young man is."

David understood. He rose and covered his face and wept, and going up to the water tower above the gate cried out bitterly with anguish: "O my son Absalom, Absalom, my son! Would to God that I might die for thee, Absalom, my son, my son Absalom!"

At the very end of his life, when he was weak and ill, another son rebelled against him and said: "I will be king." It was Adonias, the next born after Absalom. David did not rebuke him, and he began to get adherents; but Nathan, the old priest, and Bathsheba, whom he had seduced from Uriah the Hittite, came to him protesting that he had promised the succession of the crown to Bathsheba's son, Solomon.

David grieved, and while his rebel son was feasting with his young conspirators, Solomon was anointed before a multitude of people who played on their pipes and shouted with joy.

At last old David lay dying, and with his last breath his cruelty and craftiness has its say, and he incited Solomon to deal with his enemies—the kinsmen of Saul who had cursed the King on his flight from Jerusalem, and Joab, who had killed Absalom.

"Let not his hoary head go down to hell in peace," said the dying old man, forgetting how much he owed to Joab as his greatest captain, his old comrade-in-arms, who more than any other man had led his men to victory.

And young Solomon, listening to his father's words, had no mercy on Adonias his brother, nor on Joab, nor on Saul's kinsman, who had cursed the King, and they were all slain.

HALF-HERO, HALF-VILLAIN

So David slept with his fathers, half-hero and half-villain, noble and gentle in many of his acts, cruel as a tiger at other times; generous sometimes to his enemies, uplifted by a sense of divine beauty, a poet in his heart, a great lover of women, but not faithful to any one of them; sincere and humble in his reverence before the Creator of the heavens and the hills and the stars and the winds and all living things of the world, and all the tribes of men. It is impossible to judge him by modern standards of morality or by the Christian code.

He was perhaps the greatest poet that ever lived. The Psalms of David reach heights of imagination never scaled by the human mind before his time in any literature that has come down to us.

> What is man that thou art mindful of him?
> Or the son of man that thou visitest him?
> For thou hast made him a little lower than
> the angels and hast crowned him with glory and honour."

David, who wrote those words, or of whom they were written, stooped sometimes as low as the brute because of the weakness of the flesh and the wild beast in him; but he was touched with some divine flame which made him "the lamp of Israel," as his men called him.

With all that can be said against him, he stands through the mist of three thousand years heroic and human, and the young David who left his father's flocks to fight the Philistine in single combat will always be the type of heroic youth, beautiful and brave against the powers of ugliness and evil.*

✤

WATCHMAN, WHAT OF THE NIGHT?

By

Grace West Staley

CAPTAIN JOAB** waited impatiently for the King to appear. Where was David? And why didn't he do something about that vast idle army that covered the surrounding hills and valleys? Joab looked from the sea of tents to the city of the Jebusites that stood yonder on a steep hill. What was it about that great walled city that defied David's plans! Surely not its rugged hills. Why, between David and himself they had taken many walled cities. Aye, all of Israel, except this last remaining stronghold.

"If David would only restore me to my command!" cried Joab aloud.

"David will restore Joab to his command when he can once more trust him," said a voice close by on the hillside. Joab's startled eyes turned to look into the eyes of David the King.

"Have I not said I was sorry for disobeying your orders?" Joab asked. "Give me a chance, David, to redeem myself."

"What is it you would do?" asked David thoughtfully.

"Return me to my men. Let me plan a siege against the city," answered Joab.

The King shook his head. "You are hasty as always, Joab. The city of the Jebusites will not be taken by siege, but by strategy."

Joab's hopes fell. Would David never forget his mistakes and trust him? Was he to be kept at this miserable little position of watchman of the city walls?

"Then give me leave to take a message that might force the Jebusites' hand," he said.

"Why?" asked David. "What do your guards about the walls report?"

"That since the encampment of your army, no food has passed through the city

---

* From *The Sunday Chronicle*, Nov. 22, 1931. Used by special permission of the author and the publisher.
** I Chron. 11:4-7, and Isa. 21:11.

gates. Nor has any woman, servant or man sought water from the Fountain of the Virgins."

Joab pointed toward a bubbling spring where it gushed out of the rocky cavern at the foot of the hill, just below the city walls. "The Jebusites," he said, "may possibly have storehouses of food, but this spring is the only known clear water in this dry and barren neighborhood. They may be even now dying of thirst."

"Very well," said David. "Take the Jebusites the message that if they surrender now, not one life in the city will be lost, nor shall any man hunger or thirst. Go, and let me hear their reply!"

Joab walked hastily down the hill. He crossed the stream that flowed down through the little valley from the Fountain of the Virgins and made his way up the steep hill towards his guards stationed around the city walls.

"I must make David see that he can trust me," thought Joab. "If only I could take the city!"

At the city gates a guard was soon shouting Joab's message to the Jebusite sentries on top of the walls. The sentries roared with laughter. They waved their swords aloft and shouted down at him:

"Why should the Jebusites surrender so secure a city? We are so strong, the blind and the lame could defend us. Tell your King to go away. He will never take the city of the Jebusites!"

Joab turned away in disgust at this mocking reply and started on his rounds of inspection. He must hear his guards' reports and see that every position was filled.

By the time he had come clear around the city walls to the Fountain of the Virgins, Joab was not only tired but very thirsty. He removed his helmet, dipped it into the water, and was just placing it to his lips when he heard a clinking sound—like the clash of swords.

He glanced over his shoulder. Here and there he saw soldiers idly talking together, but not a sword was drawn. He looked toward the city walls. As far as his eye could see, his watchers stood at their posts. Joab looked above, thinking it might be the Jebusite sentries. Not a face could be seen on the top of the wall. Yet, *Click-clickety-click*—there it was again!

"That's strange!" Joab exclaimed, puzzled. "What is that queer sound! Where *is it* coming from!"

Joab stood by the water, quietly listening, but he did not hear the sound again. He placed his helmet back on his head with a shrug. "This water must be playing tricks on my ears," he laughed, and walked to David's tent.

"What news does my watchman bring?" asked David, as Joab entered.

"No news, David," replied Joab. "The Jebusites mock us. They say their city is invincible."

"It is as I thought," said David. "The city has food and some secret water supply within its walls."

David continued speaking in a low voice, but Joab did not hear him. The words of the King were ringing in his head. *"Some secret water supply—some secret water supply."* Suddenly he remembered the Fountain of the Virgins. That peculiar noise he had heard as he stood by the spring. Had he stumbled upon some secret of the Jebusites?

"Come Joab," said David. "Why do you loiter? The sun is already sinking. Have you forgotten your duties? Watchman, what of the night: Have you posted fresh sentries?"

With a start, Joab lifted his eyes. "The sentries have been posted," he said absently, and left the tent.

Wild hopes raced through Joab's head as he hurried back to the Fountain of the Virgins. He listened intently there, but he could hear nothing but the trickling of the water. "I cannot have imagined it," muttered Joab. "I must know what made that queer noise."

He turned to a nearby guard. "Return to your tent," he said. "I myself will relieve you of duty this night."

The surprised guard, glad to be excused, hurried off while Joab awaited the night. Then as the moon rose high in the heavens over the sleeping tents he stepped to the Fountain. *Clink, clank, clink, clank.* There, he could hear it clearly now. The sound seemed to be coming from the cavern from which the spring gushed.

Joab knew he might be facing death, yet if this was something that the King should know, he must know more. He placed his sword upon the ground, unstrapped his sandals, and stepped into the water. He waded into the cavern from which the water flowed and suddenly the water became so deep as to go over his head. There was not much room to swim or to breathe, for the water came almost to the top of the cavern. Just then he struck against the rocky wall and found it to be the end of a tunnel. Through this channel, in which shallow water was flowing, Joab crept on his hands and knees, and abruptly this dark passage way opened into a lighted cavern.

With heart that was pounding Joab looked about at the rocky walls. Here was a secret pool! This must be where the Jebusites got their water! Eagerly he looked above him and there, opening into the water was a long chimney-like shaft which led up and up through the solid rock to the city above. A bucket shaft! Joab caught his breath. It was down through this rock chimney that the Jebusite women lowered their buckets on the tell-tale jangling chain to this secret pool. It was the sound of their buckets striking the rocks that he had heard.

Joab saw instantly what the Jebusites had done. Fearing to be driven from their city by thirst, the Jebusites had dug down through the solid rock a hundred feet till they had come to the spring as it flowed through the rock on its way to the Fountain of the Virgins.

Hoping desperately to find out more, and yet fearing that every move might be heard, Joab started climbing up along the shaft. The rocks were sharp and jagged. On one of them Joab's hand was ripped open. He stopped, gasping with pain. Then slowly he struggled upward from crevice to crevice, fearing each moment to dislodge some loose particle of rock, the splash of which in the pool below might bring a Jebusite guard. Suddenly he came upon steps carved from the rock that led upward along the shaft. One step at a time he stole upward, scarcely daring to breathe. Here and there along the way he saw lanterns hanging from pegs to light the secret pool and stairway. This was the secret entrance to the city!

"The city must be asleep," thought Joab. "I have not heard or seen one bucket lowered since I found my way into the pool."

When Joab was half way up—between the pool below and the city above—he turned. "I've seen enough," he said to himself. "I must get back to the King. If only David will believe me! If only David will trust me!"

Slowly Joab made his way down the rocky steps, over the dangerous crevices and jagged rocks to the secret pool. Quickly he passed out through the dark tunnel into the cavern of the Fountain of the Virgins and into the night.

Joab looked quickly about to see if he had been missed. The stars looked peacefully down upon the silent tents. All was quiet. Hurriedly he climbed the hill to David's tent and poked the sleepy guard with his sword.

"It's Captain Joab," he said. "I must see the King at once." The guard began to argue, but Joab pushed past him into the tent.

David half rose from his couch. "Is it you, Joab? Why do you disturb me in my sleep?"

"Do not be angry, David," cried Joab, "for I bring you great news. I have found the Jebusites' secret water supply! I have found an entrance into the city!"

Instantly David rose and listened to all that Joab had seen and heard. "Joab, you have done well," said the King. "Take a small company of brave men and guide them back through the secret pool. It may be you can reach the city street before morning. And I and my army will be waiting for you at the city gates."

Joab's heart swelled with joy. David had believed him. David was trusting him. Before long he was leading a few soldiers in the daring mission. Through the Fountain and cavern he led them. Through the channel and into the secret cave. Up over the rocks the men stealthily crept after him till they reached the rocky stairway, the hanging lanterns casting their shadows on the walls like marching ghosts. Joab led his men in and out through the tunnels on the secret path until they reached the city streets above. With storehouses full of food and a secret well for water, the city of the Jebusites lay peacefully sleeping behind its rugged walls.

"Come," motioned Captain Joab to the men, "follow me!" And he silently led them through the narrow streets until they reached the city gates. Quickly they overpowered the sleeping sentinels, threw open the gates, and David and his soldiers filed silently into the city.

When the Jebusites awoke in the morning, they found their city occupied by the army of King David. Joab was soon called before the King.

"I trusted you," said David, "and you did not fail me. From this day, Joab, you will be supreme commander of my army, and rebuilder of my capital."

Joab felt that his heart would burst with happiness. "I shall make your capital stronger than all the cities of Egypt," he said; "more beautiful than the palaces of the Nile; and it shall be called Jerusalem—the city of David."*

* From *Story Art Magazine*, May-June, 1948. Used by special permission of the author.

AS PANTS THE HART

(Interpretation)

EARLY Christian worship included singing of the Psalms which had been a feature of the worship at the Temple in Jerusalem. There is a record in Mark 14:26 that after Jesus and the apostles had sung a "hymn" they went out to the Mount of Olives. This "hymn" may have been the Hallel, Psalms 113-118. Paul and Silas "sang praises unto God" during their imprisonment in Philippi. In Paul's letter to the Colossians (3:16) he recommends the singing of "psalms and hymns and spiritual songs." All this reflects the importance of singing, especially of the Psalms, among early Christians.

The singing of the Psalms or arrangements from them has continued in Christian worship. The theme of the hymn, "As Pants the Hart," is to be found in the 42nd Psalm:

As Pants the Hart

"New" version   PSALM 42   Alois Kaiser

p Andante con moto

1. As pants the hart for cool-ing streams When heat-ed in the chase,
2. For Thee, my God, the liv-ing God, My thirst-ing soul doth pine,
3. Why rest-less, why cast down, my soul, Trust God who will em-ploy
4. Why rest-less, why cast down, my soul, Hope still and thou shalt sing

So longs my soul for Thee, O God, And Thy re-fresh-ing grace.
Oh, when shall I be-hold Thy face, Thy maj-es-ty... di-vine!
His aid for thee and change these sighs To thank-ful hymns of joy.
The praise of Him who is... thy Lord, Thy health's e-ter-nal spring.

* From *Union Hymnal*, No. 40. Copyright, 1932, by the Central Conference of American Rabbis. Used by special permission of the publisher.

As the hart panteth after the water brooks,
So panteth my soul after thee, O God.

My soul thirsteth for God, for the living God:
When shall I come and appear before God?

My tears have been my meat day and night,
While they continually say unto me,
        Where is thy God?

When I remember these things, I pour out my soul in me:
For I had gone with the multitude, I went with them to
    the house of God,
With the voice of joy and praise, with a multitude
    that kept holyday.

Why art thou cast down, O my soul?
And why art thou disquieted in me?
Hope thou in God; for I shall yet praise him
    For the help of his countenance.

It is easy to see how the four stanzas of this hymn have taken the thought in
the 42nd Psalm, and have made it suitable for singing today.

The first stanza stresses the thirst of the human soul for communion with God,
its Maker and Creator. The second stanza emphasizes the longing of the human
soul for face-to-face communion with God. The third and fourth stanzas speak of
the restlessness of the human heart in its search for the peace that passes all understanding, ending with the assurance that God is the eternal spring in the renewal of health and peace in human life. The music score to this hymn was
composed by Alois Kaiser.

✠

I WILL PRAY

(Interpretation)

To the Psalms, perhaps more than to any other source, we must go to discover
the inspiration of many of the most beautiful and meaningful hymns of the
Church. And it is to the 55th Psalm that we must look for the theme of William
L. Stidger's hymn-poem, "I will Pray," written in 1938 and set to an arrangement by James R. Houghton of an older tune by Wolfgang A. Mozart.

Those who are familiar with Dr. Stidger's volume, *I Saw God Wash the World,*
will note in the words of this hymn a reference to the beauty in God's world of
nature, and to the Christian's instinctive response to the beauty of the world that
surrounds us, as at dawn we raise our voices in prayerful gratitude to the Giver
of all good gifts.

The second stanza suggests that we lift our hearts in prayer at noontide also

I Will Pray

"Evening and morning and at noon, will I pray, and cry aloud;
and He shall hear my voice." Ps. 55: 17

Dr. William L. Stidger

Wolfgang A. Mozart
Adapted by James R. Houghton

I will pray when morn-ing glo-ry Gilds the east ern hills with gold,
I will pray at noon, dear Mas-ter, When all life is high with hope
I will pray dear God, when dark-ness Throws its ves-per sha-dows 'round,

When the dew has washed the tu-lip And dawn's tale of __ time is told.
And the sun has halved the cir-cle In it's might-y __ sweep and scope;
In the si-lence I will lis-ten, Kneel-ing on Thy __ ho ly ground.

I will kneel be-fore Thine al-tars And burn in-cense at Thy shrines;
When life's blood is cours-ing wild-ly In a full ma-jes-tic stream,
I will meet Thy tryst at twi-light, When the si-lent sha-dows sleep,

In-cense of the rose and li-lac, Lo-cust-bloom and wind-washed pines.
When the tide of strength is run-ning To it's dar-ing flow and dream.
And all birds and beasts and child-ren In-to dream-land soft ly creep.

when we are in the midst of the "mighty sweep and scope" of the full day's tasks and responsibilities.

The closing stanza speaks of the soul's sincere desire at vesper time "when the silent shadows sleep" to keep our twilight tryst with the God in whom we live and move and have our being. It again relates the human family to the birds and beasts that instinctively seek rest and relaxation in nighttime's dreamland of sleep.

This hymn illuminates with word pictures the three intervals for prayer during the day—"Evening, and morning, and at noon, will I pray, and cry aloud." The underlying faith in this hymn is expressed in the Psalm: "And he shall hear my voice." This faith is a heritage from the Old Testament, made real by Christ, and passed down to us through the centuries in the singing of the Church.

✛

THE KING OF LOVE MY SHEPHERD IS

(Interpretation)

ONE cannot sing this devotional hymn of the Church without recalling at least two familiar Scripture passages:

"The Lord is my shepherd; I shall not want" (Ps. 23:1).

"I am the good shepherd: the good shepherd giveth his life for the sheep. . . . I . . . know my sheep, and am known of mine. As the Father knoweth me, even so know I the Father: and I lay down my life for the sheep" (John 10:11, 14, 15).

The 23rd Psalm is without doubt one of the most widely known and best loved of all the Psalms. Its beauty of thought and diction has been quoted in "tent and tabernacle, in college and camp, in palace and temple" for more than three thousand years.

Sir Henry William Baker's (1821-1877) magnificent hymn is in reality a poetic translation of the sentiment to be found in the 23rd Psalm. He was the son of a vice admiral, and was educated at Trinity College in Cambridge. In 1859 he became a baronet.

Perhaps his greatest work was that of chairman of the committee which edited *Hymns Ancient and Modern,* popular in the Anglican Church. In 1875 thirty-three hymns from his pen were included in one of the revised editions.

The tune "Dominus Regit Me" was composed in 1868 by John B. Dykes (1823-1876). The name of the tune is the Latin title of the 23rd Psalm. The melody is accentuated to bring out such emphatic words as "King," "Shepherd," "goodness," "never," "nothing," "he," and "forever" in the first stanza.

This hymn, like the Psalm from which it is derived, expresses trust in God's unfailing providence. It abounds in details picturing the care of a shepherd for his flock. There is security, not in freedom from danger, but in remaining beside the Lord, with His cross to guide us.

The King of Love My Shepherd Is

DOMINUS REGIT ME. 8, 7, 8, 7

HENRY W. BAKER, 1868

JOHN B. DYKES, 1868

1. The King of love my Shep - herd is, Whose good - ness fail - eth nev - er, I noth - ing lack if I am his, And he is mine for - ev - er.

2. Where streams of liv - ing wa - ter flow My ran - somed soul he lead - eth, And where the ver - dant pas - tures grow With food ce - les - tial feed - eth.

3. Per - verse and fool - ish oft I strayed, But yet in love he sought me, And on his shoul - der gen - tly laid And home re - joic - ing brought me.

4. In death's dark vale I fear no ill, With thee, dear Lord, be - side me, Thy rod and staff my com - fort still, Thy cross be - fore to guide me. A-men.

5 Thou spread'st a table in my sight,
  And grace divine bestoweth,
  And O! what transport of delight
  From thy pure chalice floweth!

6 And so through all the length of days
  Thy goodness faileth never;
  Good Shepherd, may I sing thy praise
  Within thy house forever.

LITTLE DAVID

(Interpretation)

LIKE many other folk songs, spirituals are usually sung in dialect, for the American Negro acquired the language of the country of his enforced adoption by ear alone. Only a small per cent of the Negro slaves ever learned to read or write.

African languages, particularly those of the Bantu tribes from which most of the American Negroes came, are soft and musical, as almost any missionary leader will verify. It was natural, therefore, that when these imported slaves attempted to pick up by ear the English of their slave owners, that they should drop all harsh sounds, and even leave out whole syllables in order to get an effect that was pleasing to their ears. As these Negro dialects were always spoken and never written there was no accurate way of representing them on paper. For this reason there often are different versions of the same spiritual. It is better not to attempt to write them out in what might be termed proper English, for in so doing they are robbed of much of their naturalness and effectiveness. Spirituals should be sung

Little David.

May be sung in the key of G.

Lit-tle Da-vid, play on your harp, Hal-le-lu! hal-le-lu! Lit-tle Da-vid,

play on your harp, Hal-le-lu! lu!

1. Lit-tle Da-vid was a
2. Josh-u-a was the
3. Done told you once, done

shepherd boy, He killed Go-li-ath, and shout-ed for joy.
son of a Nun, He nev-er would quit till the work was done.
told you twice, There're sinners in hell for shoot-ing dice.

in the dialect language in which they were originally composed, just as are Scottish and Irish folk songs.

In his life story David, the shepherd hero of the Old Testament, provided a distinct challenge for the enslaved Negroes in the United States. They loved to hear the stories of his heroic boyhood days as he protected his father's sheep from wolves and lions. His brave fight with the giant, Goliath, fired their imagination and stirred their volatile emotions. The sweet music of David's harp and the beautiful poetic Psalms which he composed as he guarded his father's flock on distant hillsides appealed to their own love of music, poetry, and rhythm. And so they sang of David and his achievements. With a fine disregard for history, they next sang of Joshua who died more than two hundred years before David was born. The exploits of these two great leaders in behalf of their people are merely hinted at, but this hint serves to show up the unworthiness of the playing with dice and gambling of many of their own race.

This spiritual, "Little David," which sometimes appears under the full title of the first line, "Little David, Play on Your Harp," is one of the best-loved and most frequently sung of all these "songs of the spirit."

O My Soul, Bless God, the Father

STUTTGART. 8, 7, 8, 7.

United Presbyterian Book of Psalms
U. S. A., 1871

Psalmodia Sacra, 1715

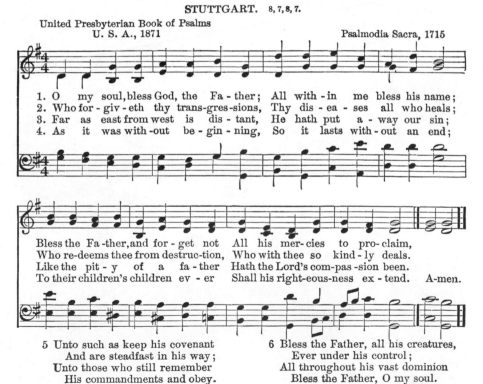

1. O my soul, bless God, the Fa-ther; All with-in me bless his name;
2. Who for-giv-eth thy trans-gres-sions, Thy dis-ea-ses all who heals;
3. Far as east from west is dis-tant, He hath put a-way our sin;
4. As it was with-out be-gin-ning, So it lasts with-out an end;

Bless the Fa-ther, and for-get not All his mer-cies to pro-claim,
Who re-deems thee from destruc-tion, Who with thee so kind-ly deals.
Like the pit-y of a fa-ther Hath the Lord's com-pas-sion been.
To their children's children ev-er Shall his right-eous-ness ex-tend. A-men.

5 Unto such as keep his covenant
And are steadfast in his way;
Unto those who still remember
His commandments and obey.

6 Bless the Father, all his creatures,
Ever under his control;
All throughout his vast dominion
Bless the Father, O my soul.

O MY SOUL, BLESS GOD, THE FATHER

(Interpretation)

THIS rich inspirational hymn is from the *United Presbyterian Book of Psalms,* published in 1871. Its tune, "Stuttgart," is from *Psalmodia Sacra,* which dates back to 1715. The hymn itself is a metrical version of parts of Psalm 103.

The six stanzas that comprise this great prayer hymn are definitely devotional in character and appeal. They are a plea to all "followers of the Way" to "bless God, the Father, and . . . all his mercies proclaim."

The loving nature of the Eternal God in forgiving the transgressions of men, in healing their diseases, and in redeeming them from destruction is clearly portrayed in the second and third stanzas.

The fourth stanza emphasizes the enduring everlasting love of our Heavenly Father.

In the fifth stanza God's followers are assured of the steadfastness of His covenants to all those who remember and obey His commandments.

The last stanza urges all creatures under His vast universal domain to continue to "bless the Father" of all earth's children.

CONTENTS

PART III   SECTION 3

THE KINGDOM OF SOLOMON

✜

And they made Solomon the son of David king . . . and anointed him unto the Lord to be the chief governor, and Zadok to be priest. Then Solomon sat on the throne of the Lord as king instead of David his father, and prospered; and all Israel obeyed him.—I CHRONICLES 29:22-23

✜

THE JUDGMENT OF SOLOMON

By

Raphael Sanzio

(Interpretation)

SOLOMON, the son of David and Bathsheba, was, according to the book of I Kings, the wisest of all of Israel's kings because the Lord had given him a double portion of wisdom. The story of how this came about is told in I Kings 3:5-12.

Soon after Zadok the priest anointed Solomon king of Israel the new king went up to Gibeon to offer a sacrifice to the Lord. And there God "appeared to Solomon in a dream by night and God said, 'Ask what I shall give thee?' And Solomon said, . . . 'O Lord my God, thou hast made thy servant king instead of David my father; and I am but a little child; I know not how to go out or come in. And thy servant is in the midst of thy people which thou hast chosen, a great people, that cannot be numbered nor counted for multitude. Give therefore thy servant an understanding heart to judge thy people, that I may discern between good and bad; for who is able to judge this thy so great a people?'

"And the speech pleased the Lord, that Solomon had asked this thing. And God said unto him, 'Because thou hast asked this thing, and hast not asked for thyself long life; neither hast asked riches for thyself, nor hast asked the life of thine enemies; but hast asked for thyself understanding to discern judgment; behold, I have done according to thy words: lo, I have given thee a wise and an understanding heart; so that there was none like thee before thee, neither after thee shall any arise like unto thee.' "

Solomon was often to remember that dream and God's assurance that to him had been given the gift of just and righteous judgment.

Raphael's picture, "The Judgment of Solomon," is an exquisite illustration of one of those wise and just judgments. One day not long after Solomon's return from Gibeon there came to him two women who lived in the same household. Two children had been born, one to each of these two women, at the same time. One of these children died; the other lived. In the nighttime, the woman whose child had died stole the child of the other woman, while she slept, and took it into her own bed. When the morning came she claimed that the living child was hers, and that the dead child belonged to the other woman.

A quarrel arose that could not be settled amicably. So the two women sought King Solomon, and asked him to decide to whom the living child belonged. He listened to each woman with great patience and then said: " 'Bring me a sword.' And they brought a sword before the king. And the king said, 'Divide the living child in two, and give half to the one, and half to the other' " (3:24-25).

When the true mother of the living child heard this decision, her heart yearned for the life of her son, even though it meant that she might lose him forever to the other woman. And she said to the king: " 'O my lord, give her the living child, and in no wise slay it.' But the other said, 'Let it be neither mine nor thine, but divide it' " (3:26).

Then King Solomon knew who the real mother of the living child was, and he said to his servant: " 'Give her the living child, and in no wise slay it: she is the mother thereof.' And all Israel heard of the judgment which the king had judged; and they feared the king: for they saw that the wisdom of God was in him, to do judgment" (3:27-28).

Raphael's painting of this wise judgment appears in the twelfth arcade in the Loggie in the Vatican in Rome. On the throne sits Solomon wearing his crown. His right hand is raised as he pronounces judgment. Before him stands his servant holding up the living child by his feet and preparing to divide the child in half with the knife grasped in his powerful right hand. The real mother rushes forward impetuously to stay the knife while she turns frantically toward Solomon pleading with him to spare the life of her child even if that meant giving it to the other woman. Between the feet of the servant lies the dead child. His mother kneels in the foreground and her gesture shows clearly that she is satisfied with Solomon's judgment to divide the living child.

Raphael has given a sense of depth to the flat surface on which this picture is painted by depicting the true mother rushing forward, her scarf floating off behind her. To oppose and contain this motion harmoniously within the picture he has introduced a strong diagonal line of interest from the living child's feet in the upper left corner to the knees of the second woman in the lower right corner. It is interesting to observe with what subtlety Raphael has arranged these figures in depth. Nearest to us is the kneeling woman who looks inward toward Solomon. The king, in turn, continues this inward motion as he looks toward the true mother who stands at the greatest depth. With her the motion in depth turns outward toward the servant in whom the motion turns inward again to the living child.

✛

GIANT TREES FOR SOLOMON'S TEMPLE

By

Paul Gustave Doré

(Interpretation)

PAUL GUSTAVE DORÉ (1832-1883) was without doubt one of the most popular of the nineteenth-century French illustrators. When he was only fifteen years old and still attending school in his native city of Strasbourg in Alsace, his father decided that his talented son was wasting too much time in mere picture illustrations. He therefore took him, with his brother, to Paris to enroll them in the Ecole Polytechnique. But young Paul was so delighted with beautiful, gay Paris that when he was given a forty-eight hour choice between attending school at

THE JUDGMENT OF SOLOMON—*RAPHAEL*

the Polytechnique or returning with his father to Alsace, he decided that he
would do neither.

Instead he secretly made some sketches illustrating "The Labors of Hercules"
and submitted them to a Paris publisher without his father's knowledge or consent. They were so well drawn that at first the publisher doubted that one so
young had really done this excellent work. However, an actual demonstration of
young Doré's ability assured him. He immediately signed a contract with the
young man to remain with him for three years at an annual salary of five hundred francs, and the additional provision that the boy would agree to attend an
art school for four hours each day. At the end of the first fortnight, however,
these visits to the art school were discontinued for young Doré felt that he already knew more than his teachers about sketching and drawing.

This artist's unusual facility in drawing was in reality his greatest handicap.
Since he was able to execute such successful pictures without formal study and
training, he never really mastered the fundamentals of his art. He depended too
much on his own imagination. Then, too, he could earn so much money without
the technical training that others had so meticulously to acquire, that he spent
the major portion of his artistic career as an illustrator. In rapid succession he
illustrated Balzac's *Contes,* Dante's *Inferno,* The Bible, *Don Quixote,* Milton's *Paradise Lost,* the *Fables* of La Fontaine, and the works of Rabelais.

His Bible pictures attracted so much attention in London that a company was
formed, agents sent to Paris to confer with young Doré, and forty huge canvases
were contracted for on the payment of three hundred thousand dollars. The artist
was so excited over this contract that he rushed home to tell his mother. She rejoiced with him, at the same time urging him to "apply his talent to pure art"
instead of mere illustrations, lucrative though they were.

The Doré Gallery which was established in London proved a great success; but
Paris refused to applaud with the same heartiness that characterized the English
response, and Doré became dispirited in spite of his mother's encouragement. She
reminded him that after all "he was only a little more than forty years old, and
that a great many artists had not been recognized at all until a much later date."
He had already overworked himself by too much hastily executed work and his
spirits never rallied. After his mother died in 1881, he soon followed her to the
grave. Thus, what might have been a long artistic career, was cut short while Doré
was yet in the prime of life.

In "Giant Trees for Solomon's Temple" Doré has focused our attention on trees
rather than on men. These are no ordinary trees, but the giant cedars of Lebanon
which grew, and still grow, on protected slopes and in the valleys of the Lebanon
mountains. These mountains formed the eastern boundary of Phoenicia which extended in a narrow strip along the Mediterranean north of Israel. During the time
of David and Solomon, Phoenicia was controlled from her seaport city of Tyre
where King Hiram ruled. He was a friend and ally of both David and Solomon
and he entered into trade contracts with them. One such contract is mentioned in
the Bible:

"Now Hiram the king of Tyre had furnished Solomon with cedar trees and fir

GIANT TREES FOR SOLOMON'S TEMPLE—*DORÉ*

trees, and with gold, according to all his desire, that then king Solomon gave Hiram twenty cities in the land of Galilee" (I Kings 9:11).

These are the cedar trees which Hiram furnished Solomon for building the Temple in Jerusalem. As to the cities Solomon gave in exchange to Hiram, "Hiram came out from Tyre to see the cities which Solomon had given him; and they pleased him not . . . and he called them the land of Cabul" [meaning "good as nothing"] (9:12-13).

The artist's imaginative genius is splendidly shown in this picture. Men of Tyre labor to cut and carry away the giant trees. The dark background shows the forest itself with several standing giants clearly portrayed. Hordes of men strain at ropes to bring down these great trees. In the middle distance are stumps of trees now being borne away on four-wheeled carts pulled by teams of eight and ten horses. The entire scene is alive with sound: the neighing of horses, the shouts of men, the crack of whips, the creak of heavily-laden carts, the ring of axes, the distant chanting of men as they pull on the ropes, and the premonitory cracking of the falling tree. Amid all these noises the rustle of leaves in the dark forest and the songs of birds nesting in the branches would be inaudible.

✣

SOLOMON BUILDS THE TEMPLE

By

Julius Schnorr von Carolsfeld

(Interpretation)

KING SOLOMON'S Temple in Jerusalem was the most important architectural achievement of the monarchy. It was patterned after the Tabernacle, but its general dimensions were double those of the latter. Its furniture and decorations were also on a much grander scale. The Temple proper was about a hundred feet long and thirty feet wide. It was built of white limestone dressed at the quarry, and it was roofed with cedar. The floors were of cypress overlaid with gold and the walls were lined with cedar overlaid with gold so that no stone was seen. (I Kings 6:2, 7, 15, 18, 20, 22, 30; II Chron. 3:5.)

The Holy of Holies, where the invisible presence of the Lord dwelt, was a chamber about thirty feet square. In it were two cherubim of olive wood, adorned with gold, each about fifteen feet high. (I Kings 6:16-28; II Chron. 3:13.) The Ark of the Covenant stood on the floor between them. The Holy of Holies was separated from the Sanctuary by a curtain, chains of gold, and two doors of olive wood.

The Holy Place or Sanctuary was about sixty feet long, thirty feet wide, and forty-five feet high. (I Kings 6:17.) There were narrow windows in its walls, probably near the roof. It contained the Altar of incense, which was of cedar overlaid with gold, ten candlesticks, and ten tables, and was entered through doors of cypress. (I Kings 6:33-34.)

Against the two sides and rear of the Temple were three stories of rooms for

SOLOMON BUILDS THE TEMPLE—*VON CAROLSFELD*

officials and for storage. (I Kings 6:5-6, 8, 10.) In front was the entrance portico before which stood the brazen (burnished copper) pillars called Boaz and Jachin, forty feet high with lotus-shaped capitals. (I Kings 7:15-22; II Chron. 3:15-17.)

The courts of the Temple were two—the great court for Israel, and the inner or upper court for the priests—walled off by a parapet, and containing a brazen altar, a brazen sea standing in four groups of three oxen each, and ten lavers of brass. (I Kings 7:23-39; II Chron. 4:6.)

Solomon built his Temple on Mount Moriah which forms the eastern side of Jerusalem. The spot was the threshing floor of Araunah, purchased by David, and it was here that Abraham, centuries before, offered up Isaac. It is interesting to note that Calvary, which lies outside Jerusalem on the north, was formerly the northern end of Mount Moriah. Hence the cross stood on the same mountain as did the Temple and the altar of sacrifice.

This engraving by Julius Schnorr von Carolsfeld entitled "Solomon Builds the Temple" shows the king with two of his counselors inspecting the work of his architects, craftsmen, and workmen. Only the man in the upper right-hand corner who leans upon his ax pauses in his labor to watch Solomon pass by. In the center of the picture the king stops and raises his head and hands in a gesture of prayerful expectancy. A ray of light is directed from heaven toward Solomon and is symbolic of the Lord's voice which came to him, saying:

"Concerning this house which thou art in building, if thou wilt walk in my statutes, and execute my judgments, and keep all my commandments to walk in them; then will I perform my word with thee, which I spake unto David thy father; and I will dwell among the children of Israel, and will not forsake my people Israel" (I Kings 6:12, 13).

The German artist, Julius Schnorr von Carolsfeld (1794-1872), who designed this picture for *Die Biebel im Bildern,* is well known for his Bible engravings and frescoes, and for the stained-glass windows he designed for churches and cathedrals. His style is that of the pre-Raphaelite artists of Germany.

✤

THE DEDICATION OF THE TEMPLE

By

William Hole

(Interpretation)

THIS beautiful scene in the courtyard of Solomon's Temple in Jerusalem was painted by William Hole for his *Old Testament History, Retold and Illustrated.* There is much here that is faithful to the descriptions of the Temple in the Bible. We are standing in the open courtyard facing the great altar of sacrifice rising from its platform. To the left is a huge metal bowl, about fifteen feet in diameter, standing on a decorative base of bulls cast in metal. This is the "molten sea . . . and under it

THE DEDICATION OF THE TEMPLE—*HOLE*

was the similitude of oxen" which are described in II Chronicles 4:2 and 3. Beyond the altar can be seen the entrance to the white limestone Temple flanked by the two metal pillars called Jachin and Boaz, only one of which is pictured here. Beyond the entrance, in the Temple proper, but invisible from our position, is the vestibule porch, the main chamber or Holy Place, and the Holy of Holies where, it was believed, the Lord dwelt "between the cherubim" above the sacred Ark.

The event William Hole portrays is no ordinary Temple sacrifice but Solomon's impressive dedication of this building planned by his father David and now completed by himself. In the foreground stands the orchestra with their stringed instruments and their horns, while in front of them is the conductor. Part of the huge crowd that assembled to witness this first sacrifice in the new Temple can be seen in a corner of the courtyard.

In the center the priests wait on the steps leading up to the great altar. Solomon stands directly in front of the burning sacrifice, his arms raised in prayer to God. The account of this event in the first Book of Kings in the eighth chapter is impressive:

"Then spake Solomon, 'The Lord said that he would dwell in the thick darkness. I have surely built thee an house to dwell in, a settled place for thee to abide in for ever.'

"Then the king turned his face about and blessed all the congregation of Israel (and all the congregation of Israel stood); and he said, 'Blessed be the Lord God of Israel, which spake with his mouth unto David my father, and hath with his hand fulfilled it.'"

Then Solomon "stood before the altar of the Lord in the presence of all the congregation of Israel, and spread forth his hands to heaven" and prayed his long prayer which, in the history of Israel, stands with Abraham's intercession for Sodom and Gomorrah, with Moses' prayer for the children of Israel, with David's thanksgiving for God's promise concerning his heirs, and with Solomon's own prayer for wisdom. At the dedication of the Temple Solomon said, in part:

"Lord God of Israel, there is no God like thee, in heaven above, or on earth beneath, who keepest covenant and mercy with thy servants that walk before thee with all their heart. . . . Behold the heaven of heavens cannot contain thee; how much less this house that I have builded? Yet . . . hearken unto the cry and to the prayer, which thy servant prayeth before thee today; that thine eyes may be open toward this house night and day. . . . And hearken thou to the supplication of thy servant, and of thy people Israel, when they shall pray toward this place; and hear thou in heaven thy dwelling place, and when thou hearest, forgive."

After Solomon's prayer, "the king, and all Israel with him, offered sacrifice before the Lord. . . . So the king and all the children of Israel dedicated the house of the Lord."

William Hole was born in 1846 in England in the cathedral town of Salisbury. He belonged to an old Devonshire family who for generations had been squires and parsons. After his marriage he made his home in Edinburgh. There he met and became a friend of Robert Louis Stevenson. He was a master of etching and his work as a painter, illustrator, and decorator became well known. In 1901 he went to Palestine to study the land and its people in preparation for his series of illustrations for the life of Christ. He made sketches, took photographs, and collected native garments and household objects. All these he brought home and used to enrich the backgrounds and add authenticity to his paintings. The New Testament series was such a success that he went to Palestine again in 1912 to prepare for his Old Testament pictures. William Hole died in 1917 after completing seventy-five Old Testament scenes.

✛

SOLOMON RECEIVES THE QUEEN OF SHEBA

By

Pellegrino da Modena

(Interpretation)

PELLEGRINO ARETUSI who painted "Solomon Receives the Queen of Sheba" in the twelfth arcade in the Vatican, was commonly known as Pellegrino da Modena in honor of the Italian city of his birth. He was first instructed in painting by his father, Giovanni da Modena, who flourished in this quaint Italian city during the latter part of the fifteen century.

In 1509 the son painted an altar piece for the hospital of Santa Marie de Pattu, which gained for the young artist a genuine reputation. The fame of Raphael, then at its height in Rome, drew young Pellegrino to that city. There he enrolled in the Raphael School of Artists in Rome.

At that time Raphael was engaged in painting the great frescoes in the Vatican. He soon recognized Pellegrino's talent and had him assist in this great project. Pellegrino was entrusted to paint, from designs furnished by Raphael, the story of Jacob, and also of Solomon and the Queen of Sheba. Both were executed to the entire satisfaction of his great master.

After Raphael's death Pellegrino returned to his native city of Modena. He was employed on several public edifices including the church of San Paola where his celebrated picture, "The Nativity of Christ," will be found.

Pellegrino was killed suddenly in 1523 while attempting to save the life of his son in a quarrel with a companion. Pellegrino's untimely death cut short the career of one of Italy's really great artists.

A fascinating story of Solomon's reign concerns the visit of the Queen of Sheba of which our Lord makes mention one thousand years later. Her kingdom, the exact location of which is not known, was probably in the southern portion of Arabia. She journeyed to Jerusalem with a large caravan laden with gifts for Solomon: gold, precious stones, and spices. So amazed was she with Solomon's Temple and palaces, and by the magnificence of his court that "there was no more spirit in her." But what impressed her most was the wisdom of Solomon. She asked him many "hard questions" and when he answered them all, she declared: "Behold the half was not told me: thy wisdom and prosperity exceedeth the fame which I heard" (I Kings 10:7).

In this painting the young Queen of Sheba advances with a quick, light spring up the steps toward Solomon's throne to embrace the aged monarch. The king, wearing his crown, rises to greet this other crowned ruler who has come from her distant kingdom to do him honor and to bring him lavish gifts. Gold in flat, cookylike disks is being poured out at Solomon's feet or borne high in a basin on the shoulder of a servant. The jars which strong men struggle to carry seem too heavy to be jars of spices. In the background is the lovely figure of a girl walking so lightly that she seems almost to float into the room. There can be no doubt that the gifts she carries are precious stones.

✤

AN ANNIVERSARY PRAYER

We come unto thee, O God our Father,
At this anniversary time,
Seeking Thy guidance on the Road ahead.

Our hearts are gladdened
As we look at the year behind us
And see the areas where we have made Progress;
Where we have worked together in real Unity;
Where Thou hast granted us
The wisdom to know the right
And the courage to undertake it.

Our hearts are troubled, Father,
By the memory of our offenses;
Of that which we ought to have done
But have not done;
Of that which we ought to have spoken
But have not spoken;
Of our misjudgement of Values;
Of our Impatience with those
Who have differed with us;
Of our Failure to hear Thee
In the still small voices.

Of these things
And all our sins remembered and forgotten
We repent.
And turn to Thee.

We ask, Dearly Beloved, for a faith in our Cause
Great enough to inspire that faith in all;
For a true sense of the Brotherhood of man

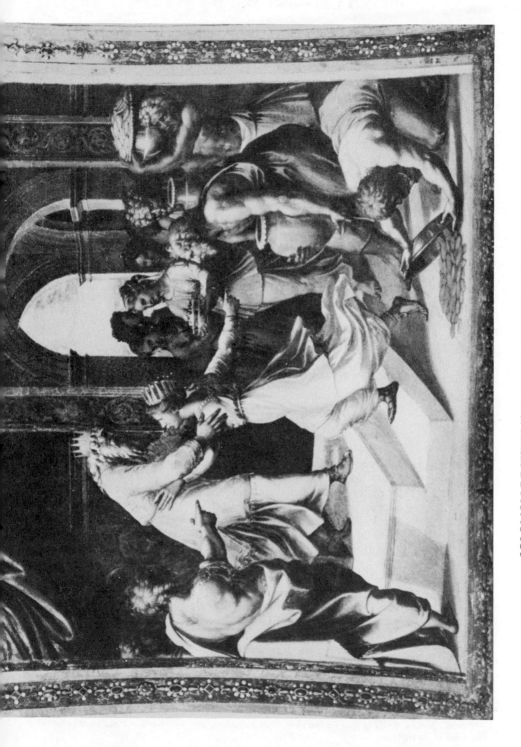

SOLOMON RECEIVES THE QUEEN OF SHEBA—*DA MODENA*

And the courage to practice it;
For patience and kindness toward all mankind,
And even when we differ,
May we do so in love.

Help us to know
That if this thing for which
We are working is of God
It cannot fail.

We pray earnestly that each one of us
May grow in an Awareness of Thee
Until we become clear channels of Thy Love;
Until each one of us has become a tool
To be used by Thee
To bring Thy kingdom on earth,
Truly the Peace
That passeth all understanding.

Help us to walk steadfastly and uprightly
Before Thee all our days,
Keeping our eyes on the vision of True Community,
Creating it,
And our hearts alive with Thee.
Amen.*

—Alma Shoemaker

HURRICANE

Unheralded, tumultuous it fell
Like prisoned lions bursting from their lair
Like demons out on holiday from hell
Like cataract translated into air
Titanic powers battled to the death;
Before the wind's onleaping cruel lash
Trees of a century gave up their breath
To fall to earth in agonizing crash.

When swept a storm from Lebanon's lofty peaks
To shake the cedars stripping forests bare
The Psalmist cried "The voice of Yahweh speaks—
All earth a temple and God's glory there!"

And still above the fury and discord
There speaks the potent grandeur of the Lord.**

—Georgia Harkness

* Adapted from *The Christian Community* (July, 1951). Used by special permission of the author and of the International Council of Community Churches.

** From *The Glory of God* by Georgia Harkness, p. 41. Copyright, 1943, by Abingdon Press. Used by special permission of the publisher.

BUILD ME A HOUSE

Build me a House,
　　Said God;
Not of cedar-wood or stone,
Where at some altar-place
Men for their sins atone.
To me, your only sin
Is to build my House too small:
Let there be no dome
To shut out the sky,
Let there be no cumbering wall.
Build me a House, a Home,
In the hearts of hungering men—
Hungering for the bread of hope,
Thirsting for faith, yearning for love,
In a world of grief and pain.
Build me a House!

Build me a World,
　　Said God;
Not with a navy's strife,
Nor with a host in arms,
Compassing death, not life.
Build me a World, said God,
Out of man's fairest dreams;
Heaven must be its dome,
Lighted by prophet-gleams;
Justice shall be the stones
On which my World shall rise;
Truth and Love its arches,
Gripping my ageless skies.
Out of dreams, on the earthy sod,
Build me a World,
　　Said God.*

—Thomas Curtis Clark

THE COMMANDMENT AND THE REWARD. A SONNET.

My son, forget not my law;
But let thine heart keep my commandments:
　　For length of days, and years of life,
　　And peace, shall they add to thee.
Let not mercy and truth forsake thee:
Bind them about thy neck'
Write them upon the table of thine heart:

So shalt thou find favour,
  And good repute in the sight of God and man.
Trust in the Lord with all thine heart,
And lean not upon thine own understanding:
In all thy ways acknowledge him,
  And he shall direct thy paths.
Be not wise in thine own eyes;
Fear the Lord, and depart from evil :
  It shall be health to thy navel,
  And marrow to thy bones.
Honour the Lord with thy substance,
And with the firstfruits of all thine increase:
  So shall thy barns be filled with plenty,
  And thy vats shall overflow with new wine.*
                              —*Proverbs 3:1-10*

COMPANION GOD

Hear Thou my prayer, O God,
  For inner light.
I would not ask to have
  The way all bright.
Dark shall not thwart my steps
  If Thou be guide.
O Thou Companion God.

Hear Thou my prayer, O God,
  For inner power.
My weakness well I know
  When storm clouds lower.
Quicken my flagging zeal;
  Guard me from fear;
Give me Thy courage, Lord;
  Be ever near.

Hear Thou my prayer, O God,
  For inner peace.
When turmoil buffets me,
  Grant Thou release.
I shall walk steadfastly
  On to the goal,
If Thou, Companion God,
  Strengthen my soul.**

                              —*Georgia Harkness*

* From *The Modern Reader's Bible* edited by Richard G. Moulton, pp. 904-5. Copyright, 1935, by The Macmillan Company. Used by special permission of the publisher.
** From *The Glory of God* by Georgia Harkness, p. 65. Copyright, 1943, by Abingdon Press. Used by special permission of the publisher.

THE SIXTY-SEVENTH PSALM

(A Response to the High Priestly Benediction)

THE HIGH PRIEST

The Lord bless thee,
  And keep thee;
The Lord make his face to shine upon thee,
  And be gracious unto thee;
The Lord lift up his countenance upon thee,
  And give thee peace!

THE PEOPLE

God be merciful unto us, and bless us,
  And cause his face to shine upon us;
That thy way may be known upon earth,
  Thy saving health among all nations.
    LET THE PEOPLES PRAISE THEE, O GOD,
    LET ALL THE PEOPLES PRAISE THEE.

O let the nations be glad,
  And sing for joy:
For thou shalt judge the peoples with equity,
  And govern the nations upon earth.
    LET THE PEOPLES PRAISE THEE, O GOD,
    LET ALL THE PEOPLES PRAISE THEE.

The earth hath yielded her increase:
  God, even our own God, shall bless us.
God shall bless us:
  And all the ends of the earth shall fear him.
    LET THE PEOPLES PRAISE THEE, O GOD,
    LET ALL THE PEOPLES PRAISE THEE.*

SOLOMON AND THE SOWER

In open field King Solomon
Beneath the sky sets up his throne;
He sees a sower walking, sowing,
On every side the seed-corn throwing.

"What dost thou there?" exclaimed the king;
"The ground can here no harvest bring,
Break off from such unwise beginning;
Thou'll get no crop that's worth the winning."

* From *The Literary Study of the Bible* by Richard G. Moulton, p. 198. Published by D. C. Heath & Company. Used by special permission of the publisher.

The sower hears; his arm he sinks,
And doubtful he stands still, and thinks;
Then goes he forward, strong and steady,
For the wise king this answer ready:—

"I've nothing else but this one field;
I've watched it, labored it, and tilled.
What further use of pausing, guessing?
The corn from me,—from God the blessing."
          —*Friedrich Ruckert; translated by N. L. Frothingham*

SOLOMON

They hewed him cedar trees of Lebanon,
     And in his golden courts the people bowed
     When through the seraphim a burning cloud
Covered the Temple of great Solomon;
But now the glory of the Lord is gone—
     Moloch and Astoreth, the ivory-browed,
     Feast on the holy mountain which he vowed
To Javeh* from the horns of Gibeon.

Yet he whose wisdom turns to weariness
     Had heard once more the mighty Voice that came
     When Javeh held the King's heart in His hand;
And though about the throne his tribesmen press,
     Over their heads he sees the sword of flame
     And Israel scattered through an alien land.**
          —*Thomas S. Jones, Jr.*

SONNET

The Creator Has Made Wisdom the Supreme Prize

My son, despise not the chastening of the Lord;
Neither be weary of his reproof:
For whom the Lord loveth he reproveth;
Even as a father the son in whom he delighteth.

     Happy is the man that findeth wisdom,
     And the man that getteth understanding.
     For the merchandise of it is better than the merchandise of silver,
     And the gain thereof than fine gold.
     She is more precious than rubies:
     And none of the things thou canst desire are to be compared unto her.

* Javeh is the sacred Hebrew word for Jehovah, God.
** From *Shadow of the Perfect Rose: Collected Poems of Thomas S. Jones, Jr.,* edited with a Memoir and Notes by John L. Foley. Copyright, 1937, by Rinehart & Co., Inc. Used by special permission of John L. Foley, literary executor for Thomas S. Jones, Jr.

Length of days is in her right hand;
In her left hand are riches and honour.
Her ways are ways of pleasantness,
And all her paths are peace.
She is a tree of life to them that lay hold upon her:
And happy is every one that retaineth her.

The Lord by wisdom founded the earth;
By understanding he established the heavens.
By his knowledge the depths were broken up,
And the skies drop down the dew.*

—Proverbs 3:11-20

THE SLUGGARD. A SONNET

Go to the ant, thou Sluggard;
Consider her ways, and be wise:
   Which having no chief,
   Overseer,
   Or ruler,
Provideth her meat in the summer,
And gathereth her food in the harvest.

How long wilt thou sleep, O Sluggard?
When wilt thou arise out of thy sleep?
   "Yet a little sleep,
   A little slumber,
   A little folding of the hands to sleep"—
So shall thy poverty come as a robber,
And thy want as an armed man!**

—Proverbs 6:6-11

THE FIELD OF THE SLOTHFUL. A SONNET

I went by the field of the Slothful,
And by the vineyard of the man void of understanding;
   And, lo, it was all grown over with thorns,
   The face thereof was covered with nettles,
   And the stone wall thereof was broken down.
Then I beheld,
And considered well:

I saw,
I received instruction.
   "Yet a little sleep,
   A little slumber,
   A little folding of the hands to sleep"—

* From *The Modern Reader's Bible* edited by Richard G. Moulton. p. 905. Copyright, 1935, by The Macmillan Company. Used by special permission of the publisher.
** *Ibid.,* p. 909.

So shall thy poverty come as a robber;
And thy want as an armed man.*

—*Proverbs 24:30-34*

THE STARRY HEAVENS AND THE MORAL LAW

(Psalm 8)

"How excellent thy name in all the earth,
Jehovah God!" the Psalmist cried. He saw
The jeweled sky, the moon and stars, the birth
Of God-created things, and bowed in awe.
He could but kneel before such majesty,
Bereft of pride, as finite humans must;
Too great a thing it seemed, for God to be
Akin to man, and lift him from the dust.

Again he looked: he saw the holy God,
And then—O miracle!—it seemed he stood
Only a step below—no human clod,
But *man!* man glorified, divine, wise, good!
He pondered long how God and man were kin,
And glimpsed the bond—the moral law within.**

—*Georgia Harkness*

WISDOM'S CRY OF WARNING. A MONOLOGUE

Because I have called, and ye refused;
I have stretched out my hand,
And no man regarded;
But ye have set at nought all my counsel,
And would none of my reproof:
I also will laugh in the day of your calamity;
I will mock when your fear cometh;
When your fear cometh as a storm,
And your calamity cometh on as a whirlwind;
When distress and anguish come upon you.
Then shall they call upon me,
But I will not answer;
They shall seek me diligently,
But they shall not find me.
For that they hated knowledge,
And did not choose the fear of the Lord:
They would none of my counsel;
They despised all my reproof:

---

* *Ibid.,* p. 941.
** From *Holy Flame* by Georgia Harkness, p. 37. Copyright, 1935, by Bruce Humphries, Inc. Used by special permission of the author and the publisher.

Therefore shall they eat of the fruit of their own way,
And be filled with their own devices.
For the backsliding of the simple shall slay them,
And the prosperity of fools shall destroy them.*

—Proverbs 1:24-32

·|·

HOW THE TEMPLE WAS BUILT

By

Margaret J. Wiggins

"ARE here all thy children?" The old Prophet, Samuel, looked straight into the eyes of Jesse, the Bethlehemite, who stood beside the door of his rude hut.

"There remaineth yet the youngest. He is watching the sheep," Jesse answered.

"Send and fetch him. We will not sit down till he comes," commanded the Prophet.

Samuel had been sent by the Lord to anoint a son of Jesse. The Lord was weary of the sins of Saul who was King and he wished to anoint a new King to take the throne.

"Take oil in thy horn and go to Jesse the Bethlehemite. They will fear thee, so take a heifer for a sacrifice and call all of the sons of Jesse to sanctify themselves and I will show thee whom to anoint," the Lord had commanded.

And now, the heifer was slain, the seven manly sons of Jesse had knelt before the Prophet, all fine men and courageous, but the Lord had not spoken.

Waiting in the firelight, the men watched the old Prophet and he watched them. He had not told them why he was there nor why they were called to the sacrifice. This was not to be told yet; the Lord would show the meaning at the right time.

Suddenly the door was thrown open and a boy stood in the glow of the firelight—ruddy and bright and beautiful to look upon.

"Rise up, Samuel, and anoint him. This is he whom I have chosen," commanded the Lord.

So, Samuel anointed David, the youngest son of Jesse. Then, after the sacrifice had been made, Samuel wrapped his mantle about him and started out the door. He turned and said in his deep, terrible voice:

"Let no word of what has transpired here tonight be spoken. The Lord will reveal His will in His own time."

So David returned to his sheep and the other brothers returned to the camps of Saul. Only Jesse, the man of Bethlehem, knew that he and his sons had found favor with the Lord God.

David, the shepherd boy, had a harp on which he played while tending the sheep. He sang songs and played sweet harmonies in the long days and in the night watches, so that before long many other shepherds brought their flocks to graze on the hills about Bethlehem so that they might be near to David and listen to his music.

Now Saul, the King of the Israelites, had lost favor with the Lord because he disobeyed the Lord and sinned. All the wars of the Israelites had turned into slaughter, and the King lost more battles than he gained. His armies went against him and even his own household despised him. Saul became a madman, sleepless and refusing to eat, trusting only his servant Abner to come near him.

Abner had heard that music has power to calm a mad mind so he persuaded Saul to let him get someone to make music for him hoping that it would soothe and quiet the sick man. Saul agreed, and Abner, who had heard of David and his harp, sent a messenger to Jesse asking that his son, David, be sent to the court of Saul to sing for the sick King.

Jesse gladly made ready a basket of fine fruits from his garden and sent David to Saul with the offering. And when David sang and played his harp beside the throne of the great King Saul, the poor sick mind, freed of tension, slept.

As the days passed and Saul became strong and well everyone was happy and the whole household of the King rang with praises to the shepherd boy and his harp. Saul kept David with him constantly, and in the times when the evil spirit would come back to torment him, he would have the boy sit beside him on the throne and sing him to sleep.

Then, when the King dozed, David still sat beside the King through the long night watches, dreaming of the time when he should be king, for he knew in his heart that he had been anointed to that end.

His dreams were not of the conquest of many nations. Instead he thought of all he could do for the people of Israel and the desire of his heart was to praise the Lord for all His goodness.

"I will build a temple for the Ark of the Covenant, the grandest Temple in the world, a house for the dwelling place of the Lord God," he vowed to himself, and he sang a new song to the stirring King. And the new song was this:

"I will praise thee, O Lord, with my whole heart; I will show forth all thy marvelous works. I will be glad and rejoice in Thee; I will sing praise to Thy name, O Thou most High."

When Saul died, David was made the King to rule over all the tribes of the Israelites. Saul had been at war with all the countries round about and his army was tired and desired rest. But David, who had known all the trials and distress of war, still kept his army ready to subdue any attacks that might be made.

He did not forget that he had dreamed of peace and that the tribes should be made into the greatest nation on earth. He had fought and had seen victory, and the spoils of war were brought to the court of the King where some of the best materials had been stored to be used when needed.

But one night David the King could not sleep. He remembered that time long ago when he had sat singing to Saul and had dreamed that when he was king he would build a Temple to the Lord. He left his bed and walked about, his thoughts on the old promise he had made to himself to make a beautiful house for the Ark of the Covenant.

The next day, Nathan, who was now the Prophet in Israel since Samuel had died, came to David and said,

"Do all that is within thy heart to do, for the Lord is with thee. He hath told me to say to thee that thou art His chosen one to build His house that He may dwell in it and no longer walk in a tent and a tabernacle. 'Thou dwellest in a house, why not build me a house of cedar?' the Lord had asked. 'I have taken thee from the sheep cote to be ruler over my people; I have been with thee and have made a name for thee greater than the great names of the earth. I have cut off thine enemies from troubling thee and they shall trouble thee no more. Thy house and thy kingdom shall be established forever. Thou shalt build me a Temple to dwell in, in the place I shall appoint.'"

So David began to get ready to build the Temple for the Lord. Hiram, King of Tyre, was David's friend. In that country were the great cedars, and David said that he would build the Temple of the cedars of Lebanon, and King Hiram promised to give him all he would need.

The houses of the treasury filled with the spoils of war were opened and the jewels were sorted and the finest set aside. The cups of gold and the bowls and other ornaments were put in another place to be used to make the house of the Lord beautiful beyond the dream of any who had ever seen temples to the heathen gods.

All the tribes were preparing to help with the building. Artisans and wood carvers were preparing to work on the pillars and the other ornamental designs. The goldsmiths and silversmiths were preparing to make the cups and plates and lamps for the inner courts and the weavers were testing their looms and the dyers were preparing their dyes. Everyone was interested and happy to be working for the Lord.

But David sinned. He shed blood needlessly. He angered the Lord. And the Lord spoke to him and said:

"I raised thee up. I set thee on the throne of Israel. I gave thee all that thou hast. But now thou hast sinned secretly and hast shed innocent blood. From this time on the sword shall never leave thine house. There shall be wars and pestilence and all the greatness of thy kingdom shall pass away. Thy sons shall turn against thee, and thy enemies shall prevail over thee. Thy hand shall not build my house, but thine own house shall be filled with evil."

All that the Lord had said to David came swiftly to pass. Wars and bloodshed, pestilence and death were everywhere. The enemies of David and Israel came from their hiding places and there was no peace.

David grew old and sick, and as he lay upon his bed he worried and fretted constantly about his sons. Which, he kept wondering, would be the one to build the Temple that he had dreamed of building for the Lord, to praise Him for all His goodness and tender mercies.

The Prophet Nathan saw the thing that was troubling the old King, and he also saw that David's eldest son was already taking the government of the people into his hands. So Nathan, who knew that Solomon, the son of Bath-sheba for whom David had sinned, was the one to be King; sent Solomon's mother to David with the message that would bring Solomon to David's mind.

"Thou didst swear that Solomon, my son, should sit on thy throne after thee. Thou didst swear that before the Lord."

And the Prophet Nathan went to the King and told of how the eldest son was making sacrifices for the people but that neither he nor Solomon, nor any of his other sons had been called to the feasts. He suggested that Solomon should be appointed to rule when David could no longer serve as King. And David listened to all that the Prophet said for him to do, and proclaimed that Solomon should be King upon his death.

Solomon was ready to hear all that his father could tell him of his dreams of the Temple. Day after day David described to him how the House of the Lord should be built. He told him of the cedars already waiting at Lebanon; of the jewels and gold and silver and precious stones waiting in the treasuries. He told him of the beautiful pieces of woven linen and the embroideries, the carvings and the lamps, the marble pillars and the measurements of the courts. David knew them all by heart, so that he could tell his son, Solomon, his dream without difficulty.

When David died, Solomon was made King and sat on the great throne of his father. Jerusalem was a great city then, rich merchants and caravan owners, beggars and thieves, slaves and free men walking the streets together. The beautiful palaces of the officers and priests of Israel, the olive groves on the hills, the great gates where the constant incoming and outgoing caravans passed, all made a maze of color and noise that never ceased.

David had taken many slaves captive in the last years of his life, so Solomon gave orders that they were to work on the great building which he was to build to the glory of the Lord. The goldsmiths and silver workers became busy with the work that had been begun in King David's time. The weavers and embroiderers finished the work that had been put aside when the Lord forbade David to build the Temple.

Solomon sent messengers to King Hiram, of Tyre, asking him to send the great cedars that David had asked to have cut for the House of the Lord. Solomon sent thousands of men to the mountains to hew and square stones for the foundation of this great building. Hiram caused the cedars all to be hewn and perfected before they were sent to Jerusalem, and everything that was used in the building was made ready before it was placed, so that there was "neither hammer nor ax nor any tool heard in the house while it was building."

And when the house was finished it was threescore cubits in length, and the breadth was twenty cubits. It was thirty cubits high, with a porch as long as the house. There was a great outside court where the people were to stand. There was the inner court where the altar stood, with troughs for the water and blood of the sacrifices.

Back of the inner court was the Holy of Holies, the place of the Ark of the

Lord. Here the High Priest could enter once a year to talk to the Lord God, and no one else could enter in. Before the oracle Solomon had made two cherubim of olive wood, each ten cubits high. Their wings were stretched out to meet each other over the oracle and to touch the walls on either side. These were overlaid with gold.

Hiram of Tyre made all the vessels to be used in the Temple, of gold he made them, casting them on molds so that they would all be alike.

When all was finished in the House of the Lord, Solomon assembled the elders of Israel and all the heads of the tribes. They were to come to the city of David, to the King of the Israelites, so that the Ark of the Lord might be brought to the Temple, the House of the Lord that Solomon had built.

When all were assembled, the priests brought the Ark of the Covenant of the Lord to the most holy place, into the oracle under the wings of the golden cherubim. Then the priests drew off the staves and there was nothing in the Ark except the two tables of stone which Moses put there when he brought the children of Israel out of Egypt.

But when the priests came out of the holy place, a cloud filled the house, and the priests could not minister the sacrifices because of the cloud, for the glory of the Lord filled the house.

Then the King turned to the people, and all the people stood to hear the words of their King, as he said:

"The Lord said unto my father, David, Whereas it is in thine heart to build an house unto my name, thou didst well. Nevertheless thou shalt not build my house, but thy son, he shall build the house in my name.

"And I am risen up, as the Lord hath performed his word. I sit on the throne of Israel, as the Lord promised, and have built an house for the name of the Lord God of Israel."

And Solomon turned to the altar and spread his hands toward heaven, saying:

"Lord God of Israel, there is no God like unto thee in heaven above or on the earth beneath, who keepest covenant with thy servants who walk with thee. But, will God indeed, dwell on the earth? Behold, the heavens and the heaven of heavens cannot contain thee; how much less this house that I have builded!"

And the King and all Israel with him offered sacrifice to the Lord. And Solomon offered a sacrifice of peace. So the King and all the children of Israel dedicated the House of the Lord as David had planned.

The feasting and the sacrificing continued for fourteen days; then they all blessed the King and went to their homes, joyful and glad for all the goodness that the Lord had done for David, His servant, and for Israel His people.

Thus, one of the greatest buildings that the world has ever known was built from a dream, a desire to worship the Lord and to give Him glory and honor and praise.*

* Used by special permission of the author.

KING SOLOMON AND THE BEE

A Hebrew Tale

ON A bright summer's day, when the sun beat down fiercely on the heads of the people, King Solomon sought the shade of one of his favorite gardens. But even where the trees were so thick that the sun's rays could not penetrate, it was hot. Not a breath of air fanned the monarch's cheek; he lay down on the thick grass and gazed through the branches of the trees at the blue sky.

"This great heat makes me weary," said the king, and in a few minutes he had fallen into a deep sleep.

All was still in the beautiful garden, except for the flutter of a few humming-birds and the buzzing of the bees. Even these sounds died out as the day grew hotter and hotter. Only one tiny bee was left moving in the garden. It flew from flower to flower, sipping the honey, until at length it also began to be overcome by the heat.

"Oh, dear! I wonder what is the matter with me," buzzed the little bee. "This is the first time I have come out of the hive. How queer I feel! I hope I am not going to faint."

It was giddy, and after flying round and round dizzily for a few minutes, it dropped plop! on King Solomon's nose. Immediately the king awoke with such a start that the little bee was frightened almost out its wits and flew straight back to the hive.

King Solomon sat up and looked around to see what had awakened him so rudely. He felt a strange pain on the tip of his nose. He rubbed his nose with his finger, but the pain increased. Attendants came rushing toward him and asked him what was the matter.

"I must have been stung by a bee," said the king angrily. "Send for the Lord High Physician and the Keeper of the Court Plaster without delay. I must not have a blister on the end of my nose. Tomorrow I am to be visited by the Queen of Sheba, and it will not do to have a swollen nose tied up in a sling."

The Lord High Physician came with his many assistants, each carrying a box of ointment, or lint, or some other preparation which might be needed. King Solomon's nose, especially the tip of it, was examined most carefully.

"It is almost nothing," said the Lord High Physician—"just a tiny sting from a little bee. It will be healed in an hour or two, and tomorrow the Queen of Sheba will not notice that anything has befallen thee."

"Meanwhile it hurts," said King Solomon; "and I am vexed with this little bee. How dared it sting me, King Solomon, monarch of all living things on earth, in the air, and in the waters!"

The pain soon ceased, but his majesty did not like the odor of the ointment on his nose and determined to have the bee before him for trial.

"Place the impudent creature under arrest at once," he commanded, "and bring it before me, so that I may hear what it has to say."

"But I do not know it," said the Lord High Chamberlain, to whom the command was given.

"Then, summon the queen bee before me in an hour and bid her bring the culprit," answered the monarch. "Tell her that I shall hold all the bees guilty until the little wretch is brought into my presence."

The order was carried to the hive by one of the butterflies, and it spread terror among the bees. Such a buzzing there was that the butterfly said, "Stop making that noise. If the king hears, it will make matters worse."

The queen bee promised to obey King Solomon's command, and in an hour she appeared in state before the great throne. She was escorted by a bodyguard of twelve bees, who cleared the way before her, walking backward and bowing, with their faces to her.

The queen bee approached the throne and made a low bow to King Solomon. "I, thy slave," she buzzed, "am here at thy bidding, mighty ruler, great and wise. Command, and thou shalt be obeyed."

"It is well," replied King Solomon. "Hast thou brought with thee the culprit, the bee that dared to attack my nose with its sting?"

"I have, your majesty," answered the queen bee. "It is a young bee that left the hive for the first time this day. It attacked not your majesty wilfully, but on account of giddiness caused by the heat. It surely injured thy royal nose but little, since it left not its sting in the wound. Be merciful, O King."

"Fear not my judgment," said the king. "Bid the bee stand forth."

Tremblingly the little bee stood at the foot of the throne and bowed three times to King Solomon.

"Knowest thou not," asked the king, "that I am thy royal master, whose person must be held sacred by all living things?"

"Yes, gracious majesty," buzzed the bee. "Thy slave is aware of this. The happening was but an accident. It is the nature of the bee to thrust forth its sting when in danger. I thought I was in danger when I fell."

"So was I, for I was beneath thee," returned King Solomon.

"Punish me not," pleaded the bee. "I am but one of your majesty's smallest and humblest slaves, but even I may be of service to thee some day."

These words made the whole court laugh.

"Silence!" commanded the king sternly. "There is naught to laugh at in the bee's answer. It pleases me well. Go; thou art free. Some day I may have need of thee."

The little bee bowed its head three times before the king and flew away, buzzing happily. Next day it kept quite close to the palace.

"I wish to see the procession when the Queen of Sheba arrives," it said; "and also I must be near the king in case his majesty should need me."

In great state, the beautiful Queen of Sheba, followed by hundreds of handsomely robed attendants, approached King Solomon. He was seated on his throne, surrounded by all his court.

"Great and mighty King," she said, curtsying low, "I have heard of thy great wisdom and would like to put it to the test. Hitherto thou hast answered all questions without difficulty; but I have sworn to puzzle thy wondrous wisdom with my woman's wit. Be heedful."

"Beautiful Queen of Sheba," returned King Solomon, rising and bowing in return for her curtsy, "thou art as witty as thou art fair. If thou art successful in puzzling me, thy triumph shall be duly rewarded. I will load thee with rich presents and will proclaim thy wit and wisdom to the whole world."

"I accept thy challenge," replied the queen; "and at once."

Behind her majesty stood two beautiful girl attendants bearing flowers. The queen, taking a bouquet in each hand, said to King Solomon, "Tell me, thou who art the wisest man on earth, which of these bunches is real and which artificial."

"They are both beautiful, and their fragrance is delicious," replied King Solomon.

"Ah!" said the queen, "but only one bunch has fragrance. Which is it?"

King Solomon looked at the flowers. Both bunches seemed exactly alike. From where he sat, it was impossible to notice any difference. He did not answer at once, but knit his brows as if puzzled. The courtiers also looked troubled. Never before had they seen the king hesitate.

"Is it impossible for your majesty to answer the question?" the queen asked.

Solomon shook his head and smiled. "Never yet have I failed to answer a question," he said. "Thou shalt be answered."

"And at once," demanded the queen.

"So be it," answered King Solomon, gazing thoughtfully around and raising his scepter.

He alone had heard the faint buzzing of the little bee, which had settled on one of the window panes.

"Let that window be opened," he commanded, pointing to it with his scepter, "that the bee may enter."

When the window was opened the little bee flew in. Straight to the Queen of Sheba it went, and without hesitation, settled on the bouquet in her left hand.

"Thou has my answer, fair Queen of Sheba," said King Solomon rising, "given by one of the tiniest of my subjects. It settled on the flowers that are natural. The bouquet in thy right hand was made by human hands."

The whole court applauded the monarch's wisdom in bidding the little bee to help him out in his difficulty.

"O King!" said the queen humbly, "I had heard of thy wisdom, but believed not. Lo! the half hath not been told."

SOLOMON VISITS THE PLAINS WHERE HIS FATHER WATCHED SHEEP

By

John Erskine

WHEN Magsala asked Solomon why he didn't seize the quiet interval and visit the region where his father had once tended sheep, he said that on second thought he could find no justification for such a pleasure-trip.

"Here I am with the taxes and a restless people, problems the like of which not even my father had to face, and they call for study. The day of mere courage has gone by. There are no more giants. I don't need a sling-shot, I need knowledge."

She leaned back in the long settee, in the cool of her room, under the window, and clasped her hands over her stately head.

"Not a sling, but whatever belongs to you, your poetry perhaps."

"Poetry? How would that help?"

"Does a poet ask? My dear! We had a poet in Egypt, three thousand years ago, who wrote—if I can remember—it's a famous passage—oh, this is it: we may busy ourselves with people, or we may busy ourselves with ideas, but in the end we busy ourselves with people."

Solomon stood beside her, walked up and down, came back to admire those companionable eyes.

"Very fine!" he concluded. "I wish I could study it in the original."

"My translation was rough," she admitted, "but that's the sense."

"To be frank," said he, "I don't quite get it."

"Why, everything depends on the person you are. Men may agree with your thoughts, but if they remain friends it's because they like *you!* Let others learn about taxes and such matters; you can employ their knowledge. For yourself, see to it you're a man your people will admire! It's a simple rule for all kings."

"What kind of man?"

She was amused at him. "Yourself, my dear—you can't be anything else, but unluckily you can fall short of that. You think your father became a wonderful ruler because he first watched the flocks, day and night, and so had leisure to learn the beautiful outside of the world—mountains, brooks, trees, stars—till life sang through him. You think if you made the same approach, you'd come at the same power. Since you think so, I say you ought never to forgive yourself if you don't hurry down there and try it."

He was eager to be convinced, but it seemed more intelligent to give in slowly.

"I doubt if everything depends on the person, aside from his ideas. A man might appear like nothing at all and yet be wise."

"In that case," she laughed, "someone else will get credit for the wisdom, someone who was charming or magnificent, and therefore easy to remember."

He took the theory under consideration. "Really, I'd rather be remembered for my brains."

Her lips almost smiled, but she spared him. "It can't be done, my dear! Earn a name for wisdom, and they'll call you wise, but they'll hand on the story of some brave thing you did, or the splendor of your house, or your manners in public, or even the number of horses in your stable. Ask them to repeat one sage idea, and they will have forgotten. That father of yours, for example, a king above kings—already they mention chiefly the giant and the pebble."

"I don't want it to be that way!"

"It's the way men are," she insisted, "and I like it! Wisdom may be shared or handed on, but power is yourself."

So Solomon went to Bethlehem in search of power. Benaiah took him most of the journey in a chariot, they two alone, and set him down within easy distance of the sheep-covered hills, and told him where to find the farmers, from one of whom he would ask employment. Benaiah had secured for him a suitable costume, a wretched shirt, breeches belted around the middle, a crude staff. Under the belt he hid a small purse, against need, and in the purse, besides gold, he had packed a bit of parchment and a colored chalk, against inspiration, but in all else he was a poor man, to the life. For complete disguise Benaiah had warned him not to wash. His feet were naked.

To face the world thus, after the softness of his youth, was at once a soul-lifting adventure. The sound of the chariot rattling back to the stable was a blessing to his ears. The sun bathing him, the air touching his body—why had he let this freedom go unused? And why did men, with this privilege, complain? Jeroboam was a fraud! The common folk couldn't really be unhappy. He who works with his hands and walks barefoot, even though he lacks possessions, or because he lacks them, can breathe health and peace, and at night, his weariness being wholesome, he can sleep.

The sap of poetry, he observed with thankfulness, was already flowing. As he hurried along the road, he composed. A short thing, to be remembered when convenient.

> The sleep of a working man is sweet,
> Whether he eat little or much.

He liked the rhythm, and the thought had unity, but perhaps the end was feeble. The last words should sustain what went before, and you couldn't rest a poem on hunger. Why not reverse the lines?

> Whether he eat little or much,
> The sleep of a working man is sweet.

The hunger still got in the way. Why not distribute the thought over a wider area, dilute it perhaps? Or establish a contrast which would put even hunger in a favorable light? Ah, that would do it!

> The sleep of a working man is sweet,
> Whether he eat little or much,
> But the abundance of the rich
> Will not suffer him to sleep.

He said it out loud to fasten it down. One of his best things! So far as he was concerned, the second two lines weren't strictly true; he usually slept from one end of the night to the other. But the poem might be taken relatively. His sleep would be still sounder as soon as he became a working man.

Before night, however, he learned to his amazement how difficult it is to get at your work. Apparently you could be born to a throne but not to a job. A ragged fellow told him so, outside the door of a hut, the first he stopped at.

"I've sheep, to be sure, but you look little like a man who could buy any."

"Not buy but tend them," explained Solomon. "I'm a shepherd."

"And who isn't?" said the fellow. "Especially if you come from the city, as I wouldn't swear you don't. When they starve yonder, with the sort of king we have, they drop down here and call themselves shepherds. One for every sheep, if we took them all on!"

"Try me for a day and a night!"

"Listen to this," said the fellow, "we let the children do it, now the weather is pleasant, and there aren't enough flocks for the large families we have. If you were familiar with sheep, you wouldn't be asking, a grown man like you!"

Of course David had been very young—Solomon was discouraged when he recalled how young. With diminished spirits he inquired of the next house, and the next, and had the same answer. No one hired a shepherd in that country— they all gave the task to the youngest and least useful, and they all had many children.

At the last door Solomon begged the favor of a bed, and since it was a charitable home, they let him sleep in the yard on straw. Perhaps because he hadn't yet worked, he didn't sleep well.

Since there was no hope of employment, and therefore no inspiration for poetry, he decided to shorten his visit, but before he departed from the neighborhood he wished to look at the very field in which David, Jesse's youngest son, once filled the duties which the local children still monopolized.

"Just over the far hill it was," said the man who provided straw. "You go straight to the southeast a mile, then turn left."

"Northeast!" corrected his wife from the inside of the hovel. "Didn't my uncle, of the same age, have the nearest flock to him? He's told me many a time!"

"Me too," replied the husband, "and it was a good story up to twenty years ago, when his memory gave out. Now, my own father's elder brother was in the army the day the lad ran at Goliath—"

"But that wouldn't be here!"

"Did I say it was? I'm explaining to this wayfarer how my father's elder brother knew better than your uncle just where the flocks were when David came up for a look at the camp and resolved to run at the giant."

Solomon abandoned them to their history, and tried southeast with a turn to the left, but since the road was harder on the feet today than it had been yesterday, he soon perceived the folly of investing effort in random explorations. Turning, he plodded back toward the little city itself, trusting fragments of his father's talk, vaguely recalled. There was a well which gave the best water on earth. It was near a gate. Solomon skirted the walls looking for the well, and he found two. In each case the proud citizens swore theirs was the authentic one. He drank from both and went on.

To the east the land fell away in a series of orchards, rich with many kinds of fruit but chiefly olives, and under the trees he saw a group of children with three goats. He walked faster. Below spread the plains, squared off in wheat-plantings, or left open for grazing. He caught sight of creatures in groups, slow-moving. The flocks! There was the pasture he looked for! Whether a little more this way or that, north or south, did it matter? That landscape from some angle had filled his father's eyes!

Stirred deep, he walked from flock to flock, creeping up behind the lads to observe them at their happy work. He expected a youthful vigilance, shot through with heroic promise. That is, he expected too much. These were no Davids. Their habit, it seemed, was to stretch out under a cypress or an olive tree and doze, with the crook resting on their legs. By way of variation, two boys were busy with a game, tossing a knife. Solomon concluded that at least one flock was watching itself.

Though he pushed on, his ardor flagged, and he asked himself what he was seeking. The past was not here, nor was the future. Noon approached, the sun grew hot, he was hungry. "Whether he eat little or much"—he was in no mood to compose poetry!

Yet he chanced on one pleasant picture, worth storing up—a boy and a girl sitting in the shade of a rock, eating fruit. As he came near, the boy was singing, between bites.

"Did you find that fruit in yonder orchards?"

The boy nodded, his mouth being full.

"Would I be permitted to feed myself from the same place?"

Simply, without hesitation, the boy counted off a third of what remained in his basket, and handed it over. Not a handsome child, not clean, not—if one judged by the features—full-witted, but Solomon sat down and ate.

At that moment he felt as little a king as on the day when he rode the mule, yet here on the plains his humility was neither timid nor baffled, as it had been during his progress through the city streets, while watching the back of Benaiah's head and the mule's ears. In a short time he had come far. The dirty boy and the awkward girl were kind to the stranger within their gate. The rock-shadow was the gate; he didn't mind being the stranger. They were themselves, as Magsala would say, perfect according to their ability, and there was justice in the gift of food, and in his acceptance of it, since they were at home in their world, as he was not yet in his.

Was it ungenerous to notice, even while he honored these children, that the life of a shepherd no longer prepared you for wisdom, valor, conquest? One look at that boy, and you'd know he'd remain as he was, unless he shrunk to something less admirable. A dull animal, with good manners, as you might rate a dog of medium quality.

Perhaps it wasn't the shepherd's life that made David become David!

Nor any other occupation!

Perhaps you must *be David* to start with!

We may say that at the stroke of this truth Solomon's education was complete. Here began the full flow of that wisdom with which his name, as Magsala foresaw, is now somewhat loosely associated. We need not stop to argue against those busy commentators who would assign to other pens his best poems and his meatiest aphorisms. Magsala foresaw this also. But the point is, he loved his father and wished to imitate his greatness, and here among the flocks he discovered the only way. Magsala had told him, but here he learned it for himself.*

✛

THE QUEEN OF SHEBA**

By

Norah Lofts

AT the beginning of the tenth chapter of the first Book of Kings there are thirteen comparatively short sentences which relate as undecorated, unromantic a story as any in the world, yet it is doubtful whether any similar amount of flat reporting in the whole history of time has ever given rise to so many legends, by-words, imaginative speculations.

Solomon was a great king; he built a great Temple for his God and a great palace for himself in Jerusalem: he had a reputation for wisdom. And one of his fellow monarchs—a woman—was curious enough about him, his buildings and his wisdom to make a long journey in order to visit him. She was satisfied that reports had not exaggerated anything; she gave him presents and received presents in return and went back to her own country. Surely one of the simplest stories ever written. One suspects that its very simplicity is responsible for its fertility. There must, said the later historians, have been more in it than that; and so the legends began.

In the first place there was a mystery about the woman and the country she ruled. The Old Testament calls her "the queen of Sheba," and the historian who first set down her story would know exactly where and what Sheba was, and would know that the term would be equally intelligible to all its contemporary readers. Sheba was then as well established, as apparently permanent as Babylon or Egypt. Hundreds of years later Christ, referring to her, called her "the queen of the south"; Josephus says that she was queen of Egypt and Ethiopia: his commentator says definitely that she was queen of Sabea in South Arabia.

Where then was Sheba, a country that allowed itself to be ruled by an inquisitive, headstrong woman?

One of the legends comes down in favour of Ethiopia and says that one of the things she took back with her was a son in her womb and that from him and his

* Abridged from *Solomon, My Son* by John Erskine, pp. 280-88. Copyright, 1935, by John Erskine. Published by Bobbs-Merrill Company. Used by special permission of the author and the publisher.
** I Kings 10:1-13.

offspring is derived the Semitic strain still visible in the ruling class of Abyssinia. But the Book of Kings is praiseworthily frank about Solomon and his women; he "loved many strange women, together with the daughter of Pharaoh, women of the Moabites, Ammonites, Edomites, Zidonians and Hittites"; why, if he had loved the queen of Sheba, should the historian have shown this unusual reticence?

Of Egypt she was not queen. Solomon had married Pharaoh's daughter. Nor was Egypt then regarded as "the utmost parts of the earth."

Whether then she ruled in Ethiopia or in Arabia is not of importance. Sheba has gone, its name by virtue of this one story has outlived its geographical identification. The story matters; not because of the legends that have mossed themselves over it, nor because "the half was not told me" and "there was no more spirit in her" have become phrases current amongst many who could not tell their origin, but because, in her own way, this queen of the south is an example of a certain type of female psychology.

She was a woman who was performing satisfactorily what was considered to be a man's job. Queens in their own right were rare in that day, and who knows what intrigues, what prejudices this woman had met and overcome in order to be, and to remain, "queen of the south"? The material success had spelled disaster for the female in her; Elizabeth Tudor is a parallel case. Driving force and enterprise and combativeness are not natural feminine traits, and the women in whom they are born or engendered by circumstances are never wholly happy or at one with their world.

This queen of Sheba's approach to Solomon was antagonistic. In her own country she had heard of his glory; to his great inheritance he had added the final subjection of the Canaanite tribes; he had allied himself by marriage to the ruling house of Egypt; he had built—with the help of Phoenician labour and material—such a Temple and such a palace as had never been seen before. And he was wise; even in his own day his knowledge of philosophy and of what we now call psychology was legendary. His existence and his reputation were a challenge to this queen in her own right. She could not—because she did not wish to—believe the reports she had heard about him. Secretly she thought that having made, or maintained herself queen of Sheba she was the shrewdest and most glorious monarch in the world. Nor were her claims empty; Josephus says "she was inquisitive into philosophy and one that on other accounts also was to be admired."

She could not resist the challenge of Solomon; so she came from her far country "to prove him with hard questions." And she arrived in Jerusalem with "a very great train, with camels that bare spices and very much gold and precious stones." Woman militant, possessive, exhibitionist. Competition between kings can be extravagant enough as the Field of the Cloth of Gold, that meeting between Henry VIII and Francis of France, proves, but when a subtle sexual element is added extravagance knows no bounds. One can imagine her, half confident, half diffident, rigging out her attendants so that her lowest menial, she hopes, will exceed Solomon in all his glory; she hopes, she almost believes. And all the gold and all the spices and all the precious stones, they are to be given to this great king of Israel, not out of generosity alone, but out of an oblique egoism.

Her impressive train and the gifts that were in it are described, but of the "hard questions" the Old Testament tells us nothing. Did she dress eight children, four boys and four girls, in identical clothes and demand that Solomon detect their sex? And did he call for bowls of water and say, "Wash your hands," and did they thus betray themselves? Who shall say?

And did Solomon, crafty in his turn, order that between the throne and the entry to the throne-room a stream of water should flow so that the queen of Sheba, approaching him, must perforce lift her skirts and show whether the rumor of a deformed foot were true or not? No one can say that either. But it is interesting to note that about these queens in their own right this hint of a physical deformity hangs. Elizabeth Tudor again, "her mind is as crooked as her carcase," someone said. Was it Sheba's deformed foot, with its implied bar to ordinary feminine attractiveness and achievement that had turned her towards an interest in philosophy? Another unanswerable question.

We only know that Solomon received her graciously and answered all her questions. For at Gibeon, before ever the Temple settled on the throne, God had appeared to him in a dream and asked him what he most wished for and Solomon had chosen wisdom, "an understanding heart." And there can be no doubt that he understood, not merely the questions which this woman set him, but the motives and far-reaching reasons for her visit. He probably both respected and pitied her, for that is the male attitude towards women of her kind. He respected her rank and her wealth and her intelligence, and he pitied her because he had no desire to add her to the seven hundred women, wives and concubines who ministered to his pleasure. And she, who had intended to impress him with her entourage and her wit, was completely deflated. "There was no more spirit in her"; and the completeness of that deflation betrays, albeit unconsciously, the scope and malice of her original intention. Had she come from curiosity that would have been appeased; from admiration, that would have been increased; from friendliness, that would have been cemented. But she had come out of the intellectual pride and vainglory to which unfeminine women are prone, and gently, without effort or ostentation, Solomon had reduced her.

Yet in the end she is an admirable, not pitiable figure. She is saved by her own integrity. Very frankly she told him that she had not believed the reports which she heard, "I believed not the words, until I came and mine eyes have seen it, and behold, the half was not told me. . . . Happy are thy men, happy are thy servants which stand continually before thee and that hear thy wisdom. . . ." A sweeping, generous, most unfeminine speech. In itself it denies the legend that this woman ever bore Solomon's son, for the child of Sheba and Solomon would have left his mark on history and not depended upon the shape of the Abyssinian nose for a memorial to his existence.

Having made her speech, she presented Solomon with the gifts which she had brought in her train, gifts which had seemed so overwhelmingly splendid when they were loaded upon the camels outside the forgotten palace in her nameless, unidentifiable capital, and which now seemed meagre and poor when offered to this great king in whose realm silver was nothing thought of, and whose drinking vessels were all of gold, and whose navy at Tharshish returned every three years from fantastic, fabulous voyages to far places, bringing "gold and silver, ivory, apes and peacocks." Solomon accepted her presents courteously and in return gave her gifts, "whatsoever she asked," which probably means anything she had chanced to admire, a custom which holds in some Eastern places until this day.

And so she turned and went back to her own country, one of the first women on record to have pitted her wits and her wealth against that of a man in a similar position; one of the first women to learn that there is only one way in which —circumstances being roughly even—women can subjugate men, and that not by wit or wealth.

The humiliation would pass, of course. To the end of her reign, to the end of her days (and we hope that such ends were coincidental) she would remember that she had visited Solomon the Great, and the glamour of her visit would hang about her. And before she reached the end of her journey to her own country there is little doubt that some of her forceful, intrepid spirit would have come back to her and she would be able to think of one question which Solomon had not answered completely, or of one question which, had she thought of it in time, might have defeated him entirely.

Solomon, busy with his women and his kingdom and his poetry would remember her seldom, and then only as the woman who gave him a greater store of spices than any subsequently seen in Israel, and—they say—the balm or balsam tree which her visit introduced into his kingdom, for women who are "inquisitive into philosophy" seldom mark the hearts of the men they encounter. Yet, of the seven hundred wives and princesses and of the three hundred concubines that graced the great king's harem, what trace remains? Whereas Sheba, in its day a rich and powerful country, though lost beyond imaginative recall, has, in the story of its queen and her journey, an undying memorial.*

☩

HOLY, HOLY, HOLY

(Interpretation)

CHURCHES of different denominations often sing this hymn to the Triune God either as an introductory or processional hymn at Sunday service. The words were written by Reginald Heber (1783-1826).

Its universality is undoubtedly due to its perfectness for corporate worship. Men and women everywhere and in every age worship something. It may be an African fetish, or a totem pole. It may be the living God or some idol made of

* Abridged from *Women in the Old Testament* by Norah Lofts, pp. 134-39. Copyright, 1949, by Norah Lofts. Published by The Macmillan Company. Used by special permission of the publisher.

Holy, Holy, Holy

Reginald Heber, 1783-1826

NICÆA
John B. Dykes, 1823-1876

HYMN, 1826   TUNE, 1861   METER, 11.12.12.10.

With exaltation

1. Ho - ly, Ho - ly, Ho - ly! Lord God Al - might - y!
2. Ho - ly, Ho - ly, Ho - ly! All the saints a - dore thee,
3. Ho - ly, Ho - ly, Ho - ly! Though the dark - ness hide thee,
4. Ho - ly, Ho - ly, Ho - ly! Lord God Al - might - y!

Ear - ly in the morn - ing our song shall rise to thee;
Cast - ing down their gold - en crowns a - round the glass - y sea;
Though the eye of sin - ful man thy glo - ry may not see,
All thy works shall praise thy Name, in earth and sky and sea;

Ho - ly, Ho - ly, Ho - ly! Mer - ci - ful and Might - y!
Cher - u - bim and ser - a - phim fall - ing down be - fore thee,
On - ly thou art ho - ly; there is none be - side thee
Ho - ly, Ho - ly, Ho - ly! Mer - ci - ful and Might - y!

God in Three Per - sons, bless - ed Trin - i - ty!
Who wert, and art, and ev - er - more shalt be.
Per - fect in power, in love, and pu - ri - ty.
God in Three Per - sons, bless - ed Trin - i - ty! A - MEN.

wood, stone, or ivory. But the need to worship is deeply planted in the human heart and it finds many ways to express itself from age to age. The more perfect the object, the higher the order of worship is; and when the being worshiped is the Holy God, Father of the Universe, man's worship reaches its highest level.

Centuries ago Israel sang the "Tersanctus." The heavenly choir sang "Holy! Holy! Holy!" And today His Church continues to sing this great hymn of adoration, the "Tersanctus" by Reginald Heber, one of England's foremost hymn writers.

This Trinity hymn of adoration is based on the rhythm of the Apocalypse (Rev. 4:8). It also echoes the song Isaiah heard the seraphim sing in the Temple during his vision of the sovereignty and majesty of God (Isa. 6:1-4). It has been more universally used than any other hymn of the Church. It is said that Tennyson regarded this hymn as one of the finest ever written.

Reginald Heber's father was a minister and a man of means and wide scholarship. His son was given every opportunity. In 1800 he entered one of the several colleges at Oxford, and during his first year won a prize for the best Latin poem. Just a year later he won the Newgate prize for the best English poem entitled "Palestine." In 1807 he was ordained priest in the Church of England and began his ministry in Shropshire. Sixteen years later he became Bishop of Calcutta, but his devotion to his work in the trying climate of India affected his health and he died in 1826.

He wrote a variety of hymns of unusually high literary quality and covering a wide range of topics. The publication of his hymns in 1827 introduced a new era in hymn writing. He gave us one of our finest missionary hymns, "From Greenland's Icy Mountains," the great Epiphany hymn, "Brightest and Best of the Sons of the Morning," the famous hymn on the Eucharist, "Bread of the World, in Mercy Broken," and two stirring hymns, "Hosanna to the Living Lord" and "The Son of God Goes Forth to War," all these in addition to our greatest hymn of adoration, "Holy! Holy! Holy!"

This hymn of adoration is invariably sung to John Bacchus Dykes' tune "Nicaea" composed in 1861. He was a clergyman of the Church of England, born at Hull in 1823 and educated at Cambridge. His musical career began early as the organist for his grandfather's church when he was only ten. He helped to form the University Music Society at Cambridge, and for a number of years was Minor Canon and Precenter in Durham Cathedral.

It is as a composer of nearly three hundred hymn tunes, however, that he is most widely known. Most present-day church hymnals contain anywhere from twenty to fifty hymns that are set to his tunes because of their rich melody and singableness.

GOD'S LAW IS PERFECT, AND CONVERTS
(Interpretation)

THE 19th Psalm, verses 7 to 11, is the inspiration for this magnificent devotional hymn from the *Scottish Psalter* (1650):

> The law of the Lord is perfect,
>   converting the soul:
> The testimony of the Lord is sure,
>   making wise the simple.
> The statutes of the Lord are right,
>   rejoicing the heart:
> The commandment of the Lord is pure,
>   enlightening the eyes.
> The fear of the Lord is clean,
>   enduring for ever:
> The judgments of the Lord are true
>   and righteous altogether.
> More to be desired are they than gold,
>   yea, than much fine gold:
> Sweeter also than honey
>   and the honeycomb.

God's Law Is Perfect, and Converts
ST. BERNARD. C.M.

Psalm 19
Scottish Psalter, 1650

Tochter Sion, (Cologne, 1741)
Arr. by J. RICHARDSON, 1863

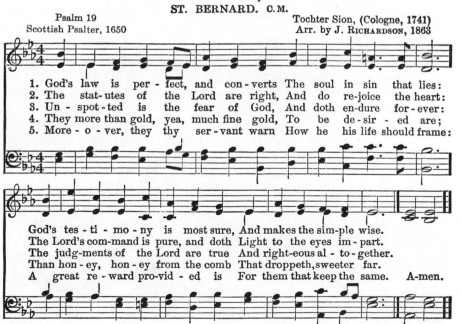

1. God's law is per - fect, and con - verts The soul in sin that lies:
2. The stat - utes of the Lord are right, And do re - joice the heart:
3. Un - spot - ted is the fear of God, And doth en - dure for - ever:
4. They more than gold, yea, much fine gold, To be de - sir - ed are;
5. More - o - ver, they thy ser - vant warn How he his life should frame:

God's tes - ti - mo - ny is most sure, And makes the sim - ple wise.
The Lord's com - mand is pure, and doth Light to the eyes im - part.
The judg - ments of the Lord are true And right - eous al - to - gether.
Than hon - ey, hon - ey from the comb That droppeth, sweeter far.
A great re - ward pro - vid - ed is For them that keep the same. A - men.

Moreover by them is thy servant
warned:
And in keeping of them there is great
reward.

This hymn is sung to the tune "St. Bernard" as arranged in 1863 by J. Richardson from a tune dating back to 1741.

✛

JERUSALEM THE GOLDEN

(Interpretation)

BERNARD of Cluny was born in the twelfth century at Morlas, France, of English extraction. He became a monk in the famous Abbey of Cluny, perhaps the wealthiest and most influential of all the French monasteries.

Three of the great hymns of the Church were taken from Cluny's longer poem containing some three thousand lines. Although translators have taken liberties in changing its expressions, its spirit has been preserved.

The translator of this hymn, John Mason Neale (1818-1866), was born in London. His father was a clergyman. He attended Trinity College at Cambridge, and was regarded as the leading scholar of his class. His knowledge of both English and Latin made him an excellent translator of verse, his most noteworthy contribution to the Church being "Jerusalem the Golden" from Bernard's longer poem.

The first and second stanzas present a paean of praise to Jerusalem in the golden days of its magnificence, crowned with glory and "decked in glorious sheen." The third stanza sings of Jerusalem, the seat of David's throne during the days of his glorious reign. The fourth stanza sings of this sweet and blessed country, "the home of God's elect," and compares it with the "land of rest" where the saints of Israel and the Christians of a later age shall abide with God the Father and in his Spirit be "ever blest."

The tune "Ewing" was composed by Alexander Ewing (1853). Mr. Ewing was born in Aberdeen, Scotland. He was educated for the law, but because of his special love for and interest in music, he later became a member of the famous Harmonic Choir of Aberdeen. At a rehearsal of this great Choir he was inspired to write a hymn tune, and "Ewing" was the result. To sing this tune is to recognize its genuine merit and spirit.

✛

SEND DOWN THY TRUTH, O GOD

(Interpretation)

EDWARD ROWLAND SILL (1841-1887) was born in Windsor, Connecticut. He graduated from Yale University, and then went West, becoming a professor of English at the University of California.

Jerusalem the Golden

EWING. 7, 6, 7, 6, D.

BERNARD OF CLUNY, c. 1145
Tr. JOHN M. NEALE, 1851

ALEXANDER EWING, 1853

1. Je - ru - sa - lem the gold - en, With milk and hon - ey blest,
2. They stand, those halls of Zi - on, All ju - bi - lant with song,
3. There is the throne of Da - vid, And there, from care re - leased,
4. O sweet and bless - ed coun - try, The home of God's e - lect!

Be - neath thy con - tem - pla - tion Sink heart and voice op - pressed.
And bright with man - y an an - gel, And all the mar - tyr throng.
The shout of them that tri - umph, The song of them that feast;
O sweet and bless - ed coun - try, That ea - ger hearts ex - pect!

I know not, O I know not, What joys a - wait us there,
The Prince is ev - er in them; The day - light is se - rene;
And they, who with their Lead - er, Have con - quered in the fight,
Je - sus, in mer - cy bring us To that dear land of rest,

What ra - dian - cy of glo - ry, What bliss be - yond com - pare!
The pas - tures of the bless - ed Are decked in glo - rious sheen.
For - ev - er and for - ev - er Are clad in robes of white.
Who art, with God the Fa - ther And Spir - it, ev - er blest! A - men.

He wrote this hymn soon after the close of the Civil War (1867), and it was first published in *The Hermitage*. It pleads that God will "send down" His truth that it may heal the hurt resulting from this senseless war between the North and South. It pleads for God's truth, His free Spirit, His love, and His peace to cleanse this, our land, of further hate and strife engendered by the Civil War.

The spirit and sentiment of all great hymns are, as a rule, both timeless and timely. There is need now, as then, for the free spirit of true religion to unite the warring peoples of the world in a universal peace that can come only through faith in, and obedience to, the everlasting "God of Peace." The hymn reminds us of what the gifts of love and brotherhood can do for all nations. It is a hymn to be sung in every age and by all peoples.

The melody to which this hymn is usually sung, "St. Michael" is an old one, dating back to *Este's Psalter* (1592). It is also sung to the tune "St. Thomas" by Aaron Williams (1763) from the English hymnal.

Send Down Thy Truth, O God

ST. MICHAEL. S. M.

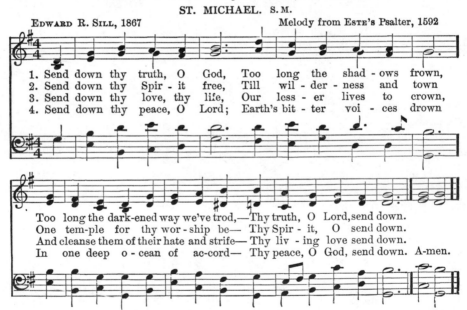

EDWARD R. SILL, 1867

Melody from ESTE'S Psalter, 1592

1. Send down thy truth, O God, Too long the shad - ows frown,
2. Send down thy Spir - it free, Till wil - der - ness and town
3. Send down thy love, thy life, Our less - er lives to crown,
4. Send down thy peace, O Lord; Earth's bit - ter voi - ces drown

Too long the dark-ened way we've trod,—Thy truth, O Lord, send down.
One tem-ple for thy wor-ship be— Thy Spir - it, O send down.
And cleanse them of their hate and strife— Thy liv - ing love send down.
In one deep o - cean of ac-cord— Thy peace, O God, send down. A-men.

PART IV

HIGH LIGHTS OF THE KINGDOM OF ISRAEL

The Two Kingdoms

CONTENTS

PART IV SECTION 1

THE NORTHERN KINGDOM

✛

How long halt ye between two opinions? If the Lord be God, follow him: but if Baal, then follow him.—I KINGS 18:21

✛

Music:

ELIJAH FED BY THE RAVENS

By

Charles M. Relyea

(Interpretation)

THERE came to the throne of the Northern Kingdom of Israel in the first half of the ninth century B.C. King Ahab, son of Omri the Great. The twenty-two years of Ahab's reign were marked by a crucial struggle between the worship of Baal and the worship of God. In this struggle the prophet Elijah was the chief champion for the Lord God of Israel.

When Ahab, influenced by his wife, Jezebel, a Sidonian princess from the city of Tyre, threatened to suppress the worship of the Lord by building an altar for Baal and by making Baal worship the court religion, Elijah suddenly appeared before the king and prophesied a long drought as punishment. During the three-year period of this drought Elijah, according to the word of God, hid himself by the brook Cherith in a crevice in the rocks near the Jordan River. There he drank the water of the brook and was fed by ravens that brought him bread and flesh in the morning and in the evening. (I Kings 17:1-6.)

It is this incident of Elijah, clad only in the skins of wild animals and sitting on a rocky ledge near the brook Cherith, that the American artist, Charles M. Relyea, has portrayed so realistically in his painting of "Elijah Fed by the Ravens."

At the prophet's feet is an earthen water bottle, while near by on the stone ledge is a scroll from which the prophet has, no doubt, been reading in the lonely watches of the day. Three ravens, black as the proverbial raven's wing, may be seen flying about around Elijah's head and feet. On the stony ledge a fourth raven has a twig of berries in his beak while he waits for the prophet to notice him and to refresh himself with red-ripe berries.

In the background is a wall of rock of huge proportions. The entire scene is barren and isolated. The prophet's eyes are fixed on the far horizon as if he were in the act of communion with his heavenly Father, and awaiting His guidance in the important decision that he soon must make.

Through the efforts of Elijah Baal worship was effectually checked in Israel. In the famous section beginning "Let us now praise famous men" found in the book of Ecclesiasticus in the Apocrypha there are twelve verses devoted to Elijah (48: 1-12). This is an indication that later Jews held his memory in high esteem. No other prophet is so often mentioned in the New Testament. The prophet, Malachi, prophesied the return of Elijah before the day of the Lord. This prophecy was literally interpreted in Israel (Matt. 16:14, 17:10, 27:47-49; Mark 6:15; John 1:21, 25). The evangelists and our Lord show that it was fulfilled in John the Baptist (Matt. 11:14, 17:10). In the transfiguration of our Lord, Elijah appears as the representative of the prophets, beside Moses, the representative of the Law (Matt. 17:3).

ELIJAH FED BY THE RAVENS—*RELYEA*

ELIJAH CARRIES THE LIVING BOY BACK TO HIS MOTHER

By

Ford Madox Brown

(Interpretation)

FOR a time during the famine in Israel and after his return from the brook Cherith Elijah, the prophet, lived in the home of a widow. Though the meal in her barrel was so low that she knew she and her son would soon die of hunger, this good woman had been kind to the prophet and had shared with him her scanty food.

But the Lord rewarded the widow's merciful deed by saying to her, through the prophet, Elijah, "Thus saith the Lord God of Israel, 'The barrel of meal shall not waste, neither shall the cruse of oil fail, until the day that the Lord sendeth rain upon the earth' " (I Kings 17:14). And the prophet's message came true.

One day after the drought had ended, and the grass was green again, and the famine was over, the widow's only son became ill with a strange disease. His breathing seemed to have stopped, and his mother was convinced that her son was dying. She appealed to God's prophet, Elijah, and he said to her, "Give me thy son." And he carried the lad into his own room in the widow's home and laid him upon the bed.

"And he cried unto the Lord, and said, 'O Lord my God, hast thou also brought evil upon the widow . . . by slaying her son?' And he stretched himself upon the child three times, and cried unto the Lord, and said, 'O Lord my God, I pray thee, let this child's soul come into him again' " (17:20-21).

And the Lord heard Elijah's prayer. The child began again to breathe rhythmically, and the color came back into his ashen face and lips. Then Elijah carried the boy back to his mother, who received him with joy and thanksgiving.

In this picture designed by Ford Madox Brown and engraved by Thomas Dalziel the aged prophet is portrayed returning the boy to his mother. She is kneeling at the foot of the stairs leading to the prophet's room on the housetop, and is saying: "Now by this I know that thou art a man of God, and that the word of the Lord in thy mouth is truth" (17:24).

Thomas Dalziel the famous English artist-engraver was born in 1823 and died in 1906. He and his brother established the Dalziel Brothers, wood engravers, in London during the nineteenth century. Among their many artistic endeavors was one to illustrate the Bible by engravings. It was called *Dalziel's Bible Gallery*. This venture was a financial failure, but it brought together such distinguished English artists as Frederick Leighton, Ford Madox Brown, Holman Hunt, Edward J. Poynter, and others, who combined their knowledge, skill, feeling, and imagination in creating these illustrations of Biblical themes.

Ford Madox Brown who designed this picture was born in 1821 in Calais, France, and studied art in Bruges and Antwerp. Sincerity was the great contribution he made to the art of his period. Every detail in his pictures was made a part of the whole composition for he was not interested in empty show. He was allied with the pre-Raphaelites, especially Rossetti. He died in 1893 in London.

✛

ELIJAH BRINGS DOWN FIRE FROM HEAVEN

By

Hans Holbein

(Interpretation)

WHILE the long drought which he had foretold still persisted, Elijah the prophet went to see Ahab the king. The story is dramatically narrated in the eighteenth chapter of the First Book of Kings. Confronted once more by the Lord's prophet, Ahab asked him in dismay: "Art thou he that troubleth Israel?"

Elijah replied: "I have not troubled Israel; but thou and thy father's house, in that ye have forsaken the commandments of the Lord, and thou has followed Baalim".

Elijah knew that the time had now come for the people to choose between Baal and the Lord God of Israel. He demanded that Ahab summon all the people to Mount Carmel where, in the name of the Lord, he would challenge all the prophets of Baal.

"How long," shouted Elijah to the people, "halt ye between two opinions? If the Lord be God, follow him; but if Baal, then follow him." But the people made no reply.

Then two altars were built one for Baal and one for the Lord, and on each altar was laid wood and a bullock to be a burnt offering. Elijah commanded the prophets of Baal:

"Call ye on the name of your gods, and I will call on the name of the Lord; and the God that answereth by fire, let him be God."

Whereupon the prophets of Baal began to call on their god, "O Baal, hear us!" But there was no answer. From morning to evening they cried and danced in frenzy around their altar, but "there was neither voice, nor any to answer, nor any that regarded."

Finally Elijah came forward and dug a ditch around the Lord's altar. Barrel after barrel of water was poured over the wood and the sacrifice upon the altar until they were soaked and the water ran down and filled the encircling trench. Then Elijah prayed, saying: "Lord God of Abraham, Isaac, and of Israel, let it be known this day that thou art God in Israel, and that I am thy servant, and that I have done all these things at thy word. Hear me, O Lord, hear me! that this people may know that thou art the Lord God."

As Ahab, and the prophets of Baal, and all the people watched and waited "the fire of the Lord fell, and consumed the burnt sacrifice, and the wood, and the

ELIJAH CARRIES THE LIVING BOY BACK TO HIS MOTHER—*BROWN*

stones, and the dust, and licked up the water that was in the trench. And when all the people saw it they fell on their faces."

A great cry rang out, for the people saw that the Lord had triumphed and they shouted: "The Lord, he is the God! The Lord, he is the God!"

This is the incident portrayed by Hans Holbein in "Elijah Brings Down Fire from Heaven." In the background the priests of Baal fruitlessly call on their god as they march about the unburned sacrifice on their altar. Flanking the Lord's altar are all the people of Israel, the kneeling prophet, Elijah, and King Ahab. Fire falls from heaven and consumes the sacrifice on the altar and licks up the water in the encircling ditch.

This is one of Hans Holbein's ninety-two woodcuts of Old Testament history, which since their publication in 1538 have been considered one of the great achievements of the graphic art. In a very small space, for the originals of these woodcuts are much smaller than this reproduction, Holbein tells an entire story clearly and convincingly. He succeeds in conveying, without a single false note, the emotions inherent in the whole dramatic scene.

✣

JEZEBEL'S THREAT

By

George J. Tobirz

(Interpretation)

JEZEBEL, wife of King Ahab, was by birth a Sidonian princess from the thriving seaport city of Tyre. She was so vindictive and hateful, so lacking in the gracious qualities that are usually the distinctive charm of royalty, that her name has become a synonym for *wicked woman*. She was a fanatical adherent of Baal and brought to her worship of this pagan god all her imperious self-will and determination which stopped at nothing to accomplish what she desired.

Jezebel introduced the worship of Baal into the Northern Kingdom of her husband, Ahab, and had altars built and dedicated to this idol. There were more than four hundred and fifty prophets of Baal who officiated at these heathen altars. Jezebel did not stop with this, but began to persecute the prophets of the Lord when they protested against the immoralities of her religion. Many of the prophets were killed; others escaped and hid in a cave. Meanwhile, the altars where the God of Israel was worshiped were destroyed.

So far Jezebel pursued her policy unopposed. But after the years of famine Elijah the prophet reappeared as the champion of the Lord. The story of how Elijah challenged the heathen prophets of Baal on Mount Carmel is one of the most dramatic in Biblical history. As a result of the contest on Mount Carmel the people of Israel pledged anew their loyalty to God, crying: "The Lord, he is the God! the Lord, he is the God!" (I Kings 18:39). All of the prophets of Baal were put to death at Elijah's command.

ELIJAH BRINGS DOWN FIRE FROM HEAVEN—*HOLBEIN*

When Ahab told Jezebel all that Elijah had done, and how he had had all the prophets of Baal slain with a sword, Jezebel, undaunted by defeat, sent the following threat to Elijah: "So let the gods do to me, and more also, if I make not thy life as the life of one of them by tomorrow about this time" (19:2).

Elijah knew that Jezebel's threat was no idle one. He therefore fled for his life through Judah, the Southern Kingdom, and on into the wilderness to Mount Horeb. There he remained for more than forty days until a messenger from the Lord appeared to him in the "still small voice" with encouragement and definite instructions.

"Jezebel's Threat" by George J. Tobirz captures the character of this wanton, wicked, and imperious queen whose union with Ahab left an indelible mark on the history of the Northern Kingdom. The scowling face, the clenched hand, the snakelike bracelet on her arm, the black shadow of hate hovering over her right shoulder, the black robe covering her left hand—all these accentuate the hatred and vindictiveness of Jezebel. Everything about her suggests that she was a powerful and dangerous opponent.

Little is known of the life of the artist of this comparatively modern painting.

✝

ELIJAH AT THE MOUTH OF THE CAVE

(Woodcut)

Artist Unknown

(Interpretation)

THE name of the prophet, Elijah, means "Jehovah is God." He was a native of Tishbeh who sojourned at Gilead. The story of his life and work is recorded in I Kings, chapters seventeen through nineteen and chapter twenty-one, and in II Kings, chapters one and two. His prophetic ministry belongs to the Northern Kingdom during the reigns of Ahab and Ahaziah.

After the prophets of Baal had been slain by Elijah, Jezebel threatened the prophet's life. He therefore fled southward in the direction of Mount Horeb. While resting under a juniper tree at the end of the day, an angel of the Lord appeared to him, saying, "Arise and eat, because the journey is too great for thee." Thereupon he arose, and ate the food provided by the angel and received strength for the forty days and nights of his flight to Mount Horeb.

The inspiration for this woodcut of Elijah comes from the nineteenth chapter of I Kings. There is narrated the awesome story of how the Lord manifested Himself to Elijah. When Elijah reached Mount Horeb, he came to the mouth of a cave and went in and lodged there. "And, behold, the word of the Lord came to him, and he said unto him, 'What doest thou here, Elijah?'"

Elijah replied: "I have been very jealous for the Lord God of hosts; for the children of Israel have forsaken thy covenant, thrown down thine altars, and slain

JEZEBEL'S THREAT—*TOBIRZ*

thy prophets with the sword; and I, even I only, am left; and they seek my life to take it away."

Then the Lord spoke again to Elijah: " 'Go forth, and stand upon the mount before the Lord.'

"And, behold, the Lord passed by, and a great and strong wind rent the mountains, and brake in pieces the rocks before the Lord, but the Lord was not in the wind; and after the wind an earthquake, but the Lord was not in the earthquake; and after the earthquake a fire, but the Lord was not in the fire; and after the fire a still small voice."

Hearing the voice, Elijah covered his face with his mantle and went out of the cave to meet his God.

"And the Lord said unto him, 'Go, return on thy way to the wilderness of Damascus; and when thou comest, anoint Hazael to be king over Syria; and Jehu the son of Nimshi shalt thou anoint to be king over Israel; and Elisha the son of Shaphat . . . shalt thou anoint to be prophet in thy room. . . . Yet I have left me seven thousand in Israel, all the knees which have not bowed unto Baal, and every mouth which hath not kissed him.' "

In this woodcut Elijah has wrapped his face in his mantle after hearing the voice of the Lord. He has prostrated himself at the entrance to the cave which had been his dwelling place. The wind, the earthquake, and the fire have passed. Elijah hears the still small voice distinctly. In the background of the picture there are evidences of the passing wind and fire; while behind the prophet may be seen the entrance to the cave. In the foreground appears the Lord surrounded with the radiance of His glory. The rays of His light are like the sun of a new day that is dawning in the world and in the heart of Elijah.

From his sublime experience at Mount Horeb, Elijah returned to his work as a prophet, confident that the Lord was with him. He was strengthened and renewed by this period of solitude and prayer. He had gained insight into God's purposes and plans. He had learned that the Lord is to be found, not in the violent upheavals of nature, but in "a still small voice."

✝

AHAB AND ELIJAH

By

Francis Bernard Dickee

(Interpretation)

FRANCIS BERNARD DICKSEE was born in 1855 in London. In 1876 he exhibited for the first time in the Royal Academy, and was made a member in 1891. His paintings include a large number of legendary, historical, and poetic themes.

Among his most distinguished Biblical pictures is that of Elijah denouncing the wicked King Ahab and his equally unscrupulous consort, Jezebel, who had had Naboth slain so that her husband might come into possession of Naboth's vine-

ELIJAH AT THE MOUTH OF THE CAVE—*ARTIST UNKNOWN*

yard which the king coveted because it bordered the grounds of his palace. The twenty-first chapter of I Kings records the event as follows:

"And it came to pass after these things, that Naboth the Jezreelite had a vineyard, which was in Jezreel, hard by the palace of Ahab king of Samaria. And Ahab spake unto Naboth, saying 'Give me thy vineyard, that I may have it for a garden of herbs, because it is near unto my house; and I will give thee for it a better vineyard than it; or, if it seem good to thee, I will give thee the worth of it in money.' And Naboth said to Ahab, 'The Lord forbid it me, that I should give the inheritance of my fathers unto thee.' And Ahab came into his house heavy and displeased because of the word which Naboth the Jezreelite had spoken to him; for he had said, 'I will not give thee the inheritance of my fathers.' And he laid him down upon his bed, and turned away his face, and would eat no bread.

"But Jezebel his wife came to him and said unto him, . . . 'Dost thou now govern the kingdom of Israel? Arise, and eat bread, and let thy heart be merry. I will give thee the vineyard of Naboth the Jezreelite.' "

Jezebel plotted to have Naboth put to death. "And it came to pass, when Jezebel heard that Naboth was stoned, and was dead, that Jezebel said to Ahab, 'Arise, take possession of the vineyard of Naboth the Jezreelite, which he refused to give thee for money; for Naboth is not alive, but dead.' "

While Ahab was on his way to Naboth's vineyard the word of the Lord came to Elijah the prophet saying, "Arise, go down to meet Ahab king of Israel, which is in Samaria. Behold, he is in the vineyard of Naboth, whither he is gone down to possess it. And thou shalt speak unto him."

The Lord instructed Elijah to deliver these words to Ahab: "Hast thou killed, and also taken possession? . . . In the place where dogs licked the blood of Naboth shall dogs lick thy blood, even thine."

When the king saw the prophet confronting him he said to Elijah, "Hast thou found me, O mine enemy?"

The prophet replied, "I have found thee, because thou hast sold thyself to work evil in the sight of the Lord."

Dicksee portrays Elijah realistically, uttering a forceful denunciation of Ahab and Jezebel. The prophet is clad in a tunic and has a mantle of animal skins over his shoulder. His penetrating eyes look directly into the face of King Ahab. One hand grasps his staff; the other is thrust out in a condemnatory gesture toward Ahab as he delivers the Lord's message. In the background a servant reins in his horse startled by the loud voice of the prophet, while another servant listens with awe to the denunciation spoken so fearlessly to the king. The soldier's hand hovers uncertainly near the handle of his sword.

The haughty and vindictive Jezebel stands in the foreground clad in costly and elaborate garments. One hand plays with the jewels at her neck, but this is her only gesture of uncertainty. There is no trace of fear in her expression nor in her proud bearing as she gazes at God's prophet with insolent disdain. Her husband, meanwhile, draws back, his body twisted as though he had just received an unexpected, physical blow. He shows no sign of preparing to defend himself. Rather,

AHAB AND ELIJAH—DICKSEE

the thoughtful, solemn expression of his profile shows that the prophet's words have struck home.

The Bible records that "it came to pass, when Ahab heard those words, that he rent his clothes, and put sackcloth upon his flesh, and fasted . . . and went softly." Then the Lord said to Elijah: "Because he humbleth himself before me, I will not bring the evil in his days; but in his son's days will I bring the evil upon his house."

✛

AHAB SHOT BY A CHANCE ARROW

By

Julius Schnorr von Carolsfeld

(Interpretation)

AHAB, the son of Omri, was king of the Northern Kingdom of Israel for twenty-two years. His reign is chiefly memorable for his frequent clashes with the uncompromising prophet, Elijah. But Ahab faced political difficulties also. Twice he defeated Ben-hadad, king of Damascus, the last time in an outstanding victory at Aphek. He later made a treaty of alliance with Ben-hadad to resist the advance of the Assyrians. Shalmaneser III, king of Assyria, in his monolithic rock inscription refers to the two thousand chariots and ten thousand men Ahab sent against him, but claims to have defeated Ahab and Ben-hadad with other kings at Karkar on the Orontes in 853 B.C.

Soon after this Ahab renewed the war with his old enemy Ben-hadad. Ahab allied himself with King Jehoshaphat of the Southern Kingdom of Judah and their purpose was to regain Ramoth-gilead east of the Jordan from Ben-hadad. At Ramoth-gilead the battle was joined with the Syrians. While Ahab stood in his chariot directing his men a chance arrow pierced him between the plates of his armor and he died in the evening (I Kings 22:29-40).

Heroic though he was in battle he left behind him a name with a dark shadow upon it, for he permitted his wife, Jezebel, to introduce the worship of Baal into his kingdom and he accepted from her the vineyard obtained by the murder of Naboth.

Julius Schnorr von Carolsfeld, the German painter and engraver, has taken the incident of King Ahab's death as given in I Kings 22:34-38 as his theme for this engraving.

"And a certain man drew a bow at a venture, and smote the king of Israel between the joints of the harness. Wherefore he said unto the driver of his chariot, 'Turn thine hand, and carry me out of the host; for I am wounded.' And the battle increased that day; and the king was stayed up in his chariot against the Syrians, and died at even; and the blood ran out of the wound into the midst of the chariot. And there went a proclamation throughout the host about the going

AHAB SHOT BY A CHANCE ARROW—*VON CAROLSFELD*

down of the sun, saying, 'Every man to his city, and every man to his own country.'

"So the king died, and was brought to Samaria; and they buried the king in Samaria. And one washed the chariot in the pool of Samaria; and the dogs licked up his blood; . . . according unto the word of the Lord which he spake."

In this graphic portrayal by Schnorr von Carolsfeld King Ahab wears a helmet and armor to protect his body. He is directing the course of a fiercely fought battle against the Syrians. While he is standing in his chariot, he is shot by a chance arrow that pierces his body between "the joints of his armor." He reels back in pain, letting his spear slip from his grasp as he tries to brace himself in order to remain standing. The four-wheeled chariot drawn by two magnificent horses is about to crush one fallen hero as it moves furiously onward. In the upper left-hand corner stands the archer whose arrow has just pierced the king's body.

The lines in this picture cross each other chaotically giving an impression of the tumultuous action of this desperate battle. The figures of the soldiers are crowded together in the corners and background where fierce hand-to-hand encounters are taking place. Only in the foreground has the artist cleared a space for the beholder to see the heroic death of King Ahab.

Julius Schnorr von Carolsfeld was born in Leipzig in 1794. There he received his earliest instructions in painting from his father. In 1818 he followed the German pre-Raphaelite painters to Rome. He made one hundred and eighty designs for a series of Bible picture engravings entitled *"Die Bibel im Bildern."* His broad, unsectarian point of view won wide acceptance for his pictures throughout the Christian Church. Schnorr made the designs for stained-glass windows in St. Paul's Cathedral, London, and the Cathedral in Glasgow. He died in 1872.

✣

THE DEATH OF JEZEBEL

By

Wenceles von Vacslaw de Brozik

(Interpretation)

JEZEBEL was one of the most colorful and yet most vicious and vindictive characters in the Old Testament. As the consort of King Ahab she was responsible for many of the evils of his reign. Her name has come down to us through the centuries as a symbol of wickedness and sin.

Jezebel, daughter of Ethbaal, king of the Sidonians, was a Baal worshiper through whose influence her husband Ahab, the son of Omri, also became a worshiper of this heathen idol, and turned deaf ears to the warnings of both Elijah and Elisha, the Lord's prophets. Before long many in Samaria, the capital of the Northern Kingdom of Israel, became worshipers of Baal like their king.

It was on Mount Carmel, at the instigation of Elijah, that the contest between the god Baal and the Lord, the true God of the Hebrew people, occurred. And it was there on an altar erected under Elijah's command that a water-soaked bullock, offered to God, was consumed by a heaven-sent fire in the presence of the wicked, disobedient Baal worshipers.

Jezebel never forgot nor forgave the humiliation to her favorite god Baal. She threatened the life of the Lord's prophet with such vindictiveness that he fled in terror to Horeb.

Later, however, after Jezebel had commanded her servants to kill Naboth, and then had urged Ahab to take possession of Naboth's vineyard, Elijah came again to Ahab at the command of the Lord. He denounced the king's sin, and told him that his kingdom would be taken from his descendants and that Jezebel, who had instigated this crime, would be killed. The prophet said: "The dogs shall eat Jezebel by the rampart of Jezreel" (I Kings 21:23). All this came to pass at the end of Jehoram's reign. This story and the events that led up to it are narrated in the ninth chapter of the second Book of Kings.

Jezebel's son Jehoram (or Joram) became king of Israel after the death of his father, King Ahab, and his older brother. Jehoram went to the royal city of Jezreel to recover from wounds received in battle and there his nephew, Ahaziah, who was at that time king of Judah, came to see him. News was brought to the two kings that Jehu, a captain in the army, was driving furiously in his chariot toward the city of Jezreel. Not knowing that his army had revolted against him and that Jehu had been proclaimed king of Israel in his place, the sick King Jehoram together with his nephew went forth in their chariots to meet Jehu. They thought Jehu came to bring tidings from the battle, not to usurp the throne. The three men met in the place that had once been Naboth's vineyard.

King Jehoram called to Jehu, asking, "Is all well?"

Jehu replied, "How can anything be well while your mother Jezebel is alive with all her wickedness!"

When King Jehoram heard this he knew Jehu was his enemy and crying, "There is treachery!" he turned to flee. But Jehu shot him with an arrow and he fell down dead in his chariot. King Ahaziah of Judah was also killed and Jehu now became undisputed King of Israel.

When Jezebel heard of this in her palace in Jezreel and learned that Jehu was speeding toward the city, she knew that her end had come. Like a queen she met it boldly. "She painted her face, and tired her head, and looked out at a window."

She waited until Jehu's chariot had come through the gate and was in the palace court below her. Then she shouted a threatening challenge to Jehu. Angered by this he looked up and cried: "Who is on my side?"

Several of Jezebel's frightened servants were only too glad to make their peace with this usurper. When Jehu shouted to them, "Throw her down!" they hurled her from her balcony to the pavement below and dogs ate her as had been predicted.

It is this incident of Jezebel being thrown from her window to the pavement below that the artist Wenceles von Vacslaw de Brozik has so graphically portrayed in his "The Death of Jezebel."

De Brozik was a painter of religious and historical scenes. He was born at Tremosyna, near Pilsen, Bohemia, in 1851. At the beginning of his art career he was a pupil in the School of Beaux Arts at Prague, and later continued his studies under the influence of Piloty's School.

In 1876 he first came to Paris to live. The following year his first pictures were exhibited in the Paris Salon. In July of 1884 he was decorated with the Legion of Honor, being promoted to the rank of officer in July of 1890. Previously in 1878 he had been given a second-class medal by the Emperor of Austria. He died in 1900.

His "The Death of Jezebel" is a fine illustration of the artist's style in composition and execution. In the background of the massive pillars which frame the balcony from which Jezebel has been watching Jehu's entrance into Jezreel may be seen the buildings of the city. In the near foreground his soldiers and inhabitants of the city may be seen milling around. Three of Jezebel's servants have obeyed Jehu's command to hurl her to the pavement below. We see the vindictive Jezebel being overpowered by three of her disloyal servants who are in the act of violently pushing this wicked consort of King Ahab from the balcony.

✛

A BIBLE STORY QUIZ

He had many brothers;
His father loved him best;
He was sold into Egypt
But withal he stood the test.

Answer—Joseph

Faithful and true to her mother-in-law,
She left the land of her birth
To glean in the fields of Boaz
And was loved by this man of great
    worth.

Answer—Ruth

A faithful little lad of old—
He heard God's voice one night;
When Eli bade him tell the truth,
He gave the message right.

Answer—Samuel

He thought more of the present
Than the future, it is said;
When his brother asked for his birth-
    right,
He chose the pottage instead.

Answer—Esau

On a journey far from home,
He dreamed and saw in the air

A ladder stretched from earth to sky
And angels walking there.

Answer—Jacob

A fervent man of faith was he—
His son he would have slain,
Obedient to the vision,
Had not God called his name.

Answer—Abraham

Brought up in the king's palace
But trained to know his God,
He was chosen to lead his people
Away from Pharaoh's rod.

Answer—Moses

He killed the giant Goliath
With only three stones and a sling;
Not only could he fight so well,
But many songs he did sing.

Answer—David

A handsome lad with golden hair—
He broke his father's heart.
He met his death by hanging
And was pierced by a fiery dart.

Answer—Absalom

THE DEATH OF JEZEBEL—*DE BROZIK*

"Every inch a king!" we read—
He gave promise of great worth,
His sinning brought his downfall—
The saddest tale on earth.

Answer—Saul

"Riches, fame, or wisdom?"
He chose the latter one.
The Queen came with her questions,
And he answered everyone.

Answer—Solomon*
—Grace Ordway Spear

AN ANTHEM OF PRAISE

I was glad when they said unto me,
Let us go into the House of Jehovah.
My feet shall stand within thy gates,
  O Jerusalem!
Jerusalem is built a compact city,
House joins to house within it.
Thither the tribes go up, the Tribes of Jehovah,
To the memorial feast for Israel,
To praise the majesty of Jehovah.
There stand the thrones of Judgment,
The thrones which the King hath established.
Pray for the peace of Jerusalem,
They shall prosper that love thee.
Peace be within thy walls,
And tranquility within thy palaces:
For my brethren and companions' sakes,
I will say, Peace be within thee;
Because of the Temple of our God,
I will seek thy good.**

A PREFATORY PSALM

Blessed is the man that walketh not in the counsel of the wicked,
  Nor standeth in the way of sinners,
  Nor sitteth in the seat of the scornful.
But his delight is in the law of the Lord;
  And in his law doth he meditate day and night.

And he shall be like a Tree planted by the streams of water,
  That bringeth forth its fruit in its season,
Whose leaf also doth not wither;
  And whatsoever he doeth shall prosper.
The wicked are not so;
  But are like Chaff which the wind driveth away.

Therefore the wicked shall not stand in the judgment,
  Nor sinners in the congregation of the righteous.

* From *Story Art Magazine*, May-June, 1951. Used by special permission of the author.
** Herder's paraphrase.

For the Lord knoweth the way of the righteous:
  But the way of the wicked shall perish.*

—Psalm 1

MORNING SONG

At the dawn, I seek Thee,
    Refuge and rock sublime,—
Set my prayer before Thee in the morning,
    And my prayer at eventime.

I before Thy greatness
    Stand, and am afraid:—
All my secret thoughts Thine eye beholdeth
    Deep within my bosom laid.

And withal what is it
    Heart and tongue can do?
What is this my strength, and what is even
    This the spirit in me too?

But verily man's singing
    May seem good to Thee;
So will I thank Thee, praising, while there dwelleth
    Yet the breath of God in me.**

—Solomon ibn-Gabirol; translated by Solomon B. Freehof

NATURE AND THE SCRIPTURES

(Psalm 19)

Behold, the lofty sky
    Declares its maker God;
And all his starry works on high
    Proclaim his power abroad.

The darkness and the light
    Shall keep their course the same;
While night to day, and day to night,
    Divinely teach his name.

In every different land,
    Their general voice is known;
They show the wonders of his hand,
    And orders of his throne.

---

* From *The Modern Reader's Bible* edited by Richard G. Moulton, p. 747. Copyright, 1935, by The Macmillan Company. Used by special permission of the publisher.

** From *The Small Sanctuary* by Solomon B. Freehof, p. 251. Copyright, 1942, by Riverdale Press. Used by special permission of the publisher.

Ye Christian lands, rejoice,
  Here he reveals his word;
We are not left to nature's voice,
  To bid us know the Lord.

His statutes and commands
  Are set before our eyes;
He puts his gospel in our hands,
  Where our salvation lies.

His laws are just and pure,
  His truth without deceit;
His promises forever sure,
  And his rewards are great.

Not honey to the taste
  Affords so much delight;
Nor gold that has the furnace passed,
  So much allures the sight.

While of thy works I sing,
  Thy glory to proclaim;
Accept the praise, my God, my King,
  In my Redeemer's name.

                                  —Isaac Watts

PEACE

If sin be in the heart,
The fairest sky is foul, and sad the summer weather,
The eye no longer sees the lambs at play together,
The dull ear cannot hear the birds that sing so sweetly,
And all the joy of God's good earth is gone completely,—
If sin be in the heart.

If peace be in the heart,
The wildest winter storm is full of solemn beauty,
The midnight lightning-flash but shows the path of duty,
Each living creature tells some new and joyous story,
The very trees and stones all catch a ray of glory—
If peace be in the heart.

                               —Charles F. Richardson

SERVANT OF GOD

O would that I might be
A servant unto Thee,

Thou God of all adored!
Then, though by friends outcast,
Thy hand would hold me fast,
And draw me near to Thee, my King and Lord.

Spirit and flesh are Thine,
O Heavenly Shepherd mine;
My hopes, my thoughts, my fears, Thou seest all,
Thou measurest my path, my steps dost know
When Thou upholdest, who can make me fall?
When Thou restrainest, who can bid me go?
O would that I might be
A servant unto Thee,
Thou God by all adored.
Then, though by friends outcast
Thy hand would hold me fast,
And draw me near to Thee, my King and Lord.

Fain would my heart come nigh
To Thee, O God on high,
But evil thoughts have led me far astray
From the pure path of righteous government,
Guide Thou me back into Thy Holy way,
And count me as one impenitent.
O would that I might be
A servant unto Thee,
Thou God, by all adored!
Then, though by friends outcast,
Thy hand would hold me fast,
And draw me near to Thee, my King and Lord.

So lead me that I may
Thy Sovereign will obey;
Make pure my heart to seek Thy truth divine,
When burns my wound, be Thou with healing near!
Answer me, Lord! for sore distress is mine,
And say unto Thy servant, I am here.
O would that I might be
A servant unto Thee,
Thou God, by all adored!
Then, though by friends outcast,
Thy hand would hold me fast,
And draw me near to Thee, my King and Lord.*

—Jehuda Halevi; translated by Israel Zangwill

* From The Standard Book of Jewish Verse translated by Israel Zangwill, p. 436. Reprinted in The Small Sanctuary by Solomon B. Freehof. Copyright, 1942, by Riverdale Press. Used by special permission of the publisher.

SOMEBODY

Somebody did a golden deed;
Somebody proved a friend in need;
Somebody sang a beautiful song;
Somebody smiled the whole day long;
Somebody thought, " 'Tis sweet to live."
Somebody said, "I'm glad to give";
Somebody fought a valiant fight;
Somebody lived to shield the right;
    Was that somebody you?

—Author Unknown

THE CONSECRATED LIFE

Lord, who shall sojourn in thy tabernacle?
Who shall dwell in thy holy hill?

He that walketh uprightly,
And worketh righteousness,
And speaketh truth in his heart.

He that slandereth not with his tongue,
Nor doeth evil to his friend,
Nor taketh up a reproach against his neighbour.

In whose eyes a reprobate is despised;
But he honoureth them that fear the LORD.

He that sweareth to his own hurt, and changeth not,
He that putteth not out his money to usury,
Nor taketh reward against the innocent.

He that doeth these things shall never be moved.*

—Psalm 15

THE PATHWAYS OF THE HOLY LAND

The pathways of Thy land are little changed
    Since Thou wert there:
The busy world through other ways has ranged,
    And left these bare.

The rocky path still climbs the glowing steep
    Of Olivet,

Though rains of two millenniums wear it deep,
   Men tread it yet.

Still to the gardens o'er the brook it leads,
   Quiet and low;
Before his sheep the shepherd on it treads,
   His voice they know.

The wild fig throws broad shadows o'er it still,
   As once o'er thee;
Peasants go home at evening up that hill
   To Bethany.

And as when gazing thou didst weep o'er them,
   From height to height
The white roofs of discrowned Jerusalem
   Burst on our sight.

These ways were strewn with garments once, and palm,
   Which we tread thus;
Here through thy triumph on thou passedst, calm,
   On to thy cross.

The waves have washed fresh sands upon the shore,
   Of Galilee;
But chiselled in the hillsides evermore
   Thy paths we see.

Man has not changed them in that slumbering land,
   Nor time effaced:
Where thy feet trod to bless we still may stand;
   All can be traced.

Yet we have traces of thy footsteps far
   Truer than these;
Where'er the poor and tried and suffering are,
   Thy steps faith sees.

Nor with fond sad regrets thy steps we trace;
   Thou art not dead!
Our path is onward, till we see thy face,
   And hear thy tread.

And now, wherever meets thy lowliest band
   In praise and prayer,
There is thy presence, there thy Holy Land,
   Thou, thou art there!

—Elizabeth Rundle Charles

THE TIME FOR PRAYER

When is the time for prayer?
With the first beams that light the
  morning sky.
Ere for the toils of day thou dost
  prepare,
  Lift up thy thoughts on high;
Commend thy loved ones to his watchful
  care
  Morn is the time for prayer!

And in the noontide hour,
If worn by toil or by sad care oppressed,
Then unto God thy spirit's sorrows
  pour,
  And he will give thee rest:
Thy voice shall reach him through the
  fields of air:
  Noon is the time for prayer!

When the bright sun hath set,
Whilst yet eve's glowing colors deck
  the skies,
When with the loved, at home, again
  thou'st met,
  Then let thy prayers arise.
For those who in thy joys and sorrows
  share:
  Eve is the time for prayer!

And when the stars come forth—
When to the trusting heart sweet hopes
  are given
And the deep stillness of the hour gives
  birth
  To pure bright dreams of heaven—
Kneel to thy God; ask strength life's ills
  to bear:
  Night is the time for prayer!

When is the time for prayer?
In every hour, while life is spared to
  thee—
In crowds or solitude—in joy or care—
  Thy thoughts should heavenward flee.
At home—at morn and eve—with loved
  ones there,
  Bend thou the knee in prayer!

—Author Unknown

TRUST IN JEHOVAH

Thou wilt keep him in perfect peace, whose mind is stayed on thee: because he trusteth in thee.—ISAIAH 26:3

Say to this mountain, "Go,
  Be cast into the sea";
And doubt not in thine heart
  That it shall be to thee.
It shall be done, doubt not His word,
Challenge thy mountain in the Lord!

Claim thy redemption right,
  Purchased by precious blood;
The Trinity unite
  To make it true and good,
It shall be done, obey the Word,
Challenge thy mountain in the Lord!

Self, sickness, sorrow, sin,
  The Lord did meet that day
On His beloved One,
  And thou art "loosed away."
It has been done, rest on His Word,
Challenge thy mountain in the Lord!

Compass the frowning wall
  With silent prayer, then raise—
Before its ramparts fall—
  The victor's shout of praise.
It shall be done, faith rests assured,
Challenge thy mountain in the Lord!

The two-leaved gates of brass,
  The bars of iron yield,
To let the faithful pass
  Conquerors in every field.
It shall be done, the foe ignored,
Challenge thy mountain in the Lord!

Take then the faith of God,
  Free from the taint of doubt;
The miracle-working rod
  That casts all reasoning out.
It shall be done, stand on the Word,
Challenge thy mountain in the Lord!

—Author Unknown

TWO VOICES

"Hear, O Israel! The Lord our God is one,
And thou shalt love Him with thy soul and might,"
So wrote within the Law some nameless son
Of Israel who spoke and passed from sight.
Another came—a Galilean Jew—
A carpenter who bade men love their God
With all their minds and hearts, and love men too—
One's neighbor as oneself. The path he trod:
He lived in love and died, to show the way,
Upon a cross with nails in feet and hands.
As Jewry says the great Shema today,
So Christians still repeat his love commands.
Across the years two Jewish voices sound:
They stir men's hearts to make God's love abound.*

—*Georgia Harkness*

"WHEN I THINK OF THE HUNGRY PEOPLE"

I have a suit of new clothes in this happy new year;
    Hot rice cake soup is excellent to my taste;
But when I think of the hungry people in this city
    I am ashamed of my fortune in the presence of God.

—*O-Shi-O, 18th-century Japanese scholar*

✠

GENEROSITY REWARDED

By

Mayme Rolf Leonard

MANY many years ago, in a far-off land, there came a great famine. Day after day the sun shone, but no rain fell. The grass and the flowers withered and died, and the grain in the fields lay parched under the withering sun. . . .

Throughout the land the famine was beginning to make itself felt keenly, in the villages as well as in the cities. And so it happened that a poor widow, living in one of the villages, saw that her supply of food was getting lower each day, and she realized that soon she would have no food at all. She was not surprised one day when she took out the jar in which she kept her flour to find that she had just enough left to make a few small cakes—one more meal for her little son and herself. She wondered if she had enough oil to mix with the flour, for she

---

couldn't make the little cakes without oil. Alas, the cruse was almost empty, for when she poured the oil in a dish there were only a few spoonfuls left.

The poor widow stood there sadly for a few moments, looking at the little heap of flour that was to provide their last meal. Then she went outside to gather a few sticks, so that she could make a fire. She wanted these cakes to be the best she had ever made, for it might be the last meal she and her son might ever eat. She did not know where she could get more flour, and she had no money to buy it, even if she had known.

Tired and weak, it took her a long time to find the sticks necessary for the fire. When she thought she had enough gathered and was turning back toward home, she heard someone call to her. She looked and saw a strange man standing close by. He was very tall, and his long hair flowed over his shoulders and about his faded, dusty garments. He looked tired and worn.

When he said, "Fetch me a little water in a vessel, that I may drink, I pray you," the woman felt so sorry for him that she forgot how tired and hungry she was, and went at once to her house to get the water. When his thirst was slaked he looked up at her with imploring eyes, and said, "Bring me, I pray you, a morsel of bread in thine hand."

The poor widow did not know what to say. This man was a stranger to her. He was asking her to share the little flour and oil that was hardly enough for herself and her son; but she had to speak honestly and frankly. She sighed and said: "Oh, sir, as the Lord thy God liveth, I have not a cake, but a handful of meal in a barrel, and a little oil in a cruse; and behold, I am gathering these few sticks that I may go in and prepare it for me and my son, that we may eat it and die."

The stranger looked at the woman as if he understood. Then he smiled gently and said: "Fear not; go and do as thou hast said; but make me thereof a little cake first, and bring it unto me, and after that make for thee and thy son."

Now, although this man was not a friend of hers, and had asked for what was most precious to her, she could not forget that he, too, was tired and hungry. So she bade him enter her home, and prepared to share her last loaf with him.

When her guest was made comfortable she kindled the fire, scraped the last bit of flour from the jar and poured in the last drop of oil from the cruse. When the cakes were baked she generously shared them, and she, her son, and her guest had plenty to eat.

When she arose the next morning the poor widow wondered what she would give her guest to eat, for he had tarried with them for the night. Despairingly she took out the jar and the cruse, as if hoping to find that she had left just a little in them. And, lo! a miracle had happened! The jar and the cruse contained just as much flour and oil as had been in them the night before.

Her guest, who was watching her, said smilingly: "Thus saith the Lord, God of Israel: The barrel of meal shall not waste, neither shall the cruse of oil fail, until the day that the Lord sendeth rain upon the earth."

And it came to pass as the stranger, who was Elijah, the great prophet, had said. For in the three years the stranger lived in the house of the widow the meal and the oil never failed her, and they had plenty to eat, while there was famine all around them.*

✦

JEZEBEL, ISRAEL'S WICKED QUEEN

By

Grace Ordway Spear

ABOUT the middle of the ninth century B.C., a baby girl was born one day in the city of Sidon on the shore of the Mediterranean Sea. The little princess grew up amid the beauty of the rich gardens of Sidon and the wooded cliffs of Lebanon. She spent her childhood exposed to the ancient culture of the city, with its poetry and art, and the wild beauty of the countryside round about. Little Jezebel loved to watch the mariners on their ships as they went about their trade with near-by towns and merchants. The child loved her father, King Ethbaal, and often walked with him, hand in hand, along the shore and among the trees. King Ethbaal had come to the throne through the murder of his brother Phelles; but if his daughter knew of this evil deed, then or later, it meant nothing to her—it was merely an incident of the many that came to her ears and attention. Her father could do no wrong—she idolized him. She had heard him rail at the Hebrews, who worshiped the *One God* whom they could not *see*—a very foolish religion, to Jezebel's thinking. She had absorbed the heathen nature worship of Baal and Ashtoreth. At least, they could *see* the gods to whom they prayed. Jezebel seemed to feel that this was a less stern, and more kindly religion; and in time, the princess, now grown to womanhood, assumed the role of missionary to the more expansive civilization represented by the worship of these two heathen gods.

The years came and went with wars and rumors of wars—until Ahab, son of Omri, came to the throne of Israel. If Omri had been an evil king, Ahab was worse, and wrought more evil against the Lord God, than all the previous kings in Israel. Seeking the beautiful princess, Jezebel, Ahab took her to wife and soon found in her not only a co-partner in the worship of Baal and the other heathen gods, but an abetter and encourager of his wicked deeds. Jezebel had no real love for Ahab, and the little respect she had, at first, soon left her, as she discovered her power over him and her ability to sway him—as well as his own wavering weakness and indecision in matters that came to him as King for settlement. She remembered her father's words to her as they walked together by the shore and in the wooded grove: "Do well whatever you do, Jezebel—lead, do not follow." And his counsel concerning Ahab upon her marriage to him. "Jezebel, my daughter, you will always be a lonely woman even though you have a husband. Ahab will be gallant and courteous, but he will never be thy true mate, nor will he ever be the real king. You will always overpower him in your thinking,

* From *The Children's Hour* by Mayme Rolf Leonard, pp. 27-29. Copyright, 1939, by The Standard Publishing Company. Used by special permission of the publisher.

and will be able to bend him to your will." It soon began to be very easy for Jezebel to assume the leadership, even in affairs of the kingdom, for Ahab evaded responsibility whenever he could and disliked making decisions. She derived a certain satisfaction from her power over her husband, but, womanlike, it soon palled on her to have him so weak and vacillating; and in time, she came secretly to despise Ahab.

Elijah, the Tishbite, prophesied in Israel, during the reign of Ahab and Jezebel. One day he came to Ahab and said: "As the God of Israel liveth, before whom I stand, there shall not be dew or rain in the land for three years, according to my words." And Elijah went and dwelt by the brook, Cherith, and the ravens were sent by the Lord to feed him. And when the brook dried up, because there had been no rain in the land, Elijah found refuge in the house of a widow woman who fed him for many days. For the Lord had said to the woman: "Thy barrel of meal shall not waste nor shall thy cruse of oil fail, until the day I will send rain upon the earth."

The famine throughout the land was desperate, and the inhabitants called upon Elijah, the prophet, to help them get food. But they would not listen to his words nor forsake the worship of their heathen gods. Jezebel, finding that there could be no compromise between the worship of Baal and that of the *One God* of the Israelites, sought by fierce persecution to bring the people of the realm to her will. Ahab made no objection, and the Queen called to the palace Obadiah, the governor of the household, saying: "Hear my word, for I shall slay all the prophets that trouble our land and cause insurrection among the worshippers of Baal. I command you to go out and put them all to death. They are weak and will be easily conquered."

"True, O Queen Jezebel," answered Obadiah; "of themselves they may be weak, but with their God to help them, no enemy can prevail against them."

"Fine words!" scornfully replied Jezebel; "but there is no sense to them! What power has a prayer such as they make to a God they cannot *see?*"

"What their God can do," replied Obadiah, "He alone knoweth. But I fear they have a strength which we cannot match."

"Enough of such talk!" vehemently cried the Queen. "Are we not of Sidon which first taught the mariners to fix their eyes upon and guide their vessels by the polar star?"

"But it was the God of Israel," answered Obadiah, "who first lit the polar star; and 'twas He who spoke the word, and the green grass appeared upon the earth."

"Enough, I say!" cried Queen Jezebel. "No wonder we have traitors in the streets when there are such thoughts in the palace."

Ahab, who had silently listened to the conversation, now interposed. "Peace, my Queen! Obadiah is no traitor. He is merely voicing the fears he has heard from others in the streets. Give him your orders, and he will fulfill them."

But when Jezebel ordered that the heads of the prophets of the Lord God be cut off, Obadiah secretly took one hundred of them and hid them in caves. Unknown to the Queen, he fed them with bread and water so that their lives were spared.

Now Elijah, the prophet, came again to Ahab, the King. And the latter said unto him. "Art thou he that troublest Israel?" And Elijah answered the King, "I have not troubled Israel. It is thou, thyself, and thy father's house; for ye have forsaken the commandments of the Lord God and hast followed Baal. But if thou will bring to me all the prophets of Baal and all the prophets of Astoreth, I will show thee which is the true God."

Ahab summoned the four hundred and fifty prophets of Baal as Elijah had said. But Jezebel commanded the four hundred of Ashtoreth to remain in the groves. When all had assembled on Mount Carmel, the heathen prophets called upon their gods from morning even until noon and pleaded with them to send rain to ease the famine; but they received no answer from Baal, nor any evidence that their prayers were heard.

Then Elijah repaired the altar which the prophets of Baal had, in their anger, destroyed; and he prepared the sacrifice and prayed: "Hear me, O Lord, that this people may know that thou art the Lord God!" And the fire of the Lord fell and consumed the burnt sacrifice and the stones and the wood and the dust, and licked up the water that was about the altar.

And when the people saw this, they fell on their faces and cried, "The Lord, He is God! The Lord, He is God!" Then Elijah slew all the prophets of Baal.

Ahab, the King, reported to Queen Jezebel all that Elijah had done; and how he had slain the prophets of Baal. And Jezebel sent a messenger to Elijah saying, "So let the gods do to me and more, also, if I make not thy life as the life of one of them by the morrow." But Elijah went and hid in a cave; and the Lord came unto him in the still, small voice, and told him what he should do.

Now there lived near the palace of Ahab and Jezebel a man named Naboth who had a vineyard. And Ahab said unto Naboth, "Give me thy vineyard that I may have it for a garden of herbs, because it is near my house. And I will give thee a better vineyard for it, or I will give thee the worth of it in money." But Naboth refused the King, saying, "The Lord forbid that I should give thee the inheritance of my fathers!"

Ahab returned to the palace, heavy-hearted and displeased; he laid himself upon his bed, turned away his face and would not eat. Jezebel, his wife, came in unto her husband and said, "Why is thy spirit sad, and why wilt thou not eat?" Then Ahab told her what Naboth had said. An expression of pity and scorn came into the Queen's face as she looked down upon Ahab; there was sarcasm in her tone as she put the question: "Dost thou govern Israel, or not? Arise and eat, and forget thy sadness. *I* will get thee the vineyard of Naboth."

Then Jezebel plotted against Naboth and secured witnesses against him; so that Naboth was judged guilty before the people, and they carried him out of the city and stoned him to death. Then Jezebel, the wicked queen, said to Ahab, her husband, "Arise, take possession of the vineyard, for Naboth is no longer alive or able to refuse thee."

When Elijah, the Tishbite, heard of this, he came again unto Ahab, and said: "Because, Oh King, thou hast sold thyself to work evil in the sight of the Lord, behold, He will bring evil upon thee and will take away thy posterity and destroy thee and thy kingdom."

Then Elijah went in unto Jezebel, the Queen, and said unto her: "Queen Jezebel, I have a message for thee." The Queen's eyes flashed fire, and she spoke angrily: "I defy thee, thou prophet! Begone, or I shall have slaves whip thee from the palace!"

But the prophet stood firm in his place and said quietly: "Queen Jezebel, hear the word of the Lord God. Do not defy Him! I see the secret fear in thine eyes, and the quivering of thy lips!"

Jezebel changed her tone : "Tell me, then, thou prophet of Israel, why thou hast always sought to thwart me and to overthrow the gods I worship?"

And Elijah answered her: "Because, O Queen, thou, from the first day of thy reign, didst seek to kill the worship of the One God in the heart of all the people and to force them to worship the idols of Baal!"

"I never forbade the worship of Israel's God," replied the Queen. "I merely commanded that Baal and Ashtoreth be supremely honored throughout the land."

"That, no true worshiper of the One God can do," replied the prophet. "O Jezebel, hadst thou listened to the voice of God when, still young, thou camest from Sidon to reign over Israel, how much good thou couldst have done as Queen! But the hour is past and thou dost not repent. Therefore, God hast sent me to tell thee thy punishment. Not only hast thou sinned thyself, but thou hast stirred thy husband, the King, to more wickedness. Hear now thy doom! From that same tower which has witnessed thy many murders, thou shalt be hurled and the dogs shall feed upon thy flesh and drink thy blood!"

When Ahab, the King, heard the words of the prophet, Elijah, he rent his clothes and put sackcloth upon him, and went softly. And Elijah said, "Seest thou how Ahab hath humbled himself before the Lord and repenteth of his sins? Therefore the Lord forgiveth him, and will not let evil befall him."

But Jezebel cried out defiantly: "Have I asked for mercy, oh thou God of Israel?"

After the death of Ahab, his successor king Jehu set out to destroy all of Ahab's family. He ordered Jezebel to be flung from the window of the tower. Her body lay where it fell, while the dogs came and devoured it as Elijah, the prophet, had predicted.

Thus ended the life of Israel's wicked Queen—Jezebel!*

✛

THE TEST ON MOUNT CARMEL

By

Florence M. Earlle

ELIJAH sat in the door of the cottage of the widow of Zarephath and looked toward the land of Israel. It had been almost three years since he had stood before

* Used by special permission of the author.

King Ahab and told him there would be no rain or dew till he should say so. He wondered how much longer God would punish the evil of the land with famine.

There was famine in this land, too; but God had kept the meal and the oil from wasting, according to His promise; so there had been enough food for him and the widow and her son. Then Elijah bowed his head and prayed.

"How long, O Lord? How long will you punish your people?"

Then he heard the voice of God speaking to him. "Arise, go to Israel and do the thing before the people that I will show you. Be not afraid of Ahab."

So Elijah bade good-by to the widow and started.

Now the famine in the land of Israel was so severe that Ahab called his trusted servant, Obadiah, and said, "You take half the cattle and I'll take half. You go in one direction, and I'll go in the other. Perhaps we can find some brook or pasture that has not dried up, and we may save some of the beasts."

And as Obadiah was going toward the land of Zarephath, he met Elijah. He could scarcely believe his eyes.

"Is it—is it really you?" he stammered. "Where have you been? King Ahab has hunted you throughout all the land and taken an oath of each city that you were not there. And now you suddenly appear and command me to go tell the King that you want to see him. While I am gone, the spirit of the Lord will snatch you away, and Ahab will kill me. I believe in God. I have hidden one hundred of the prophets when the Queen would have killed them."

"It is really I myself," said Elijah. "And you need not be afraid to tell King Ahab I am here. I have work to do before the people. I won't disappear."

When Ahab came, he was angry, yet fearful.

"Is it you, you trouble-maker?" he said.

"I am not the trouble-maker," said Elijah calmly. "You are the one who is causing Israel to be punished by God. You and your wicked Queen, Jezebel. Now do what I command you. Call all the people together at Mount Carmel. We will have a test there to prove whether the Lord is God or the sun-Baal, as you call him. See that all the prophets of Baal are present for the test."

And Ahab, because he feared, did as Elijah had commanded him.

Now Mount Carmel was on the seacoast, and had once had an altar to God, although now it was in ruins.

When all the people had gathered, Elijah said, "How long are you going to waver between Baal and God? If Baal be your god, worship him; but if the Lord is God, then worship Him."

The people did not answer him, so he went on. "Today we will test whether your god is really a god. I am only one, but the prophets of Baal are four hundred. Therefore let them prepare the sacrifice. Let there be brought two oxen, one for each altar. Build your altar, and cut the ox in pieces and bring wood for the burning; but put no fire under it. I will do the same. Then the god that answers by fire from heaven to burn up the sacrifice, will be the real god."

"That will be a good test," the people answered. "Our sun god will send the flames."

So the prophets of Baal prepared their altar with its sacrifice. Around and around it they walked, chanting as they did so, "O Baal, hear us! O Baal, hear us! O Baal, hear us!"

But there was no response from heaven.

All morning the chanting and the marching continued. At noon Elijah began to make fun of them.

"Where is your god?" he mocked. "Is he meditating? Is he talking with some other god? Perhaps he has gone hunting or on a journey; or maybe he is asleep. Cry louder and waken him."

Angered, the Baal prophets leaped upon the altar. They cut themselves with knives so that their streaming blood might attract the attention of their god. When they were exhausted, they prophesied that Baal would hear them at the time of the evening sacrifice. But, of course, there was no sign from heaven; no voice; no response of any kind. The sun moved serenely on his course, but no fire came to burn the sacrifice.

At sunset, Elijah said to the people, "Draw near. I will rebuild this altar," and he used twelve stones to represent the twelve tribes. After he had prepared the sacrifice, he did a peculiar thing; he said, "Dig a trench about this altar. Make it deep enough to hold about two bushels of seed."

When that was done, he commanded, "Now go down to the sea, and bring water enough to drench the sacrifice." And the people did so. And Elijah said, "Do it again, and again!"

The water not only drenched the sacrifice, but ran down in the trench till it was full. There could be no possible chance of trickery on Elijah's part.

His prayer was very brief. He said: "Lord God of Abraham, Isaac and Israel, let it be known now that you are God, and that I as your servant, have done this thing at Your command. Hear me, O Lord, hear me, that this people may know that you are God, and cause them to turn their hearts back to you again."

He said not a word about sending fire, but as he finished praying, the fire fell from heaven. It not only burnt the sacrifice and the wood, but it licked up all the water even in the trench. Then the people fell on their faces in awe, and cried, "The Lord! The Lord! He is the God!"

Then Elijah said, "Take the prophets of Baal; don't let any of them escape." And to Ahab he said, "Get down to your palace and feast till I call you, and send you word of the rain."

Then Elijah called a young man from the people and said, "Come with me; I need you."

Together they climbed to the very top of Mount Carmel. Elijah sat down, and putting his head between his knees, he prayed. Then he said to the lad, "Go look toward the sea."

The boy returned saying, "There is nothing there."

Before long, Elijah sent him a second time, and again the boy reported, "There is nothing there."

Five times more, Elijah sent him, and the seventh time, he returned and reported, "There is a little cloud rising out of the sea; but it isn't bigger than a man's hand."

"Go quickly to Ahab. Tell him to get his chariot ready for a journey to his palace in Samaria; tell him to hurry or the rain will stop him."

And even while the boy ran to the King, the heavens grew black with clouds and wind, and rain began to fall. Elijah threw aside his cloak, tucked up the ends of his garment in his belt, and ran before the chariot of Ahab as herald, crying: "Clear the way! The King is coming!"

Thus he took him to the gates of the city, while the rain that the people had not seen for three years ran in torrents, filling the streams and valleys of all the land of Israel.*

✛

ELIJAH, A CHARACTER STUDY

By

Kyle M. Yates

IN Jewish tradition the prophet Elijah takes first place. Through all the years he has continued to hold his high place as one of the truly great men of Israel. His life is filled with interesting adventures that urge the imagination to run riot. Such color calls for a careful study of the man, his age, his contemporaries, his message, and his influence.

THE BACKGROUND

After the death of Samuel the newly formed kingdom of Israel suffered severely at the hands of the Philistines. Their greatest invasion resulted in the death of Saul and his son Jonathan. David came to the throne of the tribe of Judah for a few years and then was elevated to be king over all Israel. Solomon followed him in a long and prosperous reign. Wealth, luxury, foreign cults and fashions were brought in. The kingdom was enlarged to include the greater part of Palestine.

In 931 B.C. the division came. Rehoboam, failing in a crisis, was left with the smaller of two adjacent kingdoms. In the North Jeroboam led the people into idolatry and pagan worship. After fifty years of disaster and turmoil Omri came to the head of the government to stop anarchy, conquer Moab, establish a monarchy, build the city of Samaria, make a treaty with Syria, and marry Ahab to the daughter of Ethbaal of Tyre. Omri was one of the strongest rulers of the entire lot. During this period in the land of Moab, Mesha ruled over a powerful kingdom. The famous Moabite Stone was set up to commemorate the deliverance from Israel.

Ahab, the successor to Omri, might have been more popular and famous if he could have lived apart from the influence of Jezebel. The sacred historian did not see some of the finer things which he did because of his close affinity with Baalism and other heathen religions.

Jezebel, the daughter of the priest of Melkart, was a powerful figure. She was

---

* Used by special permission of the author.

a passionate missionary who sought by all means available to make her religion dominant in the land. Under her vigorous leadership a real crisis arose. It was a genuine life-and-death struggle. Not only did she build her own temple and import hundreds of her own alien prophets but she set out to cut off all the prophets of Yahweh* and to turn the people away from Yahweh worship.

Assyria began to show signs of life during this period after years of comparative quiet. In the year 854 B.C. Shalmanezer III of Assyria came against the people of Palestine. The battle of Karkar settled the fate of the Westland for many years. Ahab had an army in that battle.

In Judah (the southern kingdom) Rehoboam, Abijah and Asa ruled over the remnant of David's domain. Two serious invasions from the south by Shishak and Zerah proved serious blows to the struggling kingdom. Jehoshaphat, who was king in Jerusalem during Elijah's ministry, did much to restore some of the glory of David's reign.

The land of Israel suffered greatly during the days of anarchy and invasion. As a result of the tragic turmoil of those days, living conditions were intolerable. Omri put an end to the internal disturbances but was forced to fight surrounding nations. In his vast building operations at Samaria it was necessary for him to force his people to give of their time and labor and resources until a duplicate of Solomon's dilemma must have faced him. A severe drought added to the want, the misery and the suffering of the people. While the king's court was able to maintain luxury and extravagance, the people slaved.

Jezebel, with her imported priests and prophets, introduced a new element into the life of the people. It was quite an undertaking to support these men and their elaborate worship programs. A more serious matter, however, grew out of Jezebel's conception of property rights. She had no scruples whatever about the execution of a property owner and the confiscation of the land for her own desires. Fear, hatred, distrust, and active disloyalty created a serious state of affairs in the kingdom. The work started by Omri was largely ruined by the coming of this Tyrian princess.

Elijah stood in the midst of a serious crisis in Israel. The people had lost practically all the finer appreciation of the Law and the principles of religion enunciated by Moses and Samuel. They had learned to know the gods of the surrounding peoples and had gradually adopted toward them an attitude of toleration that bordered dangerously on syncretism.

The marriage of Ahab to Jezebel was the fatal blow that introduced into Israel the cult which threatened to destroy the very existence of the Yahweh religion. Jezebel was not content to allow her religion to have a small place in the capital city (as the foreign wives of Solomon had done) but set about to accomplish the utter extermination of prophets and principles. Farley says: "To please his strong-minded queen, Ahab built in Samaria a temple to 'the Baal,' and also made 'the Asherah,' so that the Phoenician worship was now established in its entirety. The Baal worship was essentially the worship of mere power—of power as distinguished

---

* From this hybrid spelling came the divine name *Jehovah* current in English and other modern languages.

from righteousness—and the worship of power by a regular and logical process becomes literally the worship of evil. Not without reason did the Jews of later days designate this Tyrian deity the 'Prince of Devils.' "*

Along with these practices came the most hideous immorality imaginable. Moral standards were lowered and the religious life of the people fell to an alarming state. The prophets of Yahweh were persecuted. Many of them were killed. Others were compelled to hide in caves and holes or were soon silenced. The great mass of the people were "limping" along unable to distinguish between Baal and Yahweh. It was a dark day for the true religion. The leaven of Baal was working secretly throughout the entire land.

Elijah was a sturdy, virile, daring man from the wilds of Gilead. His iron constitution, his austere spirit, his majestic bearing, his flaming indignation, his consuming zeal, and his courageous nature set him forth as a man of mystery and romance. He was so strong and yet so weak. His zeal was limitless as his energy. His tremendous grip on God gave him unusual power in prayer. His faith in God was so strong that it beggars description. He hated false religions, pagan practices and ungodly treatment of the people's rights. In most instances he displayed a remarkable unselfishness and an utter disregard of personal safety. He was merciless and cruel in his treatment of the prophets of Baal when circumstances demanded a complete victory. Literally on fire for God, he gladly burned himself out doing the will of God.

He was Yahweh's champion in a dark day of crisis when true religion was practically driven from the earth. The people could not serve two gods. They were challenged to choose between Yahweh and the Tyrian Baal. It was his task to deal the deathblow to Baal in the land of Israel.

Just as truly was he a champion of the people in their fight against Jezebel's dictatorship. The ancient laws of prophecy were the true foundation of the people's rights. Yahweh was revealed as the God of fair play. Righteousness was the ruling attribute of the God of Elijah. Religion and morality were closely blended in his religion. He set forth justice as an elemental requirement. No generation will ever forget the tragic story of Naboth's vineyard and Elijah's flaming denunciation of the sin of Ahab and Jezebel.

He was a teacher of Elisha and the other young men of the "schools of the prophets." These years of quiet work with his religious successors bore rich fruit. It is difficult to evaluate the contribution of one who transmits to his pupils the store of spiritual knowledge gained through his long years of study. Elijah gave to Elisha the knowledge, the vision, the challenge to serve, and the courage to finish the work begun so dramatically.

In some strange way Elijah has taken his place in the literature of the world and in men's thoughts as a truly remarkable character. The New Testament has more reference to him than to any other prophet. At every Passover the Jews look for him and keep an extra chair for his use. Mountains are named for him

---

* *The Progress of Old Testament Prophecy in the Light of Modern Scholarship* by William J. Farley (now out of print), p. 36.

in Greece. The order of Barefooted Carmelites in the Roman church looks back to Elijah as its founder.

He was a man of God. Always there was about him something of the divine presence. When men saw him they were awed by the realization that God's man was in their midst.

He was a man of prevailing prayer. Where else do we find such a mighty man of prayer? The two instances of his praying on Mount Carmel literally lift him out of the ordinary into the sublime.

He was a man of faith. His unwavering faith in Yahweh made it possible for him to prevail in prayer and to continue the relentless fight against false religions and pagan behavior. Step by step he moved under the guidance and protection of God.

In that desperate hour of crisis he was the human agent whom God used to pull the tottering theocracy back from seeming defeat. One shudders to think of the narrow escape. God's man was put forward, clothed with supernatural power, to undertake the impossible, that the divine purpose might be fulfilled.*

✠

FATHER ALMIGHTY, BLESS US WITH THY BLESSING

(Interpretation)

THIS nineteenth-century hymn is from the *Berwick Hymnal,* published in 1886. Nothing is known of the author of the words.

The first stanza is a plea to the "Father Almighty" to bless His children; to hear the spoken and unspoken supplications of His earthly family, and in His loving-kindness to answer their need.

The second stanza is a petition to the Shepherd of men's souls to guard the inhabitants of this earth, and to guide their ways beside peaceful waters, leading them like a shepherd into paths of duty and love. It echoes the thought of the 23rd Psalm.

The third stanza appeals to the Heavenly Father to guard the children of the earth individually from every evil in every hour of every day. It expresses the hope that the "Infinite Spirit" will give only good to the children of men.

The tune "Integer Vitae" was composed in 1810 by Friedrich F. Flemming.

* Abridged from *Preaching from the Prophets* by Kyle M. Yates, pp. 23-28. Copyright, 1942, by Kyle M. Yates. Published by Broadman Press. Used by special permission of the author and the publisher.

Father Almighty, Bless Us with Thy Blessing

INTEGER VITÆ. 11, 11, 11, 5

Berwick Hymnal, 1886   Friedrich F. Flemming, 1810

1. Fa - ther Al - might - y, bless us with thy bless - ing, An - swer in
2. Shep - herd of souls, who bring - est all who seek thee To pas - tures
3. Fa - ther of mer - cy, from thy watch and keep - ing No place can

love thy chil - dren's sup - pli - ca - tion; Hear thou our prayer, the
green be - side the peace - ful wa - ters; Ten - der - est guide, in
part, nor hour of time re - move us; Give us thy good, and

spo - ken and un - spo - ken; Hear us, our Fa - ther.
ways of cheer - ful du - ty, Lead us, good Shep - herd.
save us from our e - vil, In - fi - nite Spir - it.   A - men.

HYMN OF GLORY

(Interpretation)

The Hebrew words of this hymn by an unknown thirteenth-century writer were translated by Alice Lucas. It is sung to the traditional melody, "Omnom Kayn."

The six stanzas present a paean of praise to the God of Abraham, Isaac, and Jacob. One cannot read the words without feeling a surge of the faith and trust that has kept Jewish belief in the God of their fathers a vital, life-renewing power through many centuries of hate and persecution. To Him their songs of praise and thanksgiving daily ascend, for in "Him they live, and move, and have their being." By day and by night men and women in all ages affirm their faith and

Hymn of Glory

Alice Lucas,—Tr. fr. the Heb., Author unknown, 13th Cent.   Traditional "Omnom Kayn"

1. Sweet hymns and songs will I re - cite To
2. How doth my soul with - in me yearn Be -
3. And e'en while yet Thy glo - ry fires My
4. O Thou whose word is truth al - way, Thy
5. O may my words of bless - ings rise To
6. My med - i - ta - tion day and night, May

sing of Thee, by day and night, Of Thee, who art my
neath Thy shad - ow to re - turn, Thy se - cret mys - ter -
words, and hymns of praise in - spires, Thy love it is my
peo - ple see Thy face this day, O be Thou near them
Thee, who throned a - bove the skies, Art just and might - y,
it be pleas - ant in Thy sight, For Thou art all my

soul's de - light, Of Thee, who art my soul's de - light.
ies to learn, Thy se - cret mys - ter - ies to learn.
heart de - sires, Thy love it is my heart de - sires.
when they pray, O be Thou near them when they pray.
great and wise! Art just and might - y, great and wise!
soul's de - light, For Thou art all my soul's de - light.

trust in God as they seek to know His will and to reflect His will in all their dealings with the children of men.

This great devotional hymn composed many centuries ago is still a challenge to the devout of all faiths, creeds, and nations to join in thanksgiving and glory to the God of all nations and races of mankind. "Let all the people sing" this great hymn of aspiration, yearning, and praise.

✛

LET ISRAEL TRUST IN GOD ALONE
(Interpretation)

THE history of the Hebrews is familiar to most of us, not so much because of their importance as a people, as through the influence which they have had on the later history of the world. Someone has said. "The Jews did not make history; history made them." After their slavery in Egypt, they settled on a narrow strip of land which borders on the Mediterranean Sea between Egypt and Assyria. Thus their country was on the natural highway between these two great powers. Their significance resulted from the fact that, influenced by these great civilizations to the south and east, they produced a written literature covering the history of the world which records their developing concept of God. It consists of a collection of laws, songs, and religious rites, all of which were incorporated into the Bible and thus have become the heritage of the entire Christian world.

The Israelites were distinguished for their love of music. Paul Henry Lang in *Music in Western Civilization* says: "They were forbidden to make images, but, as if to compensate, they developed poetry and music to the highest degree. Gen. 4:21 mentions Jubal as 'the father of all such as handle the harp and organ.' "

This hymn, "Let Israel Trust in God Alone," translated by James K. Gutheim from the *Hamburg Temple Hymnal,* the melody of which was composed by William Lowenberg, is a fine illustration of Jewish music. It should be sung with spirit.

The first stanza emphasizes the trust of Israel in God alone, recalling to our minds the first of the Ten Commandments, "Thou shalt have no other gods before me." It urges devout Jews everywhere to rely on God's power, for if they abide in Him, and are faithful to His word, His counsels will stand forever, and all the nations will eventually come to obey His commands.

The second stanza urges Israel to strive for truth alone, to bless mankind through the force of love expressed in human brotherhood, knowing that through love the world will ultimately be brought into one accord, and will then acknowledge and obey the Lord, living together in love and peace as children of a common Father.

Let Israel Trust in God Alone

James K. Gutheim
Tr. from the Hamburg Temple Hymnal

Wm. Lowenberg

1. Let Is - rael trust in God a - lone And in His pow'r con - fide, For He is faith - ful to His word, If we in Him a - bide; His coun - sels must for - ev - er stand, All na - tions bow to His com - mand.

2. Let Is - rael strive for truth a - lone, In love to bless man - kind, And in the bonds of broth - er - hood All na - tions soon to bind, So that they all with one ac - cord, Ac - know - ledge and o - bey the Lord.

O for a Faith That Will Not Shrink

BEATITUDO. C. M.

WILLIAM H. BATHURST, 1831   JOHN B. DYKES, 1875

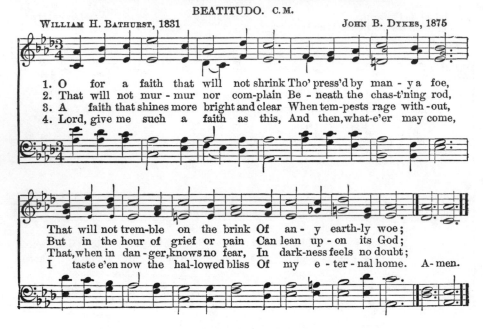

1. O for a faith that will not shrink Tho' press'd by man - y a foe,
2. That will not mur - mur nor com-plain Be - neath the chas-t'ning rod,
3. A faith that shines more bright and clear When tem-pests rage with - out,
4. Lord, give me such a faith as this, And then, what-e'er may come,

That will not trem-ble on the brink Of an - y earth-ly woe;
But in the hour of grief or pain Can lean up - on its God;
That, when in dan - ger, knows no fear, In dark-ness feels no doubt;
I taste e'en now the hal-lowed bliss Of my e - ter - nal home. A- men.

O FOR A FAITH THAT WILL NOT SHRINK

(Interpretation)

"O For a Faith That Will Not Shrink" by William H. Bathurst (1831) is another of those magnificent hymns of faith, written more than a hundred years ago, that have continued to challenge Christians everywhere to renew their faith and continue their struggle in the face of every foe.

The four stanzas present a petition to our Heavenly Father to give us, through Jesus Christ, such a strong and abiding faith that we will neither "murmur nor complain beneath the chast'ning rod," but instead "lean upon God" in the dark hours of trouble, grief, and pain. With such a faith we can here on earth experience the "hallowed bliss of my eternal home."

The music score "Beatitudo" was composed in 1875 by John B. Dykes.

✛

WALK IN THE LIGHT: SO SHALT THOU KNOW

(Interpretation)

IN 1826 Bernard Barton wrote the words to this hymn, which has its emphasis in the opening phrase of each of its four stanzas, "Walk in the Light." This recalls the words of Isaiah to the house of Jacob: "Let us walk in the light of the Lord" (Isa. 2:5).

The first stanza exhorts the worshiper to "walk in the light" of God's Holy Spirit where he will find the "fellowship of love."

The second stanza again urges the worshiper to walk in God's light that his heart may truly belong to God in whom there is "no darkness."

The third stanza assures the worshiper that walking in the light will banish the darkness of his earthly life.

The fourth stanza stresses that whoever walks in the light will find that even if his path is a difficult, thorny one it is nevertheless bright, for God who is Light dwells in his heart.

The tune "Nox Praecessit" was composed in 1875 by J. Baptiste Calkin.

Walk in the Light; So Shalt Thou Know

NOX PRÆCESSIT. C.M.

BERNARD BARTON, 1826   J. BAPTISTE CALKIN, 1875

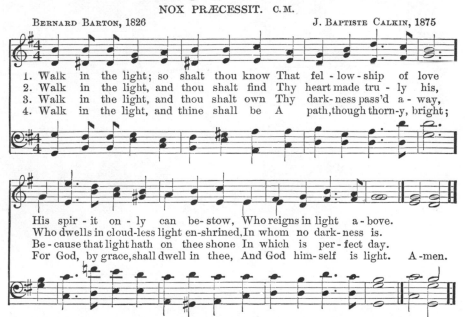

1. Walk in the light; so shalt thou know That fel - low - ship of love
2. Walk in the light, and thou shalt find Thy heart made tru - ly his,
3. Walk in the light, and thou shalt own Thy dark - ness pass'd a - way,
4. Walk in the light, and thine shall be A path, though thorn - y, bright;

His spir - it on - ly can be - stow, Who reigns in light a - bove.
Who dwells in cloud-less light en-shrined, In whom no dark-ness is.
Be - cause that light hath on thee shone In which is per - fect day.
For God, by grace, shall dwell in thee, And God him - self is light.   A - men.

CONTENTS

PART IV   SECTION 2

PROPHETS OF THE NORTHERN KINGDOM

✦

And the Lord took me as I followed the flock, and the Lord said unto me, Go, prophesy unto my people Israel.—AMOS 7:15

✦

ELIJAH CASTING HIS MANTLE ON ELISHA
Artist Unknown
(Interpretation)

THE name Elisha means "God is salvation." He was the son of Shaphat and a disciple and successor of Elijah to whom he was related much as Joshua was to Moses. His prophetic work belongs to the reigns of four kings of Israel: Jehoram, Jehu, Jehoahaz, and Joash, and the story of his life is recorded in II Kings, chapters two through nine and chapter thirteen.

He first enters the Biblical record during the reign of King Ahab when Elijah the prophet journeyed home after his experience at Mount Horeb. There the Lord had commanded Elijah saying: "Elisha the son of Shaphat . . . shalt thou anoint to be prophet in thy room" (I Kings 19:16).

At this time Elisha was a young man helping on his father's large farm. One day during the plowing season as Elisha drove one of the twelve yoke of oxen, Elijah passed by. Seeing Elisha, the prophet stopped and put his mantle on the young farmer's shoulders as a sign that henceforth Elisha would be his follower and successor.

Elisha understood what this act meant and he said: "Let me, I pray thee, kiss my father and my mother, and then I will follow thee."

The prophet replied: "Go back again, for what have I done to thee?"

After Elisha had made a farewell feast for his family and neighbors, "he arose and went after Elijah and ministered to him."

Elisha's years of service to the older prophet made him famous. In later years he was known as the man who "poured water on the hands of Elijah" (II Kings 3:11).

The picture by an unknown artist-engraver portrays the first recorded meeting of Elijah and Elisha. Young Elisha stands with one hand on the plow of the last team of oxen. Behind him the great prophet, Elijah, is about to put his mantle upon the young man's shoulders. In the background are some of the eleven other teams of oxen with their drivers tilling the huge field. Low clouds overhang the horizon and birds hover in the sky.

As a spiritual guide to his people, young Elisha showed the same opposition to the idolatrous court and priesthood of his times that had motivated Elijah; and he was a faithful servant to the Lord as was his great teacher before him. His ministry lasted for fifty years during the reigns of Joram, Jehu, Jehoahaz, and Joash. He became very popular and earned such a reputation for wisdom that Israel's kings came to him for counsel.

ELIJAH CASTING HIS MANTLE ON ELISHA—*ARTIST UNKNOWN*

ELIJAH AND THE CHARIOT OF FIRE
By

Caspar Luyken

(Interpretation)

THE story of how Elijah ascended into heaven is told in the second chapter of the Second Book of Kings. When Elijah's prophetic mission was completed, he said to Elisha: "Tarry here, I pray thee, for the Lord hath sent me to Bethel."

But Elisha would not leave his aged master. "As the Lord liveth, and as thy soul liveth, I will not leave thee," he declared. So together they set forth and came to Bethel.

There a group of men called the "sons of the prophets" came out to meet them. Taking Elisha aside they asked him: "Knowest thou that the Lord will take away thy master from thy head today?"

Elisha replied, "Yea, I know it. Hold ye your peace."

Twice more the aged prophet tested the loyalty of his follower, telling him to remain behind while he went on, first to Jericho, next to the Jordan, but each time Elisha refused to remain behind and continued on with his master. Following behind them from Jericho to the Jordan were fifty "sons of the prophets" who knew that the time had come for Elijah to be taken up into heaven.

On the banks of the Jordan Elijah took his mantle and rolled it up and struck the water with it. Thereupon the waters parted and the two prophets crossed to the opposite shore on dry ground.

When they had passed over the older prophet said to his followers, "Ask what I shall do for thee, before I be taken away from thee."

Elisha replied, "I pray thee, let a double portion of thy spirit be upon me."

"Thou hast asked a hard thing," answered Elijah, "nevertheless, if thou see me when I am taken from thee, it shall be so unto thee. But if not, it shall not be so."

As they continued walking and talking together along the bank of the Jordan, suddenly "there appeared a chariot of fire, and horses of fire, and parted them both asunder. And Elijah went up by a whirlwind into heaven."

Elisha saw him going up and he cried: "My father! my father! the chariot of Israel and the horsemen thereof!" At this moment Elisha knew that the old prophet had defended Israel as powerfully as chariots and horsemen.

Then Elisha "took hold of his own clothes, and rent them in two pieces. He took up also the mantle of Elijah that fell from him, and went back, and stood by the bank of Jordan. . . . And when the sons of the prophets which were to view at Jericho saw him, they said, 'The spirit of Elijah doth rest on Elisha.' And they came to meet him, and bowed themselves to the ground before him."

This picture, "Elijah and the Chariot of Fire," was designed by Caspar Luyken and engraved by Christophoro Weigelio. It appears as one of the beautiful illustrations in a large volume of Old Testament stories entitled *Historiae Celebriores Veteris Testamenti* published in 1712.

In the foreground Elisha kneels upon one knee, grasping in his right hand the mantle which has fallen from Elijah, while with his left hand he gestures toward the chariot and horses of fire carrying the prophet up to heaven in a whirlwind. Beneath the blazing chariot run the placid waters of the Jordan. On the opposite bank are the sons of the prophets who have come forth out of Jericho, but do not see Elijah's miraculous translation into heaven. Between the walls of Jericho and the beautiful foliage of the trees growing in the Jordan valley can be seen the bare uplands and mountains of Judah.

✛

ELISHA AND THE SHUNAMMITE'S SON

By

Julius Schnorr von Carolsfeld

(Interpretation)

THE Biblical story of Elisha and the Shunammite's son is found in II Kings 4:8-37. There lived in the town of Shunem a great and good woman. One day she said to her husband: "Let us make a little chamber, I pray thee, on the wall; and let us set for him there a bed, and a table, and a stool, and a candlestick. And it shall be, when he cometh to us, that he shall turn in thither" (4:10). Thus it was that when Elisha, the prophet, passed through Shunem, there was always a room prepared for him in advance and a welcome in this home of the Shunammite woman.

Later this good woman had a son. When the child was grown, he went with his father, one day, to the fields with the reapers. During the morning the son said to his father: "My head, my head!" His father said to a servant: "Carry him to his mother." When the servant brought him to his mother he sat on her lap until noon, and then died. The frantic mother laid him on the bed in the room which had been set aside for the prophet. Then she called her husband and said: "Send me, I pray thee, one of the young men, and one of the asses, that I may run to the man of God."

When Elisha saw her coming afar off, he said to Gehazi his servant, "Behold, yonder is that Shunammite. Run now, I pray thee, to meet her, and say unto her, 'Is it well with thee?'"

When she reached Elisha at Mount Carmel she caught hold of his feet and bewailed the death of her son. Gehazi tried to thrust her away; but the prophet of God said: "Let her alone, for her soul is vexed within her; and the Lord hath hid it from me, and hath not told me. . . . Gird up thy loins, and take my staff in thine hand, and go thy way. If thou seest any man, salute him not; and if any salute thee, answer him not again. And lay my staff upon the face of the child."

Elisha arose, and followed the mother of the child. "And Gehazi passed on

ELIJAH AND THE CHARIOT OF FIRE—*LUYKEN*

before them, and laid the staff upon the face of the child; but there was neither voice, nor hearing. Wherefore he went again to meet him, and told him, saying, 'The child is not awaked.'

"And when Elisha was come into the house, behold, the child was dead, and laid upon his bed. He went in therefore, and shut the door upon them twain, and prayed unto the Lord. And he went up, and lay upon the child . . . and the flesh of the child waxed warm. Then he returned, and walked in the house once to and fro; and went up, and stretched himself upon him. And the child sneezed seven times, and the child opened his eyes. And he called Gehazi, and said, 'Call the Shunammite.' So he called her. And when she was come in unto him, he said, 'Take up thy son.' Then she went in, and fell at his feet, and bowed herself to the ground, and took up her son, and went out." (II Kings 4:19, 22, 25-37.)

This picture portrays the story of Elisha and the Shunammite's son. The aged prophet, Elisha, has just performed the miracle of raising the child from apparent death, and has returned him to his mother alive. The child and his mother are now leaving the prophet's room. The lad looks up into his mother's face and puts his arm about her as if to assure her that he has recovered. With her arms about his shoulders, the mother gazes fondly into the face of her only child. She seems to find it difficult to believe that he is indeed alive. In the doorway stands the father, his hands about to be clasped in a prayer of thanksgiving, as his son moves toward him. Behind the mother and child the prophet raises his left hand in a blessing on them. With his right hand he offers thanks to the Lord through whose power this miracle has been wrought.

Schnorr von Carolsfeld who designed this engraving was a German artist (1794-1872) whose Bible pictures were widely accepted by Christians of many denominations.

✛

AMOS, THE SOCIAL REFORMER

By

Saul Raskin

(Interpretation)

THE prophet, Amos, was born in Tekoa, a small town on the edge of the wilderness of Judah. From his childhood home he could see the little town of Bethlehem to the north, some six miles away, from which David, Israel's second king, had come. Toward the east and only eighteen miles away were the blue waters of the Dead Sea lying more than thirteen hundred feet below the level of his home in Tekoa. The austerity of the rugged country in which Amos grew to manhood shaped not only his everyday life, but also the development of his soul. The sternness of the desert about him was in his very blood.

Like David and his own nomadic ancestors, Amos was a herdsman and raised sheep. He also tended a few sycamore fig trees along the coast of the Dead Sea,

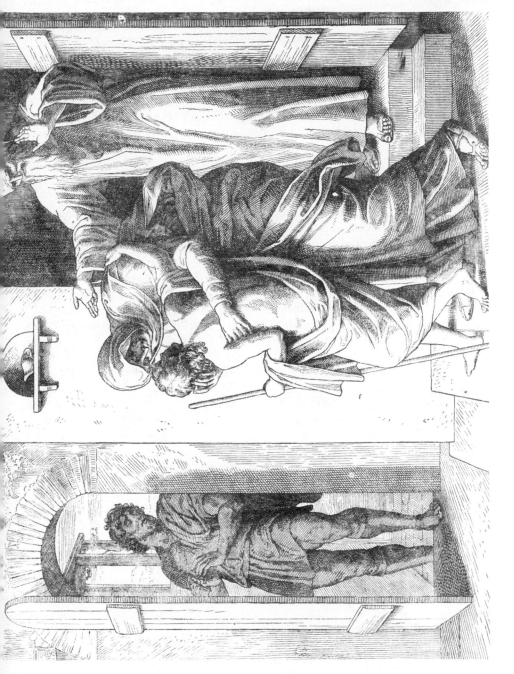

ELISHA AND THE SHUNAMMITE'S SON—*VON CAROLSFELD*

pruning them that they might bear earlier and better fruit. The Judean markets for his wool and figs were Beer-sheba, Bethlehem, Hebron, and Jerusalem; but even greater and better markets were to be found some twenty miles or more away in Gilgal and at Samaria, the capital city of the Northern Kingdom.

Amos was not deceived when he saw the pomp surrounding rulers nor by the brilliancy of Hebrew society in Jerusalem and Samaria and other cities of the Northern and Southern Kingdoms. Beneath this display he knew that the leaders of the Hebrew people, and many of the people themselves, were corrupt in their hearts. Prosperity had made them complacent. They were blind to their own wrongdoing. They offered elaborate sacrifices to the Lord instead of serving Him by living decent, good lives. Amos knew that the Lord was a righteous God who expected His people to live righteous lives. As he followed his flocks he brooded over the continual exploitation of the poor. Finally he left his flocks in order to preach the Lord's message in Israel. He declared that the Lord had spoken to him as he tended his flock, and had said to him: "Go, prophesy unto my people Israel" (Amos 7:15).

Though a native of the Southern Kingdom of Judah, he journeyed northward to Bethel in the Northern Kingdom of Israel where his great predecessors, Elijah and Elisha, had prophesied a hundred years earlier. He began his prophetic utterances, first with a stinging denunciation of the enemies of Israel, thereby gaining the attention of the leaders of Israel. Pleased and fascinated by his denunciations of their enemies, they hung on his every word. He hurled the judgment of the Lord against the slave trading of the Philistines, the brutality of the Ammonites, and the ruthless irreverence of the Moabites. Then, when he had the undivided attention and interest of the leaders of Israel, he brought his prophetic utterances to a dramatic climax by condemning the proud people of Israel themselves. "Thus saith the Lord," he cried:

> After crime upon crime of Israel
> I will not relent,
> for they sell honest folk for money,
> the needy for a pair of shoes,
> they trample down the poor like dust,
> and humble souls they harry . . .
> they loll on garments seized in pledge,
> by every altar,
> they drink the money taken in fines
> within the temple of their God.
> Yet it was I who brought you up
> from Egypt's land . . .
> You alone, of all men, have I cared for;
> therefore I will punish you for all your misdeeds.*
>
> [Amos 2:6-11, 3:2]

It is this stern, denouncing prophet, Amos, that Saul Raskin portrays in his etching. In the left background behind the prophet stands a slave trader with

* From *The Bible: A New Translation* by James Moffatt. Copyright, 1935, by Harper & Brothers. Used by special permission of the publisher.

AMOS, THE SOCIAL REFORMER—RASKIN

upraised lash ready to strike heads bowed in prayer and hands raised in supplication. In the right background Raskin portrays a self-indulgent Israelite standing before a horribly grinning idol whom he worships by draining the cup of wine to its last dregs.

Dominating the center of this etching stands the towering form of Amos, the social and religious reformer. Below him is a shepherd's crook, laid aside as he fulfills the Lord's command to prophesy against Israel. One arm clutches his robe close against his heart, while the other arm upraised with clenched fist is ready to strike, with the fierce and jagged suddenness of the lightning that plays about him, at the very heart of Israel's corruption, wickedness, and sin. Even the trees bend with the storm of his fiery accusations against God's chosen people who have betrayed Him and carried their nefarious sins even into the Temple dedicated to His holy name.

✛

HOSEA AND ISRAEL, THE UNFAITHFUL WIFE

By

Saul Raskin

(Interpretation)

ABOUT five or ten years after Amos, the Judean prophet, delivered his stirring messages at Bethel, Hosea, a native of Israel, began to preach there to his countrymen. The geographical and historical references in the book that bears his name as well as his intense sympathy for the Northern Kingdom leave little doubt that Hosea was a Northerner, and probably a Galilean. He loved Israel's hills and fields, her people, and her God.

Hosea was at heart a poet, yet he could not stand idly by while Israel was unfaithful to the worship of her own true God. He began his prophetic career a little before 740 B.C. at a time when the social, political, and religious evils which his predecessor, Amos, had pointed out so clearly had already begun to sap the strength of the state. Only the strong hand of Jeroboam II held the kingdom together (Hos. 1:1). Because of this the Israelites did not realize how near they were to national ruin, which both Amos and Hosea repeatedly proclaimed in their messages.

The years immediately following the death of Jeroboam II revealed the fatal weaknesses of Israel, and the people soon became vassals of their dreaded foe, the Assyrians. Private as well as public honor was lost and Israel began openly to practice the debasing cutoms of their pagan Canaanitish neighbors. Assyria continued to advance upon Israel. Before the final blow came, which ended Israel's national life in 722 B.C., the prophet Hosea's voice was silenced either by heartbreak or martyrdom; for throughout the closing chapters of the book of Hosea there is no reference to the closing scenes of this great tragedy.

The absorption of the Northern Kingdom by Assyria had already begun in

HOSEA AND ISRAEL, THE UNFAITHFUL WIFE—*RASKIN*

Hosea's time. Its prestige as a nation was gone. Blind to the warnings of its prophets it rushed headlong into the hands of Assyria and sought to strengthen the decline of its power by entering into alliances with foreign nations, in a vain attempt to escape the judgment of the Lord.

Hosea did his utmost to secure the return of Israel to the love and devotion of the Lord the only true God, pleading:

"O Israel, return unto the Lord thy God; for thou hast fallen by thine iniquity. Take with you words, and turn to the Lord. Say unto him, 'Take away all iniquity, and receive us graciously . . . Asshur shall not save us; we will not ride upon horses; neither will we say any more to the work of our hands, "Ye are our gods"; for in thee the fatherless findeth mercy' " (Hos. 14:1-3).

Hosea taught that God was full of compassion and love for His people. He loved them as a father loves his own children. "When Israel was a child, then I loved him" (11:1). God loved Israel as a husband loves his wife. But Israel had become an unfaithful wife, for she had abandoned the worship of the true God to offer sacrifices to heathen idols. Hosea told a story of an unfaithful wife whose husband continued to love her. This may be a reference to the prophet's own personal experience, or it may be merely a parable by which he sought to make his message clear to the people. In spite of Israel's unfaithfulness the Lord still loved her and Hosea proclaimed "the love of the Lord toward the children of Israel, who look to other gods" (3:1).

The pleading, earnest, loyal prophet has been portrayed in an etching by Saul Raskin of Hosea and of Israel as the unfaithful wife. In the left background is the unfaithful wife, clasping the hand of her lover. Her face betrays no feeling of shame or remorse for her faithlessness. To the right is the "calf of Samaria," one of the idols that many in Israel worshiped as their god. To this calf hands are everywhere lifted in worship, and one mother even holds her child up for the idol's blessing.

The background is as black as the fate of Israel. The only hope is in the face of Israel's prophet. Though he knows that Israel cannot escape the doom to which her corruption inevitably leads, Hosea holds fast to his faith in God's love.

✛

THE FRIEZE OF THE PROPHETS

By

John Singer Sargent

(Interpretation)

HOSEA AND LATER PROPHETS

AT the extreme left end of the mural, "The Frieze of the Prophets," John Singer Sargent has placed the four prophets: Hosea, Obadiah, Joel, and Zephaniah. Among all the prophets, not only in this portion, but in the entire frieze, Hosea

THE FRIEZE OF THE PROPHETS (LEFT END)—*SARGENT*

was the artist's favorite. One can see with what care and insight he portrayed the character of this ancient prophet of the Northern Kingdom.

The facts of Hosea's life are obscure and there is no clear-cut indication of a definite summons to prophesy. Some Old Testament scholars believe that he married Gomer either without knowing that she was a harlot, or that she was not a harlot at the time of their marriage. It is apparent that he lived happily with her for some years, while prophesying the doom and destruction of Israel. After the birth of their third child, Hosea discovered his wife's infidelity. His first inclination was to treat her as any adulteress—that is, expel her and allow her to be stoned to death according to the Hebrew law. But the command of the Lord came to him, saying: "Go yet, love a woman beloved of her friend, yet an adulteress, according to the love of the Lord to the children of Israel, who look to other gods, and love flagons of wine" (Hos. 3:1).

This divine decree gave Hosea an entirely new insight into the nature of God. He believed that it was his duty to continue to love Gomer, notwithstanding her infidelity, just as the Lord had continued to love the Israelites not only during their wanderings in the wilderness, but also during their continued disobedience and infidelity to His commands after reaching the promised land. Amos had already taught that the Lord is upright and righteous in all His dealings with Israel. Hosea now discovered an amazing new truth: that God is a loving Father to Israel.

Crouched at Hosea's feet in this section of "The Frieze of the Prophets" is Obadiah who lived several centuries after Hosea. As nothing is known about the life of this prophet, John Singer Sargent has left his face obscure. Obadiah prophesied the doom of Edom, one of Judah's traditional enemies. His cry for vengeance over Edom is not in keeping with the teachings of the greatest prophets.

Next to Obadiah stands Joel, turning away and hiding his face in his mantle. He, like Obadiah, lived long after Hosea, and nothing is known of his life. His description of a locust plague is famous. The book bearing his name contains only three chapters calling Judah to repentance with fasting and mourning, and promising the outpouring of God's spirit. The day of vengeance against the heathen was at hand when all nations would be gathered in the valley of decision and judged by the Lord.

Zephaniah was one of the more important of the minor prophets of Judah. He was a descendant of King Hezekiah and lived during the reign of Josiah, son of Amon, king of Judah. He prophesied about a hundred years after Hosea. He foretold the day of the Lord's wrath coming upon Judah, the punishment of Judah's enemies, the devastation and destruction of Jerusalem, and the final restoration and security of Israel.

While it is true that of this group of four prophets only Hosea may be regarded as among the greatest prophets, it is also true that all these men preached what they believed to be the Lord's message to His people. While their messages were often discouraging, these prophets do reflect the unshakable faith of Israel and Judah that their Lord is God and that He is watching over His people.

ISRAEL CARRIED AWAY INTO ASSYRIAN CAPTIVITY

By

William Hole

(Interpretation)

THE children of Israel in their homeland, whose capital city was Samaria, had forsaken the Lord and worshiped idols notwithstanding the frequent warnings of their prophets Amos and Hosea. Many of the Israelites had married pagans from the nations living around them, and had ceased to worship the Lord "in the beauty of holiness."

Finally, the Assyrians encamped against them, and the Ten Tribes which constituted the Northern Kingdom were overcome and carried away into captivity by the Assyrians. Only a few of the poorest families were left to cultivate the soil and to care for the vineyards and the olive groves. The king of Assyria established a protectorate over the Northern Kingdom and brought into the land which had belonged to the Ten Tribes many of the pagan peoples from the nations round about, who took possession of the land to till it, and to pay tribute to Assyria.

The Assyrian conquest of the Northern Kingdom of Israel was completed by the capture of the city of Samaria. This event is shown in this painting by William Hole. In the background are the walls of Samaria which was besieged for three years by the Assyrian army of Shalmaneser V and his successor, Sargon. Large wooden structures, like that on the right, were placed close to the walls as a protection for the attacking soldiers. Inside these wooden shelters the Assyrians could not be reached by the arrows shot at them by the Israelites on the walls. When Samaria was finally unable to withstand any longer the Assyrian onslaughts against her she surrendered. This was the end of Israel as a nation.

In this painting the Israelites are already being driven out of their city and starting on the long road to captivity in a foreign land. In the foreground a family group is endeavoring to stay together and bring with them a few of their household goods. A small boy drives the family's goats before him. An old man holding his grandchild in his arms rides on a rough cart while behind him rides his daughter with her baby. The father, injured in the fighting, walks beside them. A terrified girl draws away from one of the Assyrian soldiers. Beside him is a scribe keeping count of the captives as they pass.

Behind this family group, so clearly and movingly depicted, comes a large crowd of Israelites led by a man whose bowed head and dejected attitude indicate his feelings as a captive. The victorious soldiers, in contrast to the Israelites, are shown as swaggering, indifferent, and cruel and those riding horses have the arrogant pride of conquerors.

William Hole created this scene so convincingly that when we look at it we seem to be witnessing the hour when the Kingdom of Israel perished. The Ten Tribes of Israel were scattered abroad and finally mingled with other races until they became lost to history. They were often spoken of as "the lost ten tribes of Israel," and their dispersion was regarded as a penalty for their disobedience of the Law of the Lord.

✛

ALL MEN ARE SINNERS

(Psalm 14)

Fools, in their hearts, believe and say,
    That all religion's vain;
"There is no God who reigns on high,
    Or minds the affairs of men."

From thoughts so dreadful and profane,
    Corrupt discourse proceeds;
And in their impious hands are found
    Abominable deeds.

The Lord, from his celestial throne,
    Looked down on things below,
To find a man who sought his grace,
    Or did his justice know.

By nature all are gone astray,
    Their practice all the same:
There's none who fears his Maker's hand;
    There's none who loves his name.

Their tongues are used to speak deceit,
    Their slanders never cease;
How swift to mischief are their feet,
    Nor know the paths of peace.

Such seeds of sin, that bitter root,
    In every heart are found;
Nor can they bear diviner fruit,
    Till grace refine the ground.

—Isaac Watts

WINE AND WOE. A RIDDLE SONNET

Who hath woe?
Who hath sorrow?
Who hath contentions?
Who hath complaining?

ISRAEL CARRIED AWAY INTO ASSYRIAN CAPTIVITY—*HOLE*

Who hath wounds without cause?
Who hath redness of eyes?

They that tarry long at the wine;
They that go to seek out mixed wine.

Look not thou upon the wine
When it is red,
When it giveth its colour in the cup,
When it goeth down smoothly:

At the last it biteth like a serpent,
    And stingeth like an adder.
Thine eyes shall behold strange things,
    And thine heart shall utter froward things.
Yea, thou shalt be as he that lieth down in the midst of the sea,
    Or as he that lieth upon the top of a mast!
"They have stricken me,
    And I was not hurt;
They have beaten me,
    And I felt it not;
When shall I awake?
    I will seek it yet again."*

—*Proverbs 23:29-35*

AMOS, THE PROPHET OF JUSTICE

For three sins, and a fourth, God's wrath was stirred.
His chosen people wallowed in the dust;
They laughed at justice, served the gods of lust,
Oppressed the poor, and scorned his Holy Word.
But there was one who reverenced the good,
Who worshipped God and tried his will to do—
The herdsman Amos, simple, plain and true.
Said God: "Go say their sin is understood."
So Amos :"God, the mighty Lord of earth,
Hast known your sins and ye shall reap reward
For all your wrongs. A strong and cruel horde
Shall devastate your land. In bitter dearth
Ye shall abide, and from your homes shall go
To alien realms, a land of wrath and woe."**

—*Thomas Curtis Clark*

* From *The Modern Reader's Bible* edited by Richard G. Moulton, p. 939. Copyright, 1935, by The Macmillan Company. Used by special permission of the publisher.
** Used by special permission of the author.

THE COMING OF THE EVIL DAYS. A SONNET

Remember also thy Creator in the days of thy youth:
  Or ever the evil days come,
  And the years draw nigh,
    When thou shalt say, I have no pleasure in them:

  Or ever the sun
    And the light,
    And the moon,
    And the stars,
  Be darkened,
  And the clouds return after the rain:

  In the day when the keepers of the house shall tremble,
  And the strong men shall bow themselves,
  And the grinders cease because they are few,
  And those that look out of the windows be darkened,
  And the doors shall be shut in the street;
  When the sound of the grinding is low,
  And one shall rise up at the voice of a bird,
  And all the daughters of music shall be brought low;

  Yea, they shall be afraid of that which is high,
  And terrors shall be in the way;

  And the almond tree shall blossom,
  And the grasshopper shall be a burden,
  And the caper-berry shall burst:

Because man goeth to his long home,
And the mourners go about the streets:

  Or ever the silver cord be loosed,
  Or the golden bowl be broken,
  Or the pitcher be broken at the fountain,
  Or the wheel broken at the cistern:

  And the dust return to the earth,
    As it was;
  And the spirit return unto God
    Who gave it.*

—Ecclesiastes 12:1-7

* From *The Modern Reader's Bible* edited by Richard G. Moulton, pp. 1019-20. Copyright, 1935, by The Macmillan Company. Used by special permission of the publishers.

COMPENSATION

God, I have known joy—
A curly-headed doll waited for me one Christmas
    morning,
A surprise party at sixteen, where eager young friends
Bounded in like playful puppies falling over each other;
Someone I loved mumbled incoherent words one night
In a lovely park, enchanted by silver moonlight;
I have held in my arms a tiny soul I brought into the
    world—
Great joy has been mine.

God, I have known loneliness—
The days have crawled by like tiny ants dragging
    cumbersome grasshoppers,
My soul has cried out for the nearness of another
    understanding heart;
I have stood alone on a bleak world, where threatening
    clouds
Scudded through a desolate sky,
Where shrieking winds howled and laughed fiendishly
    at my utter aloneness.

Too, I have known laughter—
Childhood was sweet. I lived near a meadow, where
    lazy cows
Dozed in the shade of cool maples;
Summer nights were made of friendly dark with
    diamond glow-worms;
A song came easy to eager young lips—
I had no cares—when I knew laughter.

God, I have known sorrow—
I have stood by helplessly, as fate like a madly rushing,
    rising river,
Sullen and ruthless, swept from me everything worth
    buying at life's mart;
Baby eyes, slowly clouding with death, have pleaded
    for life,
And I stood by anxious and sorrowing, but oh! how
    helpless.
Sorrow has squeezed my heart dry of all emotion,
Even the tears are gone from my eyes,
I smile—I smile, but God, I have known sorrow.

You have been kind, dear God, for I have known
    love—
Not mere white, hot passion, but a love so possessing,

Consuming, that no sacrifice was too great to keep it;
A love that hid me from every hurt, taking me in its
    strong tender arms
Up to a land peopled with fairies, and carpeted with
    pale hyacinths.
I willingly bear the loneliness—the sorrow—
Since I have known love.*

              —*Ruby Berkeley Goodwin*

"ESTABLISH JUSTICE"

(Amos 5:10-15, 21-24)

How bright the human soul can shine,
With radiance more than half divine!
That soul will pierce the darkness dense,
Until his onward moving radiance,
Makes it seem the earth has won,
A brighter than celestial sun.

So Amos is; and so his path,
As he goes northward in his wrath,
An orb of greatest worth he is;
With whom go moral certainties.

He hasted with the needed word,
To a people who had erred;
Heat oppressed, he did not halt,
Till the altar whose deep fault
Had planted rot at the nation's core,
Was the Evil he stood before.**

              —*Harry Trumbull Sutton*

THE MAN WITH THE HOE†

God created man in his own image, in the image of God created he him.—GENESIS 1:27

Bowed by the weight of centuries he leans
Upon his hoe and gazes on the ground,
The emptiness of ages in his face,
And on his back the burden of the world.
Who made him dead to rapture and despair
A thing that grieves not and that never hopes,
Stolid and stunned, a brother to the ox?

---

* From *From My Kitchen Window* by Ruby Berkeley Goodwin, pp. 28-29. Copyright, 1942, by Ruby Berkeley Goodwin. Used by special permission of the author.

** From *Poems* by Harry Trumbull Sutton, p. 21. Copyright, 1939, by Harry Trumbull Sutton. Used by special permission of the author.

† Written after seeing Millet's world-famous painting of a brutalized toiler in the deep abyss of labor.

Who loosened and let down this brutal jaw?
Whose was the hand that slanted back this brow?
Whose breath blew out the light within this brain?

Is this the Thing the Lord God made and gave
To have dominion over sea and land;
To trace the stars and search the heavens for power;
To feel the passion of Eternity?
Is this the dream He dreamed who shaped the suns
And marked their ways upon the ancient deep?
Down all the caverns of Hell to their last gulf
There is no shape more terrible than this—
More tongued with censure of the world's blind greed—
More filled with signs and portents for the soul—
More packed with danger to the universe.

What gulfs between him and the seraphim!
Slave of the wheel of labor, what to him
Are Plato and the swing of Pleiades?
What the long reaches of the peaks of song,
The rift of dawn, the reddening of the rose?
Through this dread shape the suffering ages look;
Time's tragedy is in that aching stoop;
Through this dread shape humanity betrayed,
Plundered, profaned, and disinherited,
Cries protest to the Judges of the World,
A protest that is also prophecy.

O masters, lords and rulers in all lands,
Is this the handiwork you give to God,
This monstrous thing distorted and soul-quenched?
How will you ever straighten up this shape;
Touch it again with immortality;
Give back the upward looking and the light;
Rebuild in it the music and the dream;
Make right the immemorial infamies
Perfidious wrongs, immedicable woes?

O masters, lords and rulers in all lands,
How will the Future reckon with this man?
How answer his brute question in that hour
When whirlwinds of rebellion shake all shores?
How will it be with kingdoms and with kings—
With those who shaped him to the thing he is—
When this dumb terror shall rise to judge the world,
After the silence of the centuries?*

—*Edwin Markham*

* From *Shoes of Happiness* by Edwin Markham. Copyright, 1920, by Edwin Markham; 1946, by Virgil Markham. Used by special permission of Virgil Markham.

FAITH

Lord, give me faith!—to live from day to day,
With tranquil heart to do my simple part,
And, with my hand in Thine, just go Thy way.

Lord, give me faith!—to trust, if not to know;
With quiet mind in all things Thee to find,
And, child-like, go where Thou wouldst have me go.

Lord, give me faith!—to leave it all to Thee,
The future is Thy gift, I would not lift
The veil Thy Love has hung 'twixt it and me.*

—John Oxenham

GOD IS LOVE

God is love; his mercy brightens
   All the path in which we rove;
Bliss he wakes, and woe he lightens;
   God is wisdom, God is love.

Chance and change are busy ever;
   Man decays, and ages move;
But his mercy waneth never;
   God is wisdom, God is love.

E'en the hour that darkest seemeth
   Will his changeless goodness prove;
From the gloom his brightness streameth;
   God is wisdom, God is love.

He with earthly cares entwineth
   Hope and comfort from above:
Everywhere his glory shineth;
   God is wisdom, God is love.

—Sir John Bowring

ISRAEL'S REBELLION AND PUNISHMENT
(Psalm 78, Part 2)

O what a stiff, rebellious house
   Was Jacob's ancient race!
False to their own most solemn vows,
   And to their Maker's grace.

* Used by special permission of Miss Erica Oxenham.

They broke the covenant of his love,
 And did his laws despise;
Forgot the works he wrought, to prove
 His power before their eyes.

They saw the plagues on Egypt light,
 From his revenging hand;
What dreadful tokens of his might
 Spread o'er the stubborn land!

They saw him cleave the mighty sea,
 And marched with safety through;
With watery walls to guard their way,
 Till they had 'scaped the foe.

A wondrous pillar marked the road,
 Composed of shade and light;
By day it proved a sheltering cloud,
 A leading fire by night.

He from the rock their thirst supplied
 The gushing waters fell,
And ran in rivers by their side,
 A constant miracle.

Yet they provoked the Lord Most High,
 And dared distrust his hand:
"Can he with bread our host supply,
 Amidst this desert land?"

The Lord with indignation heard,
 And caused his wrath to flame;
His terrors ever stand prepared
 To vindicate his name.

       —Isaac Watts

SUMMER WORSHIP

I worship the God of the grasses,
 Of the quivering elms and the sea,
And every stray breeze that passes
 Is laden with wisdom for me.
I find Him in sky-topping mountains,
 In deep, shaded valleys of fern;
He sings in the crystalline fountains
 And broods as the autumn fires burn.

How vainly they seek for His glory
 In creeds that are musty with age!

Why will they not welcome His story
  On Nature's all-scintillant page?
I worship the God of the grasses,
  The Lord of the dawn-tinted skies,
And every stray breeze that passes
  Brings news of some near paradise.*

— *Thomas Curtis Clark*

THE TWILIGHT IS TURNED INTO TREMBLING

(Isaiah 21)

The twilight is turned into trembling,
The watchers see horsemen abreast,
The day is filled with confusion,
The night yieldeth dark, but not rest.

A voice crieth out of the darkness,
"O watchman, what of the night?"
From the tower the oracle soundeth,
"Inquire ye, turn to the light!"

Abroad are destruction and weeping,
In revels men lightly rejoice;
But the twilight is turned into trembling,
For the signs of the times are His voice.**

— *Georgia Harkness*

VISION

God is not little
  Petty
  Small,
God is BIG
  TOO big
  To bind
And hold with one man's creed
  Or ten
  Or Millions!

Some see a different view
  From you.
  Yet true,
As far as their short sight
  Can see.

And so
Condemn not others' views!
You may use
Theirs and yours
To see more of God!

—*Mamie Gene Cole*

I FIND THEE, LORD

I find Thee, Lord,
In every creature Thou hast made.
Not least, nay, sometimes most
In those my brethren of the lower planes
Who have no speech nor language but their own.
Full oft Thy silent things
With finer voices speak to my soul's need,
Than man with all his wondrous utterances.
A tiny flower, a soaring peak,
A shapely tree, a shimmering silver lake,
An amber stream, a sailing argosy of white-piled cloud,
These speak of Thee to Thee in me, with eloquence
    beyond all speech,
And lift me nearer Thee.
And the deep faithful eyes of horse and dog
With no equivocations, no reserves,
See Thee in me as men but rarely see
And trust me unreservedly.*

—*John Oxenham*

ELISHA, SON OF SHAPHAT

By

Grace Ordway Spear

How long halt ye between two opinions? If the Lord be God, follow him; but if Baal, then follow him.—I KINGS 18:21

THE ringing voice of the wilderness prophet came again and again to the inner consciousness of Elisha, son of Shaphat, as he plodded behind his twelve yoke of oxen in his father's field. He heard it in the night hours as he lay on his rough-hewn cot; it seemed to waken him from a dead slumber: "If the Lord be God, Follow Him!"

He had heard the prayer of the prophet Elijah on Mount Carmel: "Hear me, O Lord, hear me, that this people may know that thou art the Lord God!" He

---

* From *Scrap-Book of J. O.* by Erica Oxenham, p. 108. Copyright, 1946, by Longmans, Green and Company, New York 3, N. Y. Used by special permission of Miss Erica Oxenham.

had witnessed the fire fall from heaven and consume the burnt sacrifice and the wood and the stone and the dust, and lick up even the water that was in the trench. He, too, had marveled, but he had not joined in the cries of the crowd as they shouted: "The Lord, he is the God! The Lord, he is the God!" He knew well the fickleness of the people, and how easily they could be swayed by a spectacular demonstration. But—IF THE LORD BE GOD, then he must follow Him. And what a change might not that make in his life?

Elisha spent a restless night. But, when morning came, though weary in body from lack of quiet sleep, he was at peace in his soul; and he rose, as usual, and made ready to go to the fields. "Why hast thou no words this morning?" inquired his father. "Art thou ill in body, my son?" asked his mother, looking at him anxiously. Never a man of many words, Elisha had a strong affection for his parents, and there was a close bond between the three. He looked at them now, and wished he could find words to convey to them his thoughts and his new conviction. But none came, and they finished the simple meal in silence.

Once at the field, Elisha walked behind the oxen in deep meditation. "THE LORD, HE IS THE GOD: I WILL FOLLOW HIM!" he said earnestly to himself.

"Elisha, son of Shaphat, hear ye the word of the Lord God of Israel!" The voice roused him from his meditation, and, turning, he saw standing beside him, Elijah, the wilderness prophet, looking at him searchingly. "He hath commanded me to anoint thee prophet in my stead to carry on His work among the Children of Israel," and he cast his mantle about the shoulders of the plowman.

Elisha's face lighted. "Let me, I pray thee, return to my father's house, and kiss my mother and father farewell. Then I will come and follow thee."

And the prophet replied: "Go back and do as ye have just said, and come again hither."

The days and weeks and months ahead saw the two men always together, and a deep affection for the wilderness prophet grew in the heart of Elisha—aye, almost a reverence—as they went about among the people, proclaiming, "The Lord He is God!" and strengthening their faith.

One day, Elijah, knowing that his time was near at hand, and knowing what the parting would mean to Elisha, said to him: "Tarry here, I pray thee, for the Lord hath sent me to Bethel." But Elisha made answer: "As the Lord liveth, and as my soul liveth, I will not leave thee!" Elijah said no more, and the two men went down to Bethel together.

And again, Elijah said unto Elisha: "Tarry ye here, I pray thee, for the Lord hath sent me to Jericho." But Elisha answered as before: "As the Lord liveth, and as my soul liveth, I will not leave thee!" So they both went to Jericho together.

And Elijah said unto him a third time: "Tarry ye here. I pray thee, for the Lord hath sent me to the Jordan." But a third time, the other replied: "As the Lord liveth, and as my soul liveth, I will not leave thee!" So they continued on till they came to the Jordan River. Then Elijah took his mantle and wrapped it together and smote upon the waters so that they divided hither and thither, and the two men walked over on dry ground. And when they were crossed over, the prophet turned to Elisha and said: "Ask what I shall do for thee." And Elisha replied earnestly: "I pray thee, let a double portion of thy spirit be upon me!"

"Thou hast asked a hard thing," said the prophet; "nevertheless, if thou see me when I am taken from thee, it shall be unto thee."

And behold, as they went down the road in silence, each, sensing a separation soon to be, suddenly a chariot and horses of fire appeared out of the heavens, and parted them asunder, and Elijah went up by a whirlwind into heaven. And ELISHA SAW IT! He stood for a long time in silent thought—then taking up the mantle that fell from the shoulders of Elijah, he went back and stood by the banks of the Jordan. And the waters parted for him as they had for Elijah, and he crossed over on dry ground. As the sons of the prophets saw him coming, they said: "The spirit of Elijah doth rest upon Elisha"; and they came to meet him and bowed themselves to the ground before him. But when they would send men to seek for the prophet Elijah, Elisha commanded them, saying: "Ye shall not send!" knowing that God had taken him up into heaven by a whirlwind and a chariot of fire. And the spirit of the wilderness prophet did indeed fall upon Elisha, man of God, and he did mighty works for the Lord in Israel.

A certain woman of the wives of the prophets came to Elisha one day in deep distress and said unto him: "My Lord, my husband is dead; thou knowest he was a man who feared the Lord. Now my creditor is come to take my two sons and myself away as bondsmen." Elisha said unto the woman: "What hast thou in thy house?" And she answered: "Naught but a pot of oil." And Elisha said, "Borrow all the vessels ye can from neighbors and friends." And she did so, till there was not one vessel more to be had. Then said Elisha unto the woman: "Shut the door of thy room, and pour oil into all the vessels," and she did this. "Now sell the oil and pay thy debts, and live thou and thy children on the rest," commanded the man of God; and she did so.

One day as Elisha went on his way preaching to the people, he stopped at the house of a woman of Shunem, and she gave him bread to eat. And she said unto her husband, "Behold, I perceive that this is a holy man of God which passeth us continually." And they fitted up a room with a bed for him and a table and a stool and a candlestick. And whenever the man of God came by that way, he stopped at the house of the Shunem woman and her husband, and stayed in the chamber they had made ready for him. Now the Shunem woman conceived and bore a son, and he became ill and died. The mother gathered up her son in her arms and laid him on the bed in the chamber she kept for the man of God, and she sent for him to come to them. When Elisha came to the house, he shut the door of the room and prayed to the Lord God. And stretching himself upon the child he breathed upon him—and the child opened his eyes, and Elisha restored him to his mother.

In this country, there lived a captain of the hosts of the King of Syria, Naaman by name. He was a man of mighty valor, but he was a leper. A little captive maid lived in Naaman's house and waited upon his wife. "Would God, my lord were with the prophet Elisha in Samaria, for he would heal him of his leprosy," she said to her mistress one day. And the King of Syria heard this, and said unto Naaman: "I will send letters and ten talents of silver, and six thousand pieces of gold, and ten changes of raiment; and get you down to Samaria, that this prophet may heal you of this leprosy." And Naaman came unto Elisha with all the horses and chariots, the letters and gifts, and stopped at the door of his house. Elisha sent out a messenger to Naaman, saying, "Go, wash in the Jordan seven times, and thy flesh shall come again to thee, and thou shalt be clean."

When the message was brought to Naaman, he was wroth and cried: "Behold, I surely thought he would come out unto me. Are not the Abana and the Pharpar, rivers of Damascus, better than the rivers of Jordan?" And he went away in a rage. But his servant said unto him, "My father, if the prophet had bidden thee to do some great thing, wouldst thou not have done it? How much rather shouldst thou do it when he bids thee to 'wash and be clean'?" So Naaman went down and dipped seven times in the Jordan River as the man of God had said. And lo, his flesh came again unto him like unto the flesh of a little child, and he was clean. And Naaman returned to Elisha and said unto him: "Behold, now I know that there is no God in all the earth but the Lord God of Israel," and he would have given the prophet great gifts, but Elisha would have none of them.

Now Jehoahaz, the son of Jehu, began to reign over Israel in Samaria, and he reigned seventeen years. But he did evil in the sight of the Lord and followed the sins of Jeroboam which made Israel to sin. And the anger of the Lord was kindled against him, and he delivered him into the hands of his enemies. And Jeroboam cried unto the Lord, and the Lord heard him and came unto him. Nevertheless, Jehoahaz and his people again departed from the way of the Lord and followed again the sins of their fathers. When Jehoahaz died, Joash, his son, reigned in his stead.

Now, Elisha was fallen sick, and Joash, king of Israel, came down unto him, and wept over his face and said: "O my father, the chariot of Israel and the horsemen thereof!" And Elisha said unto Joash: "Take bow and arrows, and put thy hand upon the bow." And Joash did so. Then Elisha put his hands upon the king's hands, and he said: "Open the window eastward and shoot." And he shot. And Elisha said: "The arrow of the Lord's deliverance, and the arrow of deliverance from Syria; for thou shalt smite the Syrians in Aphek till thou has consumed them."

And the Lord was gracious unto the people of Israel and had compassion upon them, because of his covenant with Abraham, Isaac, and Jacob, and would not destroy them, yet.

And Elisha, the man of God, died of his sickness, and they buried him in the sepulcher.*

* Used by special permission of the author.

NAAMAN, THE SYRIAN CAPTAIN HEALED

By

Marian MacLean Finney

And Elisha sent a messenger unto him, saying, Go wash in the Jordan seven times, and thy flesh shall come again to thee, and thou shalt be clean.—II KINGS 5:10

FROM the city of Samaria to the banks of the Jordan was some thirty-five miles, considerably more than a day's journey each way. It lacked an hour of noon when they started, so Naaman's party was obliged to encamp over night, and it was late the following afternoon when they finally reached their destination. With an eagerness that knew no faltering, no uncertainty, Isaac had led the way. Now, finding a shallow spot in the turbulent river near one of the fords, a spot warmed for hours by the summer sun, Naaman had dipped seven times, as directed, the seventh turning vague hope into joyous certainty. He was healed every whit! Joy knew no bounds. The king's representatives had embraced him and each other. Israel was saved! The Syrian embassy was scarcely less contained. Even the camel drivers from the desert and the lowest of the servants shouted with loud voices and great enthusiasm and Naaman beamed upon them all, but it was Isaac to whom his first words of relief and happiness had been addressed, and Isaac upon whom he smiled with tenderness and even affection.

With hearts attuned to see the wonderful yellows and browns of the Valley of Jezreel in late summer, their horses' hoofs had again pattered its long expanse, the laden camels and asses driven in the rear. One more night they had encamped and now they came straggling up the hill they had descended three days before. But the young leader had made a slight error in judgment as to the time of arrival. It was shortly after sunset, a few minutes past the hour when the city closed its gates—and no man came to open! Lemuel, companion of Isaac's old scouting days, approached him with respect so profound that its sincerity was patent.

"Sir, there be not room among this crowd of mendicants," glancing contemptuously at other belated travelers, "to spread our camping equipment with due regard to our importance, and without it we shall find the night-dews too heavy to be pleasant. I pray thee have the gates opened without delay that thy servants may render thee the honor due so great a captain."

Annoyed, Isaac ceased thundering at the gates and became aware of the murmuring among his own party and the derision of the merchants and others who, like themselves, seemed doomed to spend the night with only the city walls for a covering while the chill air of the mountains penetrated even the thickest of garments. The voice of Naaman commanded silence. He spoke compassionately to Isaac.

"My son, he at whom the multitude throws roses feels mostly the thorns. He who by any act becomes more noticeable than his fellows is the target of their envy. Only a brave man can afford to be prominent. Do I not know, I, the veteran of a hundred wars and judged of all? Courage in the peril of battle I know thou hast, Isaac, for with mine own eyes have I beheld, but courage in the peril of success, hast thou fortitude sufficient for this?"

The Syrian party had unconsciously drawn closer together, away from the motley crowd of late-comers who were striving to make themselves comfortable in the shadow of the walls and were fighting energetically for the best places. . . . Lemuel again drew near Isaac, this time in hurried pompousness.

"Answer thou wisely," he said in an undertone. "He meaneth to reward thee. Remember that I have been thy friend, thy companion since boyhood, intimate enough for such jesting as I had with thee a moment ago."

Isaac shook off the counsel impatiently. His action had been inspired with no thought of reward, save in the joy of the little maid, yet Naaman was rich and generous and a gift not unlikely. If given a choice, he knew what he should ask. He had considered the matter, but the plan did not include Lemuel. . . . Naaman, amiable in the delight of physical relief, gave a few brief directions and his party settled down to waiting with whatever calmness they could muster. . . . At last, on top of the city's wall, a watchman was seen approaching from the tower at the far corner. . . . He finally stood near enough to the gate to survey the assemblage outside. With unsympathetic eye he viewed the poor travelers and the belated merchants, but a change came over his countenance as he beheld the king's representatives and the Syrian embassy. Instantly he disappeared within the city and the party without drew a sigh of content.

Yet the gate was not opened; that is, not the great gate. A smaller one within the larger was flung wide and the watchman appeared with obsequious interest: "Behold the needle's eye. Enter thou and thy beasts."

The men could get through readily, and even the horses could with difficulty, but hard is it indeed for a camel to go through the eye of a needle! They were made to kneel and then, with much tugging and cursing and shouting their drivers at last succeeded in getting them through its narrow space. The asses required almost as much effort, having to be unladen and their burdens strapped upon them once more on the city-side of the gate. . . .

The next morning Naaman's company again stood before the abode of Elisha. Again was it surrounded by gaping throngs. Again had the city of Samaria cause to be both curious and joyful. Did not all wish to gaze upon this great foreign diplomat, who had been healed in the Jordan? Did not his recovery mean that war had been averted from Israel? What would he say to the prophet and what part of his goodly treasure would he leave behind? . . .

Naaman's visit to the prophet, however, had an even greater significance than the crowd surmised. In fact, his errand was threefold. First, he had come back to bring a thank-offering. Second, he wished to make public confession of his belief in that Jehovah who, though Israel's national God, should now be his own. Third, he desired greatly to have the prophet's advice on a matter which weighed heavily upon his mind. This time he was not required to deal with the servant, Gehazi. Instead, with all the elaborate courtesy of the East, Naaman was received by Elisha in person. . . .

"Behold, now know I that there is no God in all the earth but in Israel; now therefore, I pray thee, take a blessing of thy servant," and Naaman stretched forth his hand toward the camels laden with treasure, those rich stores of which Damascus was proud and which, brought in this form, was the current idea of wealth.

Elisha demurred. "As the Lord liveth, before whom I stand, I will receive none."

Naaman stared. Surely he did not mean it. This was merely the usual reluctance, the hypocritical hesitancy which might be expected. All over the Orient it was customary to give presents to the various holy men who were successful interpreters of the wills of their respective gods, and none ever refused. This man had a different manner: a courtesy without servility, an assurance without bigotry, self-respect without self-esteem, but he was human! Once and again Naaman urged acceptance of the offering, but Elisha was firm. A murmur of surprise ran through the ranks of the Syrians and Naaman turned impatiently, commanding their withdrawal that he and the seer might converse in private. . . .

Finding insistence useless, Naaman with fine feeling ignored the benefit he had thought to confer and begged instead that a favor be granted him. "Shall not then, I pray thee, be given to thy servant two mules' burden of earth?" From the land Jehovah was supposed especially to bless Naaman would take sufficient holy ground to erect in heathen Syria an altar to this new God. "For thy servant will henceforth offer neither burnt-offering nor sacrifice unto other gods but only unto Jehovah."

The prophet graciously gave consent and dispatched Gehazi with servants of their visitor to see that proper attention be given to the matter.

Naaman's brow clouded as his host stood waiting in dignified civility. Drawing nearer, he spoke in tones which betrayed his agitation of mind. "In this thing, however, the Lord pardon thy servant; that when my master, the king, goeth into the House of Rimmon to worship there (for thou knowest that my master, the king, leaneth upon the hand of thy servant) and I must needs bow myself in the House of Rimmon as its worship requireth; when I bow myself I make request that the Lord pardon thy servant this thing."

For a moment the prophet did not speak and Naaman waited anxiously. His was not a nature which could practice deception or tolerate it in others, yet between his own religious convictions and his official duties as a member of the Syrian Court was a great gulf fixed. Elisha's answer fell upon his hungry heart like a refreshing shower on parched ground.

"It is well. Go thou in peace."

The great soldier prostrated himself before the seer, who politely bade him rise, and their farewells over . . . the Syrian embassy turned its face homeward, wondering greatly at what it had seen and heard.

Through the gate of the house just left peered a frowning face. Gehazi, servant to the prophet, had regarded his master's decision concerning the gift with some displeasure. True, Elisha was not poor, but to allow wealth to pass as lightly through his fingers as a man openeth his hand and droppeth seed in sowing time! But stay, should not his own servants be rewarded with a little, a very little indeed, of what this foreignor was reluctantly carrying away? His eyes, lighted with cupidity, grew cautious as they searched the apartments within for trace of his master. In a moment he had shut the gate softly and stepped outside.

Isaac, hearing behind them the footsteps of a runner, looked backward curiously, checking his horse. Naaman, hearing at the same moment, commanded his charioteer to stop while he dismounted. Walking a few steps toward the runner, whom he perceived to be the prophet's servant, he greeted him anxiously.

"Is all well?"

The man assured him. "All is well, but my master hath sent me, saying, 'Behold even now there be come to me from Mount Ephraim two young men of the Sons of the Prophet. Give them, I pray thee, a talent of silver and two changes of garments!'"

In answer to this request, Naaman generously insisted upon giving more than was desired: "Be content, take two talents," and although Gehazi objected with well simulated humility there was in his tones no such decisive finality as had been present in the voice of his master.

Calling two of the servants, Naaman saw to it that they bore before the messenger the heavy silver, cut and weighed, and the two changes of fine raiment. Well satisfied that at least something of all he had taken had been accepted, the Syrian captain re-entered his chariot and the party waited for the return of the burden bearers. Isaac looked after the trio questioningly. "There be many Sons of the Prophet," he reasoned with himself, "would their leader, the Man of God, honor two above the rest? Nay, it seemeth not so to me. Somehow I like not this man Gehazi. Never once, in all of our dealings, hath he looked my master or me straight in the eye!"

At the same time another mind was dealing with the same problem. Gehazi, elated at Naaman's generosity, had been likewise perplexed. To receive a present was one thing, to dispose of it quite another, especially in view of the two servants who carried the treasure and before whom he must act the part of Elisha's messenger as he had represented himself to be. At the tower in the vineyard at the foot of the hill he dismissed the men and took the burden himself, staggering under its weight. Within the house he hastily disposed of his new possessions and betook himself to his master, wondering if his absence had been noted and striving to assume an air of innocence by busying himself about necessary tasks.

Elisha's keen eye rested upon the guilty countenance: "Whence comest thou, Gehazi?"

"Thy servant went no whither."

The prophet's righteous indignation was kindled at the falsehood. "Went not my heart with thee when the man turned back from his chariot to meet thee?"

The fear in the craven face opposite told its own story. The prophet's wrath overflowed. To have upheld the honor of the Lord of Hosts and then this misrepresentation! "Is it a time to receive money and to receive garments and oliveyards and vineyards and sheep and oxen and men servants and maid servants? The leprosy therefore of Naaman shall cleave unto thee and unto thy seed forever."

Gehazi cowered, weeping and pleading, but the stern edict had gone forth. Already he knew himself to be the loathsome object Naaman had once been, and at the same hour when Isaac lay down to sleep with a smile upon his face, Gehazi rent his garments and cried aloud outside the gate through which Greed had driven him.*

✛

THE TRANSLATION OF ELIJAH

By

Florence M. Earlle

WHEN Elijah had been so discouraged that he asked to die, God gave him more work to do, not the least important of which was to train his successor. He was to find Elisha, the son of Shaphat. The young man was plowing with twelve yoke of oxen when Elijah passed by and threw his mantle over him. The sign was well known, and Elisha ran after Elijah, and asked that he might stay at home long enough to make a feast for his friends, and bid his parents good-by. Elijah consented.

How Elisha served Elijah, we do not know; but long enough to learn the power of the prophet, his dependence on, and his absolute obedience to, God. And Elisha not only ministered gladly to Elijah, but learned to love him as his own father.

But now the time had come that Elijah's request, made at the time of the test on Mount Carmel, was to be granted. The two men started on the circuit as they were accustomed to do. They went first to Gilgal, the old home of Samuel. And Elijah said, "Stay here, Son, for the Lord wants me to go to Bethel."

But Elisha answered, with the oath that was customary if one wanted to be very emphatic, "As the Lord lives, and your soul lives, I will not leave you!"

And the sons of the prophets came to Elisha when they reached Bethel, and said, "Do you know that Elijah will be taken away from you today?"

And he answered, "Yes, I know it; keep still!" for his heart was heavy.

Then said Elijah again, "Wait here, for the Lord has sent me to Jericho."

And again Elisha answered, "As the Lord lives and as your soul lives, I will not leave you!"

When they arrived in Jericho, Elisha was again told by the sons of the prophets that Elijah was to leave him that day, and these too, he asked to be silent.

Then said Elijah, "The Lord has sent me to Jordan; will you wait here?"

And again Elisha refused.

When they reached the Jordan River, fifty sons of the prophets stood on the bank of the river to watch as the two men approached. And Elijah took his cloak,

* Abridged from *In Naaman's House* by Marian MacLean Finney, pp. 185-95. Copyright, 1922, 1950, by Marian MacLean Finney. Published by Abingdon Press. Used by special permission of the author.

called a mantle, and rolling it together, struck the water. The waves divided and the two walked over on the sand of the river bed.

On the other side, Elijah said, "Ask what I shall do for you before I leave you."

And Elisha answered, "Let me have what you would give me if I were really your son."

And Elijah said, "You have asked a hard thing," for he knew that what Elisha wanted was the courage, the steadfastness, the faith in God at all times that he had tried to have. He did not mean that he wanted to be twice as great a prophet as Elijah himself had been. "You have asked a hard thing," repeated Elijah. "Yet if you are with me, and see me go, you shall have it."

Suddenly, as they talked, there appeared a chariot of fire and horses of fire, and Elijah was separated from Elisha by a whirlwind that lifted him into the heavens, and Elisha saw him no more. Elisha cried out, "My father! My father! The chariot of Israel and the horsemen thereof!"

Years later, when Elisha was an old man, he was to pray that the eyes of his servant might be opened that he could see the chariots and horsemen of fire that surrounded the city—God's defense of Israel. But today he felt that the defense of Israel had been withdrawn with the departure of Elijah, and he took hold of his own robe and tore it—the oriental way of expressing intense grief.

Elijah was gone. The sky showed no sign of what had happened. As Elisha turned to go back across the Jordan, there lay at his feet the mantle of Elijah. Reverently he folded it over his arm.

When he came to the Jordan, he rolled the mantle as he had seen Elijah do, and said, "Where is the God of Elijah?" and struck the waters. They parted, even as they had done before, and Elisha knew that what Elijah had promised him, the double portion of his spirit—was true. Others knew it too, for when he came to Jericho, the fifty sons of the prophets met him and said, as they bowed before him, "The mantle of Elijah rests upon Elisha."*

✢

AMOS, THE HERDSMAN FROM TEKOA

By

Dorothy Clarke Wilson

PART I

THE market place was not so deserted as he had expected. Most of the merchants were already in their booths and setting out their wares in preparation for the hour of sunset when the sabbath would be officially over. Prospective buyers were beginning to gather in large numbers. There were advantages in arriving at just this time, Ben Sered soon discovered. A couple of caravans had come into the city just before the sabbath, and he was able to inspect the new wares before they had been all picked over. He found several gifts which took his fancy—a small cedar chest with gold inlays of lotus flowers, a conch shell of remarkable

* Used by special permission of the author.

iridescence, a piece of real Mycenaean pottery—and he kept one eye fixed on them and the other on the slowly sinking sun. The leisurely deliberation with which it settled slowly toward the housetops was maddening. Even after it disappeared it would be necessary to wait for the signal from the high place which indicated its disappearance below the true horizon.

The signal came at last—three clear bugle notes—and almost instantly the market place burst into its customary confusion. Bargaining rose to shrill and rapid crescendos. Salesmen barked their wares. Children and dogs darted underfoot. Pushcarts and ox wagons creaked and groaned. Slaves were hoisted to the auction block and put through their paces. The whole noisy, rumbling, lumbering machine was again in motion. Ben Sered was able to buy only two of the three things he desired, the conch shell and the pottery. A rival buyer got the chest first. Thinking he might be able to bargain with him, Ben Sered set out after him in hot pursuit. But he could make little headway. The crowds seemed to be surging in one direction, and he was caught in the middle of them. Too small of stature to see what was the disturbance or attraction which drew them, he struggled mightily but to no avail, losing his precious conch shell in the process.

Then suddenly he ceased to struggle, and he forgot his conch shell. For somewhere up in front of the crowd, in the region of the farmer's bazaar, a voice was speaking. It cut through the confusion sharply like a blade, leaving a great swath of silence.

> Listen to this!
> You who crush the needy
> And take bread from the mouths of the poor!
> You who mutter, "When will the feast be over,
> That we may sell our grain?
> When will the sabbath be past
> That we may put our goods on sale?"
> You who make your measures small and your
>   weighing stones large
> And cheat by tampering with your scales!
> You who sell the very refuse of your grain
> To people who are hungry,
> Who account a handful of silver
> More important than a human being!

There was a moment's hush, like a long-drawn breath, then the voice continued:

> Yahweh has sworn by the pride of Jacob:
> "I never will forget what you have done.
> Do I love you any better than the Ethiopians,
> You people of Israel?
> To be sure, I brought you up out of Egypt;
> But I brought the Philistines also from Crete,
> And the people of Damascus from Kir.
> Listen to me, Israel!
> I am keeping my eyes on your sinful kingdom,
> I will destroy it from the face of the earth!"

Silence hung over the market place like a solid, palpable substance, even after the voice had ceased.

"He's gone!" someone shouted hysterically, and the spell was broken. Gradually the crowd broke its tight, compact unity. Ben Sered moved through it automatically, oblivious of the excited comments which were bursting about him. The voice still rang in his ears. He had a queer sensation that he had heard it, not just a few moments previously, but yesterday, perhaps, or the day before, or even longer, much longer ago; that it had been ringing in his ears with the same sharp, imperative insistency for a very long, long time. Was it this impression of timelessness, he wondered, which had made it seem so strangely familiar?

Ben Othni appeared suddenly at his side, smiling. His large white teeth seemed to have grown in size until they looked oddly like tusks. "You see?" he demanded triumphantly. "You understand now how dangerous this man is?"

"Yes," said Ben Sered. . . .

"We must stop him!" Ben Sered did not recognize his own voice, it sounded so harsh and unnatural. "He must be seized at once—arrested—"

Over his head Ben Othni and Obed Shebna exchanged a quick glance of triumph.

"It has already been done," the former assured him. "When he left the market place, the *gibborim* were ready to seize him. At this moment, we hope, he is in my house waiting for us."

A considerable crowd of dignitaries was assembled in the inner courtyard of Ben Othni's house. There were seats for the three commissioners among the judges who had been summoned hastily from their positions in the city gate. All had proceeded according to schedule. The arrest had been made quietly, outside the market place, without the knowledge of the rabble, who were disposed to herald the stranger as a divine messenger. He was at this moment in a small anteroom in charge of two burly *gibborim*.

"This is just an informal questioning," Ben Othni told the assembled dignitaries smoothly. "It is not in any sense a legal trial. Hence there need be no witnesses for the defense. If we decide to take action, it will be in effect a royal edict given by the king's deputies in his absence and enforced by his private police force, the *gibborim*." He gestured curtly to an attendant. "Have the man brought in."

At sight of the tall, straight figure towering at least a hand-breadth above the heads of the two burly *gibborim,* Ben Sered started violently. It was the man he had seen standing in the farmers' bazaar beside the booth occupied by the herdsmen of Tekoa. He could see his whole face now, not just the profile. With sudden intentness he studied the arresting features, thrown into bold relief by the flaring lamps in Ben Othni's courtyard: high, broad forehead; straight lips and sensitive nostrils and determined chin; protruding brows and high cheek bones, apparently designed by nature as a protective frame for the wide-spaced, brilliant eyes. Only in one person had he ever seen eyes of that particular brilliance and color, neither brown nor black nor gray—

Ben Sered trembled. The eyes met his, and a flicker of something more than recognition—sympathy, might it be, or perhaps pity?—passed between them. The blood moved in a rushing tide through his body, beating like hammers against his temples. His lips, grown suddenly stiff and cold, silently mouthed one word.

"Amos!"

The inquisition began, conducted by the most venerable of the judges, who took all his cues from Ben Othni and Obed Shebna.

"Treason . . . heresy . . . people have heard him say . . . duty of loyal citizens in the king's absence . . . insults to noble-women . . . Yahweh's own people . . . city's most respected merchants . . . words and antics of a mad man."

Ben Sered did not listen. Words—fragments of sentences—swept over him, like waves over a motionless rock, but they had no meaning for him. He was being stirred and shaken by emotions which for years he had believed dead. One fact alone possessed reality: Amos. The man he had seen standing in the bazaar was Amos. The voice he had heard in the market place had been Amos' voice. The tall, straight figure quietly facing his accusers here in the courtyard of Ben Othni—

"My son," he said to himself over and over. "Amos, my son, my beloved son."

"Well? What have you to say for yourself?" a voice asked coolly.

The tall, straight figure seemed to straighten itself and become even taller. "Nothing for myself," replied the man quietly, "but much in the name of Yahweh." He leveled an accusing finger at the judges.

> You who make a farce of justice,
> And interpret the law as your selfishness dictates,
> Who hate any man who exposed you
> And loathe all those who tell you the truth!
> You takers of bribes, who browbeat honest men
> And defraud the poor of justice!

The dark eyes swept the rows of faces like a flail.

> Because you have crushed the poor
> And taken bread from the hungry,
> Though you build yourselves houses of hewn stone,
> You shall not live in them;
> Though you plant vineyards for yourselves,
> You shall drink no wine from them.

> For thus Yahweh has spoken:
> "In your city squares there shall be moaning,
> And cries of anguish in all your streets.
> Even the peasants shall mingle their wails
> With the dirges of professional mourners,
> When I, Yahweh, shall sweep through your midst!"

Shrill and penetrating, cutting through the courtyard like a chilling wind, the voice rose and fell in the familiar, funereal rhythm of the mourner's dirge.

> Fallen, never again to rise.
> Is virgin Israel;
> Forsaken on her land she lies,
> With none to raise her!

In the stunned silence which followed his words the tall, straight figure turned and walked quietly, unhurriedly from the courtyard. His accusers sat motionless, staring after him; even the *gibborim* seemed powerless to move. Then one of them snapped into action.

"Follow him!"

"Did you hear what he said—about *us?*"

"Punish him for contempt of court!"

"Yahweh deliver us! The man is mad!"

"Send the *gibborim* after him!"

"No, no! Don't follow him. *Let him go!*"

Again stricken silent, they stared now at Ben Sered, who had risen to his feet and addressed them with such imperative sternness that even the *gibborim,* who had started out in the wake of their amazing prisoner, stopped uncertainly.

Feeling their gaze upon him, Ben Sered wavered. Remembering that his natural stature was unenhanced at the moment by its usual stiff linen bolster, he felt himself shrinking visibly. He flushed and stammered.

"After all, the f-fellow is quite harmless. Wh-what I mean is, wouldn't it be better to consider more carefully just what course we should pursue? Of course, with the king absent, we have no power over life and death. We would have to give careful consideration to the proper punishment—"

Ben Othni gave him a long, shrewd, contemptuous glance. "Very well," he replied. "Suppose we do just that. Will you honor my poor abode by taking your seats again, gentlemen? And you need have no fear," he continued smoothly, with a swift, narrowed glance at Ben Sered. "The prisoner will be quite safe. There are other *gibborim* waiting outside. We will know exactly where he is and what he is doing."

Ben Sered cautiously groped his way along the dark, narrow street. When the figures of two *gibborim* loomed toward him out of the shadows, he hastily drew the folds of his headdress across his face.

"The house of Ephraim ben Esdras," he muttered.

One of the *gibborim* pointed toward a dark hole in the wall. Ben Sered groped his way into it and stumbled up an interminable flight of steps before he saw in front of him a square of light, framing the small, hunched figure of a man squatted on a mat before a low table, writing. He cleared his throat, and the man put aside his clay tablets and writing tools and came forward.

"Peace be to you, sir. The blessing of the Eternal rest upon you as you enter the humble dwelling of Ben Esdras."

"Amos?" demanded Ben Sered eagerly, after the greeting had been acknowledged. Then, seeing the keen dark eyes narrow cautiously, he added quickly, "I am Simon ben Sered."

"Yes." The eyes did not relax their caution. "I know."

"I came to warn him. His life is in danger. I sat with the judges in council not an hour ago, and they plan to seize him early in the morning. We must get him out of the city immediately."

"And you? Are you not also of the council?"

"I tried to save him, believe me I did, even though I think he's probably the most dangerous man alive in Israel." Lifting the sleeve of his coat, Ben Sered passed it across his dripping face. "But I love him. He's like a son to me. I—I'd endanger the whole nation to insure his safety."

The caution faded. "Amos is already gone," said the little hunchback simply. "He believes his work in Samaria is finished."

"But—the *gibborim*—"

"There are other ways of leaving the city than by its towered gate. We who live close to the wall—"

Ben Sered sank down weakly on a mat, feeling in his sudden relief as if the life had gone out of him. The heat in the small room was stifling. But even after the strength came flowing back into his body, he felt a strange reluctance to leave.

"What are you writing?" he asked, indicating the unfinished clay tablet. Then he noticed that there were other tablets, many neat piles of them, stacked both on the table and in stone niches along the sides of the room, which looked like a small cavity scooped out of the great city wall. Was it through one of those niches, he wondered, that Amos escaped?

"I am rewriting the story of our people," said Ben Esdras simply. "It is nearly a hundred years since it was written, or perhaps, compiled, in Judah, and it has never been done in Israel. In a century the religious beliefs of a people change, and new light is constantly being shed upon past events. I have many sources here which have never been put in connected form."

Ben Sered stared. Then a strange excitement began to possess him. He touched the clay tablet reverently. "A history of our people—written in Israel! Of course! Why has no one ever thought of it? But you haven't the materials here or the proper place to work. This stinking hole—" His excitement suddenly waning, he eyed the young scholar suspiciously. "I forgot. You are Amos' friend. Have you written any of these mad ideas of his in your story?"

"No," said Ben Esdras. "Amos and I are friends, but we do not agree. We have had many arguments since he has been here these last weeks. Down there by himself on the edge of the wilderness he seems to have developed some strange and, I am sorry to say, heretical ideas. He believes the temple ritual is unimportant, and, worse than that, he seems to doubt the protecting power of the Eternal One himself, making him a weak, unreliable deity who cares for other nations as well as Israel."

"Then you don't think Israel is in danger?"

The dark eyes flashed. "How could she be, with the Eternal to protect her?"

"And you don't believe Amos received his messages from Jahweh, as he claimed?"

"How could he have done so? Did the Eternal speak to him as he did to Moses? Did he appear to him in visions or in dreams?"

"Then why," asked Ben Sered, almost convinced, "did you help him escape?"

"For the same reason," returned Ephraim ben Esdras, "that you would have done so. And because I believe in the right of every man to try to discover the truth for himself."

Ben Sered stayed in the small, hot room late into the night making practical plans for the completion of the young scholar's gigantic project. A quiet room should be set aside for him in Ben Sered's own house. Papyrus should be imported from Egypt and scribes secured to hasten the task of copying. Ben Sered should pay all the expenses, asking nothing in return except a share in the honor of the achievement.

When finally he descended the stairs, stepping cautiously over the forms of the two sleeping *gibborim,* and made his way home through the dark, ill-smelling streets, Ben Sered was filled with conflicting emotions of excitement and regret. Amos was safe. He had not even needed to betray his convictions to save Amos. And he himself, Ben Sered, had acquired a new interest in living. He was to share in an achievement which would startle all Israel and set her feet in the old comfortable paths of truth and piety, as well as win considerable honor and distinction, perhaps even a bit of immortality, for himself.

He had only two regrets. One was that it was an obscure, ugly hunchback called Ben Esdras who would make this contribution to his people's progress, whose name would be long remembered. It would have been so easy for Amos to achieve something great, so that the nation in years to come, perhaps even other nations, might have known and revered his name.

The other regret: He would have given his entire profit from the last increase in taxes, the last two increases, if he could have been in the queen's banquet hall that night and heard Amos call Bilhah and the other women, "cows of Bashan."*

✝

AMOS, THE HERDSMAN FROM TEKOA
By
Dorothy Clarke Wilson

PART II

THE road left to the east led unquestionably to danger. The road south led to home and safety. Unhesitatingly Amos took the left-hand road which climbed the hill toward Bethel.

It was a crowded road, filled with pilgrims from all over southern Israel journeying to the royal sanctuary for the annual Feast of Weeks. Every family, even the poorest, carried his offering of first fruits, the two loaves of finely ground and leavened meal which, containing as they did the very essence of life, would strengthen Yahweh and aid him in the renewal of vegetation. Many carried also other offerings: lambs and goats to be slain for the sacrifice, unusually perfect specimens of vegetables, herbs in such varieties as might have grown in a king's

* Abridged from *The Herdsman* by Dorothy Clarke Wilson, pp. 314-26. Copyright, 1946, by Dorothy Clarke Wilson. Published by The Westminster Press. Used by special permission of the author.

spice garden, great baskets piled high with apricots, pomegranates, figs, and, occasionally, bunches of red-purple grapes from an early bearing vineyard.

One of these, borne proudly on the head of a well-dressed pilgrim whose carefully tended hands had obviously not shared in the task of bringing the luscious burden to its present perfection of fruition, fascinated Amos. Unconsciously he fell into step behind the proud landowner, keeping his eyes fixed so intently on the lavish, colorful display that its rich golds and reds and purples swam together in grotesque confusion.

"Kaitz," he said to himself, "a basket of *summer fruit.* Ripe, perfect, luscious. But already dying, because it has been plucked from the source which gave it life. How soon—how very soon—it will be *ketz*—an *end!* Like Israel."

*Kaitz—ketz—*The words began to beat through his mind with a dull persistence, subduing all other sounds to their steady, relentless rhythm. The shuffling of feet, the pounding of hoofs, the creaking of ox carts, even the beating of his own heart seemed to fall in step with the grim, pulsating crescendo. *Kaitz—ketz —kaitz—ketz—*on and on, for centuries. Cities rising gloriously out of other cities' dust and ashes, only to be themselves leveled into rubble. Nations rearing their proud thrones of supremacy on the crumbling ruins of other thrones, only to make their own swift contribution to the vast, growing pile of debris. People climbing endlessly over the broken bodies of their weaker fellows, only to be themselves crushed and broken by stronger and more ruthless climbers whom they had taught to follow them. *Kaitz—ketz—*Must it go on interminably? Would no city, no nation, no people ever arise which would not blindly build into its structure, into its very being, the elements of its own destruction?

Yahweh in heaven, was there no one but him to tell them that the seeds they had planted were already ripening to a harvest of destruction! No, not Yahweh in heaven, Yahweh here! Yahweh standing on a wall—*in Bethel!*

He clambered suddenly to the wall beside the workman and held up his hand. "Listen, people of Israel!"

They listened, as other crowds had done all over southern Israel in the past seven weeks, in silence at sight of the dark, towering figure, at the first sound of the arresting, penetrating voice. Many of them had heard him before. Most of the rest had heard of him. During the journey into Bethel some had recognized him and passed the word to others, so that many were anticipating some excitement. Even the workman on the wall swallowed his oath and gaped up at him spellbound.

> This is what Yahweh showed me:
> A basket of ripened fruit.
> And he said to me,
> "Amos, what do you see?"
> And I said,
> "A basket of ripened fruit."
> Then Yahweh said to me:
> "The *end* has come to my people Israel.
> I will never pardon them again."

A faint ripple passed over the crowd as one after the other caught the subtle play on words. Then, seeing that he had more to say, they again fell silent.

> This is what Yahweh showed me:
> He himself standing upon a wall,
> A plumb line in his hand.
> And Yahweh said to me,
> "Amos, what do you see?"
> And I said, "A plumb line."
> Then Yahweh said,
> "With a plumb line I am testing my people.
> I will never pardon them again."

Another ripple passed, swelling this time into a tumultuous wave of wonder, derision, and protest. Two *gibborim,* lolling against the city wall, straightened their big, hulking bodies and tightened their hands on their sword hilts. A priest moving inward from the gate stopped, pursed his lips, and stood watching the scene with narrowed eyes. But the voice cut effortlessly as the prow of a ship through the waves of confusion.

> Can horses race on bare rock,
> Or oxen plow the sea?
> No more is it possible
> For a nation to live without justice!
> You are so proud of Lodebar,
> And boast how you captured Karnaim!
> But thus says Yahweh:
> "I will rise up a nation against you
> Which shall crush you from the pass of Hamath
> Even to the Valley of the Arabah!
> And into exile they shall send you
> Far beyond Damascus!
> The high place of Jacob shall be devastated,
> Your temples laid in ruins,
> And I will rise up against the house of Jeroboam
> With a sword!"

The wave became movements now as well as sound, swept forward as if to beat itself against the wall and wash from its eminence the amazing figure who had dared defy the ruling house of Israel, but with conflicting purposes: both to destroy him and to raise him triumphantly on its crest.

"Traitor!"

"Angel sent from Yahweh!"

"Heretic!"

"Savior!"

"Messenger of evil!"

"Another Elijah, come to deliver!"

"Down with him, speaker of lies!"

"Up with him, friend of the oppressed!"

"Look! Where is he?"

"Gone!"

"*Where?*"

The workman squatted on the top of the wall could have told them where, for he had seen the tall figure drop with amazing agility into the alley on the other side and disappear with firm and unhurried steps into one of the narrow, littered streets. But he did not choose to do so. Anybody who could jump on and off a wall like that had a right to do what he pleased. He himself had grunted enough getting up there!

"Amos! I heard you—back there—in the gate! I followed you—"

"Eben!"

"I knew it was you, knew all the time, even last spring at the festival! And I knew you'd come back. I've been waiting for you, getting ready."

"Getting—ready?"

"You must come to my house quickly! It won't be safe for you in the streets, not for a while, anyway. I saw those *gibborim* and the priest—Come on! Around this corner, remember?"

Amos permitted himself to be led by a new, strangely excited Eben, from whose lips words tumbled so fast as to be disjointed and almost inarticulate, around the corner into the small house in the familiar street. . . .

Later, after they had partaken of a frugal supper and the lamp had been lighted, Eben revealed to his boyhood friend the reason for his new exuberance. It had begun the day seven weeks before when he had heard Amos speak his words of bold denunciation before the temple. At last, he knew, the oppressed of Israel had found a champion to defend them. Sudden hope had swept through the crowded hovels of the city's poor like flame through tinder. Eben, known for many years as a bold but helpless agitator, had become their natural leader. A secret organization had been formed, most of its members former small landowners like himself, who had been swallowed up by the politically and commercially powerful holders of great landed estates.

"Now at last we're ready." Eben's voice, once so melodious, was still hoarse and rasping as when Amos had heard it almost a year before in the market place. He coughed often as he talked, a hard, dry cough which produced a faint rattling sound in his chest. His great muscles had become flabby. The flesh, once so firm and ruddy, hung loosely on his massive, thickset frame, and it was a pale, unhealthy color . . .

"What do you plan to do?" asked Amos, who had listened so intently that the shadow of his tall, straight figure, elongated grotesquely like a hovering bird, hung absolutely motionless on the wall and ceiling.

"That's just it," rasped Eben eagerly. "We don't know. We've been waiting for you to tell us."

"Me?" The shadow moved then, lifted its wings as if startled.

"Of course. You! You know the will of Yahweh. You say he's a just God, who protects the weak and punishes oppression. All over southern Israel the poor have heard your voice. If you lead them, they will be ready to follow. For years

I have been telling the people it could be done if enough of us would only get together. Now we've really begun it. There aren't many of us yet, of course, but there will be more. . . . Tomorrow night those whom I have trained as leaders are coming here. You will meet them and talk with them. You will tell us what to do."

"I?" repeated Amos slowly. "But—how, Eben, I don't know myself. How could I tell you what to do?"

In Eben's square, homely face the light of confidence shone unfalteringly. "Because you're the prophet of Yahweh," he said simply.

"I? A prophet?"

"Of course. You're like Moses. Or like Elijah. You know the will of Yahweh, don't you? He has spoken to you, as he did to Moses and Elijah. Only you know his will better than they ever did."

"You—really believe that?"

"Certainly I believe it. And I'm not the only one. There are hundreds of oppressed people all over Israel who are waiting, like us—."

"Waiting for me to tell them what to do."

Amos rose from his mat and walked back and forth along the narrow *mastaby*. . . . He stopped suddenly and looked down at Eben.

"You don't realize the power of the forces of injustice," he said earnestly. "Even though you are many, if you fling yourselves against them, you will surely be broken, and not only you but your children. I've lived in Samaria. I've seen the *gibborim* and the armies of Obed Shebna at work, and I know. Believe me, Eben! I'm only trying to think what is best. I know life is already well-nigh unendurable for the poor, but—is death any better?"

Eben returned his gaze steadily, the shining confidence in his eyes unfading. "You forget," he said simply. "Yahweh himself is on the side of justice. You yourself have said so."

It was past noon on the first day of the feast, and the rays of the summer sun were like the hot brightness of an oven into which dry fuel has been continually fed. But the worship of Yahweh, God of Israel and patron of her prosperity, continued unabated. The treasury boxes into which the people paid their tithes and fines were emptied, refilled, and emptied again with machinelike regularity. . . . On the bare hillside the crowds still swarmed so densely that at no spot was the earth visible.

In his appointed place between the altar of sacrifice and the altar of incense Hosea meticulously discharged his duties as second priest, but his mind was not on his task. His muscles were tensed for some impending danger which he feared but could not define. . . .

He knew that Amos was in the city and that he had spoken in the gate. He knew also that on the previous evening Amaziah had dispatched a message by swift courier to Jeroboam in the north. He had even persuaded the scribe to show him the text of the message.

"A man called Amos is plotting against you here in your own royal city. He is threatening the very safety of the nation. This is what he says: 'Jeroboam is to die by the sword, and Israel is to go into exile, far from its own country.' I have set *gibborim* on his trail to arrest him if he makes further disturbance. But I have no authority to silence him permanently."

Last night Hosea had gone to his home hoping to find Amos there, that he might warn him. But the herdsman of Tekoa had not been near the place. . . .

Now, however, as the hottest period of the day approached, when the high priest would withdraw into his apartment for his noon siesta and the people would of necessity disband to seek shelter from the sun, he began to breathe more freely. Perhaps Amos had foreseen the danger to himself. Perhaps even now he was in the cottage with Beeri waiting for him to come. As soon as his duties for the morning were completed, he would send a messenger—

And then suddenly it came, with no excited tremor as a warning. Just a voice rising without apparent source, clear and vibrant and commanding, above the restless movement of the crowd, above the melody of songs and harps and cymbals, above the anguished cries of dying lambs and goats, compelling every other sound to silence:

> Listen, Israel, to the voice of the Eternal:
> "I hate, I abhor your feasts,
> I scorn your sacred assemblies!
> Pile high your sacrifices!
> I will not smell them.
> Bring your cakes of fine meal!
> I will not taste them.
> Offer your fatted cattle!
> I will not look at them.
> Sing hymns and play your harps!
> I will not listen to them.
> Rather let justice roll forth like a fountain
> And righteousness as an ever-living stream!"

Even while his flesh froze with a sudden startled awareness of danger, Hosea thrilled to the very core of his being. For he knew that he had just listened to the most daring words which had ever been uttered in Israel, perhaps in any nation. For Amos had not only struck at the very heart of the accepted religious beliefs of his people. He had defied the sacred traditions of all time. He had propounded an utterly new, utterly revolutionary religion of the spirit.

Hosea was not surprised when later he entered the high priest's apartment to find Amos already there in the custody of two burly but dull-looking *gibborim.* They had time to exchange only a brief glance of understanding before the high priest himself appeared. . . .

"Bring him here," he ordered curtly.

"So you are this dreamer, this visionary who has been stirring up all the trouble." The contempt in the high priest's voice was tinged unconsciously with respect. . . . The fellow was a little overpowering with that towering frame, those enormous, deep-set eyes which looked as if they could gaze straight through a man's body. "They tell me you come from Judah."

"Yes," replied Amos, "from Tekoa."

"Then why don't you be off to Judah where you belong?" demanded the high priest petulantly. . . . "Can't you earn a good enough living there among your own *nabis,* that you have to come up here to get another handout for your babblings?"

"No prophet am I," replied Amos swiftly. "No son of a prophet am I. But a herdsman am I and a tender of sycamore trees."

"Then get back to your sheep and your sycamore trees where you belong!" retorted Amaziah irritably. "And whatever you do don't do any more of your babblings here at Bethel, where the king has his royal sanctuary. If you're so mad you must prophesy, then do it against some other nation than Israel."

"So you say I am not to prophesy against Israel. I am to do no more raving against the house of Isaac. Very well, then. Listen to what Yahweh has to say about *you.*" Beginning with a deadly quietness, the voice swept swiftly into stern crescendos. "Your wife shall be ravished in this very city, your sons and daughters shall be slain, your big landed estates shall be divided up, and you yourself shall die in a foreign land. For Israel is surely going into exile, far from its own country."

Amaziah's hard, thin features tightened like a vise. The blood mounted to his cheeks until his pale, soft flesh looked like an old goatskin swelling with new wine and ready to break. . . . Abruptly he motioned to the two *gibborim.*

"Put him in a dungeon," he ordered curtly, "one of the good strong ones under the royal palace. And keep him there. This is a matter which demands the attention of the king himself."

When the tall figure had disappeared silent now but unbowed, Amaziah sank back among his cushions relieved. . . .

His relief from worry was short-lived. For before evening a band of peasants, armed with a humble but formidable array of farm implements, had attacked and looted the warehouses of a rich landowner named Jahaz. As if this had been a prearranged signal, other small revolts took place swiftly all over the city. . . . By nightfall, it seemed that half the city was in revolt. . . . The *gibborim,* taken unawares and in various stages of drunkenness, entered the fray lustily enough but with stupid indiscrimination, generally adding to rather than mitigating the disorder.

Amaziah was at his wits' end. . . . He knew that the king, more tolerant always of any other vice than weakness, would hold him responsible. Yet the situation was quite out of his control. The contingent of soldiers which was always sent down from Samaria for the feast days had not arrived.

By midnight the revolt had been quelled. . . . But Amaziah had not forgotten his terror of the night. His conviction remained firm that the prisoner in the dungeon had cast an evil spell over the city. He dared not let him remain in Bethel. . . .

Before dawn he summoned his second priest, Hosea, and ordered him to see that the prisoner was released.

"Only for heaven's sake get him out of the city! See for yourself that he goes across the border into Judah, and take plenty of *gibborim* with you for protection."

"I shall need no *gibborim,*" said Hosea. "If he is willing to be released, he will go of his own volition."

"If he is *willing—*"

Hosea explained simply. "If I judge him correctly, he is the kind of man who might prefer imprisonment to silence. However, I shall try to do your bidding. And—I shall not return. I am withdrawing, my lord, from the priesthood."

It was nearing evening when Amos reached Bethlehem. But instead of stopping overnight at an inn, he went straight through the town and out by the southwest road, which plunged abruptly toward the Wilderness of Judah. He had had enough of cities in the past few weeks. He wanted more than anything else to bathe his spirit in vastness and solitude. . . .

To Amos this wild, inhospitable country was home. He breathed deeply of the dry, thin air, drew it into his soul as well as his body, and let it wash away a little of the heaviness of his spirit. He was profoundly sick at heart. No good, only evil, seemed to have resulted from the thing he had done. His words had not caused the unjust to repent. They had but added to the suffering of the oppressed. For the blood of the revolt, he felt, was on his hands. . . .

His work in Israel was ended. He had obeyed the strange, inner compulsion which had filled him, driven him like a consuming flame. Now the fire had died to a heap of blackened embers. He had nothing more to give.*

✛

GOD'S GLORY IS A WONDROUS THING
(Interpretation)

FREDERICK WILLIAM FABER (1814-1863) was born in Yorkshire, England. He was graduated from Balliol College, Oxford, and the following year was ordained and became the rector at Eton. He was active in the early years of the Oxford Movement in England.

He was a close friend of John Henry Newman, and in 1846 followed him into the Roman Catholic Church. When Frederick Faber revealed to Wordsworth his intention of uniting with the Roman Catholic Church, the latter replied: "I do not say you are wrong, but England loses a poet." The magnificent poetry which Frederick Faber left to humanity confirms Wordsworth's judgment. It is frequently quoted in public addresses, and much of it has become proverbial.

The one hundred and fifty hymn-poems from his pen evidence great poetic genius. His language overflows with words bearing unusual meanings, but the spirit of his hymns is always easy to understand. While the hymn, "God's Glory is a Wondrous Thing," is not one of Frederick Faber's greatest poems, it does reflect his character and his ability. It is a song of praise to the wondrous glory of God, urging men to "learn what God is like" so that "in the darkest battlefield" He will show them where to strike. This hymn closes with the affirmation that "right is right, since God is God," so that in the end the right will prevail:

* Abridged from *The Herdsman* by Dorothy Clarke Wilson, pp. 326-42. Copyright, 1946, by Dorothy Clarke Wilson. Published by The Westminster Press, Philadelphia, Pa. Used by special permission of the author.

To doubt would be disloyalty,
To falter would be sin.

In 1832 Heinrich C. Zeuner composed the tune "Hummel" to which this hymn is sung.

God's Glory Is a Wondrous Thing
HUMMEL. C.M.

FREDERICK W. FABER, 1814–1863   HEINRICH C. ZEUNER, 1832

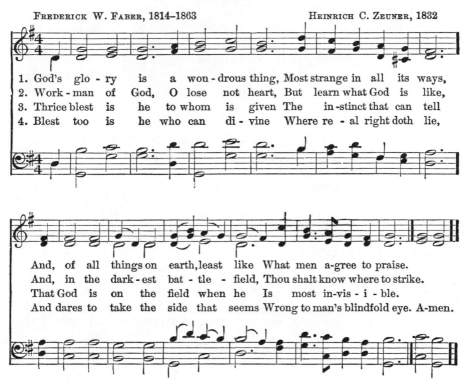

1. God's glo - ry is a won - drous thing, Most strange in all its ways,
2. Work - man of God, O lose not heart, But learn what God is like,
3. Thrice blest is he to whom is given The in - stinct that can tell
4. Blest too is he who can di - vine Where re - al right doth lie,

And, of all things on earth, least like What men a - gree to praise.
And, in the dark - est bat - tle - field, Thou shalt know where to strike.
That God is on the field when he Is most in - vis - i - ble.
And dares to take the side that seems Wrong to man's blindfold eye. A-men.

5 For right is right, since God is God,
    And right the day must win;
  To doubt would be disloyalty,
  To falter would be sin

GOD OF THE NATIONS, NEAR AND FAR
(Interpretation)

JOHN HAYNES HOLMES was born in 1879 in Philadelphia. In 1902 he graduated from Harvard University. Later he received the degree, Doctor of Divinity, not only from the Jewish Institute of Religion but from St. Lawrence University and

Meadville Theological School as well. In 1904 he was ordained by the Third Religious Society of the Unitarian fellowship in Dorchester, Massachusetts, and in 1907 he became pastor of the Church of the Messiah, now the Community Church in New York City.

He has served as president of the Unitarian Fellowship for Social Justice, as vice-president of the National Association for the Advancement of Colored People, as president of the All World Gandhi Fellowship, and other organizations. Many of his hymns have been included in church hymnals in the United States, England, and Japan. Dr. Holmes is a frequent contributor to various publications on the religious and ethical problems of today. He is also widely known for his religious poetry.

"God of the Nations, Near and Far" is a fine illustration of his poetic genius. This hymn, written after the outbreak of World War I, reflects Dr. Holmes' reaction to that overwhelming disaster. "I was completely unprepared for this wild outbreak of violence and hate," he writes. Its recurring theme is the universality of God's supreme rule and the quest of the human heart to find the paths of peace. The poet acknowledges that "the clash of arms still shakes the sky"; but this hymn voices the hope that through the years scientists, seers, wise statesmen, and pioneers will help to bring about a permanent peace. The movement toward World Brotherhood when "labor's teeming throngs" repeat in many

God of the Nations, Near and Far

ST. AGNES. C. M.

JOHN HAYNES HOLMES, 1914

JOHN B. DYKES, 1866

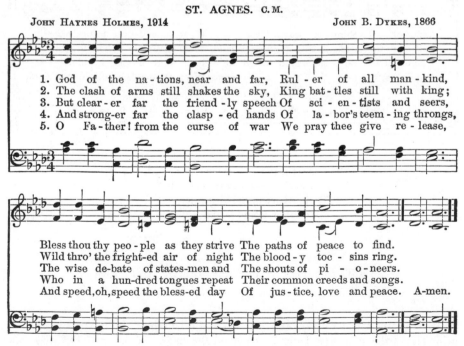

1. God of the na-tions, near and far, Rul-er of all man-kind,
2. The clash of arms still shakes the sky, King bat-tles still with king;
3. But clear-er far the friend-ly speech Of sci-en-tists and seers,
4. And strong-er far the clasp-ed hands Of la-bor's teem-ing throngs,
5. O Fa-ther! from the curse of war We pray thee give re-lease,

Bless thou thy peo-ple as they strive The paths of peace to find.
Wild thro' the fright-ed air of night The blood-y toc-sins ring.
The wise de-bate of states-men and The shouts of pi-o-neers.
Who in a hun-dred tongues repeat Their common creeds and songs.
And speed, oh, speed the bless-ed day Of jus-tice, love and peace. A-men.

languages "their common creeds and songs" will also be a factor in the achievement of permanent peace.

The hymn leaves us with no doubt as to "the curse of war" and the universal longing for peace among the peoples of the world. It closes with a prayer for release from war and the ushering in of the day of justice, love, and peace.

The tune "St. Agnes" was composed in 1866 by John B. Dykes.

✢

GOD OF THE PROPHETS

(Interpretation)

THE prophets in Bible times played an important role as messengers of God to recreant rulers and wayward peoples. It is not surprising, therefore, that a hymn should be written emphasizing the ministry of God's prophets in the affairs of men.

The first stanza of this nineteenth-century hymn by Denis Wortman (1884) recalls the transfer of Elijah's spiritual leadership to the young prophet, Elisha, when the older prophet cast his mantle on the shoulders of this youth. Every age has its own solemn task to face and every succeeding age needs the counsel of nobler and stronger prophets.

The second stanza recalls the anointing of prophets such as Elisha to consecrate them for their lifework. The anointed prophets heard God speak and, knowing the needs of men, announced God's message to them. The prophets preached righteousness and the breaking away from evil.

The third stanza speaks of the anointing of priests who became strong "intercessors" for the pardoning of man's sins. They pray, too, for love among men and for peace in the world.

The fourth stanza urges the anointing of kings and the rulers of the earth that they, too, may be conscious of God's leadership in their lives.

The fifth stanza prays that these anointed prophets, priests, and kings may become apostles of Christ and go forth to all parts of the world to proclaim the good news of God's grace.

The hymn ends with a plea for the return of an age of truth and faith when rulers are God's spokesmen and when the sublime reign of Christ begins.

This prophetic hymn is sung to the tune "Toulon" composed in 1551 by Louis Bourgeois.

God of the Prophets

TOULON. 10, 10, 10, 10

Denis Wortman, 1884

Louis Bourgeois, 1551

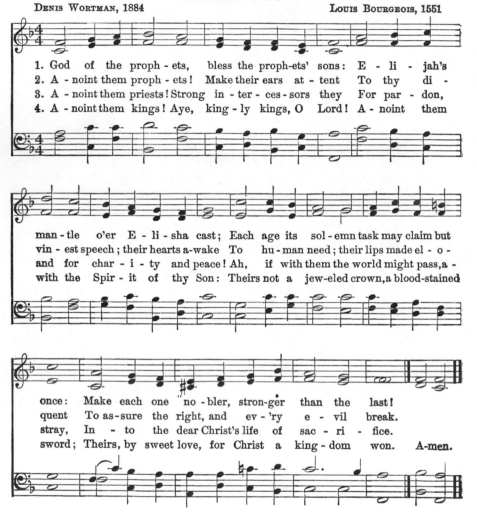

1. God of the proph-ets, bless the proph-ets' sons: E - li - jah's
2. A - noint them proph - ets! Make their ears at - tent To thy di -
3. A - noint them priests! Strong in - ter - ces - sors they For par - don,
4. A - noint them kings! Aye, king - ly kings, O Lord! A - noint them

man - tle o'er E - li - sha cast; Each age its sol - emn task may claim but
vin - est speech; their hearts a-wake To hu - man need; their lips made el - o -
and for char - i - ty and peace! Ah, if with them the world might pass, a -
with the Spir - it of thy Son: Theirs not a jew-eled crown, a blood-stained

once: Make each one "no - bler, stron-ger than the last!
quent To as-sure the right, and ev - 'ry e - vil break.
stray, In - to the dear Christ's life of sac - ri - fice.
sword; Theirs, by sweet love, for Christ a king - dom won. A-men.

5 Make them apostles! Heralds of thy cross,
  Forth may they go to tell all realms thy grace;
  Inspired of thee, may they count all but loss,
  And stand at last with joy before thy face.

6 O mighty age of prophet-kings, return!
  O truth, O faith, enrich our urgent time!
  Lord Jesus Christ, again with us sojourn;
  A weary world awaits thy reign sublime! Amen.

While Thee I Seek, Protecting Power

FIRST TUNE. BRATTLE STREET. C. M. D.

HELEN M. WILLIAMS, 1786   ARR. from IGNAZ J. PLEYEL, 1791

1. While thee I seek, pro-tect-ing Pow'r, Be my vain wish-es stilled;
2. In each e-vent of life how clear Thy rul-ing hand I see,
3. When glad-ness wings my fa-vored hour, Thy love my tho'ts shall fill;

And may this con-se-crat-ed hour With bet-ter hopes be filled.
Each bless-ing to my soul more dear Be-cause con-ferred by thee.
Re-signed, when storms of sor-row low'r, My soul shall meet thy will.

Thy love the pow'rs of thought bestowed, To thee my tho'ts would soar;
In ev-'ry joy that crowns my days, In ev-'ry pain I . . bear,
My lift-ed eye with-out a tear The low'r-ing storm shall see;

Thy mer-cy o'er my life has flowed, That mer-cy I a-dore.
My heart shall find de-light in praise, Or seek re-lief in prayer.
My stead-fast heart shall know no fear, That heart will rest on thee. A-men

WHILE THEE I SEEK, PROTECTING POWER

(Interpretation)

THIS deeply devotional prayer hymn was written in the eighteenth century by Helen M. Williams (1786).

The first stanza acknowledges that the suppliant has had in the past the "protecting Power" of the infinite God, and entreats the continued favor of His righteous hand.

The second stanza expresses the conviction that in each event of our life we can see the hand of God conferring blessings on us. In every joy we praise God, and in every pain we find relief in prayer.

The third stanza promises that in hours of gladness our hearts shall be filled with love for God; when sorrow comes to us we will bow to God's will; and when danger threatens we will face it unafraid for our hearts are at rest in God's protecting care.

The melody to which this hymn is usually sung is "Brattle Street," arranged from a composition written in 1791 by Ignaz J. Pleye. It is also sung to the tune "St. Peter" composed in 1836 by Alexander R. Reinagle.

✟

HAPPY HE WHO WALKETH EVER

(Interpretation)

Blessed is the man that walketh not
in the counsel of the ungodly,
Nor standeth in the way of sinners,
Nor sitteth in the seat of the scornful.

But his delight is in the law of the Lord;
And in his law doth he meditate
day and night.

And he shall be like a tree planted
by the rivers of water,
That bringeth forth his fruit in his season;
His leaf also shall not wither;
And whatsoever he doeth shall prosper.

The ungodly are not so:
But are like the chaff which the
wind driveth away.

Therefore the ungodly shall not
stand in the judgment,

Happy He Who Walketh Ever

PSALM 1

Jacob Voorsanger

H. Fabisch

Allegro moderato

1. Hap - py he who walk - eth ev - er In the ways of God, our Lord;
2. He shall flour - ish like a flow - er, Plant - ed by the wa - ter - side;

Hap - py he who sin - neth nev - er 'Gainst the teach - ings of His word;
God will give him grace and pow - er, In his vir - tue to a - bide.

Whose de - light is Him to serve, Day by day and year by year;
By the help of God, most tender, Shall he pros - per in his ways;

From His pre - cepts ne'er to swerve; Un - to peace shall he be near.
Vir - tue shall be his de - fend - er, Bless - ed shall be all his days.

> Nor sinners in the congregation
> of the righteous.
>
> For the Lord knoweth the way
> of the righteous:
> But the way of the ungodly shall perish.
>
> [Ps. 1]

One cannot read the words of this great hymn by Jacob Voorsanger, the music by H. Fabisch, without recalling the words of the first Psalm on which it is based.

What a debt of gratitude we owe to the people of all ages who have couched in beautiful rhyme high sentiments and emotions that constantly challenge human hearts to "delight in the law of the Lord and in his law . . . meditate day and night."

Through the centuries this great body of poetic literature known as the Psalms has been a continuing challenge to men everywhere to live their lives in the light of God's teachings, and to crown with glory and usefulness this being who is made in the image of God, his Maker. To sing this great canticle is to reaffirm one's faith and trust in righteous, upright living and being.

✛

GOD IS LOVE; HIS MERCY BRIGHTENS

(Interpretation)

JOHN BOWRING, the author of this magnificent hymn, was born in Exeter, England (1792-1872). He was the son of Charles Bowring, a woolen manufacturer. The son was educated for the purpose of carrying on his father's business, and with this aim in mind he was encouraged to study foreign languages. At sixteen young Bowring could both write and speak Spanish, Italian, Portuguese, French, and German, as well as his native tongue.

On reaching his maturity John Bowring entered the commercial career of his father, obtaining a large contract for supplying the British army. Because of his fluency in languages, he made many translations of poetry from the Bohemian, Bulgarian, and other Slavic tongues. As a result of his literary attainments he was honored with a degree by the University of Groningen in Holland. Some years later he was elected as a Radical from Kilmarnock to the English House of Commons. He also served for a time as Governor of Hong Kong, and in 1854 was knighted. At his death in 1872 his wife had engraved on his tombstone the words: "In the Cross of Christ I Glory."

Although he was engaged in both business and politics, he found time to write hymns and it is upon these that his lasting fame rests. Several of the hymns he composed are to be found in most Protestant hymnals.

"God is Love, His Mercy Brightens" was composed in 1825. Each of its four stanzas closes with the affirmation, "God is wisdom, God is love"; and each stanza emphasizes some virtue of the everlasting God.

The first stanza stresses God's mercy and love. The second stanza emphasizes the lasting quality of God's mercy in contrast to the transitory nature of man. The third stanza speaks of God's "changeless goodness" in the darkest hour and in the midst of earth's greatest gloom. The fourth stanza calls attention to the fact that hope and comfort come from above and entwine themselves in and through all man's earthly care and trials.

The melody "Cross of Jesus" was composed in 1887 by John Stainer.

God Is Love; His Mercy Brightens

CROSS OF JESUS. 8, 7, 8, 7

JOHN BOWRING, 1825

JOHN STAINER, 1887

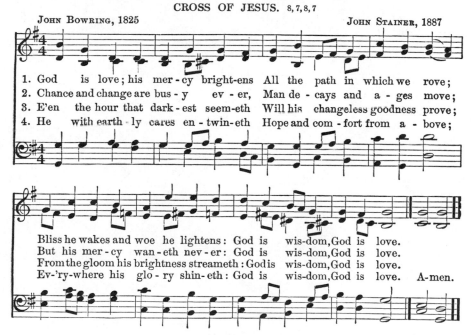

1. God is love; his mer-cy bright-ens All the path in which we rove;
2. Chance and change are bus-y ev-er, Man de-cays and a-ges move;
3. E'en the hour that dark-est seem-eth Will his changeless goodness prove;
4. He with earth-ly cares en-twin-eth Hope and com-fort from a-bove;

Bliss he wakes and woe he lightens: God is wis-dom, God is love.
But his mer-cy wan-eth nev-er: God is wis-dom, God is love.
From the gloom his brightness streameth: God is wis-dom, God is love.
Ev-'ry-where his glo-ry shin-eth: God is wis-dom, God is love. A-men.

PART V

HIGH LIGHTS OF THE KINGDOM OF JUDAH

CONTENTS

PART V SECTION 1

THE SOUTHERN KINGDOM

✠

Woe is me! for I am undone; because I am a man of unclean lips, and I dwell in the midst of a people of unclean lips: for mine eyes have seen the King, the Lord of hosts.—ISAIAH 6:5

✠

REHOBOAM AND THE DIVISION OF THE KINGDOM

By

Julius Schnorr von Carolsfeld

(Interpretation)

REHOBOAM was the son of Solomon, Israel's wisest king, and the natural successor to his father's throne. Upon the death of his father he went to Shechem, for all Israel were gathered together there to make him king. The story of what happened there is told in I Kings, chapter 12.

In Egypt at this time there lived a certain Jereboam who had fled there from the wrath of King Solomon against whom he had "lifted up his hand." Hearing that King Solomon had died and that his son Rehoboam was to be proclaimed king, Jereboam returned from Egypt and went to Shechem. There he joined himself to the people of the northern tribes of Israel. These people had been dissatisfied with the rule of Solomon and they came to Rehoboam to make their grievances known. Jereboam acted as their spokesman. He said to Solomon's son:

"Thy father made our yoke grievous. Now therefore make thou the grievous service of thy father, and his heavy yoke . . . lighter, and we will serve thee."

The young king needed time to think over this demand, so he replied: "Depart yet for three days, then come again to me."

First King Rehoboam went to the old men who had been advisers to his father during his reign, and asked: "How do ye advise that I may answer this people?"

The old men gave him wise counsel: "If thou wilt be a servant unto this people this day, and wilt serve them, and answer them, and speak good words to them, then they will be thy servants for ever."

This counsel displeased Rehoboam and he went to the young men with whom he had grown up. They were inexperienced in the arts of ruling and ignorant of the responsibilities of kingship and they advised Rehoboam: "Thus shalt thou speak unto this people . . . 'Whereas my father did lade you with a heavy yoke, I will add to your yoke. My father hath chastised you with whips, but I will chastise you with scorpions.'"

On the third day when the people came to hear the decision of their new king he foolishly disregarded the counsel of the experienced counselors and answered them in the words of the young men. He threatened heavier burdens and harsher punishments.

When the northern tribes of Israel saw that the young king had no intention of improving their lot, they rebelled against the house of David and Solomon and shouted a defiant song:

What portion have we in David?
  Neither have we inheritance in the son of Jesse.
To your tents, O Israel!
Now see to thine own house, David!

517

Then Israel sent for Jereboam and made him their king and "there was none that followed the house of David, but the tribe of Judah only."

This engraving is one of the series of Bible pictures designed by the German artist, Julius Schnorr von Carolsfeld, for his *Die Biebel im Bildern*. It shows Rehoboam at Shechem soon after his crowning as king of Solomon's realm. There is a defiant, surly expression on his face as he turns his back upon all that is happening in the distance and prepares to mount his horse. In the middle distance one of his aged counselors holds up a warning finger. He seems to be saying to the young king: "You see what happens when you spurn our wise advice and threaten the people with heavier burdens than even your father imposed on them!"

Crowds are streaming away from Rehoboam toward a distant hill where Jereboam is being crowned king of Israel. Horns are blown in exultation as Israel rebels from the hated rule of Rehoboam and the united kingdom of Solomon becomes the divided kingdoms of Israel and Judah. While the biblical story does not specifically say that Jeroboam was crowned within sight of King Rehoboam, nevertheless the 12th chapter of I Kings does indicate that Jeroboam was crowned "king over all Israel" immediately after King Rehoboam had refused to listen to the counsel of the old men.

Never again was the kingdom united. Instead, the two divided kingdoms struggled along for a period of years under various kings, some wise and good, others vicious and unworthy, until finally all were lost as captives either to Assyria or Babylonia.

✛

ATHALIAH AND THE CORONATION OF JOASH

By

William Hole

(Interpretation)

ALTHOUGH Jehoshaphat, king of Judah, was a good man and in many respects a wise and just ruler, he brought trouble upon the house of Judah by marrying his son Jehoram to Athaliah, the daughter of Israel's wicked King Ahab and Jezebel.

When Jehoshaphat died, Jehoram his son became king of Judah, but Jehoram's wife Athaliah led him and many of the people of Judah to worship Baal as her mother Jezebel before her had done in Israel.

After reigning only eight years King Jehoram died and was buried in the city of David, but not in the sepulcher of the kings. Ahaziah, his son, succeeded him, but reigned only one year in Jerusalem. He also did evil in the sight of the Lord, and was slain by Jehu when he revolted against Ahab's house and killed Ahab's wife Jezebel and his son Jehoram and made himself king of the Northern Kingdom of Israel.

In the Southern Kingdom of Judah the queen mother, Athaliah, was so enraged when she heard of her son's death that she rose up and destroyed all the princes of the royal house of David, even her own grandsons, and made herself

REHOBOAM AND THE DIVISION OF THE KINGDOM—*VON CAROLSFELD*

the reigning queen of Judah. She thought that there was no one left to dispute her right to the throne, for she believed she had killed all the royal princes. However, a daughter of King Jehoram, now the wife of Jehoiada, the high priest, took her baby nephew Joash, one of Ahaziah's sons, and hid him in the house of God for six years. He was in reality the only rightful heir to the throne of Judah.

When young Joash was seven years old his aunt and her husband, the high priest Jehoiada, believed the time had come to supplant the usurping queen, Athaliah, and put Joash on the throne which was his by right. Accordingly, Jehoiada summoned all the civil and military authorities of the land to the Temple court. There he showed them the little boy Joash who was their rightful king. The strong men of the kingdom entered into a covenant to protect the boy king. In the second Book of Kings in the eleventh chapter is the dramatic story of Joash's coronation.

"And the guard stood, every man with his weapons in his hand, round about the king, from the right corner of the temple to the left corner of the temple. . . . And he [Jehoiada] brought forth the king's son, and put the crown upon him, and gave him the testimony. And they made him king, and anointed him. And they clapped their hands, and said, 'God save the king.'"

Hearing the shouts of acclamation coming from the Temple, Queen Athaliah hurried there and "when she looked, behold, the king stood by a pillar, as the manner was, and the princes and the trumpeters by the king, and all the people of the land rejoiced, and blew with trumpets."

But filled with anger, Athaliah tore her clothes and cried, "Treason! Treason!"

The queen was swiftly seized by order of Jehoiada "and they laid hands on her; and she went by the way by the which horses came into the king's house: and there she was slain."

This painting by William Hole captures the dramatic moment of this incident. Outside in the blazing sun the boy king stands crowned upon the steps of the Temple. The defiant queen stands with her foot poised on the threshold of the courtyard. Her fist is clenched and there is hate on her face. She has just cried "Treason!" and is tearing her clothes as the guard rushes toward her to seize her and so protect their young and rightful king.

✛

THE RABSHAKEH DEMANDING THE SURRENDER OF JERUSALEM

By

José Cordero Villegas

(Interpretation)

JOSÉ CORDERO VILLEGAS was born in Seville, Spain, in 1848. He was a pupil of Mariano Fortuny, the artist, whose manner he copied. He also studied in Rome. His principal works are: "The Christening," "Dreams of the Arabian Knights,"

ATHALIAH AND THE CORONATION OF JOASH—*HOLE*

"Bull Fighters," "Poultry Market in Gangier," "Cairo Clipper Merchant," and "Rose Vase." He died in 1921.

The only known Old Testament picture from his brush is "The Rabshakeh Demanding the Surrender of Jerusalem." Its theme is found in II Kings 18:17-33 which records the challenge which the Rabshakeh, or general of the Assyrian army, delivered to three representatives of Hezekiah, king of Judah. The three men who came outside Jerusalem's walls to meet the Rabshakeh and his armed guard were Eliakim, son of Hilkiah, who was the head of Hezekiah's household; Shebnah, the scribe; and Joah, the son of Asaph, the recorder.

To these men the Rabshakeh, in a clever attempt to undermine their confidence in their God and in their king, delivered the message of his master the great king of Assyria: "What confidence is this wherein thou trusteth? . . . Now on whom dost thou trust, that thou rebellest against me?"

The Rabshakeh next attempted to bribe them: "Now therefore, I pray thee, give pledges to my lord the king of Assyria, and I will deliver thee two thousand horses, if thou be able on thy part to set riders upon them" (II Kings 18:23).

Eliakim, Shebnah, and Joah, fearful of the effect these words might have upon the people listening from the walls, said to the Rabshakeh: "Speak, I pray thee, to thy servants in the Syrian language; for we understand it; and talk not to us in the Jews' language, in the ears of the people that are on the wall."

But the Rabshakeh cried in a loud voice in the language the people understood a message from the king of Assyria: "Let not Hezekiah deceive you, for he shall not be able to deliver you out of his hand; neither let Hezekiah make you trust in the Lord, saying, 'The Lord will surely deliver us, and this city shall not be given into the hand of the king of Assyria.' Hearken not to Hezekiah. . . . Make an agreement with me by a present, and come out to me; and then eat ye every man of his own vine, and every one of his fig tree, and drink ye every one the waters of his cistern. . . . Hearken not unto Hezekiah when he persuadeth you, saying, 'The Lord will deliver us.' Hath any of the gods of the nations delivered at all his land out of the hand of the king of Assyria?" (II Kings 18:29-33).

In the background of this painting is the stone wall, high and apparently impregnable, surrounding the city of Jerusalem, upon which the guards of Judah pace to and fro. Immediately before the Rabshakeh stand the three representatives of King Hezekiah, king of Judah, in whose presence the Assyrian general has just offered his bribe to the soldiers to desert and surrender without resistance to the demands of Assyria. Ignoring the request of Hezekiah's representatives that he speak to them, and through them to their king, in the Syrian language, so that the guards on the wall might not overhear what is said, the Rabshakeh shouts in the Hebrew tongue his bribe and dire threat.

But Eliakim, the son of the chief of Hezekiah's household, Shebnah, the scribe, and Joah, the son of the recorder, are not influenced by this bribe nor scared by the threat. Like Hezekiah, their king, they have put their trust in the Lord God of their people; and when the interview is over they will return in quiet dignity to their king to warn him of the impending invasion of Sennacherib's army.

Note that the armored headdress, the sword, spears, and shields of Sennacherib's

THE RABSHAKEH DEMANDING THE SURRENDER OF JERUSALEM—*VILLEGAS*

general and his men are in sharp contrast to the white-robed, unwarlike costumes of the representatives of Hezekiah, king of Judah. The first man on the left has closed his eyes and placed his hands on his breast in an attitude of quiet prayer. The middle one points upward to the guards on Jerusalem's high walls, while the third clenches his hands at the Rabshakeh's insolent mockery of their faith in the Lord. Yet all of them seem unafraid of the Rabshakeh's words and undismayed by the might of Sennacherib's army and its danger to their city of Jerusalem.

The painting is alive with the quiet strength and poise of these men who continued to rely on their God and their king in the very presence of a general whose army is far greater in strength and power than the army of Judah.

✛

HEZEKIAH SPREADING THE LETTER BEFORE THE LORD

Artist Unknown

(Interpretation)

THE name Hezekiah means "Jehovah strengtheneth." According to the story of this king's reign over the Southern Kingdom of Judah as recorded in the eighteenth, nineteenth, and twentieth chapters of II Kings, he was true to the meaning of his name.

Hezekiah was the son of Ahaz, one of the evil kings of Judah who "did not that which was right in the eyes of the Lord, his God" (II Kings 16:2). His son was twenty-five years old when he began to reign, and he reigned twenty-nine years in Jerusalem. Unlike his father, he was a good king and faithful to the Lord. Yet his reign, although a long one, was not without its difficulties and dangers.

The kingdom of Judah was threatened by Sennacherib, king of Assyria, to whom Ahaz had paid tribute for protection. The Rabshakeh, chief of Sennacherib's princes and general of Assyria's army, demanded the surrender of Jerusalem. But the Lord, in whom Hezekiah trusted, advised him through the prophet Isaiah, saying: "Be not afraid of the words which thou hast heard, with which the servants of the king of Assyria have blasphemed me. Behold, I will send a blast upon him, and he shall hear a rumor, and shall return to his own land; and I will cause him to fall by the sword in his own land" (19:6, 7).

Some months later the Rabshakeh again sent messengers to Hezekiah with a letter, saying: "Let not thy God in whom thou trustest deceive thee, saying, 'Jerusalem shall not be given into the hand of the king of Assyria.' Behold, thou hast heard what the kings of Assyria have done to all lands, by destroying them utterly; and shalt thou be delivered? Have the gods of the nations delivered them which my fathers have destroyed?" (19:10-12).

It is this incident of Hezekiah with the letter from the messengers of Assyria that is so vividly portrayed in this picture.

The letter contained a threat to destroy utterly the city of Jerusalem, the capital of the Southern Kingdom. When King Hezekiah received it, he took it into the house of the Lord, spread it before the Lord on the altar, and prayed: "O Lord

HEZEKIAH SPREADING THE LETTER BEFORE THE LORD—*ARTIST UNKNOWN*

God of Israel, which dwellest between the cherubims, thou art the God, even thou alone, of all the kingdoms of the earth; thou hast made heaven and earth. Lord, bow down thine ear and hear; open, Lord, thine eyes, and see; and hear the words of Sennacherib, which hath sent him to reproach the living God. Of a truth, Lord, the kings of Assyria have destroyed the nations and their lands, and have cast their gods into the fire; for they were no gods, but the work of men's hands, wood and stone; therefore they have destroyed them. Now, therefore, O Lord our God, I beseech thee, save thou us out of his hand, that all the kingdoms of the earth may know that thou art the Lord God even thou only" (19:15-19).

The winged figures of the cherubim can be seen in the carved woodwork behind the altar. A seven-branch candlestick is at the left of the kneeling king. Pomegranates, similar to those which were embroidered on the high priest's robe, form a carved decoration for the railing. There is beauty in the king's benevolent face and his open-eyed trust is apparent as he kneels before the altar of his God. The significance of Hezekiah's name, "Jehovah strengtheneth," is apparent in every line of this beautiful picture.

✛

ISAIAH

By

Michelangelo Buonarroti

(Interpretation)

WHILE Amos and Hosea were prophesying in the Northern Kingdom of Israel the messages entrusted to them by the Lord, a young man was growing up in Jerusalem in the Southern Kingdom, who was destined to become one of the great prophets. This young man was Isaiah.

The Southern Kingdom of Judah was prosperous and outwardly happy during Isaiah's boyhood and youth in King Uzziah's long and successful reign. Uzziah encouraged agriculture and the raising of cattle and some men became rich and built up large estates. Commerce flourished and horses and chariots imported from Egypt were seen everywhere. King Uzziah had strengthened his kingdom's defenses and had won back one of Solomon's ports on the Red Sea. Crowds of worshipers thronged the Temple in Jerusalem and offered incense and sacrifices, confident that in so doing they found favor with the Lord. Judah was prosperous, powerful, and secure.

But Isaiah looked on at all this and was filled with foreboding. He had studied the prophecies of Amos and Hosea and he knew that their denunciations of Israel applied equally well to Israel's southern neighbor, Judah. Isaiah saw that the wealth of a few was obtained by the oppression of many. Great luxury and miserable poverty went hand in hand. Injustice and violence flourished. Religion had become a matter of observing the correct outward forms, instead of a thing of the understanding and the heart. All this Isaiah saw and he knew that Judah had become so self-complacent and satisfied with material things that she had all but forgotten her dependence upon the Lord her God.

One day during the year of King Uzziah's death while Isaiah was worshiping in the Temple in Jerusalem, he saw a vision which changed his whole life. In the sixth chapter of the Book of Isaiah he wrote of this great experience:

"In the year that king Uzziah died I saw also the Lord sitting upon a throne, high and lifted up, and his train filled the temple. Above it stood the seraphims; each one had six wings. With twain he covered his face, and with twain he did fly. And one cried unto another, and said, 'Holy, holy, holy, is the Lord of hosts; the whole earth is full of his glory. . . .'

"Then said I, 'Woe is me! For I am undone, because I am a man of unclean lips, and I dwell in the midst of a people of unclean lips; for mine eyes have seen the King, the Lord of hosts.'

"Then flew one of the seraphims unto me, having a live coal in his hand, which he had taken with tongs from off the altar. And he laid it upon my mouth and said, 'Lo, this hath touched thy lips; and thine iniquity is taken away, and thy sin purged.'

"Also I heard the voice of the Lord, saying, 'Whom shall I send, and who will go for us?' Then said I, 'Here am I! Send me.' And he said, 'Go, and tell this people.'"

With this vision of the holiness of God and his call to prophesy, Isaiah's prophetic mission in Judah began. His messages were often unpopular. They fell upon deaf or uncomprehending ears. The priests and rulers opposed him. He believed that it was useless for Judah to depend upon help from foreign allies, for it was the Lord alone who was her real defense. When a delegation of Judean diplomats went to Egypt to obtain her help, Isaiah poured out the Lord's condemnation in verse:

> "Woe to the rebellious children," saith the Lord,
> "That take counsel, but not of me . . .
> That walk to go down into Egypt,
> And have not asked at my mouth;
> To strengthen themselves in the strength of Pharaoh,
> And to trust in the shadow of Egypt!
> Therefore shall the strength of Pharoah be your shame,
> And the trust in the shadow of Egypt your confusion."
>
> [30:1-3]

Throughout the reigns of three kings, Isaiah continued to warn the people of Judah that no amount of sacrifices would atone for their lack of righteous conduct. When King Hezekiah came to the throne and instituted reforms Isaiah was encouraged. He began to look forward to a day when there would be justice for all, when righteousness would flourish, and when there would be peace. In that happy day

They shall beat their swords into plowshares,
And their spears into pruninghooks;
Nation shall not lift up sword against nation,
Neither shall they learn war any more.   [2:4]

This is the prophet which Michelangelo has portrayed in one of the sections of
his mighty Sistine Chapel frieze. Isaiah sits on a stone bench resting a large book
beside him. He seems to have been reading from this volume when a thought or
inspiration arrested him. With his right hand he holds his place in the book, while
his body and head turn majestically as if to listen to the animated little figure symbolizing inspiration behind him. Clearly it is no ordinary thought that is in the
prophet's mind, for the noble pose of his head and the grave, withdrawn expression of his face show him to be listening with the inner ear of faith to a message
from the Lord. Michelangelo understood so profoundly the nature of prophetic
inspiration that he was able not only to depict here a particular prophet, Isaiah,
but to suggest all prophets who listen and who hear the word of God.

✣

MICAH, THE PROPHET

By

Saul Raskin

(Interpretation)

MICAH was born in Morsheth, a rural community near the city of Gath. Gath had
been under the control of the Philistines for many years until King Uzziah of
Judah conquered it and annexed it to the Southern Kingdom. This city had been
fortified by Rehoboam, Solomon's son, and since Rehoboam's time had been inter-
mittently under the control of the Philistines and the Southern Kingdom. King
Uzziah was king of Judah during Micah's infancy and early childhood, but he was
stricken with leprosy, and the reins of government had passed to the hands of his
son, Jotham, who became regent. During Micah's lifetime five different kings ruled
the throne of Judah—Uzziah, Jotham, Ahaz, Hezekiah, and Manasseh.

Micah was the son of a peasant farmer and loved the community of his birth.
Throughout his long life he was convinced that it was the common people in any
community, the shepherds and the farmers, who were the backbone of a nation's
strength and power. He had learned through conversations with other farmers
about the courageous herdsman-prophet, Amos of Tekoa, who preached to the
Israelites in Samaria, the capital of the Northern Kingdom.

During his young manhood he had known Isaiah and heard his fearless denunciations of the religious and political leaders in Jerusalem. In his own heart Micah
felt the inner flame of prophetic zeal. The more he listened, the more he became
convinced that he, too, would be one of the Lord's prophets.

When he began to prophesy, he warned all nations of the approaching last

ISAIAH—*MICHELANGELO*

judgment when God would come in a great cataclysm. He felt, however, that the city most in need of hearing the voice of the Lord was Samaria; and so his early prophecies were against this center of life in the Northern Kingdom. While the kingdom of Israel had thus far withstood the shock of the Assyrian invasion, all the prophets of Micah's time knew that sooner or later Israel would have to succumb to the Assyrian hordes.

The collapse of Samaria, which Micah and other prophets had predicted, occurred probably two years before King Hezekiah began to reign in Judah. It came when Sargon of Assyria captured the city in 722 B.C.

With the downfall of the Northern Kingdom Micah turned his prophetic voice toward the people of his own land, Judah. He denounced the rich who in their covetousness seized the homes and farms of the poor and sold the women and children of Judah into slavery:

> Woe to men who on their beds
> some mischief plan,
> and carry it out when morning comes,
> because they can!—
> coveting fields and seizing them,
> coveting houses and snatching them,
> crushing yeomen and their homes,
> smallholders and their livings.*
>
> [Micah 2:1, 2]

Next Micah turned to the leaders of the people and in flaming indignation poured out his denunciations:

> Leaders of Jacob, listen to this,
> you judges over the house of Israel,
> who spurn at justice and twist equity,
> who build your Sion up with bloodshed
> and Jerusalem on crime,
> judges passing verdicts for a bribe,
> priests pattering oracles for pay,
> prophets divining for money
> and all the while relying on the Eternal,
> saying, "Surely the Eternal is among us;
> no evil can befall us!"**
>
> [Micah 3:9-11]

In the book of Micah's prophecies can be found the question men of faith ask, What does the Lord require of me? The simple, profound answer sums up the teachings of all the prophets: "To do justly, and to love mercy, and to walk humbly with thy God?" (Micah 6:8).

It is this peasant-prophet that Saul Raskin portrays with such insight and clarity. Commanding the center position stands Micah, the farmer, lifting his eyes

---

* From *The Bible: A New Translation* by James Moffatt. Copyright, 1935, by Harper & Brothers. Used by special permission of the publisher.
** *Ibid.*

MICAH, THE PROPHET—*RASKIN*

from the fields to look toward the distant hills and Jerusalem, center of the religious and political life of his day. In the background is the slave driver of a wealthy landowner with lash raised against those who labor throughout the heat of the day for heartless, grasping landlords. Micah stands between the evils of the country and the corruption of the city, weighed down by the wrongs everywhere committed against his fellow countrymen. He is a powerfully built man, but his shoulders are bent beneath his invisible burden. He begins to raise his right hand as if in entreaty to the Lord. Behind him shines the rising sun, as bright as the hope with which the book of Micah closes: "He will turn again; he will have compassion upon us; he will subdue our iniquities. And thou wilt cast all their sins into the depths of the sea. Thou wilt perform the truth to Jacob, and the mercy of Abraham, which thou hast sworn unto our fathers from the days of old" (7:19-20).

✛

KING JOSIAH AND THE BOOK OF THE LAW

By

Julius Schnorr von Carolsfeld

(Interpretation)

JOSIAH was only eight years old when he succeeded his father, Amon, on the throne of Judah. During the reigns of his grandfather, Manasseh, and of his father, Amon, the worship of strange gods had been introduced into the country. Altars had been built to Baal and images set up in the very Temple at Jerusalem. Men worshiped the sun and moon and stars and made sacrifices to the evil god Molech. But when Josiah was old enough to rule the land himself all this was changed. He chose the Lord God of his mighty ancestors and he served the Lord faithfully throughout the thirty-one years of his long reign.

While Josiah's workmen were repairing the Temple they found an old book which the priest Hilkiah sent to the king. Josiah desired to know what the strange book contained, so his scribe, Shaphan, began reading it aloud to him. It proved to be the Book of the Law and it contained the Laws of God which He had given to Moses but which the people had been disobeying for many years.

"And it came to pass, when the king had heard the words of the book of law, that he rent his clothes" (II Kings 22:11). Josiah was filled with sorrow for the sins of his father and his people and he was alarmed lest the Lord punish them for all their disobedience.

Immediately he set out to reform his kingdom. "And the king sent, and they gathered unto him all the elders of Judah and of Jerusalem. And the king went up into the house of the Lord, and all the men of Judah and all the inhabitants of Jerusalem with him, and the priests, and the prophets, and all the people, both small and great. And he read in their ears all the words of the book of the covenant which was found in the house of the Lord" (II Kings 23:1, 2).

KING JOSIAH AND THE BOOK OF THE LAW—*VON CAROLSFELD*

Then Josiah stood up beside a pillar of the Temple and made a promise for himself and his people: "to walk after the Lord, and to keep his commandments and his testimonies and his statutes with all their heart and all their soul, to perform the words of this covenant that were written in this book" (II Kings 23:3). To ratify their covenant with God all the people stood up.

The king commanded all the altars to foreign gods to be destroyed. Idols were pulled down and burned; the worship of heavenly bodies was forbidden; priests of the pagan cults were ousted; and wizards and soothsayers were banished. Josiah "turned to the Lord with all his heart, and with all his soul, and with all his might, according to all the law of Moses." It was said of him that "like unto him was there no king before him . . . neither after him arose there any like him" (II Kings 23:25).

This engraving from Julius Schnorr von Carolsfeld's *Die Biebel im Bildern* shows the Book of the Law being read to King Josiah. This book comprised most of Deuteronomy. Shaphan the scribe has put his quill pen in his belt and is bending over the old book as he reads. The king has risen from his throne and there is grief on his face as he begins to tear his garments in a gesture of remorse. Outside in the streets of Jerusalem a celebration to the heathen gods is in full swing. People dance, trumpets blare, an image of the sun god is carried in procession, and obeisance is made to a golden calf. The king will soon put an end to all this idolatry and heathen worship. Josiah's efforts to bring his people back to the worship of the true God is one of the inspiring chapters in the history of the Southern Kingdom.

✛

SONG IN THE LAND OF JUDAH

We have a strong city;
Salvation will he appoint for walls and bulwarks.
Open ye the gates,
That the righteous nation which keepeth truth may enter in.
Thou wilt keep him in perfect peace,
Whose mind is stayed on thee, because he trusteth in thee.
Trust thee in the Lord for ever:
For in the LORD JEHOVAH is a Rock of Ages.

For he hath brought down them that dwell on high, the lofty city:
He layeth it low, he layeth it low, even to the ground;
He bringeth it even to the dust.
The foot shall tread it down;
Even the feet of the poor,
And the steps of the needy.

The way of the just is uprightness:
Thou that art upright dost direct the path of the just.
Yea, in the way of thy judgments, O LORD,
Have we waited for thee;

To thy name and to thy memorial
Is the desire of our soul.

With my soul have I desired thee in the night;
Yea, with my spirit within me will I seek thee early:
For when thy judgments are in the earth,
The inhabitants of the world learn righteousness.
Let favour be shewed to the wicked,
Yet will he not learn righteousness;
In the land of uprightness will he deal wrongfully,
And will not behold the majesty of the LORD.*

HOLY FLAME

Isaiah mourned the passing of the king,
And to the temple came to muse and pray.
Dark was the kingdom's future on that day,
Beset with greed and every evil thing.
No spokesman of the Lord was there to sting
The conscience of the mob, or lead the way
To gallant victories in Jehovah's fray
With sin and strife, with self and suffering.

God gave Isaiah then the vision high;
His unclean lips were purged with sacred fire;
Out of the smoke a Voice in challenge came;
Unhesitant, he answered, Here am I.
Again the days are dark, the outlook dire;
Lord, touch Thy prophets now with holy flame.**

—Georgia Harkness

ISAIAH

He mounts on eagle wings with power to span
    The ages' dream, and from his song there grows
    A mighty vision, lovelier than those
The shepherd saw in Rocky Midian,—
A Form that skyward gaze alone can scan,
    Above whose Brow, the star of morning glows,
    Who makes the desert blossom like the rose,
By God begotten, yet the Son of Man.

Watchman on walls of high Jerusalem
    Break into singing, where a throng shall start
    To mock the Beauty of the Sacrificed;

* From *The Literary Study of the Bible* by Richard G. Moulton, p. 420. Published by D. C. Heath and Company. Used by special permission of the publisher.
** From *Holy Flame* by Georgia Harkness, p. 13. Copyright, 1935, by Bruce Humphries, Inc. Used by special permission of the author and the publisher.

Bowed are the cypress and the cedar stem;
  For carrying the lambs against His heart,
  Upon the holy mountain dawns the Christ!*

                                         —*Thomas S. Jones, Jr.*

ISAIAH

Of noble rank, a patriot past compare,
He saw his people grovel in the mire,
By pagan nations dragged to vice and shame;
They knew not God, for truth they had **no** care.
This the world he knew. And yet, above the slime
Of deeds corrupt and thoughts of alien birth,
He raised his eyes and glimpsed a vision high:
Jerusalem redeemed! In some far time
The House of Jacob set upon a hill,
And all the nations thronging to its gates
To learn the way of God, the God of love;
Night should be gone as all men learned His will.
His people could not see that mighty dream
Which held Isaiah with its heavenly gleam.**

                                    —*Thomas Curtis Clark*

LEGISLATORS

Woe unto them that decree unrighteous decrees, and that
  write grievousness which they have prescribed; to
  turn aside the needy from judgment, and to take
  away the right from the poor of my people, that
  widows may be their prey, and that they may rob the
  fatherless!
And what will ye do in the day of visitation, and in the
  desolation which shall come from far? to whom will
  ye flee for help? and where will ye leave your glory?

                    —*Isaiah, Hebrew prophet, 8th century* B.C.

"YOUR HANDS ARE FULL OF BLOOD"

Hear the word of the Lord, ye rulers of Sodom; give ear
  unto the law of our God, ye people of Gomorrah.
To what purpose is the multitude of your sacrifices unto
  me? saith the Lord. . . . Bring no more vain oblations. . . .
When ye spread forth your hands, I will hide mine eyes

from you; yea, when ye make many prayers, I will not
hear: your hands are full of blood.

—Isaiah, Hebrew prophet, 8th century B.C.

SUPPORTED BY GOD

I will carry, and will deliver.—ISAIAH 46:4

The heathen made their gods of stone and gold,
And carried them about as burdens borne;
While prophets told of God that would uphold
And carry man in comfort through the storm.
Is life a painful journey made alone
Across the desert wastes of time and space?
Or is it sweet companionship at home
With God, who carries man in fond embrace?
We ought to know with life we cannot cope
With man-made tools, without some help divine,
Our destiny is wrought by faith and hope,
Permitting God to lead, the way enshrine.
It's joy to carry on the service quest,
When you know God supports you with His best.*

—Henry C. Spear

CHORUS OF WATCHMEN

How beautiful upon the mountains are the feet of him
   That bringeth good tidings, that publisheth peace,
   That bringeth good tidings of good, that publisheth salvation:
That saith unto Zion, Thy God reigneth!

The voice of thy Watchmen! they lift up the voice,
   Together do they sing,
   For they shall see, eye to eye,
How the LORD returneth to Zion.

Break forth into joy, sing together,
   Ye waste places of Jerusalem:
For the LORD hath comforted his people,
   He hath redeemed Jerusalem.

The LORD hath made bare his holy arm
   In the eyes of all the nations;
   And all the ends of the earth
Shall see the salvation of our God.

* From *Sermon Sonnets* by Henry C. Spear, p. 19. Used by special permission of the author.

Depart ye, depart ye, go ye out from thence,
   Touch no unclean thing;
Go ye out of the midst of her;
   Be ye clean, ye that bear the vessels of the LORD.

For ye shall not go out in haste,
   Neither shall ye go by flight;
For the LORD will go before you,
   And the God of Israel will be your rearward.*

                                 —*Isaiah 52:7-12*

THE DESTRUCTION OF SENNACHERIB

The Assyrian came down like the wolf on
   the fold,
And his cohorts were gleaming in purple and
   gold;
And the sheen of their spears was like stars
   on the sea,
When the blue wave rolls nightly on deep
   Galilee.

Like the leaves of the forest when summer is
   green,
That host with their banners at sunset were
   seen;
Like the leaves of the forest when autumn
   hath blown,
That host on the morrow lay withered and
   strown.

For the Angel of Death spread his wings on
   the blast,
And breathed in the face of the foe as he
   passed;
And the eyes of the sleepers waxed deadly
   and chill,
And their hearts but once heaved, and forever
   grew still!

And there lay the steed with his nostrils all
   wide,
But through them there rolled not the breath
   of his pride:
And the foam of his gasping lay white on the
   turf,
And cold as the spray of the rock-beating surf.

* From *The Modern Reader's Bible* edited by Richard G. Moulton, pp. 527-28. Copyright, 1935, by The Macmillan Company. Used by special permission of the publisher.

And there lay the rider distorted and pale,
With the dew on his brow and the rust on his
    mail;
And the tents were all silent, the banners
    alone,
The lances uplifted, the trumpet unblown.

And the widows of Ashur are loud in their wail,
And the idols are broke in the temple of Baal;
And the might of the Gentile, unsmote by the
    sword,
Hath melted like snow in the glance of the
    Lord!

—Lord Byron

GOD'S VENGEANCE

Saith the Lord, "Vengeance is mine";
    "I will repay," saith the Lord;
Ours be the anger divine,
    Lit by the flash of his word.

How shall his vengeance be done?
    How, when his purpose is clear?
Must he come down from the throne?
    Hath he no instruments here?

Sleep not in imbecile trust,
    Waiting for God to begin;
While, growing strong in the dust
    Rests the bruised serpent of sin.

Right and wrong,—both cannot live
    Death-grappled. Which shall we see?
Strike! Only justice can give
    Safety to all that shall be.

Shame! to stand faltering thus,
    Tricked by the balancing odds;
Strike! God is waiting for us!
    Strike! for the vengeance is God's.

—John Hay

THE LORD'S LEADING

Thus far the Lord hath led us, in dark-
    ness and in day.
Through all the varied stages of the
    narrow homeward way;

Long since he took that journey—he
  trod that path alone;
Its trials and its dangers full well
  himself hath known.

Thus far the Lord hath led us; the
  promise hath not failed.
The enemy, encountered oft, has never
  quite prevailed.
The shield of faith has turned aside, or
  quenched each fiery dart,
The Spirit's sword in weakest hands has
  forced him to depart.

Thus far the Lord hath led us; the
  waters have been high,
But yet in passing through them we felt
  that he was nigh.
A very present helper in trouble we
  have found,
His comforts most abounded when our
  sorrows did abound.

Thus far the Lord hath led us; our need
  hath been supplied,
And mercy hath encompassed us about
  on every side;
Still falls the daily manna; the pure
  rock-fountains flow;
And many flowers of love and hope
  along the wayside grow.

Thus far the Lord hath led us; and will
  he now forsake
The feeble ones whom for his own it
  pleases him to take?
Oh, never, never! earthly friends may
  cold and faithless prove,
But his is changeless pity and everlasting
  love.

Calmly we look behind us, our joys and
  sorrows past,
We know that all is mercy now, and
  shall be well at last;
Calmly we look before us; we fear no
  future ill,
Enough for safety and for peace, if *Thou*
  art with us still.

Yes, they that know thy name, Lord,
  shall put their trust in thee,
While nothing in themselves but sin and
  helplessness they see.
The race thou hast appointed us with
  patience we can run,
Thou wilt perform unto the end the
  work thou hast begun.

—Author Unknown

THE PILGRIM

(Psalm 84)

"O Lord, how amiable Thy dwelling-place!
How bright Thine altars gleam!" The pilgrim trod
With weary feet the Judean dust to trace
Again the path to Zion and to God.
His soul athirst, and fainting in the way,
He longed for Zion's courts. There he would rest,
At home like sparrow at the close of day,
At home like mother swallow on her nest.

"How blessed is the man whose strength is Thine,"
The traveler cried. "O Lord, how blessed he
Within whose heart are highways! Though as brine
The vale of woe he treads, springs flow from Thee!"
Refreshed and singing joyously, he came
To where the altars glowed with living flame.*

—Georgia Harkness

THE TAUNT-SONG OF SENNACHERIB

(2 Kings 19:21-28)

I. *The Translation*

Jerusalem laughs at thy threats, thou blasphemer of the Holy One of Israel. (2 Kings 19: 21-24)	She laughs at thee, despises thee, The virgin daughter of Zion; She only shakes her head at thee, Jerusalem's fair daughter.
	Whom hast thou scorned and whom blasphemed, Against whom hast thou raised thy voice, And lifted up thine eyes on high? The Holy One of Israel!

* From *Holy Flame* by Georgia Harkness, p. 40. Copyright, 1935, by Bruce Humphries, Inc. Used by special permission of the author and the publisher.

By messengers thou hast provoked
Yahwe, and said: "I will ascend
With chariots the mountains high,
The deepest woods of Lebanon:

"Its cedars tall, its choice fir-trees,
Its farthest lodge I will cut down;
Strange waters I will dig and drink,
Will with my foot dry Egypt's stream.

Didst thou
not realize
that thou
art my tool?
(2 Kings 19:
25, 26)

"Hast thou not heard it from afar,
What I have done in ancient times?
I bring about what I have planned:
Thou shouldst make cities into heaps.

"The dwellers in them have no power,
They wither up like the field's herbs,
The green grass, on house-top the flower,
The field of grain, when east wind blows.

I will sum-
marily turn
thee back.
(2 Kings 19:
27, 28)

"Thy sitting down, thy going out,
Thy coming in, I know it well.
Because thy raging against me,
Thy pride has come into my ears.

"My hook I will put in thy nose,
Will place my bridle in thy lips,
Will turn thee back the self-same way,
By which thou camest to this place."*

SIMPLE TRUST

I do not know why sin abounds
    Within this world so fair,
Why numerous discordant sounds
    Destroy the heavenly air—
I can't explain this thing, I must
    Rely on God in simple trust.

I do not know why pain and loss
    Oft fall unto my lot.
Why I must bear the heavy cross
    When I desire it not—
I do not know, unless 'tis just
    To teach my soul in God to trust.

I know not why the evil seems
    Supreme on every hand:

Why suffering flows in endless streams
   I do not understand—
Solution comes not to adjust
   These mysteries. I can but trust.

I do not know why grief's dark cloud
   Bedims my sunny sky,
The tear of bitterness allowed
   To swell within my eye—
But, sorrow-stricken to the dust,
   I will look up to God and trust.

                                    —*R. F. Mayer*

A SONG OF TRUST

I cannot always see the way that leads
   To heights above;
I sometimes quite forget that he leads on
   With hands of love;
But yet I know the path must lead me to
   Immanuel's land,
And when I reach life's summit
   I shall know and understand.

I cannot always trace the onward course
   My ship must take,
But, looking backward, I behold afar
   Its shining wake
Illumined with God's light of love;
   and so, I onward go,
In perfect trust that he who holds the
   helm the source must know.

I cannot always see the plan on which
   He builds my life;
For oft the sound of hammers, blow
   on blow, the noise of strife,
Confuse me till I quite forget he knows
   And oversees,
And that in all details with his good
   plan my life agrees.

I cannot always know and understand
   The Master's rule;
I cannot always do the tasks he gives
   In life's hard school;
But I am learning with his help, to solve
   Them one by one,
And, when I cannot understand, to say,
   "Thy will be done."

                          —*Gertrude Benedict Custis*

WISDOM AND DISCIPLINE

Whate'er my God ordains is right;
   His will is ever just;
Howe'er he orders now my cause
   I will be still, and trust.
      He is my God,
      Though dark my road,
He holds me that I shall not fall,
Therefore to him I leave it all.

Whate'er my God ordains is right;
   He never will deceive;
He leads me by the proper path,
   And so to him I cleave,
      And take, content
      What he hath sent;
His hand can turn my grief away,
And patiently I wait his day.

Whate'er my God ordains is right;
   He taketh thought for me;
The cup that my Physician gives
   No poisoned draught can be,
      But medicine due;
      For God is true;
And on that changeless truth I build
And all my heart with hope is filled.

Whate'er my God ordains is right;
   Though I the cup must drink
That bitter seems to my faint heart,
   I will not fear nor shrink;
      Tears pass away
      With dawn of day;
Sweet comfort yet shall fill my heart,
And pain and sorrow all depart.

Whate'er my God ordains is right;
   My Light, my Life, is he,
Who cannot will me aught but good;
   I trust him utterly;
      For well I know,
      In joy or woe,
We soon shall see, as sunlight clear,
How faithful was our Guardian here.

Whate'er my God ordains is right;
   Here I will take my stand;

Though sorrow, need, or death make earth
  For me a desert land
    My Father's care
    Is round me there;
He holds me that I shall not fall,
And so to him I leave it all.

                  —*S. Rodigast*

THE MESSAGE OF MICAH

Woe to them that devise iniquity and work evil.—MICAH 2:1

A peasant from Jerusalem to the sea
Declared to Isr'el transgression and sin;
Proclaimed God hurt by immorality;
Pronounced the doom he saw was surging in.
What was the sin of old Jerusalem?
It was the grandeur, ground out of the poor;
Devisers of iniquity, condemn!
The mills of God grind slowly, but so sure.
"What doth a holy God require of thee?"
(But princes, prophets, priests knew not their God)
"It's justice, kindness, and humility,"
That stays Almighty's disciplining rod.
Those who cry, "Peace," and then prepare for wars
Will not be in the remnant that restores.*

                  —*Henry C. Spear*

THE PROMISE OF MICAH

What doth the Lord require of thee, he said,
But justice, kindness, and to walk with God?
Thus Micah spake. But proud Jerusalem
Had deafened ears and hearts of stone. The head
Of Israel was bloody; hate and greed
And violence were hers. Samaria
And Judah should strong nations devastate.
And yet, a remnant! Out of it a seed
Should grow. From Bethlehem should dawn bright hope;
And in the mountains should be set the House
Of God; all people there should worship Him,
The Lord of all the earth. Men should not grope
In sin and night. Then lasting peace should be,
And God should rule His realm from sea to sea.**

                  —*Thomas Curtis Clark*

* Used by special permission of the author.
** Used by special permission of the author.

THE FOOLISH YOUNG KING

By

Florence M. Earlle

KING SOLOMON had died and the people had made a great mourning for him as was the custom. Yet many in their hearts were glad, for the king had laid such a heavy burden of taxation upon them that it was almost unbearable. They knew that the young prince, Rehoboam, did not have the wisdom of his father. They knew, too, that there would be no building of a palace or a wonderful Temple. They were proud, of course, of the Temple—the building of which King David had planned and gathered materials, and which his son Solomon had built—but it had been costly and taxation was constantly increased. Perhaps Rehoboam would be merciful and lighten their taxes.

Now there had been in the kingdom a young man named Jeroboam. He had been appointed by Solomon as an overseer of the building of the city of Millo and of the repairing of the breeches of the walls about Jerusalem. But one day a spy brought word to the king of the peculiar action of the prophet, Ahijah.

He said: "I saw him catch a new cloak from the shoulders of Jeroboam as the two were in the field together. The prophet tore it into twelve pieces. Ten of these he handed back to Jeroboam. I did not hear what he said, but I did hear Jeroboam answer, 'What, for me to rule over?'"

Solomon knew at once what had happened. God had warned him over and over that if he turned to idol worship, he would lose his kingdom. In the last warning, He had said: "Because you have not kept my covenants and laws, I will surely take the kingdom away from you and give it to your servant. For your father David's sake, I will not take it away from you; but I will from your son. Yet still for David's sake, I will let your son keep a part of the kingdom—a small part."

So Solomon tried to kill Jeroboam, for he was certain that he was the servant God had meant. But the young man fled to Egypt. Now, upon learning of the death of Solomon, Jeroboam returned; and the people were glad to see him, for he was a man of valor. They did not know there was any prophecy concerning him, but they did think he would be a good man to present their request to the young king for the reducing of their taxes.

All the tribes went to Shechem to crown Rehoboam king. When the elaborate ceremonies were over, and Rehoboam was seated upon his throne, Jeroboam appeared before him.

"O King, live forever! I have a petition to present. The people are weary of the heavy taxes which your father placed upon them. It is hard for a man to grow a field of grain and be forced to give up more than half of it to support the court. It is bitter to have to give up more than two-thirds of all the cattle he raises to feed the king's household. We beg of your majesty that you will be merciful to your servants and demand less taxes of us. Then we will serve you loyally and joyfully."

The king hesitated. Then he said. "I must have time to think these things over. Go to your homes and return in three days and I will answer you then."

For the people the three days were full of doubt and speculation. "Do you think he will grant our request?"

"He had better. What good is living if we have nothing to live for but to support the king and his court?"

"What shall we do if he doesn't?"

"Do? We'll rebel!"

"Oh God forbid! We must have a king, no matter how cruel he is."

"Oh yes, we will have a king, but it need not be Rehoboam."

"Do you mean he will be killed?"

"No, I have a plan. Keep this a secret. Do you know that several years ago the prophet Ahijah told Jeroboam that he would be king over the ten tribes? Solomon tried to kill him. That is why he fled to Egypt."

A secret? Not for long, for Jeroboam had quietly started that report. Before long all Israel knew that they would rebel if Rehoboam refused their plea.

Meanwhile the young king called together his father's counselors.

"Heed them, O King," they pleaded. "If you will lighten the taxes, they will be loyal and serve you. You know that the taxes are exceedingly heavy. There is no need now for such since the palace and the Temple have been built. Be wise and grant the people their request."

"I'll think over what you have said," answered the young king. Then he dismissed them and called the "wise men" he had chosen. These were young men near his own age.

"What do you think I should do?" he asked.

They answered, "You are the king. If you heed the request of the people now, they will be forever asking you to do something for them. If you make the taxes lighter, you won't be able to keep up the court as it was in your father's time. You don't want other nations to say that you are not as great as your father. Tell them that as your father beat them with whips, you will beat them with more cruel ones. Tell them that your little finger shall be heavier on them than your father's whole body would have been. You are the king! Make them know it!"

"You are right!" said Rehoboam. "I am the king!"

When the people returned at the end of three days, the young king said, "My father made your yoke heavy, but I will add to it. He chastised you with whips, but I will chastise you with scorpions."

And when the people understood that the new king planned to be far harder on them than Solomon had been, and that he would show no mercy, they rebelled.

Jeroboam, who had picked men in all the tribes to lead the revolt if their request was not granted, raised the cry of rebellion—"To your tents, O Israel! What part do we have in the inheritance of David? Neither will we follow any longer a descendant of Jesse. To your tents, O Israel!"

So all the tribes except Judah and Benjamin deserted Rehoboam and returned to their homes in anger. Then they called Jeroboam and made him their king.

These tribes thereafter came to be known as the kingdom of Israel, while those remaining under Rehoboam and his descendants were called the kingdom of Judah.*

✝

THE GOOD KING JEHOSHAPHAT

By

Florence M. Earlle

JEHOSHAPHAT had succeeded his father Asa on the throne of Judah. He followed in the ways of Asa, taking away the high places of the idol shrines and worshiping God instead of Baal. And the Lord prospered him. In the third year of his reign, he appointed his priests and Levites to go throughout the land and teach the people the fear of God.

Then he made an alliance with Ahab, king of Israel. After several years, he went to visit Ahab. The king of Israel made a great feast for his guests, for Jehoshaphat had taken many of the members of his court and part of his army with him. Then Ahab said to Jehoshaphat,

"Will you go up with me to Ramoth-Gilead and fight the king of Syria?"

"Yes," said Jehoshaphat. "You and I are one and my people and your people are one. We will be with you in war. But wait. Let us inquire of the Lord about this battle."

Ahab gathered before him four hundred prophets and said to them, "Shall we go up to battle with Syria, or shall we stay here?"

All four hundred said, "Go up. God will deliver the enemy into your hands."

But Jehoshaphat was not satisfied.

"Isn't there another prophet of the Lord that we might inquire of him?"

"Oh yes, there is one, named Micaiah. He is the son of Imlah; but I hate him, for he has never prophesied anything but evil for me."

"Oh, don't say that; please call him."

So Ahab gave orders that Micaiah should come before the king. The messenger who went for the prophet said, "All the other prophets declare good to the king. If you are wise, you will agree with them."

"What God tells me to speak, I'll speak," answered Micaiah. When he was ushered into the presence of the king, Ahab said,

"Shall we go up to Ramoth-Gilead, or shall we not?"

Micaiah answered in a mocking tone, "Of course! Go up and prosper. The enemy will be delivered into your hands."

Ahab demanded angrily, "How many times do I have to command you to tell the truth? Tell me now, 'in the name of the Lord,' shall we go up or not?"

"I saw all Israel scattered upon the mountain like sheep having no shepherd. The Lord said, 'These have no master; let them return in peace every man to his own house!'"

* Used by special permission of the author.

Ahab turned to Jehoshaphat. "Did I not tell thee that he would not prophesy anything but evil for me?"

But Micaiah was not done speaking.

"Hear the word of the Lord. I saw Him sitting on His throne, surrounded by the hosts of heaven. And He said, 'Who will entice Ahab that he may go up to Ramoth-Gilead and die there?' Several suggestions were made. Then a spirit came and stood before the Lord. 'I will entice him. I will go out and be a lying spirit in the mouths of all his prophets.' And the Lord said, 'Go!' "

Then one of the prophets of Israel stepped out and slapped the cheek of Micaiah.

"Which way went the spirit of the Lord from me to speak to you?" he sneered.

Micaiah answered, "You will see him on that day when you run into an inner room to hide yourself."

Ahab turned to his servants. "Take this man to Amon, the governor of the city and to my son, Joash. Tell them to keep him and feed him on bread and water till I return in peace."

Micaiah turned away. "If you ever do return in peace," he said, "the Lord has not spoken by me!"

In spite of the prophet's warning, Jehoshaphat went with Ahab to Ramoth-Gilead. Then Ahab suggested, "You put on my robes. I am going to disguise myself when I go into the battle," and Jehoshaphat foolishly agreed.

Now the Syrian commander had ordered that the soldiers concentrate on killing the king of Israel. Consequently, when they saw the royal chariot, they thought it contained Ahab, and surrounded it. Jehoshaphat cried out, "I am not Ahab!" and the soldier who had drawn his sword, turned back. But the captain saw that one certain chariot was speeding for the gate of the city. It looked suspicious and he ordered that the man in that chariot be shot at. The arrow reached its mark, and Ahab sank down wounded. He said to his driver, "Take me out of the host." All day the battle raged, and Ahab braced himself against the side of the chariot and watched. But at sunset he died.

Jehoshaphat returned to his house in Jerusalem and was met by the prophet, Jehu:

"Why should you help the ungodly and love them that hate God? Therefore God is angry with you. Nevertheless because you have destroyed the idols in the land, He will not forsake you."

After this Jehoshaphat restored the order of worship throughout his kingdom. He set up a system of judges charging them to fear God and to serve Him with perfect hearts.

Near the end of his reign the Moabites and the Ammonites joined forces and came up against Jerusalem. The king was terrified. He proclaimed a fast and gathering the people together in Jerusalem, he went to the Temple and prayed for help. And God sent a prophet to him with the message: "Thus saith the Lord— the battle is not yours, but God's. Do not be afraid by reason of this multitude. Go down to the battle, but you need not fight. Stand still and see the salvation of the Lord for He will be with you."

Jehoshaphat bowed his face to the ground and worshiped, and all the people did likewise. It was as the prophet had said, for the armies fought among themselves and destroyed each other. For Judah there was the spoil of battle, and it was so great, that they were three days collecting it from the battlefield.

And Jehoshaphat reigned twenty-five years, and he did that which was right in the sight of Jehovah.*

✦

HEZEKIAH THE DEVOUT

By

George Matheson

HEZEKIAH is one of the Jewish heroes. There is no picture in the Old Testament Gallery on which his countrymen have so prolonged their gaze. He shines out as the second David, as the nearest approach to the glory of the nation's age of gold. And yet all this is an illusion. When we scrutinise the picture, the impression is not sustained. There is no real analogy between Hezekiah and David. In one sense, there is a contrast. David is a natural genius illuminated by grace; Hezekiah is a commonplace mind illuminated by grace. David is inherent beauty rendered more attractive by dress; Hezekiah is inherent plainness to which dress imparts a beauty. David is a rich nature intensified; Hezekiah is a meagre nature enriched.

What, then, shall be our inscription on the life of this king? Shall we call him great? No; he did not really arrest the decadence of his country. Shall we call him brave? No; we shall see that, naturally, he was deficient in courage. Shall we call him wise? No; we shall find that, in his own strength, he exhibited a shallow policy. But it is quite a common thing to see a soul transformed by the advent of a great love into qualities the opposite of its own. Love makes the timid brave, love makes the foolish wise. So was it with Hezekiah. There came to him at a certain moment of his life the sense of a great love. I know not when it broke upon him; judging from the concluding verse of 2 Chron. XXIX, I should say its influence was sudden—dating from the solemn hour of his coronation. What was this mighty love which entered the soul of Hezekiah? It was no earthly passion, no sensuous attachment, no worldly preoccupation of the heart. It was that form of love which is found in saints and martyrs—the love of God. Yet upon this man it had the same effect as any earthly passion—it transformed him . . . made a new creature of him. It gave firmness to a vacillating nature; it lent energy to a weak will; it inspired boldness in a naturally shrinking spirit. Hezekiah is, in truth, a type of the man under the influence of a religious revival. He represents the commonplace mind possessed by a new emotion. He stands as the symbol of that exaltation which may come to a very ordinary life when fired by Divine enthusiasm. He typifies that empire over which he rules—an empire humanly insignificant, slenderly endowed, meagrely furnished, inadequately equipped for a struggle with surrounding forces, yet rearing a proud head and presenting a brave front, through the promises and the potencies of a unique religious faith.

* Used by special permission of the author.

Hezekiah, then, is essentially the devout man—the man of God; this is his distinctive characteristic; apart from this he is nothing. As I study his portrait in the Great Gallery, four successive scenes rise into view. I will call them metaphorically the four hours in Hezekiah's day—the hour in the street, the hour on the sea, the hour in the vale, and the hour on the hill. Each reveals a separate aspect of the religious life—an aspect as familiar to modern England as it was to the heart of ancient Israel. Let us consider these four manifestations of the Divine life as exhibited in the experience of Hezekiah.

The first scene opens in the street—amid the surging of the crowd. Hezekiah is seen gazing on that crowd. He is twenty-five years old; he has been called to the throne by the death of his father Ahaz. And suddenly it occurs to him that by the fact of his kinghood he stands to that multitude in a new relation. It seems to him that he has become this morning the man responsible for the sins of the people, the man on whose shoulders must fall the burden of all the evil they may do. He feels himself lifted to a high moral altitude—a height which makes him dizzy with its terrible suggestions of a fall. In the eyes of the young king the fall, so far as the multitude are concerned, is already an accomplished fact. He sees a city wholly given to idolatry—the idolising of pleasures which are not pure. He sees that the life of his father has been the cause of this badness, that the crowd have taken their morals from the crown. He sees that the crown must give back to the people that virtue of which it has despoiled them, that it has fallen to him to make atonement for his father's sins. He feels that the attractions to an irreligious life must be suppressed at all hazards and by the most drastic means. The people must be drawn from the worship of the world to the worship of God, and they must be drawn by the shutting of the world's gates. Let their pleasures be prohibited! Let their carnal haunts be closed! Let their gaming-tables be broken! Let their drinking orgies be forbidden! Let their luxury in dress be restrained and their extravagant expenditure moderated! Put out the world's street-lamps and leave its votaries in the dark; then, perhaps, will they seek the kingdom of God!

So closed Hezekiah's first hour—the hour in the street. When he next appears before us, the scene is changed. If his morning hour is in the street, his forenoon hour is, metaphorically, on the sea. There has come a storm. The ship of the Jewish State is lashed with foam and her timbers are creaking. That storm is Sennacherib. Sennacherib is coming with all the host of Assyria—Sennacherib the impious, the terrible. He is coming to ravage the City of God—to destroy the dwelling-place of the Most High. Who shall withstand the day of his appearing? Already have the surrounding nations sunk before him. Even the land of Samaria has fallen— the twin sister of Judah, the twin daughter of Jacob. What will Hezekiah do? Any ancient gallery but that of the Bible would, in the interest of a national hero, have concealed what follows. Any ancient gallery but that of the Bible would have depicted its Hezekiah as coming forth to die—hopeless of the fight, yet ready for the martyr's doom. But the Bible has an artistic purpose to fulfill far beyond the flattering of national patriotism. It shows Hezekiah as he was. It represents him in the first instance as frightened, trembling, panic-struck. He flies to the temple. He gathers the silver which had been stored there. He strips the doors and the pillars of the gold with which he had beautified them. He dismantles that house of God which he had just adorned; he despoils it of its treasures. He brings out these treasures. He sends them as a tribute to Sennacherib. He prostrates himself in vassalage. He purchases peace by the wealth meant for the Lord.

Are you surprised that I regard this exposure of Hezekiah's weakness as a stroke of art? Do you not see that, if a man is to be painted whose strength is in God alone, it must be shown that he has no natural strength? What is the problem which the Bible artist has here before him? It is the depicting of a life that shall be timid by nature and brave by grace. Could anything be better done, more artistically done? We see at the outset the man Hezekiah as nature made him—a most unheroic figure, an abject, trembling figure. We see a soul paralysed with terror in the presence of his foe, speechless and prostrate before a danger which he is powerless to avert and impotent to face. But even as we gaze upon the humiliating spectacle we feel that it is to be but the dark background of a great glory. We feel that it is meant to intensify something which the pencil is about to produce. That something is a delineation of what can be done by the unaided grace of God. You have seen a conjurer offer to put articles into an empty box through supernatural channels. The first thing he does is to make you quite sure that the box is empty. "Look at it!" he says, "be certain there is nothing in it!" So it is with this artist of Divine things. He says, "I am going to show you that God can put treasures into a vacant mind. Be quite certain at the outset that this mind *is* vacant! Look at this poor creature Hezekiah! See how empty he is, how barren he is, how useless he is! See what a poor, shivering, trembling soul he is by nature—how unable to be a man, how unfit to be a king! Truly the box is empty!"

By and by the box is shut; and when next it is opened, a startling spectacle presents itself—the vacant space has been filled! We see nothing to account for the change. No hand has been visible at work, no process of replenishment has been observed. . . . In a short time after the manifestation of his abject terror, Hezekiah appears before us full of courage, radiant with hope. . . . There is no more ground for natural hope now than there was when he lay grovelling in fear. Sennacherib has not departed. The Assyrian host had not declined. The resources of Judah have not increased. . . .

Whence, then, came this transformation of Hezekiah? From within. It was a strengthening of the mind. He has sought a place of prayer in the interval, and that place had made a man of him. He had gone in, a coward; he came out, a hero. The whole art of the picture is made to center in the breath of God. Hezekiah in himself is nothing; he is only strong in the presence of the Lord. The triumph of the Divine Spirit, as exhibited by this artist, does not lie in the destruction of Sennacherib's host. It lies in the transformation of Hezekiah. It lies in the fact that the breath of God can make a coward brave, a craven bold, a pessimist hopeful, a mourner joyous, a croucher kingly. That was the real victory over the power of Sennacherib.

The third scene comes. It is Hezekiah's hour in the vale. It is a distinctly different experience from the other two. These had one thing in common—they were both public scenes. The danger in the street and the danger in the storm were dangers which Hezekiah shared with his *people*. But now there has dawned for him an hour of solitary trouble—that kind of trouble hardest to bear. He is prostrated on a bed of sickness—on what to all appearance is a bed of death. And here we are confronted by a paradox—one of those touches of artistic originality which are peculiar to the Gallery of the Bible. It is no uncommon thing to find men shrink back from the dark valley. But what causes them to shrink back is commonly supposed to be the sense of their own unworthiness. Here, we have an extraordinary combination of the sense of fear with the sense of rectitude—a blending of feelings to which I can recall no parallel. At one and the same moment Hezekiah experiences an intense shrinking from death and an intense conviction of having done his duty. He had displayed timidity before the host of Sennacherib; but on that occasion he had forgotten the presence of God. Here, he displays the same timidity in the full view of God's presence. He is quite conscious that God is beside him; he is quite certain that his soul is in a right attitude towards God. Yet, in spite of his sense of rectitude, in spite of the approving voice of his own conscience, he is filled with deepest loathing for the Valley of the Shadow. We can account for the *bad* man's terror in the hour of death; we can account for the sadness at such an hour from the sense of a work unfulfilled; but how are we to explain such a combination as this—"I beseech Thee, O Lord, remember now how I have walked before Thee in truth and with a perfect heart, and have done that which is good in Thy sight. And Hezekiah wept sore."

I explain it by an appeal to sober fact. I say it is on the spiritualized nature that death bears most heavily. What else does Paul mean when he says, "If in this life only we have hope, we are of all men most miserable"?! He means that a man who, like Hezekiah, is without the hope of immortality will at the approach of death be sad just in proportion to the spiritual height of his nature. . . . To a man with such a conviction death, if it comes without the hope of immortality, must come as a foe. I have been greatly struck with one of the utterances of a Psalmist of Israel when lying under the shadow of the dark valley, "In death there is no remembrance of Thee; in the grave who will give Thee thanks!" His one sigh was for parting with *God;* his one lament was for losing the presence of God; his one tear was for cancelling the soul's remembrance of God. He does not say, "I grieve to quit the flowers and woods and hills." He does not cry, "I mourn to leave the purple and fine linen and sumptuous fare of the world's day." All these are forgotten in one poignant pain, "In death there is no remembrance of Thee."

I come to the fourth hour—the hour on the hill. For the first time in his life Hezekiah has an unclouded prospect. His days have been prolonged; he has been restored to health and strength. The enthusiastic devotion of his people has welcomed him back from the gates of death. Rich offerings of thanksgiving pour into the treasury. At home and abroad the hearts of men are opened to signify their gratitude for his restoration, and from all quarters costly gifts flow in. It is the only moment of his reign in which Hezekiah has been free from struggle.

All the preceding scenes had been scenes fraught with fear; this is a mountain view, a cloudless view, the view given by a summer day.

And now comes the strange thing. This hour of prosperity, this hour on the hill, is the only hour in which Hezekiah suffers actual loss. He has passed through the furnaces of sorrow and got no hurt; but he is singed by the blaze of prosperity. "Singed" is indeed the word. He is not burned, he is not scorched, he is not disabled; it is but a grazing of the wing; yet it dims the wing's beauty. The bird does not fall from the sky; but he flies lower. Hezekiah does not commit a great sin. What he reveals is a petty weakness—a pride of material display. He is like a child with a new toy. He throws open his treasures to the inspection of the king of Babylon. In thus tempting the Babylonian he prepares a fall for his own descendants; but it is not in this I see his loss. His loss is from within. He has dropped something of the *inner* gold; he has become proud of the wrong thing. He has become satisfied, also, with the wrong security. When told that his conduct will bring ruin to his successors, he says, in effect, "Never mind, there will be peace in *my* time." This jars upon us. A king should not only be his own keeper, but his brother's keeper. He is meant to be more than the custodian of his personal power; he is set to guard the power of those who come after him. Is it not a pity we have this parting blot in the narrative! Should not art have secured a cloudless ending! Why bring Hezekiah triumphantly through his actual troubles, and obscure the glory of that hour when his troubles have passed away!

Now, I say that the art has been beautiful, consummate. It supplies the one lesson that Judaism needed. . . . That a man should be tarnished in the street, that a man should be shaken on the sea, that a man should be depressed in the vale—all this was felt to be natural. But that a man should be corrupted on the hill, that the hour of *prosperity* should be an hour of moral danger—this was a new thing. Men had learned to pray, "In all time of our tribulation, in the hour of death, and in the day of judgment, good Lord deliver us!" but they had not learned to pray, "Deliver us in all time of our *wealth!*" They could see the need for a rod and staff in passing through the Valley of the Shadow; but to cry for a rod and staff in passing through the green pastures and standing by the quiet waters—that was a strange prayer. And that was the prayer taught by Hezekiah's hill. It told the Jew not to limit his dread to the precipice. It told him to beware of the *flowers.* It bade him seek God in his sunshine. It revealed that the thorn was not man's greatest calamity. It inspired distrust of the rose, distrust of the summer day. It taught that the shade was required as well as the shining. It exhorted the human spirit not to despise the shadows cast by the tree of life. That was the high lesson proclaimed by Hezekiah's hill.*

* Abridged from *Representative Men of the Bible* (Second Series) by George Matheson, pp. 242-63. Published by Hodder & Stoughton, Ltd. Used by special permission of the publisher.

KING HEZEKIAH AND THE ASSYRIAN CONQUEST

By

Grace Ordway Spear

AHAZ, son of Jotham, a young prince of twenty years of age, had come to the throne in Judah. There was every reason why his reign should be a prosperous one, for he had come of a goodly heritage; both his father and his grandfather (King Uzziah) had been good kings and had set him an example in righteous living. Ahaz, however, did not follow in the ways of his father, but did evil against the Lord God. Not only did he erect heathen idols of wood and stone and worship them himself; he also succumbed to the abominable practice of the Baal worshipers and burned his own sons on the altar fires.

At this time Rezen, king of Syria, came with his armies to attack Jerusalem and besieged Ahaz and carried away a great multitude of his people as captives. Ahaz sent messengers to the king of Assyria, saying: "Come up and deliver me from the hand of the king of Syria and from the hand of the king of Israel." He also sent by the messengers rich gifts for him—gold and silver which he found in the temple and in his treasure house. The king of Assyria received the messengers and the gifts which they brought. After listening to Ahaz's plea, he went up to Damascus, captured the city and carried away the inhabitants, and killed Rezen, the king of Syria.

Then Ahaz, king of Judah, went up to meet Tiglath-pileser, king of Assyria, whom he had besought to come to his aid. While at Damascus, Ahaz saw the altar that was in the heathen temple, and he was greatly attracted to it. He secured the pattern of the altar and sent a model to Urija, the priest in his own temple in Judah, with all instructions for making one like it. Urija immediately set to work and had the altar finished when Ahaz, the king, arrived home. Ahaz removed the bronze altar of the Lord to one side and gave the new heathen altar the place of prominence in the temple. He also ordered all the sacrifices and offerings of the people to be made at the altar modeled after the one at Damascus. He also commanded Urija, the priest, to receive them there. Ahaz reasoned within himself—"Because the gods of the king of Syria helped them, therefore I will sacrifice to them that they may help me, also."

Meanwhile, Hoshea ruled over Samaria, and that country, too, was attacked by Shalmaneser, king of Assyria. Hoshea was taken captive and ordered to pay heavy tribute to Shalmaneser. Hoshea did this for many months; then he formed a plot against the Assyrian king and stopped paying the tribute moneys. King Shalmaneser learned of the conspiracy against himself, and took Hoshea and shut him up in prison; and he carried all the people of Israel as captives into Assyria and placed them in the city of the Medes.

Now the children of Israel had sinned against the Lord their God and followed after Baal. They forgot the goodness of God in bringing them up out of the land of Egypt and rescuing them from the cruel slavery of Pharaoh. They again built heathen idols and offered sacrifices to them, cursing the Lord God and heeding not His words: "Thou shalt have no other gods before me!" Yet God remembered that they were His children. He loved them in spite of their evil ways, and He sought, through His prophets and seers, to bring them to repent and to return unto Himself. Again and again He pleaded with them, saying, "Turn from your evil ways and keep my commandments!"

But the people would not listen to God's voice and continued to reject His laws. Moreover, they failed to keep the promises their fathers had made to God. They became proud and haughty; they made molten images and worshiped them instead of God. They ceased to train their sons and daughters in the ways of the Lord, and encouraged them to worship the heathen god—Baal. Seeking no longer to serve Jehovah, they fell into the hands of their enemies and were carried away out of their own country into the land of Assyria, and other peoples took possession of their cities.

Far away from their homeland, the captive Israelites had time to think and to repent of their wickedness. They remembered their disloyalty to God and wanted the people remaining in Judah to walk in the way of the Lord. So they besought the king of Assyria to send a priest to teach them God's law. The king granted their plea and sent a priest to instruct the people in Samaria. The people received the priest and listened to his words; they were willing to accept belief in the One God of Israel, but they had so long worshiped their heathen gods that they could *see* and *touch,* that it was difficult—yes, well-nigh impossible—for them to give up these heathen customs entirely. Therefore, the religion in Samaria became a confusion of the idol worship of Baal and the worship of the true God, and thus it has remained for them and their children even unto this day.

When Hezekiah became king of Judah, he promised to be a good king. He put his trust in Jehovah and kept His commandments. He broke down the altars of the heathen gods and cleansed the temple, and led the people of his kingdom in the ways of the Lord. His reign was propsperous, and the country was no longer subservient to the king of Assyria, for God was with Hezekiah in all that he did.

In the fourteenth year after he came to the throne, Hezekiah's faith was severely tested. Sennacherib, now king of Assyria, came up against all the fortified cities of Judah, intending to take them. When Hezekiah saw that Sennacherib had come determined to attack Jerusalem, he held a council of his princes and the leading men of his kingdom. They decided to stop up the water of the fountains that were without the city, for said Hezekiah, "Why should we let the Assyrians come and find abundant water?" The people all fell to work and stopped up all the fountains outside the city. They also, at the king's command, built up the city wall that had been torn down, and made another outside wall. Moreover, they replenished their stock of weapons and their shields. King Hezekiah then set commanders of war over the people, gathered them together in the open space at the gate of the city, and spoke to them thus: "Be strong and of good courage, my people! Fear not, neither be dismayed because of the king of Assyria, nor of his great armies. For there is One greater with us than with him. The Lord, our God is with us and He will help us to fight our battles!"

After this, Sennacherib, king of Assyria, sent messengers to Jerusalem with a letter, taunting King Hezekiah and his people, saying: "What confidence are you trusting now to save you from the hand of the king of Assyria? Do you still say, 'Our God will surely deliver us!'? Know you not what I and my fathers have done to all the peoples of all the lands we have conquered? Do not let Hezekiah deceive you. There is no god of any nation or kingdom who has been able to deliver his people from our hands—neither shall your God deliver you!" And the Assyrians shouted in a loud voice to the people on the wall to frighten and terrify them that they might take the city.

But Hezekiah prepared himself and went into the house of the Lord and prayed: "O Lord, the God of Israel! Thou art God, even thou alone, over all the kingdoms of the earth. Thou hast made the heavens and the earth. Incline Thine ear, O Lord, and hear my prayer! The Assyrian is at our doors to lay waste our land. But now, O Lord, deliver us, I pray Thee, from his hand that all the kingdoms of the earth may know that Thou, O God, art God alone!"

And Jehovah heard Hezekiah's prayer in the temple and sent unto him his prophet, Isaiah, saying: "God hath heard thy prayer, Hezekiah, and He will be with thee in thy trouble. For the king of Assyria shall not enter this city, for I will defend it, for the sake of my servant David." And in that same night, one hundred and eighty-five thousand of the Assyrians were slain in their camp outside the city; and Sennacherib returned to his own country where he dwelt in Nineveh until he met his death as he was worshiping in the temple of his own heathen god—Nisroch.

After this, Hezekiah, the king, became ill and was at the point of death. Then the word of the Lord came unto him saying, "Set your house in order, Hezekiah, for you are surely going to die." And Hezekiah turned his face to the wall and prayed: "Remember now, I beseech Thee, how I have conducted myself before Thee in truth and with a perfect heart, and have done that which was good in Thy sight." And the Lord spoke to him again through His prophet Isaiah, and said: "Hezekiah, prince of my people—I have heard your prayer, and I will heal you. Moreover, I will add fifteen years to your life. On the third day, you shall go up to the house of the Lord and I will defend this city and deliver you from your enemies."

Now the king of Babylon, hearing that King Hezekiah was ill, sent eunuchs to him bearing a gift. While Isaiah was speaking, the eunuchs stood without the city. Hezekiah made them welcome and showed them all his treasure-house—the silver, the gold, the rich spices, the fine oils, his armory, and all that was found among his treasures. He had enormous wealth, for God had given him great riches.

When the visitors had seen all of the king's treasures, the prophet asked: "What did these men say, Hezekiah? And from whence do they come?"

Hezekiah replied: "They have come from a distant land—from Babylon."

"What did they see in your house?" inquired Isaiah.

"They saw all that is in my house; there is nothing among all my treasures that I did not show them."

Then Isaiah, the prophet, said to King Hezekiah: "Hear the word of the Lord God, Hezekiah! The time has come when all that is in thy house and which thy fathers have stored up to this day, shall be carried to Babylon. And your sons shall be eunuchs in the palace of the king of Babylon."

When Hezekiah heard the words of the prophet, he bowed his head and made answer: "Good is the word of the Lord."

And Hezekiah, the good king of Judah, slept with his fathers—and Manasseh, his son, took the throne in his stead.*

✢

THE SHADOW THAT RETREATED

By

Florence M. Earlle

HEZEKIAH, son of Ahaz, began to reign in the kingdom of Judah when he was twenty-five. Although his father had been a wicked king, leading the children of Israel into the worship of many gods, destroying the temple furniture and furnishings and allowing the building to fall into decay, Hezekiah had been reared by a good mother. His first act was to clean and repair the temple. Then he re-established the work of the priests and Levites, and celebrated again the feast of the Passover. He gave orders that all the heathen altars were to be destroyed, and that all the groves of trees in which such worship had been carried on should be cut down.

His reign was not peaceful for Sennacherib, king of Assyria, came and captured all the walled cities of Judah. Then he came up and encamped against Jerusalem. But Hezekiah, trusting in God, was told by the prophet, Isaiah, that the conqueror would not attack the city. "He will flee back to his own land." And it was so, for a plague swept through Sennacherib's camp, killing so many that the king returned to Assyria with his depleted army without making an attack.

But now in the fourteenth year of his reign, Hezekiah is ill. A boil has appeared, and the intense pain causes him to walk the floor in agony. A servant entering bowed low:

"My Lord, the prophet Isaiah is without."

He swept aside the curtain and Isaiah entered. His face was sad as he spoke.

"Set your house in order, for the Lord has said that you shall die."

He left without another word. Hezekiah was stunned. That he should die! Why he had reigned but fourteen years? He was only thirty-nine, and life was sweet. He threw himself down upon his bed, the pain of the boil forgotten in the greater realization that it would bring his death. Then he prayed.

"O Lord, remember how I have tried to do right. I have not worshiped false

* Used by special permission of the author.

gods; I have taken away the altars that the people might not sin against you. I have obeyed you as well as I knew how. Oh, spare my life, spare my life!" and Hezekiah wept.

Then to Isaiah, walking slowly through the outer court, came the word of God again.

"Return and tell the king that his prayer has been heard. I will increase his life by fifteen years."

Joyfully, Isaiah hurried back. He waited for no servant to announce him, and burst into the room where the king lay weeping.

"The Lord has heard your prayer," he cried. "He will give you fifteen more years, and in three days from now, you shall go to the temple and worship."

Hezekiah could scarcely believe the news. The change from grief to joy was too great.

"How?" faltered Hezekiah, "How shall I know that I shall live and worship in the temple in three days? Give me some sign that I may be sure."

And Isaiah said, "Come to the window. Look at the sun dial on the pavement of the court. Shall the shadow go forward ten degrees or backward?"

"It is the usual thing for the shadow to go forward. Let the shadow go backward."

And while the two watched, slowly the shadow that had begun to slip down, began to creep back. Slowly, slowly, it climbed back: one—five—seven—eight—nine—ten degrees and then stopped. Then said Isaiah, "Lay a lump of figs on that boil, and it will burst and heal."

Three days later, Hezekiah walked up the steps of the temple, and stood before the altar of incense in the outer court. In the evening, the priest would offer a sacrifice of thanksgiving for him; but now he wanted to be alone and thank God. His prayer was in the words of his ancestor, David:

"The King shall joy in Thy strength, O Lord, for Thou hast given him his heart's desire. He asked of Thee life, and Thou gavest it him; even length of days. Be exalted, Lord! So will I sing Thy praise forever."*

✛

ISAIAH THE PHILANTHROPIST

By

George Matheson

IN the portrayal of its patriarchs, in the description of its judges, in the presentation of its warriors, in the exhibition of its kings, in the disclosure of its family circles, the Gallery displays a graphicness which is unique. But as we pass from these spheres into the sphere of the prophets, we see a great change. Here, we are ushered into a compartment of the Gallery which, in the estimation of the Jew, is the main compartment. We should expect it to be distinguished from the

* Used by special permission of the author.

others by a greater fulness of detail. On the contrary, we find a desertion of detail altogether. The figures become mere outlines, and the outlines themselves are shadowy. We see no more the tracing of a life from dawn to eve. Neither morning nor evening is there, nor is there a clear revealing of the midday. A silhouetted form stands before us whose face is hid, whose expression veiled, whose very attitude is but dimly recognized. Contrast the portraits of an Abraham, an Isaac, a Jacob, a Joseph, with the portraits of an Amos, an Isaiah, a Jeremiah, an Ezekiel, and you will see the full force of the difference. The former are almost modern in the interest they awaken; the latter seem far away. The former are men; the latter are shadows. The former suggest the living world; the latter come like voices from the dead.

How are we to account for this? Is it accident? No, it is too methodical for that; a thing which pervades one class exclusively cannot be accidental. Is it ignorance on the part of the delineator? No, why should the artist know less of Isaiah than of Abraham; Isaiah belonged to an age when knowledge was more easily transmitted than it was in the days of Abraham. Is it the uneventfulness of a prophet's life in comparison with a ruler's life? No, for the facts we wish to learn are just the common uneventful facts which environ men of every day— the place of birth, the home circle, the training influences, the worldly circumstances, the struggles for survival, the loves and hates and shadows of human life. This is what we want to know; this is what is not revealed.

Is there any explanation which can be suggested for this biographical reticence? I think there is. I believe it originates in the notion that a man's religious message has more power when separated from his personal circumstances. This is not a feeling peculiar to the Jew. It lies at the root of clerical celibacy; it forms the basis of religious asceticism. There has ever been a widespread impression that familiarity with the teacher of sacred things weakens the force of his message. How often you and I are disappointed when we have realized our wish to meet some distinguished educator of the race. We have figured to ourselves the joy of that meeting—how our hearts will burn, how our souls will be enlightened. And we have found the man a very ordinary individual, with the average amount of human frailties and perhaps more than the average amount of human foibles. The man who habitually lives on the mountain is apt to find himself not at home on the plains. . . . The Jew felt this and sought to obviate it. He withdrew the everyday life of his prophets from common observation. He placed his Isaiah in the mist. He shrouded his form and features. He hid his environment. He concealed his domestic altar. He threw a veil over his circle and his circumstances. He allowed only his *voice* to be revealed. He would not let us look, but he bade us listen. He sent a cloud to the eye, but he lifted a curtain from the ear.

To the ear, then, let us appeal. Let us listen to the voice of this man Isaiah. Hundreds have listened to that voice for the purpose of doctrine, for messages of prophecy, for exercises of criticism. But for none of these objects would I be here an auditor. I am not in search of the prophet, but of the man. I wish to see whether the knowledge which has been shut out by one entrance has been admitted by another. If we adopt the modern limits to the authorship of Isaiah, we have thirty-nine chapters recording his literary utterances. Are these utterances wholly impersonal! Do they reveal only the destiny of nations, the fate of despots, the fall of potentates! Do they lift merely the veil of history! Do they not lift a veil also from the prophet's own life and give us some notes of an autobiography!

We have not read far ere we are arrested by a note of autobiography. It is a note of a very peculiar kind. When a man gives a record of his life he usually begins by telling when and where he was born. Isaiah begins by telling where he was "born again." To him his real birth was the birth of his spirit. His natal day was the day of his conversion. He is conscious of one crisis moment—a moment which rises above the level of the sea—a drastic moment, a dreadful moment, a moment when, like Jacob, he saw the ladder between earth and heaven. It seemed to him that he stood in the temple of God—not the human temple at Jerusalem but the great Temple above. He received one glimpse of the burning purity before which cherub kneels and seraph bows and angel veils the face. And as he gazed on that everlasting fire the most commonplace fact of human experience broke upon him as a revelation. In the light of God he saw for the first time the dark spot on his own soul. No earthquake, no volcano, no rush of mighty waters ever appalled a man as Isaiah was appalled by the sight of his own heart. It was as if a deformed creature had received the present of a looking-glass and for the first time beheld his misshapenness. In the glass of the Divine glory Isaiah beheld, not only the deformity of himself, but the deformity of the world. His first vision of sin came from a sight of holiness; he got his earliest glimpse of corruption when he gazed into the face of God.

What was this deformity which Isaiah saw in the world and in himself? No man beholds sin in the abstract; it is always a special form of sin. What is that special form of sin which Isaiah sees? It is human selfishness—the unbrotherhood of man to man. I could bring the whole Book of Isaiah to substantiate this point. From first to last the man is a humanitarian. The keynote of his message is philanthropy. The cry which rises into his ears is the cry of stricken humanity—the cry of the poor and needy, the cry of the sad and weary. The burning coal which touched his lips is the pain of human want, the parching of human thirst, the heat of human toil. He hears God calling him to lash the sins of the nation; but to him all the sins of the nation are forms of a single sin—*selfishness*. Does he deplore idolatry; it is because the idols of man are images of man's own glory. Does he repudiate extravagance in dress, and luxury in living; it is because this outlay of wealth might have been for the sake of the destitute. Does he vociferate against foreign alliances in the time of danger; it is because to him the evil is not without but within, and can only be cured from within—by cultivating the barren spots in the life of the community. The burden of Isaiah is the burden of human compassion. It is the desire to right the wrongs which man has done to his brother, to kindle into flower the withered branch, to light the Valley of the Shadow, to bring the sons of darkness under the dome of day.

That was the call of Isaiah—the call to be a humanitarian preacher. We have, I think, a wrong idea of this man. We figure him as a man praying amid a world of atheists. . . . The preparation *he* proposed for meeting God was not the attendance at the temple, not the observance of the Sabbath, not the keeping of any feast whatever, but the sympathy of the heart with the wants and woes of man.

Now, in what way did Isaiah propose to inaugurate this sympathy? His initial cry was, "Get the heart of a little child within you!" It seemed to him that before a man could begin to think of others, he must cease to think of himself—must become self-unconscious. Isaiah had a great admiration for the nursery; it was to him the type of spiritual regeneration. His idea was that the men who wish to become philanthropists must begin by emptying themselves, by losing consciousness of themselves.

The man who attached such importance to the training of the nursery must have been a most domesticated man. I think we have generally had a contrary impression. We have figured him as the reverse of homey. The Isaiah that has floated before our eyes has been commonly a stately form treading the upper circles, walking amid courts and breathing the air of kings. The dignity of his rhythm has seemed incompatible with a modest sphere; the strength of his denunciations has appeared to imply the voice of one who moved upon the mountains. But look beneath the surface and you will change your view. There will stand before you a new Isaiah, a humble-minded Isaiah, an Isaiah whose heart is in the valley. His very house was in the valley—in the lower part of Jerusalem. Men called the spot "the Valley of Vision"—perhaps by way of a sneer. The Jewish prophets were never on the social heights; they were against the fashion and therefore out of fashion. Down in his Valley of Vision Isaiah lived, far from the madding crowd—divorced from public sympathy, almost in social ostracism. But not divorced from family life. No—there the brightness comes in. Isaiah had the joy of wedded happiness. He had a wife whose mind was in tune with his own. She was familiarly called "the prophetess"—a great compliment to her, and a great testimony to her unity with her husband. And there were two sons born to them—sons who gave Isaiah his experience of the nursery, sons whose names he had fondly recorded. Was there a vague hope in his heart that one of these might prove to be the Messianic Child—the Child who, when He reached the years of understanding, should become that ministrant Man for whom the world waited?

For, never forget that Isaiah started his spiritual life with the motto, "Wanted —a ministrant Man." This was *his* Messianic hope. . . . It is significant that the heart of Isaiah sought its refuge from the blast in something human, "a *man* shall be a hiding-place from the storm and a covert from the tempest." . . . He wants to see humanity healed of its wounds; why not summon cherubim and seraphim to be ministering spirits? It is because in him ministration has struck a new note of development. He has made a discovery. He says in effect: "Hitherto we have looked to the *angels* for the succour of human woes; henceforth man shall be the hiding-place of man. Hitherto we have sought a covert from the tempest under an angel's wing; henceforth we shall see it in the heart of a brother man." That is what Isaiah meant to say when he spoke of a man as our hiding-place. He was dismissing with a wave of the hand the whole celestial army. He had learned from experience that in the hour of sadness no angelic sympathy will suffice. He had learned by human fatherhood, by the earthly tie of husband, by the response of filial devotion, that nothing but the human can sympathetically help the human. . . . His cry is for a Son of Man who shall seek and save the *lost,* who shall stimulate the barren fig-tree, who shall gather in even those whom the world has cast out, who shall cleanse the lepers for whom earth itself is too pure, who shall waken from the grave humanity's dead.

It is by the philanthropy of Isaiah that I explain a phase of his mind which I have always felt to be very peculiar—its strange mixture of severity and tenderness. There have been severe men, and there have been tender men, and there have been men who have revealed one type yesterday and the other to-day. But it is a rare thing to see the two revealed at the same moment. That spectacle appears in Isaiah. He is like one of those days in which we have simultaneous rain and sunshine; and we do not know whether to weep or smile. Nothing can explain the blast of his anger; it is withering, annihilating. But, even while he denounces, there is a quivering in the voice which speaks volumes on the other side. In one and the same chapter we have the touch of Esau and the voice of Jacob. It is not that the rainbow comes *after* the flood. The mystery lies in the fact that the flood and rainbow exist together, and that the peaks of Ararat never cease to be visible even while the ark tosses on the face of the waters.

I would direct special attention to the fact that in all his exhortations he professes to be calling Judah back to her former self. He summons her to no new life of untried capacities; his cry is "Return!" He feels that she *can* be better because she once *was* better. He points her to no speculative height; he bids her to be true to her first traditions. He tells her to resume her original level of humanitarian sympathy. He declares that the spirit of philanthropy was her starting-point, that the dawning of her day was the breath of brotherhood. It is not as a reformer that he preaches the charity of man to man; it is as a conservative. He claims the life of human sympathy as the original life of the nation. He tells his countrymen that if they want to see their true glory they must not look to the future but to the past, "Thine ear shall hear a voice *behind* thee, saying, This is the way; walk ye in it." To him the philanthropic age was indeed the age behind him. Had not the service of man been the first motive of the commonwealth! Was it not this that had stimulated an Abraham! Was it not this that had inspired a Moses! Was it not this that had quickened a Boaz! Was it not this that had given wings to a David and wisdom to a Solomon! Was it not this that lay at the origin even of religious forms! Was not the Sabbath for man's rest, circumcision for man's health, sacrifice for the sanctifying of man's food! No wonder Isaiah's cry is "Return!" The ministrant Man for whom he had looked had been the Man of his country's morning. The future he beheld for her was the reflex of an idealized past. He believed in her to-morrow because he believed in her yesterday. Her Messianic day was no foreign day. It was her time of revival, her hour of rehabiliment. The Man who was to be her hiding-place from the storm, the Man who was to be her covert from the tempest, was the same who under the shadows of Peniel had wrestled with Jacob until the breaking of the day.*

✛

JOSIAH, THE BOY KING WHO TURNED HIS NATION TOWARD GOD

By

Florence M. Earlle

JOSIAH was only six when his grandfather, King Manasseh, died. But two things had been impressed on his childish mind by that time. One was hearing about the battle in which his grandfather had been taken captive to Babylon. He had missed the king during those long months of his absence, and was delighted when he had returned. The other thing was the reform that the king had made when he came back. He had destroyed the idol shrines in the land, tearing them down and commanding that thereafter the people should worship only Jehovah. Then when the work of destruction was all over, he had taken Josiah on his knee and talked with him.

"Someday," he had said, "you will become king. You must see to it that the people worship God alone. Never allow the shrines of the idols to be rebuilt. Remember," he had warned solemnly, "God is our God and powerful. He will punish us if we fail to worship Him. The first law that Moses gave us was that we were to have no other gods but Him. All the troubles that our people have had have come because we did not obey this command. Remember this, my child, as long as you live." And the boy had promised.

Not long afterward Manasseh died, and his son, Amon, father of Josiah, came to the throne. During the two years of his reign, he rebuilt the shrines for idol worship, and the Temple worship of Jehovah was forsaken and forgotten.

"It won't be that way when I am a man and become king," the child promised himself. But when he was only eight, his father was assassinated, and Josiah, the boy, was crowned king.

It was hard, at first, to know just what to do. He had little knowledge of God, but he wanted to restore His worship. He tried to collect about him the men who did worship God and to learn from them.

When he was twelve, he decided the time had come to clean the land from idol worship. Gathering about him his court, and the workmen who would do the actual work, the king went first to the great temple of Baal, the sun god. It was situated on a high hill outside Jerusalem in a grove of trees, as were all heathen shrines. Within the temple were images of Baal and of his wife Ashtaroth, the moon goddess. Some of these gods were of metal, molten or carved, and some were of wood.

"Break down the altars," the king commanded. "Destroy the images. Burn the wooden ones and break the metal ones into fine pieces. Then grind the pieces to dust."

* Abridged from *Representative Men of the Bible* (Second Series) by George Matheson, pp. 265-85. Published by Hodder & Stoughton, Ltd. Used by special permission of the publisher.

The people watched in silence, doubtless many of them expecting fire to fall upon them for their desecration, for Baal was the sun god. But nothing happened. When the work of destruction was complete, the dust from the images was strewed on the graves of the priests who had served the temple, thus desecrating them forever.

"Now tear down the temple and cut down the trees!"

That too was desecration in the eyes of the people for trees were precious in the land. Yet with them down, the temptation to rebuild the temple would be less.

When the destruction of the Baal temple on the outskirts of Jerusalem was complete, Josiah went farther in his kingdom. Wherever he found a temple, he stopped and ordered it destroyed. Sometimes he wondered if his grandfather could know and approve of what he was doing. This work took time, for there were many temples dedicated to the worship of foreign gods, and there was other work that the king must do. So it was not until the eighteenth year of his reign that Josiah felt sure that all signs of idolatry throughout his kingdom had been destroyed.

While he had been rooting out the heathen worship, he had ordered the people to bring their money, formerly devoted to the idols, to the priests for the repairing of the Temple in Jerusalem. Now he called Hilkiah, the chief priest, and asked that all the money be turned over to him. There was much to be done, for the former king who had worshiped idols had taken some things from the house of God and destroyed others. Wood had to be secured for new floors and couplings, and stone hewn for pillars and partitions. But the workmen were honest. They were not required to give an account of the money spent.

In cleaning out the rubbish one day, the high priest found tucked down behind a pillar, a scroll of the law of Moses. How long it had lain there neglected, he had no idea. He had never seen it before. He called Shapan, the scribe, asking that he report to the king what had been found.

Now the scribe was the only one who could read, so he must read the law before the king. The day was appointed, and Josiah held court. Then Shapan stood up and began to read. He read of the laws for observing the three great feasts, Pentecost, Tabernacles, and the Passover. He read of the observance of the Sabbath and of the year of Jubilee, and the laws regarding the use of the land. Then near the end of the scroll he began to read the warnings if the laws of God were not kept, especially that warning about worshiping idols.

"If ye despise my statutes and break my commandments, I will also do this to you: [Five chastisements were given.]

"I will set my face against you and you shall be slain before your enemies. I will break the power of your pride and your land shall not yield its increase. I will send wild beasts among you that shall rob you of your children and your highways shall be desolate. I will send pestilence among you. I will destroy your high places and make your cities waste."

Then finally Shapan read: "I will scatter you among the heathen and your cities shall be laid waste and your land shall be desolate!"

And the king rent his clothes and burst into weeping, for he knew that his forefathers had disobeyed and that he, himself, had not done all he could to make the people worship God. Then he sent Hilkiah, Shapan and others to inquire of the Lord for him, for he said, "The anger of God is kindled against us, for the evil we have done and the good that we have failed to do."

The men went to Huldah, the prophetess, and she warned them of what was to befall the nation in these words:

"Thus saith the Lord, God: tell the man who sent you that all the evil spoken of in the book shall come upon the land; for the people have forsaken me and burned incense to strange gods. But to the king himself, say, 'Because your heart is humble, and because you have wept before me, I have heard your prayers. The evil shall come upon this land; but you shall not live to see it.'"

Josiah gathered all the people together and had read before them the book of the law. Then he made a covenant with the Lord to keep His commandments and walk in His ways. And all the people agreed to the covenant. Then came Hilkiah, the high priest, and said to the king, "O king, live forever! You have destroyed the heathen temples in many places in the land, but not in the house of God."

"What do you mean?" inquired Josiah.

"That in the courts and even in the place of the altar of sacrifices there are articles that belong to the worship of Baal and other gods."

The king was horrified. He had not been in the Temple, for he knew that no worship could be held there while the repairs were going on. He had left inspection of the work to the high priest. Now he commanded that all the vessels that were made for the use of Baal worship, or that of any other god, be brought out and destroyed. He discovered when he went to the Temple, that a small portion of metal had been made to house a Baal shrine and set up in the outer court of the building. This he carried down to the brook Kidron, and had it burned. He found that close beside the Temple were some houses that looked suspicious. Investigation proved that these were the homes of the women who wove the hangings of the temples of Baal.

"Tear them down!" commanded the king.

There were two altars in the courts of the Temple that Josiah did not know about. "Who put these here?" he demanded. "Are they for heathen worship or do they belong to Jehovah?"

"Your grandfather, Manasseh, made them," said Hilkiah. "He never used them after he returned from Babylon, but he did not destroy them. And your father ordered sacrifices burned upon them to Molech."

"Destroy them! Beat them to powder and throw the dust in the Kidron. And Molech! That worship must be absolutely rooted out. Let us go to the valley of the children of Hinnon. I will defile Tophet, so that never again will any of my subjects cause his son or daughter to pass through the fire to Molech."

On the way, Josiah discovered the horses that his father had given to Baal, in the stables of the chamberlain Nathan-melech.

"Send them to my court," ordered the king, "and bring out the gold chariot and grind it to powder."

The valley of Hinnon he defiled by burning dead men's bones and by ordering that hereafter it should be used as a place to burn the refuse of the city of Jerusalem.

After this Josiah went throughout his kingdom again, seeking shrines that he might have missed in the first reform, or that had been secretly rebuilt. He journeyed to the extreme end of his kingdom—Bethel—and there found the high place and altar that Jeroboam, when he became king, had had set up that his people might not go down to Jerusalem to worship. These he broke down and ground to powder, burning the grove of beautiful trees that had grown up during the years. He also gave orders that the heathen priests were to be put to death.

And it is written of Josiah that like unto him there was no king before him that turned to the Lord with all his heart, and with all his soul, and with all his might; neither after him, rose there any like him.*

✛

GREAT GOD, WE SING THAT MIGHTY HAND

(Interpretation)

PHILIP DODDRIDGE (1702-1751) was one of the great hymn writers of the eighteenth century. He was a contemporary of Charles Wesley, although he was born in London a few years before Wesley.

His father was a staunch and devout layman of the Independent Church. Philip was the youngest of a large family but displayed such promise as a child that the Duchess of Bedford, appreciating his talents, offered to educate him at either Oxford or Cambridge. He declined, however, preferring to remain among the Dissenters, and received his education for the ministry in the non-Conformist Seminary at Kibworth instead.

After his ordination he received many calls from Presbyterian congregations, but finally accepted the call of the Independent Church at Northampton. He also taught in the theological academy, where he prepared many young candidates for the ministry.

Although Philip Doddridge lived only forty-nine years he was a voluminous writer of both prose and poetry. Many of his hymns appear in modern church hymnals. It was said that he was "a man of God who always walked closely with his God," and the hymn, "Great God, We Sing That Mighty Hand," reflects the piety and fervor of this man.

The hymn is sung to a melody entitled "Truro," ascribed to Charles Burney (1726-1814), published in 1789 in the *Psalmodia Evangelical.*

* Used by special permission of the author.

Great God, We Sing That Mighty Hand

TRURO. L. M.

Philip Doddridge, 1702–1751

Psalmodia Evangelica, 1789

1. Great God, we sing that might-y hand By which sup-
2. By day, by night, at home, a-broad, Still are we
3. With grate-ful hearts the past we own; The fu-ture,
4. In scenes ex-alt-ed or de-pressed, Thou art our

port-ed still we stand: The ope-ning year thy mer-cy shows;
guard-ed by our God, By his in-ces-sant boun-ty fed,
all to us un-known, We to thy guard-ian care com-mit,
joy, and thou our rest; Thy good-ness all our hopes shall raise,

That mer-cy crowns it till it close.
By his un-err-ing coun-sel led.
And, peace-ful, leave be-fore thy feet.
A-dored through all our chang-ing days. A-men.

LORD GOD OF HOSTS, HOW LOVELY

(Interpretation)

THIS hymn is from the *United Presbyterian Book of Psalms* published in 1871 in the United States. The author of the words is unknown; but the sentiment expressed is a free interpretation of the 134th Psalm.

A comparison of the lines of this hymn with the Psalm which appears below is revealing:

> Behold, bless ye the Lord, all ye servants of the Lord,
> Which by night stand in the house of the Lord.
> Lift up your hands in the sanctuary,
> And bless the Lord.
> The Lord that made heaven and earth
> Bless thee out of Zion.

The tune "Lincoln" to which this hymn is sung was composed in 1604 by Melchior Vulpius.

Lord God of Hosts, How Lovely

LINCOLN. 7, 6, 7, 6

Psalm 134
United Presbyterian Book of Psalms,
U. S. A., 1871

MELCHIOR VULPIUS, 1604

1. Lord God of Hosts, how love - ly   The place where thou dost dwell!
2. My soul is long - ing, faint - ing, Je - ho - vah's courts to see;
3. Be - hold, the spar - row find - eth A house in which to rest,
4. And where, se - cure - ly shel - tered, Her young she forth may bring:
5. Blest who thy house in - hab - it! They ev - er give thee praise.

Thy tab - er - na - cles ho - ly In pleas-ant - ness ex - cel.
My heart and flesh are cry - ing, O liv - ing God, to thee.
The swal-low hath dis - cov - ered Where she may build her nest;
So, Lord of hosts, thy al - tars I seek, my God, my King.
Blest all whom thou dost strength-en, Who love the sa - cred ways! A-men.

NOT ALONE FOR MIGHTY EMPIRE

(Interpretation)

THE words of this patriotic hymn were written in 1909 by the late Rev. William Pierson Merrill, pastor of the Brick Presbyterian Church of New York City. It is usually sung to a much older tune, "Austrian Hymn," composed by Franz Joseph Haydn. While not one of the older hymns of the Church, the power and significance of its message have grown with the years.

The four stanzas, expressing as they do praise and thanksgiving for past mercies and blessings, voice also the hope and prayer of men and women of all nations and races that "strife of class and faction" shall pass away and that nations shall be free indeed.

The passion and patriotism of this hymn make it an ideal song for patriotic days and occasions in the life of the Church Universal. Men and women of the "living present" raise their voices in praise to God for temporal blessings, for the deeper "things unseen" that determine the destiny of nations and races, and for the heritage of freedom by which they rule themselves in lands that are truly free.

For the prophet leaders of the people and their love and loyalty to God's living word; for all those "heroes of the spirit" in this and every land praise and thanksgiving are given. The hymn closes with a prayer that the faith of people in "simple manhood" shall remain strong, till in the end it shall find "fruition in the Brotherhood of Man."

✠

O GOD, UNSEEN BUT EVER NEAR

(Interpretation)

SAMUEL LONGFELLOW (1819-1892) was the younger brother of Henry Wadsworth Longfellow, America's eminent New England poet. He was born in Portland, Maine, graduated from Harvard University, and later finished a divinity course.

He was recognized for his outstanding literary ability and with his classmate, Samuel Johnson, prepared a hymnbook for the Unitarian Church. Later the two men published another collection of hymns entitled *Hymns of the Spirit.*

Samuel Longfellow became pastor of the Second Unitarian Church in Brooklyn; there he inaugurated a Vesper Service which became unusually popular.

His best-known hymn is "Holy Spirit, Truth Divine." Many others from his pen will be found in the new *Pilgrim Hymnal* and in *Hymns for the Living Age.*

This hymn, "O God, Unseen but Ever Near," was written in 1864. It is in reality a liberal paraphrase of an older hymn by Edward Osler (1836).

Its four brief stanzas recognize the Unseen God as the refuge of all those who put their trust in Him and who, soiled and weary, seek shelter from the heat and

Not Alone for Mighty Empire

Austrian Hymn 8 7 8 7 D

WILLIAM P. MERRILL (1867-   ) 1909

FRANZ JOSEPH HAYDN, 1797

1. Not a - lone for might - y em - pire, Stretch-ing far o'er land and sea,
2. Not for bat - tle - ships and for - tress, Not for con-quests of the sword,
3. For the ar - mies of the faith - ful Lives that passed and left no name,
4. God of jus - tice, save the peo - ple From the war of race and creed,

Not a - lone for boun-teous har - vests, Lift we up our hearts to Thee.
But for con - quests of the spir - it Give we thanks to Thee, O Lord;
For the glo - ry that il - lu - mines Pa - triot souls of death-less fame,
From the strife of class and fac - tion, Make our na - tion free in - deed;

Stand - ing in the liv - ing pres-ent, Mem - o - ry and hope be-tween,
For the her - i - tage of free-dom, For the home, the church, the school,
For the peo - ple's proph-et - lead-ers, Loy - al to Thy liv - ing word,
Keep her faith in sim - ple man-hood Strong as when her life be - gan,

Lord, we would with deep thanksgiving Praise Thee more for things un-seen.
For the o - pen door to man-hood In a land the peo - ple rule.
For all he - roes of the spir - it, Give we thanks to Thee, O Lord.
Till it finds its full fru - i - tion In the Broth-er - hood of Man. A-men.

O God, Unseen But Ever Near

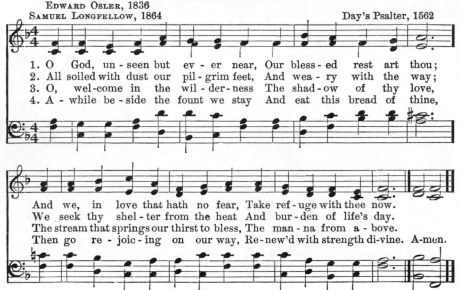

ST. FLAVIAN. C.M.

EDWARD OSLER, 1836
SAMUEL LONGFELLOW, 1864

Day's Psalter, 1562

1. O God, un-seen but ev-er near, Our bless-ed rest art thou;
2. All soiled with dust our pil-grim feet, And wea-ry with the way;
3. O, wel-come in the wil-der-ness The shad-ow of thy love,
4. A-while be-side the fount we stay And eat this bread of thine,

And we, in love that hath no fear, Take ref-uge with thee now.
We seek thy shel-ter from the heat And bur-den of life's day.
The stream that springs our thirst to bless, The man-na from a-bove.
Then go re-joic-ing on our way, Re-new'd with strength di-vine. A-men.

burden of the day. This hymn acknowledges our Father God as the source from which all earth's blessings come. He is our refuge and our shelter. His love is like a shadow in the burning wilderness, or a spring of water when we thirst, or manna when we hunger. Man needs constantly to seek God's sustaining gifts in order to renew his strength.

The melody "St. Flavian" to which this hymn is sung was published in 1562 in *Day's Psalter.*

✛

GOD IS MY STRONG SALVATION

(Interpretation)

JAMES MONTGOMERY (1771-1854) was born in Ayrshire, the birthplace of Scotland's great lyric poet, Robert Burns. He was the son of a Moravian minister. When he was just a small lad his parents were sent as missionaries to the West Indies, where they passed away, leaving their young son at a Moravian school in Yorkshire.

Even as a boy, young Montgomery began to write verse. Because he was not particularly studious, he was apprenticed to a grocer near Wakefield; but he ran away. During all the trying years that followed he continued to write poetry, but was unsuccessful in getting a London publisher to print his verse.

Later he secured a position as assistant on the *Sheffield Register.* His employer, the editor-in-chief, was later persecuted because of his political writings and fled

God Is My Strong Salvation

CHENIES. 7, 6, 7, 6, D.

JAMES MONTGOMERY, 1822

TIMOTHY R. MATTHEWS, 1855

1. God is my strong sal - va - tion; What foe have I to fear?
2. Place on the Lord re - li - ance, My soul, with cour - age wait;

In dark - ness and temp - ta - tion, My light, my help, is near.
His truth be thine af - fi - ance, When faint and des - o - late.

Tho' hosts en - camp a - round me, Firm to the fight I stand.
His might thine heart shall strength - en, His love thy joy in - crease,

What ter - ror can con - found me With God at my right hand?
Mer - cy thy days shall length - en, The Lord will give thee peace. A - men.

* Tune used by special permission of Novello & Company, Ltd.

to America leaving the paper in the hands of his assistant. Thus young Montgomery became the owner of a publication and at an early date changed its name to *Sheffield Iris*. His own reforms in the paper, however, did not merit the approval of the local authorities, and he was fined and imprisoned for six months.

This persecution, however, along with the continued publication of his poems increased his fame. He lectured far and wide for religious and missionary organizations; and although he was never acclaimed as a great hymn writer, he did win recognition as one of the ablest literary critics of his times. He wrote many lyrics and became one of the largest contributors to the hymnal of his day and succeeding generations.

His best hymn is based on the 72nd Psalm. "God Is My Strong Salvation" is also numbered among his best. In two brief stanzas it acclaims that God is the strong Saviour of men in times of temptation and terrors. It urges man to place reliance upon God, for God's mercy will lengthen his days and "the Lord will give thee peace."

In his old age James Montgomery won admiration for his poetic writings which attracted the attention of such outstanding writers as Byron, Wordsworth, Southey, and Moore. His noble character was an influence for good among his fellow men. The government gave him an annual pension of two hundred pounds. When he died in 1854 the residents of Sheffield erected a bronze statue to his memory.

The melody "Chenies" was composed in 1855 by Timothy R. Matthews.

CONTENTS

PART V SECTION 2

THE PROPHETS OF JUDAH

✛

For I know that my redeemer liveth, and that he shall stand at the latter day upon the earth.—JOB 19:25

✛

THE PROPHET ZEPHANIAH

By

Saul Raskin

(Interpretation)

THE name of the prophet, Zephaniah, means "Jehovah has hidden." He was born in Jerusalem about the middle of Manasseh's reign. He was of royal blood, for his great-great grandfather was Hezekiah, king of Judah. He prophesied in the time of Josiah before the reforms which Josiah instituted in 621 B.C.

There was much in Judah at this time which merited condemnation. The Baal worship which King Manasseh had encouraged began to flourish again. Many people had adopted the Assyrian religion and worshiped the planets, especially the sun and moon and the planet Venus. The king's approval of this worship had given prestige to the worship of heavenly bodies on Judean housetops, and had led many of the Hebrew people to offer sacrifices to these pagan gods. The life of both princes and merchants in Jerusalem bore the marks of a godless civilization, and Zephaniah knew that these leaders must eventually feel the cruel weight of the Lord's judgment. It was the invasion of the Scythians into Palestine that revealed to Zephaniah that the Lord was calling him to be a prophet. King Josiah had been the ruling monarch in Judah only eleven years when these barbarian hordes began to pour into Asia Minor and Palestine. Young Zephaniah had witnessed the devastation left by these raiding, sacking hordes, and he was convinced that soon Judah also would be overthrown. He warned Judah and Jerusalem that the great day of the Lord's judgment was near when the neighboring nations would be judged and destroyed.

Judah herself could not escape the Lord's judgment in the approaching great day. Zephaniah warned them to repent. But the people still believed themselves secure from danger and were indifferent to the Lord's judgments on their conduct. They said, "The Lord will not do good, neither will he do evil" (1:12). It was to people like this that Zephaniah preached of the approaching day of judgment, warning them in vivid language to prepare for its coming:

> The great day of the Lord is near,
> It is near, and hasteth greatly,
> Even the voice of the day of the Lord:
> The mighty man shall cry there bitterly.
> That day is a day of wrath,
> A day of trouble and distress,
> A day of wasteness and desolation,
> A day of darkness and gloominess,
> A day of clouds and thick darkness,
> A day of the trumpet and alarm
> Against the fenced cities,
> And against the high towers.

And I will bring distress upon men,
That they shall walk like blind men,
Because they have sinned against the Lord.

[1:14-17]

It is this prophet, Zephaniah, that Saul Raskin has portrayed. With a candle in
his hand and his arms flung out, he goes about searching for those who are loyal
to the Lord. He said, "I will search Jerusalem with candles" (1:12). In the background jagged streaks of lightning hover over this wicked, disobedient city. At
the left fires may be seen flaring over the Temple, while on the right altars with
their heathen images are falling down.

✛

HABAKKUK, THE SKEPTIC

By

Saul Raskin

(Interpretation)

HABAKKUK grew to young manhood in Jerusalem at a time when his country
was at peace with surrounding nations, during the reign of the good king, Josiah,
who had established an era of justice and righteousness. The king had inaugurated many reforms, and the Temple and the worship of the Lord, the true God,
had been given a new strength and dignity.

From boyhood Habakkuk loved the beautiful Temple in the capital city of his
nation, and was especially attracted to the teachers of God's law who thronged
its courts. However, it was not to the priests in the Temple that he felt most
drawn. Rather, it was to the prophets of his day, who spoke out fearlessly against
entrenched wrongs, at times denouncing even formal worship when it was sub-
stituted for purity in the inner life and justice and social righteousness in dealing
with one's friends and neighbors.

The death of King Josiah, following closely upon the battle of Megiddo
against the Egyptians, left Judah bereft and stricken. His younger son, Jehoahaz,
was placed upon the throne, but his nation's fortunes began to wane and within
three months Pharaoh Necho conquered the land, banished the young king,
placed his two-year-old brother, Jehoiakim II, upon the throne, established a protectorate, and demanded a heavy tribute of gold and silver from the people of
Judah.

This Egyptian protectorate was short lived. Soon the Chaldeans from Babylonia gained control of Judah. Upon the death of Jehoiakim, his eighteen-year-
old son, Jehoiachin, was placed upon the throne. He ruled but three months
when Nebuchadnezzar, king of Babylonia, besieged and took Jerusalem, carrying
not only the young king, but the queen mother, royal officials, many soldiers,
craftsmen, and important people into captivity in Babylon.

THE PROPHET ZEPHANIAH—*RASKIN*

Unable to understand why the Lord allowed the ruthless cruelty of these conquering hordes Habakkuk cried out, saying:

"O Lord, how long shall I cry, and thou wilt not hear, even cry out unto thee of violence, and thou wilt not save? Why dost thou show me iniquity, and cause me to behold grievance? For spoiling and violence are before me; and there are that raise up strife and contention. Therefore the law is slacked, and judgment doth never go forth; for the wicked doth compass about the righteous; therefore wrong judgment proceedeth" (1:2-4).

Long and earnestly Habakkuk brooded over the punishment of his people by the wicked and barbaric Chaldeans. He could not, like Jeremiah, accept the domination of his country by Nebuchadnezzar, nor share Jeremiah's counsel that Judah accept it in friendly submission. It was not in keeping with God's loving-kindness to allow a nation like that of the "bitter and hasty" Chaldeans to triumph. He saw them "march through the breadth of the land, to possess the dwelling places that are not theirs. They are terrible and dreadful . . . their horses also are swifter than the leopards, and more fierce than the evening wolves" (1:6-8).

Against the wrongs done by the conquering Chaldeans Habakkuk cried out in bitterness of heart and soul. He pronounced a series of woes against this enemy of Judah. These pronouncements are recorded in the second chapter of the Book of Habakkuk. They are fierce and taunting words from a prophet of a conquered people against their conquerors. He denounced their lustful plunder and spoliation, their unscrupulous greed and selfish gain, their cruelty and violence, their shameful drunkenness and its attendant debauchery, and their idolatry.

Habakkuk believed that this savage nation of the Chaldeans was being used by the Lord to punish Judah and he dared to cry out his question to his God: "Thou art of purer eyes than to behold evil, and canst not look on iniquity; wherefore lookest thou upon them that deal treacherously, and holdest thy tongue when the wicked devoureth the man that is more righteous than he?" (1:13).

In Saul Raskin's etching, "Habakkuk, the Skeptic," the prophet seems to be asking this question. He stands in the center of a circle of doubt and despair from which there seems to be no escape. He points to the darkness of a world overrun by Chaldean armies. Clouds of hate and war and destruction arise on all sides. His uplifted hand and questioning eyes seem to say: "O Lord, how can you permit this?"

In his watchtower, waiting to hear the Lord's reply, Habakkuk finally received the divine answer. The overthrowing of evil will eventually take place: "Though it tarry, wait for it, because it will surely come" (2:3). Meanwhile, the righteous man who remains loyal to God shall continue to live, for "the just shall live by his faith" (2:4). In the end he will see God's glory established, "for the earth shall be filled with the knowledge of the glory of the Lord, as the waters cover the sea" (2:14).

At last Habakkuk's doubts are at an end as he says: "The Lord is in his holy temple; let all the earth keep silence before him" (2:20).

HABAKKUK, THE SKEPTIC—RASKIN

THE FRIEZE OF THE PROPHETS

By

John Singer Sargent

(Interpretation)

Right Center Section

In this section of Sargent's "Frieze of the Prophets" stand Jeremiah, Jonah, Isaiah, and Habakkuk. Jonah, standing somewhat apart from the group behind Isaiah, wears a turban on his head. The Book of Jonah, unlike those of the other prophets, does not contain prophecies, but it delivers its message by means of a story about a prophet. The artist has suggested this by portraying Jonah with downcast eyes reading from an unrolled scroll.

Disobedient to the Lord's command to go to Nineveh and preach there, Jonah embarked on a ship bound for a distant port in the opposite direction. A great storm arose and Jonah was cast overboard and swallowed by a great fish. The story continues with Jonah's repentance, his miraculous escape from the fish, and his preaching in Nineveh. The whole city turned to God, but Jonah was displeased, for he did not want to see the heathen enjoying God's mercy. When a worm ate his gourd vine and Jonah became filled with grief and self-pity, the Lord told him that He would feel grief at the destruction of Nineveh.

Isaiah, Habakkuk, and Jeremiah were real prophets whose messages from the Lord to His people were part of the history of their turbulent period. Isaiah was the earliest of the three, receiving his call to be the Lord's spokesman "in the year that king Uzziah died," which was about 740 B.C. He stands in Sargent's "Frieze of the Prophets" with uplifted arms and eyes raised to heaven as he must have stood in the Temple when he saw his vision of "the Lord sitting upon a throne, high and lifted up, and his train filled the temple. Above it stood the seraphims. . . . And one cried to another and said, 'Holy, holy, holy, is the Lord of hosts: the whole earth is full of his glory'" (Isa. 6:1-3).

Isaiah heard the Lord say: "Whom shall I send, and who will go for us?" Then Isaiah answered: "Here am I; send me" (6:8). For nearly forty years, while Assyria threatened Judah from the north and Egypt threatened her from the south, Isaiah delivered his message of trust in God.

Habakkuk lived about a hundred years after Isaiah, when Assyria had been vanquished by the Chaldeans ruling in Babylon. It was the cruel Chaldeans who now threatened Judah. Sargent portrays Habakkuk deeply troubled because he cannot understand why the Lord allows Judah to be punished by the far more wicked Chaldeans.

The Chaldeans, or Babylonians as they were also called, advanced nearer to Jerusalem. Jeremiah, who was a contemporary of Habakkuk, lived and prophesied in Jerusalem while the city was being subjugated and finally destroyed by the

THE FRIEZE OF THE PROPHETS (RIGHT CENTER SECTION)—*SARGENT*

Babylonians in 587 B.C. More is known of Jeremiah than perhaps of any other character in the Old Testament except David, for Jeremiah left a record of his life and his thoughts in the book bearing his name. Although he lived through one of the most disastrous periods of his people's history, he was courageous and he remained loyal to his own deepest convictions. Here he is pictured as a man bowed down by the sorrows of his country, yet standing steadfast as a valiant prophet of the Lord.

✛

JOB IN HIS ADVERSITY

By

Julius Schnorr von Carolsfeld

(Interpretation)

THE Book of Job is named after the man whose story forms its subject. No one knows when it was written nor by whom. Its author must have been a philosopher as well as a poet. He wrote this superb poem in an effort to explain the problem of the suffering of the righteous. Prophets like Habakkuk grappled with this question of why the wicked flourish and the good man often suffers, but none of them entered so fully into so many aspects of the problem as the Book of Job.

Job had been a rich man in former days, possessing many sheep, oxen, asses, and camels. He lived in a beautiful home and his many sons and daughters were a great joy to him. He had been a good, upright man, using his wealth to help the poor, the fatherless, and the widows.

Now all is changed. Suddenly all his wealth vanished: his oxen and asses were stolen; his sheep together with their shepherds perished in a fire; his camels were driven away. Then, as all his sons and daughters feasted in their house, a great wind destroyed the building and all Job's children were killed. Finally Job himself fell ill and his cup of woe was filled to overflowing. "He sat down among the ashes," for he could do nothing but endure, as best he might, hours of pain and suffering.

His wife came to him and said: "Curse God, and die." But he replied: "Thou speakest as one of the foolish women speaketh. What? shall we not receive good at the hand of God, and shall we not receive evil?" (2:10).

When Job's three friends heard of all his misfortunes they came "to mourn with him and to comfort him." Eliphaz, Bildad, and Zophar all "lifted up their voice, and wept. And they rent every one his mantle, and sprinkled dust upon their heads toward heaven. So they sat down with him upon the ground seven days and seven nights, and none spake a word unto him, for they saw that his grief was very great" (2:12, 13).

This engraving, "Job in His Adversity," shows a man bowed down by misfortunes almost too great to bear. In his hand he holds a broken bit of pottery. His wife stands in the doorway urging him to "curse God, and die." In the back-

JOB IN HIS ADVERSITY—*VON CAROLSFELD*

ground flames still rise from the ruined house where all his sons and daughters perished.

Julius Schnorr von Carolsfeld who designed this engraving portrays one of Job's friends sunk in gloom with his hat pulled down over his eyes. On the face of another is pictured real sympathy that causes him to suffer with his friend. The third man is standing and attempting to explain to Job why all this suffering has come to him.

Job's friends believed that affliction points to sin and that it is a sign of God's disfavor, just as prosperity is a sign of His favor. But Job's own conscience was clear, for he knew of no sins to account for his unexampled sufferings. Job answered his friends when they declared that his suffering was a punishment for his sins or a trial to improve his character. He declared that he was innocent.

Through all the arguments between Job and his friends who proved to be "miserable comforters," Job continued to trust God and remain faithful to Him. "Though he slay me, yet will I trust in him" (13:15), Job declared.

At length in a dramatic climax the Lord Himself answered Job out of the whirlwind. He reminded Job of the great mysteries of the universe and man's limited understanding. In the end Job found comfort in the knowledge that God cared for him. He was content to accept his sufferings, for he trusted in God's power and wisdom.

✤

JEREMIAH DENOUNCING JERUSALEM

By

Max Lieberg

(Interpretation)

JEREMIAH, the prophet, was of priestly descent. His prophetic career began at an early age in the thirteenth year of King Josiah, 626 B.C., and covered the period of Judah's increasing weakness until the fall of Jerusalem and the Babylonian Exile. He was the leader of a small minority in Judah, and prophesied against three great wrongs: the religious apostasies of his people, their neglect of justice, and the false patriotism that led them to break faith by repeated revolts against Babylon.

Again and again Jeremiah denounced the evils practiced in Jerusalem and spoke the Lord's message: "Moreover I will deliver all the strength of this city, and all the labours thereof, and all the precious things thereof. And all the treasures of the kings of Judah will I give into the hand of their enemies, which shall spoil them, and take them, and carry them to Babylon" (20:5).

All who had been faithless to the Lord, whether king or prince, priest or prophet, men of Judah or dwellers in Jerusalem, all were condemned by Jeremiah in the words of the Lord:

"For this city hath been to me as a provocation of mine anger and of my fury

JEREMIAH DENOUNCING JERUSALEM—*LIEBERG*

from the day that they built it even unto this day; that I should remove it from before my face, because of all the evil of the children of Israel and of the children of Judah, which they have done to provoke me to anger, they, their kings, their princes, their priests, and their prophets, and the men of Judah and the inhabitants of Jerusalem. For they have turned unto me the back, and not the face; and though I taught them, rising up early and teaching them, yet they have not hearkened to receive instruction. But they have set their abomination in the house which is called by my name, to defile it. And they built the high places of Baal, which are in the valley of the son of Hinnom" (32:31-35).

Jeremiah's prophecies were not popular. One day as Jeremiah finished a stern warning of the approaching fate of Jerusalem, "the princes of Judah heard these things, then they came up from the king's house unto the house of the Lord, and sat down in the entry of the new gate of the Lord's house." A crowd had gathered and the priests and prophets addressed the people, saying: "This man is worthy to die, for he hath prophesied against this city, as ye have heard with your ears" (26:11).

Then Jeremiah arose and made his own defense before the princes and priests and all the people: "The Lord sent me to prophesy against this house and against this city all the words that ye have heard. Therefore now amend your ways and your doings, and obey the voice of the Lord your God. And the Lord will repent him of the evil that he hath pronounced against you. As for me, behold, I am in your hand. Do with me as seemeth good and meet unto you" (26:12-15).

This is the Biblical incident which provided the inspiration for the painting, "Jeremiah Denouncing Jerusalem," by Max Lieberg, the German artist (1856-1912).

The setting of this painting is an open place in Jerusalem outside the new gate of the Temple. On a stone platform stands Jeremiah, who is denouncing Jerusalem and all her people for their evil ways. The scene is typically Oriental. On the ground before the prophet a mixed crowd has gathered. Some listen intently to the prophet's words. Some are moved to anger; and one has seized a stone in readiness to hurl it at the prophet. At the right two shepherds appear to have wandered in from the neighboring fields. In the left foreground stand two troubled priests. A haughty prince standing near the platform expresses his disapproval by not looking at the prophet. Everywhere there are angry faces. Clubs are brandished, hands are flung up accusingly. "This man is worthy to die" shouts the mob in the background. Dominating this scene which is about to break out into violence is the calm figure of the Lord's fearless prophet, Jeremiah. He delivers his unpopular message to the people and braves their wrath, for God's word was like a fire burning in his bones and he must prophesy.

THE MESSAGE OF ZEPHANIAH

The day of Jehovah is at hand! And they
Who violate the sacred places shall die.
Their wealth shall vanish and their land
Shall be despoiled, their houses desolate.
Gaza, Ashkelon shall be forsaken;
Ashdod and Ekron shall be rooted up;
And the lords of wrath shall be no more.
Jehovah hath spoken!

Nineveh, that bloody city which said,
I am, and there is none beside me,
Shall be a place for beasts to lie in.

Sing, O daughters of Zion, my people;
Be glad and rejoice, for Jehovah thy God
Hath cast out the enemy. And I,
The God of Israel, am in thy midst.
And I will make you a name and a praise
When I bring back your captivity.
Thus saith Jehovah!*

—*Thomas Curtis Clark*

WOE TO JERUSALEM AND THE NATIONS

This is the joyous city
  That dwelt carelessly,
  That said in her heart, I am,
  And there is none else beside me:
How is she become a desolation,
A place for beasts to lie down in!
Every one that passeth by her shall hiss,
And wag his hand.

Woe to her that is rebellious and polluted,
To the oppressing city!
  She obeyed not the voice;
  She received not correction;
  She trusted not in the LORD;
  She drew not near to her God.
Her princes in the midst of her are roaring lions;
Her judges are ravening wolves;
They leave nothing till the morrow.
Her prophets are light and treacherous persons:
Her priests have profaned the sanctuary,
They have done violence to the law.

* Used by special permission of the author.

The LORD in the midst of her is righteous;
He will not do iniquity;
Every morning doth he bring his judgment to light,
He faileth not;
But the unjust knoweth no shame.*

Zephaniah 2:15, 3:1-5

THE DAY OF THE LORD

The great Day of the LORD is near:
  It is near and hasteth greatly!
Even the voice of the Day of the LORD;
  The mighty man crieth there bitterly!

That Day is a day of wrath,
  A day of trouble and distress,
A day of wasteness and desolation,
  A day of darkness and gloominess,

A day of clouds and thick darkness,
  A day of the trumpet and alarm
Against the fenced cities,
  And against the high battlements.**

—*Zephaniah 1:14-16*

SEEK YE THE LORD

Gather yourselves together, yea, gather together,
O nation that hath no shame;
  Before the decree bring forth,
  Before the day pass as the chaff,
  Before the fierce anger of the LORD come upon you,
  Before the Day of the LORD's Anger come upon you.

Seek ye the LORD, all ye meek of the earth,
Which have wrought his judgment;
  Seek righteousness,
  Seek meekness:
  It may be ye shall be hid
  In the Day of the LORD's Anger.†

—*Zephaniah 2:1-3*

---

* From *The Modern Reader's Bible* edited by Richard G. Moulton, pp. 727 28. Copyright, 1935, by The Macmillan Company. Used by special permission of the publisher.
** *Ibid.*, p. 726.
† *Ibid.*, p. 727.

SONG OF REJOICING

Sing, O daughter of Zion; shout, O Israel;
Be glad and rejoice with all the heart, O daughter of Jerusalem.
  The LORD hath taken away thy judgements,
  He hath cast out thine enemy:
  The king of Israel, even the LORD, is in the midst of thee:
  Thou shalt not fear evil any more.

In that day it shall be said to Jerusalem, Fear thou not:
O Zion, let not thine hands be slack.
  The LORD thy God is in the midst of thee,
  A mighty one who will save:
  He will rejoice over thee with joy, he will rest in his love,
  He will joy over thee with singing.*

                                              —*Zephaniah 3:14-17*

WALL STREET, 600 B.C.

They take up all of them with the angle, they catch them
  in their net, and gather them in their drag; therefore they sacrifice unto their net, and burn incense
  unto their drag; because by them their portion is
  fat, and their meat plenteous.
                          —*Habakkuk, Hebrew prophet, 6th century* B.C.

Woe to him that coveteth an evil covetousness to his house, that
  he may set his nest on high, that he may be delivered
  from the power of evil! Thou hast consulted shame to
  thy house by cutting off many people, and hast sinned
  against thy soul. For the stone shall cry out of
  the wall, and the beam out of the timber shall answer
  it.
                          —*Habakkuk, Hebrew prophet, 6th century* B.C.

"BE STILL AND KNOW THAT I AM GOD"

Be still and know that I am God,
Ye who with fret and fear are worn;
Who hear no voice when tempests beat;
Who faint, by sorrows overborne;
Who dwell in shadows of defeat.

Be still and know that I am God;
The world is mine—the shine, the storm;

Your life is mine—your hopes, your fears;
The sun is mine, to keep you warm;
I guard your days, your distant years.

Be still and know that I am God;
Let not the fires of war appall!
Fear not the demons of the seas!
The kings who build on blood shall fall;
I rule the nations' destinies.

Be still and know that I am God;
Mine only is the conquering sword;
What can avail the tyrant's boasts,
If I oppose, who am the Lord?
Fear only Me, the Lord of Hosts?*

—*Thomas Curtis Clark*

THE DIVINE PATIENCE

God strives.
Before the firmament was formed, the Eternal One
Envisaged all, and saw a battle to be won.
Through countless aeons of creative pain and toil
A struggling God has labored with untiring moil.
God strives.

God feels.
The God who hears the gunfire of eternal war,
And smells the stench of sin, must suffer with and for
Humanity. The God who heals with conquering power
Must know himself the pangs of grief when shadows
    lower.
God feels.

God waits.
Man lights a torch: in feverish haste he goes about
His task. He sees the light burn low: it flickers out.
The ever-striving, ever-suffering God relights
The torch, and labors on through age-long nights.
God waits.**

—*Georgia Harkness*

---

* Used by special permission of the author.

** From *Holy Flame* by Georgia Harkness, p. 71. Copyright, 1935, by Bruce Humphries, Inc. Used by special permission of the author and the publisher.

HE KEEPS THE KEY

For God will bring every work into judgment, with every hidden thing, whether it be good, or whether it be evil.—ECCLESIASTES 12:14

Is there some problem in your life to solve,
  Some passage seeming full of mystery?
God knows, who brings the hidden things to light.
    He keeps the key.

Is there some door closed by the Father's hand
  Which widely opened you had hoped to see?
Trust God and wait—for when He shuts the door
    He keeps the key.

Is there some earnest prayer unanswered yet,
  Or answered not as you had thought 'twould be?
God will make clear His purpose by-and-by.
    He keeps the key.

Have patience with your God, your patient God,
  All wise, all knowing, no long tarrier He,
And of the door of all thy future life
    He keeps the key.

Unfailing comfort, sweet and blessed rest,
  To know of EVERY door He keeps the key.
That He at last when just He sees 'tis best,
    Will give it thee.
                    —*Author Unknown*

IF WE KNEW

If we knew the cares and sorrows
  Crowded round our neighbor's way,
If we knew the little losses
  Sorely grievous, day by day,
Would we then so often chide him
  For the lack of thrift and gain,
Leaving on his heart a shadow
  Leaving on our hearts a stain?

If we knew the clouds above us,
  Held by gentle blessings there,
Would we turn away, all trembling
  In our blind and weak despair?

Would we shrink from little shadows
   Lying on the dewy grass
While 'tis only birds of Eden
   Just in mercy flying past?

Let us reach within our bosoms
   For the key to other lives,
And with love to erring natures
   Cherish good that still survives;
So that when our disrobed spirits
   Soar to realms of light again,
We may say, "Dear Father, judge us
   As we judged our fellow men."

—*Author Unknown*

LIFE OWES ME NOTHING

Life owes me nothing. Let the years
Bring clouds or azure, joy or tears,
   Already a full cup I've quaffed;
   Already wept and loved and laughed,
And seen, in ever endless ways,
New beauties overwhelm the days.

Life owes me naught. No pain that waits
Can steal the wealth from memory's gates;
   No aftermath of anguish slow
   Can quench the soul-fire's early glow.
I breathe, exulting, each new breath,
Embracing Life, ignoring Death.

Life owes me nothing. One clear morn
Is boon enough for being born;
   And be it ninety years or ten,
   No need for me to question when.
While Life is mine, I'll find it good,
And greet each hour with gratitude.

—*Author Unknown*

"O STRENGTH AND STAY"

O Strength and Stay upholding all creation,
Who ever dost Thyself unmoved abide,
Yet day by day the light in due gradation
From hour to hour through all its changes guide;

Grant to life's day a calm unclouded ending,
An eve untouched by shadows of decay,

The brightness of a holy death-bed blending
With dawning glories of the eternal day.

Hear us, O Father, gracious and forgiving,
Through Jesus Christ, Thy co-eternal Word,
Who, with the Holy Ghost, by all things living,
Now and to endless ages art adored.

—Attributed to St. Ambrose, 340-397

REVELATION

I made a pilgrimage to find the God:
I listened for his voice at holy tombs,
Searched for the print of his immortal feet
In dust of broken altars; yet turned back
With empty heart. But on the homeward road,
A great light came upon me, and I heard
The God's voice singing in a nestling lark;
Felt his sweet wonder in a swaying rose;
Received his blessing from a wayside well;
Looked on his beauty in a lover's face;
Saw his bright hand send signals from the suns.*

—Edwin Markham

VICTORY

Ye that have faith to look with fearless eyes
    Beyond the tragedy of a world at strife,
And know that out of death and night shall rise
    The dawn of ampler life:
Rejoice, whatever anguish rend the heart,
    That God has given you the priceless dower
To live in these great times and have your part
    In Freedom's drowning hour,
That ye may tell your sons who see the light
    High in the heavens—their heritage to take—
"I saw the powers of darkness take their flight;
    I saw the morning break."**

—Author Unknown

* From *The Shoes of Happiness and Other Poems* by Edwin Markham. Copyright, 1915, by Edwin Markham, 1943, by Virgil Markham. Used by special permission of Virgil Markham.
** Found on the body of an Australian soldier.

I WILL NOT DOUBT

Though he slay me, yet will I trust in him.—JOB 13:15

I will not doubt, though all my ships at sea
   Come drifting home with broken masts and sails;
   I will believe the Hand which never fails,
From seeming evil worketh good for me.
    And though I weep because those sails are tattered,
    Still will I cry, while my best hopes lie shattered,
        "I trust in Thee."

I will not doubt, though all my prayer return
   Unanswered from the still, white realm above;
   I will believe it is an all-wise love
Which has refused these things for which I yearn;
    And though at times I cannot keep from grieving,
    Yet the pure ardor of my fixed believing
        Undimmed shall burn.

I will not doubt, though sorrows fall like rain,
   And troubles swarm like bees about a hive.
   I will believe the heights for which I strive
Are only reached by anguish and by pain;
    And though I groan and writhe beneath my crosses.
   I yet shall see through my severest losses
        The greater gain.

I will not doubt. Well anchored in this faith,
   Like some staunch ship, my soul braves every gale;
   So strong its courage that it will not quail
To breast the mighty unknown sea of death.
    Oh, may I cry, though body parts with spirit,
    "I do not doubt," so listening worlds may hear it,
        With my last breath.

—Author Unknown

PROSPERITY

Thou hast taken a pledge from thy brother for nought, and
   stripped the naked of their clothing. Thou hast
   not given water to the weary to drink, and thou
   hast withholden bread from the hungry.
But as for the mighty man, he had the earth; and the
   honourable man dwelt in it.
Thou hast sent widows away empty, and the arms of the
   fatherless have been broken.

—Job 22:6-9

"SHALL WE RECEIVE GOOD—AND NOT EVIL?"

(JOB 2:1-13)

You say this Job be sometime dead;
Or that he lived two thousand years ago.
His question lives; and it is fed
By almost every trembling hand of woe.

Some questions gain a mocking health;
They borrow immortality from pain;
They live a cruel life by stealth,
Then startle by a dread, un-lost refrain.

"Why do the righteous suffer so?"
Ah me, the millions who have deeply said it!
Would God not send some overflow
To pious roof, or barn, or worthy basket?

Forbear, nor be as some, unwise;
God's office? Not to soften nor to shield;
Nor part the cloud so trouble flies;
But this, to make him stand who else had reeled.*

—*Harry Trumbull Sutton*

✢

ZEPHANIAH, A CHARACTER STUDY

By

Kyle M. Yates

THE Prophets represented God as both severe and tender. His nature expresses itself in contrasting ways. Severity and tenderness are constantly manifesting themselves as we watch the divine dealing with men. This contrast is especially clear in the message of Zephaniah. He presents the terror and tenderness of divine love. In 1:2 God says: *"I will utterly consume all things from off the face of the ground."* And in 3:17 He says: *"The Lord thy God is in the midst of thee, a mighty one who will save; . . . he will rest in his love; he will joy over thee with singing."*

Zephaniah lived in an hour of decay and dissolution in the midst of a rapidly changing world order. The savage horde of Scythians pouring down from the plains of South Russia threw fear and consternation into the hearts of the people of Palestine. They were cruel, bloodthirsty, fearless, ruthless ruffians who drove relentlessly on as far as Egypt. Their merciless behavior created a panic in the hearts of men. The great Assyrian power that had held absolute sway since the

---

* From *Poems* by Harry Trumbull Sutton, p. 35. Copyright, 1939, by Harry Trumbull Sutton. Used by special permission of the author.

rise of Tiglath Pileser in 745 B.C. was fast losing its hold on the world. When Assurbanipal died in 626 B.C. the death knell of Assyria was sounded. The power-ful Babylonian kingdom under Nabopolassar was now in position to take over the supremacy of the East. Nineveh was not destroyed until 612 B.C. Babylon was really the mistress of the nations. The union of the armies of the Medes, the Scythians and the Babylonians caused a mighty upheaval in the world. It is not a small thing to watch the death of one world empire and the coming into life of another. As a young man Zephaniah witnessed these epoch-making happenings.

Josiah came to the throne in Jerusalem following the death of Manasseh and Amon. It would be difficult to describe the tragic effects of the long reign of Man-asseh. The nation was converted into heathenism, with foreign fashions, practices, worship and behavior the order of the day. The pure worship of Yahweh* was banished.

The effect of the lower ethical standards showed up in the behavior of the people. The princes of Judah had become so corrupt that justice was impossible. Injustice, oppression and violence were the natural results of the sort of court life that Josiah found. He could not hope to do much as a lad in the midst of a group that had thrown off restraints and turned pagan. Two generations had grown up since the good days of Isaiah and Hezekiah. No prophets had been allowed to speak of the deep things of God. The entire life of the court was opposed to the sort of preaching that God's chosen prophet would bring. The people had been stimulated by so many false things that they had become callous to any stimulus. They were "settled on their lees." In Zephaniah's indictment of Jerusalem he pic-tures the people as unteachable, the rulers as predatory, the courts as merciless, the prophets as traitors, and the priests as profane. It was a dark day for God's land.

Josiah set out to clean up the Temple and to turn the people back to Yahweh worship. In the course of the repairs on the Temple a book was found that made a profound impression on king and people. The book was a part of the Penta-teuch that gave directions for the behavior of God's people in the chosen land. The youthful king realized at once something of the significance of the book. Huldah, the prophetess, was consulted and God's word was brought to the king. As a result of the reading of the Law a definite effort at reform was undertaken. Idols, images, groves, high places, pagan altars and other abominations were broken down. An effort was made to force upon the people a nation-wide reform. It was a great undertaking and did much for the kingdom. It failed only in that the reforms could not go deep enough to transform individual hearts and lives. Outwardly it was a great success. Too much credit cannot be given to the zealous young king.

We cannot be sure what part Zephaniah and Jeremiah played in the reform movement. They were both vitally interested in cleaning up the land and in a genuine turning to God. . . . We may be sure that Zephaniah and Jeremiah en-couraged Josiah in his worthy ambitions and that they helped as far as possible in stirring up the people to carry out the king's orders. It is perhaps best to date the activities of Zephaniah from 625 B.C.

---

* From this hybrid spelling came the divine name Jehovah current in English and other modern languages.

The Hebrew prophets were usually in sympathy with the poor so that their messages became strong indictments of the nobles who possessed wealth and lands. Zephaniah was an aristocrat who did not pose as a spokesman of the peasant. With justifiable pride he traced his lineage back to Hezekiah. It must have given him standing with princes and rulers as he stepped out to proclaim his stern denunciations.. He was probably the same age as Josiah and Jeremiah.

His book reveals an exceptionally accurate knowledge of Jerusalem itself. He must have spent all his days in that city. His grim, austere, sober nature has gained for him the name "puritan" or "protestant." He seemed obsessed with a terrible conception of the doom that was coming upon the wicked world about him. No hope was in sight, for the certain doom was richly deserved and must come on friend and foe alike.

Zephaniah reminds us of Isaiah in his broad understanding of the guilt and needs of other nations. He thought of his civilization as incurably corrupt. All the surrounding nations were equally enmeshed in sin and guilt. His own beloved land was involved and must suffer the cruel tortures of a just God who could do no other thing in the light of men's behavior. Yahweh was to sweep away, as with a devastating flood, all the nations; and Judah must suffer the full severity of the onslaught. A new era of peace, plenty and happiness was to follow in the wake of the destruction.

Zephaniah was not a poet. He was deeply impressed with the fact that God had laid His hand on him and that he must warn his beloved people of the impending calamity. He was sensitive to the faintest whisper of God. Imagination and emotion play a large place in his preaching. He was a flaming evangelist who spoke with fury and effectiveness a burning message of rebuke to a people who were rapidly losing all power to respond to such serious challenges. . . . Some have called him fanatical. However this may be, he was vitally concerned with the proclamation of the divine denunciation.

Zephaniah's book is made up of several brief oracles delivered during the early days of Josiah's preparation for the reformation. In scathing language he announces the coming day of wrath and destruction for all who have sinned against the holy God of Hosts.*

✣

THE MORNING STARS SANG

By

Lillian Breazeale Mitchell

JOB stood in the door of his black tent in the land of Uz, watching the restless movement of his sheep and goats, watching the uneasy swaying of his camels, and seeing his oxen for some unknown reason increase the speed of their slow steps. Even Bani, the dog by his side, barked with sharp, fearful tones. It was as

---

* Abridged from *Preaching from the Prophets* by Kyle M. Yates, pp. 163-66. Copyright, 1942, by Kyle M. Yates. Published by Broadman Press. Used by special permission of the author and the publisher.

though the gray sky above unfolded an atmosphere of apprehension all about Job.

But even as he watched a rift came in the gray sky, the warm sun pushed through bringing its tranquil brightness. Job sensed peace dispersing before his eyes. He did not know that Satan, who had been lingering there, at that moment had gone away—gone, to stand before the Lord; nor did he know that a council was being held in heaven, concerning the man called Job, who lived in the land of Uz.

Straightway the Lord asked in council, "Whence cometh thou?" And Satan answered, "From going to and fro in the earth, and from walking up and down in it."

"Has thou considered my servant Job? for there is none like him in the earth, a perfect and upright man," asked the Lord.

Tinged with sinister suggestion in the tone of his voice, Satan quickly answered, "Doth Job fear God for nought? Hast not thou made a hedge about him, and about his house, and about all that he hath, on every side? Thou hast blessed the work of his hands, and his substance is increased in the land. But put forth thy hand now, and touch all that he hath, and he will renounce thee to thy face."

And God, for reasons that reached out into eternity, answered Satan, and said, "Behold, all that he hath is in thy power; only upon himself put not forth thy hand."

From that meeting in heaven with an undisguised motive, Satan quickly turned toward Uz again. There Job's oxen plowed the fields—five hundred yoke of oxen. His asses, hundreds of them, quietly ate the grass. The camels which he owned were three thousand in number. Seven thousand sheep moved in black waves over the pastures. All spoke of the wealth of Job.

Far above the riches that surrounded him, Job valued his seven sons and his three daughters. His keen eyes radiated joy with the knowledge of their happiness. In the dawn of each new day, he rose up to bring them in his heart before the Lord, lest they should be without a sacrifice for their sins. Then was Job's life filled with the elements of contentment even as the desert near him was filled with its grains of sand.

Thus, another day dawned—like all other days in the household of Job—calm and peaceful. His sons and daughters met in the home of their eldest brother for their usual feast together. Job sat before the door of his tent with joy shining in his keen eyes and spoke to his dog, "Bani, the Lord made this day. It is perfect." And Bani folded his front paws around his head and dozed peacefully.

But at that moment, Satan surveyed the household of Job and coolly schemed against it. Before long Job looked into the distance and saw a black speck against the blue of the southern sky, which grew as it approached him. He watched the figure come with the speed of a runner, for he was one of Job's own servants. At last he stood before his master, and with his message, shattered the peace of Job. "While the oxen plowed, and the asses ate the grass of the field, the Sabeans fell upon us," he cried. "They have taken the oxen and the asses and they have slain thy servants. I am the only one left to bear the message to you."

As a strong wind speeds on its way, so Satan moved with great haste against Job. Even before the servant finished speaking, another servant arrived. Quickly he spoke, "Out of the black clouds lightning flashed against us and burned the sheep and the goats, and the shepherds—even as they tended the sheep. I was the only one left," and his trembling voice revealed the horror of his message.

Scarcely did he pause before another servant came to speak. "Three armies of Chaldeans closed around your camels and took them away," he said. "They left me alone to bear the message to you."

A fourth messenger rushed up and in his eyes was the look of one who suffered as he spoke. "A great whirlwind dashed across the desert," he said. "It beat the corners of the house until it fell—the house, which held thy sons and thy daughters. They are dead," he added, and sorrow etched itself on his tired face.

Job arose and rent his mantle, even as his heart was torn. He threw himself down with his forehead upon the dust. Grief poured from his honest heart as pure water runs from the depth of the earth. Then, after a time, tranquillity filled the heart of Job, and he spoke again, "God gave the sheep and the goats to me, and the asses, and the camels." For a moment Job was silent, then he added, "Yes, God gave my children to me. I took all these blessings from Him. Have I any right to say He cannot take them away?"

As water pours from the earth to become a blessing, so the grief of Job turned into praise. "Blessed be the name of the Lord," said Job.

With evil in his eyes, Satan quickly left the land of Uz and went to stand before the Lord again; and again the Lord spake the same words concerning His servant Job, and these words the Lord added, "And still Job holdeth fast his integrity."

With alertness, Satan quickly answered, "Yea, all that a man hath will he give for his life. But put forth thine hand now, and touch his bone and his flesh, and he will curse thee to thy face."

And God, for reasons that reached out into eternity, answered Satan, and said, "Behold he is in thine hand, but save thou his life."

Turning again toward Uz, Satan said to himself, "I will wreck his body and the foundation of Job will fall." Then with a twisted grin on his face, Satan smote Job with boils—many, many boils, loathsome and full of pain.

A grotesque figure was the Job who turned to sit on an ash mound in his grief. Bani lay near by keeping his eyes on his master in silent sympathy.

But Job's wife longed to speak. She had watched him prosper through the years. She was mindful that his keen eyes shone with joy when their seven sons and three daughters were happy; and she knew that Job rose early in the morning to carry them in his heart before the Lord. All these things went into the growth of Job's household, even as a sapling grows into a tree with limbs, and foliage, and blossoms ready to produce fruit. Now she saw Job as she would see a tree cut down to a mere trunk, stripped of every limb, and leaf, and blossom— bleeding from its wounds and seemingly ready to die. "Death—that is all the Lord has left for Job," she thought. Then she turned to him, and with hopelessness in her heart, she cried, "Dost thou still retain thine integrity? Curse God, and die."

Job listened to her words as he saw the travelers pass and stare at him—the man, who had been the most prosperous one among them. But in spite of his pain and humiliation, Job sat up straighter and looked at his wife in surprise. "What?" he asked. "Shall we receive good at the hand of God and refuse to receive evil?"

Not only did the people of Uz know of Job's affliction but the bad news spread even to distant lands. On a gray and gloomy day he sat on the mound of ashes and Bani lay beside him. Suddenly Job became conscious of three people approaching —friends, whose station, each in his own country, was like unto his own in Uz. And behold, they rent their beautifully embroidered mantles and cried with loud voices as they came. They threw ashes into the air above their heads, for to them the suffering Job scarcely resembled the Job of great prosperity. So Eliphaz, Bildad, and Zophar—Job's three friends—climbed the mound and sat in the ashes to mourn with him and to comfort him. Nor did they speak for a season, for so great was the suffering of Job.

After a long silence Job poured his sorrow into the silent sympathy of his friends. "Let the day perish wherein I was born," he cried, as his thin hands rubbed the tears from his tortured eyes. "Would that I could rest as kings do in their tombs, and as princes do when they lay down their gold and silver and sleep in peace," and his voice was full of longing.

Job's friends exchanged glances of disappointment. They held in their hearts molds for their religious beliefs—three identical molds—into which they placed every man's religious experience. Each man had made his mold with this, his own formula: "The man who sows wickedness reaps evil in his harvest, and the righteous man reaps good—always."

Eliphaz turned his clear eyes toward Job, and said, "Behold, you have taught many who needed teaching." He paused, and then calmly asked, "Did you ever see an innocent man perish, Job? Is not every righteous man rewarded, and every wicked man punished?"

The weight of affliction was upon Job, an upright man, and he cried, "My grief . . . would be heavier than the sand of the sea." Then his voice tightened as he added, "You, my friends, have deserted me—even as the brook deserts the place where it runs, under the heat of the sun." Bani arose, rubbed against his master, and with a soft bark of approval moved even closer to him.

Bildad's sharp voice seemed to match the features of his face as he firmly said to Job, "God will not punish an upright man; if you were upright God would bless you." Then as though he spoke with the wisdom of the ages, he added: "A flag never grows without water, neither does a man prosper without righteousness."

Annoyed by his friends, Job declared, "God sends affliction not only to the wicked but to the righteous." Then his quick voice cried, "Would that I had not lived to see the sun." But even after his tense cry, Job declared with calm assurance, "Though He slay me, yet will I trust Him."

Zophar's lips drew straight as he fastened his gaze on Job with the conviction that he had sinned in secret. "God has not punished you as much as you deserved," he alleged. "But stretch your hands toward the Lord and He will make you shine as the morning." Then he held the formula for the mold, with which he measured the work of the Lord, before Job again. "The righteous are always rewarded," he said sternly.

Job pressed his hand against his forehead as he uttered an appeal for himself, "Surely—I desire to reason with God." Then he murmured, "God hath destroyed me on every side . . . He counteth me unto Him as one of His enemies." But like a candle sending out its light, faith penetrated the darkness in the heart of Job, and made him exclaim, "For I know that my redeemer liveth. . . ."

The friends of Job looked from one to the other, for no word of understanding had passed from them to Job. Elihu, a young man who had stopped to listen, straightened and stepped forward to offer a solution to close the heated discussion, but neither did his words solve the motive for the suffering of Job.

Clouds suddenly gathered over the mound of ashes. A whirlwind began to blow; a voice came from the wind—God's voice, speaking to Job. Listening to the voice, Job heard of the Creator, who laid the cornerstone for the foundation of the earth, while the morning stars sang together; the Creator who knew the treasures of the snow and hail, who sent the drops of dew by night; and who made it rain in desert places where no man lived; the Creator of hoary frost; who listened to the cry of the young raven and called it prayer; who told the eagle to place her nest on the height of the cliff; of the Creator whose voice the universe obeyed.

Then Job said to the Lord, "I know thou canst do everything." And facing God, Job saw himself, and cried, "I have uttered words I did not understand . . . I repent in dust and ashes," and with his words peace came to his eyes. Bani arose and stood by the side of his master with his head high, proudly facing the wind.

And God spoke to Job's friends that they might offer gifts to him, and He spoke to Job that he might bring them in his heart before the Lord. Job was given twice as much as he had lost; but far above the riches that surrounded him, he valued the seven sons and the three daughters who came to bless his home.

The suffering of Job, God permitted for reasons that reach into eternity, beyond the ken of man. But Job's face was radiant as he said, "I have seen the Glory of the Lord." And somehow the memory of the suffering of Job was lost in that Glory, while the morning stars sang together.*

✛

JEREMIAH, THE VOICE OF THE LORD

By

Florence C. Porter

IN about the year 645 B.C., in the village of Anathoth, four miles northeast of Jerusalem, Jeremiah was born. He was of the priestly family of Hilkiah, descended from Eli, the high priest.

* Used by special permission of the author.

As a youth, Jeremiah must have wandered up and down the rocky hills near his home and viewed the desolate places about which he later wrote. He was, no doubt, a keen observer and enjoyed the things of nature. Perhaps at times he watched the speckled birds and noted the migration of the stork, of the turtle, of the crane and of the swallow. Of them he wrote that although they obeyed the times appointed by the Lord, the people would not heed His judgment.

As a boy, he may have talked to the shepherds in the valleys about the destruction that can come to the flocks. A lion might come out to slay them, or a wolf in the evenings spoil them, or a leopard tear them to pieces. These dangers Jeremiah later used as a comparison to show the judgment that would come upon the people that had forsaken their God.

Jeremiah lived in a troubled time in the land of Judah. The Assyrians had conquered Israel: Judah had become a vassal state; and many of the people had turned away from the worship of Jehovah and had adopted the religious practices of their overlords. To a young man, reared in a religious home as was Jeremiah, and possessed of a highly sensitive nature, this turning away from God brought great sorrow.

When the son of Hilkiah was less than twenty years of age, the word of the Lord came to this young man, saying: "Even before thou wert born, I chose thee for a prophet unto the nations."

And young Jeremiah answered, "Ah, Lord God! behold I cannot speak: for I am but a child."

"Say not, I am a child: for thou shalt go to all that I shall send thee, and whatsoever I command thee thou shalt speak. Be not afraid: for I am with thee to deliver thee," the Lord made answer.

Then the Lord put forth his hand and touched Jeremiah's mouth as he said, "Behold, I have put my words in thy mouth. See, I have this day set thee over the nations and over the kingdoms, to root out, and to pull down, and to destroy, and to throw down, to build and to plant."

So came Jeremiah's commission to him from the Lord God; and from that time forth the son of Hilkiah became truly, "The Voice of the Lord."

Then, moreover, there came a vision to Jeremiah. "What seest thou?" said the Lord. And the young prophet answered, "I see a rod of an almond tree."

Then the Lord said, "Thou hast well seen: for I will hasten my word to perform it."

A second time the Lord spoke, saying, "What seest thou?" And Jeremiah answered: "I see a seething pot; and the face thereof is toward the north."

Then said the Lord, "Out of the north an evil shall break forth upon all the inhabitants of the land. And I will utter my judgments against those who have forsaken me, and have burned incense unto other gods, and worshipped the work of their own hands. Arise thou, therefore, gird up thy loins, and speak unto them all that I command thee, but they shall not prevail against thee; for I am with thee to deliver thee."

Jeremiah obeyed the Lord God and, leaving his home, to Jerusalem he went. There he gave the people message after message introduced by the words, "Thus

saith the Lord." Mingled with the words denouncing the people for their wickedness and their backsliding, he urged them, both of the land of Israel and Judah,
to return to the Lord with their whole hearts, and he held out to them this
promise: "For I am merciful," saith the Lord, "and I will not keep my anger
forever." Jeremiah also spoke hopefully of the future, saying: "And all the nations shall be gathered unto the throne of the Lord, and to the name of the Lord,
to Jerusalem."

But the people heeded not. Jeremiah believed that if a man's heart was right
toward God, such a man must live a clean life and must deal rightly with his
fellow men. But the rich men of his times made slaves of their own people in
the land of Judah, nor did they grant freedom to their servants in the seventh
year of their servitude. These actions were not in accordance with the laws that
the Lord had given by Moses. Moreover, the people appeared to worship the
Lord with their sacrifices and with their lips, but not in their hearts.

At one time the word of the Lord came to the prophet saying, "Go and get
thee a linen girdle and put it on thy loins, but put it not in water."

Jeremiah obeyed. Then came a second message telling the prophet to take the
girdle that he had on his loins and go to the Euphrates where he was to hide the
girdle in a hole in the rocks. This the prophet did.

Then, after many days, again the Lord said, "Arise, go to the Euphrates, and
take the girdle from thence which I commanded thee to hide there."

The prophet went to the Euphrates, where he dug and found the girdle where
it had been hidden, but the girdle was marred and was good for nothing.

The message of this experience to Jeremiah was that thus the Lord would mar
the pride of Judah and of Jerusalem, for although the Lord had drawn close to
him the people that they might be a pride and a glory to him, they would not
hear or heed his commands.

At another time there came a command to the prophet that he was to arise
and go to the potter's house, and there receive the word from the Lord. Obedient
to the command, Jeremiah went and observed the work of the potter. He saw the
lump of clay being turned on the wheel and, being obedient to the potter's hand,
becoming a beautiful vessel.

But one vessel that he was shaping became marred in the hand of the potter;
hence it became a lump of shapeless clay which the potter placed again on his
wheel and shaped by his hand till it too became a vessel that seemed good in
the maker's sight.

Then said the Lord, "O house of Israel cannot I do with you as this potter?
Behold, as the clay is in the potter's hand, so are ye in my hand, O house of
Israel."

Again a potter's vessel was used—this time to bring a message to the elders of
the people and to the priests. The prophet was told to take with him an earthen
vessel and go with the elders to the valley by the east gate of the city wall and
there bring to them words of the evil that would come to the city.

The faithful Jeremiah went and told them that their enemies would destroy them by the sword, that their city would be made desolate, and that they would be subjected to siege and famine. The earthen vessel was broken and then came the message, "Thus saith the Lord: Even so will I break this people and this city, as one breaketh a potter's vessel that cannot be made whole again."

Then the prophet stood in the court of the Lord's house and spoke in a like manner to all the people.

When Pashur, the chief governor in the house of the Lord, heard of the prophecies of Jeremiah, he smote the prophet and put him in the stocks that were in the high gate of Benjamin by the house of the Lord. Even though the obedient prophet was released the next day, thus was God's messenger put to shame for bringing to the people the word of the Lord.

During the reign of Josiah, the good king, he made a covenant with the Lord after the book of the law had been found in the house of the Lord. Moreover, he ordered that the vessels of Baal and Ashtoreth be burned, the groves cut down, the images and altars broken to pieces, and the priests of Baal in the high places slain. Then the king commanded that all the people keep the passover. According to the records, there had not been such a passover held since the days of the judges in Israel.

But after a reign of thirty and one years, Josiah went to fight against the king of Egypt who wished to go through the land of Judah to fight against Assyria at the Euphrates River. At Megiddo the forces of Egypt and Judah met, and Josiah the king was slain.

From the death of Josiah to the time of the captivity, there ruled three kings; and the record of each one of them is summed up in the words, "And he did that which was evil in the sight of the Lord." Their history was one of making treaties with other countries and not keeping them, of paying tribute to Egypt and Assyria, and of using bribery and treachery.

Jeremiah, being ever true to his commission of being "the voice of the Lord," became at enmity with both the kings and people; but they continued to harden their hearts nor would they listen to nor heed his prophecies. It was only his immediate prophecies that foretold punishment upon the rulers and people, for Jeremiah still envisioned a blessed future when Jehovah would "arise up unto David a righteous Branch" and "a king should reign and prosper, and should execute judgment and justice in the earth."

In the beginning of the reign of Jehoiakim, the son of Josiah, Jeremiah was told to stand in the court of the Lord's house and speak unto all the cities of Judah which came to worship in the Lord's house. The words which the Lord commanded his prophet to speak were those that gave the people a choice. They might repent and turn every man from his evil way with the promise that the Lord would turn back from the evil which he purposed unto them, or they might refuse to hearken to the Lord and thereby suffer punishment for themselves and their city. But the priests and the prophets and all the people rose up against the faithful messenger of the Lord saying, "Thou shalt surely die. Thou hast prophesied that our city shall be desolate."

When the princes of Judah heard these things, they came from the king's house unto the house of the Lord. Unto them the priests and the prophets repeated their charge against Jeremiah: "This man is worthy to die; for he has prophesied against this city."

In a simple and straightforward way Jeremiah answered their charge in these words: "The Lord sent me to prophesy against this house and against this city all the words that ye have heard." And again he repeated the Lord's promise to them if they would repent and mend their evil ways.

Then the princes and all the people spoke thus to the priests and the prophets on Jeremiah's behalf, saying: "This man is not worthy to die: for he has spoken to us in the name of the Lord, our God." Therefore was the life of the prophet spared.

Then came the word of the Lord to Jeremiah that he was to make bonds and yokes, wear them on his own neck, and send them to each of the kings of the surrounding countries as a symbol of servitude to the king of Babylon. And with this command from the Lord there came His words that all the nations would serve Babylon and that the nation which would not put its neck under the yoke of Nebuchadnezzar would be punished by the sword, by famine, and with pestilence until it was consumed.

But Hananiah, a false prophet, prophesied that the Lord had broken the yoke of the king of Babylon, and that in two years the vessels of the Lord's house would be returned to Jerusalem with all the captives of Judah. Furthermore, Hananiah took the yoke from Jeremiah's neck and broke it. And the prophet Jeremiah went his way.

Then came the word of the Lord to his Prophet to tell Hananiah: "Thou hast broken the yoke of wood, but thou shalt make for them yokes of iron. I have put a yoke of iron upon the neck of all these nations that they shall serve Nebuchadnezzar king of Babylon." And that same year Hananiah, the false prophet, died.

Now as Nebuchadnezzar king of Babylon became stronger in his kingdom, he began to threaten the land of Judah and the other near-by countries. Jeremiah thought of Nebuchadnezzar as an agent of the Lord God in bringing about the punishment of the people of Judah for turning from him and heeding not his words.

Because of the enmity of the king, the prophets, the priests and the people against Jeremiah, the prophet of the Lord had to go into hiding. Jeremiah must have been a very lonely man. He had left his home and his family in Anathoth to come to Jerusalem as "the voice of the Lord." Sometime after he received his commission from the Lord, another command had come to him. The prophet was not to take a wife nor to have sons or daughters of his own. But he did have a friend upon whom he could call—Baruch, the son of Neriah.

In the fourth year of Jehoiakim the king, the word of the Lord came to Jeremiah, saying: "Take thee a roll of a book and write therein all the words that I have spoken unto thee against Israel, and against Judah, and against all the nations from the days of Josiah even unto this day."

Then Jeremiah called Baruch who acted as his scribe and he wrote on a roll of a book the words of the Lord as spoken by the Lord's prophet. When the roll was finished, Jeremiah commanded Baruch to read it in the Lord's house upon the fasting day the words of the Lord in the ears of the people of Judah.

When the princes were told of the reading of Baruch, they sent for him to read all the words of the roll in their ears. When they had heard all the words, they were afraid and said unto Baruch: "We will surely tell the king of all these words." Then when Baruch told them that he had written the words as spoken by Jeremiah, they warned him, "Go, hide thee, thou and Jeremiah, and let no man know where ye be."

So the roll was laid in the chamber of the scribe and the king was told all the words. Then Jehoiakim the king sent Jehudi to bring the roll and read it in the presence of the king and all the princes. Now the king sat in the winter house and there was a fire burning on the hearth. When Jehudi had read three or four leaves, the king cut the roll with his penknife and cast it into the fire where it was all consumed. Then the king gave orders to take Baruch the scribe and Jeremiah the prophet; but the Lord had hid them.

Again came the word of the Lord to Jeremiah to take another roll and write in it all the former words that were in the first roll. With the help of Baruch, the scribe, all the words of Jeremiah were written on another roll, and there were added besides them many like words.

Though the people refused to believe the prophecies brought to them by Jeremiah in the latter part of Jehoiakim's reign, Judah became a vassal state under Nebuchadnezzar. "The Voice of the Lord" was not stilled, but from that time on till the final siege of the city and the carrying away of the people as captives to Babylon, the message was that they should yield to Babylon with the hope of saving the city and the remaining vessels of the house of the Lord.

In the events leading directly to the siege and the final captivity of Judah, the hardships of Jeremiah and the failure of the people to understand the warnings of the Lord's prophet became greater and greater; but never once did the faith of the prophet fail nor did he cease to voice the message of the Lord God. To the end of his life the prophet continued to be, in word and deed, "the Voice of the Lord."*

✠

GOD OF THE NATIONS, WHO FROM DAWN OF DAYS

(Interpretation)

WALTER RUSSELL BOWIE (1882——) was born in Richmond, Virginia. In 1904 he took his B.A. degree at Harvard and the following year his M.A. degree. Later he received doctor's degrees from Richmond College, Virginia Theological Seminary, and Syracuse University.

In 1909 he was ordained by Bishop Gibson and that same year married Jean Laverack of Buffalo, New York. His first rectorate was in Greenwood Parish in Virginia, and in 1911 he became rector of St. Paul's Episcopal Church in Richmond, the city of his birth. Later he accepted a call to Grace Church in New York City. For a number of years he was a professor at Union Theological Seminary in New York City.

* Used by special permission of the author.

God of the Nations, Who from Dawn of Days

TOULON. 10, 10, 10, 10

W. RUSSELL BOWIE, 1913   LOUIS BOURGEOIS, 1551

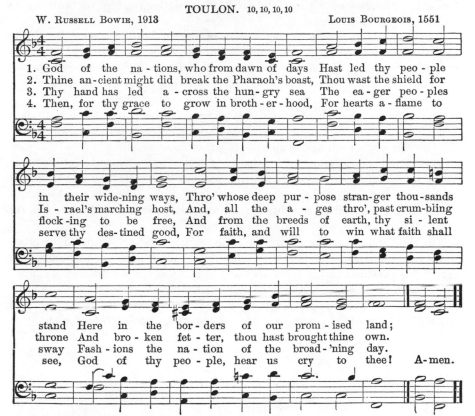

1. God of the na - tions, who from dawn of days Hast led thy peo - ple
2. Thine an - cient might did break the Pharaoh's boast, Thou wast the shield for
3. Thy hand has led a - cross the hun - gry sea The ea - ger peo - ples
4. Then, for thy grace to grow in broth - er - hood, For hearts a - flame to

in their wide-ning ways, Thro' whose deep pur - pose stran-ger thou-sands
Is - rael's marching host, And, all the a - ges thro', past crum-bling
flock -ing to be free, And from the breeds of earth, thy si - lent
serve thy des - tined good, For faith, and will to win what faith shall

stand Here in the bor - ders of our prom - ised land;
throne And bro - ken fet - ter, thou hast brought thine own.
sway Fash - ions the na - tion of the broad - 'ning day.
see, God of thy peo - ple, hear us cry to thee! A - men.

*Words copyright, 1914, 1942, by Harper & Brothers. From *Social Hymns of Brotherhood and Aspiration* edited by Mabel Hay Burrows Mussey. Used by special permission of the publisher.

He has written a number of valuable books for young people and adults. One of the best, *The Master,* was published in 1928. Dr. Bowie is an outspoken leader on such subjects as social justice and political problems and issues.

This hymn was first published in 1914. The melody to which it is sung, "Toulon," was composed in 1551 by Louis Bourgeois.

✠

O GOD, THE ROCK OF AGES

(Interpretation)

EDWARD HENRY BICKERSTETH (1825-1906) was one of the renowned Bickersteth family. He was born in Islington, and was the son of the Reverend Edward Bickersteth, rector at Watton and secretary for the Church Missionary Society.

Edward, Jr. was graduated from Trinity College, at Cambridge, and early distinguished himself as a poet and a writer. He was deeply interested in charitable and social movements, and soon after his graduation became vicar of Christ Church at Hampstead, where he labored arduously for thirty years both for his parish and for foreign missions.

At sixty years of age he became Bishop of Exeter, England, where he contin-ued his vigorous leadership and activities for another fifteen years. He won fame for his poetry and published a book of hymns, *From Year to Year,* which contained a great many hymns written to emphasize important events in the Christian year.

This hymn is one of his best and was included in his book. It was written in 1860 and is a hymn of peace to "God, the Rock of Ages," who has forever been the "dwelling place serene" of all who put their trust in Him.

The second stanza compares the changing experiences of men to "shadows on sunny hills," "grasses in the meadows that blossom but to die." To Edward Henry Bickersteth life was like "a sleep, a dream, a story, by strangers quickly told," reminding us, one and all, that life is transitory, that all things pass away like the glory which vanishes when things become old.

The third stanza recognizes the enduring nature of God, "Whose light grows never pale," and who will if we but allow Him "teach us aright to number our years" that goodness and mercy shall shine in and through us, making our hearts bright because they are blessed by the Spirit of God.

The tune to which this hymn is sung, "Miriam," was composed in 1865 by Joseph P. Holbrook. It is also sung to a Welsh tune entitled "Meirionydd."

✛

UNTO THE HILLS

(Interpretation)

THE 121st Psalm has been the inspiration of countless thousands of discouraged, struggling pilgrims along life's highway. Through the centuries men and women have found comfort and a renewal of their strength and courage in its lofty sentiments.

In the long ago, David may have sung it on the hillsides of Judea as he guarded his father's flocks in the lonely watches of the night. Kings and emperors have found surcease from care and responsibility in its fervent devotional message of faith and trust. Soldiers in far countries, as they watched the movements of their enemies from some distant mountain peak, have repeated its assuring sentiments. Sailors in the midst of boisterous waves on the high seas, as they toiled with the ship's machinery and rigging, have voiced their faith and trust in God by repeating its strength-restoring words, as they prayed to the God of their fathers for protection, help, and strength.

It is small wonder, therefore, that Hebrew authors should include among their canticles of praise to the God of Abraham, Isaac, and Jacob this beautiful Psalm that has brought strength and comfort to many.

O God, the Rock of Ages

MIRIAM. 7, 6, 7, 6, D.

EDWARD H. BICKERSTETH, 1860

JOSEPH P. HOLBROOK, 1865

1. O God, the Rock of A - ges, Who ev - er - more hast been,
2. Our years are like the shad - ows On sun - ny hills that lie,
3. O Thou who canst not slum - ber, Whose light grows nev - er pale,

What time the tem - pest rag - es, Our dwell - ing place se - rene,
Or grass - es in the mead - ows That blos - som but to die;
Teach us a - right to num - ber Our years be - fore they fail;

Be - fore thy first cre - a - tions, O Lord, the same as now,
A sleep, a dream, a sto - ry, By stran - gers quick - ly told,
On us thy mer - cy light - en, On us thy good - ness rest,

To end - less gen - er - a - tions, The ev - er - last - ing thou.
An un - re - main - ing glo - ry Of things that soon are old.
And let thy Spir - it bright - en The hearts thy - self hast blessed. A - men.

Unto the Hills

Alice Lucas PSALM 121 Jacob Beimel

Andante

1. Un - to the hills I lift mine eyes, Whence
3. He is thy rock, thy shield and stay, On

comes my help that lies in God, Who is en-throned a -
thy right hand a shade al - way, The sun ne'er smit - eth

bove the skies, Who made the heav - ens and earth to be.
thee by day, The moon at night ne'er troub - les thee.

Unto the Hills
Continued

2. He guides thy foot o'er moun - tain steeps, He
4. The Lord will guard thy soul from sin, Thy

slum - bers not, thy soul He keeps, Be - hold He slum - bers
life from harm with - out, with - in, Thy go - ing out and

not, nor sleeps, Of Is - ra - el the guard - ian He.
com - ing in, From this time forth e - ter - nal - ly.

This hymn should be sung slowly, smoothly, and with true devotional fervor. Thus the heart will respond to its mood of faith in the guidance of the Heavenly Father, and will trust in His sustaining care.

We are indebted to Alice Lucas and Jacob Beimel for the English words and the music of this rich, devotional canticle.

✛

WE PRAISE THEE, O GOD

(Interpretation)

THE words of this great hymn were composed in 1902 by Julia Bulkley Cady. Little is known of the life of this pious woman, but the spirit of this hymn is clearly in its three brief stanzas.

We Praise Thee, O God

KREMSER. 12, 11, 12, 11

JULIA BULKLEY CADY, 1882–   Netherlands Folk Song, 1625

1. We praise thee, O God, our Re-deem-er, Cre-a-tor, In grate-ful de-
2. We wor-ship thee, God of our fa-thers, we bless thee; Thro' life's storm and
3. With voic-es u-ni-ted our prais-es we of-fer, To thee, great Je-

vo-tion our trib-ute we bring. We lay it be-fore thee, we
tem-pest our Guide hast thou been. When per-ils o'er-take us, es-
ho-vah, glad an-thems we raise. Thy strong arm will guide us, our

kneel and a-dore thee, We bless thy ho-ly name, glad praises we sing.
cape thou wilt make us, And with thy help, O Lord, our bat-tles we win.
God is be-side us, To thee, our great Redeemer, for-ev-er be praise. A-men.

The first stanza is a tribute of love, praise, and devotion to "God, our Redeemer, Creator."

The second stanza is a recognition of the "God of our fathers," who, through the centuries, has been the guide, protector, and stay of men, helping them to win life's battles.

The third stanza expresses the united praise of all "followers of the way" to God, whose "strong arm will guide us," and whom in gratitude we praise as our great Redeemer.

The melody to which this hymn is sung is entitled "Kremser." It was arranged by Edward Kremser from a Netherlands folk song dating back to 1625.

✢

THE MAN WHO ONCE HAS FOUND ABODE

(Interpretation)

THE 91st Psalm was the inspiration for the writing of this great hymn from the *United Presbyterian Book of Psalms* (1871). Its theme is found in the Psalmist's assurance that there is "security for him who trusts in the Lord."

The first stanza of this hymn is in reality a poetic translation of the first verse of the 91st Psalm, which reads:

> He that dwelleth in the secret place
> of the most High
> Shall abide under the shadow of the
> Almighty.

The second stanza is a liberal phrasing of the second stanza of this Psalm:

> I will say of the Lord, He is my
> refuge and my fortress:
> My God; in him will I trust.

The third stanza emphasizes the truth that the Lord

> Will deliver thee from the snare
> of the fowler,
> And from the noisome pestilence.

The fourth stanza assures His followers that

> He shall cover thee with his feathers,
> And under his wings shalt thou trust.

The fifth stanza is a paraphrase of the fifth stanza of this Psalm:

> Thou shalt not be afraid for the
> terror by night;
> Nor for the arrow that flieth
> by day.

The Man Who Once Has Found Abode

TALLIS' CANON. L. M.

Psalm 91
United Presbyterian Book of Psalms
U. S. A., 1871

THOMAS TALLIS, 1560

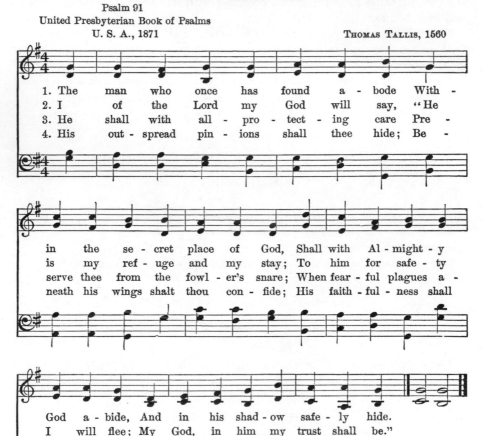

1. The man who once has found a - bode With -
2. I of the Lord my God will say, "He
3. He shall with all - pro - tect - ing care Pre -
4. His out - spread pin - ions shall thee hide; Be -

in the se - cret place of God, Shall with Al - might - y
is my ref - uge and my stay; To him for safe - ty
serve thee from the fowl - er's snare; When fear - ful plagues a -
neath his wings shalt thou con - fide; His faith - ful - ness shall

God a - bide, And in his shad - ow safe - ly hide.
I will flee; My God, in him my trust shall be."
round pre - vail, No fa - tal stroke shall thee as - sail.
ev - er be A shield and buck - ler un - to thee. A - men.

5 No nightly terrors shall alarm,
    No deadly shaft by day shall harm,
    Nor pestilence that walks by night,
    Nor plagues that waste in noonday light.

6 Because thy trust is God alone,
    Thy dwelling-place the Highest One,
    No evil shall upon thee come,
    Nor plague approach thy guarded home.

The sixth stanza broadly interprets in poetic form the lines:

> Nor for the pestilence that walketh
> in darkness;
> Nor for the destruction that wasteth
> at noonday.

The melody to which this poetic translation is of the 91st Psalm is sung is entitled "Tallis' Canon." It was composed about 1567 by Thomas Tallis.

PART VI

HIGH LIGHTS OF THE FALL OF JUDAH, THE EXILE, AND THE RETURN

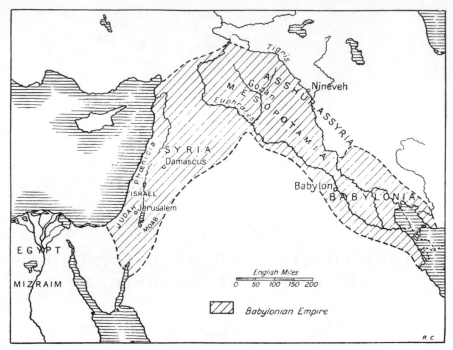

The Babylonian Empire in the time of Nebuchadrezzar

THE EXILE

NEBUCHADNEZZAR treated the Jews leniently, as ancient conquerors went. The lowest estimate of those deported to Babylon is that of Jeremiah 52:28-30, which gives a total of 4,600. If these were fighting men, and women, children, and old men were included proportionately, the number may have reached 20,000 in all. But they were the leaders of the nation and the skilled men. A Jew of the moderate party, Gedaliah, was appointed governor. He set up his headquarters at Mizpah, where he was assassinated by conspirators who came from Ammon, against whom he had refused to take precautions. A considerable number of Jews fled to Egypt, probably fearing indiscriminate reprisals, and the Dispersion began in earnest. Those who were left, deserted by their leaders and disheartened by the pressing in of Edomites into their territory, led a miserable existence.

The Jews in Babylon found a leader in Ezekiel, a priest who had gone with the 597 party. When in 586 his continued prophecies of final disaster were fulfilled, his influence became great and he and his followers with wonderful faith and tenacity began to plan for the future. As Jeremiah 29 and Ezekiel show, communications between Babylonia and Judea were kept open. Jeremiah's advice to build houses and plant gardens shows that the prospects of the exiles were fair. Indeed, materially, they had little cause to complain.*

* Both map and excerpt are from *Concise Bible Commentary* by W. K. Lowther Clarke, pp. 17-18. Copyright, 1953, by The Macmillan Company. Used by special permission of the publisher.

CONTENTS

PART VI SECTION 1

THE BABYLONIAN CAPTIVITY

✛

And in . . . the nineteenth year of king Nebuchadnezzar king of Babylon, came Nebuzaradan, captain of the guard, a servant of the king of Babylon, unto Jerusalem. And he burnt the house of the Lord. . . . And all the army of the Chaldees, that were with the captain of the guard, brake down the walls of Jerusalem round about. Now the rest of the people that were left in the city, and the fugitives that fell away to the king of Babylon . . . did Nebuzaradan the captain of the guard carry away.—II KINGS 25:8-11

✛

MUSIC:

THE PEOPLE CARRIED CAPTIVE FROM JERUSALEM

By

Julius Schnorr von Carolsfeld

(Interpretation)

THE Biblical material which the German artist Schnorr von Carolsfeld used as the inspiration for this engraving is found in II Kings 25:8-15. It reads: "In the fifth month, on the seventh day of the month, which is the nineteenth year of king Nebuchadnezzar king of Babylon, came Nebuzaradan, the captain of the guard, a servant of the king of Babylon, unto Jerusalem. And he burnt the house of the Lord, and the king's house, and all the houses of Jerusalem, and every great man's house burnt he with fire. And all the army of the Chaldeans, that were with the captain of the guard, brake down the walls of Jerusalem round about. Now the rest of the people that were left in the city, and the fugitives that fell away, . . . did Nebuzaradan the captain of the guard carry away. But the captain of the guard left of the poor of the land to be vinedressers and husbandmen.

"And the pillars of brass that were in the house of the Lord, and the bases and the brasen sea that was in the house of the Lord, did the Chaldeans break in pieces, and carried the brass of them to Babylon. And the pots, and the shovels, and the snuffers, and the spoons, and all the vessels of brass wherewith they ministered, took they away. And the firepans, and the bowls, and such things as were of gold, in gold, and of silver, in silver, the captain of the guard took away."

The subjugation of Jerusalem by Nebuchadnezzar began during the reign of Jehoiachin and was completed under Zedekiah, who was twenty-one years old when he began to reign and who reigned eleven years. It was the king of Babylon who had made him king, and who changed his name from Mattaniah to Zedekiah. Nevertheless, after nine years of domination by Babylon, Zedekiah rebelled; and no sooner had his rebellion been recognized than Nebuchadnezzar himself, with all his army, came against Jerusalem and besieged it until the eleventh year of Zedekiah's reign. By that time the famine in Jerusalem was great for there was no bread at all for the people in the city. The destruction of Jerusalem foretold by Jeremiah, the prophet, was at hand.

A breach was made in the city's wall, and all King Zedekiah's soldiers fled by night by way of the gate between the two walls which was by the king's garden. The army of the Chaldeans surrounded the city. They pursued the king and his men, overtook them on the plains of Jericho, and carried them captive to the king of Babylon. They killed the sons of Zedekiah before his very eyes, and put out the eyes of Zedekiah and carried him captive to Babylon.

Zebuzaradan, the captain of the guard, the servant of the king of Babylon, came into Jerusalem on horseback, surrounded by soldiers of the Chaldean army. He gave orders to break down the fortifications of the city and to drive the Hebrews out of the city and into exile in Babylon.

In the background of Schnorr von Carolsfeld's portrayal of this incident Neb-uzaradan appears on his horse giving orders to his soldiers. Some of them are tearing down the walls of Jerusalem. In the foreground the Hebrews are being brutally driven from their homes by their conquerors. Fear and agony are reflected in their faces. They are now going into exile in a foreign land. The two women and their children in the foreground and the man carrying his possessions from a stick on his shoulder are about to join the long line of sorrowing people stretching at the left of the picture into the far distance. For them the Babylonian Exile has already begun.

✛

JEREMIAH

By

Michelangelo Buonarroti

(Interpretation)

JEREMIAH was born, near the end of Manasseh's reign, in Anathoth, a small village about four miles northeast of Jerusalem on the very edge of the wilderness of Judah. Between it and the northern end of the Dead Sea there was nothing except barren hills.

His father, Hilkiah, was the village priest, and among his ancestors were priests who once guarded the sacred symbols of their ancestral Hebrew religion in Shiloh.

Jeremiah was not yet twenty years old when he began to feel the inner leading toward the holy calling of a prophet. When that call came, Jeremiah heard the voice of the Lord, saying: "Before thou camest forth out of the womb I sanctified thee; and I ordained thee a prophet unto the nations" (1:5).

As the Lord's prophet Jeremiah was not understood by his contemporaries. Some of his trials and persecution were caused by members of his own family; some by designing priests and prophets; and others by princes and the people as well.

His lamentation over Josiah's death (II Chron. 35:25) indicates that he may have enjoyed a long and intimate friendship with the king. No doubt he was a valuable adviser to that good monarch, whose twelve-year reign was one of the brightest in Judah's history.

Jeremiah's writings show his unshrinking courage and the pathos of his position. Parts of his writings are vivid and picturesque. The prophet had the ability to describe the miseries of his people with pathetic tenderness. With courage he calls Judah to repentance; he sets forth her sins; and he appeals to the people to remember the Lord's covenants. He also foretells their rejection and captivity. With clarity he prophesies the doom of Jerusalem because of her wickedness; the destruction of foreign nations; and the restoration of the remnant.

When Jerusalem was captured and many of her people were sent as exiles to Babylon, Jeremiah wrote them a letter, saying:

THE PEOPLE CARRIED CAPTIVE FROM JERUSALEM—*VON CAROLSFELD*

"Thus saith the Lord of hosts, the God of Israel, unto all that are carried away captives, whom I have caused to be carried away from Jerusalem unto Babylon:

" 'Build ye houses, and dwell in them; and plant gardens, and eat the fruit of them. Take ye wives, and beget sons and daughters . . . that ye may be increased there, and not diminished. And seek the peace of the city whither I have caused you to be carried away captives, and pray unto the Lord for it, for in the peace thereof shall ye have peace. . . . After seventy years be accomplished at Babylon I will visit you, and perform my good word toward you, in causing you to return to this place' " (29:4-7, 10).

Jeremiah lived through the terrible days of Jerusalem's capture in 598 B.C. and its total destruction eleven years later. Finally he and Baruch, his companion and secretary, were forced to flee to Egypt with a group of escaping Hebrews. There he probably died not long after 586 B.C.

In this part of the Sistine Chapel frieze Michelangelo has portrayed Jeremiah brooding over the tragedy of Jerusalem's destruction. He sits with head bowed upon his uplifted hand, deeply pondering. On his shoulders seem to rest the afflictions of all his people and even of all humanity. This figure of Jeremiah is one of the most famous of all Michelangelo's prophets, not only because he is portrayed with consummate technical skill, but because he expresses all men's sorrows and their attempts to understand the ways of God with man.

Behind Jeremiah two small figures can be seen which show the substance of the prophet's thoughts. On the left the woman with bowed head and downcast eyes hopelessly laments the complete ruin of Judah. But the woman on the right seems animated by resolution. She wears a robe and hood as if prepared for a long journey. Momentarily she glances backward as she sets forth toward a new life in exile. She symbolized Jeremiah's hope and prophetic insight concerning the future. The Lord revealed to Jeremiah that He would make a new covenant with His people, which would not be based on their prescribed national laws, for the nation had been destroyed. The new covenant would be based on the inner response of each human heart to the word of the Lord. Whether a person lived in Jerusalem and worshiped in the Temple, or mourned in exile beside "the waters of Babylon," his Lord was God if he kept His covenant. For people facing a long period of exile this new prophecy of Jeremiah's was a message of hope. It is recorded in Jeremiah 31:33-34:

"But this shall be the covenant that I will make with the house of Israel. After those days, saith the Lord, I will put my law in their inward parts, and write it in their hearts; and will be their God, and they shall be my people. And they shall teach no more every man his neighbor, and every man his brother, saying, 'Know the Lord,' for they shall all know me from the least of them unto the greatest of them, saith the Lord; for I will forgive their iniquity, and I will remember their sin no more."

JEREMIAH—*MICHELANGELO*

"BY THE RIVERS OF BABYLON"

By

Herbert G. Schmalz

(Interpretation)

THE nineteenth-century artist, Herbert G. Schmalz, was born in London in 1856. He displayed his art in both the Royal Academy of Fine Arts and the Grosvenor Gallery in 1881 to 1896.

The theme of this beautiful painting will be found in Psalm 137:1-4. In poetic form it reads:

> By the rivers of Babylon,
> There we sat down, yea, we wept,
> When we remembered Zion.
> We hanged our harps
> Upon the willows in the midst thereof.
> For there they that carried us away captive
> required of us a song,
> And they that wasted us required of us mirth, saying:
> Sing us one of the songs of Zion.
> How shall we sing the Lord's song
> In a strange land?

This picture tells its own story of the heartache and sorrow which is the fate of captive peoples in times of war in every land and in every age. Family ties have been broken, in many instances never again to be restored. Means of livelihood are no longer assured. A strange land, strange faces, strange customs, even a strange language provide almost insurmountable barriers to establishing homes in this country to which they have been carried as captives.

The captive daughters of Judah are seated along the bank of "the rivers of Babylon." The picture might well be entitled "The Death of Hope," for every expression and attitude of these exiles is one of fright, despair, and hopelessness. Never again will they see their beloved Jerusalem, the city of Zion. How can they be xepected to sing the "songs of Zion" or to provide mirthful entertainment with dancing and music for their captors? Their hearts are heavy with the memories of happier days which will never return.

On either side near the top of the steps to the palace entrance stand armed soldiers guarding any possible escape of these prisoners of war; while at the top of the steps, in the center, the king's courtiers look scornfully on these despondent exiles and demand of them "songs of Zion" and "mirth."

At the top of the gleaming white steps may be seen the figures of two giant serpents coiled ready to strike. They are symbolic of the heathen worship in Babylon, and also of its wickedness and sin. The architectural background of the

BY THE RIVERS OF BABYLON—*SCHMALZ*

picture as well as the costumes of its characters indicate the artist's familiarity with the history and customs of ancient Babylon.

✛

THE VISION OF EZEKIEL

By

Raphael Sanzio

(Interpretation)

WE do not know the exact date of Ezekiel's birth, but it must have been about 620 B.C. The city of Jerusalem was in all probability the place of his birth. In the Book of Ezekiel he describes himself as the son of Buzi (1:3) and a member of one of the aristocratic, priestly families of Judah who were in charge of the Temple in Jerusalem.

He lived as a youth in Jerusalem during the reign of the wicked king, Jehoiakim. He undoubtedly knew Jeremiah and heard him prophesy during the years prior to the fall of the city.

In 597 B.C. while he was still a young man, he was among the more than ten thousand captives carried away from Jerusalem in the first deportation ordered by Nebuchadnezzar, king of Babylon. It was in Babylonia, living among his fellow captives by the river Chebar, that he received his call to be a prophet. This was in 593 B.C. and he continued his prophetic ministry until 571 B.C. The word Ezekiel means "God strengthens," and indicates the source of the prophet's power to encourage the exiles of the Babylonian captivity.

The Book of Ezekiel opens with Ezekiel's overpowering vision of the glory and majesty and holiness of God and with his call to be a prophet. Ezekiel tells his story thus:

"Now it came to pass in the thirteenth year, in the fourth month, in the fifth day of the month, as I was among the captives by the river Chebar, that the heavens were opened, and I saw visions of God. In the fifth day of the month, which was the fifth year of king Jehoiachin's captivity, the word of the Lord came expressly unto Ezekiel the priest, the son of Buzi, in the land of the Chaldeans by the river Chebar; and the hand of the Lord was there upon him.

"And I looked, and, behold, a whirlwind came out of the north, a great cloud, and a fire infolding itself, and a brightness was about it, and out of the midst thereof as the colour of amber, out of the midst of the fire" (Ezek. 1:1-4).

This storm heralded the approach of a manifestation of God. What Ezekiel saw was to him "the appearance of the likeness of the glory of the Lord." First he saw four living creatures: a man, a lion, an ox, and an eagle. They bring to God the praises of all creation, singing: "Blessed be the glory of the Lord" (3:12).

Ezekiel's description of the four creatures is not entirely clear, but it conveys a sense of the cosmic power and majesty of God. He wrote: "Also out of the midst

THE VISION OF EZEKIEL—*RAPHAEL*

thereof came the likeness of four living creatures. And this was their appearance: they had the likeness of a man; and every one had four faces, and every one had four wings. And their feet were straight feet; and the sole of their feet was like the sole of a calf's foot; and they sparkled like the color of burnished brass. And they had the hands of a man under their wings on their four sides; and they four had their faces and their wings. Their wings were joined one to another; they turned not when they went; they went every one straight forward.

"As for the likeness of their faces, they had the face of a man; and they four had the face of a lion on the right side; and they four had the face of an ox on the left side; they four had also the face of an eagle. . . . And they went every one straight forward: whither the spirit was to go, they went, and they turned not when they went. As for the likeness of the living creatures, their appearance was like burning coals of fire, and like the appearance of lamps. It went up and down among the living creatures; and the fire was bright, and out of the fire went forth lightning. And the living creatures ran and returned as the appearance of a flash of lightning" (1:5-14).

Next Ezekiel saw strange wheels and finally above the firmament there was the likeness of a sapphire throne on which sat the likeness of a man. "This was the appearance of the likeness of the glory of the Lord. And when I saw it, I fell upon my face, and I heard a voice of one that spake" (Ezek. 1:28).

The voice bade him stand on his feet and go to the rebellious children of Israel with a message from the Lord. Such was Ezekiel's call to be a prophet.

Raphael translates the difficult, confused imagery of Ezekiel's vision into a superb picture. Above a beautiful landscape, storm clouds are lowering and lightning strikes downward toward earth. In the midst of the storm cloud is a luminous amber sky in which fly the four living creatures of the vision. Above them, His upraised arms supported by cherubim, rises the majestic figure of the Lord.

The four living creatures who appeared to Ezekiel were like those seen centuries later and described in Revelation 4:7 as giving glory to God in heaven.

Like all of Raphael's paintings, "The Vision of Ezekiel" excels in composition. The picture presents a rounded group, alive with motion, but concentrated as one big mass against a luminous sky. The harmonious color scheme of the original is also characteristic of Raphael. This painting hangs in the Pitti Palace in Florence, Italy.

Raphael was born in Urbino, Italy, in 1483, the son of a distinguished painter. At the age of twenty-two he visited Florence, where he met many of the noted artists of his day and saw many masterpieces of painting and sculpture. In 1506 he returned to Florence, remaining there two years, during which time some of his finest pictures were painted.

In 1508 he was summoned to Rome by Pope Julius II. There he was given a contract to paint the walls and ceilings of four halls in the Vatican known as the Stanze. He remained in Rome until his untimely death in 1520, at the early age of thirty-seven.

EZEKIEL, AND HIS VISION OF THE VALLEY WITH DRY BONES

By

Saul Raskin

(Interpretation)

THE prophet, Ezekiel, was, according to a recent writer, "the most interesting personality in the group of the great prophets." He certainly deserves a place of highest rank among the prophets. His prophetic ministry began in the fifth year of Jehoiachin's exile (593 B.C.), and continued for more than twenty years.

The Book of Ezekiel may be readily divided into two sections. The first twenty-four chapters are devoted to the teachings and actions of the prophet prior to the final destruction of Jerusalem in 586 B.C. The latter half of the book has a three-fold arrangement: Chapters 25-32 contain a collection of predictions against various nations; chapters 33-39 contain a collection of comforting messages to Ezekiel's fellow exiles; and chapters 40-48 contain his vision of a reconstructed Temple and city of Jerusalem. This was "a book destined to exercise an incalculable influence on the history of his people and indirectly on Western nations."*

Ezekiel is the connecting link between the old and the new covenants. He stands, as Dr. R. H. Pfeiffer says, "between the national religion of the prophets and the personal religion of the Psalms." He knew and loved his people, but he was a close student of history and he realized that the years under the old covenant were at an end. The exile was a period of transition, a time of preparation for the larger future which he was confident was to come. He helped to prepare for that future by teaching that God judges each indivdual soul. His people could be reborn as a nation only after each individual turned to the Lord in penitence.

He was dominated by zeal for the Lord and he lived under the spell of God's holiness and glory. The visible world became no less real to him than the invisible. He saw visions and heard voices. Out of his creative imagination came the dream of the heavenly Jerusalem, more perfect and dazzling than any earthly city.

His fellow exiles, to whom he preached in Babylonia, found it difficult to believe that their nation would ever be restored and Jerusalem rebuilt. There was a saying among them: "Our bones are dried, and our hope is lost." As Ezekiel brooded on this saying he had a vision of a valley filled with dry bones. The Lord commanded him to prophesy to these bones. "So," declares Ezekiel, "I prophesied as I was commanded. And as I prophesied there was a noise, and behold a shaking, and the bones came together, bone to his bone. And when I beheld, lo, the sinews and the flesh came up upon them, and the skin covered them above. . . . And the breath came unto them, and they lived, and stood up upon their feet, an exceeding great army" (37:7, 8, 10).

The Lord explained to Ezekiel that "these bones are the whole house of Israel"

---

* From *Introduction to the Old Testament* by Robert H. Pfeiffer, p. 565. Copyright, 1941, by Harper & Brothers. Used by special permission of the publisher.

which He would bring to life from their graves in Babylonian exile and establish as a nation in their own land.

His vision of the valley with dry bones has been popularized in song, story, and art (37:1-14). It is this prophetic vision which Saul Raskin has chosen as the theme for his picture of Ezekiel, the prophet. In the center foreground stands the prophet, one hand upraised and the other outstretched toward forms in the process of being reborn to living flesh and blood. Behind him are the trumpets of the Lord, as well as the branches of the tree of life for the healing of the nations. Staunch and unafraid the prophet stands surrounded by these shadowy skeleton forms, his eyes alight with the vision of the new day for Israel.

☩

"IN THEIR HEARTS WILL I WRITE IT"

(JEREMIAH 31:31-37)

Upon each heart his law—the tracery of God;
Upon the conscience felt, the touch of mercy's rod;
Thus Heaven does descend as rain upon the clod.

Is this why man is man, or lacking, beast is beast?
Is beast, while men partake as of celestial feast.
Thus God would mark between the greatest and the least.

Bid heart to love this law; bid God to write it deep;
Its holy passions bid your soul and body keep;
That joy exceed the roes' which on the mountains leap.*
—*Harry Trumbull Sutton*

JEREMIAH

The "weeping prophet"! For his people, lost
In pagan wanderings, forgot their God,
The God of Israel and Judah, who
Had made for them a home at such great cost.
They walked no more His ways; deceit and lies,
Oppression of the poor, provoked His wrath,
And dire destruction should be their reward.
God's prophet wept, but lifted up his eyes.
All is not lost, he cried, if ye forsake
Your pagan ways and walk the path of right.
They heard but did not heed. Great Babylon
Swept down and took them. Yet, the prophet spake
From his dark dungeon: "Still thy God is near,
And He will save if only ye will hear!"**
—*Thomas Curtis Clark*

* From *Poems* by Harry Trumbull Sutton, p. 28. Copyright, 1939, by Harry Trumbull Sutton. Used by special permission of the author.

** Used by special permission of the author.

EZEKIEL, AND HIS VISION OF THE VALLEY WITH DRY BONES—*RASKIN*

PROPHET OF DOOM

Appointed of God to root out and destroy
The heathen worship of an evil day,
Heroic Jeremiah, God's employ,
With eloquence and pathos had his say.
He saw a God who stressed the moral law
With personal responsibility;
And ceremony all alone a flaw,
Religion without nationality.
For forty years his warning voice was heard,
Condemning gross oppression and deceit,
So "Babylon's" supporters were disturbed,
"Jerusalem" seemed headed for defeat.
There's no salvation in a temp'ral state,
Ignoring God men bow to tragic fate.*

—*Henry C. Spear*

THE BURDEN OF EGYPT

(ISAIAH 19)

Behold, Jehovah rideth on the storm
To come to Egypt, sunk in strife and sin.
Each smiteth each his brother: war's alarm
Has put to flight all counsel, and within
The fertile meadows is dry, driven dust.
The Nile yields naught. Confusion takes its toll,
For wisdom dies, struck down by fear and lust,
And they that work for hire are grieved in soul.

But though destruction stalk, an altar to the Lord
Shall bring to men salvation in that day.
No longer need they smite with lifted sword
For enemies shall walk in one highway.
That nation shall be blessed whose inner light
Makes clear the pathway for God's healing might.**

—*Georgia Harkness*

EXILE

"They that wait upon the Lord renew their strength;
On eagles' wings they mount up to the skies;
When in the race they scan the highway's length
They faint not, and unwearied, gain the prize."

* Used by special permission of the author.
** From *Holy Flame* by Georgia Harkness, p. 42. Copyright, 1935, by Bruce Humphries, Inc. Used by special permission of the author and the publisher.

In Babylon men heard a prophet's voice,
Afire with God's supernal majesty.
Amid their tears they could again rejoice:
They heard him say, "My people, comfort ye!"

No exile has been mine, save that I made.
My soul moved out and left the holy fires;
No conquering armies, but a deepening shade
Hid from my sight the gleaming temple spires.
And when I yearned for home, I heard God say,
"Wait ye upon the Lord, and find the way."*

—Georgia Harkness

EZEKIEL, PROPHET OF THE EXILE

And Jehovah spake unto Ezekiel:
I have set Jerusalem among the nations,
And she has rejected mine ordinances,
And is worse than Sodom and Gomorrah;
She is a useless vine.
Behold, I shall make her a desolation
And a reproach
Among the nations round about her.

Israel, my people, will not hearken;
They are a rebellious house.
I will bring a sword upon her
And will destroy her high places;
And her false prophets shall be slain.
For I am Jehovah.

Ammon, Moab, Edom and Philistia;
Tyre, that dwellest at the entry of the sea;
I will bring terrible nations upon them
And they shall bring them down to the pit.

Pharaoh of Egypt,
The monster in the midst of the rivers,
Hath said, I am god.
His land will I give unto Babylon;
And all the nations shall know
That I am Jehovah.

And Jehovah spake unto Ezekiel:
Yet will I leave a remnant of my people;
And they shall take away the abominations
From Jerusalem and Israel;
And I will give them a new heart.

* *Ibid.,* p. 44.

I will search for my sheep
And I will bring them into their own land;
And I will feed them with good pasture.
My tabernacle shall be with them
And I will be their God;
And they shall be my people.
And all the nations shall know
That I am Jehovah.*

—*Thomas Curtis Clark*

EZEKIEL

He thunders from the cherubs' glowing wheels,
And in proud cities shaken by the tread
Of Asshur's horsemen cloaked in blue and red.
The leopard crouches and the gray wolf steals;
Before that voice the prince of Tyrus reels,—
His purple tissues deck the dark sea-bed
Where ships of Ophir rust, with sails outspread
And green gold dripping through the cloven keels.

He speaks, and captives of the willowed rim
Of Chebar hear the holy river run
Where idols stained their broken altar-stone,
And know that He who rides the cherubim
Above the fallen summits of the sun
Is Lord of Israel and God alone.**

—*Thomas S. Jones, Jr.*

HE COMETH LATE

The strings of camels come in single file,
    Bearing their burdens o'er the desert sands.
Swiftly the boats go plying on the Nile—
    The needs of men are met on every hand,
But still I wait
For the messenger of God who cometh late.

I see a cloud of dust rise on the plain.
    The measured tread of troops falls on my ear.
The soldier comes, the empire to maintain,
    Bringing the pomp of war, the reign of fear.
But still I wait
For the messenger of God who cometh late.

* Used by special permission of the author.
** From *Shadow of the Perfect Rose: Collected Poems of Thomas S. Jones, Jr.* edited with a Memoir and Notes by John L. Foley. Copyright, 1937, by Rinehart & Co., Inc. Used by special permission of John L. Foley, literary executor for Thomas S. Jones, Jr.

They set me watching o'er the desert drear,
   Where dwells the darkness, as the deepest night;
From many a mosque there comes the call to prayer—
   I hear no voice that calls on God for light.
But still I wait
For the messenger of God who cometh late.

—Author Unknown

IN THE MARKET-PLACE

In Babylon, high Babylon,
   What gear is bought and sold?
All merchandise beneath the sun
   That bartered is for gold;
Amber and oils from far beyond
   The desert and the fen,
And wines whereof our throats are fond—
   Yea! and the souls of men!

In Babylon, gray Babylon,
   What goods are sold and bought?
Vesture of linen subtly spun,
   And cups from agate wrought;
Raiment of many-colored silk
   For some fair denizen,
And ivory more white than mild—
   Yea! and the souls of men!

In Babylon, sad Babylon,
   What chattels shall invite?
A wife whenas your youth is done,
   Or leman for a night.
Before Astarte's portico
   The torches flare again;
The shadows come, the shadows go—
   Yea! and the souls of men!*

—George Sterling

THE LAMENT OF THE CAPTIVES

By Babylon's waters we sat, and we wept,
As we thought upon Zion.
There on the willows within her
We hung our harps.
For there our captors demanded
The language of song!
Our plunderers asked of us mirth!
"Sing us one of the songs of Zion."

* From *Beyond the Breakers.*

How can we sing Yahweh's* songs
In land of strangers?
Could I forget thee, O Jerusalem,
My right hand should forget!
My tongue should cleave to my palate
If unmindful of thee!
If I set not Jerusalem higher
Than best of my joy!

Remember, Yahweh, to the sons of Edom
The day of Jerusalem,
Who said, "Lay bare! lay bare!
To the foundation with it!"
Happy be he who repayeth it,
What thou didst deal us.
Happy be he who seizeth and dasheth thy little ones
Against the rock!**

—Psalm 137

MAN-MAKING

We are all blind until we see
    That in the human plan
Nothing is worth the making if
    It does not make the man.

Why build these cities glorious
    If man unbuilded goes?
In vain we build the work, unless
    The builder also grows.†

—Edwin Markham

STAND STILL AND WAIT

Thine ears shall hear a word behind thee, saying, This is the way, walk ye in it; when ye turn to the right hand, and when ye turn to the left."—ISAIAH 30:21.

"STAND STILL," my soul, for so thy Lord commands:
E'en when thy way seems blocked, leave it in His wise hands;
His arm is mighty to divide the wave.
"Stand still," my soul, "stand still" and thou shalt see
How God can work the "impossible" for thee,
For with a great deliverance He doth save.

* The American Revised Version prints the word Jehovah which is not a real word, being made up of the consonants in *Yahweh* and the vowels in *Adonai*.

** See Kings, Briggs and McLaren in *Expositor's Bible,* for rendering.

† From *Poems of Edwin Markham* selected and arranged by Charles L. Wallis. Copyright, 1950, by Virgil Markham. Published by Harper & Brothers. Used by special permission of Virgil Markham.

Be not impatient, but in stillness stand,
Even when compassed 'round on every hand,
In ways thy spirit does not comprehend.
God cannot clear thy way till thou art still,
That He may work in thee His blessed will,
And all thy heart and will to Him doth bend.

"BE STILL," my soul, for just as thou art still,
Can God reveal Himself to thee; until
Through thee His love and light and life can freely flow;
In stillness God can work through thee and reach
The souls around thee. He then through thee can teach
His lessons, and His power in weakness show.

"BE STILL"—a deeper step in faith and rest.
"Be still and know" thy Father knoweth best
The way that leads His child to that fair land,
A "summer" land, where quiet waters flow;
Where longing souls are satisfied, and "know
Their God," and praise for all that He has planned.

—*Author Unknown*

THESE ARE NOT LOST

The look of sympathy; the gentle word
Spoken so low that only angels heard;
The secret act of pure self-sacrifice,
Unseen by men, but marked by angels' eyes;
    These are not lost.

The silent tears that fall at dead of night
Over soiled robes that once were pure and white;
The prayers that rise like incense from the soul,
Longing for Christ to make it clean and whole;
    These are not lost.

The happy dreams that gladdened all our youth,
When dreams had less of self and more of truth;
The childhood's faith, so tranquil and so sweet,
Which sat like Mary at the Master's feet;
    These are not lost.

The kindly plans devised for others' good,
So seldom guessed, so little understood;
The quiet, steadfast love that strove to win
Some wanderer from the ways of sin;
    These are not lost.

Not lost, O Lord! for in Thy city bright
Our eyes shall see the past by clearer light,
And things long hidden from our gaze below
Thou wilt reveal, and we shall surely know
    They are not lost.

—Author Unknown

ULTIMATE

Now each man knows a different God!
Each for himself doth see
A shape of doom; a vengeful Judge—
    A fearsome mystery—
Or, blessed hope! A Strength, a Friend—
    Beloved utterly.

A Shadow, brooding and malign—
    Or sanctuary blest.
No thing man knows so well as this—
    The God within his breast.
The God he makes—and fears; or loves—
    His soul's most precious guest!

Yet, spent and stark, into the night
    How like men always go!
Each staring back upon a Cross
    Of matchless love, and woe:
And all men clutch that seamless robe,
    Both God's friend, and his foe!*

—Laura Simmons

"SEEK YE THE LORD"

(Isaiah 55:6-11)

Seek ye the Lord—he may be found;
Call ye upon him—he is near;
The wicked need but turn around;
Unrighteous change despite to fear.

So near and open is the way
To that vast store called "every blessing."
Injustice turn, make this your day,
And with it very life possessing.

How will ye see your land defiled;
Jerusalem as a virgin stripped;
Your eyes, are they so gold-beguiled,
They'd see sons hewn, and mothers ripped?

* Printed in *The Christian Century;* also the *Literary Digest.* Used by special permission of *The Christan Century.*

Is God unseen of robe and crown?
Or is his throne of truth too plain?
He will be seen with awful frown
When blood from blood must not refrain.

O seek, O call, be glad God's near;
Let mercy fill and guide your hand;
So in his House with joy appear;
God's not too hard to understand.*

—Harry Trumbull Sutton

GOD NEVER FORSAKES

Leave God to Order all thy ways,
    And hope in him whate'er betide,
Thou'lt find in him, in evil days,
    Thy all-sufficient strength and guide.
Who trusts in God's unchanging love
Builds on the rock that naught can move.

What can these anxious cares avail,
    The never-ceasing moans and sighs?
What can it help us to bewail
    Each painful moment as it flies?
Our cross and trials do but press
The heavier for our bitterness.

Only thy restless heart keep still,
    And wait in cheerful hope, content
To take whate'er his gracious will,
    His all-discerning love, hath sent.
Nor doubt our inmost wants are known
To him who chose us for his own.

He knows when joyful hours are best;
    He sends them as he sees it meet;
When thou hast borne the fiery test,
    And now art freed from all deceit,
He comes to thee all unaware
And makes thee own his loving care.

Nor in the heat of pain and strife
    Think God has cast thee off unheard,
And that the man whose prosperous life
    Thou enviest is of him preferred.
Time passes, and much change doth bring
And sets a bound to everything.

* From *Poems* by Harry Trumbull Sutton, p. 25. Copyright, 1939, by Harry Trumbull Sutton. Used by special permission of the author.

All are alike before his face;
　'Tis easy to our God most high
To make the rich man poor and base,
　To give the poor man wealth and joy;
True wonders still by him are wrought
Who setteth up and brings to naught.

Sing, pray, and swerve not from his ways,
　But do thine own part faithfully;
Trust his rich promises of grace,
　So shall they be fulfilled in thee.
God never yet forsook at need
The soul that trusted him indeed.

—George Neumarck

SOMETIME

Sometime when all life's lessons have been learned,
　And sun and stars forevermore have set,
The things which our weak judgments here have spurned,
　The things o'er which we grieved with lashes wet,
Will flash before us, out of life's dark night,
　As stars shine most in deeper tints of blue;
And we shall see how all God's plans are right,
　And how what seemed reproof was love most true.

And we shall see how, while we frown and sigh,
　God's plans go on as best for you and me;
How, when we called, He heeded not our cry,
　Because His wisdom to the end could see.
And even as wise parents disallow
　Too much of sweet to craving babyhood,
So God, perhaps, is keeping from us now
　Life's sweetest things, because it seemeth good.

And if, sometimes, commingled with life's wine,
　We find the wormwood, and rebel and shrink,
Be sure a wiser hand than yours or mine
　Pours out this potion for our lips to drink;
And if some friend we love is lying low,
　Where human kisses cannot reach his face,
Oh, do not blame the loving Father so,
　But wear your sorrow with obedient grace!

And you shall shortly know that lengthened breath
　Is not the sweetest gift God sends His friend;
And that, sometimes, the sable pall of death
　Conceals the fairest boon His love can send.
If we could push ajar the gates of life,
　And stand within and all God's workings see,

We could interpret all this doubt and strife,
    And for each mystery could find a key!

But not to-day. Then be content, poor heart!
    God's plans like lilies pure and white unfold.
We must not tear the close-shut leaves apart;
    Time will reveal the calyxes of gold.
And if, through patient toil, we reach the land
    Where tired feet, with sandals loosed, may rest,
When we shall clearly see and understand
    I think that we will say, "God knew the best!"*

—*May Riley Smith*

✛

THE WEEPING PROPHET

By

Florence M. Earlle

FOR years the prophet, Jeremiah, had been proclaiming to the kings of Judah that destruction would come upon them if they did not forsake their idol worship and turn back to God. But his message fell on deaf ears.

Zedekiah, the king, was much pleased when the Chaldeans who were besieging Jerusalem, hearing that Egypt was coming, withdrew. But Jeremiah came to the king and said, "Thus says the Lord; Do not deceive yourself, saying that the Chaldeans will surely not return, for they will. They will take the city and burn it with fire."

But Zedekiah paid no attention.

Then Jeremiah left Jerusalem to go into the land of Benjamin. But at the city gate, he was arrested and accused of planning to go to the Chaldeans. The princes beat him and put him in prison where he remained for several weeks. Then, one day, the king took him out secretly and brought him to the palace.

"Is there any word from the Lord?" he asked.

"Yes," answered Jeremiah, "there is. It is what I have already told you. You will be delivered to the Chaldeans. But what is my offense that I have been put in prison? Do not send me back or I shall die there."

And Zedekiah, fearing Jeremiah, yet refusing to listen to him, ordered that he be kept in court and fed with a piece of bread each day so long as there was bread in the city.

But when Jeremiah spoke to the people, telling them that the city would be destroyed, and that only if they surrendered could it be saved, the princes came to Zedekiah and demanded that Jeremiah be put to death.

He is weakening the morale of the people and of the few fighting men we have. He isn't seeking the welfare of the people in telling them such things."

And weak-kneed Zedekiah said, "He is in your hands; the king will do nothing against you."

* From *A Gift of Gentians*.

So the princes took Jeremiah and put him in the dungeon that was in the court of the prison. They let him down with ropes. There was no water in the dungeon, but mud, and Jeremiah sank down into it up to his knees. And there they left him.

But there was in the court a servant who believed that Jeremiah was telling the truth. Taking his life in his hands, for it was almost unheard of that a servant should approach the king unasked, the man said, "My Lord, the king, the princes have done an evil thing to Jeremiah the prophet. They have put him in the dungeon of the court and he will die there, as there is no bread in the city. I beg of you, do something about him."

Then said Zedekiah, "You take thirty men and get Jeremiah up out of the dungeon."

So the servant took men to help him and went to the dungeon. They threw down pieces of cloth for Jeremiah to pad his armpits. Then they lowered a rope and drew him up.

When the king knew that he was out of the dungeon, he sent for him: "Tell me," he said, "what word is there from the Lord. Hide it not from me."

"If I tell you, you will put me to death," said Jeremiah. "Neither will you listen if I give you good advice."

"I swear that I will not put you to death," said Zedekiah. "And I will not turn you over to the princes. Only tell me!"

"Thus says the Lord: If you will go to the Chaldean prince you shall live, and the city will not be burned with fire. But if you do not, then it will be burned, and you shall not escape out of their hands."

And Zedekiah said, "I am afraid some of my own people have gone over to the Chaldeans. They will betray me."

"They will not betray you, but I beg of you to obey and save this city and your life."

The king arose. "Don't let anyone know that you have told me these things. If the princes find out and question you, as to what you said and what I said, tell them that you begged me not to return you to the dungeon."

For two years, the city of Jerusalem was besieged. At last when there was famine and the Chaldeans had cut off the water supply, the king and his court fled by night through a postern gate. But their enemies pursued them to the plain and captured them. Zedekiah was blinded and taken in chains to Babylon. The city was burned. The temple was not spared, nor the palace, nor any great house. All the metal of the temple, the pillars of brass, the moulton sea, the fire pans, the bowls and all the silver and gold articles were carried away. And only the poor of the land were left. The rest were carried away to Babylon as Jeremiah had prophesied.

As for Jeremiah, when the Chaldean captain found that he had foretold all that had come to pass, he regarded him with awe. He gave him the choice of going to Babylon with the court and the great men, or of staying on the land with the poor. They were left so that the land might not return to desert. And Jeremiah said, "I will stay." So he lived on with the small remnant that remained in Jerusalem; and later he was taken with others down to Egypt where he died.*

* Used by special permission of the author.

"BY THE RIVERS OF BABYLON"

By

Florence M. Earlle

IT had been such a long hard journey from Jerusalem to Babylon. The Jewish captives had tramped wearily along in silence for the most part, although now and then a few had broken into wailing. Their Babylonian captors had not been unkind. They had allowed time for rest, time for food, and made camp when the days were hot. But the people could not forget the horror of the last days of the siege of Jerusalem: the fact that their princes had been killed before the very eyes of the king, and that the king himself was in the procession, tied to the wheels of the conqueror's chariot, and blinded.

But at last it was over. The king had been taken to prison after he had walked in the triumphal entry of the Babylonian ruler, Nebuchadnezzar. The people were given lands and huts in which to live. But they did not know what to do. Babylon was all so strange from their own arid and rocky country. Here green fields waved in the sun and wind, and water flowed plentifully in the rivers. They were beautiful rivers, although not one of the captives would have compared them favorably with their own Jordan. But still it was the rivers that made them think most of home. It was on their banks that they met on the Sabbath Day and wept for their lost land.

Here and there among the temple singers, one had managed to keep his harp and hide it among his few possessions. But they had no heart to sing. When they met, the singers mournfully hung their harps on the willows that lined the banks, and joined in the wailing of the people over their lost land. Too late they realized that their prophet, Jeremiah, had been right in his advice to them. Over and over he had begged the king and the princes to surrender to Nebuchadnezzar and save the city. But they had refused to follow his suggestions. He had warned them that their worship of idols would bring destruction; but they simply could not believe that God would allow Jerusalem, His own city and the city of the great king David, to be taken.

One Sabbath one of the overseers came out to the river bank where the Jews were gathered, and saw their harps hanging on the willow branches. Now all the other nations knew that the Jews were a musical people; that they loved to sing and had beautiful songs that their great King David had written.

"Why be so unhappy?" he said to them. "Sing! Sing some of your songs of Zion."

Wails broke out afresh.

"How can we sing the Lord's songs in a strange land?" they cried. "How can we sing praises to our God when He has forsaken us?"

The overseer shrugged his shoulders and walked away.

"Ungrateful!" he muttered. "Our king gives them land to live on and a chance to be independent. He lets them live without demanding tribute and does not make slaves of them. They could work, but they refuse to do anything but wail for their lost city."

But God had not forsaken them, nor had His prophet, Jeremiah. Although he had remained with the poor of the land around Jerusalem, he was still interested in the exiles. Before long he sent them a message:

"This is what God has to say to you of the captivity:

" 'Build houses for yourselves and plant gardens and fruit trees. Carry on a normal life, letting your sons and daughters marry and rear families. And seek the peace and prosperity of Babylon, praying for it; for in its peace, shall also be your own. Do not listen to anyone who claims to be a prophet or a dreamer of dreams that I have sent. He is false; I have not sent him. And here is hope. Seventy years from now, I will bring you back to Jerusalem. If you will seek me with your whole hearts, I will be found of you. When you pray, I will answer you. Keep this hope, for it will become a reality that your children and your grandchildren, yes, and some of you too, shall return and rebuild Jerusalem.' "

And God kept His word. Seventy years later, Cyrus, king of Persia (for Babylon had fallen to the Persians), made a proclamation throughout his kingdom. He also put it in writing that whoever wished could go back to Jerusalem and rebuild the city. And there were among those who returned, some who had followed the same road seventy years before as captives.

✛

EZEKIEL AND THE EXILES

By

John Paterson

EZEKIEL makes his first appearance among the exiles by the river Chebar in the fifth year of the captivity of Jehoiachin (July 593 B.C.). At that time "the heavens were opened, and I saw visions of God" (1:1), and "the hand of Jehovah was there upon him" (1:3). From that date until April, 571 B.C. (29:17 ff.) we have dated oracles from the prophet.

The appearance of the prophet is significant not only to the exiles but to himself. For it showed clearly that the word of God could be revealed in Babylon as well as in Jerusalem. But the message which Ezekiel proceeds to deliver must have sounded strange and harsh to his hearers. It is a message in the manner and tone of Amos, and it is delivered in pre-emptory tones.

"They, whether they will hear, or whether they will forbear (for they are a rebellious house), yet shall know that there hath been a prophet among them" (2:5).

If the prophet could not speak another word than judgment there would have been no further development of Jewish religion. History and the events had vindicated the prophet, and now the time had come for another word. For under the impact of hostile circumstances men may lose heart and become desperate or wholly debilitated. Hitherto Ezekiel had been mastered by the thought of judgment (chaps. 1-24), but after the fall of the city he is mastered by the thought of restoration. Like Deutero-Isaiah the prophet recognizes that men require to be comforted, and that word "comforted" is to be interpreted in the sense of its Latin original which means "made strong, fortified." This is perhaps the most difficult type of preaching the preacher is called upon to do, and it is too often neglected with the result that men lose heart and become spiritually depressed.

Here Ezekiel displays some of his richest imagery. No more eloquent expression of Israel's hope could be found than that in chapter 37, the vision of the Valley of Dead Bones.

And he said unto me, Son of man, can these bones live? And I answered, O Lord Jehovah, thou knowest. Again he said unto me, Prophesy over these bones, and say unto them, O ye dry bones, hear the word of Jehovah. Thus saith the Lord Jehovah unto these bones: Behold I will cause breath to enter into you, and ye shall live. And I will bring up flesh upon you and cover you with skin, and put breath in you, and ye shall live; and ye shall know that I am Jehovah. [37:3-6]

Or like Hosea Ezekiel will vary metaphor and simile and speak of the good shepherd.

As a shepherd seeketh out his flock in the day that he is among his sheep that are scattered abroad, so will I seek out my sheep; and I will deliver them out of all places whither they have been scattered in the cloudy and dark day. And I will bring them out from the peoples, and gather them from the countries, and will bring them into their own land; and I will feed them upon the mountains of Israel, by the watercourses, and in all the inhabited places of the country. . . . I myself will be the shepherd of my sheep, and I will cause them to lie down, saith the Lord Jehovah. I will seek that which was lost, and will bring back that which was driven away, and will bind up that which was broken, and will strengthen that which was sick. [34:12, 13, 15, 16]

Nor is the hope limited to the members of the southern kingdom: the banished brethren of the north also shall be brought back (chap. 36). Mythological features enter here, and we are reminded of such thoughts as appear in Isaiah 11:1 ff., and here, too, we hear echoes of Jeremiah.

> A new heart also will I give you,
> And a new spirit will I put within you,
> And I will take away the stony heart
> out of your flesh,
> And I will give you a heart of flesh. [36:26]

All this is in line with the thought of earlier prophets but Ezekiel introduces novel ideas of a theological nature and gives us a more dogmatic idea of God. Like Isaiah he feels the sublimity of God, and his recurring phrase, "Son of man," which is equivalent to "earth-born creature," emphasizes the great gulf between the creature and the Creator. Like Isaiah, too, he is overwhelmed by the vision of the divine glory which is the outward revelation of the inward holiness of God. The simple restrained manner of Isaiah gives place here to strange and bizarre details (chaps. 1, 9) derived from his Babylonian environment. In Isaiah we have a spiritual emphasis but in Ezekiel we are more impressed with the physical.

These strange creatures that crowd the vision of Ezekiel are the precursors of the later Jewish angels, and here we have the initial stages of what later became a full-blown angelology. The old thought of the *near God* who walks and talks with men in the early traditions of Genesis is passing away and giving place to the new thought of the *far God* who can communicate with his worshipers only through intermediaries. The theologian has superseded the story-teller.

Ezekiel's thought of individualism must not be set in total isolation from his thought of the redeemed community. The first twenty-four chapters are mainly concerned with judgment and what follows thereafter, including the oracles against the various nations, concerns the future salvation. It may be that Ezekiel himself is divided in his own personality and that this division is reflected in his book. In the earlier part of his career the prophetic impulse prevails over the priestly, but in the later stages of his career it would seem that the priestly element overrides the prophetic impulse: this is particularly so in the last nine chapters, which are frequently denied to Ezekiel by critics. But the strange variety of the book may be due to the strangely composite personality of Ezekiel as prophet and priest.

In the thought of salvation Ezekiel differs from the earlier prophets, for the motivating force of Ezekiel is not the divine love and mercy but *the thought of the divine honor.* . . .

Such a thought is clearly related to the doctrine of monotheism and issues directly from the thought of the divine majesty symbolized in the inaugural vision. It may be expressed in gross mythological form and accompanied with all the fantastic imagery of Apocalypse, but the thought itself is not gross. . . .

Chapters 40-48 give in detail Ezekiel's description of the new Jerusalem. In accord with the Hebrew genius the ideal is made real, and here we have the priestly blueprint of Utopia. It would seem, if we assume Ezekiel's authorship, that here most prominently the original priestly heritage of Ezekiel is finding expression. Prophecy is passing over into ecclesiasticism. The prophet, who earlier took such lofty imaginative flights and soared on wings of strange fantasy here comes down to earth and becomes very practical and prosaic. Precise measurements and delimitations take the place of dreams, visions, and grotesque fancies. That is Ezekiel, and that must be borne in mind as we judge him. . . .

The ideal of Ezekiel is a religious community fenced and guarded by physical and spiritual sanctions. Inasmuch as we may not draw too much from these chapters, in view of uncertainty of authorship, we need not follow all the details of the elaborate scheme. The principle of theocracy introduced by Deuteronomy is carried to new heights, and the religion of the book is firmly established. Judaism is emerging; ritualism and sacerdotalism are in the ascendant. The hierarchy has ousted the monarchy, and the people who were once a nation have now become a church. A holy God, a holy people, a holy land—these are the pillars on which the whole structure rests. No thought of missionary expansion is here but only a hard rigid exclusivism.

Thus saith the Lord Jehovah, no foreigner, uncircumcised in heart and uncircumcised in flesh, shall enter into my sanctuary, of any foreigners that are among the children of Israel. [44:9]

A wall of partition had been erected which later was strengthened and consolidated by Ezra and Nehemiah (Ezra 10:10 ff.; Nehemiah 9:2 ff.), and it was not thrown down until Paul went to Antioch and liberated the full Christian Gospel (Acts 15).

There can be no mistaking the zeal of Ezekiel. Like Elijah he is very zealous for the Lord Jehovah. "Back of all the crude, prosaic, uncouth actions that frequently offend our aesthetic feeling we feel the glow of a holy consuming fire."* Amid all the grotesque imagery this zeal for Jehovah shines forth. In the period in which he was called to minister no quality was more required, for he was called to reanimate a community who had lost hope and become dispirited. . . .

This zeal for Jehovah is mainly responsible for the harsh note in his message as it is responsible also for his one-sided emphasis on the divine honor. Luther, Calvin, and John Knox did not speak soft words, and were frequently as brusque as Amos himself. There are times when the spirit of man must be stabbed awake and Ezekiel and the Reformers lived in such times. . . . Men had first to be made aware of the real nature of sin and brought into contact with a reality that transcended their current thought. This also Ezekiel did for his people, and this also is no mean service.

It is easy to see how he failed in his thought of individualism. The thought of the individual and God should have led straight to the thought of universalism but Ezekiel could not disengage this thought from the thought of Israel as the people of God. And thus he presents us with the thought of a universal God without a universal religion. Israel after the flesh did not give way to an Israel after the spirit, but Ezekiel here with his fractional insight was preparing the path which the apostle Paul was to tread. The thought, too, of a God of love who does not desire the death of any, but that all should turn to Him for life was a seminal thought that ripened in the Gospel. And the thought of the prophet as one who watches for men's souls added the conception of pastor to that of preacher.

Ezekiel's emphasis on physical holiness, separation in space and time, may appear a throw-back to ideas of a much earlier time. It led to an emphasis upon cult and ritual, and involved the danger that the ethical may be thrust to the background. That this was a real danger is obvious from the history of Judaism, and we see it taking shape in succeeding centuries.

Every movement that is really vital has elements of danger and possibilities of misdirection. The Roman Catholic Church and the Protestant Church, in all its varieties and schisms, alike stem from the Apostolic Church, but one need not charge the Apostles with responsibility for the crudities of the Douk-hobors or the ecstatic on-goings of the Holy Rollers. Nor may we attribute Scribism and Pharisaism to Ezekiel, though the possibility of such developments was present. Other developments were also possible. Ezekiel was attempting to realize the prophetic ideals, and sought to bring them into the region of daily life. The ritual may be the expression of the ethical, and for most people the ethereal atmosphere of pure spirituality is simply not possible. Ezekiel is practical though

* Ernest Sellin, *Der alttestamentliche Prophetismus* (1912), p. 79.

his practicalness led to grave abuses. But the abuses are not due to Ezekiel but to the hardness of men's hearts.

Moreover, it had to be so. For if Judaism was to survive and preserve its precious heritage it could only be in this way. The hard shell of Judaism had to form around the kernel of divine truth that it might be safeguarded and kept against "the fullness of times." The law was our tutor to lead us to Christ. The "father of Judaism" is a term frequently applied to Ezekiel but it need not be taken as a term of abuse. For Judaism paved the way for the Gospel and prepared "a highway for our God."*

✝

ALL PEOPLE THAT ON EARTH DO DWELL

(Interpretation)

THIS four-verse hymn based on the 100th Psalm dates back to the middle of the sixteenth century. It was first published in 1561 in *Day's Psalter,* and has since been included in nearly every hymnbook of the Church. Around it, therefore, is gathered a host of traditions and memories.

In the 100th Psalm the Church has always acknowledged that "the Lord is God indeed" and that we are His people. We praise the Lord and offer thanks-

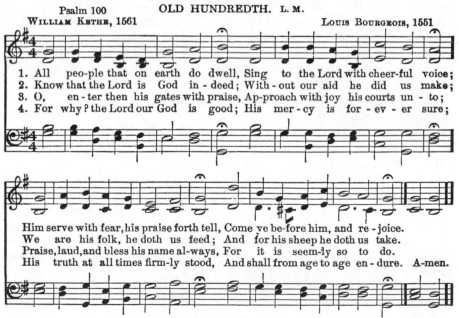

All People That on Earth Do Dwell

Psalm 100
WILLIAM KETHE, 1561

OLD HUNDREDTH. L. M.

LOUIS BOURGEOIS, 1551

1. All peo-ple that on earth do dwell, Sing to the Lord with cheer-ful voice;
2. Know that the Lord is God in - deed; With-out our aid he did us make;
3. O, en-ter then his gates with praise, Ap-proach with joy his courts un - to;
4. For why? the Lord our God is good; His mer-cy is for - ev - er sure;

Him serve with fear, his praise forth tell, Come ye be-fore him, and re - joice.
We are his folk, he doth us feed; And for his sheep he doth us take.
Praise, laud, and bless his name al-ways, For it is seem-ly so to do.
His truth at all times firm-ly stood, And shall from age to age en - dure. A-men.

* Abridged from *The Goodly Fellowship of the Prophets* by John Paterson, pp. 165-78. Copyright, 1948, by Charles Scribner's Sons. Used by permission of the publisher.

giving for His goodness, His mercy, and His truth which endure from generation to generation.

The author of the hymn, William Kethe (?-1593) was a Scottish minister exiled for his faith during the stormy period when freedom of thought was struggling for existence. The following picture of the exiles in Geneva is revealing: "A most interesting sight is offered in the City on week-days, when the hour for service approaches. As soon as the first sound of the bell is heard, all shops are closed, conversation ceases, business is put on one side, and from all parts the people hasten to the nearest church. Arrived there, each one draws from his pocket a small book which contains some psalms with notes, and thus the congregation sings before and after the sermon, while everyone testifies how great consolation is derived from this custom."

It was in this fashion that the Genevan congregation sang to the tune "Old Hundredth," composed in 1551 by Louis Bourgeois, William Kethe's version of the 100th Psalm. In 1541 the composer of the tune followed Calvin to Geneva where he became master chorister and musical editor of the *Genevan Psalter*. History indicates that he was exempt from guard duty and other work so that he might spend his time teaching children, young people, and adults to sing, and writing and arranging musical compositions.

✟

O GOD, WHOSE LAW FROM AGE TO AGE

(Interpretation)

THIS magnificent hymn of the Church is from the pen of one of America's outstanding liberal clergymen, John Haynes Holmes, and was composed in 1910 while Dr. Holmes was pastor of the Church of the Messiah, now the Community Church in New York City.

Dr. Holmes has held several important positions of leadership among Christian organizations. He served as president of the Unitarian Fellowship for Social Justice for a number of years. In 1929 he went to Palestine on a special mission for the Jews. Because of his interest in Gandhi, Dr. Holmes went to India in 1947 and conferred with the great Indian leader. His book *My Gandhi,* published in 1953, reveals why Dr. Holmes considered him to be "the greatest man in the world."

He is a prodigious author for various present-day publications, writing on religious subjects and the problems of our times. He is probably better known, however, for his religious poetry. Not a few of his stirring poems have been set to music and are regularly sung in many Protestant churches.

This four-stanza hymn, "O God, Whose Law from Age to Age," recognizes God's law is changeless and His love abides "while eons come and go." In the midst of our earthly life with its strife, and doubts, and fears we flee to Him and put our trust in Him.

The second stanza acknowledges that the winds obey God's will and are

O God, Whose Law from Age to Age

ST. LEONARD. C.M.D.

JOHN HAYNES HOLMES, 1910

HENRY HILES, 1867

1. O God, whose law from age to age, No chance or change can know,
2. The winds, thy faith-ful mes-sen-gers, Are guid-ed by thy hand,
3. Thy ho-ly pur-pose moves be-fore The na-tions on their way,
4. Dear Fa-ther, we would learn to trust The do-ing of thy will,

Whose love for-ev-er-more a-bides, While e-ons come and go;
Thy min-is-ters, the flames of fire, O-bey thy stern com-mand;
And leads the stum-bling hosts of men From dark-ness in-to day.
And in thy per-fect law of love Our doubts and fears would still.

From all the strife of earth-ly life, To thine em-brace we flee,
The seas re-sound with-in the bound Where thy do-min-ion reigns,
No cap-tain's sword, no proph-et's word, But thy great mer-cy prove;
Help us to know, in joy or woe, Thy ways are al-ways best,

And 'mid our crowding doubts and fears Would put our trust in thee.
And wheel-ing plan-ets seek the paths Thy might-y will or-dains.
No clime or kin-dred but at-test Thy prov-i-dence of love.
And we, thy chil-dren ev-er-more, By thy great good-ness blest. A-men.

* Words used by special permission of Dr. John Haynes Holmes.

guided by His hands as are the "flames of fire" which are His ministers and obey His stern command. Even the seas obey God's sovereign will, "and wheeling planets seek the paths" ordained by the will of God.

The third stanza recognizes God's holy purpose and plan as He guides "the nations on their way," and His leadership of the "stumbling hosts of men from darkness into day."

The fourth stanza voices the appeal of the humble in heart who "would learn to trust the doing of thy will," and who in and through God's "perfect law of love" learn to still their "doubts and fears." It reveals that whether they bring "joy or woe" God's ways are best for us His children who are blessed by His great goodness.

The tune "St. Leonard" to which this hymn is sung was composed in 1867 by Henry Hiles.

☩

O LOVE OF GOD MOST FULL

(Interpretation)

ONE of the great nineteenth-century hymns of the Church was composed by Oscar Clute (1840-1901). It is entitled "O Love of God Most Full" and is a paean of praise to God for His love "most full" and "most free" toward the children of men.

The first stanza compares the love of God in the hearts of men to the warmth of the glowing sun that shines upon, strengthens, and warms God's earthly family.

The second stanza acknowledges man's utter safety in the eternal love of God. Just as long as that love continues "no foe can cast me down" nor fear cause man to flee in terror. Because God's "love is near" sorrow cannot overwhelm us, storms are calmed, tempests do not cause fear, and "the darkest night is full of light."

The third stanza expresses the conviction that it is in and through this faith in, and dependence upon, God's love that mankind is able to triumph over sin, to put temptations aside, and to strive "to win the victor's crown."

The closing lines are an entreaty that the "love of God most full" and the "love of God most free" come to warm man's heart and to fill man's soul, and in the end to lead man to God.

Alfred J. Caldicott composed the tune "Pastor Bonus" in 1875.

O Love of God Most Full

PASTOR BONUS. S.M.D.

Oscar Clute, 1840–1901

Alfred J. Caldicott, 1875

1. O Love of God most full, O Love of God most free,
2. No foe can cast me down, No fear can make me flee,
3. I tri - umph o - ver sin, I put temp-ta - tion down;

Thou warm'st my heart, thou fill'st my soul, With might thou strengthenest me;
No sor - row fill my life with ill; Thy love sur-round - eth me.
The love of God doth give me strength To win the vic - tor's crown.

Warm as the glow - ing sun So shines thy love on me,
The wild - est sea is calm, The tem - pest brings no fear,
O love of God most full, O love of God most free,

It wraps me round with kind-ly care, It draws me un - to thee.
The dark-est night is full of light, Be-cause thy love is near.
Come warm my heart, come fill my soul, Come lead me un-to thee! A - men.

THEY WHO SEEK THE THRONE OF GRACE

(Interpretation)

In this hymn by Oliver Holden (1835) we have another of those prayer hymns that emphasize in the closing line of each stanza that "God is present ev'ry-where." His boundless love is available to the children of men at all times and in all places if only they will seek His throne and avail themselves of His boundless grace.

The first stanza stresses that God is always present to those who seek access to Him. All those "who seek the throne of grace" find that "God is present ev'ry-where."

The second stanza assures the suppliant that whether one seeks God's throne of grace in sickness or in health, in want or in wealth, he will find that God is also searching for him, for the Eternal "God is present ev'ry-where."

The third stanza urges the continuance of earnest prayer even when earth's comforts fail and the "woes of life prevail," for God is present in His world and will answer in His own good time the seeking heart of all those who put their trust in Him.

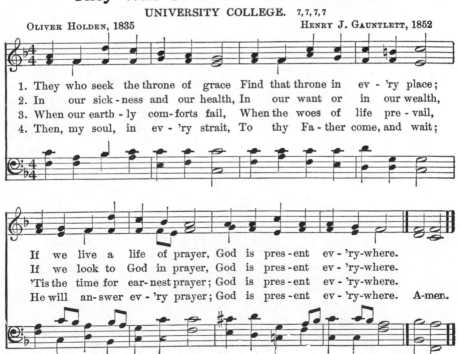

They Who Seek the Throne of Grace

UNIVERSITY COLLEGE. 7,7,7,7

OLIVER HOLDEN, 1835   HENRY J. GAUNTLETT, 1852

1. They who seek the throne of grace Find that throne in   ev - 'ry place;
2. In   our sick - ness and our health, In   our want or   in   our wealth,
3. When our earth - ly com - forts fail, When the woes of life pre - vail,
4. Then, my soul, in   ev - 'ry strait, To   thy   Fa - ther come, and wait;

If   we live a   life of prayer, God is pres - ent   ev - 'ry-where.
If   we look to   God in prayer, God is pres - ent   ev - 'ry-where.
'Tis the time for ear - nest prayer; God is pres - ent   ev - 'ry-where.
He will an - swer ev - 'ry prayer; God is pres - ent   ev - 'ry-where.   A-men.

The fourth stanza summarizes the constant care of the Heavenly Father by urging all suppliants to wait before God because in "ev'ry strait" no matter how unsolvable the problem "He will answer ev'ry prayer."

The tune "University College" was composed in 1848 by Henry J. Gauntlett.

CONTENTS

PART VI SECTION 2

THE RETURN OF A REMNANT TO JERUSALEM

✛

Now in the first year of Cyrus king of Persia . . . the Lord stirred up the spirit of Cyrus . . . that he made a proclamation throughout all his kingdom, and put it also in writing, saying, . . . "All the kingdoms of the earth hath the Lord God of heaven given me; and he hath charged me to build him an house in Jerusalem, which is in Judah. Who is there among you of all his people? The Lord his God be with him, and let him go up."—II CHRONICLES 36:22-23

✛

MUSIC:

THE RETURN OF THE EXILES

By

William Hole

(Interpretation)

THE Biblical material which provides the theme of the painting, "The Return of the Exiles," by the English artist William Hole, is found in the Book of Ezra.

Seventy years have elapsed since the tribes of Judah and Benjamin were carried away as captives into Babylon. Nebuchadnezzar has died and the Babylonian Empire, overthrown by the Persians, is now ruled by Cyrus, the great Persian king. Soon after coming to the throne he issued a proclamation ending the seventy years of captivity for the Hebrews and allowing all those who so desired to return to Jerusalem. The Book of Ezra records the story as follows:

"Then rose up the chief of the fathers of Judah and Benjamin, and the priests, and the Levites, with all them whose spirit God had raised, to go up to build the house of the Lord which is in Jerusalem. And all they that were about them strengthened their hands with vessels of silver, with gold, with goods, and with beasts, and with precious things, beside all that was willingly offered. Also Cyrus the king brought forth the vessels of the house of the Lord which Nebuchadnezzar had brought forth out of Jerusalem, and had put in the house of his gods; even those did Cyrus king of Persia bring forth by the hand of Mithredath, the treasurer, and numbered them unto Sheshbazzar, the prince of Judah. . . . All these did Sheshbazzar bring up with them of the captivity that were brought up from Babylon unto Jerusalem" (1:5-11).

"Now these are the children of the province that went up out of the captivity of those which had been carried away, whom Nebuchadnezzar the king of Babylon had carried away unto Babylon, and came again unto Jerusalem and Judah, every one unto his city. [Then follows a list of the names of the families.] . . . The whole congregation together was forty and two thousand three hundred and threescore, beside their servants, and their maids, of whom there were seven thousand three hundred thirty and seven; and there were among them two hundred singing men and singing women. Their horses were seven hundred thirty and six; their mules, two hundred forty and five; their camels, four hundred thirty and five; their asses six thousand seven hundred and twenty" (2:1, 64-67).

This painting by William Hole shows one small section of the returning band of exiles. By focusing our attention on only a few people and portraying them as distinct individuals the artist helps us understand the whole joyful journey from exile in Babylonia back to Jerusalem. The people are skillfully and dramatically grouped.

In the foreground a young family comprising a father, mother, and sleeping baby, looks forward in happy expectation toward a new life in their own city of Jerusalem which they have never seen before. Behind them kneels a man who has just caught his first glimpse of the distant skyline of the Holy City and prostrates himself on the ground in a prayer of thanksgiving. In his joy he has dropped his few possessions tied in a bundle on his staff. An old man and woman gaze in incredulous wonder at the familiar outlines of Jerusalem which during their long years in exile they had not even hoped to see again. A donkey wearing gay trappings is led forward by an eager boy. In the background people rest in an overnight shelter; a donkey is led by his master; horns are blown to signal the approaching end of the long journey.

The landscape of the background is no imaginary scene but a faithful portrayal from actual studies made by the artist in Palestine. Sir George Adam Smith, author of *Jerusalem* and the *Historical Geography of the Holy Land,* said that William Hole was "so fine an artist, so competent a master of the landscapes of the Holy Land and of the hardly altered figures, habits, and crafts of its peoples" that he made the life of those ancient days live before our eyes.

✛

MOURNING OVER THE RUINS OF JERUSALEM

By

Paul Gustave Doré

(Interpretation)

THIS engraving designed by Paul Gustave Doré, the nineteenth-century French artist, is typical of his unusual ability as an illustrator of Biblical scenes and events. It portrays the mourning of a group of older Hebrew exiles on their return from the Babylonian captivity. They found the walls of that ancient capital city in ruins, and the beautiful Temple of Solomon, the pride and glory of the Hebrew nation, completely destroyed.

The rebuilding of the second Temple, or Zerubbabel's Temple, was begun in the second year after the return of the exiles from Babylon. To Zerubbabel and his associate, Jeshua, fell the task of overseeing this tremendous undertaking. They began their work by calling together in Jerusalem all the priests and the Levites, and "all they that were come out of the captivity unto Jerusalem." They were organized so that each man had a definite task and responsibility. When they laid the foundation stone of the second Temple, the priests were dressed in their priestly apparel and provided with trumpets; and the Levites, the sons of Asaph, were provided with cymbals so that they might praise the Lord. They praised and gave thanks to God "because he is good, for his mercy endureth for ever toward Israel" (Ezra 3:11).

Of course there were tears of regret also, for many of the older exiles, who in their youth had been carried away into Babylonian captivity, remembered the magnificence of Solomon's Temple that had been so ruthlessly destroyed by Nebuchadnezzar's army. Ezra tells the story of their grief in this way:

"But many of the priests and Levites and chief of the fathers, who were an-

THE RETURN OF THE EXILES—*HOLE*

cient men, that had seen the first house, when the foundation of this house was laid before their eyes, wept with a loud voice; and many shouted aloud for joy. So that the people could not discern the noise of the shout of joy from the noise of the weeping of the people; for the people shouted with a loud shout, and the noise was heard afar off" (3:12-13).

These sorrowing exiles as portrayed by Doré mourn the bygone days of Jerusalem's splendor. The great Temple built by Solomon is gone forever. No doubt that the new Temple will suffice as a place of worship; but it can never take the place of the one in which they had worshiped in the days of their youth, in the days of the greatest strength and magnificence of the Hebrew nation. The sound of their grief is co-mingled with shouts of joy by the younger exiles, most of whom were born in Babylon during the seventy years of their exile and thus did not know the glory of Jerusalem.

✛

THE FRIEZE OF THE PROPHETS

By

John Singer Sargent

(Interpretation)

The Hopeful Prophets

At the extreme right end of Sargent's "Frieze of the Prophets" is the last section of this remarkable mural. This group is often referred to as the "Hopeful Prophets" because all but Micah are looking forward to the dawn of a new day for Israel.

Micah, a younger contemporary of Isaiah, lived in a little village in southwestern Palestine. He was a peasant, but did not hesitate to denounce the social wrongs of his people. He is credited with being the author of at least the first three chapters of the Book of Micah, and may have been the author of the book in its entirety. He was courageous in his preaching, and his writings show that he possessed real literary ability.

He is the only one of this group of "Hopeful Prophets" who is not portrayed by the artist, John Singer Sargent, as looking forward with hope to the future. Micah stands with averted head, his hand covering his eyes as he ponders the wrongdoing of men and nations. Yet it was Micah who prophesied in clear and unmistakable words the coming of a new day and the coming of a new leader for Israel. "But thou, Bethlehem Ephratah, though thou be little among the thousands of Judah, yet out of thee shall he come forth unto me that is to be ruler in Israel; whose goings forth have been from of old, from everlasting. . . . And he shall stand and feed in the strength of the Lord, in the majesty of the name of the Lord his God; and they shall abide: for now shall he be great unto the ends of the earth." (5:2, 4).

Standing at the right of Micah is Haggai. The Book of Haggai contains only

MOURNING OVER THE RUINS OF JERUSALEM—*DORÉ*

two brief chapters. Haggai lived during the reign of Darius, king of the Medes and Persians, and he exhorted his people to rebuild the Temple in Jerusalem. Zerubbabel and Jeshua were moved by his exhortations and set about the task of rebuilding, but the people were indifferent and Haggai rebuked them for their halfheartedness.

Sargent has robed Haggai entirely in white. His arms are uplifted and there is a look of hope on his aged, wrinkled face.

Immediately at the right of Haggai is Malachi, who lived two generations after Haggai and is the last of the prophets and the author of the book placed last in the Old Testament. Its message stresses the Lord's love of Jacob, rebukes the impious priests, condemns conjugal sin, urges the support of God's house by the bringing in of the whole tithe, and admonishes the children of Israel to remember the law of Moses and to obey its statutes and ordinances. This prophecy ends with a note of hopeful anticipation of a better day to come.

Malachi wears a rich wine-colored robe with a headdress that ends in a stole. He stands with one arm uplifted and with an expression of hope on his face.

The last in this group of "Hopeful Prophets" is Zechariah who prophesied in Jerusalem while Haggai was preaching there. Like Haggai he inspired the Hebrews to rebuild the Temple, still in its ruins as late as 520 B.C. He was more, however, than a prophet of "stones and timber" for he recalled to the people the teachings of the great prophets.

This prophet is robed entirely in white. His face is turned with a strong, hopeful look to the future when "many people and strong nations shall come to seek the Lord of hosts in Jerusalem, and to pray before the Lord."

✢

THE REBUILDING OF THE TEMPLE

By

Paul Gustave Doré

(Interpretation)

THE second Temple, or Zerubbabel's Temple as it is more often referred to, was erected by the Hebrew exiles under the leadership of Zerubbabel after their return from captivity in Babylon. This Temple had the same general plan as Solomon's Temple although it was less magnificent. The rebuilding was begun on September 24, 520 B.C. (Ezra 6:3-4) and completed on March 5, 515 B.C. (Ezra 6:15).

The name Zerubbabel means "dispersed" or "born in Babylon." He was a descendant of the kings of Judah, and was born during the exile. In 538 B.C., while he was a young man, he was permitted by Cyrus the Great, king of Persia, to lead the Hebrew exiles back from their years of captivity in Babylon to Jerusalem.

The Book of Ezra records the story of the rebuilding of the Temple as follows:

THE FRIEZE OF THE PROPHETS (RIGHT END SECTION) —SARGENT

"Now in the second year of their coming unto the house of God at Jerusalem, in the second month, began Zerubbabel the son of Shealtiel, and Jeshua the son of Jozadak, and the remnant of their brethren the priests and the Levites, and all they that were come out of the captivity unto Jerusalem; and appointed the Levites, from twenty years old and upward, to set forward the work of the house of the Lord. . . . And when the builders laid the foundation of the temple of the Lord, they set the priests in their apparel with trumpets, and the Levites the sons of Asaph with cymbals, to praise the Lord, after the ordinance of David king of Israel" (3:8, 10).

The work of rebuilding the Temple had not progressed far, however, before the enemies of the Israelites began to trouble them. The Biblical account reads:

"Now when the adversaries of Judah and Benjamin heard that the children of the captivity builded the temple unto the Lord God of Israel; then they came to Zerubbabel, and to the chief of the fathers, and said unto them, 'Let us build with you: for we seek your God, as ye do; and we do sacrifice unto him since the days of Esarhaddon king of Assur, which brought us up hither.' But Zerubbabel, and Jeshua, and the rest of the chief of the fathers of Israel, said unto them, 'Ye have nothing to do with us to build an house unto our God; but we ourselves together will build unto the Lord God of Israel, as king Cyrus the king of Persia hath commanded us.' Then the people of the land weakened the hands of the people of Judah, and troubled them in building, and hired counsellors against them, to frustrate their purpose, all the days of Cyrus king of Persia, even until the reign of Darius king of Persia" (4:1-5).

This engraving by Paul Gustave Doré shows something of the tremendous labor that the rebuilding of the Temple by the returned Hebrew exiles entailed. In the foreground a group of faithful Hebrews push and pull a four-wheeled cart on which is loaded a huge stone for the Temple. Above them stands Zerubbabel pointing with his outstretched hand and index finger to the place where the stone is to be set. Ladders and scaffolds in the background indicate that the building is far from complete, but one of the Hebrews is kneeling on a foundation pier and stretching out his arms in thanksgiving to God. Below him the guard, armed with spears, arrows, and shields files out to protect the city during the approaching night. In the lower left-hand corner other men strain at the ropes of a second cart, hastening to bring up its load before the darkness overtakes them.

✣

ZACHERIAS

By

Michelangelo Buonarroti

(Interpretation)

THIS painting of the prophet, Zacherias, whose name is now usually spelled Zechariah, is from Michelangelo's stupendous fresco on the ceiling of the Sistine

THE REBUILDING OF THE TEMPLE—*DORÉ*

Chapel in Rome. This figure occupies the space between two of the corner span-
drels of the ceiling.

Zechariah was a priest by birth, being the son of Iddo, the head of a priestly
family which returned to Jerusalem with Zerubbabel from Babylon. Like Haggai,
he began to prophesy during the second year of the reign of Darius (520 B.C.).
Haggai urged the returned exiles to rebuild the Temple of the Lord in Jerusalem.
His "twin" prophet, Zechariah, called the people to repentance and to the spiritual religion of the great prophets.

He was a young man when he began to prophesy (2:4), and his prophetical
ministry seems to have extended far beyond the time of the dedication of the
second Temple in Jerusalem. In all probability he, himself, collected his own
messages and put them in permanent written form years later.

There is a decided transition between the eighth and ninth chapters of the
Book of Zechariah, that causes scholars to believe that chapters one through
eight, and chapters nine through fourteen, were written during different periods.
Chapters one through eight were undoubtedly written by Zechariah in the sixth
century B.C. Chapters nine through fourteen may be pre-exilic because of the
allusions found therein to Damascus, Ephraim, Philistia, Assyria, and Egypt.
However, allusions in these chapters to the many Jews scattered among the nations lead most scholars to date this part of the Book of Zechariah neither in the
Babylonian nor the Persian, but in the Greek period, in the third century B.C.

This second part of the Book of Zechariah by some unknown prophet living
in a later day contains poetical oracles that seem to refer to Christ. The following
poem is an example:

> Rejoice greatly, O daughter of Zion!
> Shout, O daughter of Jerusalem!
> Behold, thy King cometh unto thee.
> He is just, and having salvation;
> Lowly, and riding upon an ass,
> And upon a colt the foal of an ass . . .
> And he shall speak peace unto the heathen;
> And his dominion shall be from sea even to sea,
> And from the river even to the ends of the earth.
>
> [9:9, 10]

The first eight chapters of the Book of Zechariah by the sixth-century prophet
himself are full of visions. Among the visions he describes are: the four horsemen of the Lord patrolling the earth, a man with a measuring line, the candlestick and olive trees, the flying scroll, the four chariots.

Zechariah looked forward to a happy time when the Lord would again "dwell
in the midst of Jerusalem." Then would come to pass what the Lord had promised through His prophet, Zechariah: "They shall be my people, and I will be
their God, in truth and in righteousness" (8:8).

It is this prophet, Zechariah, that Michelangelo has portrayed. He is shown as
a venerable man who has probed beneath the surface of things to discover the
ways of God and man. Here he is reading a book intended to represent his own
prophecies. His strong hands and shoulder indicate a vigorous man, while the

ZACHERIAS—*MICHELANGELO*

restless movement of his robes and the poised position of his foot show him to be a man of action as well. Behind him stand two lively children playing some game. They symbolize the coming time of joy Zechariah foretold for Jerusalem when "the streets of the city shall be full of boys and girls playing in the streets thereof" (8:5).

✢

A NEW SONG

A poem for the seventh day of the Passover, the anniversary of the crossing of the Red Sea.

> The day the saved of God
> Traversed the deep dryshod,
> *Then a new song*
> *Sang Thy redeemed throng.*
>
> Lo, sunken in deceit
> The Egyptian daughter's feet,
> But lo, the Shulamite (i.e., Israel)
> Went shod in fair delight.
> *Then a new song*
> *Sang Thy redeemed throng.*
>
> Thy banners Thou will set
> O'er those remaining yet
> And gather those forlorn
> As gathering ears of corn.
> *Then a new song*
> *Sang Thy redeemed throng.*
>
> Ah, take her as of yore,
> And cast her forth no more
> Let sunlight crown her day
> And shadows flee away.
> *Then a new song*
> *Sang Thy redeemed throng.**
> —*Jehuda Halevi; translated by Nina Salaman*

BEHAVIOR OF BUILDERS

I am doing a great work, so that I cannot come down.—NEHEMIAH 6:3

> To see a need and take it as your own,
> To lose yourself in some heroic task,
> Is placing love upon the motive throne,

* From *The Small Sanctuary* by Solomon B. Freehof, pp. 253-54. Copyright, 1942, by Riverdale Press. Used by special permission of the publisher.

By giving help before the needy ask.
To turn deaf ears on ridicule and jest,
Be unafraid at threats of violence,
Gives victory to efforts of the best,
Assures the aid of righteous Providence.
To stay aloft at tasks of service great,
And not come down to parley with the crowd,
To be above self-seeking forms of hate,
Will line with silver every threat'ning cloud.
Devotion of a builder building high,
Will cause the things of low estate to die.*

                                        —*Henry C. Spear*

BOOK OF ECCLESIASTES

Let's call the class together for a chat;
Just how life should be lived will be our theme;
Before the end we should know where we're at,
It's wasting time to make of life a dream.
Those who have sampled pleasure, wealth, and fame
Have been paid off in gloom and dark despair;
To feast on wisdom only makes a name
Unless with others all our truth we share.
Eternity is in the heart of man!
There is no answer if the grave's the end,
Rejoice in labor and share what we can,
Obey our God whose laws do not offend.
Life is not vain unless for self we live,
There's joy, when men as well as God, forgive.**

                                        —*Henry C. Spear*

STRENGTH AND SUBLIMITY

Lift up your heads, O ye gates;
And be ye lifted up, ye everlasting doors;
And the King of glory shall come in.
Who is this King of glory?
The Lord strong and mighty,
The Lord mighty in battle.
Lift up your heads, O ye gates;
Even lift them up, ye everlasting doors;
And the King of glory shall come in.
Who is this King of glory?
The Lord of Hosts, he is the King of glory.

                                        —*Psalm 24*

* From *Sermon Sonnets* by Henry C. Spear, p. 8. Used by special permission of the author.
** Used by special permission of the author.

THE HOUSE OF THE LORD

I was glad when they said unto me
Let us build again the House of the Lord,
Let us make strong the walls of Zion,
Let us fashion with beauty the Place of Prayer,
The Holy Place of God's Appearing.

The House of the Lord is clothed in white;
Holiness becometh her, like a garment of praise.
The tower thereof appeareth unto heaven
And her foundation goeth down to the strength of the
    earth,
The abiding strength of the hills of God.

Within thy walls, O Church of God,
The voice of praise shall rise to heaven above;
To God shall prayer be made continually;
His truth proclaimed to all mankind;
And love and joy and peace shall worship Him.

Before thine altar let every heart be bowed in humble
    consecration.
The Place of Prayer shall become the place of spiritual
    transformation: as
Darkening skies grow azure in the royal light of God's
    own house,
Gray shadows trace weird arabesques of delicate beauty
    upon its pillared whiteness, may
The peace of God which passeth all understanding invade
    the sanctuary of the troubled soul,
The deepening blue of vesper light
Shed from above the benediction of love
Upon all who worship here.

Peace be within Thee.
O House of God, we seek thy good.
Teach us, O God, to worship Thee
In the beauty of holiness.*

—*Ernest F. McGregor*

JERUSALEM

Fair shines the moon, Jerusalem,
    Upon the hills that wore
Thy glory once, their diadem
    Ere Judah's reign was o'er:

* From *Occasional Hymns and Songs of Worship and Praise* by Ernest F. McGregor, p. 2. Copyright, 1942, by Ernest F. McGregor. Published by A. S. Barnes & Company, Inc. Used by special permission of Mrs. Ernest F. McGregor.

The stars on hallowed Olivet
  And over Zion burn,
But when shall rise thy splendor set,
  Thy majesty return?

The peaceful shades that wrap thee now
  Thy desolation hide;
The moonlit beauty of thy brow
  Restores thine ancient pride;
Yet there, where Rome thy temple rent,
  The dews of midnight wet
The marble dome of Omar's tent,
  And Aska's minaret.

Thy strength, Jerusalem, is o'er,
  And broken are thy walls;
The harp of Israel sounds no more
  In thy deserted halls:
But where thy kings and prophets trod,
  Triumphant over death,
Behold the living Son of God,—
  The Christ of Nazareth!

The halo of his presence fills
  Thy courts, the ways of men;
His footsteps on thy holy hills
  Are beautiful as then;
The prayer, whose bloody sweat betrayed
  His human agony,
Still haunts the awful olive shade
  Of old Gethsemane.

Woe unto thee, Jerusalem!
  Slayer of prophets, thou,
That in thy fury stonest them
  God sent, and sends thee now:
Where thou, O Christ! with anguish spent,
  Forgav'st thy foes, and died,
Thy garments yet are daily rent,
  Thy soul is crucified!

They darken with the Christian name
  The light that from thee beamed,
And by the hatred they proclaim
  Thy spirit is blasphemed;
Unto thine ear the prayers they send
  Were fit for Belial's reign,
And Moslem scimitars defend
  The temple they profane.

Who shall rebuild Jerusalem?
    Her scattered children bring
From earth's far ends, and gather them
    Beneath her sheltering wing?
For Judah's septre broken lies,
    And from his kingly stem
No new Messiah shall arise
    For lost Jerusalem!

But let the wild ass on her hills
    Its foal unfrightened lead,
And by the source of Kedron's rills
    The desert adder breed:
For where the love of Christ has made
    Its mansion in the heart,
He builds in pomp that will not fade
    Her heavenly counterpart.

—*Bayard Taylor*

MALACHI, THE MESSENGER

Of Judah and her treachery he spake
The messenger of God. On tables vile
Her priests made tainted offerings
And every law of truth and good they brake.
To foreign gods they turned, and pagan vice
Was seen among the people whom God loved.
But there would come a messenger with wrath
Upon his lips. Their heartless sacrifice
Should burn as by a grim refiner's fire.
And they should be redeemed! And God would bless.
No longer would he curse their offerings,
But as a father give them food. His ire
At last should pass, and he, the mighty God,
Would smite the spoilers from his sacred sod.*

—*Thomas Curtis Clark*

THE MESSAGE OF HAGGAI

My house lieth waste, saith Jehovah,
And ye live in ceiled houses.
And Zerubbabel the governor heard,
And Josiah the high priest heard,
And the people heard.
Consider your ways, saith Jehovah;
Go up to the mountain and bring wood
And build my house.

* Used by special permission of the author.

Thus spake Jehovah through Haggai the prophet.
And Zerubbabel and Josiah and the people
Were stirred and did build God's house.

Then saith Jehovah:
Consider my house as it was
In its former glory.
But be ye strong, O Zerubbabel and Josiah.
I will shake the nations
And the precious things of all the nations
Shall come.
And I will fill this house with glory.
And the latter glory of the place
Shall be greater than the former.
For the silver is mine and the gold is mine.
Be ye strong, O Judah and Jerusalem,
For I have chosen thee.*

—*Thomas Curtis Clark*

"THE DESIRE OF ALL NATIONS SHALL COME"

(Haggai 1:2-12)

Come, let us build. Most noble word!
A temple school, or home, or state;
It seems the voice of Heaven's heard,
When men so speak, "Come, let us make."

The centuries await that hour;
Seems winter's past and spring is here,
When patient time bestows her dower;
Or blossoms on her tree appear.

Let us! (how vivid is the task;
Twice vivid when we work as one)
Together, so our natures ask;
How else shall noble work be done?

Such building shall the nations shake;
They shall be more than somewhat roused;
The house of Mammon wide shall quake;
And God's own poor be fed and housed.**

—*Harry Trumbull Sutton*

* Used by special permission of the author.
** From *Poems* by Harry Trumbull Sutton, p. 31. Copyright, 1939, by Harry Trumbull Sutton. Used by special permission of the author.

WHO WILL BUILD THE WORLD ANEW?

Who will build the world anew?
    Who will break tradition's chains?
Who will smite the power of gold?
    Who will chant the spirit's gains?

War and hatred, let them go!
    Caste and creed have had their day;
Pride and lust will lose their power—
    Who will find the better way?

Who will preach that might is weak?
    Who will teach that love is power?
Who will hail the reign of right?
    This his day and this his hour!

Faithless priests and warring lords
    Are as Babylon and Tyre,
Making way for prophet hosts
    Shouting truth in words of fire.

Who will live to slay the false?
    Who will die to prove the true?
Who will claim the earth for God?
    Who will build the world anew?*

—*Thomas Curtis Clark*

WORLD BROTHERHOOD

My country is the world;
My flag with stars impearled
    Fills all the skies
All the round earth I claim
Peoples of every name;
And all inspiring fame
    My heart would prize.

Mine are the lands and seas
All flowers shrubs and trees
    All life's design;
My heart within me thrills
For all uplifted hills
And for all streams and rills;
    The world is mine.

And all men are my kin
Since every man has been
   Blood of my blood;
I glory in the grace
And strength of every race
And joy in every trace
   Of brotherhood.

The days of pack and clan
Shall yield to love of man
   When war-flags are furled;
We shall be done with hate
And strife of state and state
When man with man shall mate
   O'er all the world.

                              —Author Unknown

GOD KNOWS

God knows—not I—the devious way
   Wherein my faltering feet may tread,
Before into the light of day,
   My steps from out this gloom are led,
And, since my Lord the path doth see,
   What matter if 'tis hid from me?

God knows—not I—how sweet accord
   Shall grow at length from out this clash
Of earthly discords which have jarred
   On soul and sense; I hear the crash,
Yet feel and know that on his ear
   Breaks harmony—full, deep, and clear.

God knows—not I—why, when I'd fain
   Have walked in pastures green and fair,
The path he pointed me hath lain
   Through rocky deserts, bleak and bare.
I blindly trust—since 'tis his will—
   This way lies safety, that way ill.

He knoweth, too, despite my will
   I'm weak when I should be most strong.
And after earnest wrestling still
   I see the right yet do the wrong.
Is it that I may learn at length
   Not mine, but his, the saving strength?

His perfect plan I may not grasp,
   Yet I can trust Love Infinite,

And with my feeble fingers clasp
    The hand that leads me into light.
My soul upon his errands goes,
    The end I know not—but God knows.

—Author Unknown

A DAY LOST OR WON

If we sit down at the set of sun
And count the things that we have done,
    And counting find
One self-denying act, one word
That eased the heart of him who heard,
    One glance most kind,
That fell like sunshine where it went,
Then we may count the day well spent.

But if through all the livelong day
We've eased no heart by yea or nay;
    If through it all
We've nothing done that we can trace
That brought the sunshine to a face,
    No act most small
That helped some soul, and nothing cost,
Then count that day as worse than lost.

—Author Unknown

HYMN OF THANKFULNESS

My God, I thank Thee who hast made the earth so bright;
So full of splendor and of joy, beauty and light;
So many glorious things are here, noble and right.
I thank Thee, too, that Thou hast made joy to abound;
So many gentle thoughts and deeds circling us round;
That in the darkest spot of earth some love is found.
I thank Thee more that all our joy is touched with pain;
That shadows fall on brightest hours; that thorns remain;
So that earth's bliss may be our guide, and not our chain.
For Thou, who knowest, Lord, how soon our weak heart clings,
Hast given us joys, tender and true, yet all with wings;
So that we see, gleaming on high, diviner things.

—Adelaide A. Proctor

SOWING AND REAPING

He that goeth forth with weeping,
    Bearing precious seeds in love,
Never tiring, never sleeping,
    Findeth mercy from above.

Soft descend the dews of heaven,
  Bright the rays celestial shine;
Precious fruits will thus be given,
  Through an influence all divine.

Sow thy seed, be never weary,
  Let no fears thy soul annoy;
Be the prospect ne'er so dreary,
  Thou shalt reap the fruits of joy.
Lo, the scene of verdure brightening,
  See the rising grain appear;
Look again, the fields are whitening,
  For the harvest time is near.

                              —Thomas Hastings

GOD MEANS US TO BE HAPPY

God means us to be happy;
  He fills the short-lived years
With loving, tender mercies—
  With smiles as well as tears.
Flowers blossom by the pathway
  Or, withering, they shed
Their sweetest fragrance over
  The bosoms of our dead.

God filled the earth with beauty;
  He touched the hills with light;
He crowned the waving forest
  With living verdure bright;
He taught the bird to carol,
  He gave the wind its voice,
And to the smallest insect
  Its moment to rejoice.

What life hath not its blessing?
  Who hath not songs to sing,
Or grateful words to utter,
  Or wealth of love to bring?
Tried in affection's furnace
  The gold becomes more pure—
So strong doth sorrow make us,
  So patient to endure.

No way is dark and dreary
  If God be with us there;
No danger can befall us
  When sheltered by his care.
Why should our eyes be blinded
  To all earth's glorious bloom?

Why sit we in the shadows
   That falls upon the tomb.

Look up and catch the sunbeams!
   See how the day doth dawn!
Gather the scented roses
   That grow beside the thorn!
God's pitying love doth seek us;
   He leads us to his rest;
And from a thousand pathways
   He chooses what is best.

—*Author Unknown*

ZECHARIAH, THE PROPHET OF THE RESTORATION

I will return to Zion, saith the Lord;
And I will dwell in Jerusalem,
Which shall be called "The faithful city."
And her mountain, "The holy mountain";
And her people, and the people of Judah,
Shall be my people, and I their God.
Thus spake Jehovah,
Who had been indignant over Zion
And had been aroused to wrath over her.

Exult greatly, O Zion!
Lo, your king comes to you,
Humble and riding upon an ass;
And his domination shall be from sea to sea.

Thus spake Jehovah,
Who remembered no more
His enmity toward Jerusalem.

And it shall come to pass that the nations
Which warred against Jerusalem
Shall go up to her mountain
To worship the King, the Lord of hosts;
And all shall say, "Holy to the Lord."

Thus spake Jehovah,
Who had forgotten his wrath
And had restored his people
To Jerusalem and to Judah.*

—*Thomas Curtis Clark*

* Used by special permission of the author.

RAMERI AND THE SCRIBES

By

Marie E. Aenis

LONG AGO, two hundred years before Christ was born, there lived in Egypt a boy whose name was Rameri. He did not live in the dusty city. He lived in the country near the papyrus marshes.

Rameri's father, Big Peru, made papyrus scrolls. He sold them to the scribes in order to support his family.

It was important to be near enough to the marshes to gather fresh stems for this work. Some of the scrolls were thirty feet long and that took a lot of papyrus.

Although Rameri was only fourteen, he helped his father make the scrolls. Rameri's three sisters—Elissa, Naida, and Deida—helped, too.

Early in the morning, Rameri took his three sisters to the marshes to gather the tall stems. As the children came near the marshes, they could smell the pleasant fragrance of the papyrus plant. They could see the feathery flower that looked like a bell and the tall, stiff stems of the plant. They looked into the water and saw the long, pointed leaves that were growing near the creeping root of the plant.

Then Rameri took a long, sharp knife and began to cut through the thick, pithy stems.

Elissa, who was the oldest and the little mother of the family, laid the stems in bundles and tied them together.

Naida and Deida played with the feathery flowers and watched the birds rise from the marshes, until it it was time to go home.

Then Rameri tied the bundles of stems on his sisters' backs and carried a bundle himself.

Little Deida giggled, "The stems are taller than we are, but the bundle is not very heavy. See—I can dance with mine." The merry child hopped up and down and twirled and fell flat on her pretty face.

Elissa and Naida cried, "Oh—oh, Deida!"

Rameri picked up his little sister. When they saw that she was unharmed and laughing instead of crying, they all laughed.

Rameri glanced at the shrinking shadows. "Come," he said to his sisters. "We must hurry. Father will wonder where we are, and there is work to do."

Soon the children were home again. When they came into the yard, they saw their frail mother sitting in the shade of the date palm tree. She was playing with the baby, Little Peru. They saw their father stirring a big pot of sticky water.

Big Peru looked up as his children came toward him with their bundles of papyrus. "Thou art late," he said sternly. "The sun is rising high. We have work to do."

The children hung their heads for they knew that they had not hurried. They were sorry.

Naida and Deida were too young to cut the stems. They sat under the palm tree with their mother and Little Peru and watched.

Elissa sorted the stems and cut them into fairly even lengths.

Rameri sliced the stems into long, flat pieces.

Big Peru laid the flat pieces down side by side. He laid others across these pieces and wet them all with the sticky water. Then Big Peru put a flat, heavy stone over the papyrus page. He let it dry under pressure.

Then Elissa, Rameri and their father started over and made another page.

It took a long time for the pages to dry. When the pages were dry, Rameri piled them on top of one another. He rubbed each one with a smooth shell.

When there were enough pages, Big Peru would fasten them together, side by side, and make a long scroll.

It was upon this type of scroll that the scribes wrote about Noah and Moses and Christ.

Young Rameri looked up from his work. He studied the pile of papyrus pages. "Father," he said seriously, "why could not we fasten the pages one on top of the other like these? It would be much easier to carry to market than the big long scrolls."

Big Peru threw back his head and roared with laughter. "Son, thou art a fool. How wouldst thou roll them, dreamer."

Rameri's eyes sparkled. "Thou wouldst not need to roll them, father, see." He held a pile of pages with one hand and lifted the open side with the other.

Rameri's father watched but shook his head. "The scribes would say we had all gone mad."

"Let us try, father," begged Rameri, always eager to try something new.

Big Peru laughed. "Try if thou like, son. But be sure to tell the scribes that I, Big Peru, had nothing to do with the strange-looking scroll."

Rameri rubbed the pages faster than ever with the shell. Then he piled them all just so and fastened one side.

Even Big Peru agreed that the pages turned well and that it was easier to hold than the scrolls.

When all was ready, Rameri gathered his father's long scrolls and his new book, bade good-by to his family and walked to the dusty city. When the young boy came to the market place, he found the scribes waiting to buy Big Peru's fine scrolls. Bravely Rameri showed the scribes his new idea for papyrus pages.

The scribes, like Big Peru, roared with laughter.

But one scribe, Bartholomew, did not laugh. He held the strange book in his hands. He turned the pages. Then Bartholomew took out his coins. "I will buy this," he said to the amazed boy.

The other scribes stopped laughing. They crowded around Bartholomew.

Rameri did not wait. He took all of his coins for the scrolls and the book and hurried all the way home. "I sold it! I sold it!" the triumphant boy shouted to his father.

Big Peru, who was bouncing Little Peru on his knee, looked at his son with amazement. "Who bought it—not a scribe?"

"Yes," cried Rameri. "Bartholomew bought it." The boy threw himself on the ground to rest.

In a little while, a group of men came into the yard. They were the scribes from the dusty city."

"Thou hast a great son, Big Peru," said Bartholomew. "We want more papyrus pages fastened like these."

For a moment the amazed father stared at the scribes. Then Big Peru put his hand on Rameri's shoulder and said proudly, "My son!"

And so, perhaps it was because of Rameri that in the second century B.C. the scribes began to write in papyrus books, instead of on cumbersome scrolls.*

✠

REBUILDING THE TEMPLE

By

Cynthia Pearl Maus

THE city of Jerusalem was destroyed in 587 B.C. by Nebuchadnezzar, and many of the Hebrews were carried away as captives to Babylon. In 561 B.C. Nebuchadnezzar died, and in 538 B.C. Babylonia was conquered by King Cyrus of Persia. Earlier the Israelites of the Northern Kingdom had been carried away as captives by Assyria and their identity was lost among the races in whose midst they were sent. But the Hebrews carried away by Nebuchadnezzar, principally descendants of the tribes of Judah and Benjamin, kept themselves as a separate group, and were never absorbed by the Chaldeans, the Babylonians, and the Persians among whom they lived.

These exiles in their loneliness and depression of mind and spirit turned once more to the worship of the invisible God of the Hebrews; and their leaders concentrated on and encouraged them to make a careful study of the Hebrew writings. Their hope for the future was found in the prophecies of Jeremiah, who had encouraged them to believe that if they turned their hearts back to God and worshiped Him only, they would, one day, be allowed to return to Jerusalem and the Promised Land.

When Babylon was captured by Cyrus, the Persian, the thrill of a new hope was born in the hearts of these homesick captives. Cyrus was an Aryan of the same stock as the Greeks and Romans. Not only was his language different, but his religion also was entirely unlike the idol worship of the Babylonians. It was natural, therefore, that the Hebrews should hail King Cyrus.

Cyrus knew that the once prosperous land west of the Jordan with its coast line on the Mediterranean sea was a natural highway from Egypt to the north. He knew also that Jerusalem, its capital, had been demolished and its Temple de-

* From *Story Art Magazine*, May-June, 1950. Used by special permission of the author and the publisher.

stroyed. And he thought that the easiest way to restore it to its former strength and power would be to let a host of these industrious Hebrew exiles return to the land of their nativity to restore its capital and to rebuild its Temple. And so in the very first year of his reign, he issued the following proclamation:

"Thus saith Cyrus king of Persia, 'The Lord God of heaven hath given me all the kingdoms of the earth; and he hath charged me to build him an house at Jerusalem, which is in Judah. Who is there among you of all his people? his God be with him, and let him go up to Jerusalem, which is in Judah, and build the house of the Lord God of Israel . . . which is in Jerusalem. And whosoever remaineth in any place where he sojourneth, let the men of his place help him with silver, and with gold, and with goods, and with beasts, beside the freewill offering for the house of God which is in Jerusalem.' " (Ezra 1:2-4)

None of the Hebrews was compelled to return; only those who wanted to go were to be among the returning exiles. But Cyrus did urge those who remained in Babylon to help those who went to Jerusalem by giving them gifts of gold, silver, cattle, and other needed material and equipment. As their king, Cyrus collected from the idol temple in Babylon the vessels of gold and silver which Nebuchadnezzar had taken from the Temple in Jerusalem, and through his treasurer he handed these over to a prince of Judah named Sheshbazzar, and they were brought safely back to Jerusalem.

It was indeed a joyous procession when the caravan of exiles set forth from Babylon. The journey took almost four months and there were hardships on the way; nevertheless, they returned with joy to the land of their hopes and longings. The city was still in ruins, but the site was there and they had returned to rebuild their capital and its Temple and to make it and their nation worthy again to receive the blessing of their God.

The Books of Ezra and Nehemiah tell us stories of how these returned exiles rebuilt, not only the Temple, but also the walls surrounding Jerusalem. And each of the prophets Haggai, Zechariah, and Malachi tell interesting stories of this work of rebuilding and restoration.

On their return, the exiles gathered together immediately to worship the Lord, according to the Law. There was no Temple, but they hastily built an altar, probably on the site of the old altar in Solomon's Temple, and here they offered sacrifices regularly.

It was nearly a year after their return before they were actually able to start the rebuilding of the Temple. Arrangements had to be made with Tyre and Sidon to furnish the needed cedars of Lebanon. These had to be floated down on rafts to Joppa, and then hauled overland to Jerusalem. Masons and carpenters had to be hired to fit and trim materials for the place they were to occupy. When the wonderful day actually came, and the builders were ready to lay the foundation stone of the Temple, the priests and Levites appeared in their official robes with trumpets and other musical instruments, and there was singing and rejoicing as well as tears of sadness and regret.

The Samaritans and other neighboring tribes hindered the work of rebuilding the Temple, from time to time, and a famine in the land postponed its completion for nearly fifteen years. The new Temple was finally completed, however, but not until after King Cyrus had died and Darius ruled in his stead.

✠

ALMIGHTY GOD, BENEATH WHOSE EYE

(Interpretation)

JOHN HAYNES HOLMES was born in 1879 in Philadelphia. In 1902 he graduated from Harvard University, and two years later was ordained by the Unitarian Church (Third Reformed Society) in Dorchester, Massachusetts. Since 1907 he has been minister and later minister emeritus of the Church of the Messiah, now the Community Church in New York City.

Dr. Holmes has served as author for various publications, writing on the problems of the day and on religious subjects. His challenging religious poetry is widely known and his hymns are sung in the United States, England, and Japan.

"Almighty God, beneath Whose Eye" is one of his best known hymns. The melody was composed in 1653 by Praxis Pietatis Melica and is reprinted from the *English Hymnal*.

The five stanzas need no interpretation. The poem is an appeal to the Eternal God of the Ages, "beneath whose eye no sparrow falls in vain," to guide the will

Almighty God, Beneath Whose Eye

NUN DANKET ALL. C. M.

JOHN HAYNES HOLMES, 1910   Praxis Pietatis Melica, 1653

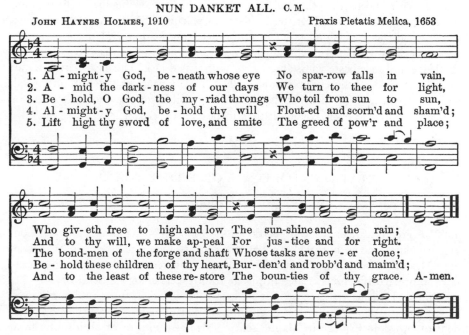

```
1. Al - might-y  God,  be - neath whose eye   No spar-row falls  in   vain,
2. A - mid  the  dark - ness  of   our days   We turn  to thee  for  light,
3. Be - hold,  O  God,  the  my - riad throngs Who toil from sun  to  sun,
4. Al - might-y  God,  be - hold thy will   Flout-ed and scorn'd and  sham'd;
5. Lift  high thy sword of  love, and smite  The greed of pow'r and  place;
```

```
Who  giv - eth free  to  high and low  The  sun-shine and  the   rain;
And  to  thy will,  we make ap-peal  For  jus - tice and  for  right.
The  bond-men of  the forge and shaft Whose tasks are nev - er  done;
Be - hold these children  of  thy heart, Bur - den'd and robb'd and maim'd;
And  to  the least  of  these re - store  The boun-ties of  thy  grace. A-men.
```

---

* Words used by special permission of Dr. John Haynes Holmes.

of men toward justice and right, and to protect all those who labor and "whose tasks are never done." It asks God to smite the forces of greed and restore to the least of His children the bounties of His grace.

✣

CLEAR THE WAY FOR THE ETERNAL

(Interpretation)

THE source of inspiration for this hymn, written by William L. Stidger in 1939 and set to a musical melody arranged by James R. Houghton from an older melody by Rowland H. Prichard, will be found in the Book of Isaiah (40:3), Moffatt translation. Isaiah's cry, with which this hymn opens, was also the cry of John the Baptist preparing the way for Christ (Mark 1:3).

This hymn-poem presents a distinct challenge to the Church today to "clear the way for the Eternal" God. Of this the prophets spoke, and for this martyrs suffered, and God's Only Begotten Son gave His life on the Cross, leaving to His disciples the affirmation, "I am the way, the truth, and the life. No man cometh unto the Father save through me."

It is an appeal to the missionaries of the Cross and to church leaders everywhere to take up the challenge of the unfinished task of building a redeemed world order of society in which men and women will reflect the will of the Eternal in all they think, say, do, and are.

This hymn throbs with the heartbeat of a man who gave his life to the training of young men and women for the ministry of teaching, preaching, and evangelizing a world that still blunders on in ignorance, superstition, and sin.

Sing it, young men and women, with passion and purpose as you take up its challenge and rededicate yourselves to the unfinished task. This is a martial hymn of dedication to all those who would walk in the footsteps of the Almighty God, and who believe with Jesus Christ that it is possible for all who follow in His train to "be perfect even as your Father in heaven is perfect."

✣

CREATION'S LORD, WE GIVE THEE THANKS

(Interpretation)

THE Reverend William DeWitt Hyde (1858-1917), an outstanding American Congregationalist, the author of this twentieth-century hymn, was born in Winchendon, Massachusetts. He graduated from Harvard University in 1879 and four years later completed his ministerial training at Andover Theological Seminary.

William Hyde served as pastor at Paterson, New Jersey, from 1883 until 1885. Then, only three years after the beginning of that ministry, he was elected president of Bowdoin College in Maine, serving also as professor of philosophy from 1886 until the time of his death in 1917.

Clear the way for the Eternal

"Hark! there is one calling, 'Clear the way for the Eternal!'"

William L. Stidger

Rowland H. Prichard
Arranged by James ·R. Houghton

"Clear the way— for the E - ter-nal!" 'Twas of this the prophets spake,
"Clear the way— for the E - ter-nal!"Church of God a - cross the land.
"Clear the way— for the E - ter-nal!" In— the mine and field and mart,

'Twas for this— the martyrs suf-fered Hangman's noose and fie - ry stake.
Here we have—the great com-mis-sion, Here we— hear the great command!
So - cial jus - tice for the workman, Com-rade-ship of— mind and heart.

"Clear the way for the— E - ter-nal!" 'Twas for this—that Je - sus came—
"Clear the way for the— E - ter-nal!" Mis-sion-ar - y proph-et, priest,—
"Clear the way for the— E - ter-nal!"Cleave the brush and till the sod; —

To our mor - tal life and liv - ing; To— im-mor-tal death and shame.
Through the for - ests and the jun - gles North and south and west and east. A-men.
Clear the way for the E - ter - nal Footsteps of Almight-y God!

He was often spoken of as "the Boy President" because of his youth. Nevertheless, he was a wise counselor to the students, an able administrator, and a much-loved and honored citizen of his community. He wrote several books on religious and educational subjects and gave a series of lectures at Harvard, Chicago, and Yale Universities.

"Creation's Lord, We Give Thee Thanks" was written as a challenge to the college students whose recognized leader he was. Its message bears a constant challenge to young men and women to forsake their own petty affairs and become a part of the nation's life, entering the "marshal'd ranks" of those who work for the moral principles that "alone can make a nation great" and who see a vision of "the blessed kingdom of the right."

The first stanza is a prayer of thanks to the Eternal God for having given to

Creation's Lord, We Give Thee Thanks

ROCKINGHAM. L. M.

WILLIAM DE WITT HYDE, 1903

EDWARD MILLER, 1790

1. Cre - a - tion's Lord, we give thee thanks That this thy
2. That thou hast not yet fin - ished man, That we are
3. Be - yond the pres - ent sin and shame, Wrong's bit - ter,
4. What though the King - dom long de - lay, And still with
5. Since what we choose is what we are, And what we

world is in - com - plete; That bat - tle calls our
in the mak - ing still, As friends who share the
cru - el, scorch - ing blight, We see the beck - 'ning
haugh - ty foes must cope? It gives us that for
love we yet shall be, The goal may ev - er

mar-shal'd ranks, That work a - waits our hands and feet;
Mak - er's plan, As sons who know the Fa - ther's will.
vi - sion flame, The bless-ed king-dom of the right.
which to pray, A field for toil and faith and hope.
shine a - far; The will to win it makes us free. A - men.

* Words used by special permission of Mrs. George R. Hyde.

mankind an incomplete world, and for the commission in Genesis 1:28 to take this incomplete world and "subdue it: and have dominion over" it.

The second stanza voices the author's thanks that mankind is incomplete. Individuals as well as the races of men are in the process of becoming. The youth of today, grasping the finest education that Christian colleges can provide, can help to complete God's dream of a perfected world society.

The third stanza changes to a meditation relative to present-day conditions and the challenge that these times offer to youth for a life investment that can and will change the world.

The fourth stanza emphasizes the "field for toil" that is offered to youth in which they may invest their lives in helping to usher in the goal of a redeemed world order of society.

The fifth stanza challenges youth to choose not only what they are, but what under God's guidance they yet may be. This goal forever shines before youth's pathway. The "will to win it [that goal] makes us free."

The tune "Rockingham" was composed in 1790 by Edward Miller.

✛

O, WHERE ARE KINGS AND EMPIRES NOW?

(Interpretation)

According to Julian's *History of Hymnology* (1891 edition), Arthur Cleveland Coxe was the son of the Rev. Samuel H. Coxe, a Presbyterian minister. He was born

O, Where Are Kings and Empires Now
ST. ANNE. C. M.

ARTHUR CLEVELAND COXE, 1839   WILLIAM CROFT, 1708

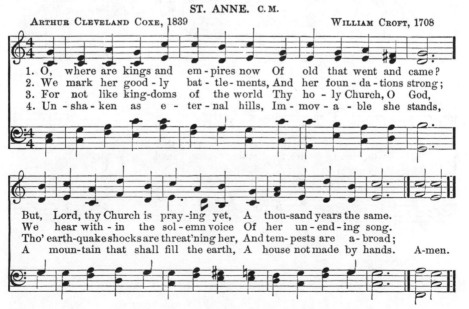

1. O, where are kings and em - pires now Of old that went and came?
2. We mark her good - ly bat - tle - ments, And her foun - da - tions strong;
3. For not like king - doms of the world Thy ho - ly Church, O God,
4. Un - sha - ken as e - ter - nal hills, Im - mov - a - ble she stands,

But, Lord, thy Church is pray - ing yet, A thou - sand years the same.
We hear with - in the sol - emn voice Of her un - end - ing song.
Tho' earth - quake shocks are threat'ning her, And tem - pests are a - broad;
A moun - tain that shall fill the earth, A house not made by hands. A - men.

at Mendham, New Jersey, May 10, 1818. He became a member of the Protestant
Episcopal Church and was ordained in 1841. He was rector of Grace Church, Balti-
more, and of Calvary Church in New York, later being consecrated Bishop of the
Western Diocese of New York. Bishop Coxe is credited with writing seventeen
hymns, of which the tenth is "O, Where Are Kings and Empires Now?"

This challenging hymn is indeed worthy of a place in present-day church hymnals,
and the sentiment of the hymn speaks for itself. Its four stanzas present an inquiry
into the fate of kingdoms and empires that have long since ceased to exist. These
are contrasted with the Church of God which, through the passing centuries, continues to pray and sing "her unending song." In spite of earthquakes and tempests

These Things Shall Be

TRURO. L. M.

JOHN A. SYMONDS, 1880   Psalmodia Evangelica, 1789

1. These things shall be,— a loft - ier race Than e'er the
2. They shall be gen - tle, brave, and strong To spill no
3. Na - tion with na - tion, land with land, In - armed shall
4. New arts shall bloom of loft - ier mould, And might - ier

world hath known shall rise With flame of free - dom in their souls,
drop of blood, but dare All that may plant man's lord - ship firm
live as com - rades free; In ev - 'ry heart and brain shall throb
mu - sic thrill the skies, And ev - 'ry life shall be a song,

And light of knowl - edge in their eyes:
On earth, and fire, and sea, and air.
The pulse of one fra - ter - ni - ty.
When all the earth is par - a - dise. A - men.

the Church stands on her strong foundations, unshaken, immovable.

To read the words of this magnificent hymn is to rejoice in the endurance and vitality of Christianity, and to thrill anew with love and loyalty to Christ, the head of the Church, whose redeeming mission shall finally cause it to spread throughout the world.

The familiar tune "St. Anne" was composed in 1708 by William Croft.

✟

THESE THINGS SHALL BE

(Interpretation)

THE author of the words to this nineteenth-century hymn, John A. Symonds, was born in 1840 in Bristol, England. He was educated in Harrow School, later attended Balliol College at Oxford, and in 1862 became a Fellow of Magdalen College at Oxford. He was the author of two volumes of verse, as well as many scholarly works in prose among which is his *The History of the Italian Renaissance.* He died in 1893.

The four stanzas of this prophetic hymn of aspiration were selected from a seventeen-stanza poem, written by the author in 1880 under the title "The Vista." They emphasize the prophecy of a new and better day to which Isaiah 2:4 refers: "And they shall beat their swords into plowshares, and their spears into pruning-hooks; nation shall not lift up sword against nation, neither shall they learn war any more." One cannot sing the words of this great hymn of faith and triumph without feeling a surge of hope for that better day to come when war shall be outlawed and the sons of men shall learn to live together in peace as children of a common Heavenly Father.

The tune "Truro" is from *Psalmodia Evangelica* published in 1789.

CONTENTS

PART VI SECTION 3

STORIES OF THE PERSIAN PERIOD

---✛---

So this Daniel prospered in the reign of Darius, and in the reign of Cyrus the Persian.—DANIEL 6:28

---✛---

DANIEL INTERPRETS THE DREAM OF NEBUCHADNEZZAR

By

William Hole

(Interpretation)

THE name Daniel means "judge of God," that is, "one who judges in God's name." The brief story of this young man, related in the twelfth chapter of the Book of Daniel, reveals how well the meaning of his name fits his life and character.

The Book of Daniel is a collection of stories about Daniel and his friends and of the visions he saw. During the Babylonian captivity Daniel held a high place in the courts of Nebuchadnezzar, Cyrus, and Darius in spite of all the plots of his scheming rivals. In the second chapter of the Book of Daniel is the famous story of how Daniel interpreted King Nebuchadnezzar's dream. It was in the second year of his reign that the king began to dream dreams which troubled him greatly and caused him to lose much sleep. "Then the king commanded to call the magicians, and the astrologers, and the sorcerers, and the Chaldeans, for to shew the king his dreams. So they came and stood before the king."

The king told them about his dream and desired to know its interpretation. Then the Chaldeans spoke with confidence: "O king, live for ever! Tell thy servants the dream, and we will shew the interpretation."

Nebuchadnezzar warned the wise men of his decree: "The thing is gone from me: if ye will not make known unto me the dream, with the interpretation thereof, ye shall be cut in pieces. . . . But if ye shew the dream, and the interpretation thereof, ye shall receive of me gifts and rewards and great honour."

The wise men found the king's dream impossible to interpret and they said: "There is not a man upon the earth that can shew the king's matter. . . . And it is a rare thing that the king requireth, and there is none other that can shew it before the king, except the gods, whose dwelling is not with flesh."

The king was furious with them and commanded that all the wise men of Babylon be destroyed. Daniel and his friends were among those whom the king ordered to be slain.

When Daniel learned of the king's decree from Arioch, the captain of the king's guard, he prayed to the Lord and in a vision the secret of the king's dream was revealed to him. Then Daniel said: "Blessed be the name of God for ever and ever. . . . I thank thee, O thou God of my fathers, who hast given me wisdom and might, and hast made known unto me now what we desired of thee, for thou hast now made known unto us the king's matter."

When Arioch heard that Daniel could interpret the king's dream, he brought him in haste to Nebuchadnezzar. Seeing Daniel, one of the captives from Judah, standing before him the king asked: "Art thou able to make known unto me the dream which I have seen, and the interpretation thereof?"

Daniel replied: "The secret which the king hath demanded cannot the wise men, the astrologers, the magicians, the soothsayers, shew unto the king. But there is a God in heaven that revealeth secrets, and maketh known to the king Nebuchadnezzar what shall be in the latter days."

This painting showing Daniel interpreting the king's dream is one of the colored illustrations in *Old Testament History, Retold and Illustrated* by William Hole. The artist made a careful study of all the available material concerning life at the court of King Nebuchadnezzar in ancient Babylon before he undertook to paint this picture. It shows the distant skyline of the city, the broad, peaceful-flowing Euphrates, and the king's throne room open on one side to cool breezes from the river. Marble pillars, rich draperies, a patterned carpet leading up to the throne all indicate the luxury surrounding the king. He is guarded by a foreign slave armed with a sword. An aged counselor stands at the king's left. Some of the wise men, who with all their strange drawings and crystal balls were unable to interpret the king's dream, stand or kneel before the king. Daniel kneels below the throne, his head uplifted as he tells Nebuchadnezzar the meaning of his dream. He comes not in his own strength, but with the devout faith that the interpretation he makes is a revelation of the Lord his God. Daniel's whole bearing indicates his confidence that it is the God of the Hebrews who is the source of his wisdom. The intent expression on the face of the king shows that he is convinced Daniel's interpretation is a true one.

✛

DANIEL DISCOVERED AT PRAYER

By

Sir Edward John Poynter

(Interpretation)

DANIEL was a man who remained faithful to God against desperate odds. In his youth he had been among the captives taken to Babylon by Nebuchadnezzar. There he kept the laws of his religion and continued to worship the Lord God of Israel. God gave him "knowledge and skill in all learning and wisdom; and Daniel had understanding in all visions and dreams" (Dan. 1:17). Like Joseph in Egypt, centuries earlier, Daniel's unusual ability was recognized and he rose to important positions in the kingdom.

When Darius the Persian conquered Babylon he divided his new empire into one hundred and twenty provinces each ruled by a satrap. Darius appointed three presidents to be over the one hundred and twenty satraps and he chose Daniel to be one of these presidents. But that was not all, for new honors and responsibilities awaited Daniel. "An excellent spirit was in him, and the king thought to set him over the whole realm"(6:3).

Jealous of his growing power, the satraps and other presidents tried to find some ground of complaint against Daniel, but they could find none. They said to each other: "We shall not find any occasion against this Daniel, except we

DANIEL INTERPRETS THE DREAM OF NEBUCHADNEZZAR—*HOLE*

find it against him concerning the law of his God" (6:5). They knew of his faithfulness to the Lord his God and with this in mind they laid their plot.

"Then these presidents and princes assembled together to the king, and said thus unto him: 'King Darius, live for ever!'" They persuaded the king "to establish a royal statute, and to make a firm decree, that whosoever shall ask a petition of any God or man for thirty days, save of thee, O king, he shall be cast into the den of lions."

Flattered that his governors and counselors had put him on the level of a god, Darius failed to perceive that this was a trap and he signed the decree so that it became an unalterable law of the Medes and the Persians.

But a decree of the Medes and the Persians could not prevent a God-fearing man from praying. "Now when Daniel knew that the writing was signed, he went into his house; and his windows being open in his chamber toward Jerusalem, he kneeled upon his knees three times a day, and prayed, and gave thanks before his God, as he did aforetime. Then these men assembled, and found Daniel praying and making supplication before his God" (6:10, 11).

This story was the inspiration for Sir Edward John Poynter's engraving, "Daniel Discovered at Prayer." In his elaborately decorated chamber Daniel kneels before his window toward Jerusalem and the Temple of his God. He has removed his shoes, remembering the Lord's injunction to Moses: "Put off thy shoes from off thy feet, for the ground whereon thou standest is holy ground" (Ex. 3:5). According to the custom of his people Daniel wears a head covering. In the background the curtain has been drawn aside by one of those in the plot against him.

Everyone knows the end of the story: how he was thrown into the lions' den where the fearful king found him the next day alive and unhurt. And Darius decreed that everyone should worship the God of Daniel, "for he is the living God, and stedfast for ever, and his kingdom that which shall not be destroyed, and his dominion shall be even unto the end" (6:26).

✛

DANIEL IN THE LIONS' DEN

By

Luke Yuan Tu Chen

(Interpretation)

DANIEL and his three friends, Shadrach, Meshach, and Abednego, were among the Hebrew exiles who were carried as captives to Babylonia. Their loyal devotion to the living God of the Hebrews resulted in their being placed in positions of great honor and responsibility throughout the reigns of Nebuchadnezzar and of Belshazzar, his successor.

After Belshazzar was slain and Darius, king of the Medes and Persians, came into power, he put Daniel into a position of authority over the hundred and

DANIEL DISCOVERED AT PRAYER—*POYNTER*

twenty princes of the kingdom, but the princes became jealous of Daniel's power and plotted to overthrow him. They persuaded the unsuspecting king to sign a decree "that whosoever shall ask a petition of any God or man for thirty days . . . he shall be cast into the den of lions" (Daniel 6:7).

"Now when Daniel knew that the writing was signed, he went into his house; and his windows being open in his chamber toward Jerusalem, he kneeled upon his knees three times a day, and prayed, and gave thanks before his God, as he did aforetime" (6:10).

Daniel's enemies found him praying and reported to the king that Daniel had defied the decree. But the king was "sore displeased with himself, and set his heart on Daniel to deliver him." His efforts were of no avail, for his decree, being a law of the Medes and the Persians, was irrevocable. The king could find no way to circumvent this nefarious scheme to trap Daniel.

Daniel was therefore cast into a den of lions. A stone was brought and laid upon the mouth of the cave, and the king unwillingly sealed it with his own personal signet.

On the following morning King Darius hurried to the cave, hoping against hope that Daniel's God had preserved him from these ferocious lions. He called to Daniel, saying: "O Daniel, servant of the living God, is thy God, whom thou servest continually, able to deliver thee from the lions?" (6:20). And Daniel answered: "O king, live for ever. My God hath sent his angel, and hath shut the lions' mouths, that they have not hurt me" (21-22).

The king was overjoyed and commanded that Daniel be taken up out of the lions' den. This was done. The king then decreed that the God of Daniel should be worshiped throughout his kingdom "for he is the living God, and stedfast for ever."

It is this Biblical inicident that Luke Yuan Tu Chen, the Chinese artist, has painted in his "Daniel in the Lions' Den." In the midst of these hungry, ferocious beasts stands the serene figure of Daniel, his eyes lifted to heaven as he prays to the Lord that his life may be spared so that the Persian king may know that the God in whom he trusts is really able to save and preserve those who believe in him.

These hungry lions look on and even sniff at the feet of this defenseless man, yet they make no attempt to devour him. Sheer walls of stone rise high on all sides, offering no hope of escape other than the miraculous power of God who is Lord not only of the Hebrew people, but also of all men and women everywhere and in all ages.

The upturned face of the lion facing Daniel seems almost to speak, as his eyes raised in curious questioning seem to say: "He trusts in a power higher than we know. His life is guarded by the God who created all of us, men and animals, and who holds our destinies in His hands. Daniel is our friend and brother, we cannot destroy him. He knows no fear of us because he trusts in the Lord, Creator of the universe, and the Guardian of all created life."

DANIEL IN THE LIONS' DEN—*TU CHEN*

THE FRIEZE OF THE PROPHETS

By

John Singer Sargent

(Interpretation)

LEFT CENTER SECTION

IMMEDIATELY at the left of the center section of Sargent's "Frieze of the Prophets" stand the figures of Amos, Nahum, Ezekiel, and Daniel, grouped together not because their life and work covered the same period in Hebrew history but because there is a similarity in the ideas and ideals they promulgated.

From Amos on the prophets were all monotheists, that is, they believed that there was only one God, the Lord. He was the planner of the universe and the controller of the history and destiny of man. He manifested His power and glory in nature as well as in man, controlling and using both to serve His great purposes. He was the God, not only of the nation, but of the individual as well—a God of both wrath and mercy, of justice and love.

The prophets affirmed that God is a spiritual person; that He controls a universe governed by moral and spiritual laws; and that He punishes men for breaking these laws. According to the prophets, God expects men to behave toward Him and toward one another as though they were children of a common Creator. Men are expected to be like the God who created them, not in power, but in the basic essence of their characters.

Before the time of Amos, the first of the great prophets, many of the children of Israel thought that the Lord might do immoral, even irrational things, merely because He was deity and all-powerful. But the prophets from Amos on down to the time of Jesus insisted that God is moral, and thus has a right to make moral demands of His people.

According to James Philip Hyatt, professor of Old Testament history, and chairman of the Graduate School of Religion at Vanderbilt University:

"While the prophets were always interested in proclaiming truer ideas of God, they were more concerned to call men to deeper experiences of the living God and to summon them to submit themselves more unreservedly to His authority. They taught that God is sufficient for all the various needs of man. Half-gods and false idols must go, so that the true and living God may rule. The only way of salvation for men and nations is the way of obedience to the God of justice and mercy, of nature and history.

"The prophets believed that sin is rebellion against a sovereign God and rises from corruption of the heart. Their view of sin was serious because their view of God's nature was serious. To them sin often involves maltreatment of one's neighbor and wrong social relations, but it is basically an offense against God and a flaunting of His authority."*

* From *Prophetic Religion* by James Philip Hyatt, p. 176. Published 1947 by Abingdon Press. Used by special permission of Stone and Pierce.

THE FRIEZE OF THE PROPHETS (LEFT CENTER SECTION)—*SARGENT*

Amos, on the extreme right in this section of the mural, was a poet-prophet of unusual ability. His only public appearance which is definitely recorded (Amos 7:10-17) seems to have been at Bethel in the Northern Kingdom, during the reign of Jeroboam, king of Israel. It is possible, however, that the book bearing his name represents excerpts from a number of prophetic messages delivered in various cities at different times.

Even less is known of the life and work of Nahum, the Elkoshite, since the book bearing his name contains only three short chapters. He prophesied the overthrow of the city of Nineveh and its utter destruction; and also of the goodness and severity of the Lord's judgments of men and nations.

The Book of Ezekiel has provoked more discussion among Old Testament students than almost any other of the prophetic books. The Babylonian setting of the book would seem to indicate that it is the work of a prophet who lived between 550 and 500 B.C. He was a prophet of ethical insight and highly indignant over the social and religious practices of his people.

Ezekiel's vision of the four living creatures and the four wheels has been popularized in the Negro spiritual "Ezekiel Saw the Wheel." It is known that he prophesied the siege and destruction of Jerusalem and the punishment of the Hebrew nation for its wickedness. He also prophesied the restoration and renewal of the nation and the land of Israel.

The Book of Daniel, although grouped in the Old Testament among the prophets, is not, properly speaking, a book of prophecy. In the Hebrew Bible it is classified among the writings. Nevertheless, it does contain some prophecies, visions, and interpretations of prophetic dreams. The book portrays the life of Daniel during the reign of Jehoiakim, king of Judah, at a time when the kingdom was overthrown by Nebuchadnezzar, king of Babylon. Daniel was among the youths selected because of their skill, education, and abilities to be among those who served the king. These conquered sons of the kingdom of Judah were given Babylonian names. The Book of Daniel tells how they remained true to the God of the Hebrews; and it narrates the problems that resulted from their loyalty to their faith.

These four prophets, living in widely different periods of Hebrew life and history, Sargent has grouped together in his mural, "The Frieze of the Prophets." They were alike only in their belief in God's essential goodness, love, justice, and mercy; and of the necessity of man's response with like character qualities if he is to receive the Lord's blessing and continued guidance.

VASHTI DEPOSED

By

Ernest Normand

(Interpretation)

THE story of Vashti, the beautiful Persian queen who dared to disobey the king's command, is one of the tragedies of the Old Testament. The peculiar incident that occasioned the queen's rebellion is narrated in the opening chapter of the Book of Esther. It describes in detail how notable and important was the festival which Queen Vashti spurned.

In the magnificent palace of Shushan, in the third year of the reign of King Ahasuerus over the kingdom of the Medes and Persians, whose empire in all of its richness and glory extended from India to Ethiopia, the king held a courtly festival to which all the princes in all the provinces of his vast empire were invited. The festivities lasted for one hundred and eighty days; and the purposes of this prolonged *fiesta* was to impress the princes and servants of the king's court with all the richness and magnificence of his empire.

Near the end of all this feasting and entertainment the king gave a great public feast to all the people, both great and small, princes and servants, in his palace. It was held in the king's court, which was beautifully decorated for the occasion with hangings of white, green, and blue cloth fastened with cords of linen and purple to silver rings and pillars of marble. The guests all drank from vessels of gold, and royal wine flowed in abundance.

Vashti, the queen, also made a feast for the women of the royal court. On the seventh day of this feast, when the king was himself mellow with wine, he commanded his seven chamberlains to bring Vashti, the queen, before the king dressed in her royal robes and wearing her royal crown that all his guests might see how beautiful she really was, for "she was fair to look upon."

But Queen Vashti refused to come at the king's command, and his majesty, the king, was very angry. In his burning anger he sought the advice of the wise men of his court who counseled him on matters of state. They advised that the disobedient queen should be set aside as an example to all the other women of the kingdom that they should never disobey their husbands. Their advice that Vashti be deposed and her place given to another, and younger, woman, who would be more gracious and submissive than her predecessor, was followed. The king of the Medes and Persians signed a royal decree that was published throughout all the kingdom, as an object lesson to the women of the land that all wives, henceforth, great and small, should give honor and obedience to their husbands.

Ernest Normand's portrayal of this tragedy shows the beautiful Queen Vashti stretched on her couch in despair. She has just received the king's decree. Her clenched hands, one clasping the cover on her couch and the other supporting her head, are eloquently expressive of her feelings. The architecture and elaborate hangings are displayed in rich colors and lighted from above in an artistic effect. Near Vashti's feet kneels one of her devoted and sorrowing slaves; for even this slave knows that her fate is sealed, since the laws of the Medes and Persians are irrevocable.

✛

ESTHER BEFORE KING AHASUERUS

By

Giustino Menescardi

(Interpretation)

THE story of Esther, the Hebrew girl who became queen of the Persian Empire when Queen Vashti was deposed, is one of the most dramatic accounts in the Old Testament.

The Hebrew people during Esther's lifetime were captives in Babylonia which had been overpowered and was now a part of the great Persian Empire whose duration extended from approximately 536 B.C. to 323 B.C.

Vashti's refusal to come into the king's court that her marvelous beauty might be seen and appreciated by the court had resulted in her banishment. A search was made among other beautiful young women of the Empire for a new queen. Esther, a Hebrew maiden of unusual beauty, was finally selected by the king above all others to take Vashti's place.

Haman, chief adviser to King Ahasuerus, hated the Hebrews, and particularly Mordecai, Esther's uncle, because he refused to make obeisance to him, or to worship the gods of the Medes and Persians. So he set a trap whereby not only Mordecai, but all the Hebrew captives who were faithful to the Lord might be put to death.

Mordecai heard of this scheme and prevailed on Esther, his niece, to go to King Ahasuerus, without summons, to plead for her own life and that of her people. After many days of fasting, prayer, and purification, and realizing that to go before the king without his summons might mean instant death, Esther finally decided to hazard a personal appearance.

She knew she would have to be clever to prevent Haman, the king's adviser, from suspecting her intention. The story of the ruse by which she eventually won not only the life of her people, but also a just punishment for wicked Haman, is recorded in the ten-chapter Book of Esther.

The theme of this picture is Esther's courageous appeal to the king. The beautiful queen approached, without previous summons, the king's throne. Elaborately gowned and attended by three of her ladies-in-waiting, Esther made her unheralded approach not knowing what fate might be in store for her. When the king held out to her his golden scepter she almost fainted with relief.

Interest and attention are focused upon the lovely young queen as she swoons and is supported by her worried attendants. Haman, the king's evil adviser, rolls his

VASHTI DEPOSED—*NORMAND*

scheming eyes toward his master and raises his hand as if counseling Ahasuerus to pay no attention to Esther. But it is too late for that, for the king has already risen from his throne and is preparing to assist the queen. At the right Esther's uncle, Mordecai, knowing the risk Esther is taking to make her appeal to the king, clasps his hands in prayer for her success and the deliverance of all the Hebrew people.

Giustino Menescardi, a Venetian painter who belongs to the period of Tiepolo, painted the picture from which this detail is taken. It is skillfully designed and has an attractive vitality. In it the heroic style blends gracefully with a naturalistic treatment.

✠

BELSHAZZAR

Midnight came slowly sweeping on;
In silent rest lay Babylon.

But in the royal castle high
Red torches gleam and courtiers cry.

Belshazzar there in kingly hall
Is holding kingly festival.

The vassals sat in glittering line,
And emptied the goblets with glowing wine.

The goblets rattle, the choruses swell,
And it pleased the stiff-necked monarch well.

In the monarch's cheeks a wild fire glowed,
And the wine awoke his daring mood.

And, onward still by his madness spurred,
He blasphemes the Lord with a sinful word;

And he brazenly boasts, blaspheming wild,
While the servile courtiers cheered and smiled.

Quick the king spoke, while his proud glance
    burned,
Quickly the servant went and returned.

He bore on his head the vessels of gold,
Of Jehovah's temple the plunder bold.

With daring hand, in his frenzy grim,
The king seized a beaker and filled to the
    brim,

ESTHER BEFORE KING AHASUERUS—MENESCARDI

And drained to the dregs the sacred cup,
And foaming he cried, as he drank it up,

"Jehovah, eternal scorn I own
To thee. I am monarch of Babylon."

Scarce had the terrible blasphemy rolled
From his lips, ere the monarch at heart was
    cold.

The yelling laughter was hushed, and all
Was still as death in the royal hall.

And see! and see! on the white wall high
The form of a hand went slowly by,

And wrote—and wrote, on the broad wall
    white,
Letters of fire, and vanished in night.

Pale as death, with a steady stare,
And with trembling knees, the king sat there;

The horde of slaves sat huddering chill;
No word they spoke, but were deathlike still.

The Magians came, but of them all,
None could read the flame-script on the wall.

But that same night, in all his pride,
By the hands of his servants Belshazzar died.*

                        —*Heinrich Heine (1820)*

DANIEL

Daniel was a godly man
    And thankful through his days . . .
He never failed to pray to God
    And give Him all the praise.

His trials were so many,
    And he was tempted sore . . .
But he was saved by righteousness,
    And the godly cloak he wore.

Interpreting the royal dreams
    Through wisdom from on high . . .
He ever gave the praise to God,
    As his life did verify.

*Translated by Charles Godfrey Leland, 1863.

In the fiery furnace
   And in the lions' den . . .
The flames were stayed, the jaws were set
   Before oppressing men.

But he emerged triumphant,
   For God was ever near . . .
He guards His children from all harm
   When danger does appear.

Through our temptations and our trials,
   On life's tempestuous ways . . .
I thank Thee, God, for Daniel,
   And for his life of praise.

Upon my knees, I pray that God,
   Will make me thankful too . . .
And worthy of His love and care . . .
   I know He'll see me through!*

                        —*Ruth Ricklefs*

DAY'S END

Day ends:
Breasting the North,
My shoulders shiver
As I onward go.
And yet,
I utterly forget
The cruel cold,
Nor feel the dark,
Because my heart
Aches with the people's woe.

Oh, let me trust
That through my tears
God's Kingdom has
One little inch drawn near!
Then what is it to me
That my weak body be
Beaten to dust?
Midnight:
I crawl from out my bed
Into the cold,
And gaze up at the stars again,
Finding God there
To help me bear
My daily load
Of grief and care,
Sorrow and pain.

* Used by special permission of the author.

Deep in the night
Our spirits meet,
And prayer is sweet!*

—*Toyohiko Kagawa*

EXILED FROM THE HOUSE OF GOD

As the hart panteth after the water brooks,
So panteth my soul after thee, O God.
My soul thirsteth for God, for the living God:
When shall I come and appear before God?
My tears have been my meat day and night,
While they continually say unto me, Where is thy God?
These things I remember,
And pour out my soul within me
How I went with the throng, and led them to the house of God,
With the voice of joy and praise, a multitude keeping holyday.

> *Why art thou cast down, O my soul?*
> *And why art thou disquieted within me?*
> *Hope thou in God:*
> *For I shall yet praise him,*
> *Who is the health of my countenance,*
> *And my God.*

My soul is cast down within me:
Therefore do I remember thee from the land of Jordan,
And the Hermons, from the hill Mizar.
Deep calleth unto deep at the noise of thy waterspouts:
All thy waves and thy billows are gone over me.
Yet the LORD will command his lovingkindness in the day-time,
And in the night his song shall be with me,
Even a prayer unto the God of my life.
I will say unto God my rock, Why hast thou forgotten me?
Why go I mourning because of the oppression of the enemy?
As with a sword in my bones, mine adversaries reproach me;
While they continually say unto me, Where is thy God?

> *Why art thou cast down, O my soul?*
> *And why art thou disquieted within me?*
> *Hope thou in God:*
> *For I shall yet praise him,*
> *Who is the health of my countenance,*
> *And my God.*

Judge me, O God, and plead my cause against an ungodly nation:
O deliver me from the deceitful and unjust man.
For thou art the God of my strength; why hast thou cast me off?
Why go I mourning because of the oppression of the enemy?

* From *Songs from the Slums* by Toyohiko Kagawa, pp. 72-73. Copyright, 1935, by Whitmore & Smith. Published by Abingdon Press. Used by special permission of the publisher.

O send out thy light and thy truth;
   Let them lead me:
Let them bring me unto thy holy hill,
   And to thy tabernacles.
Then will I go unto the altar of God,
Unto God my exceeding joy:
   And upon the harp will I praise thee, O God, my God.

   Why art thou cast down, O my soul?
   And why art thou disquieted within me?
     Hope thou in God:
   For I shall yet praise him,
   Who is the health of my countenance,
     And my God.*

                  —*Psalms 42:1-11; 43:1-5*

GLORY TO GOD ALONE

Soli Deo gloria

Here man with axe doth cut the bough in
   twain,
And without him the axe could nothing do;
Within the tool there doth no force remain,
But man it is that might doth put thereto;
   Like to this axe is man in all his deeds,
   Who hath no strength but what from God
     proceeds.

Then let him not make vaunt of his desert,
Nor brag thereof when he good deeds hath
   done,
For it is God that worketh in his heart,
And, with his grace, to good doth make him run.
   And of himself he weak thereto doth live,
   And God gives power, to whom all glory
     give!

                  —*Geoffrey Whitney (1580)*

IMPLORING DIVINE LIGHT

O Thou, whose power o'er moving worlds
   presides,
Whose voice created, and whose wisdom
   guides,
On darkling man in pure effulgence shine,
And clear the clouded mind with light divine.

'Tis thine alone to calm the pious breast
With silent confidence and holy rest;
From thee, great God, we spring, to thee we
   tend,
Path, motive, guide, original, and end!

    —Boethius; translated by Samuel Johnson

THE LESSON OF DANIEL

A proud king reigned in Babylon the great;
A pure youth dreamed, to goodness consecrate.
The youth turned eyes to Heaven, with a prayer;
The king appraised his wealth and kingdom fair.
But God disdained the kingdom—it was gone;
The humble youth prayed earnestly at dawn.
No lions' den nor furnace breathing fire
Can frighten him whom Godly thoughts inspire.
The tyrant's taunts are as the winter grim
Whose insults pass as God's bright spring comes in.
The hosts of error, clad in stern array,
Inflame the world, then glumly fade away.
Proud kings and mighty kingdoms suffer loss;
Love lives!—through Godly visions and a Cross.*

    —Thomas Curtis Clark

LIGHT SHINING OUT OF DARKNESS

God moves in a mysterious way
 His wonders to perform;
He plants his footsteps in the sea,
 He rides upon the storm.

Deep in unfathomable mines
 Of never-failing skill
He treasures up his bright designs,
 And works his sovereign will.
Ye fearful saints, fresh courage take,
 The clouds ye so much dread
Are big with mercy, and shall break
 In blessings on your head.

Judge not the Lord by feeble sense,
 But trust him for his grace,
Behind a frowning providence
 He hides a smiling face.

* Used by special permission of the author.

His purposes will ripen fast,
　Unfolding every hour;
The bud may have a bitter taste,
　But sweet will be the flower.

Blind unbelief is sure to err,
　And scan his work in vain;
God is his own interpreter,
　And he will make it plain.

— *William Cowper (1779)*

MAY GOD BE IN YOUR HEART

May God be ever in your heart. Strive to see God in all
things without exception, and acquiesce in His will with
absolute submission. Do everything for God, uniting
yourself to Him by a mere upward glance, or by the overflowing of your heart towards Him. Never be in a hurry;
do everything quietly and in a calm spirit. Do not lose
your inward peace for anything whatsoever; even if your
whole world seems upset. Commend all to God. . . . Whatever happens, abide steadfastly in a determination to
cling simply to God, trusting to His eternal love for you;
and if you find that you have wandered forth from His
shelter, recall your heart quietly and simply.*

St. Francis de Sales

PSALM 23

The Lord my pasture shall prepare,
And feed me with a shepherd's care;
His presence shall my wants supply,
And guard me with a watchful eye;
My noonday walks he shall attend,
And all my midnight hours defend.

When in the sultry glebe I faint,
Or on the thirsty mountain pant,
To fertile vales and dewy meads
My weary, wandering steps he leads,
Where peaceful rivers, soft and slow,
Amid the verdant landscape flow.

Though in the paths of death I tread,
With gloomy horrors overspread,
My steadfast heart shall fear no ill,

* From *Wise and Loving Counsels.*

For thou, O Lord, art with me still:
Thy friendly crook shall give me aid,
And guide me through the dreadful shade.

Though in a bare and rugged way,
Through devious lonely wilds, I stray,
Thy bounty shall my wants beguile;
The barren wilderness shall smile,
With sudden greens and herbage crowned,
And streams shall murmur all around.

—*Joseph Addison (1712)*

SPIRIT VERSUS MACHINERY

The spirit of the living creature was in the wheels.—EZEKIEL 1:21

We build machines to do the work of man;
We organize a framework for each task;
We think that anyone can work a plan
And run machines and never questions ask.
We've standardized and mechanized life's road,
So people have become mere bolts and cogs,
The human elements we see corrode,
The masses rise and shout, "We are not dogs."
We must put living spirit in the wheels,
And humanize the avenues of trade,
So daily tender sympathy man feels,
And longs to give to others loving aid.
God breathed His living spirit into man,
We ought to keep that spirit, and we can.*

—*Henry C. Spear*

NAHUM DOOMS NINEVEH

Of Nineveh, the proud and mighty one,
Jehovah wearied, and her end was told.
Her chariots, her horsemen, captains bold—
Their power was spent; they faced a setting sun.
For, as they raged, Jehovah, jealous God,
Planned direful death for Nineveh the great:
The bloody city, full of lies and hate,
Who on small Judah raised her vengeful rod.
What could avail the haughty men of might
Who slew Jehovah's people in their wrath?
What could avail their strength when in the path
Of conquest stood the God of truth and right?

* From *Sermon Sonnets* by Henry C. Spear, p. 14. Used by special permission of the author.

The kingdom fell—and thus all kingdoms fall
That take up arms against the Lord of All!*
—Thomas Curtis Clark

THE VISION OF NAHUM

Jehovah is mighty, and a jealous God,
And who can stand before him?
The chariots of Nineveh are strong,
Her men run like lightnings;
But Jehovah hath seen her drunkenness
And her violence toward Judah,
And he will make a full end of her,
And she shall perish from the earth.
Thus spake Nahum.
But Jehovah is good,
A stronghold in the day of trouble;
He knoweth them that take refuge
In him.
Israel and Judah, the people of the remnant,
Shall be redeemed from the hand of the spoiler,
The bloody city.
Thus spake Nahum, the prophet of God:
Behold, upon the mountains how beautiful are
The feet of him that bringeth good tidings,
That publisheth peace!**
—Thomas Curtis Clark

FOR TODAY AND TOMORROW

O God, Our Father, hear our cry
In this our hour of mortal need
Thy world is sinking in a slough
Of doubt and fear, of hate and greed.

Self-throned on high, the Powers of Ill
Turn Thy fair world to evil ways;
We claim Thy promises of old—
"Thy help, Lord, in these evil days!"

Thy Power can overcome all ill,
Before Thee all the might of man
Is wind-blown dust, and Thy vast Love
Holds all creation in its span.

* Used by special permission of the author.
** Used by special permission of the author.

The arm is mighty as of old
To smite the evil, to uphold
Thy valiant ones who hold the Faith
That Love shall vanquish sin and death.

Confound all ill, uplift the good,
Let Thy Will be man's only will,
So shall Thy Kingdom come on earth
And man at last Thy hope fulfil.*

—*John Oxenham*

✛

THE MIRACLE OF THE FIERY FURNACE

Arranged by

Cynthia Pearl Maus

THOSE who have heard Charles Laughton of motion-picture fame in his dramatic presentations of "Great Works from Literature" can never forget his dramatic interpretation of the story of Shadrach, Meshach, and Abed-nego, emphasizing, as it does, the power of *rhythm* and *repetition* in effective storytelling. In fact, many of our modern poets and storytellers have borrowed their use of this same device of *rhythm* and *repetition* of certain words and phrases in the writing of poetry and the telling of stories. This device is not new; it is as old as the Book of Daniel from which this Biblical story of the three Hebrew princes is taken.

Italics are used throughout the story which follows to indicate the recurring words and phrases in this rhythmical Bible story (Daniel 3) from ancient Hebrew history.

King Nebuchadnezzar had caused a great image to be made and had covered it with gold. This image had been set up on the plain of Dura, near Babylon, as an idol to be worshiped by all the people. It stood almost a hundred feet high and could be seen all over the plains below. When it was complete the king sent out a command for all the princes and nobles throughout his kingdom to come together for the service of dedication to this golden idol.

From far and near they came and stood at the base of this golden image. Among those who gathered to see this spectacle were three of Daniel's friends, the young Jews, Shadrach, Meshach, and Abed-nego. Daniel himself was not present. Doubtless he was busy with the work of the kingdom in some other place.

At one moment in this dedicatory service before the golden image all the musical instruments sounded, and all the people were supposed to kneel down and worship this great golden image. This is the way the Book of Daniel tells the story of this idol worship:

"Nebuchadnezzar the king made an image of gold, whose height was threescore cubits, and the breadth thereof six cubits: he set it up in the plain of Dura, in the

---

* From *Scrap-Book of J. O.* by Erica Oxenham, pp. 109-10. Copyright, 1946, by Longmans, Green and Company. Used by special permission of Miss Erica Oxenham.

province of Babylon. Then Nebuchadnezzar the king sent to gather together the *princes,* the *governors,* and the *captains,* the *judges,* the *treasurers,* the *counsellors,* the *sheriffs,* and all the *rulers* of the *provinces,* to come to the dedication of the image which Nebuchadnezzar the king had set up. Then the *princes,* the *governors,* and the *captains,* the *judges,* the *treasurers,* the *counsellors,* the *sheriffs,* and all the *rulers* of the *provinces,* were gathered unto the dedication of the image that Nebuchadnezzar the king had set up. . . .

"Then an herald cried aloud, 'To you it is commanded, O people, nations, and languages, that at what time ye hear the sound of the *cornet, flute, harp, sackbut, psaltery, dulcimer,* and all *kinds* of *music,* ye fall down and worship the golden image that Nebuchadnezzar the king hath set up; and whoso falleth not down and worshippeth shall the same hour be cast into the midst of a burning fiery furnace.' Therefore at that time, when all the people heard the sound of the *cornet, flute, harp, sackbut, psaltery,* and all *kinds* of *music,* all the people, the nations, and the languages, fell down and worshipped the golden image that Nebuchadnezzar the king had set up.

"Wherefore at that time certain Chaldeans came near, and accused the Jews. They spake and said to the king Nebuchadnezzar . . . 'Thou, O king, hast made a decree, that every man that shall hear the sound of the *cornet, flute, harp, sackbut, psaltery,* and *dulcimer,* and all *kinds* of *music,* shall fall down and worship the golden image; and whoso falleth not down and worshippeth, that he should be cast into the midst of a burning fiery furnace. There are certain Jews whom thou hast set over the affairs of the province of Babylon, *Shadrach, Meshach,* and *Abed-nego;* these men, O king, have not regarded thee: they serve not thy gods, nor worship the golden image which thou hast set up.'

"Then Nebuchadnezzar in his rage and fury commanded to bring *Shadrach, Meshach,* and *Abed-nego.* Then they brought these men before the king. Nebuchadnezzar spake and said unto them, 'Is it true, O *Shadrach, Meshach,* and *Abed-nego,* do ye not serve my gods, nor worship the golden image which I have set up? Now if ye be ready that at what time ye hear the sound of the *cornet, flute, harp, sackbut, psaltery,* and *dulcimer,* and all *kinds* of *music,* ye fall down and worship the image which I have made; *well:* but if ye worship not, ye shall be cast the same hour into the midst of a burning fiery furnace; and who is that God that shall deliver you out of my hands?' *Shadrach, Meshach,* and *Abed-nego* answered and said to the king, 'O Nebuchadnezzar, we are not careful to answer thee in this matter. If it be so, our God whom we serve is able to deliver us from the burning fiery furnace, and he will deliver us out of thine hand, O king. But if not, be it known unto thee, O king, that we will not serve thy gods, nor worship the golden image which thou hast set up.'

"Then was Nebuchadnezzar full of fury, and the form of his visage was changed against *Shadrach, Meshach,* and *Abed-nego:* therefore he spake, and commanded that they should heat the furnace seven times more than it was wont to be heated. And he commanded the most mighty men that were in his army to bind *Shadrach, Meshach,* and *Abed-nego,* and to cast them into the burning fiery furnace. Then these men were bound in their coats, their hosen, and their hats, and their other garments, and were cast into the midst of the burning fiery furnace. Therefore because the king's commandment was urgent, and the furnace exceeding hot, the flame of the fire slew those men that took up *Shadrach, Meshach,* and *Abed-nego.* And these three men, *Shadrach, Meshach,* and *Abed-nego,* fell down bound into the midst of the burning fiery furnace.

"Then Nebuchadnezzar the king was astonied, and rose up in haste, and spake, and said unto his counsellors, 'Did not we cast three men bound into the midst of the fire?' They answered and said unto the king, 'True, O king.' He answered and said, 'Lo, I see four men loose, walking in the midst of the fire, and they have no hurt; and the form of the fourth is like the Son of God.' Then Nebuchadnezzar came near to the mouth of the burning fiery furnace, and spake, and said, *'Shadrach, Meshach,* and *Abed-nego,* ye servants of the most high God, come forth, and come hither.' Then *Shadrach, Meshach,* and *Abed-nego* came forth of the midst of the fire. And the *princes, governors,* and *captains,* and the *king's counsellors,* being gathered together, saw these men, upon whose bodies the fire had no power, nor was an hair of their head singed, neither were their coats changed, nor the smell of fire had passed on them.

"Then Nebuchadnezzar spake, and said, 'Blessed be the God of *Shadrach, Meshach,* and *Abed-nego,* who hath sent his angel, and delivered his servants that trusted in him, and have changed the king's word, and yielded their bodies, that they might not serve nor worship any god, except their own God. Therefore I make a decree, That every people, nation, and language, which speak any thing amiss against the God of *Shadrach, Meshach,* and *Abed-nego,* shall be cut in pieces, and their houses shall be made a dunghill; because there is no other god that can deliver after this sort.' Then the king promoted *Shadrach, Meshach,* and *Abed-nego,* in the province of Babylon."

✛

DANIEL, A MAN OF COURAGE

By

Grace Ordway Spear

THE fighting was over, the land laid waste at the hands of the enemy, and they were preparing to return to Babylon in triumph. The people who survived the battles were huddled in desolate, pathetic groups, their homes destroyed, their loved ones killed by the sword of the conqueror, and they, themselves, knew not what the future might hold in store for them.

Ashpenaz, master of the eunuchs, recalled the last words of King Nebuchadnezzar as they left Babylon: "Bring back to me as captives, certain of the children of Israel —of noble birth, well-favored in appearance, and skillful in all wisdom and knowledge, and quick to learn; such as have ability to stand in the king's palace, that we may teach them the learning and the tongue of the Chaldeans." So Ashpenaz went about among the people and selected youths such as met the qualifications listed by the king, among them four Hebrew boys—Daniel, Hananiah, Mishael, and Azariah. Separating them from their families, he told them that they were to be taken to Babylon. It was no use to resist—the cruelities of war had taught even the children that they might expect anything. "My son," said the mother of Daniel, the most prepossessing of all the fine-looking lads, "forget not the God of thy fathers, and He will protect thee from harm! Remember the training of thy early days, and do not depart from it!" And hiding her sorrow, she watched her son and his three companions being led away captive, never to be returned to her.

King Nebuchadnezzar was well pleased when he saw the youths, and he ordered their names to be changed: Daniel became Belteshazzar—Hananiah became Shadrach—Mishael, Meshach—and Azariah, Abed-nego. He also commanded that the youths be fed with the same rich food that came to the royal table, that they might continue to improve in appearance and be fit to stand in the king's court at the end of the training period, which was three years. But Daniel, remembering his home training and his mother's last admonition, "purposed in his heart that he would not defile himself with the portion of the king's meat, nor with the wine which he drank." And Daniel spoke to the chief steward and proposed a test, saying, "Prove thy servants, I beseech thee, ten days; and let them give us pulse to eat, and water to drink. Then let our countenance be looked upon before thee; and the countenance of the children that eat of the portion of the king's meat; and as thou seest, deal with thy servants."

The test was tried; and at the end of ten days, the comparison was made; and the countenance of the four Hebrew youths who had been fed on pulse and water—Daniel, Shadrach, Meshach, and Abed-nego—appeared fairer and fatter in flesh than those who had eaten the king's rich food. So they were permitted to continue to eat the vegetables, and to drink water instead of wine. When the three years of training were completed, all the captive youths were brought in before the king, and, among them, he found none so fine as Daniel, Shadrach, Meshach, and Abed-nego—not only in appearance, but in all matters of wisdom and understanding.

In the second year of his reign, Nebuchadnezzar, the king, dreamed a dream which troubled him greatly. Not one of his magicians, or astrologers, or sorcerers, or other wise men were able to tell the king of his dream or to interpret it for him. Daniel, hearing of the king's dream and of his anger at finding none who could interpret it, went in to the king, and said: "Give me time, O King, and I will tell thee thy dream and the interpretation thereof."

Then Daniel and his three friends—Hananiah, Mishael, and Azariah—prayed to God for wisdom and for mercy (for the king had threatened to take the lives of all the wise men of his kingdom); and God answered their prayers and gave Daniel power and wisdom to reveal to the king the meaning of his dreams.

When Daniel came into the presence of the king, Nebuchadnezzar asked, "Belteshazzar, art thou able to make known unto me the dream which I have seen, and the interpretation thereof?"

And Daniel replied, "Not of myself, O King; but there is a God in heaven that revealeth secrets, and maketh known to the King what shall be in the latter days."

Then Daniel told King Nebuchadnezzar what he had seen in his dream and said: "Thou sawest in thy dream, O King, a great image. The form of it was terrible with its head of gold, its breast and arms of silver, and the rest of the body of brass. The legs were iron, and its feet were part iron and part clay. Thou sawest a stone cut out of the mountain, strike the image upon its feet and break them to pieces. The image fell, and the wind blew them away—none could tell where. Afterward, the stone that had broken the image grew to be a great mountain and filled all the earth. This is what thou sawest in thy dream, O King.

"And this is the interpretation of it. The gold, the silver, the brass, the iron, and the clay, all signify different kingdoms. The head of gold was thyself, King Nebuchadnezzar, for God hath given thee the greatest of the kingdoms and made thee greater than all the other kings upon the earth. After thou diest, new kingdoms will rise. At the last, God will set up *one* kingdom more which shall never be destroyed. Instead, it will break into pieces all those kingdoms that were before it, as the stone broke the image in thy dream."

When Daniel finished speaking, the king fell upon his face and worshiped, and said to Daniel: "Of a truth your God is the God of gods, and the Lord of kings, and a revealer of secrets." Then the king made Daniel a great man and gave him many great gifts, and made him ruler over the whole province of Babylon, and the chief of the governors over all the wise men of Babylon. And Daniel sat in the gate of the king.

And King Nebuchadnezzar again dreamed a dream and sent for Daniel to come and interpret it to him. And Daniel said to Nebuchadnezzar: "This is what God hath spoken to thee in thy dream: 'Thou hast grown great and full of power, and thy kingdom reaches to the end of the earth. But thou shalt be driven out to live among the beasts of the field until thou hast learned that God doth rule over all the nations of the earth and maketh whomsoever he will to be king.'" And all of Daniel's words came true.

When Nebuchadnezzar ceased to reign over Babylon, his son came to the throne. And Belshazzar made a great feast to one thousand of his lords and drank wine before them. And in that same hour, the fingers of a man's hand came forth and wrote upon the wall. And when none of the king's wise men could read the writing to the king, Daniel was brought in to Belshazzar. What a fine-looking man he was as he stood in the courtroom—composed and fearless, as Belshazzar, troubled and ill at ease, spoke in a loud nervous voice, saying: "Now, if thou canst read the writing and make known to me the interpretation thereof, thou shall be clothed with scarlet, and have a chain of gold about thy neck, and be the third ruler in the kingdom."

Then Daniel answered: "Let thy gifts, O King, be to thyself, and give thy rewards to another; but I will read the writing unto thee and make known to thee the meaning. *'Mene, Mene, Tekal Upharsin,'*—God hath numbered thy kingdom and finished it. Thou art weighed in the balance and found wanting. Thy kingdom is divided and given to the Medes and Persians." And in that night, Belshazzar, king of the Chaldeans, was slain, and Darius, the Median, took the throne.

King Darius immediately set over the kingdom one hundred and twenty princes who should give account of their acts to three presidents, also appointed by Darius, of whom Daniel was first, and was preferred above all the others. Daniel showed an excellent spirit toward all the people, and King Darius recognized this, as did the presidents and princes. But they could see that Daniel was growing more and more in favor with the king; and they were filled with jealousy of him and planned to entrap him. Knowing the weakness of the king, they assembled before him and cleverly made this proposal: "King Darius, live forever! Would it not be well to establish a royal statute, forbidding anyone to ask a petition of any God or man for thirty days, save of thee, O King? Think of the honor that would be thine!" And King Darius fell into the trap laid for him, and signed his name and placed his seal upon the decree, so that it could not be changed, according to the law of the Medes and Persians which altereth not. If anyone disobeyed this decree of the king, he was to be cast into a den of lions.

When Daniel heard of the law, he seemed undisturbed. It had always been his habit to kneel at his open window every morning, noon, and evening, and pray to his God, and he continued to follow this daily custom as he had done aforetime.

The jealous presidents and princes, watching for Daniel, hastened to report to the king what they had seen. Darius, realizing what he had done, sought now to make an exception of Daniel, but the men were prepared for this. "Know, O King, that, according to the law of the Medes and Persians, no decree or statute which the King establisheth may be changed?" they reminded him, and Darius knew that it was so.

With a heavy heart, the king ordered Daniel to be brought and cast into the den of lions. Before the stone was placed at the mouth of the den, marveling at the quiet fearlessness of Daniel, as he offered no resistance or made no plea, the king said, confidently: "Thy God whom thou servest continually, He will deliver thee, Daniel!"

But the King could not sleep that night for thinking of Daniel; and very early in the morning he went in haste to the den. Hardly daring to hope, he cried out in a trembling voice: "O, Daniel servant of the living God, is thy God whom thou servest continually, able to deliver thee from the lions?" And Darius was overjoyed to hear the clear voice of Daniel, reassuring him, "O, King, live forever! My God hath sent his angels and hath shut the lions' mouths that they have not hurt me," and immediately the king commanded that Daniel be taken up out of the den.

The accusers of Daniel and their families were then cast into the lions' den and were devoured by the hungry beasts. And King Darius established a new decree throughout all his kingdom saying: "I command all people in every dominion of my kingdom to fear the God of Daniel, for He is the living God." And so long as Darius held to this decree his reign was secure and strong, while Daniel continued to prosper in the kingdom.

After the death of Darius, Cyrus became king of Babylon. Daniel had prayed to God that the Jews, who had been captive so long, might return to Jerusalem and rebuild the city. While Daniel was thus praying one evening, the angel Gabriel flew by him and touched him. And the angel said, "O, Daniel, I am come to tell thee of things which shall be. Thou art greatly loved of God, and He hath heard thy prayers for thy people. They shall return to their own land, and they shall rebuild the city of Jerusalem."

And the Jews did return to their own land and built again the altar of the Lord that stood in the court of the Temple, and made ready to rebuild the Temple, also, that they might worship God therein.

And Daniel continued to prosper throughout the reign of Cyrus as he had while Darius was king.*

✢

THE HANDWRITING UPON THE WALL

By

William Stearns Davis

THERE on the wall the letters glowed, right under the torch-holder; glowed like ruddy fire, the whole dread inscription spreading in one long, terrible line under the eyes of king and nobles. While Belshazzar looked, his bronzed cheeks turned ashen. The awful hand had vanished the instant the sentence was written—gone—whither? The lord of the Chaldees gazed upon his servants, and they—back at their master, while none spoke. But the letters did not vanish; their steadfast light burned calmly on. Then came another fearful deed; for Belshazzar caught the golden cup that had fallen from his hand, and dashed it against the wall. A great square of the plaster fell, but lo! the letters were burning still. Then new silence, while every man heard the beating of his heart and thought on his unholy deeds.

But the stillness could not last forever. Belshazzar broke it. The pallor was still on his face, his knees smote together, his voice quivered; but he was kinglier than the rest, even in his fear—he at least was brave enough for speech.

"Ho! captains of Babylon! Why do we gape like purblind sheep? A notable miracle from the gods! Some new favour, no doubt, vouchsafed by Marduk!"

No one answered; all strength had fled from the stoutest sword-hand. Belshazzar's voice rose to a sterner pitch, as he faced the array of priests.

"What mean these letters? They are not the characters of the Chaldee. Their meaning? Here are learned men, wise in every tongue. Translate to us!"

Still no answer; and the king's wrath now mastered all his fears.

"Fools!" his hand was on his sword-hilt; "Marduk has not added to the miracle by smiting all dumb." He confronted the "chief of the omen-revealers," who stood close to the dais.

"Here, Gamilu, this falls within your duties. Look on the writing. Interpret without delay; or, as Marduk is god, another has your office!"

Gamilu, a venerable pontiff, lifted his head, and stared at the inscription. . . . With vain show of confidence he commenced:

"Live forever, lord of the Chaldees! A fortunate sign, on a doubly fortunate day! This is the word which Bel, the sovereign god, has sent to his dearly loved son, the ever victorious king, Belshazzar—"

. . . Here he stopped, bravado failing. Thrice he muttered wildly, then grew still. The king's rage was terrible. "Juggler! you shall learn to mock me. Nabu destroy me too, if you are living at dawn!"

The luckless man fell on his knees, tearing his beard: his one groan was, "Mercy."

* Used by special permission of the author.

Belshazzar heeded little. "You other priests—you the chief 'demon-ejector'—do you speak! The meaning?"

A second wretch cast himself before the king. "Pity, Ocean of Generosity, pity! I do not know."

The king wasted no curse. "You, Kalduin, 'master of the star-gazers,' who boast to be wisest astrologer in Babylon—look on the writing . . ."

But Kalduin also fell on his knees, groaning and moaning. . . .

"Lord! Lord!" he moaned in fear, "I know not, I cannot tell. Mercy! Spare!"

Belshazzar shook his kingly head as might a desert lion, he alone steadfast, while a thousand were trembling.

"And is there no man in all Babylon who can read this writing?" was his thunder.

There was a rustling beside him. From her chair the aged queen-mother, . . . leaned forward. "Your Majesty. . . . There is a man in your kingdom in whom is the spirit of the holy gods."

"What man?" demanded Belshazzar. Every eye was on the queen, who continued:

"The name of the man is Daniel, whom the king called Belteshazzar; now let Daniel be called, and he will show the interpretation."

But the words were like fire thrust into the king's face. He recoiled from her; the ashen gray came back to his cheeks. "Not Daniel! I will never see him! I have sworn it! Not he! Not he!"

. . . But from all the captains rose one clamour:

"Send for Daniel! He is the only hope. He alone can reveal. Send! Send!"

"Never! I will not send," cried Belshazzar. But he saw again that burning line, he grew yet paler.

"Daniel! Daniel! We are lost if the writing is longer hid. Send for the Jew!"

. . . Belshazzar addressed Mermaza. "Eunuch, go to the innermost prison and bring Daniel hither without delay."

Then there was silence once more, while monarch and servants watched those letters burning on the wall. Presently—after how long—there were feet heard in the outer court, the clanking of chains; then right into the glare and glitter came Mermaza, followed by two soldiers; and betwixt these an old man, squalid, unkempt, clothed in rags, the fetters still on wrist and ankle. But at sight of him a hundred knelt to worship.

"Help us, noble Jew! Make known the writing that we may obey heaven, and may not die!" One and all cried it. But Daniel heeded nothing until he stood before the king.

Belshazzar tried vainly to meet the piercing eye of the Jew. His own voice was metallic, while he groped for words.

"Are you that Daniel of the captive Hebrews, whom Nebuchadnezzar brought out of Judea?" Where were the king's wits fled, that he asked this of the man so long known and hated? A stately nod was his reply.

"I have heard that the spirit of the gods is in you, and light and understanding and excellent wisdom. . . . And I have heard that you can make interpretations and dissolve doubts. . . . Now, if you are able to read the writing and make known the interpretation, you shall be clothed in scarlet, and have a chain of gold about your neck, and be the third ruler of the kingdom."

The king stretched forth his hands to the Jew, imploring. The prophecy was fulfilled; Belshazzar the king supplicated Daniel the captive! The old man's form straightened; he swept his gaze around that company, every eye obedient to his. His voice was low, yet in that silence each whisper swelled to loudness.

"Let your gifts be for another, O King; give your rewards to another, but I will read the writing to the king, and make known the interpretation."

Then he told the tale all Babylon knew so well. . . .

"You, O Belshazzar, have not humbled your heart, . . . but have lifted yourself up against the Lord of Heaven; and they have brought the vessels of His house before you, and you, and your lords, and your women have drunk wine in them; and you have praised the gods of silver, of gold, of brass, iron, wood and stone, which see not, nor hear, nor know; and the God in whose hand your breath is, and whose are all your ways, you have not glorified. Then was the hand sent from Him . . . and this is the writing that was written: *'Mene, Mene, Tekel, Upharsin.'* And this is the interpretation: *'Mene'*—God has numbered your kingdom and finished it. *'Tekel'*— you are weighed in the balances and found wanting. *'Upharsin'* which is otherwise *'Peres'*—your kingdom is divided and given to the Medes and the Persians."

Then, as the king looked, lo! another wonder. The fiery words were gone, and only the shattered plaster showed where they had burned.

The King grasped a goblet once more. "By Nabu, the jest is so well played, you still wander for wits. Daniel must have reward. Ho! Mermaza; the robe of honour and the chain of gold. Off with the rags and fetters. Behold in Daniel the third prince of the kingdom. Set a new seat on the dais. A health to his Highness." He drained the cup, then in a darker tone, directly at the Hebrew: "This is the promised reward. But when at midnight I quit the feast, if your prophecy is not fulfilled, you die the perjurer's death, for mocking thus your king."

Daniel answered nothing. The eunuchs pried off his fetters, put on him the robe and the golden chain. They set him a chair beside Belshazzar, offering a jewelled goblet. He took it, tasting only once . . .

The revels were resumed. The torches flared above the king of the Chaldees and all his lords drained their liquor—beaker on beaker—in one mad, vain hope—to drown out their own dark thoughts. The fiery apparition had vanished from the plaster only to glow before the uncertain vision of each and all. Soon rose drunken laughter, more fearful than any scream or moaning.

Atossa sat on her own high seat, watching, waiting, wondering. . . Daniel was sitting by her side. Once she ventured, despite Belshazzar's frown, to speak to him.

"My father, the spirit of the holy Ahura is on you. Tell me, shall we be saved, you, and Ruth and I, from the power of these 'Lovers of Night'?"

Daniel, calm, unblenching, sober, amid a hundred gibbering drunkards, answered with a confidence not of this world: "My child, we shall be saved. Doubt it not; but whether we be saved in this body, or depart to see Jehovah's face, He knoweth, not I. But His will is ever good."

The king interrupted boisterously, with unveiled mockery:

"Give wisdom, noble Daniel. Shall I rebuild the walls of Uruk or spend the money on new canals at Sippar?"

The Hebrew made the king wince once more, as he looked on him.

"Lord of Babylon, think no more on walls and cities. Think on your past deeds. Think of the Just Spirit before whom you must stand."

Deeper the drinking, madder the revelling. From the outer palace rose the laughter of soldiers and the city folk. . . . The king's cheek was flushed, his voice was loud and high. . . . Suddenly Belshazzar's voice shouted:

"Midnight, the feast ends; and you, O Jew, have lost!"

The king was standing. The lamps were smoking; the noise of the feasters failing, as the wine accomplished its work. . . . Belshazzar addressed Mermaza. "Eunuch, deliver Daniel the Jew to Khatin for instant death. His mummery turns to his own ruin. *Now* truly let his weak god save!"

Even as he spoke there was a strange clamour rising in the palace without: a headlong gallop, a shouting, not of mirth but of alarm. Yet none heeded.

"Your Majesty," Daniel answered steadily, "suffer me only this: let me embrace my daughter Ruth."

The king nodded. "Be brief, for you have vexed me long!" Then, turning to Atossa: "Ah, lady, queen—at last! To the harem! you are my wife!"

Atossa knew she was being taken by the hand; she saw all things dimly as through darkened glass. Nearer the gallop without, louder the shouting, and through it and behind a jar and a crashing—not of the elements surely. Daniel had clasped Ruth to his breast. His words were heard only by her and another. The king gestured impatiently. "Enough! Away!" But no more; there was a panic cry at the portal, the howl of fifty voices in dismay; and right into the great hall, over the priceless carpets, through the revelling throng, spurred a rider in armour . . . Up to the very dais he thundered . . . and stood before the king.

"All is lost, lord of the Chaldees!" and then he gasped for breath. But already in the outer palace was a fearful shout. "Arms! Rescue! The Foe!"

Belshazzar tottered as he stood, caught the arm of the throne. His face was not ashen, but black as the clouds on high. "What is this, fool?" he called.

"The Persians carry all before them—hear!" and hear they did. "The foe will come and none to stay!"

"None to stay? Twenty thousand men of war in Babylon and Belshazzar be snared as a bird in his own palace?" The king drew his sword flinging far the scabbard.

"Up, princes of the Chaldees, up!" He trumpeted, above the shrieking all around. "All is not lost! We will still prove the Jew the liar!"

Yet while he cried it a second messenger panted into the great hall.

"The outer defences of the palace are forced, O King! The foe are everywhere!"

Belshazzar leaped down from the dais . . . and sprang forward. "At them, men of Babylon; all is not yet lost!"

Then a new crash that drowned all else, and the whirl of a thousand feet. Men and women, cursing, howling, were rushing back into the hall. In an instant the empty scene became a chaos of forms, all the gibbering palace folk fleeing thither.

"Lost! The gate is carried! The palace is taken!"

But the end had not yet come. Another voice was thundering in the Chaldee, Belshazzar's voice:

"Rally again! All is not lost. We will defend the palace room by room!"

Each time the Persians swept back to the charge, and still the clamour rose. . . .

For a third time the great palace quaked. The door was again darkened by many men—and in their midst they saw the king. . . .

Belshazzar was covered with blood, whether his own or the foeman's, who might say? His mantle was in tatters, the tiara smitten from his head, on his arm a shivered shield. The king staggered, then the sight of Atossa upon the dais seemed to dart new power through his veins. He steadied, swept his weapon around in command of the officers who pressed by.

"Rally again!" cried the king; "we have still thousands around the walls and throughout the city. Prolong the defence till dawn, and we may yet conquer!"

The king surveyed the room one instant.

"We can defend this hall until the garrison may rally. . . . Drive forth this rabble, and barricade the doors!"

Then came a crash of hail and rain, beating down the canopy, quenching half the lights, and adding gloom to terror. . . . Atossa leaped from her seat; despite her brave words to Ruth, more of this chaos would strike her mad. She slipped from the grasp of Khatin, and flew toward the entrance. . . .

"Darius! I come!" cried she in her Persian, and a shout without was answering, when a clutch mighty as Khatin's halted her. She was in Belshazzar's own hands.

"Take her back to the dais," shouted the king to two guardsmen; "watch her preciously; her life is dearer to us now than gold."

This time cords were knotted around her arms and she was held fast. She looked at Daniel. There he sat, serene and silent, the only calm object in that scene of furies.

"Peace, my child," he spoke mildly, yet amid that storm she heard him; "we shall full soon know what is the will of God."

The last Babylonians had been brushed from the portal, a rush of feet, a battle-cry, the loudest of the night; and right in the entrance, sword in hand and looking upon Atossa, was the son of Hystaspes, at his side Isaiah, at his back the stoutest veterans of Cyrus the conqueror.

There was silence for an instant, while the foes glared on one another. Then the Babylonish officers by sheer force drew their king behind them, and formed in close array the before the dais. The last stand!

"Stand fast, Chaldees! . . . let them touch the king only across our bodies. While he lives Babylon is not truly lost."

The Persians were entering slowly, grimly. Their prey was in their clutch; they were too old in war to let him slip by untimely triumph. . . .

Darius had advanced from his company, halfway across the hall, as if he alone would walk upon the swords of the Chaldees. He addressed the king.

"Live forever, Lord of Babylon! Live forever. I have bayed a fairer game, this night, than an aurochs or a lion; but I have brought him to the net at last. . . . Let him be wise; he will find my master merciful." . . . Yield! . . . Do not sacrifice these gallant men—"

But he ended swiftly, for the king had leaped upon the dais, and his voice sounded amid the thunder. "Look! with all your eyes look, Persians! Behold the daughter of Cyrus." Atossa had been upborne upon his strong arms and those of Khatin, and stood upon the royal couch before the gaze of all. And at sight of her a tremor thrilled through the Persians.

"The Princess in Belshazzar's clutch! . . . I say to you, that as the first arrow flies, or sword-stroke falls, the blade enters the breast of the child of Cyrus. Get you gone, and that instantly, if you would not see her die!"

But now Atossa spoke, her voice clear as Belshazzar's:

"And I, daughter of your king, command that you hold back in nothing for my sake. For to an Aryan maid of pure heart death is no great thing, when she knows behind it speeds the vengeance."

Darius had flung away his target; his hands had snatched something—a quiver, a bow. He leaped before them all, while Belshazzar's voice again was rising:

"Back, Persians; or as Bel is god of Babylon, the maid dies, and you are her murderers!" He sprang down beside her, leaving Khatin standing.

But the prince drew the shaft to the head, and sent his eye along the arrow. Did he level at Atossa's own breast? So thought she, with all the others, and her cry rang shrilly:

"Shoot! In Ahura's great name, shoot! Death at your hands is sweet!"

They saw her close her eyes, and strong men turned away their faces. . . . But Belshazzar, looking on his foe, was startled—*he had seen him shoot before.*

"Strike!" he commanded Khatin. "Swiftly!"

They saw the long blade move, and heard the whiz of the arrow. Right through the headsman's wrist sped the shaft, just as the stroke fell. The sword turned in impotent fingers, and fell upon the floor. And still Atossa stood.

"Move not! There alone is safety, where I cover you! And now—on them, men of Iran!"

The Persians had sprung upon their prey and never relaxed their death grip; but the Babylonians ringed around their king a living wall, and fought in silence, for all was near the end. . . .

Then right betwixt raging Persian and raging Chaldee sprang a figure—an old man in hoary majesty, Daniel the Jew.

"Peace!" and for that instant every man hearkened. "Your god is helpless, O Belshazzar, your idol mute. Your power is sped, but bow to the will of the Most High. He will still pity the penitent. Do not cast your life away."

But at this word the king lifted his last javelin.

"Be this my answer to your god."

The missile brushed the white lock on the old man's forehead, and fell harmless.

The Babylonians retreated sullenly to the wall, set their backs against it. Then, with death in the face of each, with the shattered plaster frowning down on them, those men who had fought so long and well to save their king and city, raised the paean of the vanquished, to the god whose power that night had passed.

At the last note the Persians closed around them, and each Chaldee as he stood fought to the end. . . . About the king the strife raged fiercest, for Darius had commanded, "Slay not! Take living!" . . . Twenty hands stretched out to seize him; he buffeted all away, leaped to one side, and before any could hinder, drew the dagger from his girdle and sheathed it in his own breast. He staggered. Isaiah upbore him. The king saw in whose arms he was, then his eyes went up to the shivered plaster. . . . A spasm of agony passed through Belshazzar's frame. . . . He cried, . . . *"Bel is dead! O God of the Jews, Thou hast conquered!"*

Soon the great court was empty, the victors gone, and the vanquished cold and still. But till dawn the tempest held its carnival above the towers of the palace. And the winds had one cry. . . .

"Babylon the Great is fallen, is fallen, is fallen! The Lady of Kingdoms is fallen, is fallen, is fallen. She will oppose the weak no more, will slay the innocent no more, will blaspheme God no more! Fallen is Babylon, the Chaldees' crown and glory."

In a greater book than this is written how Cyrus the Persian made good his vow to Isaiah, and restored the Hebrews to their own land, raising Jerusalem out of her dust and ashes. Elsewhere also is told how Darius and Atossa fared together onward until the son of Hystaspes sat on Cyrus's own throne and gave law to all nations. And to Isaiah Jehovah granted that he should become a mighty prophet among his people, and see rapt visions of the "King-who-was-to-be." But as for Babylon the Great, the traveler who wanders through the desert beside the brimming Euphrates looks upon the mounds of sand and of rubbish, then thinks on the word of the Hebrew poet and prophet of long ago:

> And Babylon, the glory of the kingdom,
> Shall be as when God overthrew Sodom and Gomorrah.
> It shall never be inhabited,
> Neither shall the Arabian pitch tent there;
> Neither shall shepherds make their fold there;
> But wild beasts of the desert shall lie there,
> And owls shall dwell there,
> And satyrs shall dance there,
> And wild beasts of the islands
> Shall cry in their desolate houses;
> Her days shall not be prolonged.*

THE REJECTED QUEEN

By

Florence M. Earlle

BIGTHAN, dancing by on slender, bare, brown feet, stopped before Roxana who was bearing a water jar on her head.

"Have you heard the good news?" she asked. "No, no! of course not," she interrupted herself. "Good Queen Vashti has but now decided. She is to give us a feast.

She says that we were so patient during that long one-hundred-and-eighty-day feast that King Ahasuerus gave, that now when his majesty has decided to give the court servants one, 'tis but fair that we too are feasted. His feast will be held in the garden"—both girls looked toward it—"with its pillars and pavement of red, blue, black and white marble. The hangings will be of blue and green and white, fastened with cords of purple and fine linen to silver rings. The gold and silver couches will be used too, and the drinking vessels will be different for each man. There will be food and royal wine in abundance; such is the king's command," said Bigthan. "I wish I were a man of the king's court."

"I thought you said that Queen Vashti was giving a feast," said Roxana.

"I did. Our feast will be held in the queen's court. It is not so gorgeous as the king's, yet I think it is beautiful too. Her flowers are so lovely, and the queen herself—oh I cannot compare her beauty to anything I have ever seen. I could just sit and gaze upon her, and never grow tired!"

"And still you have told me nothing about the feast?"

"Yes! Yes! It is to last seven days, and we, her maidens, are to be treated as royal guests. Did ever a queen show such favor to her servants before? No wonder the king loves her for her kindness, and her graciousness, and her great beauty. I am sure there never could be one equal to her!"

"Peace," said Roxana, "but we are fortunate to have such a mistress."

They looked up eagerly as Vashti, accompanied only by Hester, her favorite maid, walked slowly across the court to the royal house of the women. She had just come from the king's palace, where she had been admired, and then sent away when the wise men came. There were seven of them; men in whom Ahasuerus placed the utmost confidence. Whatever they suggested, he was likely to follow, and Vashti did not like this.

"He should have more say in his own kingdom," she thought. "He makes no decisions any more, especially since Memucan has been added to the number. I do not like him. He stares at me as if—well—as if I were not the queen. When I gave him a reproving look, he dropped his eyes, but an evil smile played around his mouth. He would not hesitate to do me harm in the king's eyes if he could. I am sure of it."

The seven days of feasting were drawing to a close. Joyous, happy days they had been in the queen's house; days of drunken revel in the king's court. It was nearing midnight of the seventh day, when royal messengers knocked at the door of the queen's palace.

"Open, in the king's name! A message for the queen! The king requires that you come with me to court."

"To the court? *Now?* Why?" asked the bewildered queen.

"He wishes to show your beauty to his guests. He commands that you dress in your royal robes, wear your crown, and come unveiled."

"But only dancing girls come to a feast. He would kill me if I came even as a dancing girl. And unveiled! the king is mad!"

Compassion showed in the face of the messenger, yet he knew that he had been given a royal command, and that disobedience on his part would mean death.

"His heart is merry with wine," he muttered; "yet you must come! A wife must obey her husband."

For a moment the bewildered queen hesitated; then she straightened herself and said, "I shall not come. The king himself will be the first to blame me if I do. He knows not what he does now; tomorrow, he will not believe that he asked such a thing."

"I dare not return without you," said the boy.

"You must!" said Vashti firmly. "I shall never obey such a command. Tomorrow, all will be well."

There was consternation in the court when the messenger returned without the queen, and rage in the heart of the king. He called his seven wise men to him.

"What shall we do to Queen Vashti according to the law, because she has not obeyed the king?" he cried.

Again an evil smile played around the mouth of Memucan. Before another could speak to sooth the king's anger, he said, "Queen Vashti hath done wrong not only to the king, but to all the princes and to all the peoples that are in all the king's provinces. This behavior of the queen will be reported to all women, making their husbands contemptible in their sight, when it shall be said, 'King Ahasuerus demanded that Queen Vashti be brought before him, but she did not come.' Even this day the princesses of Persia and Media who have heard of the queen's behavior will relate it to all the king's princes, and there will be contempt and rage. And so if it please the king, let it go forth, and let it be written in the law of the Medes and Persians that altereth not, that Vashti the queen come no more before King Ahasuerus, and that the king give her royal position to another who is better than she. And when the king's decree is published throughout the kingdom, all women will give honor to their husbands, both of high and low degree."

And the saying of Memucan pleased the king, and no one in the royal court dared make a plea for Queen Vashti.

Scribes were called, and the decrees written and sent by swift messengers to all of the one hundred and twenty provinces, and the king's anger was appeased.

Then he remembered Vashti, and what had been decreed against her, and he longed to look upon her again. Yet the law was of the Medes and Persians. What he had written he had written. She could come no more to his court. Royalty was hers no longer, but beauty was yet hers. He might go to her, and tell her farewell. Alone, he made his way to the house of the women, and Vashti was brought before him. Never had she seemed so desirable. Her sadness and her beauty tore his heart-strings.

"Vashti," he whispered, "thou art ever my queen!"

"Nay," she answered, smiling pityingly. "Queen no more—but thou art my king! and I, one of your subjects! But never again art thou my lord!"

With bowed head and stumbling steps, Ahasuerus returned to his palace. Vashti's pity had humbled his heart. The very throne was a mockery, since her place beside him would be forever empty.

Far away in a remote part of the kingdom, he built for Vashti a beautiful palace, and giving her choice of maidservants and eunuchs, he sent her away, there to live out her days.*

+

DOWN BY THE RIVERSIDE

(Interpretation)

WHEN the African Negro was brought to the United States, he carried no material possessions. He did, however, bring remembered stories, native songs, and dances. These have remained, in somewhat modified form, a true part of American Negro culture.

The songs which the American Negro sang in this new home of his enforced adoption were not the same as those he had sung in his original home in Africa. The rhythm, the melodies, the harmonic variations, it is true, were African; but the words, the sentiments, the spiritual tone were truly American—the result of the new experiences, trials, and tribulations he underwent in his new home.

After the abolishment of slavery in the United States many Negroes wanted to forget the spirituals because the conditions that produced them no longer existed. There were other Negro scholars and musicians, however, who appreciated their artistic beauty and value and aided in their preservation. One of the pioneers in the conservation of this primitive culture was Henry T. Burleigh. He was one of the first to introduce spirituals on the concert stage. As an "arranger, composer, and baritone soloist, he played the role of a path-breaking ambassador of Negro music to the musically elect." Mr. Burleigh "entered the New England Conservatory of Music while Antonin Dvořak was on the staff, and it was his singing of spirituals that attracted Dvořak to the beauty of Negro music and inspired him to use it as thematic material for his 'New World Symphony.' In 1894, Burleigh became soloist in the choir of St. George's Episcopal Church, New York, a post which he held for more than thirty years. Mr. Burleigh has published about a hundred arrangements of spirituals, among them 'Twelve Negro Spirituals' for solo voice."**

This spiritual, "Down by the Riverside," is an excellent illustration of the type of spiritual that begins with a solo, followed by a chorus response by a harmonizing group. Its inspiration undoubtedly was found in the Old Testament story of the children of Israel in bondage in Babylon, when they hung their harps on the willows and refused to sing, saying:

> How shall we sing the Lord's song
> In a strange land?
> If I forget thee, O Jerusalem,
> Let my right hand forget her cunning.
> If I do not remember thee,
> Let my tongue cleave to the roof
> of my mouth;

* Used by special permission of the author.
** From *The Negro's Contribution to Music in America* by Rose K. Nelson and Dorothy L. Cole, p. 12. Rev. ed., 1941. Used by special permission of the Service Bureau for Intercultural Education.

If I prefer not Jerusalem
Above my chief joy.
[Ps. 137:4-6]

These American Negroes were also pilgrims in a strange land, inhabitants of a new and different country and in bondage to a people whose language and customs were strangely different from that of the country from which they had come. Being in servitude there were many times when they could and did sing with fervor and conviction:

Goin't' lay down my burden,
Down by the river-side,
Down by the river-side,
Down by the river-side.
Goin't' lay down my burden,
Down by the river-side,
Goin' to study war no more.

There they were going to meet their mother and father, as well as the Hebrew children, and ultimately also Jesus, their friend and Saviour. With the prophet, Isaiah, they believed that the day would come when nations would "beat their swords into plowshares, and their spears into pruninghooks: nation shall not lift up sword against nation, neither shall they learn war any more" (Isa. 2:4). Therefore, they, the Negroes, were "Goin't' study war no more."

✛

HANDWRITING ON THE WALL

(Interpretation)

"THE main characteristic of the Negro spiritual is an insistent and lively rhythm. Once started, it is carried along by the momentum of its beat. This living, throbbing beat was the outlet for every emotion the Negro slave felt and expressed. In the spirituals, his confused reaction to a complex and alien religion was borne on the stream of this throbbing mingling of rhythm and melody. Work songs and prison songs, songs of joy and gaiety, songs of sadness and sorrow, as well as the religious songs, were all characterized by the same pulsing, rhythmic beat, and all expressed the emotions of the singer. The effect on the listener of the insistent, pulsing rhythm shows that it corresponds to a universal emotion which survives among the most primitive people. In the Negroes themselves, before they had acquired the restraints of respectability, it produced a sort of rhapsodic elation the lingering effects of which can still be observed in revivals and camp meetings. There is an irresistible inclination to bodily time-marking, a lifting of the shoulders, a swaying of the head, a tapping of the feet, and a clapping of the hands. There is a longing to let this extraordinary rhythm take possession of one's body and work its will—like the devils that were believed to enter the bodies of sinners in Puritan times. The human reaction to this rhythm is as compelling as a natural force, and

Down By the River-Side.

1. Goin't' lay down my bur-den, Down by the river-side, Down by the river-side,
2. Goin't' lay down my sword and shield, Down by the river-side, Down by the river-side,
3. Goin't' try on my long white robe, Down by the river-side, Down by the river-side,
4. Goin't' try on my star-ry crown, Down by the river-side, Down by the river-side,

Down by the riv-er-side, Goin't' lay down my bur-den, Down by the riv-er-side,
Down by the riv-er-side, Goin't' lay down my sword and shield, Down by the riv-er-side,
Down by the riv-er-side, Goin't' try on my long white robe, Down by the riv-er-side,
Down by the riv-er-side, Goin't' try on my star-ry crown, Down by the riv-er-side,

Goin' to stud-y war no more. Ain't goin't' stud-y war no more, Ain't goin't'

stud-y war no more, Ain't goin't' study war no more, ... Ain't goin't' war no more.
goin't' study war no more,

5. Goin't' meet my dear old mother.   7. Goin't' meet dem Hebrew children.
6. Goin't' meet my dear old father.   8. Goin't' meet my loving Jesus.

* From *Southland Spirituals,* No. 6. Copyright, 1936, by Homer Rodeheaver, Hall-Mack Company. Used by special permission of the publisher.

Handwriting on the Wall

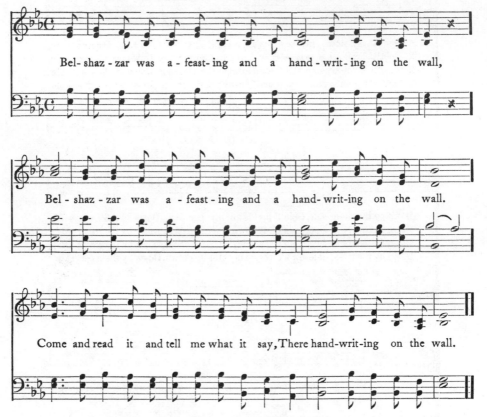

Bel- shaz - zar was a - feast-ing and a hand - writ-ing on the wall,

Bel - shaz - zar was a - feast-ing and a hand- writ-ing on the wall.

Come and read it and tell me what it say, There hand-writ-ing on the wall.

In trouble there handwriting on the wall,
In trouble there handwriting on the wall.

CHORUS
Come and read it and tell me what it say,
There handwriting on the wall.

Bring the Wise men — handwriting on the wall,
Bring the Wise men — handwriting on the wall.   CHORUS

They could read it — handwriting on the wall,
They could read it — handwriting on the wall.   CHORUS

Call Daniel — there handwriting on the wall,
Call Daniel — there handwriting on the wall.   CHORUS

* From *Old Songs Hymnal* collected by Dorothy G. Bolton and arranged by Harry T. Burleigh, No. 11. Copyright, 1945, by Fleming H. Revell Company. Used by special permission of the publisher.

Handwriting on the Wall

Daniel read it there — handwriting on the wall,
Daniel read it there — handwriting on the wall. CHORUS

Mene, Mene, there handwriting on the wall,
Your Kingdome is finished — there handwriting on the wall. CHORUS

Tekle, Tekle, there handwriting on the wall,
Weighed in the balance — there handwriting on the wall. CHORUS

Daniel read it and told me what it said,
There handwriting on the wall. CHORUS

the Negro did not resist the temptation to give in to this overwhelming rhythmic urge; he allowed it to take complete possession of him."*

It is not surprising that the dramatic story of the feast of Belshazzar from the fifth chapter of Daniel should provide a great challenge to the Negro's imagination and volatile emotions. Daniel's interpretation of the mysterious handwriting on the wall at Belshazzar's feast, where more than a thousand lords drank wine from goblets of gold in the presence of a multitude of people, naturally made a deep impression on the Negro's mind and heart. Therefore, he sang of it in the spiritual, "Handwriting on the Wall." Its several stanzas are most effective when sung as a solo followed by a harmonizing choral group singing the chorus.

This terrible inscription written on the wall with only a hand visible told its own dramatic story: and Daniel, alone, of all the wise men present was able to read and interpret its meaning. Briefly expressed this is the meaning of "MENE, MENE, TEKEL, UPHARSIN" which Daniel interpreted as follows (vv. 25-28):

MENE—"God hath numbered thy kingdom, and finished it."

TEKEL—"Thou art weighed in the balances, and art found wanting."

UPHARSIN—"Thy kingdom is divided, and given to the Medes and Persians."

✢

O MOTHER DEAR, JERUSALEM

(Interpretation)

THIS sixteenth-century hymn was arranged by David Dickson (1583-1663). The poet's picture of the New Jerusalem is portrayed in the closing book of the New Testament, the Revelation:

And I John saw the holy city, new Jerusalem, coming down from God out of heaven, prepared as a bride adorned for her husband. And I heard a great voice out of heaven saying, Behold, the tabernacle of God is with men, and he will dwell with them, and they shall be his people, and God himself shall be with them, and be their God.

* From *The Negro's Contribution to Music in America* by Rose K. Nelson and Dorothy L. Cole, p. 18. Rev. ed., 1941. Used by special permission of the Service Bureau for Intercultural Education.

And he showed me that great city, the holy Jerusalem, descending out of heaven from God, having the glory of God: and her light was like unto a stone most precious, even like a jasper stone, clear as crystal.

And I saw no temple therein: for the Lord God Almighty and the Lamb are the temple of it. And the city had no need of the sun, neither of the moon, to shine in it: for the glory of God did lighten it, and the Lamb is the light thereof.

And the nations of them which are saved shall walk in the light of it: and the kings of the earth do bring their glory and honour into it.

Revelation 21:2-3, 10-11, 22-24

In this new Jerusalem which John describes in the above verses, the saints of all times shall find a permanent harbor, where no sorrow, grief, or toil shall mar man's perfect happiness.

The third stanza speaks of the eternally green gardens of the new Jerusalem where pleasant flowers bloom continually and where living waters forever flow.

The fourth stanza sings of fellowship with God's angels in this new Jerusalem, the "happy home" where sorrows are at an end, and joys eternal abound.

The melody to which this sixteenth-century hymn is sung is entitled "Materna." It was composed in 1882 by Samuel A. Ward.

✝

WHEN WILT THOU SAVE THE PEOPLE?

(Interpretation)

EBENEZER ELLIOTT (1781-1849), the composer of this hymn, was an English Unitarian. He was an iron merchant at Sheffield. He had attended the Unitarian Sunday School, and had become an ardent agitator in one of the most important struggles that the English people ever engaged in against their government.

These reformers organized petitions, held many conferences, and founded societies to work for certain reforms in their government which they felt were right and needed. In 1840 these reform agitations reached the peak of their intensity, and Ebenezer Elliott was directly in the center of the fight. He wrote poetry that was so apt in its implications that when it appeared in local newspapers, it won for him the title of "The Corn Law Rhymer."

Among the many poems he wrote one survives. It was written in 1832 and is entitled "When Wilt Thou Save the People?" It was first published as a hymn in 1850.

The first stanza is a questioning appeal to the great God of Mercy to "save the people." The prayer is not for "kings and lords," but for nations; not for "thrones and crowns," but for men. They are the "flowers of thy heart, O God." The author prays, "Let them not pass, like weeds, away."

The second stanza inquires, "Shall crime bring crime forever?" Shall men always "toil for wrong?" The poet answers his own inquiry with the staunch faith that both the mountains and the sky say "No!" In some not too distant day the sun shall shine brightly, and God will "save the people!"

The third stanza expresses the conviction that all men are God's children, and

O Mother Dear, Jerusalem

MATERNA. C. M. D.

F. B. P., c. 16th Cent.
Alt. by David Dickson, 1583-1663

Samuel A. Ward, 1882

1. O moth-er dear, Je-ru-sa-lem, When shall I come to thee?
2. No murk-y cloud o'er-shad-ows thee, Nor gloom, nor dark-some night,
3. Thy gar-dens and thy good-ly walks Con-tin-ual-ly are green,
4. There trees for-ev-er-more bear fruit, And ev-er-more do spring;

When shall my sor-rows have an end, Thy joys when shall I see?
But ev-'ry soul shines as the sun, For God him-self gives light.
Where grow such sweet and pleas-ant flow'rs As no-where else are seen.
There ev-er-more the an-gels are, And ev-er-more do sing.

O hap-py har-bor of the saints! O sweet and pleas-ant soil!
There lust and lu-cre can-not dwell, There en-vy bears no sway;
Right thro' the streets, with sil-ver sound The liv-ing wa-ters flow;
Je-ru-sa-lem, my hap-py home, Would God I were in thee!

In thee no sor-row may be found, No grief, no care, no toil.
There is no hun-ger, heat, nor cold, But pleas-ure ev-'ry way.
And on the banks, on ei-ther side, The trees of life do grow.
Would God my woes were at an end, Thy joys that I might see! A-men.

When Wilt Thou Save the People

COMMONWEALTH. P.M.

EBENEZER ELLIOTT, 1850

JOSIAH BOOTH, 1888

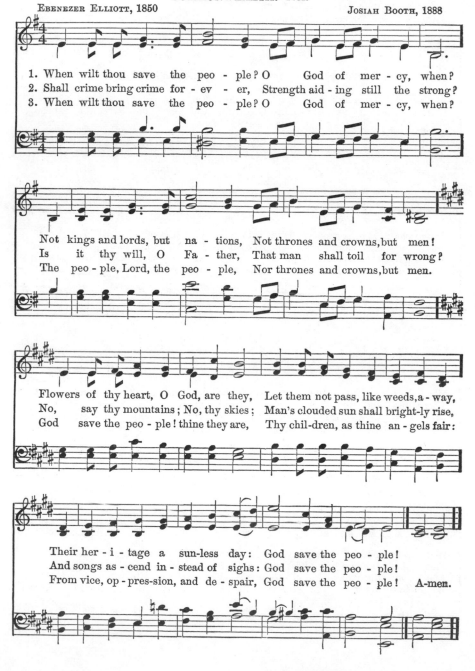

1. When wilt thou save the peo - ple? O God of mer - cy, when?
2. Shall crime bring crime for - ev - er, Strength aid - ing still the strong?
3. When wilt thou save the peo - ple? O God of mer - cy, when?

Not kings and lords, but na - tions, Not thrones and crowns, but men!
Is it thy will, O Fa - ther, That man shall toil for wrong?
The peo - ple, Lord, the peo - ple, Nor thrones and crowns, but men.

Flowers of thy heart, O God, are they, Let them not pass, like weeds, a - way,
No, say thy mountains; No, thy skies; Man's clouded sun shall bright-ly rise,
God save the peo - ple! thine they are, Thy chil-dren, as thine an - gels fair:

Their her - i - tage a sun-less day: God save the peo - ple!
And songs as - cend in - stead of sighs: God save the peo - ple!
From vice, op - pres-sion, and de - spair, God save the peo - ple! A-men.

are valuable in His sight as angels. Therefore, the poet again raises the question, "When wilt thou save the people?" and answers his own inquiry with the firm reply that God will "save the people . . . from vice, oppression, and despair" because they are His.

The theme of this hymn is an outcry against wrongs and injustices against people. Its refrain, "God save the people," is all the more significant because those who sing it are reminded of "God save the king" of the English national anthem. This hymn, however, has more than a national application, for it is concerned with the welfare of people everywhere and expresses the aspirations of the many who work for social justice in the twentieth century.

The melody to which this hymn is sung is entitled "Commonwealth." It was composed in 1888 by Josiah Booth.

CONTENTS

PART VI SECTION 4

LATER LEADERS OF JUDAISM

✛

Blow ye the trumpet in Zion, and sound an alarm in my holy mountain; let all the inhabitants of the land tremble; for the day of the Lord cometh, for it is nigh at hand.—JOEL 2:1

✛

EZRA, THE SCRIBE

By

Saul Raskin

(Interpretation)

AMONG the Hebrew colony living in Babylonia during the reign of Artaxerxes, king of Persia, was the remarkable priest Ezra. His name means "help." Not only was he a priest descended from Aaron, but "he was a ready scribe in the law of Moses" (Ezra 7:6). He was a student of the Scriptures and, in the laborious manner of his day, made copies of the Scriptures on scrolls. But Ezra was more than a Biblical scholar. He also interpreted the Scriptures to his fellow Hebrews living in Babylonia and taught them the Law of Moses. He thus became a leader in the Hebrew colony in Babylon. His whole life was directed to a single goal, "for Ezra had prepared his heart to seek the law of the Lord, and to do it, and to teach in Israel statutes and judgments" (7:10). He was thus a scholar, a good man of action, and a teacher.

To help him carry out his immense task Ezra founded a special group of men called scribes who, like himself, devoted themselves to studying the Law of Moses and teaching it to the people. Many scholars believe that the synagogue or "place of assembly" originated in Babylonia as the place where Ezra and the scribes met with small groups of people to read to them and instruct them in the Law of Moses. When many of these people returned to Jerusalem with Ezra, they established synagogues there as well.

The Book of Ezra is in reality a continuation of the Chronicles. The last sentence of the thirty-sixth chapter of II Chronicles breaks off with a sentence in which Cyrus decrees the rebuilding of the Temple in Jerusalem, which decree is completed in the opening chapter of the Book of Ezra. It tells of the restoration of Jerusalem and of the rebuilding of the Temple; then it describes the work of Ezra, the scribe.

The book contains only ten brief chapters dealing with the decree to rebuild the Temple; a list of those who returned from Babylon; the hindrances put in their way by their adversaries; a letter to Artaxerxes and his reply; the completion of the rebuilding of the Temple; the proclamation of a fast; gifts received by the Temple; Ezra's prayer concerning mixed marriages; and it closes with a listing of the names of those who had foreign wives.

It is the prophet-scribe, Ezra, that Saul Raskin has portrayed in his etching of Ezra. He is seated on a low bench and wears his prophetic robes. One hand holds open the scroll which is on his lap, while the other upraised holds the quill pen with which he has been writing down his message. This picture shows Ezra as a learned scholar and teacher of the Law. He is a man of deep thought, troubled by the present state of religion among his people, and strong and courageous enough to do something about it.

EZRA, THE SCRIBE—*RASKIN*

NEHEMIAH MAKES HIS PETITION TO ARTAXERXES

By

William Hole

(Interpretation)

NEHEMIAH was one of the Jews who lived in Susa (Shushan), the winter capital of the Persian kings at the head of the Persian Gulf. He attained the influential position of royal cupbearer which brought him often into the presence of King Artaxerxes Longimanus. Our information about Nehemiah comes from the Book of Nehemiah which contains his own memoirs.

Word had reached Nehemiah in Persia of the unhappy condition of the exiles who had returned to Jerusalem. The city was still without defensive walls and gates which could be closed at night. Lacking this protection the inhabitants were exposed to attack and had become hopeless and dispirited. Grieved by the sad state of his ancestral city, Nehemiah made a personal appeal to the Persian king. He wrote in his memoirs in the second chapter of Nehemiah:

"And it came to pass in the month Nisan, in the twentieth year of Artaxerxes the king, that wine was before him; and I took up the wine, and gave it unto the king. Now I had not been beforetime sad in his presence. Wherefore the king said unto me, 'Why is thy countenance sad, seeing thou art not sick? This is nothing else but sorrow of heart.'

"Then I was very sore afraid, and said unto the king, 'Let the king live for ever. Why should not my countenance be sad, when the city, the place of my fathers' sepulchres, lieth waste, and the gates thereof are consumed with fire?'

"Then the king said unto me, 'For what dost thou make request?'

"So I prayed to the God of heaven. And I said unto the king, 'If it please the king, and if thy servant have found favour in thy sight, that thou wouldest send me unto Judah, unto the city of my fathers' sepulchres, that I may rebuild it.'

"And the king said unto me (the queen also sitting by him), 'For how long shall thy journey be? and when wilt thou return?'

"So it pleased the king to send me; and I set him a time. Moreover I said unto the king, 'If it please the king, let letters be given me to the governors beyond the river, that they may convey me over till I come into Judah.'

"And the king granted me, according to the good hand of my God upon me."

This is the incident depicted in William Hole's painting, "Nehemiah Makes His Petition to Artaxerxes." The scene is in a room of the royal palace overlooking a large pool and a garden. Palm trees and flowering vines frame the background. The king is surrounded by all the comforts and luxuries of an emperor of the ancient east. A boy stands ready to keep insects away. A woman sits near by on a cushion. She is about to sing and accompany herself on her musical instrument. The queen leans back in her chair idly making a gesture toward a pigeon that has just alighted on the pavement. At first glance the entire scene appears to be one of leisure, tranquility, and luxury. But the king has paused, with his golden wine cup part way to his lip, and he listens intently to the request of his cupbearer, Nehemiah, bending respectfully before him. The moment is fraught with importance, not only for Nehemiah, but for the Jews and for their Holy City, Jerusalem.

Sir George Adam Smith, the Scottish divine who wrote the introduction for William Hole's *Old Testament History, Retold and Illustrated* for which this picture was painted, commented on the artist's "historic eye," the originality of his conceptions, and the skill with which the individuality of his figures is depicted. All this is well shown in this painting.

✛

REBUILDING THE WALLS OF JERUSALEM

By

William Hole

(Interpretation)

NEHEMIAH, like Ezra the scribe, was one of the outstanding restorers of Judaism after the Babylonian exile. In the royal palace in Susa Nehemiah served as cupbearer to the Persian king, Artaxerxes Longimanus. Learning of the wretched condition of Jerusalem, Nehemiah made a personal appeal to Artaxerxes to be allowed to go to his ancestral city and rebuild its ruined walls. Artaxerxes granted Nehemiah's request, appointed him governor of Judea, gave him letters of safe conduct, and ordered that the materials necessary for rebuilding the city walls be made available to him.

On his arrival in Jerusalem Nehemiah went out at night to make a secret survey of the ruined walls. Then he called the citizens of Jerusalem together and said to them: "Ye see the distress that we are in, how Jerusalem lieth waste, and the gates thereof are burned with fire. Come, and let us build up the wall of Jerusalem, that we be no more a reproach" (Neh. 2:17).

Stirred by his appeal and heartened by God's evident favor toward Nehemiah and the Persian king's offer of material help, the people enthusiastically shouted, "Let us rise up and build" (2:18).

"So," wrote Nehemiah in his memoirs, "built we the wall; and all the wall was joined together unto the half thereof, for the people had a mind to work" (4:6).

When the work of rebuilding the wall was going well, trouble threatened from Jerusalem's neighbors. Sanballat, the governor of Samaria, Tobiah, the governor of the Ammonites, and others, when they "heard that the walls of Jerusalem were made up, and that the breaches began to be stopped, then they were very wroth, and conspired all of them together to come and to fight against Jerusalem, and to hinder it. Nevertheless," commented Nehemiah, "we made our prayer unto our God, and set a watch against them day and night. . . .

"And it came to pass, when our enemies heard that it [their conspiracy] was known unto us, and God had brought their counsel to nought, that we returned all

NEHEMIAH MAKES HIS PETITION TO ARTAXERXES—*HOLE*

of us to the wall, every one unto his work. And it came to pass from that time forth, that the half of my servants wrought in the work, and the other half of them held both the spears, the shields, and the bows, and the habergeons; and the rulers were behind all the house of Judah" (4:7-9, 15, 16).

These defensive measures proved effective against Sanballat, Tobiah, and the other conspirators. Thus with Nehemiah's inspiring leadership and the people's enthusiastic work the walls of Jerusalem were rebuilt.

This painting, "Rebuilding the Walls of Jerusalem," by William Hole is a realistic portrayal of the story. William Hole went to Palestine in 1901 and again in 1912 to make studies of the landscapes, costumes, habits, and customs for his Old Testament and New Testament pictures. This picture is a skillful recreation of the building of one portion of a wall still standing in Jerusalem. The Biblical expert, Sir George Adam Smith, whose books on Jerusalem and the Holy Land are famous, comments on the true rendering of details in this painting and its "lifelike and convincing scene."

Framed under the beam of a great derrick used to lift stones into place the unfinished wall stretches away into the distance until it is interrupted by a watchtower. On the right a lifelike street of the city runs downhill. Laborers in the foreground work on the stone blocks. Mortar is being mixed in the same manner as it is done today. Nehemiah is pictured standing on the wall and pointing to some part of the work while two men near him bend over the plans. Armed with a spear a guard is posted on the wall watching for enemies who may be approaching. So must this scene have appeared had we stood in this spot in 445 B.C.

✛

JOEL

By

Michelangelo Buonarroti

(Interpretation)

JOEL is believed to have lived some time between 500 and 350 B.C. He is the last of the Hebrew prophets whose name is attached to his writings. He lived at a time when elders and priests exercised power in Jerusalem, for the monarchy had long since been abolished. In his prophecies he mentions the rebuilt Temple standing in Jerusalem and the walls which Nehemiah built.

The three brief chapters of the Book of Joel fall into two parts. In part one there is to be a "day of the Lord"—a day of His power and judgment—for Judah and Jerusalem, symbolized by a plague of locusts whose devastation is vividly described. To meet this calamity, Joe calls for repentance with prayer and fasting:

> Blow ye the trumpet in Zion,
> And sound an alarm in my holy mountain.
> Let all the inhabitants of the land tremble,
> For the day of the Lord cometh,

REBUILDING THE WALLS OF JERUSALEM—*HOLE*

For it is nigh at hand. . . .
Therefore also now, saith the Lord,
"Turn ye even to me with all your heart,
And with fasting, and with weeping, and with mourning.
Rend your heart, and not your garments."
And turn unto the Lord your God,
For he is gracious and merciful,
Slow to anger and of great kindness.   [2:1, 12, 13]

Part two (chapters 2:18 to 3:21) contains the Lord's promise of relief from famine, and of an abundance of rain and rich harvests to make up for the spoiling of the locusts (2:18-27). He is to send a new spirit upon all the people, so that, when the days of fiery trial shall come, they shall remember to call upon Him and be saved (2:28-32). The nations are to be summoned to judgment (3:1-14). In the terror of that day Jerusalem is to find refuge in its Lord, while persecuting nations shall be desolate (3:15-21).

It was a prophecy of Joel's that Peter believed was fulfilled on the day of Pentecost. Joel's words explained the wonderful things that had befallen the little company of Christ's followers. "For this," explained Peter, "is that which was spoken by the prophet, Joel:

"And it shall come to pass in the last days," saith God,
"I will pour out of my Spirit upon all flesh;
And your sons and your daughters shall prophesy,
And your young men shall see visions,
And your old men shall dream dreams;
And on my servants and on my handmaidens
I will pour out in those days of my Spirit,
And they shall prophesy.
And I will show wonders in heaven above . . .
And it shall come to pass that whosoever shall
  call on the name of the Lord shall be saved."   [Acts 2:16-19, 21]

The artist Michelangelo, in his painting entitled, "Joel," portrays a scholar seated in one of the chairs in the Temple, with a reading desk at his side. In his hands he holds a scroll with the words of the Lord. Behind him stand two youths, one of whom bears, under his arm, the book of the Law. His other hand is outstretched as if to attract the attention of the other youth without disturbing the prophet's reading and meditation. The powerful figure of the prophet, with his partly turned head, his raised arms, and firmly planted foot conveys the impression of deep thought. As we look at this prophet we feel that this is more than the representation of a particular man, Joel. In him we see all men who seek to understand the ways of God and who know that for His will to be accomplished among men God's Spirit must take possession of them.

JOEL—*MICHELANGELO*

JONAH PREACHING AT NINEVEH

Artist Unknown

(Interpretation)

IN the Book of Jonah is the story of a prophet named Jonah. He appears with a unique mission; that is, the task of preaching repentance to the great and wicked city of Nineveh. The author of this story wrote it to rebuke the exclusive spirit of Israel who believed that the Lord loved only Israel, not other nations. The lesson is the more effective because the nation the Lord showed He loved in this story was Assyria, the most dangerous foe of ancient Judah.

This Old Testament volume contains only four brief chapters. Chapter one deals with the Lord's command to Jonah to go to the city of Nineveh, the capital of Assyria. Jonah disobeyed and was punished by being swallowed by a great fish. Chapter two contains Jonah's prayer from the fish's belly and the Lord's answer to his prayer. Chapter three deals with the Lord's command to Jonah, for a second time, to go to Nineveh and preach repentance to that city. This time Jonah went to the great city, a three-day journey from his home. There he preached earnestly and with telling effect that Nineveh would be overthrown forty days hence, unless the people repented of their wickedness and sin against the Lord.

"So the people of Nineveh believed God, and proclaimed a fast, and put on sackcloth, from the greatest of them even to the least of them. For word came unto the king of Nineveh, and he arose from his throne, and he laid his robe from him, and covered him with sackcloth, and sat in ashes. And he caused it to be proclaimed and published through Nineveh by the decree of the king and his nobles, saying, 'Let neither man nor beast, herd nor flock, taste any thing: let them not feed, nor drink water. But let man and beast be covered with sackcloth, and cry mightily unto God: yea, let them turn every one from his evil way, and from the violence that is in their hands. Who can tell if God will turn and repent, and turn away from his fierce anger, that we perish not?' And God saw their works, that they turned from their evil way; and God repented of the evil, that he had said that he would do unto them; and he did it not" (Jonah 3:5-10).

This picture of "Jonah Preaching at Nineveh" by an unknown artist is striking indeed. In the background a large building of that magnificent Assyrian city may be seen. Immediately behind Jonah is a carved relief of a winged bull with a human head. This was a symbol of the Assyrian empire. In front of the prophet, men and women appear expressing interest and penitence—some kneeling, some raising their hands in acclamation, some looking with mild interest and curiosity, some prostrating themselves before the prophet in abject humiliation and repentance.

Jonah himself is shown as a heroic figure standing with upraised hand as he delivers the Lord's challenging and condemnatory message to this wicked and disobedient city.

The picture that follows, "Jonah Sheltered by the Vine," should be studied in connection with this one in order to appreciate and understand the purpose of the

JONAH PREACHING AT NINEVEH—*ARTIST UNKNOWN*

Book of Jonah in the literature of the Old Testament, for the significance of this story is found in the fourth and last chapter of this brief story of a prophet.

✛

JONAH SHELTERED BY THE VINE

(Woodcut)

Artist Unknown

(Interpretation)

THE Book of Jonah is not prophecy in the ordinary sense. Its place among the prophets is justified because it is a story with a message. Jonah is grouped with the minor prophets, who are "minor" because their collected prophecies are shorter than Isaiah, Jeremiah, Ezekiel, and Daniel.

The fourth and last chapter of the Book of Jonah records the incident on which the woodcut, "Jonah Sheltered by the Vine," is based. The prophet's disappointment when the wicked city of Nineveh repented in sackcloth and ashes was overpowering. He was more than regretful; he was actually angry because the Lord had refused to destroy the city. The real cause of his anger was that he did not want a foreign nation to enjoy the favor and forgiveness of God. This, he felt, belonged only to the Jews. This disgusted prophet went out of the city and sat on the east side, making for himself a booth to shade him from the sun while he waited to see what was to become of Nineveh.

"And the Lord God prepared a gourd, and made it to come up over Jonah, that it might be a shadow over his head, to deliver him from his grief. So Jonah was exceeding glad of the gourd. But God prepared a worm when the morning [sun] rose the next day, and it smote the gourd that it withered. And it came to pass, when the sun did arise, that God prepared a vehement east wind; and the sun beat upon the head of Jonah, that he fainted, and wished in himself to die, and said, 'It is better for me to die than to live.' And God said to Jonah, 'Doest thou well to be angry for the gourd?' And he said, 'I do well to be angry, even unto death.' Then said the Lord, 'Thou hast had pity on the gourd, for the which thou hast not laboured, neither madest it grow; which came up in a night, and perished in a night. And should not I spare Nineveh, that great city, wherein are more than sixscore thousand persons that cannot discern between their right hand and their left hand; and also much cattle?' " (Jonah 4:6-11).

In the background of this woodcut is the city of Nineveh, apparently unharmed notwithstanding Jonah's dire warning that it would be destroyed. Over it rises the morning sun, and already the vine that shelters the prophet has begun to wither because of the worm. In the foreground reclines Jonah, his hands flung out pettishly. His expression is one of self-pity as well as of unspoken rebuke to the Lord for showing His compassion on Nineveh.

Jonah's complaint against God is childish. The Lord, in using the lesson of the gourd, tries to help the despondent Jonah realize that the saving of life is of more

JONAH SHELTERED BY THE VINE—*ARTIST UNKNOWN*

importance than his prestige as a prophet. The Book of Jonah, ending in a clear message from God that He cared deeply for the people of a heathen city, was a voice raised in protest against the pride and exclusiveness of Israel after the Return from Exile.

✛

JUDAS MACCABAEUS ENTERS JERUSALEM

By

Julius Schnorr von Carolsfeld

(Interpretation)

THE Maccabees were a family of loyal Jews who opposed the introduction of Greek culture into Palestine in the second century B.C. They succeeded in winning religious and political freedom for the Jews and they ruled them from 166 to 63 B.C. The story of the uprising of the Maccabees, narrated in the First and Second Book of Maccabees in the Apocrypha, belongs to the period between the Old and the New Testaments.

The causes for the Maccabean revolt lie deeply imbedded in history. When Alexander the Great overcame the Persian Empire between 333 B.C. and 323 B.C., Syria and Palestine, which had been parts of the old Persian Empire, came under the influence and control of the Greeks. The Jews found themselves included first under the Egyptian Ptolemies, then in the empire of Seleucus, one of Alexander's brilliant generals who fell heir to a large part of the empire Alexander had won. Under the Ptolemies and later under the Seleucid emperors Greek civilization was introduced into Palestine. Greek laws, manners, and customs spread throughout the land and some of the Jews began to worship the ancient Greek gods: Zeus, Apollo, Artemis, Demeter, and Dionysus. The Jews at this time spoke Aramaic, though they continued to use Hebrew in their legal and religious writings. However, many of them now began to speak Greek also. In the city of Alexandria in Egypt where Alexander had settled many Jews Greek became the only language they could understand. It became necessary to translate the Hebrew Scriptures into Greek to meet their needs. This first Greek translation of the Old Testament is known as the Septuagint.

Judaism was severely challenged by this spread of Greek civilization, but when Antiochus IV Epiphanes, one of the Seleucid emperors, plundered the Temple in Jerusalem, forced the Jews to violate the Law of Moses, and murdered loyal Jews, a religious revolt broke out. This was the revolt led by the aged priest Mattathias and his five sons chief among whom was Judas Maccabaeus.

Judas Maccabaeus and his heroic band of followers succeeded in defeating the Syrian detachment sent against them and finally in 165 B.C. entered Jerusalem in triumph. Judas said to his soldiers: "Behold, our enemies are discomfited. Let us go up to cleanse and dedicate the sanctuary."

Thereupon they "assembled themselves together and went up into mount Sion.

JUDAS MACCABAEUS ENTERS JERUSALEM—*VON CAROLSFELD*

And when they saw the sanctuary desolate, and the altar profaned . . . they rent their clothes, and made great lamentation" (I Mac. 4:36-38).

The Temple, upon whose altar sacrifices to Zeus had been made for three years, was purified, the worship of the Lord God of Israel was restored, and the daily sacrifices were made once more.

Julius Schnorr von Carolsfeld in this stirring picture, "Judas Maccabaeus Enters Jerusalem," tells the story of how the Jews regained their beloved Temple. Judas Maccabaeus gestures toward the Temple and seems to urge his followers toward it. In front of him sit two dejected soldiers who have already seen the desecrated Temple. Others catching their first sight of the ruined building and flames rising from one of its courts are aghast. Behind Judas his trumpeter blows a blast to summon the entire army to Mount Sion. Loyal to the Lord who has been their God since He led the children of Israel out of Egypt, these heroic men prepare to "enter into his gates with thanksgiving, and into his courts with praise." They know that "the Lord is good; his mercy is everlasting; and his truth endureth to all generations" (Ps. 100:4, 5).

✢

BROTHERHOOD

The crest and crowning of all good,
Life's final star is Brotherhood;
For it will bring again to Earth
Her long-lost Poesy and Mirth,
Will send new light on every face,
A kingly power upon the race,
And till it comes, we men are slaves,
And travel downward to the dust of graves.

Come, clear the way then, clear the way:
Blind creeds and kings have had their day.
Break the dead branches from the path:
Our hope is in the aftermath—
Our hope is in heroic men,
Star-led to build the world again.
To this Event the ages ran:
Make way for Brotherhood—make way for Man.*

—Edwin Markham

THE SPIRIT OF BROTHERHOOD

The law of God is one as God is one; but we only discover it article by article line by line.

We can only rise to God through the souls of our fellowmen.

* From *Poems of Edwin Markham* selected and arranged by Charles L. Wallis. Copyright, 1950, by Virgil Markham. Published by Harper & Brothers. Used by special permission of Virgil Markham.

God is in you without doubt; but God is likewise in all men who people
    this earth;

God is in the life of all generations which were, which are and which
    are to be.

God has given you the general opinion of your fellowmen and your own
    conscience to be to you two wings with which to soar to Him.

God asks not what have you done for your soul? but what have you done
    for the brother souls I gave you?

Wherever a man suffers through the oppression of error, of injustice
    of tyranny there is your brother.

Why speak of Brotherhood and yet allow our brothers every day to be
    trampled, degraded, despised?

If error rules your brothers in some other corner of this earth and you do not
    desire and endeavor as far as lies in your power to overthrow it
    you are false to your duty.

A solemn mission is ours: to prove that we are all sons of God
    and brothers in Him.

— Joseph Mazzini

CALLING FOR GOD

Where is the God of justice?—MALACHI 2:17

God made the world both beautiful and good.
Then turned it over to His children fair,
A place to work and play in brotherhood,
To love and grow and blessings vast to share.
But what a mess man has made of God's gift!
How selfishness and hate have marred the plan!
The human race bewilderedly adrift,
The image of the God all blurred in man.
Why doesn't God assert His sovereign rights?
And make His subjects live as He desires?
His plan is seen as Jesus Christ invites
Devotion to the service love inspires.
God came to earth through Jesus Christ that is true,
He'll only come again through me and you.*

—Henry C. Spear

DEMAND FOR MEN

The world wants men—large hearted, manly men;
Men who shall join its chorus and prolong

* From *Sermon Sonnets* by Henry C. Spear, p. 21. Used by special permission of the author.

The psalm of labor, and the psalm of love.
The times want scholars—scholars who shall shape
The doubtful destinies of dubious years,
And land the ark that bears our country's good
Safe on some peaceful Ararat at last.
The age wants heroes—heroes who shall dare
To struggle in the solid ranks of truth;
To clutch the monster error by the throat;
To bear opinion to a loftier seat;
To blot the era of oppression out,
And lead a universal freedom on.
And heaven wants souls—fresh and capacious souls;
To taste its raptures, and expand, like flowers,
Beneath the glory of its central sun.
It wants fresh souls—not lean and shrivelled ones;
It wants fresh souls, my brother, give it thine.
If thou indeed wilt be what scholars should;
If thou wilt be a hero, and wilt strive
To help thy fellow and exalt thyself,
Thy feet at last shall stand on jasper floors;
Thy heart, at last, shall seem a thousand hearts—
Each single heart with myriad raptures filled—
While thou shalt sit with princes and with kings,
Rich in the jewel of a ransomed soul.

—Author Unknown

GOD'S CARE FOR ALL

There's not a bird, with lonely nest
In pathless wood or mountain crest,
Nor meaner thing, which does not share,
O God, in thy paternal care!

There's not a being now accurst,
Who did not taste thy goodness first;
And every joy the wicked see
Received its origin from thee.

Each barren crag, each desert rude,
Holds thee within its solitude;
And thou dost bless the wanderer there,
Who makes his solitary prayer.

In busy mart and crowded street,
No less than in the still retreat,
Thou, Lord, art near, our souls to bless
With all a parent's tenderness!

And every moment still doth bring
Thy blessings on its loaded wing;

Widely they spread through earth and sky,
And last to all eternity!

Through all creation let thy name
Be echoed with a glad acclaim!
And let the grateful churches sing;
With that let heaven forever ring!

And we, where'er our lot is cast,
While life and thought and feeling last,
Through all our years, in every place,
Will bless thee for thy boundless grace!

— *Baptist Wriothesley Noel (1841)*

THE GREEK ODE* FORM OF PSALM 30

Strophe 1

I will extol thee, O Lord; for thou hast raised me up,
And hast not made my foes to rejoice over me.
O Lord my God,
I cried unto thee, and thou hast healed me.
O Lord, thou hast brought up my soul from Sheol:
Thou hast kept me alive, that I should not go down to the pit.

Antistrophe

Sing praise unto the Lord, O ye saints of his,
And give thanks to his holy name.
For his anger is but for a moment;
In his favour is life:
Weeping may tarry for the night,
But joy cometh in the morning.

Strophe 2

As for me, I said in my prosperity,
I shall never be moved.
Thou, Lord, of thy favour hadst made my mountain to stand strong.

Antistrophe

Thou didst hide thy face; I was troubled.
I cried to thee, O Lord;
And unto the Lord I made supplication:

Strophe 3

"What profit is there in my blood when I go down to the pit?
Shall the dust praise thee? Shall it declare thy truth?
Hear, O Lord, and have mercy upon me:
Lord, be thou my helper."

* A Greek ode was performed by a body of singers whose evolutions as they sang a stanza carried them from the altar toward the right: then turning they performed an answering stanza, repeating the movement until its close brought them back to the altar from which they had started. The first stanza of a pair was called a *strophe,* from the Greek word meaning "a turning," its answering stanza an *antistrophe.*

Antistrophe

Thou hast turned for me my mourning into dancing;
Thou hast loosed my sackcloth, and girded me with gladness:
To the end that my glory may sing praise to thee, and not be silent.
O Lord my God, I will give thanks unto thee for ever.*

"HOW FAR, O RICH?"

How far, O rich do you extend your senseless avarice?
   Do you intend to be the sole inhabitants of the
   earth? Why do you drive out the fellow sharers
   of nature and claim it all for yourselves?

The earth was made for all, rich and poor in common.
   Why do you rich claim it as your exclusive right?
   The soil was given to the rich and poor in common
   —wherefore O ye rich, do you unjustly claim it
   for yourselves alone?

Nature gave all things in common for the use of all;
   usurpation created private rights.

Property hath no rights. The earth is the Lord's and
   we are His offspring.

The pagans hold the earth as property. They do blaspheme
   God.

                         —*St. Ambrose*

OMNIPRESENCE

I looked for God's strength,
And found it in the towering mountains;
Seeking for His humility,
I gazed upon the peaceful face of a valley;
To determine God's breadth,
I looked across a wide expanse of ocean,
And I found His beauty
In the heart of a deep, red rose.
His comforting warmth, I felt
On a breath of soft June air;
His ethereal brightness, I saw
In the center of a flame;
And His eternal tenderness
Was cradled in a mother's arms.**

                     —*Ruby Berkley Goodwin*

* From *The Literary Study of the Bible* by Richard G. Moulton. Published by D. C. Heath & Company. Used by special permission of the publisher.

** From *From My Kitchen Window* by Ruby Berkley Goodwin, p. 25. Copyright, 1942, by Ruby Berkley Goodwin. Used by special permission of the author.

PRAISE TO THE CREATOR

(Psalm 100)

Ye nations of the earth rejoice
Before the Lord, your Sovereign King,
Serve him with cheerful heart and voice;
With all your tongues his glory sing.

The Lord is God;—'tis he alone
Doth life and breath and being give;
We are his work, and not our own;
The sheep that on his pasture live.

Enter his gates with songs of joy;
With praises to his courts repair;
And make it your divine employ,
To pay your thanks and honours there.

The Lord is good; the Lord is kind;
Great is his grace, his mercy sure;
And the whole race of man shall find
His truth from age to age endure.

—Isaac Watts

SPEAK OUT

If you have a friend worth loving,
    Love him. Yes, and let him know
That you love him, ere life's evening
    Tinge his brow with sunset glow.
Why should good words ne'er be said
    Of a friend—till he is dead?

If you hear a song that thrills you,
    Sung by any child of song,
Praise it. Do not let the singer
    Wait deserved praises long.
Why should one who thrills your heart
    Lack to joy you may impart?

If you hear a prayer that moves you
    By its humble, pleading tone,
Join it. Do not let the seeker
    Bow before his God alone.
Why should not thy brother share
    The strength of "two or three" in prayer?

If your work is made more easy
    By a friendly, helping hand,
Say so. Speak out brave and truly,
    Ere the darkness veil the land.
Should a brother workman dear
    Falter for a word of cheer?

Scatter thus your seeds of kindness
    All enriching as you go—
Leave them. Trust the Harvest-Giver;
    He will make each seed to grow.
So, until the happy end,
    Your life shall never lack a friend.

                                        —*Author Unknown*

PRAYER AND PRAISE

God of the open, of dawning and starlight,
Of the sea's blue, the sun's gold, the clouds' varied pageant:
God of mountains and forests and rich, waving grasses;
Of April's fresh beauty and autumn's deep crooning;
Of the snow blast, the night wind,
The tempest, life-laden;
God of light, God of grandeur,
We adore Thee.

God of the spirit of man, emerging,
Warring against the shackles of darkness;
God of strength, of freedom, of hope everlasting;
God of history, of science, of music symphonic;
God of all Christ-souls of all ages and peoples,
Fulfilling the past, transcending the present,
Insurgent, exulting, with eyes to the eastward;
God of truth, God of progress,
We Extol Thee.

God of our hearts, Father of mercy,
Pitying, loving, craving affection;
God sacrificial, Calvary-proven;
Sun of all life, star of all peoples,
Warming, enlightening, cheering and luring;
God of humanity, God of Compassion,
Father of Christ who died for our saving,
We love Thee.*

                                        —*Thomas Curtis Clark*

* Used by special permission of the author.

A PRAYER FOR THE NEW YEAR

May it be Thy will,
Our God and God of our fathers,
That this coming year be unto all Thy people—
A year of plenty,
A year of blessings,
A year of assembly in Thy sanctuary,
A year of happy life from Thee,
A year of dew and rain and warmth,
A year in which Thou wilt bless our bread and water,
A year in which Thy mercies will be moved toward us,
A year of peace and tranquility, in which Thou
      wilt set a blessing upon the work of our hands.

—Ancient Hebrew Prayer

"THE WORD"

In the beginning was the Word,
    And the Word was with God,
    And the Word was God.
He was in the beginning with God.

All things came into being
    Through Him,
    And apart from Him
Nothing that now exists came into being.

In Him was life,
    And that Life was the Light of men.
The Light shines on in the darkness,
    And the darkness has never overpowered it.*

—John 1:15

THE MESSAGE OF JOEL

Hear ye! saith Joel the prophet:
Joy shall wither away among my people;
Every vine and tree shall be laid waste
By the worm and the locust;
A strong people whom Jehovah hath prepared
Shall overrun Judah and Israel;
And the land shall be desolate.
Jehovah hath spoken.

* *The New Testament in Modern Speech* by Richard Francis Weymouth, p. 164. Published by Harper & Brothers. Used by special permission of the publisher.

Yet, Jehovah thy God hath not forgotten thee!
The day of darkness, of cloud and gloominess,
Shall pass and be no more.
Turn again, with fasting and mourning;
Jehovah is gracious and merciful;
He will send grain and new wine;
The pastures and the wilderness shall spring,
And he will restore the years of plenty,
And ye shall eat and be satisfied.
Blow the trumpet in Zion,
For Jehovah hath done great things.
Repent, ye who dwell in Zion
My holy mountain! . . .
Then will Jehovah judge the nations
That have scourged my people.
But Judah will abide forever
And Jerusalem from generation to generation.*

—Thomas Curtis Clark

THE JOB

BUT, GOD, it won't come right! it won't come right!
    I've worked it over till my brain is numb.
The first flash came so bright,
Then more ideas after it—flash! flash!—I thought it some
New constellation men would wonder at.
Perhaps it's just a firework—flash! fizz! spat!
Then darker darkness and scorched pasteboard and sour smoke.

But, God, the thought was great,
The scheme, the dream—why, till the first charm broke
The thing just built itself while I, elate,
Laughed and admired it. Then it stuck,
Half done, the lesser half, worse luck!
You see, it's dead as yet, a frame, a body—and the heart,
The soul, the fiery vital part
To give it life, is what I cannot get. I've tried—
You know it—tried to catch live fire
And pawed cold ashes. Every spark has died.
It won't come right! I'd drop the thing entire,
Only—I can't! I love my job.

You, who ride the thunder,
Do you know what it is to dream and drudge and throb?
I wonder.
Did it come to you with a rush, your dream, your plan?
If so, I know how you began.
Yes, with rapt face and sparkling eyes,
Swinging the hot globe out between the skies,

Marking the new seas with their white beach lines,
Sketching in sun and moon, the lightning and the rains,
Sowing the hills with pines,
Wreathing a rim of purple round the plains.
I know you laughed then, while you caught and wrought
The big, swift rapturous outline of your thought.
And then—
MEN.

I see it now.
O God, forgive my pettish row!
I see your job. While ages crawl
Your lips take laboring lines, your eyes a sadder light,
For man, the fire and flower and center of it all—
Man won't come right!
After your patient centuries
Fresh starts, recastings, tired Gethsemanes
And tense Golgothas, he, your central theme,
Is just a jangling echo of your dream.
Grand as the rest may be, he ruins it.

Why don't you quit?
Crumple it all, and dream again! But no;
Flaw after flaw, you work it out, revise, refine—
Bondage, brutality, and war and woe
The sot, the fool, the tyrant and the mob—
Dear God, how you must love your job!
Help me, as I love mine.*

—Badger Clark

STORY OF JONAH

God had a job that needed to be done;
To call the Ninevites away from sin;
He chose the prophet Jonah as the one,
And sent him out the victory to win.
But Jonah ran away from duty's call,
He found the road was rough he chose to trod,
He soon was glad to give to God his all,
And went and did the job on foreign sod.
We, too, seek to evade God's just demands,
But soon we have a mess upon our hands,
And call on God to lift from us the load.
There's joy and blessing for the folks who see
The will of God as love's perfect degree.**

—Henry C. Spear

* From *Sky Lines and Wood Smoke* by Badger Clark, pp. 11-12. Copyright, 1935, by Badger Clark. Used by special permission of the author.

** Used by special permission of the author.

GOD OF THE COMMON LIFE

(Tune: *Ancient of Days*)

O God of life, by whom our lives are given.
Quicken our sight to see Thy gracious hand,
In all the good for which great souls have striven,
And help us humbly by Thy power to stand.

O God of toil, who callest us to labor
Within the common life of mills and marts;
Help us to see each human soul as neighbor;
Grant us the gift of understanding hearts.

O God of peace, in whom all men are brothers
Speak to this sundered world, by hatreds rent;
Teach us to praise Thee by our love of others,
And give us peace whose strength by war is spent.

O God of might, high over class and nation
Who dwellest in each humble contrite soul;
To Thee we look in hope and adoration;
Lead on in triumph by Thy gleaming goal.*

—*Georgia Harkness*

CATCHING UP WITH GOD

Man cannot keep pace with God—
God is walking out ahead!
　Truths He seemed so long concealing,
　Only now He is revealing.
Atom-smashing betatron,
Geiger Counters with their drone,
Isotopes that trace disease.
Pentathol that gives men ease
Under healing surgeon's knife,
Helping stretch a precious life—
Tardy men find all of these,
Marvels God has given for peace.

God of science, God of mind,
God of love for all mankind,
Help us find Thee more and more,
As we search Thy wonder-store.

In our little daily findings,
In the great world-shaking grindings,

If we can't keep pace with Thee,
Let our spirits reverent be.

Seeking, scarching, time will come
When the total plan we'll see,
And our present ignorance
Part of Thy advance will be.*

—*Madeleine S. Miller*

✜

THE REBUILDING OF THE WALL

By

Florence C. Porter

WHEN the Jews were in captivity in Persia, Nehemiah, a young Jew, served as cup-bearer to Artaxerxes, the king.

One day there entered into the palace a group of men, recently come from Judah. How glad Nehemiah was to find his brother with them! "How is it with thee and with our brethren?" he asked eagerly. "How fares our city Jerusalem?"

"Our brethren are in great sorrow," the brother gravely answered. "The wall of Jerusalem is broken down and the gates thereof are all burned with fire. The neighboring nations are hostile and over-run the city, doing mischief by day and by night."

When Nehemiah heard these words, he sat down and wept and fasted. As he thought, there came to him a plan of action. But he was a servant of the great Artaxerxes and no plan of his could succeed without the seal of the king's approval.

"O Lord God of Heaven," he prayed, "hear the prayer of thy servant. Grant that I may have mercy from the king and may find favor in his sight."

For four months he waited and planned. Then, one day, as the young cupbearer was serving the king, Artaxerxes noticed that his countenance was sad.

"Why art thou sad, seeing thou art not sick?" the king said unto him.

"O King, live forever! Why should not my countenance be sad, when the city, the home of my fathers, lieth waste and the gates thereof are burned with fire?"

Then said the king, "For what dost thou make request?"

"If it please thee, O King, that thou wouldst send me to Jerusalem, the city of my fathers, that I may build it."

"Thou hast served faithfully and well in my palace," said the king. "Return to thy native land. The king appoints thee governor of Judah during thy stay. For how long shall thy journey be? When wilt thou return?"

So it pleased the king to grant the request. Whereupon Nehemiah set a time for his return.

He made of the king a further request. "If it please thee, O King, let letters be given me to the governors beyond the river, that they may convey me over till I come into Judah, and a letter to the keeper of the king's forest that he may give me

* Used by special permission of the author.

timber to make beams for the gates of the palace and for the wall of the city, and for the house that I shall enter into."

Nehemiah felt that the God of his fathers was with him when the king granted this second request also.

Captains of the army and horsemen were appointed to take Nehemiah safely to the city of Jerusalem, for he must needs journey through the lands of people who were not friendly to the Jews. To the governors of these provinces were presented the king's letters and they could not question the right of the newly appointed governor to go through their land. But the nearer the band came to Jerusalem, the more hostile the people became. Nehemiah could see that, even with the king's commission, his task would not be an easy one.

At last they reached the city of Jerusalem. After three days' stay, Nehemiah, with a few trusted men, arose in the night, and silently, secretly, with no beast save the one he rode upon, went out to view the ruins of the wall and the gates of the city. To no one did he tell the plan that God had put into his heart.

When he had seen what work was needed, he called together the Jews, the priests, the nobles, the rulers and the rest that did the work, and said unto them: "Ye see how Jerusalem lieth waste; come, let us build up the wall of our city, that we may be again a united people. When I was a captive in a strange land, the message came to me of your great need. My prayer to God was answered when the king spake kindly to me, and granted my request to return to my native land to rebuild the city of my fathers."

Then all the people said, "Let us rise up and build."

To every one was appointed his place to work and the rebuilding was started.

As soon as the enemies without heard of the plan of Nehemiah, they sent a messenger to him. "What is this thing that ye do? We of Samaria laugh at your foolish plans," they taunted. Then they grew threatening. "Will ye rebel against the king?" they questioned.

Nehemiah sent back the message, "Our God will help us; therefore we will arise and build."

Again word came to Nehemiah that Sanballat, the chief leader of the hostile tribes, had spoken before his brethren and the army of Samaria these mocking words, "What do these feeble Jews? Will they fortify themselves? Will they sacrifice? Will they revive the stones out of the heaps of rubbish which are burned?" Another leader added, "Even that which they build, if a fox go up, he shall even break down their stone wall."

But the Jewish people had a mind to work and the work went on till all the wall was joined together unto half the height thereof.

Then their enemies planned a surprise attack, to come secretly from all sides, slay the workers, and cause the work to cease.

"Hear, O our God, and help us," the Jewish people prayed.

Nehemiah set a watch both day and night. Friends who lived outside the city kept the Jews informed of the plans of the enemies. Ten different times they gave warning of plots that had been made against Jerusalem. Nehemiah ordered the people to arm themselves with their swords, their spears, and their bows.

"Be not afraid," he encouraged them. "Remember the Lord and strive for your brethren, your sons and your daughters, your wives and your homes."

When the builders knew the enemies had learned that their plots had been made known, and that God had brought their plans to nought, they returned to the wall, each one to his work.

But from that time, half of the workers wrought in the work and the other half held the spears, the shields, and the bows. They who bore burdens with those who laded, every one with one of his hands helped in the work, and with the other, held a weapon. And the builders, every one had a sword girded by his side. The one that sounded the trumpet was by Nehemiah.

So the work continued till the wall was complete, except for the setting up of the gates. Then there came to Nehemiah a servant of Sanballat, saying, "Come, let us meet together in one of the villages." But Nehemiah could not be turned from his work.

"I am doing a great work so that I cannot come down; why should the work cease, whilst I leave it to come down to you?" he questioned.

Four times the message was brought. Each time Nehemiah's answer was the same.

A fifth time the servant came, bearing this message: "It is reported among our people that thou and the Jews think to rebel, for which cause thou buildest the wall, that thou mayest be their king. Come now, therefore, let us take counsel together."

Nehemiah returned answer. "There are no such things done as thou sayest. Thou pretendest them out of thine own heart."

Again and again he pleaded, "O God, give us strength of heart and hand that we may not be turned aside."

Steadily the work went on. In fifty and two days, not only the wall was finished, but the gates were set up in place and porters were appointed to keep watch over them. The enemies about perceived that this work was wrought of God. Nehemiah, through his unfailing faith, had worked out the task that he felt had been entrusted to him when he was a cupbearer to the king in far-off Persia.*

JONAH, THE REBEL PROPHET

By

Robert Nathan

Now the word of Jehovah came unto Jonah the son of Amittai, saying, "Arise, go to Nineveh, that great city, and cry against it; for their wickedness is come up before me." But Jonah rose up to flee unto Tarshish from the presence of Jehovah.

—JONAH 1:1-3, A.S.V.

In those days there were prophets in Israel. They lived in the desert beyond the Jordan, in caves and in rude huts made of clay and mats. There were many holy men

* From *Story Art Magazine,* May-June, 1951. Used by special permission of the author.

among them, whose ears had been pierced by the sweetness of God's voice and whose eyes had been dazzled by the fiery appearances of His angels.

In the cold night air God went to look for Jonah. Poor Jonah had not found peace after all. The lonely desert, so calm and quiet in the past, had given no rest to his thoughts.

God found him sitting wearily upon a rock, his head bowed between his hands. The Lord spoke, and the desert was silent.

"Jonah," said God in a voice like a great wave breaking, slowly, and with the peace of the sea, "Jonah, you have wept enough. . . . Now I have something for you to do."

Jonah remained seated without looking up. He seemed no longer to care what God had for him to do.

"Arise, Jonah," said God, "and go to Nineveh. Cry out against that great city for its sins."

But Jonah looked more dejected than ever. "What have I to do with Nineveh?" he asked. "Am I prophet to the Assyrians? I am a Jew. Do not mock me, Lord."

"I do not mock you," said God gravely. "Go, then, and do my bidding."

Jonah rose slowly to his feet.

"I am your God, Jonah, and where you go, there you will find Me."

Jonah sank down upon the rock again. He was not convinced. In a whisper, he said: "You are not God in Nineveh, and I will not go."

"Peace unto you, Jonah," said God in tones of divine sweetness; "take up your task, and doubt Me no more."

And He returned to heaven in a cloud. Overcome with weariness . . . Jonah fell asleep upon the ground.

. . . Silence brooded over the desert. The stars kept watch without a sound, and Jonah slept with a quiet heart.

But in the morning his doubts returned more strongly than ever. "They will mock me in Nineveh. I shall be made a laughing-stock. What power has the Light of Israel in the land of Marduk. I should count myself lucky if I escaped being stoned to death.

"For how can God destroy Nineveh? I might as well preach to the fish in the sea."

But now he had something to do, at least. He determined to flee from God. "I shall go to Tarshish," he thought, "and begin life over again. There is nothing for me here any longer. The desert will be glad to be rid of me."

He traveled swiftly, on other roads from those he had come. Late on the afternoon of the second day he crossed the Brook Kanath, and saw in the distance the white domed roofs of Joppa shining above the sea.

It was late when he came to the shore, and night was already moving upon the deep. It was the season when the mists from the ocean blow landward in the evening.

Night hung black and silent over the sea. The wings of angels leaned upon the wind which moved dark and vast between the earth and sky. The stars paled, and the sun rose like a ball of fire in the east.

In the morning Jonah found a ship bound for Tarshish. The cargo was already loaded when he made his bargain and went aboard. Bearded and singing, the seamen hoisted the sails, yellow as a slice of the moon; with a sly, tranquil motion the ship moved out of the harbor, over the blue sea. The white roofs of Joppa faded behind them in the east, lost in the gradual fog; the sea-gulls cried above them; and Jonah sat silent, dreaming, gazing at the sea.

The warmth of the sun, reflected from the sea, entered his mind and lulled his limbs. Sea-quiet took hold of him; the peace of the ocean bathed his spirit. He grew drowsier and drowsier; he began to doze. And as he fell asleep, his last thought was that he had got away from God.

In the afternoon the wind died away; an ominous haze enveloped the sky; and the sea grew oily. The sails were hastily drawn in; and the oars were made ready. Huddled together on the deck, the seamen spoke in low, anxious voices. All eyes were turned toward the east, which grew darker and darker. All was still; the air did not stir. Moved by fear, the men trembled; and as though herself frightened, the ship started to creak in all her timbers. All at once the sky uttered a moan; high above them the air began to sing. Then it seemed as if the sky fell down upon the sea, for the water rose like the hills, and the dark came down upon it. Unable to move, the ship trembled from bow to stern, lifted dizzily upon the waves, tilted in the wind, and dropped like a stone into the trough.

Pale with fear, the sailors rushed to lighten the ship by throwing the cargo overboard. Then, as the tiny vessel dashed about in the water like a cork, they fell upon their knees and prayed to their gods.

Seeing that Jonah still slept, sheltered by the deck which curved above him, the captain ran to awaken him. "Here," he said, "this is a storm. You should be more anxious, my friend. Have you a god? Then pray to him, for we need all the help we can get."

Dazed by the tumult, still half asleep, Jonah gazed in confusion at the heaving waters. "I will not pray," he said. And the captain shrank back at the sight of his face.

But the seamen, clinging to the deck, looked anxiously at Jonah, and at the great seas which broke over them without ceasing. "This is no common storm," they told each other; "some great god is angry."

And Jonah looked at them as frightened as they were. His mind reeled; had he not gotten away from God after all? Had God come after him—out there on the sea? Was there no way to flee from God?

"It is my fault," he said to the sailors proudly. "I alone am to blame. I am a Jew who has denied his God. It is my life that is wanted. Throw me overboard."

Seizing Jonah, they cast him overboard, with a prayer. "Do not lay innocent blood upon us," they said, "O god of the Jews. This is your doing, not ours."

So saying they waited, trembling.

At once the sea grew calm, the wind died away, and the sun sank tranquilly down in the clear west. The peace of evening brooded again upon the water. And the ship, with all her sails set for Joppa, fled to the east.

Jonah sank through the waters without complaint. It was the end, and he had no desire to live. But as his breath failed, his mind brought back to him the blue and shining sky, the sweet odors of the desert, the happy dreams of his youth. "No," he cried to himself, "no, I must live; I must live."

With a groan Leviathan* hurled himself through the waves and took the prophet into his mouth.

On the third day, God spoke. And the whale, lashing the waters with his tail, sped like an eager minnow, to the shore, and vomited Jonah forth upon the sand.

Jonah was let out of the whale in the north, near Arvad, and not far from Kadesh.

At Kadesh he saw statues of the river deities, Chrysonhoa and Pegai. In the sun of late afternoon their shadows pointed like great spears toward Nineveh.

At the end of the second day he began to pass the boundary stones of Assyria, set up to warn trespassers upon private property. Thinking them altars, Jonah cursed each one as he went by. The next day he passed kilns in which colored bricks were being baked.

That night he slept outside the gates of Nineveh. The city rose above him in the dark; he heard the sentries' challenge on the walls.

In the morning he entered the city with some farmers on their way to the markets. The sun was rising, gleaming upon the great winged bulls before the temples, the green and yellow lions upon the walls. Under the clear upland sky the city shone with color like *a fair*. The markets opened; the streets filled with men and women in their colored shawls and clashing ornaments.

But not for long. As the hours passed he grew weary; and as the brightness wore off, he began to think of his own life again, he began to hate Nineveh, to hate the bold colors all around him, the youth that carried itself so proudly and carelessly in the streets. "Yes," he thought, "that is all very well for you; but you know nothing about life." And, lifting his arms, he cried aloud with gloomy satisfaction, "Yet forty days, and Nineveh shall be overthrown."

The success of this remark astonished him. Without waiting to find out any more about it, the Assyrians hurried home and put ashes on their heads. Nineveh repented like a child of its sins; in an orgy of humility the city gave up its business, and dressed itself in sackcloth. The king even, left his throne, and sat down in some ashes.

Jonah was vexed. And when he learned that because of its repentance Nineveh was to be spared, his courage gave way to a flood of disappointment.

"I knew it," he said bitterly to God; "I knew You'd never do it."

And with an angry countenance he retired to an open field on the east side of the city, to see what would happen.

Then God, who was anxiously watching, spoke to Jonah from the sky. "Why are you angry?" said the Holy One. "Have I done you a wrong?"

Jonah replied, sighing, "Who will ever believe me now, Lord?"

And for the rest of the day he maintained a silence, full of reproach.

Then because the sun was very hot, and because where Jonah was sitting there was no shade of any sort, God made a vine grow up, overnight, to shelter Jonah.

"There," said God, "there is a vine for you. Rest awhile and see."

That day Jonah sat in comfort beneath his shelter. At noon a farmer brought his meal, salt and oil; he ate, was refreshed, and dozed beneath his vine.

But in the morning worms had eaten the leaves of the vine, gorged and comfortable, they regarded Jonah from the ground with pious looks. As the day progressed,

* A large unidentified ocean mammal. Anything huge.

the sun beat down upon him without pity, a strong wind blew up from the east, out of the desert, and the prophet grew faint with misery.

God, looking down on His prophet, smiled sadly. "What is a vine?" He said gently. "Was it your vine, Jonah? You neither planted it nor cared for it. It came up in a night, and it perished in a night. And now you think I should have spared the vine for your sake. Yes . . . but what of Nineveh, that great city, where there are so many people who cannot discern between their right hand and their left hand? Shall I not spare them, too, for My sake, Jonah?"

Jonah rose wearily to his feet. "Well," he said, "I may as well go home again."

And with bowed head he passed through the city, and out of the western gate. In the streets the citizens made way for him with pious murmurs and anxious looks, but Jonah did not notice them. All his courage was gone, his pride, his hope of glory, all gone down in the dust of God's mercy to others, to all but him. To him alone God had been merciless and exacting.

High among the clouds, God turned sadly to Moses. "You Jews," He said wearily, "you do not understand beauty. With you it is either glory or despair."

And with a sigh He looked westward to the blue Aegean. Warm and gold the sunlight lay over Greece.*

✠

PALESTINE UNDER THE GREEKS AND ROMANS

By

Cynthia Pearl Maus

SOMETIME between 333 B.C. and 323 B.C. Alexander the Great, according to an old Jewish tale, swept aside the rule of Persia and established a new regime throughout the length and breadth of the Persian Empire. Palestine was a part of that Empire; and so after Alexander the Great had captured the northern cities of Damascus and Tyre, he moved against Jerusalem.

The High Priest in Jerusalem had given his oath that he would not bear arms against Darius III; therefore, as soon as he heard that Alexander the Great was marching toward Jerusalem, he ordered the Hebrew people to pray and to offer sacrifices that they might be delivered from the armies of the approaching monarch.

The Lord had warned Jaddua, the High Priest, to open the gates of Jerusalem and to go out to meet the oncoming conqueror, unarmed, and clad only in his High Priestly robes. This he did, and when Alexander the Great saw this brave leader, he paid homage to the name of the Lord, the God of Israel, emblazoned in gold on the High Priest's miter. The Hebrews who witnessed this strange scene broke into cries of joyous acclamation for the Greek king and surrounded him. Alexander the Great was so impressed by this reception that he took Jaddua's arm and they entered the city of Jerusalem together in the midst of a crowd of singing, rejoicing inhabitants.

The coming of this ruler of the Greek Empire brought about a new era in Jeru-

* Abridged from *Jonah* by Robert Nathan, pp. 3, 180-212. Copyright, 1925, 1953, by Robert Nathan. Published by Alfred A. Knopf. Used by special permission of the author.

salem. The king not only offered sacrifice to the Lord in the Temple in Jerusalem, but he gave the Hebrew people wide and generous privileges.

For the first time in history the coming of this Greek monarch brought the culture of the East and West together. Soon the Greek language, Greek philosophy, and Greek manners and customs spread throughout Palestine. And while the Greeks continued to worship the gods—Zeus, Apollo, Artemis, Demeter, and Dionysus—the Hebrews were allowed to continue their worship of the God of the Israelites.

Alexander settled many of the Hebrews in a new city bearing his name—Alexandria—in Egypt; and it was to meet their needs that the first translation of the Hebrew Scriptures was made into the Greek language. We know this translation as the Septuagint.

Upon the death of Alexander the Great this mighty Greek Empire was divided among his generals; and although the Hebrews went through difficult times following the death of Alexander the Great, they continued to enjoy, for the most part, the favor of these Greek generals up until the reign of Antiochus Epiphanes about 170 B.C. He marched against Jerusalem, despoiled it, broke down its walls and even defiled the altar in the Temple in Jerusalem by offering thereon the flesh of swine. The Hebrews were forbidden to keep their Sabbath holy, and Antiochus even built altars dedicated to the worship of their Greek gods in the streets of Jerusalem.

His attempt to make the Hebrews worship these Greek gods instead of the Lord resulted in the rise of the Maccabees, a band of loyal Hebrews who fought their way to victory in 165 B.C. The Temple which Antiochus had closed was reopened, cleansed, and rededicated to the worship of God. The Maccabees established the "Feast of Dedication" which was observed annually in Jerusalem until the city and the Temple was destroyed in A.D. 70.

In 63 B.C. a Roman general named Pompey laid siege to Jerusalem, and finally after three months, and by using the strategy of violating the Hebrew Sabbath, his armies made a breach in the walls of Jerusalem and they rushed into the city. Pompey desecrated the Temple, even pushing his way into the Holy of Holies which he found empty. He refused to plunder the Temple of its sacred vessels and treasures. Instead, he ordered the Temple to be cleansed of its injured and slain, and permitted the continuation of its services of worship.

Antipater, an Edomite, was made the local ruler of the Roman government, and Herod the Great, Antipater's second son, was appointed by the Roman Empire as King of Judea. He was not a Jew, but had married a beautiful Jewess, so that his descendants represented a combination of the Hebrews and Edomites, both of which were descendants of Abraham.

Some of the Hebrew people accepted the rule of Herod the Great with pride and joy; others hated him and the Roman government under which they were held as a Roman province.

Herod the Great was very ambitious and rebuilt the Temple in Jerusalem on a much grander scale than it had ever known. He also established a theater and an amphitheater for games and the display of physical strength and dexterity. He also built many strong fortresses throughout Palestine and lavished money on his own private palace.

Herod was a monarch of strong passions, and his savage wrath was immediately pitted against any obstacle that stood in his way. So widely known was his cruelty and venomous hate that Emperor Augustus of Rome is credited with having said "that it was better to be Herod's hog than his son."

It was this Herod the Great, old now and dying of a terrible disease, who was on the throne as King of Judea, when Joseph and Mary made their historic trip from Nazareth to Bethlehem "to be enrolled," according to the King's decree, in the city of Joseph's ancestors; and with the coming of that Child of Promise we cross "History's Bridge" into the New Testament.

☩

"WHERE IS THY GOD?"

By

Margaret J. Wiggins

MONTELL was the swiftest runner of the Temple children. Many races won had given her first place among those boys and girls who spent their days in the great Temple of the Jews in the ancient city of Jerusalem. Running was the important thing in their day's work—running errands for the priests—helping clean the courts —carrying supplies to and from the city, or herding the flocks of cattle in the Temple stockade.

For days, now, there had been much running for all the children. There was fierce fighting outside the walls of the city. The army of the King's brother, Aristobulus, was trying to gain the throne from Hyrcanus, who was the son of the last of the Maccabee brothers who had kept the faith and held the Jewish tribes together against all the foes who came upon them after they had returned from the years of captivity in Babylon.

The old order was gone. There was no strong leader now, to lead the Jews into resistance. Hyrcanus was only a tool in the hands of Antipater, the father of Herod the Great. He saw the confusion of the Jews, so he placed Herod as official head of the country of Palestine, with Hyrcanus in the office of High Priest, the spiritual leader, which pleased the Jews, and he sent the rebel Aristobulus to Rome, in chains.

When, at last, the day came when the great Roman General arrived to claim the country and the old city of Jerusalem as subjects of Rome, the Jews could no longer resist, and so they bowed in submission, and relapsed into a welcome of resentful quietness.

Herod, who at the instructions of Antipater was playing both the Jews and the Romans, had given consent that the Jews could continue to worship in the Temple, and observe all the rites and ceremonies that they were accustomed to do under the laws of the High Priests. There was to be no interference from Rome as long as the Jews did not interfere with the civil laws.

So it was that at last the Temple was again quiet and the children were given a little time to relax and rest from the constant running to and fro, up and down, in and out, from city to Temple, and back to the city again, many times in the days of fighting. Montell had been the first one always to be sent out with messages, and often her life was in danger from the soldiers and the fighting in the streets. But her swift little legs carried her safely, and the High Priest and even the Roman, Antipater, had praised her for her cleverness in escaping the dangers she encountered. Her father and mother were always anxious about her, but they had dedicated her to the Temple, so she was no longer in their care. Her father was the night watchman in the Temple, walking the walls, all the hours of the night. And, sometimes, when there was fighting, Montell had walked beside him, all the night through.

The great General Pompey was the head of the Roman army placed in Palestine. He was well known for his leadership and conquests wherever the Romans had desired new territory. But Pompey was not just a soldier, thinking only of battles and victories. He had heard many tales about the great city of Jerusalem and the marvelous Temple that King Solomon had built. He knew that the Syrians had destroyed most of the original Temple, had stolen and destroyed the ornaments of gold and silver, the carvings and the candlesticks and the lamp of jewels that the Temple had been decked with.

He had also heard how the Jews, returning from the years of captivity in Babylon, had set about rebuilding the walls, and the Temple, a trowel in one hand and a sword in the other. He had heard that many of the Jews in captivity had kept some of the ornaments they had taken from the Temple in their flight, hidden all the time they were in Babylon, and when they returned there had been great joy in placing them again in their beloved and restored Temple.

"There must be something wonderful about the God of the Jews," said Pompey to himself. "He must be more lovable than the gods of the Romans—I shall see what He is like, now that I am in Jerusalem."

When all was quiet in the city, and the people were once more going about the business of living, Pompey decided to see the Temple and find out what it was that made the Jews a "peculiar people." Always, in all parts of the known world, Jews were singled out from other nations, they were "different." Now, Pompey was going to see if he could find out *why*.

One of the priests on the high wall at the back of the Temple saw a cloud of dust coming along the high road from the city. Since the sun was past noon and there were no caravans following, the dust meant that the soldiers were coming.

Watching closely, he saw the horses turn into the yard leading to the gate of the Temple. He shouted at the guard at the gate, then turning, ran to the inner court where Hyrcanus was reading the Book of the Law.

"The uncircumcised Gentile is coming into the Temple," he cried. "What can we do?"

Watching closely, he saw the horses turn into the yard leading to the gate of the Temple. He shouted at the guard at the gate, then turning, ran to the inner court where Hyrcanus was reading the Book of the Law.

Hyrcanus clapped his hands which was the signal for the children to be ready for orders. He looked down into the outer court where there usually were some people praying and making sacrifices. He called the guard. The guard said there was only one other guard, Obed, Montell's father, who could help to defend the gate.

Hyrcanus shouted, "Montell! Run! Bring thy father. Run as you have never run before!"

And Montell ran! She called to her legs, "Faster, go faster!" But it seemed that the streets were all so long—the little home so far away!

Her mother, sitting at the loom in the outer room, saw her child flying through the streets, into the passage, and wondered how she could stop, as she had been taught, before she reached the door, so she would not waken her sleeping father. But, as the door came into her line of vision, she slowed, drew her breath slowly, deeply, pressed her hands down her body to still its quivering, and stepped into the room. She whispered her errand to her mother, and asked, "Will you waken him?"

"No, swift angel, you were sent. Awaken him, and God be with you and him."

Montell stepped softly into the room where her father slept. She saw he slept with his arm above his head, with his fist clenched.

Her presence must have roused him, for he turned and opened his eyes. Swiftly, Montell was beside him.

"Father! Waken! You are needed at the Temple! The great Roman is marching with his men to destroy it and we need you."

Obed was up and putting on his clothes before she stopped speaking. "Run back, child, and stand in front of the golden curtain before the Holy of Holies. Stand there till I come!"

There was only the patter of little feet as she passed through the passage, through the court, into the street now filled with people. She fought her way through the crowd, along the side of the Temple, into the outer court, running, running, through the troughs that were to carry off the blood of the sacrifices, running through the portico, to the inner court, up the stairs to the entrance of the Holy of Holies.

There, with the golden curtain before her eyes, she again drew the long, slow breath, held her quivering body straight and still, closed her burning eyes, and moistened her dry lips with a tongue as dry. Her whole being was throbbing with the terrible exertion, but, she was at her post before the golden curtain of the Holy of Holies—and Pompey, the Roman, was at the Temple gate!

The gate had been closed since the Romans had conquered the city, and now, Pompey called for it to be opened. No one responded to his demands, so one of the soldiers beat it open, pushing aside those who would have stopped him. Pompey walked in to the outer court, looking about him in an interested way, picking up the various things that were there, setting them down again in the exact place they had been. He looked with wondering eyes at the ornaments, at the structure of the great outer court, at the carvings and the stairs. These he began to ascend, and the soldiers came along with him. At the entrance to the inner court, he paused and ordered his men to stay behind.

The crowd that had gathered watched to see what he would do. He had touched many things but had put them all back as they had been; nothing was being destroyed. There was no intent, it seemed, to destroy. The man simply was interested in seeing the Temple.

He entered the court of the priests where the great books of the Law were kept.

He took one in his hand, but soon laid it back on the desk, as he could not read Hebrew. Then, he saw more stairs, and began to go up them.

"Thou shalt not enter there!" shouted one of the priests.

"Why shall I not enter there?" Pompey asked.

"That place is the Holy of Holies, and no man enters there except the High Priest, and he can go in there only once a year."

Behind the golden curtain at the head of the stairs stood a little girl. She held her breath—she stood as tall and stiff as if she were one of the cherubim from the great court. Would the man come in—would he kill her if she tried to keep him out— would her father never come! Nearer, and nearer she heard his step! He *was* coming! Had no one stopped him?

Then—the golden curtain was snatched away from the door, the man stood before her, more astonished than she, for she had known he would be there, and he was at the point of adventure such as he had never before known—to see a God, a God that was worshiped by thousands as if life depended on their worship.

"Ho-ho!" he shouted, too amazed to say more. Then, looking all about, he said, "That is the place where they say your God is," and he reached for the door to open it.

Montell was quicker. She moved to the door, her back to it, her arms outstretched, her feet planted firmly.

"Thou shalt not enter here," she cried.

Very quietly, but firmly, the great Pompey reached his left hand out and took the child by the shoulder, drawing her behind him, at the same time pushing the door open.

Empty! Bare! Not a single thing was in the room!

Incredulous, amazed beyond speech, the Roman stepped back as if struck. He looked all about, stooping down to see if anyone could be hiding on the floor. Then, staggering, groping, he moved to the chair that was at the landing of the stairs, and, still holding Montell, he sat down and drew her to his knee.

"Where is thy God, child? Tell me, I wish to find Him. I know He is not like the Roman gods. Where is *thy* God?"

Montell looked at the great man. Dressed in the gorgeous uniform of the Romans he was handsome. Not young, and still not old, he seemed trying truly to find where the God of the Jews could be found. She thought for a moment before she said,

"Our God is not a man like the Roman gods. Our God is a Spirit whom we come into the Temple to worship and praise for His loving-kindness to us. Every day we rejoice and give Him our love and thanks, and He hears us and cares for us. Once a year only, the High Priest enters the Holy of Holies, and our God talks to Him, and instructs him how to govern us. Sometimes, we also hear His voice, and then we shout and sing, knowing that Jehovah is with us." Then, as Pompey seemed to be thinking very hard of all she had said, Montell said again,

"Our God is not a man. He is a Spirit."

Suddenly she realized that she was not alone, that her father was standing beside her, his sword in his hand, that Hyrcanus and the other priests were at the head of the stairs, and that in the courts below were hundreds of people just waiting to see what Pompey was going to do. There was no trouble, no great disturbance, not much noise, and the soldiers were also quietly waiting for orders from their general.

Pompey smiled at Montell, patted her shoulder and said, "You are a brave little girl, and I thank you for telling me about your God."

He, too, seemed suddenly to realize that there were people all about. He rose, looked again in the sacred room, and then went slowly down the stairs, called an order to his men, and was soon on his horse with the rest of the men following.

Montell was praised by all. Her father took her home and she was given homage by the Jews, with a feast and presents and a little medal to wear, showing that she was brave and true.

When she grew up she lived in the little town of Bethlehem. Sixty-five years later, she stood on the steps of the Inn, with friends, watching a Star that hung over the old hillside stable in the Inn yard. Someone said that a Baby had been born, who was to be the King of the Jews, the Promised One of Israel.

Montell suddenly thought of the great Roman General, Pompey. She wished that his seeking for the God of the Jews could lead him *now,* to this stable, where the Son of God had been born. Perhaps here he would find his answer to the question, "Where is *thy* God?"*

✝

JERUSALEM IN THE DAYS OF HEROD THE GREAT

By

Lew Wallace

IN an aperture of the western wall of Jerusalem hang the "oaken valves" called the Bethlehem or Joppa Gate. The area outside of them is one of the notable places of the city. Long before David coveted Zion there was a citadel there. When at last the son of Jesse ousted the Jebusite, and began to build, the site of the citadel became the northwest corner of the new wall, defended by a tower much more imposing than the old one. The location of the gate, however, was not disturbed, for the reason, most likely, that the roads which met and merged in front of it could not well be transferred to any other point, while the area outside had become a recognized market-place. In Solomon's day there was great traffic at the locality, shared in by traders from Egypt and the rich dealers from Tyre and Sidon. Nearly three thousand years have passed, and yet a kind of commerce clings to the spot. A pilgrim wanting a pin or a pistol, a cucumber or a camel, a house or a horse, a loan or a lentil, a date or a dragoman, a melon or a man, a dove or a donkey, has only to inquire for the article at the Joppa Gate. Sometimes the scene is quite animated, and then it suggests, What a place the old market must have been in the days of Herod the Builder! And to that period and that market the reader is now to be transferred.

Following the Hebrew system, the meeting of the Wise Men . . . took place in the afternoon of the twenty-fifth day of the third month of the year; that is, on the

Used by special permission of the author.

twenty-fifth day of December. The year was . . . the sixty-seventh of Herod the Great, and the thirty-fifth of his reign; the fourth before the beginning of the Christian era. The hours of the day, by Judean custom, begin with the sun, the first hour being the first after sunrise; so, to be precise, the market at the Joppa Gate during the first hour of the day stated was in full session, and very lively. The massive valves had been wide open since dawn. Business, always aggressive, had pushed through the arched entrance into a narrow lane and court, which, passing by the walls of the great tower, conducted on into the city. As Jerusalem is in the hill country, the morning air on this occasion was not a little crisp. The rays of the sun, with their promise of warmth, lingered provokingly far up on the battlements and turrets of the great piles about, down from which fell the crooning of pigeons and the whir of the flocks coming and going.

As a passing acquaintance with the people of the Holy City, strangers as well as residents, . . . it will be well to stop at the gate and pass the scene in review. Better opportunity will not be offered to get sight of the populace who will afterwhile go forward in a mood very different from that which now possesses them.

The scene is at first one of utter confusion—confusion of action, sounds, colors, and things. . . . Here stands a donkey, dozing under panniers full of lentils, beans, onions, and cucumbers, brought fresh from the gardens and terraces of Galilee. When not engaged in serving customers, the master, in a voice which only the initiated can understand, cries his stock. Nothing can be simpler than his costume— sandals and an unbleached, undyed blanket, crossed over one shoulder and girt round the waist. Nearby, and far more imposing and grotesque, though scarcely as patient as the donkey, kneels a camel, raw-boned, rough and gray, with long shaggy tufts of fox-colored hair under its throat, neck and body, and a load of boxes and baskets curiously arranged upon an enormous saddle. The owner is an Egyptian, small, lithe, and of a compexion which had borrowed a good deal from the dust of the roads and the sands of the desert. He wears a faded *tarbooshe,* a loose gown, sleeveless, unbelted, and dropping from the neck to the knee. His feet are bare. The camel, restless under the load, groans and occasionally shows his teeth; but the man paces indifferently to and fro, holding the driving-strap, and all the time advertising his fruits fresh from the orchards of the Kedron—grapes, dates, figs, apples, and pomegranates.

At the corner where the lane opens out into the court, some women sit with their backs against the gray stones of the wall. Their dress is that common to the humbler classes of the country—a linen frock extending the full length of the person, loosely gathered at the waist, and a veil or wimple broad enough after covering the head, to wrap the shoulders. Their merchandise is contained in a number of earthen jars, such as are still used in the East for bringing water from the wells, and some leathern bottles. Among the jars and bottles, rolling upon the stony floor, regardless of the crowd and cold, often in danger but never hurt, play half a dozen halfnaked children, their brown bodies, jetty eyes, and thick black hair attesting the blood of Israel. Sometimes, from under the wimples, the mothers look up, and in the vernacular modestly bespeak their trade in the bottles of "honey of grapes," in the jars "strong drink." Their entreaties are usually lost in the general uproar, and they fare illy against the many competitors; brawny fellows with bare legs, dirty tunics, and long beards, going about with bottles lashed to their backs, and shouting "Honey of wine! Grapes of EnGedi!" When a customer halts one of them, round comes the bottle, and, upon lifting the thumb from the nozzle, out into the ready cup gushes the deep-red blood of the luscious berry.

Scarcely less blatant are the dealers in birds—doves, ducks, and frequently the singing bulbul, or nightingale, most frequently pigeons; and buyers, receiving them from the nets, seldom fail to think of the perilous life of the catchers, bold climbers of the cliffs; now hanging with hand and foot to the face of the crag, now swinging in a basket far down the mountain fissure.

Blent with peddlers of jewelry—sharp men cloaked in scarlet and blue, top-heavy under prodigious white turbans, and fully conscious of the power there is in the lustre of a ribbon and the incisive gleam of gold, whether in bracelet or necklace, or in rings for the finger or the nose—and with peddlers of household utensils, and with dealers in wearing-apparel, and with retailers of unguents for anointing the person, and with hucksters of all articles, fanciful as well as of need, hither and thither, tugging at halters and ropes, now screaming, now coaxing, toil the venders of animals—donkeys, horses, calves, sheep, bleating kids, and awkward camels; animals of every kind except the out-lawed swine, All these are there; not singly, as described, but many times repeated; not in one place, but everywhere in the market.

Turning from this scene in the lane and court, this glance at the sellers and their commodities, the reader has need to give attention, in the next place, to visitors and buyers, for which the best studies will be found outside the gates, where the spectacle is quite as varied and animated; indeed, it may be more so, for there are superadded the effects of tent, booth, and sook, greater space, larger crowd, and more unqualified freedom, and the glory of the Eastern sunshine.

Let us take our stand by the gate, just out of the edge of the currents—one flowing in, the other out—and use our eyes and ears awhile. In good time! Here comes two men of a most note-worthy class.

"Gods! How cold it is!" says one of them, a powerful figure in armor; on his head a brazen helmet, on his body a shining breastplate and skirts of mail. "How cold it is! Dost thou remember, my Caius, that vault in the Comitium at home which the flamens say is the entrance to the lower world? By Pluto! I could stand there this morning, long enough at least to get warm again!"

The party addressed dropped the hood of his military cloak, leaving bare his head and face, and replied, with an ironic smile, "The helmets of the legions which conquered Mark Antony were full of Gallic snow; but thou—ah, my poor friend!—thou hast just come from Egypt, bringing its summer in thy blood."

And with the last word they disappear through the entrance. Though they had been silent, the armor and the sturdy steps would have published them Roman soldiers.

From the throng a Jew comes next, meagre of frame, round-shouldered, and wearing a coarse brown robe; over his eyes and face, and down his back, hangs a mat of long uncombed hair. He is alone. Those who meet him laugh, if they do not worse; for he is a Nazarite, one of a despised sect which rejects the books of Moses, devotes itself to abhorred vows, and goes unshorn while the vows endure.

As we watch his retiring figure, suddenly there is a commotion in the crowd, a parting quickly to the right and left, with exclamations sharp and decisive. Then the cause comes—a man, Hebrew in feature and dress. The mantle of snow-white linen, held to his head by cords of yellow silk, flows free over his shoulders; his robe is richly embroidered; a red sash with fringes of gold wraps his waist several times. His demeanor is calm; he even smiles upon those who, with such rude haste, make room for him. A leper? No, he is only a Samaritan. The shrinking crowd is asked, would say he is a mongrel—an Assyrian—whose touch is the robe of pollution; from whom, consequently, an Israelite, though dying, might not accept life. In fact, the feud is not of blood. When David set his throne here on Mount Zion, with only Judah to support him, the ten tribes betook themselves to Shechem, a city much older and, at that date, infinitely richer in holy memories. The final union of the tribes did not settle the dispute thus begun. The Samaritans clung to their tabernacle on Gerizim, and, while maintaining its superior sanctity, laughed at the irate doctors in Jerusalem. Time brought no assuagement of the hate. Under Herod, conversion to the faith was open to all the world except the Samaritans; they alone were absolutely and forever shut out from communion with Jews.

As the Samaritan goes under the arch of the gate, out come three men so unlike all whom we have yet seen that they fix our gaze, whether we will or not. They are of unusual stature and immense brawn; their eyes are blue, and so fair is their complexion that the blood shines through the skin like blue pencilling; their hair is light and short; their heads, small and round, rest squarely upon necks columnar as the trunks of trees. Woollen tunics, open at the breast, sleeveless and loosely girt, drape their bodies, leaving bare arms and legs of such development that they at once suggest the arena; and when thereto we add their careless, confident, insolent manner, we cease to wonder that the people give them way, and stop after they have passed to look at them again. They are gladiators—wrestlers, runners, boxers, swordsmen; professionals unknown in Judea before the coming of the Roman; fellows who, what time they are not in training, may be seen strolling through the king's gardens or sitting with the guards at the palace gates; or possibly they are visitors from Caesarea, Sebaste, or Jericho; in which Herod, more Greek than Jew, and with all a Roman's love of games and bloody spectacles, has built vast theatres, and now keeps schools of fighting men, drawn, as is the custom, from the Gallic provinces or the Slavic tribes on the Danube.

"By Bacchus!" says one of them, drawing his clenched hand to his shoulder, "their skulls are not thicker than egg-shells."

The brutal look which goes with the gesture disgusts us, and we turn happily to something more pleasant.

Opposite us is a fruit-stand. The proprietor has a bald head, a long face, and a nose like the beak of a hawk. He sits upon a carpet spread upon the dust; the wall is at his back; overhead hangs a scant curtain; around him, within hand's reach and arranged upon little stools, lie osier boxes full of almonds, grapes, figs and pomegranates. To him now comes one at whom we cannot help looking, though for another reason than that which fixed our eyes upon the gladiators: he is really beautiful—a beautiful Greek. Around his temples, holding the waving hair, is a crown of myrtle, to which still cling the pale flowers and half ripe berries. His tunic, scarlet in color, is of the softest woollen fabric; below the girdle of buff leather, which is clasped in front by a fantastic device of shining gold, the skirt drops to the knee in folds heavy with embroidery of the same royal metal; a scarf, also woollen, and of mixed white and yellow, crosses his throat and falls trailing at his back; his arms and legs, where exposed, are white as ivory, and of the polish impossible except by perfect treatment with bath, oil, brushes, and pincers.

The dealer, keeping his seat, bends forward, and throws his hands up until they meet in front of him, palm downwards and fingers extended.

"What hast thou, this morning, O son of Paphos?" says the young Greek, looking at the boxes rather than at the Cypriote. "I am hungry. What hast thou for breakfast?"

"Fruits from the Pedius—genuine—such as the singers of Antioch take of mornings to restore the waste of their voices," the dealer answers, in a querulous nasal tone.

"A fig, but not one of the best, for the singers of Antioch!" says the Greek. "Thou art a worshipper of Aphrodite, and so am I, as the myrtle I wear proves; therefore I tell thee their voices have the chill of a Caspian wind. Seest thou this girdle?—a gift of the mighty Salome—"

"The king's sister!" exclaims the Cypriote, with another salaam.

"And of royal taste and divine judgment. And why not? She is more Greek than the king. But—my breakfast! Here is thy money—red coppers of Cyprus. Give me the grapes, and—"

"Wilt thou not take the dates also?"

"No, I am not an Arab."

"Nor figs?"

"That would be to make me a Jew. No, nothing but the grapes. Never waters mixed so sweetly as the blood of the Greek and the blood of the grape."

The singer in the grimed and seething market, with all his airs of the court, is a vision not easily shut out of mind by such as see him, as if for the purpose, however, a person follows him challenging all our wonder. He comes up the road slowly, his face towards the ground; at intervals he stops, crosses his hands upon his breast, lengthens his countenance, and turns his eye towards heaven, as if about to break into prayer. Nowhere, except in Jerusalem, can such a character be found. On his forehead, attached to the band which keeps the mantle in place, projects a leathern case, square in form; another similar case is tied by a thong to the left arm; the borders of his robe are decorated with deep fringe; and by such signs—the phylacteries, the enlarged borders of the garment, and the savor of intense holiness pervading the whole man—we know him to be a Pharisee, one of an organization (in religion a sect, in politics a party) whose bigotry and power will shortly bring the world to grief.

The densest of the throng outside the gate covers the road leading off to Joppa. Turning from the Pharisee, we are attracted by some parties who, as subjects of study, opportunely separate themselves from the motley crowd. First among them a man of very noble appearance—clear, healthful complexion; bright black eyes; beard long and flowing, and rich with unguents; apparel well fitting, costly, and suitable for the season. He carries a staff, and wears suspended by a cord from his neck, a large golden seal. Several servants attend him, some of them with short swords stuck through their sashes; when they address him, it is with the utmost deference. The rest of the party consists of two Arabs of the pure desert stock; thin, wiry men, deeply bronzed, and with hollow cheeks, and eyes of almost evil brightness; on their heads red *tarbooshes;* over their *abas,* and wrapping the left shoulder and the body so as to leave the right arm free, brown woollen *haicks* or blankets. There is loud chaffering; for the Arabs are leading horses and trying to sell them; and, in their eagerness, they speak in high, shrill voices. The courtly person leaves the talking mostly to his servants; occasionally he answers with much dignity; directly, seeing the Cypriote, he stops and buys some figs. And when the whole party has passed the portal, close after the Pharisee, we betake ourselves to the dealer in fruits, he will tell, with a wonderful salaam, that the stranger is a Jew, one of the princes of the city, who has travelled, and learned the difference between the common grapes of Syria and those of Cyprus, so surpassingly rich with the dews of the sea.

And so, till towards noon, sometimes later, the steady currents of business habitually flow in and out of the Joppa Gate, carrying with them every variety of character; including representatives of all the tribes of Israel, all the sects among whom the ancient faith has been parcelled and refined away, all the religious and social divisions, all the adventurous rabble who, as children of art and ministers of pleasure, riot in the prodigalities of Herod, and all the peoples of note at any time compassed by the Caesars and their predecessors, especially those dwelling within the circuit of the Mediterranean.

In other words, Jerusalem, rich in sacred history, richer in connection with sacred prophecies—the Jerusalem of Solomon, in which silver was as stones, and cedars as the sycamores of the vale—has come to be but a copy of Rome, a centre of unholy practices, a seat of pagan power. A Jewish king one day put on priestly garments, and went into the Holy of Holies of the first temple to offer incense, and he came out a leper; but in the time of which we are reading, Pompey entered Herod's temple and the same Holy of Holies, and came out without harm, finding but an empty chamber, and of God not a sign.

This was Jerusalem as it appeared on the eve of the crossing of "history's bridge" from the Old to the New Testament; and this was the Jerusalem to which the Wise Men came on the eve of that momentous event, saying to Herod the Great, "Where is he that is born King of the Jews? for we saw his star in the east, and are come to worship him" (Matt. 2:2).*

✛

BROTHERHOOD

(Interpretation)

WILLIAM L. Stidger, for eighteen years head of the Department of Homiletics in the Boston University School of Theology and minister of the Church of All Na-

* Abridged from *Ben Hur, A Tale of the Christ* by Lew Wallace, pp. 34-43. Published by Harper & Brothers. Used by special permission of the publisher.

tions in Boston, was widely known as a radio preacher, columnist, world traveler, and author of both prose and poetry.

His *I Saw God Wash the World* is treasured by every lover of beauty in thought expressed in challenging verse; and his several volumes of *Sermon Nuggets in Stories* have found their way into the libraries of many preachers. Dr. Stidger firmly believed that "a story oft catches him whom a sermon misses"; therefore, in his *Sermon Nuggets in Stories* he has, with the skill of a trained reporter, passed on to the reader brief, effective stories about things he has heard and seen in his wide experience and travel in America and around the world. Businessmen as well as ministers find challenge and sales material in his books. Clay Doss, vice president and sales manager of Nash Motors, Detroit, says of one of these books of short stories: "I have used hundreds of the Stidger stories in my pep talks to my sales staff. They thrill an audience, carry a point with power, and lift an ordinary speech to higher levels. I listen to preachers frequently and I always feel that the average minister should know about these Fort Knox treasuries of hidden gold."

While many people know the name of William L. Stidger from his poetry and prose writings, few know of his contribution to the field of Christian hymnody. This hymn, "Brotherhood," was written in 1939 and set to music by Frank R. White. It should be sung "with spirit," as indicated by its author on the accompanying music score. It provides a constant challenge to all those who believe that human brotherhood is one of the greatest gifts that God can bestow upon His earthly family, and that the races of men are progressing, ever more surely, toward that epoch in human history when all will live in peace.

One cannot sing the two verses of this present-day hymn-poem without being conscious that "true brotherhood is comradeship of heart and soul and life and lip" between all the races and children of men. Such comradeship makes many demands upon us and offers us high ideals of conduct which can be expressed in the pattern of our daily life. The task of achieving human brotherhood is one to which every man and woman can and should make his own individual contribution. A little thoughtfulness, a little kindness, a little courtesy, a little love expressed through daily contacts by each one of us brings the goal of human brotherhood nearer and nearer as the years go by.

✣

HOW GENTLE GOD'S COMMANDS

(Interpretation)

PHILIP DODDRIDGE, the author of this devotional hymn, was born in 1702 in London, and died in 1751 in Lisbon, Portugal. His father was a devout layman of the Independent Church. As a child young Doddridge displayed unusual abilities, so much so that the Duchess of Bedford offered to educate him at either Cambridge or Oxford. He declined, however, preferring to remain among the Dissenters. His education for the ministry was taken at the non-Conformist Seminary at Kibworth, and there he first became a pastor. During the years that followed he served as min-

Brotherhood

William L. Stidger

Frank R. White

How Gentle God's Commands

Dennis S. M.

PHILIP DODDRIDGE, 1702-1751

Arr. from J. G. NAGELI, 1768-1836
by LOWELL MASON, 1792-1872

1. How gen - tle God's com-mands, How kind His pre - cepts are!
2. While Prov - i - dence sup - ports, Let saints se - cure - ly dwell;
3. Why should this an - xious load Press down your wea - ry mind?
4. His good - ness stands ap-proved, Down to the pres - ent day;

Come, cast your bur-dens on the Lord, And trust His con-stant care.
That hand, which bears all na - ture up, Shall guide His chil-dren well.
Haste to your heavenly Fa-ther's throne, And sweet re - freshment find.
I'll drop my bur - den at His feet, And bear a song a - way. A-men.

ister for several Presbyterian churches, but finally accepted a call to become the pastor of the Independent Church at Northampton.

Philip Doddridge was an outstanding author of both prose and poetry. Several of his finest poems still survive in church hymnals. "How Gentle God's Commands" is a fine illustration of the poet's faith in, and devotion to, the God he served so faithfully during his brief life span.

The four stanzas offer praise to God whose commands are gentle and whose precepts are kind. It is an appeal to all men to "cast your burdens on the Lord" and to trust implicitly His constant care. From the beginning of time God's goodness to the children of men has never failed.

The melody "Dennis" was arranged from J. G. Nageli (1768-1836) by Lowell Mason (1792-1872).

✛

LORD, WHILE FOR ALL MANKIND WE PRAY

(Interpretation)

THIS hymn, written by an Englishman, Dr. John Reynell Wreford (1800-1881), was included in his *Lays of Loyalty* composed in honor of Queen Victoria's accession to

Lord, While for All Mankind We Pray

ST. ANNE. C.M.

JOHN R. WREFORD, 1837

WILLIAM CROFT, 1708

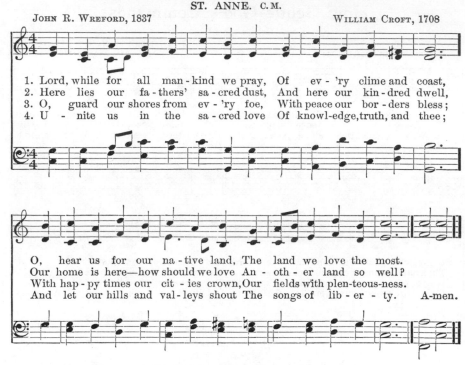

1. Lord, while for all man-kind we pray, Of ev-'ry clime and coast,
2. Here lies our fa-thers' sa-cred dust, And here our kin-dred dwell,
3. O, guard our shores from ev-'ry foe, With peace our bor-ders bless;
4. U-nite us in the sa-cred love Of knowl-edge, truth, and thee;

O, hear us for our na-tive land, The land we love the most.
Our home is here—how should we love An-oth-er land so well?
With hap-py times our cit-ies crown, Our fields with plen-teous-ness.
And let our hills and val-leys shout The songs of lib-er-ty.   A-men.

5 Lord of the nations, thus to thee
Our country we commend;
Be thou her refuge and her trust,
Her everlasting Friend.

the English throne in 1837. Nevertheless, it has found an esteemed place in many of the church hymnals published in America.

Dr. Wreford was educated at Manchester College in York and in 1826 became co-pastor of the Unitarian New Meeting in Birmingham, England. He wrote many books on theology and church history as well as several volumes of poetry, largely devotional. After several years as co-pastor of the New Meeting, Dr. Wreford was forced to resign due to serious voice difficulty. He did not belong to the modern school of Unitarians, but regarded himself, instead, as affiliated with the English Presbyterians, who regularly repudiated sectarian names and distinctions of a doctrinal nature.

The tune "St. Anne" to which this hymn is most frequently sung was composed in 1708 by William Croft.

✛

O LORD OF HEAVEN AND EARTH AND SEA

(Interpretation)

CHRISTOPHER WORDSWORTH (1807-1885) was a nephew of England's distinguished poet, William Wordsworth. He graduated with honors from Trinity College at Cambridge. In college he won a prize not only for scholarship, but also for athletics.

While he was still under thirty years of age he became headmaster of Harrow School, and later Canon of Westminster. He also served for fifteen years as Bishop of Lincoln.

Christopher Wordsworth was a prodigious worker, and among other things undertook the monumental task of writing a commentary on the entire Bible. He also arranged a series of hymns which were later published under the title *The Holy*

O Lord of Heaven and Earth and Sea

First Tune.   ALMSGIVING.   8,8,8,4

Christopher Wordsworth, 1863   John B. Dykes, 1875

1. O Lord of heav'n and earth and sea, To thee all
2. For peace-ful homes and health-ful days, For all the
3. We lose what on our-selves we spend; We have, as
4. To thee from whom we all de-rive Our life, our

praise and glo - ry be; How shall we show our
bless - ings earth dis - plays, We owe thee thank - ful -
treas - ure with - out end, What - ev - er, Lord, to
gifts, our power to give, O, may we ev - er

love to thee, Who giv - est all?
ness and praise, Who giv - est all.
thee we lend, Who giv - est all.
to thee live, Who giv - est all!   A - men.

Year. Many of these were from his own pen, and appear in several present-day church hymnals.

"O Lord of Heaven and Earth and Sea" was written in 1863. It is a song of praise to God for the manifestations of His power, love, and glory as reflected in earth, and sky, and sea. Thanksgiving also for "homes and healthful days" and "for all the blessings earth displays" is offered to God "who givest all."

The axiom that "we lose what on ourselves we spend" and keep what in God's name "we lend" is emphasized in the third stanza, while the fourth stanza acknowledges that all we have and are, "our life, our gifts, our power to give," are from the hand of the Eternal God "who givest all."

"Almsgiving," the melody to which this hymn is sung, was composed in 1865 by John B. Dykes.

✛

O GOD OF TRUTH, WHOSE LIVING WORD

(Interpretation)

THE nineteenth century was rich in the production of English hymns. Among those composed was this one from the pen of Thomas Hughes (1823-1896). Not a great

O God of Truth, Whose Living Word

FIRST TUNE.   ST. STEPHEN.   C. M.

THOMAS HUGHES, 1859   WILLIAM JONES, 1789

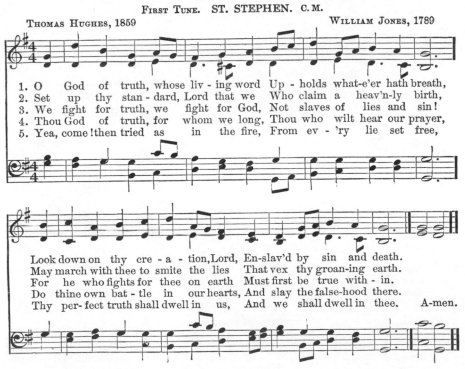

1. O   God   of   truth, whose liv - ing word   Up - holds what-e'er hath breath,
2. Set   up   thy stan - dard, Lord that we   Who claim a   heav'n-ly   birth,
3. We fight for truth, we   fight for God, Not slaves of   lies and sin!
4. Thou God of   truth, for   whom we long, Thou who wilt hear our prayer,
5. Yea, come! then tried as   in   the fire, From ev - 'ry   lie set free,

Look down on thy cre - a - tion, Lord, En-slav'd by sin and death.
May march with thee to smite the lies That vex thy groan-ing earth.
For   he who fights for thee on earth Must first be true with - in.
Do thine own bat - tle in   our hearts, And slay the false-hood there.
Thy per- fect truth shall dwell in   us, And we shall dwell in thee.   A-men.

deal is known of his life, but this hymn written in 1859 bears its own testimony concerning the spirit of the man who wrote it. Its five brief stanzas bear witness to the "God of truth, Whose Living Word" lives on from age to age.

The first stanza emphasizes the living word of God and recalls to our minds the first and second stanzas of the Gospel according to St. John:

"In the beginning was the Word, and the Word was with God, and the Word was God. The same was in the beginning with God."

The second stanza appeals to the Lord of Heaven to set up the standard for all those who claim "heav'nly birth" that they may march forward to "smite the lies that vex thy groaning earth."

The third stanza stresses the fact that "we fight for truth" and are "not slaves of lies and sin." Those who fight for God on earth know that they "must first be true within."

The fourth stanza appeals to the Heavenly Father to hear the prayer of His children on earth, that He might help them to win the battle in their own hearts and to "slay the falsehood there."

The last stanza summarizes the theme of this great hymn, for we know that if God's "perfect truth shall dwell in us," we in turn "shall dwell in thee."

This hymn is sung to the tune of "St. Stephen," composed in 1789 by William Jones, as well as to the tune of "Marlow," written in 1718 by John Chetham.

✜

THE GOD THAT TO THE FATHERS

(Interpretation)

THE Hebrew people believed that all music possessed magic power. Had not the prophet Samuel, when he anointed Saul to be king, said: "It shall come to pass . . . that thou shalt meet a company of prophets coming down from the high place with a psaltery, and a tabret, and a pipe, and a harp, before them; and they shall prophesy. And the spirit of the Lord will come upon thee, and thou shalt prophesy with them, and shalt be turned into another man." Later when an "evil spirit from God was upon Saul . . . David took an harp, and played with his hand: so Saul was refreshed, and was well, and the evil spirit departed from him" (I Sam. 10:5-6, 16:23).

This hymn, the three stanzas of which stress social progress, was composed by Minot J. Savage. The melody to which it is sung was written by Lewis M. Isaacs.

The first stanza emphasizes the continuing presence of the God of their fathers who remains with the children of Israel today, and urges all people to look, not backward to the twilight, but forward to the dawning of a new day.

The second stanza sings of the far-off vision which the forebears of the Jewish people had seen, and urges us today to glory in the dream beginning to come true as the "Golden Age" of universal brotherhood draws near.

The third stanza urges us to rejoice "in God's free spirit, the ever-broad'ning ray of truth," leading and guiding men forward to the Golden Age. It stresses the importance of faithful following of God's commands, like the pioneers of years gone by, until God's work of redeeming the human race shall be fully accomplished.

The God that to the Fathers

Minot J. Savage

Lewis M. Isaacs

1. The God that to the fa - thers Re-vealed His ho - ly will
2. 'Twas but far off, in vi - sion, The fa-thers' eyes could see
3. We trust in God's free spir - it, The ev - er broad'ning ray

Has not the world for - sak - en; He's with the chil-dren still.
The glo - ry of the king - dom, The bet - ter time to be;
Of truth, that shines to guide us A - long our for - ward way,

Then en - vy not the twi - light That glimmered on their way;
To - day, we see ful-fill - ing The dream they dreamt of yore,
Let us to-day be faith - ful, As were the pi - o - neers,

Look up and see the dawn - ing That broad-ens in - to day.
While near - er draws and near - er, The Gold - en Age in store.
Till lo, their work complet - ed, The Gold - en Age ap - pears.

* From *Union Hymnal,* No. 234. Copyright, 1932, by the Central Conference of American Rabbis. Used by special permission of the publisher.

O GOD, ABOVE THE DRIFTING YEARS

(Interpretation)

JOHN WRIGHT BUCKHAM wrote this hymn in 1916 for the Semicentenary of the Pacific School of Religion.

The first stanza appeals to the God who reigns "above the drifting years." It recognizes the truth that "the shrines which our fathers founded stand"; and it acknowledges the fact that "where the higher gain appears" we can trace the "working of God's hand."

The second stanza recalls the tireless toil and prayers of all those saints and sages of the past whose life and work have yielded a rich harvest of lasting good.

O God, Above the Drifting Years

DUKE STREET. L. M.

JOHN WRIGHT BUCKHAM, 1916   JOHN HATTON, –1793

1. O God, a - bove the drift - ing years, The shrines our
2. From out their tire - less prayer and toil E - merge the
3. The torch to their de - vo - tion lent, Light - ens the
4. Fill thou our hearts with faith like theirs, Who served the

fa - thers found - ed stand, And where the high - er
gifts that time has proved, And seed laid deep in
dark that round us lies; Help us to pass it
days they could not see; And give us grace, through

gain ap - pears, We trace the work - ing of thy hand.
sa - cred soil Yields har - vests rich in last - ing good.
on un - spent, Un - til the dawn lights up the skies.
am - pler years, To build the King - dom yet to be. A-men.

* Words written for the Semicentenary of the Pacific School of Religion and used by special permission of Miss Margaret Buckham.

The third stanza acknowledges the truth that the devotion of our fathers has lighted the darkness of the world and cast its glow upon our present age.

The fourth stanza is a prayer that we may be filled with faith like that of the saints of old, "who served the days they could not see" and that we may be given the grace "to build the Kingdom yet to be."

The melody "Duke Street" to which this hymn is sung was written in 1793 by John Hatton.

APPENDIX

ORIGIN AND CONTENT OF THE OLD TESTAMENT

Abridged from

Introduction to the Old Testament

By Robert H. Pfeiffer*

THE Old Testament owes its origin primarily to the religious aspiration of the Jews. . . . Its publication, which included the canons of the Pentateuch (400 B.C.), the Prophets (200 B.C.), and Writings (A.D. 90), resulted from the religious needs of the Jews. For the Jewish religion developed gradually through centuries of time from a purely national worship of a tribal God into a monotheistic religion with universal appeal.** . . . In regarding all parts of the Old Testament as written by inspired prophets and therefore divinely revealed, Judaism imparted to many pages of the Old Testament a profoundly religious character originally quite alien. Probably the most conspicuous instance of this trend is the devotional use of the Song of Songs.

"God, who at sundry times and in divers manners spake in time past unto the fathers by the prophets" (Hebr. 1:1), has revealed his character and his requirements in the pages of the Old Testament. By subtly ingenuous interpretation and by allegorizing the literal meaning of the text, the deepest religious truths can be detected in the most secular words of the Scriptures, the ultimate norm of faith and morals.†

The authority of the Old Testament for orthodox Christianity is scarcely less sweeping than for Judaism. Jesus did not come to abrogate the Law and the Prophets but to fulfill them (Matt. 5:17-19). To a scribe inquiring after the way to eternal life he enjoined obedience to the summary of the Law (Deut. 6:5 and Lev. 19:18), saying, "This do and thou shalt live" (Luke 10:25-28). However, Jesus did not regard the Scriptures as the complete and final revelation of God's will. In some instances, God adapted his requirements to the hardness of the human heart, and thus it happens that the Law of Moses which permits divorce is contrary to the law of God forbidding it (Mark 10:2-12, Matt. 19:3-9).

The Apostle Paul, however, took a step that Jesus had not taken: he forsook Judaism and definitely founded a new religion, based on the doctrine that Christ, through his death and resurrection, had brought salvation to those who have faith. The mystical and sacramental conception of the person of Christ advocated by Paul

---

* *Introduction to the Old Testament* by Robert H. Pfeiffer. Copyright, 1941, by Harper & Brothers. Used by special permission of the publisher.

** G. F. Moore, Judaism, Vol. I, pp. 219-34.

† *Ibid.*, pp. 235-50, on the inspiration and authority of the Scriptures.

was bound to be anathema to Palestinian Jews and should logically have led to the complete rejection of the Hebrew Scriptures. But Paul never took this step; and the Old Testament (in the Greek version called the Septuagint) remained the Bible of the early Christian Church.

For the early Christians, however, the Prophets and Psalms were of far greater importance than the Law. To justify their own faith in Jesus the Messiah, and to convert the Jews to this faith, the first Christians had only one argument at their disposal (aside from the miracles of Jesus); namely, the promises of the Old Testament fulfilled in the life, death, and resurrection of Jesus. Such a line of reasoning, out of which the first Christian theology was developed, unquestionably antedated Paul's conversion (I Cor. 15:3) and may be traced back to the risen Jesus (Luke 24:25-27, 44).

After proving that the passion and glorification of Jesus were predicted in the Old Testament, the early Christians undertook to show that, in many incidents of Jesus' birth and earthly career, the Scriptures were fulfilled. The Gospels of Matthew and John particularly emphasize the fulfillment of prophecy in the life of the Master (Matt. 1:23; 2:6, 15, 18, 23; 3:3 [Mark 1:3; Luke 3:4-6; John 1:23]; 4:15 f.; 8:17; 12:17; 13:35; 21:5 [John 12:5]; 26:31 [Mark 14:27]; 27:9 f., 35 [John 19:24], etc.; John 2:17; 3:14; 6:31; 7:42; 12:14 f., 37-41; 13:18; 15:25; 17:12; 19:36 f., etc.). Mark and Luke, if only occasionally and without emphasis, see in the life of Jesus the fulfillment of prophecy (Mark 1:2 f.; 4:12; 14:27; 15:24, 29; 15:28 is an interpolated quotation of Luke 22:37; Luke 3:4; 4:21; 7:27; 20:17; 23:35; cf. 24:25). Thus it cannot be gainsaid that the Old Testament contributed something to the biographical accounts of Jesus.

For us moderns the Old Testament is religiously significant in three ways. First of all, as inspired scripture in Church and Synagogue, it continues to be a norm of faith and conduct, a guide for the perplexed, and a source of edification for both congregations and individuals. Secondly, the religious teaching of the Old Testament is the ultimate source of the basic doctrines of Christianity as well as of Judaism. The Christian Church is indebted to the Old Testament for its faith in a unique God— the Creator of the world and the Father in heaven; for the assurance that God has revealed himself in chosen men (prophecy) and in sacred books (canonicity); for the conviction that the moral law originates in the divine mind and will; for the hope in the Kingdom of God on this earth and in the invisible world; and for the assurance that in his mercy God has provided atonement for human sin, that true repentance brings forgiveness; and that salvation is offered to all human beings. In the third place, the Old Testament is a unique record of religious progress from a religion of observance national in scope to a religion in spirit and in truth whose temple "shall be called a house of prayer for all peoples " (Is. 56:7).

THE PENTATEUCH

The first five books of the Old Testament (Gen., Ex., Lev., Num., and Deut.) were called, after their canonization about 400 B.C., "the Law of Moses" (II Chron. 23:18; 30:16; cf. 33:8) or "the book (*sepher*) of Moses" (35:12; cf. 25:4). Later, one simply said "the Law" (Hebrew *Torah*, Greek *nomos*); this term is so used by the grandson of Ben Sira, in his preface to the translation of Ecclesiasticus, and also in the New Testament (e.g., Luke 10:26), Philo of Alexandria and Flavius Josephus. The word "Pentateuch" (from the Greek *pente,* five; *teuchos,* scroll) is first found in Origen's commentary on John 4:25 ("the pentateuchal book"), but it was probably used by the Hellenistic Jews of Alexandria during the first century, as the equivalent of the Talmudic expression "the five fifths of the Law" (meaning the Pentateuch written in five volumes; when written on one scroll, it is called "the Book of the Law").

The poetry contained in the Pentateuch spans the whole period between 1200-400 B.C., but does not contain the three great masterpieces of classical Hebrew poetry (Judg. 5; II Sam. 1:19-27; Nah. 1:10-3:19). The authors of the ancient narrative sources of the Pentateuch . . . may be the authors of the poetic divine oracles, blessings, and curses, which are an integral part of their stories; but in all probability they quoted the longer poems from anthologies or from the mouth of bards (Num. 21:27). The names of two ancient anthologies are preserved, *The Book of the Wars of Jehovah* (Num. 21:14) and *The Book of the Upright* or, . . . *The Book of Poetry* (Josh. 10:13; II Sam. 1:18).

The Pentateuch is the final result of the amalgamation of five narrative sources . . . besides a number of poems and legal codes. The editorial work by which these diverse elements were combined in a single book with each unit previously subjected to revision and addition, began about 650 B.C., if not earlier, and ended about 400 B.C., when the Pentateuch was issued to the Jews in their widely scattered settlements as a definite edition of the Law of Moses.

HISTORICAL BOOKS

The sixth of the nine volumes comprising the legal and historical corpus from Genesis to Kings is called "Joshua" not after the name of its author but after that of the hero whose achievements it relates. Describing the vicissitudes of the Israelites, from the death of Moses to that of Joshua, it deals with the invasion and conquest of Canaan (1-12) and the distribution of territory among the various tribes (13-24).

The Book of Judges is a history of the period between Joshua and Samuel. Its title, which occurs already in Origen and in the Talmud . . . is taken from the name of the leaders whose stories it relates. The Hebrew word, translated "judges" (*shōphetîm*), has a wider meaning than in English. . . . It does not refer to arbitrators or to the presiding officers of a court of justice (as in 11:27), but to the men performing a twofold function. First they heroically delivered their people from the oppression of their enemies (2:16, 18; cf. I Sam. 8:20; Neh. 9:27), then they ruled dictatorially until their death without, however, founding a dynasty, except for Gideon (9:2).

The two Books of Samuel, like the two Books of Kings, were originally in Hebrew a single volume, as we know from the Talmud. . . . The division into two books was introduced in the Greek version . . . because the Greek, in which vowels are written, required one and three-quarters more space than the Hebrew, in which no vowels were used until after A.D. 600. Thus one large scroll sufficed in the Hebrew, while two were required for the Greek. The division was introduced into the Hebrew text for the first time in Daniel Bomberg's first edition of the Hebrew

Bible (Venice, 1516-1517) and thereafter became current. In the Greek and Latin Bibles, the four Books of Samuel and Kings are called I, II, III, IV "Kingdoms" ("Kings" was preferred by Jerome), respectively.

The two Books of Kings, like the two Books of Samuel . . . were originally, in the Hebrew, a single volume. They relate the history of Israel from the last days of David (about 973 B.C.) to the release of Jehoiachin from his Babylonian prison in 561 B.C.

This history is divided into three main parts: 1. Accession and reign of Solomon (I 1-11). 2. Division of the kingdom (I 12:1-24) and the reigns of the kings of Israel and Judah to the end of the Northern Kingdom (I 12:25—II 17:6), with an appendix on the mixed race and religion of North Israel (the later Samaritans) after 722 B.C. (II 17:7-41). 3. History of the kings of Judah from 722 to 561 B.C. (II 18-25).

PROPHETIC WRITINGS

Isaiah: Since J. C. Doederlein published his commentary on this book (*Esaias.* 1775; 2nd ed., 1780), it is generally recognized that it comprises two distinct works. The first is the "Book of Isaiah" (Is. 1-39), the second, now called the "Second Isaiah" (or Deutero-Isaiah), is an anonymous work written about 550 B.C. or later (Is. 40-66). The second accidentally became part of the volume of Isaiah when the prophetic oracles extant about 200 B.C. were issued in four volumes (Is., Jer., Ez., and "The Twelve" [Minor Prophets]).

This comprehensive edition of prophetic writings, called "The Latter Prophets," was copied on four scrolls of papyrus almost equal in length: only two consist of the works of individual prophets (Jer. and Ez.), with later additions; the others are anthologies. Anonymous prophecies in Is. 40-66 filled up the space left on the first scroll after the Book of Isaiah was copied. Owing to their anonymity and to the fact that Is. 1:1 was naturally taken to be the title of the complete scroll (cf. Luke 4:17), the oracles of Is. 40-66 were attributed to Isaiah despite mention of Cyrus king of Persia (Is. 44:28; 45:1), who conquered Babylon two centuries after Isaiah began his prophetic ministry.

Jeremiah: The Book of Jeremiah is divided into three parts (1-25; 26-45; 46-51) and ends with a historical appendix in ch. 52. It may be summarized as follows:

      I. The words of Jeremiah (1:25)
      II. The Biography of Jeremiah (26-45)
      III. The Oracles against Foreign Nations (46-51)
      IV. Historical Appendix (52)

The public ministry of Jeremiah, like that of Isaiah a century before (740-700), covered four dramatic decades (626-586) which were epoch-making in the political history of Judah. As in the case of Isaiah, Jeremiah's words and deeds are so intimately related to the vicissitudes of Judah and to the international political upheavals that without a knowledge of the historical background they would be incomprehensible.

Ezekiel: Superficially the Book of Ezekiel resembles, in general structure, the Book of Isaiah. Both are divided into three main parts: oracles against Judah and Israel

(Is. 1-12; Ez. 1-24). oracles against foreign nations (Is. 13-27; Ez. 25-32), oracles on the future glory of Israel (Is. 28-66; Ez. 33-48). On closer examination, however, it will be noted that, while Isaiah is an anthology of writings of diverse character and date grouped more or less arbitrarily, Ezekiel is more homogeneous and exhibits a chronological arrangement.

The Book of the Minor Prophets (Hosea, Joel, Amos, Obadiah, Jonah, Micah, Nahum, Habakkuk, Zephaniah, Haggai, Zechariah, and Malachi) is sometimes referred to as "the Book of the Twelve," and covers the period from 785 to 460 B.C.

Hosea: The prophet Hosea, son of Beeri, was called to the prophetic ministry "in the days of Jeroboam II, the son of Joash king of Israel (785-744 B.C.) . . . which makes Hosea a predecessor of Isaiah. . . . His first oracle (1:4) predicted divine punishment of Jehu's bloody deeds on the plain of Jezreel (II Kings 10:11), and Jehu's dynasty actually met its doom in the revolution of Shallum in 744 B.C.

Hosea was a Northern Israelite, and possibly a member of a priestly family like Jeremiah, as B. Duhm has suggested. He lived in the Northern Kingdom . . . and often refers to localities within its borders. . . . He addressed his oracles to "Ephraim" or "Israel" (i.e., the Northern Kingdom); references in his book to the kingdom of Judah are interpolations of Judean editors, who adapted the book for Southern readers.

Joel: Nothing is known about Joel, son of Pethuel, probably the last Hebrew prophet who attached his name to his writing. The little book bearing his name is divided into two parts: 1:1-2:27, describing the divine deliverance, after public repentance, from a visitation of locusts followed by a famine; 2:28-3:21 (H. 3-4), a vision of the outpouring of the divine spirit, of the final judgment over the heathen and of the millennium.

Amos: About 750 B.C. Amos lived in Tekoa, a mountainous village situated in the wilderness of Judah, two hours' march south of Bethlehem. He earned a meager livelihood by pasturing sheep. The barren steppe in that region is chiefly suited to pasture sheep and goats, although a limited amount of grain, grapes, and figs was also raised in favored spots.

It was while pasturing his sheep near Tekoa that Amos received the divine call to go forth and prophesy in the Northern Kingdom, even though he was not at that time a prophet and never became a member of the prophetic fraternity.

The Book of Amos is divided into three parts. The first section . . . consists of a series of brief oracles against seven nations, followed by a longer one against Israel. . . . The middle part of the book is a collection of brief addresses denouncing Israel. Three begin with "Hear this word," others with "Woe unto you that . . ." The third part of the book is a series of visions, interrupted by a biographical account of the sudden end of the prophet's public career at Bethel, and by an oracle against wealthy merchants.

Obadiah: Before the fall of Jerusalem in 586 B.C., the attitude of Judeans toward the Edomites was not unfriendly. But when, after the fall of Jerusalem, many Judeans sought temporary refuge in Edom they were not welcomed; for the Edomites were allied to Nebuchadnezzar.

The oracle of Obadiah consists of a denunciation of Edom (1:14; 15b) and of a prediction of the coming "Day of the Lord" (15a; 16:21); each main division has two subdivisions (1-9, 10-14; 16-18, 19-21); 15b is the conclusion of the first part and 15a the title of the second part.

Both parts of the book are intensely nationalistic. The first voices exultation for the plight of an unfriendly neighbor, the second a hope that he may be completely wiped off the face of the earth. This passionate cry for vengeance is diametrically opposed in spirit to the national self-sacrifice for the benefit of mankind, envisioned in one of the servant poems of the Second Isaiah (Is. 53).

Jonah: Unlike the rest of the Book of the Twelve, the Book of Jonah is not a prophetic oracle, but a story about a prophet, Jonah, son of Amittai. According to II Kings 14:25, Jonah, a Zebulonite prophet from Gathhepher, predicted the conquests of Jeroboam II; the hero of the story is unquestionably intended as that ancient prophet.

The story of Jonah is neither an account of actual happenings nor an allegory of the destiny of Israel or of the Messiah (cf. Matt: 12:40): it is fiction—a short story with a moral—like the Book of Ruth, which is much less fantastic, or the stories about Daniel. Whether the hero was identified with an actual prophet living in the time of Jeroboam II, which is not to be excluded, or was a legendary character, like Daniel, is totally irrelevant to an understanding of the book. In spite of its abrupt close, as soon as the lesson has been stated, the book is a perfectly good short story —with a beginning, a middle, and an end.

Micah: The prophet Micah was a native of Moresheth near Gath (1:1) and was a younger contemporary of Isaiah. . . . He prophesied during the reigns of Judah's kings, Jotham (740-735), Ahaz (735-720), and Hezekiah (720-692). There is no reason to doubt the accuracy of the statement of the elders of Judah (a century later) that in the days of Hezekiah Micah the Moreshite prophesied the words of Mic. 3:12. In contrast to Isaiah, an aristocrat from the capital with access to the court, Micah was, like Amos, a humble villager. His primary concern was the expropriation of the poor for the enrichment of the upper classes.

The Book of Micah consists of his own oracles (1-3) with their comforting interpolations (2:12 f.; 4:1-5:15), and a later anonymous prophecy (6:1-7:6), with its own hopeful editorial appendix (7:7-20).

Nahum: We owe the preservation of Nahum's magnificent ode to a misunderstanding. As appears in the title, this martial song was considered a prophetic oracle or prognostication against Nineveh and thus given a place in the Book of the Twelve. In reality, however, to judge from his one extant poem, Nahum was not a prophet. . . . He was a poet. Even though Jehovah himself occasionally threatens Nineveh in the course of the poem (2:13; [H2:14]; 3:5 f.), there is nothing specifically religious in this exultant outburst of joy over the inevitable downfall of the Assyrian Empire which has since 701 B.C. crushed the kingdom of Judah. Nahum was both a great poet and a great patriot; his passionate nationalism, his burning hatred for the "city of blood, filled with falsehood, abounding in violence, where rapine never ceased" (3:1), his flaming animosity for the empire that "sold nations for harlotries and peoples for witcheries" (3:4), inspire a superb paean of triumph, matchless in literary power and beauty.

Habakkuk: Like the Book of Nahum, "the burden which Habakkuk the prophet saw" (1:1) is composite: to the prophetic oracles in chs. 1-2, a psalm entitled "a prayer of Habakkuk the prophet, upon Shigionoth" (3:1), has been added in ch. 3. There is no valid reason for attributing both parts of the book to the same author.

The first two chapters are a series of five short and more or less disconnected prophetic utterances. The first (1:2-4) is a complaint because Jehovah allows violence and injustice to triumph in the land. The second (1:5-11) is a divine oracle: Jehovah is arousing the Chaldeans, "a bitter and hasty nation," who will, in their speedy advance, conquer nations and kingdoms. The third (1:12-17) is a renewed appeal to the prophet's God: if Jehovah is righteous and mighty, why does he allow the wicked to devour the righteous? The fourth (2:1-5) is the divine answer which the prophet received on his watchtower: eventually the wicked will be punished, but the righteous Jew "shall live by his faithfulness" (2:4). The fifth oracle (2:6-20, omitting 2:18, a gloss on 2:19) is called a taunting proverb and consists of five "Woes" against the conquering nation that is rapacious, unscrupulous, sanguinary, intemperant, and idolatrous.

Zephaniah: The prophet Zephaniah was a contemporary of Habakkuk and prophesied a few years before him: Josiah's reforms in 621 separate the two prophecies. . . . The genuine oracles of Zephaniah belong to the reign of Josiah (638-609), more exactly to the time of the Scythian invasion along the Mediterranean coast (between 630 and 624). . . . Zephaniah was born about one century after King Hezekiah and could . . . have been his descendant in the fifth generation.

Zephaniah, in his denunciation of religious syncretism and political corruption, applies the teaching of Isaiah to his own day and derives from Amos the dismal conception of "the Day of the Lord." His bold, positive, unflinching nature differs radically from the introspective and emotional temperament of his contemporary, Jeremiah. The message of the two is subtly different, even when both are prophesying under the appalling menace of the Scythian invasion. The earnest, sober, vigorous style of this prophet lacks the poetic brilliance of Amos and Isaiah, but his picture of the horrors of the *dies irae* (1:15 f.) has become classic.

Haggai: The Book of Haggai consists of four oracles dated exactly near the end of the second year of Darius I, King of Persia (521-485 B.C.). . . . At that time Haggai and Zechariah (cf. Ezra 4:24; 5:1 f.) induced the people to begin rebuilding the Temple of Jerusalem, which had lain in ruins since 586. The new edifice was completed four years later (Ezra 6:14 f.).

Negligible though this book appears from the point of view of literature and religion, it is of great importance, together with Zechariah, as a historical source.

Zechariah: The Prophet Zechariah, son of Iddo (Ezra 5:1; 6:14), a priest according to Neh. 12:16, was a contemporary of Haggai. The Book of Zechariah consists of eight visions of the night, interpreted by an angel and dated on the 24th day of the eleventh month of the second year of Darius . . ., with an introductory address (1:1-6) and appendix (6:9-15); oracles dealing with the observance of the fasts (7-8) close the book for Zech. 9-14 are much later.

Malachi: The Book of Malachi was originally anonymous and bore the same title as the two books Zech. 9-11 and 12-14: "An Oracle. The Word of the Lord" fol-

lowed in Zech. 12:1 with "against Israel"; and in Mal. 1:1 with "unto Israel." . . .
An editor added at the end of 1:1 the words "by the hand of Malachi," making a
proper name of *"mal'ākî"* (my messenger) in 3:1.

The book consists of a preamble (1:2-5), a denunciation of the priests that despise
God's name (1:6-2:9), four oracles against Jewish laymen (2:10-16; 2:17-3:5; 3:6-12;
3:13-4:3), and a concluding warning (4:4-6) presumably appended by the final editor of the Book of the Twelve as a parting advice to the reader.

THE WRITINGS, OR HAGIOGRAPHA

The Psalms: The English title of the Book of Psalms is derived from the Greek
title *bíblos psalmôn* (Luke 20:42; Acts 1:20). . . . In classical Greek, *psalmós* meant the
playing of a stringed instrument, and the music obtained thereby, but the LXX gave
it the meaning of a sacred song (psalm) in translating *mizmôr.* This Hebrew word
originally signified a musical composition for stringed instruments, and was later
used in the titles of fifty-seven psalms to indicate a hymn with instrumental accompaniment.

The liturgical use of psalms in Temple worship is well attested since the days of
the Chronicler (*ca.* 250 B.C.), who speaks of the musical parts of the ritual with such
expert knowledge that very likely he belonged to one of the Levitical choirs. The
Chronicler attributes to David the organization of Temple music, both instrumental
and vocal. He could not date this institution back to the time of Moses, because the
Pentateuch (canonized about 400 B.C.) knows nothing of Temple music except the
blowing of silver trumpets by the priests (Num. 10:1-10), one of the latest laws in
the Pentateuch.

The Book of Proverbs: The Book of Proverbs has the longest title of any in the Old
Testament. This title was already known to Ben Sira (Ecclus. 47:17 refers to I Kings
4:32 and to Prov. 1:6) about 180 B.C., and the last edition of the book must therefore be earlier. Ordinarily, however, the first two words of the book (*mishlê she-
lōmôh,* the Proverbs of Solomon, or only Proverbs) constitute the title by which
the book is referred to. This brief title is purely conventional, and does not charac-
terize the contents.

In the first place, the book states that Solomon is not the author of all the sections
(and had actually no more to do with the writing of this book than David with the
composition of Psalms). In the second place, even the Hebrew *māshāl,* which has a
much wider meaning than the English "proverb," does not in the least fit several
important parts. The book contains the teaching of wise men and not "proverbs"
in the sense of popular bywords or folk maxims.

The Book of Job: This book consists of the prose folk tale about Job, whose piety
withstood every test (1:1-2:10) and was rewarded by God (42:10b-17); of a discussion between Job and three of his friends on the justice of God in rewarding human
conduct (3-27, in verse; with a prose introduction, 2:11-13, and epilogue, 42:7-10a);
of a poem on divine wisdom (28); of monologues of Job (29-31); of the speeches of
Elihu (32-37, in verse except for 32:1-6a); of the speeches of Jehovah (38:1-40:2,
6-41:34) and Job's replies (40:3-5; 42:1-6).

The chief chronological problem concerning the Book of Job is the determination of the period in which its original author lived; the secondary parts of the book were added before 200 B.C., the approximate date of the final edition of the work. The folk story of Job in its oral version goes back to unknown antiquity, but the prologue and epilogue of the book in which it has been transmitted to us can hardly be earlier than the sixth century.

Nothing is known of the author except what may be inferred from the poem. Unfortunately he makes no allusions to known historical events or persons, and consequently the chronological clues are indirect, vague, and subject to various interpretations. Critical research has yielded conflicting results and the only conclusion which may be regarded as generally accepted is that the poet lived between 700 and 200 B.C. Psalms and Proverbs are the only other parts of the Old Testament the possible dating of which extends over a similar period.

The Song of Songs: According to the title, "The Song of Songs which is Solomon's" (1:1), this book of verse is the most beautiful of the 1,005 songs which legend tells us Solomon composed (I Kings 4:32 [H. 5:12]). In Hebrew the expression "song of songs," like "vanity of vanities," "holy of holies" is used to indicate the superlative. . . . The attribution of this book to Solomon's pen is no less fictitious than that of Proverbs, Ecclesiastes, Wisdom, Psalms and Odes of Solomon to this ancient and opulent monarch. The repeated mention of Solomon in the course of the book (1:5; 3:7, 9, 11,8:11 f.), which in ch. 3 definitely identifies the bridegroom with King Solomon, may have prompted the editor responsible for the title to ascribe the book to him.

Song of Songs is a short anthology of love poems of various length sung by the bride, the bridegroom, and their friends. The individual poems, whose beginning and end are not always well marked, may be the work of a number of authors and are arranged without any definite plan.

The Book of Ruth is one of the most charming short stories in Hebrew literature: Goethe assigned it a pre-eminent position among epics and idylls. The plot of the story is well known. In the days of the judges during a famine, Elimelech with his wife Naomi and his two sons Mahlon and Chilion migrated from Bethlehem in Judah to the land of Moab. After Elimelech's death, Mahlon and Chilion married Moabitic women, Orpah and Ruth, respectively. But the two husbands soon died (1:1-5). Upon hearing that the famine had ended, Naomi took leave of her two daughters-in-law, having resolved to go back to Bethlehem. Orpah returned to her father's house but Ruth said to Naomi, "Intreat me not to leave thee, . . . for whither thou goest I will go; . . . thy people shall be my people, and thy God my God: where thou diest, will I die, and there will I be buried. . . ."

The date of this book is controversial, even though its traditional attribution to Samuel (Talmud [*Baba Bathra* 14b] and Christian writers) is no longer regarded as tenable. To join Ruth and Judges (and Lam. to Jer.), as Josephus does, counting 22, instead of 24, books in the Old Testament, means to disregard the canonization of Ruth and Lamentations among the Hagiographa rather than among the Prophets.

On the whole, a postexilic date seems preferable. By placing the story "in the days of the judging of the judges" (1:1), the author discloses familiarity with the Deuteronomic edition of Judges (*ca.* 550 B.C.) rather than with the rude and barbaric period which he so gracefully idealizes in his charming romance. For it is plain that the book is fiction . . . rather than history. . . .

The Book of Lamentations: Originally this small collection of five elegies bore no title. In Hebrew editions, both manuscript and printed, the first word of three of the poems (1:1; 2:1; 4:1), *êkhah,* "Ah how!" serves as a superscription. But in the Talmud . . ., the book is named after its contents *qînôth* (dirges), and this term in translation served as title in the versions: *thrēnoi* in the LXX and *threni* or *lamentationes* in the Latin versions. . . .

The five poems constituting the book, each of which corresponds to one of the five chapters, lament the destruction of Jerusalem in 586 B.C. and its dire aftermath. . . . In the fifth poem, half a century after the calamity of 586, the congregation begs God to take note of their misery (v. 1)—their lands and homes in the hands of aliens, members enslaved or in want, women ravished, the sanctuary on Zion a pile of ruins and inhabited by jackals (vv. 2-18)—and prays for restoration (vv. 19-22).

According to tradition Jeremiah was the author of the Book of Lamentations. Thus clearly in LXX, where the book begins with these words, "And it came to pass, after Israel was led into captivity and Jerusalem laid waste, that Jeremiah sat weeping and lamented with this lamentation over Jerusalem. . . ."

The Book of Ecclesiastes: The unknown author of this book, according to 1:12, assumed the enigmatic pseudonym of *qōhéleth* (Greek *ekklēsiastès,* from which, through the Latin, we get the English title), and is regularly called so in the book.

On the whole, Ecclesiastes is written in prose except for a few poetic verses. Sometimes prose and poetry can hardly be distinguished. The author collects his reflections on a variety of subjects, without striving for either consistency of thought or logical order, particularly after he has stated his chief conclusions in the first three or four chapters, which seem more coherent than any other part.

The book closes with two editorial appendices, the first of which commends the teaching of Ecclesiastes (12:9-11), while the second, depreciating the writing of many books (such as this one) and much investigation, prefers the practice of the Jewish religion since all human actions will eventually be judged by God (12:12 f.).

The Book of Esther: This book is a brief historical novel relating the vicissitudes of Esther in the court of Persia and the origin of the Jewish festival of Purim. In the Hebrew Bible the book is included in the third canon, the Writings or Hagiographa, and is one of the "five scrolls," generally the fifth, preceding Daniel. In the Greek Bible it usually stands after the historical books (or after the poetical books), before the prophetic books: in the English Bible it is found between the historical and the poetical books.

The Book of Esther, like Ruth, Jonah, Daniel and other Hebrew or Aramaic works of fiction, purports to be the recital of actual events, and was regarded as historical by orthodox Jews and Christians of ancient and modern times. The only support for this view is to be found in the fairly accurate knowledge which the author possessed about Persian royal palaces. . . .

The majority of critics have come to the conclusion that the story of Esther is not history, but fiction. Like other books of the Old Testament whose influence was outstanding, Esther appeared at the psychological moment, both expressing and molding the fleeting mood of the day. The author's purpose was to intensify the patriotic fervor of his people, in the moment of its triumph over the Gentiles, not only by means of a dramatic tale of long ago, but also by means of an institution (Purim) destined to kindle yearly the people's pride for all time to come.

The Book of Daniel is written in two languages: Hebrew and, in 2:4b-7:28, Aramaic; a marginal rubic, at the beginning of this section ("in Aramaic," 2:4) calls attention to the sudden change of language. The contents of this book may be summarized as follows:

I. Stories: *Daniel and his friends remain true to their religion in spite of persecution* (1-6).

II. *Daniel's four visions: the end of the heathen empires and the advent of the Kingdom of God* (7-12).

Although according to the Talmud (*Baba Bathra,* 15a) the "Men of the Great Synagogue" in the time of Ezra and Nehemiah "wrote" (i.e., edited) Daniel, the traditional view in Judaism and Christianity was that Daniel wrote his book in the sixth century.

The author of the Book of Daniel was obviously a very learned man. Like the imaginary hero of his book, the author was not only a seer, but also a sage. His range of reading was wide and his knowledge of popular tales, circulating orally, quite extensive.

Despite its limitations, imposed to a great extent by the historical situation from which it arose, the Book of Daniel is a noble book, inspired by the faith that the God of Israel is the king of the universe, and that he will soon vindicate his people and usher in the new age when the Kingdom of Heaven will belong to the poor, and the meek will inherit the earth.

The Book of Chronicles: The Hebrew title of Chronicles, which like Samuel and Kings was originally a single volume, means literally "things of the days," i.e., "events of [past] time," "history." Chronicles is a history of Judaism from Adam to Cyrus (538 B.C.), running parallel to Genesis-Kings and concluded in Ezra-Nehemiah.

It is generally recognized that the Chronicler wrote between 350 and 250 B.C., or more exactly in the second half of this period. With considerable ingenuity, W. F. Albright has argued that he was no other than Ezra (400-350), who reorganized Judaism in 398 after Nehemiah's activity.

The Books of Ezra and Nehemiah: In the Hebrew Bible the Books of Ezra and Nehemiah were regarded as one volume until 1448, when, following the Vulgate, the division was introduced in a Hebrew manuscript.

The book of Ezra-Nehemiah is the sequel of Chronicles and was written by the Chronicler. It relates the history of the Jews during the century which elapsed from the edict of Cyrus allowing the Exiles to return (538 B.C.) to Nehemiah's second visit to Jerusalem (432 B.C.; Neh. 13:6 f.; cf. 5:14), and may be summarized as follows:

1. *The return of the Exiles and the rebuilding of the Temple.*
2. *The activity of Ezra.*
3. *Nehemiah's administration of Judea as Persian governor, in 444 and 432* B.C.
4. *Nehemiah's second visit to Jerusalem in 432* B.C.

The literary analysis of the Books of Ezra and Nehemiah show, beyond the shadow of a doubt, that their author is the Chronicler and that he utilized written sources. But a wide difference of opinion prevails among critics in assigning the material to the Chronicler and to his sources.

When Nehemiah wrote, the Hebrew language was gradually dying out as the vernacular of the Jews (cf. Neh. 13:23 f.) and was soon to be replaced by Aramaic. His book is therefore the last Hebrew work written while this language was still living. Although he used at least three Aramaic expressions (in 2:6; 5:7, 15), his diction and grammar are notably more classical than those of the rest of Ezra-Nehemiah, where the characteristics of the Chronicler's artificial and strenuously labored Hebrew-Aramaic diction are apparent. . . . Therefore, Ben Sira (180 B.C.) ended the summary of the Old Testament in his "Praise of the Fathers of Old" (Ecclus. 44:1-49:13) with Nehemiah, "who raised up our ruins and healed our breaches;" he ignored entirely the legendary figure of Ezra. Indeed, with Nehemiah an epoch came to its end—the heroic and tragic Hebrew period of the Old Testament—and a new one began: the Holy Congregation of Normative Judaism.

The *Italics* show the page on which the picture will be found; the Roman figures refer to the interpretation of the picture.

INDEX OF POETRY BY AUTHORS AND TITLES

INDEX OF STORIES BY TITLES AND AUTHORS

INDEX OF MUSIC AND MUSIC INTERPRETATIONS BY TITLES AND AUTHORS

The *Italics* indicate the page on which the music score will be found; the Roman figures refer to the interpretation of the music.

ACKNOWLEDGMENTS

Acknowledgment is made to Abbott Book for the loan of art prints from his collection, and for his efforts in clearing permissions on those still in copyright.

Especial help in finding pictures was given by the following individuals and organizations in New York: Elizabeth Roth and Wilson G. Duprey of the Print Room of the New York Public Library; Olivia H. Paine, Assistant Curator of Prints, Metropolitan Museum of Art; The Frick Art Reference Library; and the Library of the National Council of the Episcopal Church.

The following have granted permission to include materials as indicated:

PICTURES

Alinari for "The Fall of Jericho" and "The Sacrifice of Isaac" by Lorenzo Ghiberti; "The Statue of David" by Michelangelo; "Finding the Baby Moses" by Raffaelino dal Colle; "The Vision of Ezekiel" by Raphael Sanzio; "Samson and Delilah" by Alessandro Turchi.

Boston Public Library Trustees for "Esther before King Ahasuerus" by Giustino Menescardi.

Wm. Collins Sons & Company, Ltd., for the frontispiece "The Old Testament" from *Through the Bible* by Theodora Wilson Wilson.

Eyre & Spottiswoode, Ltd., and Providence Lithograph Company for pictures by William Hole from his volume *Old Testament History Retold and Illustrated:* "Athaliah and the Coronation of Joash," "Daniel Interprets the Dream of Nebuchadnezzar," "The Dedication of the Temple," "Israel Carried Away into Assyrian Captivity," "Nehemiah Makes His Petition to Artaxerxes," "Rebuilding the Walls of Jerusalem," and "The Return of the Exiles."

C. R. Gibson and Company for "Elijah Fed by the Ravens" by Charles M. Relyea.

The Metropolitan Museum of Art for "Esther before King Ahasuerus" by Giustino Menescardi.

Saul Raskin for nine etchings from his art subjects on the Old Testament: "Abraham," "Amos, the Social Reformer," "Ezekiel ,and His Vision of the Valley with Dry Bones," "Ezra, the Scribe," "Habakkuk, the Skeptic," "Hosea and Israel, the Unfaithful Wife," "Micah, the Prophet," "The Prophet Zephaniah," and "Samuel, the Maker of Kings."

S.V.D. Catholic Universities National Council and the Catholic Library (Peking, China) for "Daniel in the Lions' Den" and "Moses Smites Water from the Rock" by Luke Chen (Yuan Tu).

William R. Jack, designer, and Carroll E. Whittemore Associates, Inc., for reproduction of stained-glass window, "Ruth and Boaz."

The John C. Winston Company for "Ahab and Elijah" by Francis Bernard Dicksee; "Elijah Casting His Mantle on Elisha" by an unknown artist.

POETRY

Abingdon Press for "Day's End" from *Songs from the Slums* by Toyohiko Kakawa; three poems from *The Glory of God* by Georgia Harkness: "The Agony of God,"
821

"Companion God," and "Hurricane."

Sara King Carleton for "The Heavens Declare the Glory" from *Poems for Life* compiled by Thomas Curtis Clark (Harper & Row).

The Christian Century for "Ultimate" by Laura Simmons.

Badger Clark for "God Meets Me in the Mountains" and "The Job" from his book, *Sky Lines and Wood Smoke.*

Mrs. Leslie Savage Clark for four poems written especially for this anthology and three poems previously published in other publications.

Thomas Curtis Clark and Mrs. Thomas Curtis Clark for twenty-six poems, several of which were composed especially for this anthology, others of which appear in one of several anthologies compiled by him, as well as several of which appeared in *The Christian Century* under his editorship.

Stanton A. Coblentz for "Noah" written especially for this anthology.

Grace Noll Crowell for two poems written especially for this anthology: "David, the Youth" and "Hannah, Sewing."

Lola F. Echard for two poems written especially for this anthology: "Father Abraham" and "God's Chosen King."

Evangelical Publishers for two poems by Annie Johnson Flint: "Go Forward" from *Flint Poems in One Volume* and "When Thou Passest Through" from *Songs of Faith and Comfort.*

John L. Foley, literary executor for Thomas S. Jones, Jr., for five poems by Thomas S. Jones, Jr., from *Shadow of the Perfect Rose: Collected Poems of Thomas S. Jones, Jr.,* edited by John L. Foley: "A Well Side," "David, The Threshing Floor," "Ezekiel," "Isaiah," and "Solomon."

Ruby Berkeley Goodwin for two poems from her volume, *From My Kitchen Window:* "Compensation" and "Omnipresence."

Mrs. Arthur Guiterman for "The Voice unto Pharaoh" by Arthur Guiterman.

D. C. Heath and Company for poems from *The Literary Study of the Bible* by Richard G. Moulton.

Bruce Humphries, Inc., and Georgia Harkness for eleven poems from *Holy Flame* by Georgia Harkness.

Adelaide Love for "The Nearness" from *Poems for Life* compiled by Thomas Curtis Clark (Harper & Row).

The Macmillan Company for several excerpts from *The Modern Reader's Bible* edited by Richard G. Moulton.

Virgil Markham for two poems by Edwin Markham: "Brotherhood" and "Man-Making" from *Poems of Edwin Markham,* selected and arranged by Charles L. Wallis (Harper & Row); "Revelation" and "The Man with the Hoe" from *The Shoes of Happiness and Other Poems* by Edwin Markham.

Gertrude E. McGregor for "The House of the Lord" by her late husband, the Rev. Ernest F. McGregor.

Madeleine S. Miller for eight poems written especially for this anthology, and one, "Labor," previously published.

Erica Oxenham for the following poems written by her father, John Oxenham: "Faith" and "The Sacrament of Light" from *Sacraments* by John Oxenham (Pilgrim Press); "I Find Thee, Lord" and "For Today and Tomorrow" from *Scrap-Book of J. O.* by Erica Oxenham (Longmans, Green and Company); Psalm XIX" from *Modern Poet's Book of Psalms.*

Ruth Ricklefs for two poems written especially for this anthology: "Daniel" and "The Gleaners."

The Riverdale Press for "Servant of God" by Jehuda Halevi, translated by Israel Zangwill, "A New Song" by Jehuda Halevi, translated by Nina Salaman, and "Morning Song" by Solomon ibn-Gabirol, translated by Solomon B. Freehof, from *The Small Sanctuary* by Solomon B. Freehof.

Charles Scribner's Sons for five poems from *The Messages of the Poets*, Vol. II, by Nathaniel Schmidt.

Alma Shoemaker and the International Council of Community Churches for "An Anniversary Prayer" from the July 1951 issue of *Christian Community*.

The Rev. Henry C. Spear for nine poems, five of which are from his booklet *Sermon Sonnets*.

William L. Stidger and Mrs. William L. Stidger for seven poems, four of which are reprinted from Dr. Stidger's volume *I Saw God Wash the World*, and three written especially for this anthology.

Harry Trumbull Sutton for five poems interpretative of the poems previously published in his booklet *International Sunday School Lessons for 1940*.

STORIES

Abingdon Press for fourteen lines from *The Prophets Tell Their Own Story* by Elmer A. Leslie.

Marie E. Aenis for "Rameri and the Scribes" from *Story Art Magazine*.

G. Bell and Sons, Ltd., for six lines from *Raphael* by Henry Strachey in the interpretation of "Moses Striking the Rock" by Raphael Sanzio.

Bobbs-Merrill Company, Inc., for "Abram Son of Terah" from *Abram Son of Terah* by Florence Marvyne Bauer; and John Erskine for "Solomon Visits the Plains Where His Father Watched Sheep" from *Solomon, My Son* by John Erskine; for "Through the Red Sea to the Promised Land" from *The Yoke* by Elizabeth Miller.

Broadman Press for two character studies on the prophets Elijah and Zephaniah from *Preaching from the Prophets* by Kyle M. Yates.

Mrs. William Stearns Davis for "The Handwriting upon the Wall" from *Belshazzar, a Tale of the Fall of Babylon* by William Stearns Davis (The Macmillan Company).

Mrs. Warwick Deeping and *The Sunday Chronicle* for "Abraham and Isaac" by Warwick Deeping.

Sally Craft and *Story Art Magazine* for "The Forgiving Father."

Florence M. Earlle for fifteen stories, several of which were written especially for this anthology, and to Fleming H. Revell Company for source material from *Bible Character Studies* by William J. May in Miss Earlle's story "Offerings for the Tabernacle."

Marian MacLean Finney for "Naaman, the Syrian Captive Healed" from her novel *In Miriam's House*.

Sir Philip Gibbs and *The Sunday Chronicle* for "David, the Hero with the Feet of Clay" (in two parts).

Harcourt, Brace & Company for "Shepherd of Israel" from *Shepherd of Israel* by Leonora Eyles.

Harper & Row for "Origin and Content of the Old Testament" from *Introduction to the Old Testament* by R. H. Pfeiffer; for "Jerusalem in the Days of Herod the Great" from *Ben Hur, a Tale of Christ* by Lew Wallace; for two excerpts from *The Bible: a New Translation* by James Moffatt, and one from *The New Testament in Modern Speech* by Richard Francis Weymouth.

Hodder & Stoughton, Ltd., for three stories from *Representative Men of the Bible* by George Matheson: "Hezekiah the Devout" and "Isaiah the Philanthropist" (from Series II) and "Samuel, the Seer" (from Series I); for four excerpts from *Representative Men of the Bible* by George Matheson.

The Macmillan Company for "Rahab" and "The Queen of Sheba" from *Women in the Old Testament* by Norah Lofts; for two maps, "The Two Kingdoms" and "The Babylonian Empire in the Time of Nebuchadezzar," and two brief excerpts, from *Concise Bible Commentry* by W. K. Lowther Clarke.

Lillian Breazeale Mitchell for "The Morning Stars Sang" written especially for this anthology.

Robert Nathan for "Jonah, the Rebel Prophet" from his novel *Jonah* (Alfred A. Knopf).

The National Wool Growers Association and *Reader's Digest* for "The Basque Sheepherder and the Shepherd Psalm" from *The National Wool Growers.*

Florence C. Porter for "Jeremiah, the Voice of the Lord" written especially for this anthology, and "The Rebuilding of the Walls" from *Story Art Magazine.*

Dairmuid Russell and Russell-Volkening, Inc., and Lord Dunsany for "Joseph, the Poor Boy Who Saved a Country" by Lord Dunsany, from *The Sunday Chronicle.*

Charles Scribner's Sons for "Moses, the Leader of a People" from *Amid These Storms* by Sir Winston Churchill (permisson also of Oldham Press, Ltd., for British, Canadian, and world rights for this story which appeared in a volume by Sir Winston Churchill entitled *Thoughts and Adventures,* 1932); for "Ezekiel and the Exiles" from *The Goodly Fellowship of the Prophets* by John Paterson; for several brief excerpts from *Messages of the Earlier Prophets* and *Messages of the Later Prophets* by Saunders Kent in connection with various art interpretations on the prophets.

Grace Ordway Spear for four stories written especially for this anthology: "Daniel, a Man of Courage," "Elisha, Son of Shaphat," "Jezebel, Israel's Wicked Queen," and "King Hezekiah and the Assyrian Conquest;" also "A Bible Story Quiz" (in verse) from *Story Art Magazine.*

Grace West Staley for "How a Shepherd Boy Helped a King" from *Jack and Jill,* "Jabal, Jubal, and Tubal-Cain" from *Junior Language and Arts Magazine,* and "Watchman, What of the Night?" from *Story Art Magazine.*

The Standard Publishing Company for "Generosity Rewarded" from *The Children's Hour* by Mayme Rolf Leonard.

Hallie R. Thresher and *Story Art Magazine* for "How the Birds Learned to Sing."

Margaret J. Wiggins for "How the Temple was Built" and "Where is Thy God?" written especially for this anthology, and "A Legend of the Bed of Straw" from *Story Art Magazine.*

Willis Kingsley Wing and Dorothy Clarke Wilson for "Amos, the Herdsman from Tekoa" from *The Herdsman* by Dorothy Clarke Wilson, in two parts.

Bethany Press for permission to photograph "Guide Me, O Thou Great Jehovah" from *Worship and Hymns* compiled by S. W. Hutton.

Margaret Buckham for the words to "O God, above the Drifting Years" written by her father, John Wright Buckham.

Central Conference of American Rabbis (Rabbi Isaac E. Marcuson, secretary), for permission to photograph the following hymns and canticles from *Union Hymnal:* "As Pants the Hart," "Happy He Who Walketh Ever," "Hymn of Glory," "Let Israel Trust in God Alone," "The Law, 'The Torah,'" "The God that to the Fathers," "To the God of All Creation," "Unto the Hills," and "When Israel to the Wilderness."

W. E. DuBois for an excerpt from *Songs of Sorrow in the Souls of Black Folk* in connection with an interpretation of the spiritual.

Harper & Row for "God of the Nations, Who from Dawn of Days" by Walter Russell Bowie, from *Social Hymns of Brotherhood and Aspiration* edited by Mabel Hay Burrows Mussey.

Dr. John Haynes Holmes for the words "Almighty God beneath Whose Eye," "God of the Nations, Near and Far," and "O God, Whose Law from Age to Age."

Mrs. George R. Hyde for the words to "Creation's Lord, We Give Thee Thanks" by William DeWitt Hyde, from *The Pilgrim Hymnal*.

William Pierson Merrill for the words to "Not Alone for Mighty Empire."

Novello & Company, Ltd., for the tune "Chenies" by Timothy R. Matthews in the hymn "God is My Strong Salvation" by James Montgomery, and the tune "Cross of Jesus" by John Stainer in the hymn "God is Love, His Mercy Brightens" by John Bowring.

The Pilgrim Press for permission to photograph several hymns from *The Pilgrim Hymnal*.

Fleming H. Revell Company for permission to photograph seven spirituals from *Old Songs Hymnal* collected by Dorothy G. Bolton and arranged by Harry T. Burleigh: "Adam and Eve Walking in the Garden," "Didn't It Rain," "Don't God's Children Have a Hard Time?" "Handwriting on the Wall," "Joshua and Jonah," and "You'll be a Witness for the Lord;" for permission to photograph the following hymns from *Services for the Open* arranged by Laura I. Mattoon and Helen D. Bragdon: "Before Us, Father Abraham" arranged by Percy Shaw, and "O Love of God How Strong and True" by Horatius Bonar; for three brief excerpts from *Lyric Religion* by H. Augustine Smith in connection with hymn interpretations.

The Rodeheaver Hall-Mack Company for permission to photograph the following spirituals from *Southland Spirituals:* "Down by the River-side," "Go Down, Moses," and "Little David."

Charles Scribner's Sons for an excerpt from *The Gospel in Hymns* by Albert Edward Bailey in connection with a hymn interpretation.

William L. Stidger and Mrs. William L. Stidger for four hymns with accompanying music score, hitherto published in sheet music form: "Brotherhood," "Clear the Way for the Eternal," "I Will Pray," and "Some Sinai."